A book about an teacher at Second Baptist urday School for another former teacher. This book is given to the Second Baptist library in memory of another librarian who was married in Second ptist Church on June 26, 1930,

Douglas Southall
FREEMAN

Douglas Southall Freeman, 1886-1953. (Image courtesy of Dementi Studio, Richmond, Virginia.)

Douglas Southall
FREEMAN

By David E. Johnson

PELICAN PUBLISHING COMPANY
Gretna 2002

Library of Congress Cataloging-in-Publication Data

Johnson, David E., 1961-
  Douglas Southall Freeman / David E. Johnson.
    p.cm.
  Includes bibliographical references and index.
  ISBN 1-58980-021-4 (alk. paper)
    1. Freeman, Douglas Southall, 1886-1953. 2. Biographers—United States—Biography.
  3. Historians—United States—Biography. 4. Washington, George, 1732-1799—In
  literature. 5. Lee, Robert E. (Robert Edward), 1807-1870—In literature. I. Title.

  E175.5.F78 J64 2002
  973.4'1'092—dc21
  [B]
                                                                2001059802

Unless otherwise indicated, all scripture quotations are taken from the *King James Version* of the Bible.

Scriptures marked NKJV are taken from *The New King James Version* of the Bible. Copyright © 1979, 1980, 1982 by Thomas Nelson, Inc., Publishers.

Cover photo courtesy of Mary Tyler McClenahan. Original portrait by Ernest Hamlin Baker.

Printed in the United States of America
Published by Pelican Publishing Company, Inc.
1000 Burmaster, Gretna, Louisiana 70053

For Holly

Contents

Prologue

His mind is working before the alarm clock sounds. Time seldom runs away, Douglas Southall Freeman knows, "if the mind holds a check rein on it."[1]

This morning the alarm goes off at 2:30 A.M. This hour is the destination reached as the result of a gradual movement to rise ever earlier. For many years it was 4:30 A.M., then, one delightful morning, it was 3:55 A.M., a "new early."[2] After that day, the minutes retreated before a force of will determined "to sneak up a few minutes earlier."[3]

He swings his feet over the side of his bed. If he looks in the mirror as he dresses, he sees a man of medium frame, with blue-gray eyes peering from behind steel-rimmed glasses. His face is unremarkable. It is not the broken aquiline nose, the cleft chin, or balding head that draw people to him. Friends know it is the "mobility of expression" and "intensity of feeling" his face can display.[4]

Dressed in a three-piece suit, which will be rumpled by day's end, he takes a few steps from his bedroom and is now in a small chapel. A kneeling bench, a cross, and a stained-glass window set apart this closet-sized room. Here he kneels and prays to the God he had met in the Baptist church of his youth. What he had accepted in faith had been proven in living. "It works," he said, "this religion of Jesus Christ," and through it he finds his mind and spirit enlarged.[5] His mother had hoped he would enter the ministry. Instead, he rises from his home altar each day determined to set an "example of diligence, energy and service to mankind in recognition of the mercies I have had."[6]

From the third floor he goes down for an unhurried breakfast. A few miles away, the office of the editor of the *Richmond News Leader* is dark and quiet. It will not long remain so.

His car moves out of the driveway at 3:10. The city of Richmond, Virginia, is not a typical sleepy Southern town, but sleep is an acceptable condition at this hour. The drive takes Freeman down the spacious boulevard called Monument Avenue. In the distance, a figure begins to emerge. Set off on a large island in the center of the avenue, towering above treetops and stately homes, is the statue of Robert E. Lee.

Lee, who has been Freeman's companion for a longer time than even his beloved wife Inez.

Lee, who brought him fame and a Pulitzer Prize when he made the general come alive for all time in four masterful volumes.

Lee, his greatest hero.

As he drives by the equestrian statue, Douglas Southall Freeman raises his hand and salutes the general. This is a pattern of daily life.[7]

At 3:25, Freeman begins his day as editor of the *Richmond News Leader*, Richmond's afternoon newspaper. The newsroom is beginning to show signs of life. In comes young Carl, promptly at 3:30, with the morning wire dispatches.[8] Here is the first edition of the morning *Richmond Times-Dispatch*. Now current on the world's events, Freeman turns to his typewriter. Since 1915 he has traced the history of the world in two to three columns of editorial, Monday through Saturday. He has dissected the military operations of two world wars—so impressing Woodrow Wilson with his analysis of the war in Europe that the president kept Freeman's editorials on his desk.[9] Through Coolidge prosperity and Prohibition, Depression and New Deal, hot and cold wars, and Old and New Souths, he has seen the *News Leader* through years in which he knows "history is being made that will loom high."[10]

While his editorials are being blocked and set, his attention turns to managing the paper. Can a general request be made that all departments give the city editor any tips on news? Might we inquire about a staff photographer? Can we avoid references in headlines to the race of the subject? Is there a better method of coordinating news stories with editorial comment? Is the filing system adequate?[11] Turning from internal memoranda, Freeman starts on the mail of the day. During hot Richmond summers, the first letter is to Mrs. Freeman vacationing at their beach cottage. Next go letters to any of his three children out of state at camp, at school, or, in later years, at their own homes or off to war. Then come responses to governors, Cabinet secretaries, generals, chambers of commerce, daughters of the Confederacy, professors, writers, historians, and *News Leader* readers. Mail that one would expect to be received by a man who is simultaneously president of the Southern Historical Society, rector of the Board of Trustees of the University of Richmond, trustee for the Carnegie Endowment for International

Peace, and trustee for the Rockefeller Foundation. Henrietta Crump, the secretary without whom he "could not get on a day," is as likely to bring in a note from Winston Churchill as a criticism from a reader alleging unfavorable news coverage.[12] Both letters will receive the same full and courteous attention.

His eyes now sweep up to his office clock. It is 7:58 A.M. and time to leave for the morning radio broadcast. The walk to the studio is two minutes from his office. He steps up to the microphone at 8:00, and thousands of Virginians mark the beginning of their day.

The voice they hear is not a deep radio voice, but a calm, soothing, baritone with a familiar accent. They might just be beginning their day, but he has been observing the world for more than five hours and will tell them what they need to know. The news from Europe or New York or downtown Richmond. The triumphs of goose-stepping tyrannies or the trials of animals with hoof-and-mouth disease. The weather. The day in history. What proper Southerners should fix for dinner. All without a prepared script. At 8:15, he finishes his broadcast, and Richmond begins its day.

Back in his office, his staff is assembled for the morning conference. They cannot help but notice the misspelled sign prominently displayed in his office: "Time alone is irreplacable. Waste it not." A not so subtle reminder that the relaxed meeting—coined by reporters as "bringing wampum" to the "great Sachem"—must move along. News tidbits are swapped, assignments discussed, and laughter heard as the latest jokes are unveiled. One morning the room is rendered uneasily silent as a newcomer begins to explain the movements of Confederate general "Jeb" Stuart in June 1862. All eyes turn to Freeman who stops the budding historian's account with "My dear boy, in some quarters I am considered a modest authority on these matters."[13]

The conference ends at 8:32 as the *News Leader* newsroom assumes the flurry common to all city papers. Freeman can hear the "distant roar" of business manager Allen Potts raising a "grave question concerning the ancestry of seventeen individuals, four firms, and three classes."[14] In the midst of this commotion, it is time to receive visitors, make phone calls, and implement decisions. Why is it that the governor issues his press releases too late in the day for our paper? Labor disputes are always in the offing, and the "Big Boss," *News Leader* publisher John Stewart Bryan, might drop in to discuss the topic from all angles. "Forty-five mortal minutes at the very rush time of the morning" Freeman complains as a conversation drags on.[15] At noon, visitors or not, he excuses himself for another broadcast.

When he leaves the studio at 12:15, following his mid-day update of news and history, Douglas Freeman has home on his mind. His day at the paper is complete and is soon far away as he heads back down Monument Avenue—again saluting General Lee—to home and Inez.

Inez Goddin Freeman. She had taken his heart in 1908 and held it with a tenacity reminiscent of her Confederate veteran father. To her devoted husband she is ever "so poised, so just, so loving and so humble in the beauty of character."[16] They will share time in the garden. A relaxing lunch. Home news will take the stage from world news. The early afternoon belongs to them.

At 2:30 P.M., he goes back to his third-floor room for a brief nap. Sleep comes immediately and ends almost as quickly one-half hour later. A different kind of work waits.

On his desk lie notes, papers, books, letters, and manuscripts. Unconnected pieces of history. He will sift through the slightest scraps of information, determine their truthfulness, and test their veracity. Once they become organized facts, he will marshal them together with elegant prose. Here he spends almost twenty years writing the life of Lee. Here he traces the eccentric brilliance of "Stonewall" Jackson, seeks to understand the enigma of Longstreet, laughs with Stuart, and shakes his head in knowing disgust over other forgotten captains. His publisher wants one volume on Lee—he can present such a life in no less than four. The reading public clamors for a Lee-like study of George Washington, but he knows he must first honor Lee's lieutenants. Three more volumes. As if writing the history of the leadership of the Army of Northern Virginia is not in itself an all-consuming project, he writes magazine articles, speeches, book reviews, and introductions for the books of others.

"I have no idea how many introductions I have written for books or how many addresses of mine have been put in print," he says, even as more titles flow from his study.[17] *Virginia: A Gentle Dominion*; *The Last Parade*; *The South Is Still Solid*; and *Eisenhower in Great Military Tradition*. He will craft addresses to be delivered to students being grad-uated from universities and to generals being taught at war colleges. He will complain about these intrusions, but he will rarely refuse a request.

Then, with a Pulitzer for *R. E. Lee* and international acclaim for *Lee's Lieutenants*, his study becomes George Washington's home. Was ever there a more daunting figure? The least-known best-known hero in American history. Freeman will have to transport himself from the nine-teenth century back more than one hundred years to another era with its unfamiliar characters and terrain. But Washington needs a biography, and he is the only one who can write it.

He discounts the cherry tree story and finds young Washington full of "conflicts, gradations, and contradictions."[18] Two volumes on Washington's youth, then a third volume as the planter becomes a patriot. Now Freeman uncovers the hero, greater, he says, than we believed him to be.[19] The work will go past four volumes, to six in Freeman's life, and one after his death.

The work of the day is done at 6:30. He will spend the evening with his family, his dinner guests, and his favorite music. He will recount humorous stories and allow those around him to shine.

Time has marked his day. Now at 8:30 he climbs again to the third floor, his final trip of the day. As his mind winds down—even after his body is instantly asleep—he knows to be true what he has so often said: "Fully this day I have labored and honestly I have striven to make the day's work a thing of beauty."[20]

The alarm clock will sound again in six hours.

CHAPTER 1

"Plenty of Work and Opportunity"

Victory! Glorious victory belonged to them! The boys of the Fourth Virginia Artillery, only recently mustered into infantry, had come through their first fight. The morning had seen them march through the heavy underbrush and thick pines of the Virginia woods outside Richmond until they were within sight of the Union earthworks. Then, with a bayonet charge, the boys had swept the Federals from their fortifications. The ecstasy of victory, mixed with the relief of survival, filled the young soldiers as they stood in Casey's Redoubt. It was May 31, 1862, during what would be known as the Battle of Seven Pines.[1]

Douglas Southall Freeman's father, Walker Burford Freeman, looked down the line to his right and his left. All along the line he saw the flags and uniforms of Confederate general Robert Rodes's brigade. He knew nothing of what might be happening at other portions of the line, but could it be anything other than a similarly glorious report? He saw no evidence to the contrary. All around him lay dead and wounded Yankees, yet he and his comrades were amazingly intact. The bounty of their capture, eight guns and all the supplies of the overrun Federal camp, was spread before them. And now, suddenly, in their midst was General Rodes. Astride his horse, the light of battle reflecting in his face, the thirty-two-year-old, six-foot, blond brigadier looked every bit the Arthurian hero. He congratulated his men on their splendid effort and then gave a special order to the Fourth Virginia: Turn those captured guns toward the enemy and open fire! A cheer of joy erupted from Walker and the boys in the redoubt. Their training was in artillery, and their pride had not well suffered the recent switch to infantry. Now they would man the captured guns, bring their training to bear, and finish the morning's work.[2] If at this moment a wave of euphoria surged through eighteen-year-old Walker Freeman, it was merely the latest manifestation of such an emotion he had experienced in the nine months since he left the small town of Liberty, Virginia, to fight for the Confederacy.

The town of Liberty stood on an eminence in Bedford County in the midst of the rolling foothills of Virginia's Blue Ridge Mountains. Bedford was a pastoral county bounded on the north by the James River and the south by the Staunton River. Towering above the fields and streams were the Blue Ridge ranges: Headforemost Mountain, No Business Mountain, Big and Little Onion Mountains, and the twin peaks of Otter. The names of the creeks winding through the countryside bespoke a way of life: Sheep, Stony, Difficult, Goose, Crab Orchard, and Clover.[3] The land was fertile, the streams full of spotted trout, and wildflowers splashed color from the emergence of "Johnny-jump-up" in April through the end of the aster in October.[4] Walker Freeman was entranced with the beauty of Liberty, and the sight from the town looking to the west was indelibly stamped in his mind's eye.

> The great range of the Blue Ridge is in full view, standing out against the horizon, in bold outline. It is near enough to be plainly visible, and yet far enough to give the coloring and contour a dreamy tint that lulls one into thoughts of the almightiness of God and the wonders of His handiwork.[5]

Walker Freeman had been born a slight five miles from this panoramic scene. His father, Garland Hurt Freeman, had come to Liberty in the mid-1830s from a not-too-distant farm near the Meadows of Goose Creek. Then in his twenties, Garland Freeman was a powerfully built man with a "pious disposition."[6] He brought with him his young wife, Judith Holland, and established a farm in the shadow of "No Business Mountain."[7] There the two set to work—hard work—clearing the ground and sowing the first crop. Their work was rewarded in a season as the farm prospered, and their domestic bliss was increased with the birth of a son, Stephen. As was so often the case in these days on the frontier, tragedy followed soon on the heels of elation. Judith was struck with "a sudden illness" of unknown origin and died. Now a widower with a small son, Garland Freeman persevered in his farm work and soon chose a second wife, Thormuthis Burford. It was an auspicious marriage for the young successful farmer. His bride came from a prosperous Amherst County family—prosperity bred of wise land speculating.[8] With her cumbersome first name shortened to "The" (pronounced "thee"), she and

Garland began a happy and successful marriage in 1836.[9] Remembered as a gentle and devoted wife and mother, "The" Freeman bore nine children—six girls and three boys. Walker Burford Freeman, the fourth child, was born August 28, 1843.[10]

Little record exists of Walker's young life. It can be assumed that it was the typical life of a farm boy in the mid-nineteenth century. His future love of the land was no doubt established during these years. "The calm green permanence of the Peaks of Otter," Douglas Freeman would one day write, "spares men the waste and blindness of hurry. Roads wind caressingly; even the streams flow slowly."[11] When Walker was four, his father moved the family five miles north to the village of Charlemont. Walker viewed the growing community, with its tobacco factory, tannery, grist mill, and tailor shop, as "prosperous and refined."[12] His father's 301-acre farm did not reach the "prosperous" level of the surrounding thousand-acre farms, but it did contain a stable, barn, tobacco houses, and dairy. A herd of cattle grazed in its plentiful fields, and the land produced crops "sufficient for the ample maintenance of a large family."[13]

Like most similarly situated farmers, Garland Freeman owned slaves. He apparently acquired them by inheritance and not by purchase off the slave block.[14] He is reported to have opposed slavery, a sentiment not uncommon in western Virginia, though his opposition rested more on economic reasons than on moral grounds. Unlike many planters, Freeman did not rely on slaves either as an investment or a primary source of labor. He also looked on them more humanely than was often the case elsewhere. In the summer of 1848, he accepted appointment as an instructor of the "colored people." In that role, he was to meet at least once every two weeks for the purpose of providing religious instruction to area slaves.[15] He was also to encourage slaves to attend worship services on Sunday. Freeman is reported to have pledged himself to fulfill this duty "as far as practicable."[16] This interaction with slaves was nothing new for Freeman. He worked the farm with them side by side, as did his sons as they matured.[17] The work appealed to young Walker. He judged farming "a most independent life" providing "many opportunities . . . to demonstrate my manhood." Part of Walker's love for farm work was that it relieved him from the restraints of school, but his contented joy with outdoor work was genuine. "No one but a country boy," he asserted, "knows how big he feels when first he is allowed to hold the big double plow."[18]

A farm in nineteenth-century Virginia was more than merely a means of livelihood. It was an all-consuming lifestyle that shaped attitudes, customs, and values. Particularly in Thomas Jefferson's Virginia, where the agrarian life was viewed as the noblest existence of man, life on a farm left a permanent imprint. Walker Freeman felt it was "good fortune to be born and reared on the farm."[19]

> Through these years I had ample opportunity for development of physical culture in the daily practice of the various forms, than which no better have ever been devised. For constancy, variety and effect, they were ideal. There is a wide difference in taking physical exercise in a mechanical way, and that of getting it continually as the outcome of one's daily employment. One is mechanical and irregular, the other is constant and natural.[20]

Not that life was all hard work. There were horses to ride across vast fields and, as winter approached, great parties at neighboring farms. "After the dining room was cleared," Walker remembered, "men would come in with their fiddles and banjos and the dancing would continue until dawn of day."[21] Wheat harvesting and corn shucking, though serious business, were turned into "frolic and fun." The corn shucks would "fly faster and faster," Walker noted, as the workers "steamed up from the start with strong raw whiskey or neighborhood apple brandy."[22] The pious Garland drew the line at hard drink and dancing at his parties, but Walker remembered that he still enjoyed "real social pleasure" in "the good old days in old Virginia."[23]

With his farm and family prospering, Garland Freeman assumed a leadership role in the community. Liberty had no county judge, so leading citizens sat as magistrates and heard local disputes and cases. Garland served for many years as a justice of the peace on this bench.[24] A Democrat, he discussed politics "in a most spirited manner" usually with his Whig brother John. Politics was as often sport as serious discussion in rural Virginia. Walker observed that "the amateur politician, the leisurely farmers, and the men who sat around at the country store whittling sticks" lost no opportunity to express their "weighty opinions" on the issues of the day.[25] Law and politics provided Garland two means of activity and service; religion offered a third. In a grove near Charlemont stood a little frame church called Mt. Hermon. Garland became an active member and would serve through the years as a deacon, treasurer, church clerk, and Sunday School superintendent.[26] His views on religion were remembered as "rigid" and "puritanical," but he was viewed by his neighbors as considerate, unselfish, and conscientious. "Garland Freeman is a good man—one of the best men I ever knew," one local commented. "It's a great pity he is so convinced a Baptist."[27] By the mid-1840s, Garland Freeman was firmly established as a leading man in the county, a respected and successful farmer, and a happily married husband and father.

Walker Freeman approached his teen years as a husky, robust, and well-liked lad. He had grown tall and handsome, with fair hair and blue eyes.[28] His education had come first at home from his mother and elder sister, then from small schools around Charlemont, usually staffed by traveling ministers.[29] Walker's love of the outdoors, combined with the natural tendencies of a rambunctious youth, frequently landed him in trouble with his teachers. He nonetheless excelled academically and was admitted to the "select school" for young men in preparation to enter the University of Virginia.[30] As the year 1856 came to an end, Walker Freeman was walking the same successful path of his father. Events on the horizon, both close to home and across a dividing nation, would soon jolt the idyllic life of the Freeman family.

The first blow landed in 1857. Garland Freeman passed away at the age of forty-seven, apparently from an attack of typhoid. He had contracted pneumonia in December 1856 and, despite receiving the best available medical attention, was in a weakened condition when the fever struck.[31] His death left a void in the social, cultural, and religious life of Charlemont, and he was mourned by a genuinely grieved community. His obituary in the *Religious Herald* reflected the public measure of the man.

> He was active and useful in the family, and in society, and a pious devoted and valuable member of the church . . . As a husband he was tender and kind, as a father affectionate, as a master lenient, as a neighbor unselfish, as a citizen conscientious, as a Christian meek and humble, and as an officer, active, prompt and efficient . . . He was a lover of truth, and a man of irreproachable moral character and deep-toned piety.[32]

His family buried him on his farm as thirteen-year-old Walker reflected on his father's "noble example for uprightness, in service to his fellow men, and devotion to the principles of truth and righteousness."[33] The example of Garland Freeman would, his son affirmed, be "ever before me."[34]

The settling of Garland Freeman's estate proved to be a disconcerting experience. Garland's son by his first marriage, Stephen, was entitled to a share of his late father's estate, and part of the Freeman farm would have to be sold to satisfy this obligation. The timing of such a sale could not have been worse. Slow economic times, brought on by the Panic of 1857, had descended on Virginia, and an immediate sale would guarantee low prices for farm acreage. "The" Freeman would be forced to sell more land than she wanted in order to raise the sufficient share. A logical solution was to wait for an economic upturn that could benefit all parties. This logic was clear to everyone except the court-appointed trustee, Dr. Falls, who demanded an immediate sale. Arguments could not persuade him to wait until more favorable economic times, so much of Garland Freeman's farm was sold to satisfy the share of his first son.[35]

The economic crisis that depressed farm and crop prices in 1857 was followed in 1858 by a severe drought that cut short remaining crops. Farmers faced twin demons of despair: not enough crops to sell and low prices for those that would sell. To these worries were added rumors of slave insurrections. As the abolitionist movement of the North grew, whispers intensified rumors that slaves in Bedford County would soon revolt. As nerves grew raw, the town established night patrols to act as a public warning network. Walker Freeman and his brothers spent many nights on patrol "visiting" the slave quarters, but "never heard a word that indicated" any plan of uprising.[36] Still, the seed of suspicion had been sown in fertile ground, and a traveling veterinary surgeon who came through town was rumored to be none other than John Brown.[37]

The presidential election of 1860 was the fourth major upheaval in as many years to shake Walker Freeman's life. Having inherited some of Garland Freeman's political acumen, Walker watched the growing sectional tensions with a discerning eye. "The signs of the times," he concluded, pointed to "a coming conflict."[38] With the election of Abraham Lincoln, "on his platform," it became plain to Walker that "war was almost certainly to ensue."[39] Virginia did not immediately join the fledgling Confederacy in the wake of Lincoln's election or the firing on Fort Sumter. It took Lincoln's call for troops to invade the South before Virginia voted for secession and began to form military companies. By May 1861, Bedford County had sent nine companies into the service of the Confederacy, with Walker's older brother and other family members in the ranks.[40] "I just heard you were going to join the army," Walker wrote a cousin. "I wish I could go, but my folks think I am too young."[41] His family's opposition notwithstanding, Walker put aside thoughts of entering the University of Virginia and begged his mother for permission to join the fight.[42] "The" Freeman had every reason to refuse her son's entreaties: He was only seventeen years old and was the eldest of only two sons still at home to work the family farm. These were valid excuses in 1861 when the manpower needs of the Confederacy were not as acute as they would become during the course of the war. None of this swayed Walker, and his persistence on the subject did not wane. After a few weeks "The" consented—provided Walker could find a company to accept him. Heartened by success, he headed to Liberty and enlisted in a company of field artillery being raised by Capt. Alexander Jordan, a local tobacco manufacturer. Jordan's stipulations were that Walker pass a physical—no problem for the six-foot teenager—and secure his mother's written permission. Her condition of his finding a unit having been met, "The" Freeman had no choice but to sign. Walker Freeman became a member of the Piedmont Artillery.[43]

The Piedmont Artillery consisted of about one hundred men from all walks of life. The roster consisted of lawyers, doctors, teachers, students, farmers, blacksmiths, the former editor of the *Valley Virginian*, and one patriot who claimed his pre-war profession was "drinking liquor and fox hunting."[44] All through the hot Virginia summer, the company drilled, trained, and prepared for action. In August 1861, orders came to make the short trip to Lynchburg.

On the day the soldiers left for war, Liberty looked like any one of thousands of similarly situated Southern towns during the summer of 1861. The town was giving its youth to the cause of the Confederacy, and the full range of emotions—from boisterous pride to anxious fear— was on display at the station. A large crowd gathered, speeches were made, and tearful good-byes exchanged. "Flowers were heaped upon us in great profusion," Walker Freeman remembered.[45]

It seemed to me as if the train would never start. But after a while we boarded the cars and moved off amidst the waving of handkerchiefs and calling out the last farewells. A beautiful silken flag, the gift of the ever blessed Ladies, kissed the breeze as we turned the curve below the town and proceeded to Lynchburg.[46]

From Lynchburg, the company went to Staunton, thence east across the face of central Virginia and down the peninsula to Gloucester Point, across the York River from Yorktown. Two other companies joined them there and, as 1861 drew to a close, winter quarters were constructed. Walker Freeman settled down with "a happy, jolly set" eagerly awaiting spring and the opening campaign.[47]

On May 4, 1862, the Fourth Virginia Artillery, as Walker's Piedmont unit was now designated, was ordered to move west from Gloucester Point to Hanover Courthouse. The reason for this backward move was the withdrawal of Gen. Joseph E. Johnston and the Army of Northern Virginia in the face of the slow advance up the peninsula of Gen. George B. McClellan's Army of the Potomac. Johnston would, in time, pull the army back to the outskirts of the capital at Richmond. Hanover Courthouse, Walker's destination, was north of Richmond, some twenty miles from the far left of Johnston's defensive line. As excitement and anticipation filled the boys from the shadow of the Blue Ridge, Walker felt nothing but gloom. He was ill with the mumps and unable to move out with his company. His condition carried but one consequence: He was expected to look out for himself and make his own way west. With the Union Army advancing in the wake of withdrawing Confederates, Walker Freeman felt certain he would soon be a prisoner of war.[48]

Not willing to chance falling into the enemy's hands, Walker picked himself off his sick bed and, with two other recovering comrades and a black cook named Jim, set "out like Abraham, not knowing whither he went."[49] Already on the north bank opposite the enemy, the sickly band sought to speed their escape by using a skiff owned by a local operator. As they haggled over use of the craft, they heard the distant, yet unmistakable, sound of a steamer coming up the river. A few moments later, the sight was confirmed: It was a steamer bound for West Point. A plan quickly developed: The four men would board the skiff, get close to the steamer, hail it, and get on board. The strategy worked as planned until the skiff neared the steamer. Then, suddenly, a displaced wave rose, rolled toward the small craft, and forced it under. "It was," Walker admitted, "a dangerously perilous position."[50] The alert ship captain sized up the pending catastrophe and reversed his engine, calming the water. As the water settled, the four men hung to the wrecked skiff until they could be lifted to safety. A tongue-lashing from the captain for attempting so foolhardy a venture was a price the boys were willing to pay for successful escape from the clutches of the Union Army.[51]

Walker Freeman, still weak from the mumps and now wearing drenched clothing, spent a restless trip on board the steamer. He had not eaten since leaving Gloucester Point, and his prospects did not improve upon arriving at West Point. The floor in the front hall of a boarding house was the best the town could offer for a bed and, almost as soon as sleep came, enemy gunboats broke the peaceful revelry of the dawn. Chaos descended along with the Union shells. As women screamed and soldiers sought to keep order, someone yelled above the tumult that a freight train was leaving for Richmond. Moving in a daze, Walker and his companions beat a path to the railway. At first denied entry on the departing train, the soldiers pushed their way through, having to draw knives at one point to get Jim on board, and found a spot. As the train lurched slowly west to Richmond, the pilgrimage from Gloucester Point reached a blissfully uneventful end.[52]

After reaching Richmond, Walker set out for home. Nursed by "The" Freeman, he recovered "in about a week" and prepared to rejoin his unit. Before leaving home, Walker tended to one item of importance: He took time to be baptized.[53] Feeling both physically and spiritually fit, he made the trip back east and found his company encamped six miles below Richmond. Here he learned the military situation. McClellan had continued to advance up the peninsula and was now some ten miles east of Richmond. General Johnston had decided at last to turn and strike a blow. His decision was to attack the IV Federal Corps at Seven Pines before it could be reinforced.[54] The Fourth Virginia Artillery was mustered with infantry and would move toward certain action in the morning. He hadn't missed it. He would be with his company when they engaged the enemy. As Walker waited that night for the morning's work, the skies were rent by a great thunderstorm; the electrical display in the sky somehow foreshadowing what the morrow held. It was another sleepless night.[55]

At eight o'clock in the morning, the Fourth Virginia moved out. "Our route of two miles," Walker wrote, "lay through a jungle so thick with briars, thorns and vines that it was almost impossible to move." But move they did. At the edge of a slight elevation, the firing started, and the first charge was made.[56]

Thus the confluence of events and influences that placed Walker Freeman in Casey's Redoubt on May 31, 1862. Though a boy in years, he had the experiences of a man from both the farm and the military. Now he stood flush with victory as General Rodes gave the order to turn the guns on the withdrawing Federals.

Fire they did, but the guns failed to achieve the desired effect. The Federals were reforming. Rodes decided to move his brigade again forward and drive the enemy. The order came, and Walker Freeman moved forward. He instantly sensed this charge was different. The Confederates were engulfed by fire not only from the front, but also from an angle to their left. Walker now walked into volleys "that seemed to be so destructive that no human being could hope to live in the midst of it."[57] But live he did, and there was nothing to do but continue forward. He was soon 150 yards from where the charge started, and "men were falling on every hand like autumn leaves in a storm."[58] The line surged forward, faltered under a blistering volley, reformed, and charged again into "an awful tornado of death missiles." Walker found himself going forward by stepping on and over the bodies of dead and wounded soldiers. Looking down at this pontoon of human lives, he noticed blood coming from his left shoe. He was unaware until that moment that a minnie ball had passed through his left thigh. Still he pressed onward. Then a second bullet struck his right knee. Seventeen-year-old Walker Freeman dropped to the ground.[59]

Still conscious despite his wounds, Freeman was able to observe the line continue forward. Then, slowly, the distant line grew larger as it came closer to him. The army was falling back to the position from which it had launched the attack. The withdrawing troops had scant time to retrieve the wounded and, for the second time in a month, Walker Freeman faced the distinct possibility of being taken prisoner. Then he saw a friend, Jim Hopkins, and his yell pierced the air above the cries of the wounded and the dying.

"Jim! Are you going to leave me here?"[60]

"The" Freeman opened her newspaper to read the casualty list from the Battle of Seven Pines. There she saw "W. Freeman, 4th Artillery, killed." She was certain as an ambulance approached the farm that it carried the body of her dead son. But it was Washington Freeman who died at Seven Pines, and the ambulance carried home the very much alive Walker Freeman to recover from his wounds.[61] His friend had rescued him from the battlefield, and his wounds had been successfully treated in Richmond. He was weak and on crutches, but he was safe and home. "It was," he said, "heaven on earth."[62]

The months of recovery passed "swiftly and pleasantly," but not without their own difficulties. Walker's brother Gustavus died in July of typhoid, and the fever attacked the weakened Walker. Again displaying his physical resilience, and with the faithful "The" at his side, he survived typhoid and made preparations to leave home and rejoin his company. The year had left its mark—both physically and emotionally. His brother's death, his wounding, his battle with mumps and typhoid, "and the promise now of a long conflict with the enemies of our country" shaped the man who mounted his horse on New Year's Day, 1863, and started over snow-covered ground to rejoin the war.[63]

The Piedmont Artillery was now part of the Thirty-Fourth Virginia, the brigade of general, and former Virginia governor, Henry A. Wise. When Freeman arrived at the camp near Chafin's Farm outside of Richmond, he was appointed a courier for General Wise. The summer of 1863 was one of recovery and restoration for Walker, even while it was one of destruction and desolation for the Confederacy. He regained his health and enjoyed the camp with its "great brigade drills, shade and rest, with a good surrounding country to forage."[64] He observed "great revivals of religion" throughout the camps, though his Baptist faith, tested through almost two years of war, needed no revival. In September, Wise's brigade was ordered south to Charleston, South Carolina, to assist in Gen. P. G. T. Beauregard's defense of that city. The Federal Army withdrew by the time the Virginians arrived on the scene, so much of their time that fall was spent marching and countermarching in pursuit of the enemy. Vigilance turned quickly to routine, and Walker Freeman passed an uneventful winter.[65] The monotony was broken in the spring of 1864 with an order to move back to Virginia. This time, the men were told, their march would not be in vain. They were heading north to halt the advance of "the much hated" Union general Ben Butler.[66] Even as they marched, however, the stage was being set for a far greater fight than one against "Beast" Butler.

After battling Robert E. Lee across the face of central Virginia, Ulysses Grant's Federal juggernaut shifted its focus from Richmond and hurled itself toward Petersburg, Virginia. With precious few troops defending the approach to the city, Beauregard stripped his lines wherever possible and hurried his men into battle. When Walker Freeman arrived from South Carolina, there was no time for rest after the march. He immediately faced shot and shell. Could it have been only two years beyond the day of his wounding at Seven Pines? Now, as he assessed the surrounding situation, Walker saw far fewer men and only three pieces of artillery aiding his portion of the line in this desperate fight. The battle raged all afternoon until it set with the evening sun. "It was," Walker wrote, "one of the greatest battles for length of time and hard fighting I have ever witnessed."[67] The silence over the combat zone did not signal rest for the weary combatants. All night the Confederates dug trenches and improved existing lines. With the sun of June 16 came the first volley from the Federal lines.

Walker spent another day "fighting, digging, sweating and starving."[68] Now fresh seasoned troops—Winfield Scott Hancock's men—moved in opposite the ragged Confederates. The dead filled in trenches, and smoke hung over the field, but the line held. "If there ever was a place on earth that looked like the infernal region," Walker wrote, "this was the place."[69]

Assault after assault finally forced the Confederates back. Again they dug in—using bayonets and tin cups to move the dirt. Night passed with no sleep or food. Then as dawn broke on June 18, Walker saw through bleary eyes the glint of bayonets in the distance—reinforcements had arrived. He extracted himself from his dugout and moved to the rear. As he drifted off into an exhausted sleep, the final death struggle of the Confederacy, the Siege of Petersburg, began.[70]

After the seemingly relentless onslaught, a dreadful calm descended as the siege settled in. June passed into July and Walker Freeman became accustomed to a daily ritual of watching, waiting, and avoiding sniper shots. The trenches that now housed the hopes of the Confederacy were deep enough for a man to stand upright without his head emerging above the crest of the parapet. Eighteen inches from the ground was a step upon which soldiers could stand and fire. There was little water, few rations, and a nightly artillery duel. Now the torridly hot days also brought anxious rumors about Federal miners tunneling somewhere beneath Confederate lines.[71]

Shortly before dawn on July 30, 1864, Freeman was on watch on the parapet when the rumors took on life. A spectacular explosion under the center of the Confederate line shattered the morning's uneasy calm. Men and weapons were hurled through the air as eight thousand pounds of powder were detonated in an underground tunnel. Through the smoke and settling debris, Union troops moved forward to the attack. Their goal was to break the stalemate with a lighting strike. Their object was the newly created cavity, 170 feet long, 60 feet wide, and 30 feet deep. At first, the Union plan proceeded as designed. Then, as blue-clad troops entered the crater, the attack disintegrated as soldiers milled around gazing at the man-made canyon. Walker was moved to the rear of the crater to hold off the Federals until troops under Gen. William Mahone arrived to retake the captured works. By 1:00 P.M., the battle was over, and the uneasy silence returned.[72]

"Rations were continually getting smaller," Walker noted. "They now reached the bottom . . . (with) about an ounce of renoid unsmoked bacon and a very small allowance of cold corn pone."[73] The diseases of the trenches sought to do what Federal snipers did not. Walker was struck by malaria, its fever coming on in waves, then dissipating before its inevitable return. Despite his illness, he always answered duty call and was sufficiently well to take advantage of a pass into Petersburg. As he walked down the road, he recognized an unmistakable figure—Gen. Robert E. Lee.

> He was riding Traveler when we met him on the Baxter Road going towards the trenches. There were two of us in company. When he met us, he drew rein and asked how we were getting on in the trenches. He was cordial in his greeting and remarked that he hoped we were not suffering severe discomforts.[74]

Though shivering with malaria, Walker nonetheless assured Lee that he was "fit as a fiddle."[75]

The inevitable end of the siege occurred on April 2, 1865. Lee pulled his army out of the trenches and headed west toward Farmville. "We moved through the mud," Walker said, "more dead than alive."[76] During a brief skirmish with Union forces, he found himself standing close to General Lee. Walker searched the general's face for a sign of excitement or worry, but saw none. He did note that Lee was careful not to "ride over or up against" any of his exhausted men.[77] On April 8, with no food to cook or tents to pitch, the men rested in sight of the village at Appomattox Court House. Walker stood on the hill and looked out after dark. To the west, south, and east, Federal campfires lit the night. The thought came to him that "maybe even General Lee couldn't get out of that trap."[78] Lee would make one attempt to escape. There would be one more charge. Walker would be in the final desperate thrust to break through. He and his companions formed battle lines and moved forward. Yet almost as quickly as it began, "the firing ceased."[79] This silence bespoke something ominous and, in a moment, the word spread through the lines: General Lee had surrendered.

"Gloom, disappointment, sadness and sorrow" settled on Walker and his comrades. Years later, he would summarize his feelings as he stacked arms at Appomattox Court House.

> God in His mercy and boundless grace, gives us in times of deepest sorrow and distress, something always to be thankful for. The silver lining to the dark cloud that enveloped us all, was that we could now go home. "Home," that sweet word! Though we had been for four long years passing through the storms of strife and turmoil, the fires of sanguinary battles, the lonely nights on the

picket post, hearing the mournful cry of the wounded and dying, the word "home" had always been in our thoughts and had lost none of its preciousness.[80]

Walker Freeman went home. If he took self-inventory as he trudged along the westward path, his sadness at the defeat of the Confederacy was balanced by the satisfaction of what he had gained in experience. He was twenty-two years old, a twice-wounded veteran who had survived the entire war while fighting in major theaters. He was—despite the horrors of months of trench warfare—in good health and had developed a self-confidence he had previously not known. "I had learned the habit of promptness in acknowledging responsibility," he wrote, "and had been trained to respond without hesitation or mental reservation to the call of duty." He kept walking until, at length, he saw the blues and greens of the mountains of home—unaltered in their majesty even as the lives living in its shadow were forever changed. Duty now made a new demand of Walker Freeman. With his father, half-brother, and older brother dead, he was head of the Freeman family. His was the task of rebuilding not only his own life, but also that of his family.[81]

His arrival met with an auspicious start. His father's old servant, "Uncle Billy," had prepared plant beds for a tobacco crop. Seizing this opportunity, Freeman returned to the hard farm work of his youth, planting wheat, growing tobacco, and acquiring what livestock he could obtain. The first year was challenging. "Raising tobacco," Walker would later say, "is the hardest way in the world to make a living."[82] The tobacco grew that first year, and the family survived. The second year saw drought, but by the end of the third year, the farm was sufficient for the needs of the family.[83] With his family as secure as the times and nature would allow, Walker decided to try a new direction for himself. Turning his share of the farm over to his mother and family, the farm boy left the land to try his hand at business.

Dr. A. S. Thomson was a local physician who also ran a large dry goods store. Walker approached him with the idea that the two form a mercantile business. Thomson agreed, but made it clear that, due to his medical practice, the management of the venture would be Walker's responsibility. No stranger to either work or responsibility, Walker accepted the partnership terms.[84]

The Virginia in which Walker Freeman's business opened was now called "Military District No. One." Towns were garrisoned by detachments of Federal soldiers, and the commanding officers ruled with martial law authority. Most Confederate veterans were unable to vote due to the "iron clad oath" that required them to swear they had fought against the Union under duress. In addition to formal military rule, Walker observed "carpet baggers and scalawags who had come down like a swarm of vultures to pillage and rob the people."[85] It was apparent that the policy of the Federal government was to convert the South into little more than an agricultural colony for the North. With the political situation so situated, Walker turned his attention to economic recovery and, by 1868, his mercantile partnership was prospering.

Like his father before him, Walker assumed a leadership role in the community. To supplement his income, he secured an appointment as a part-time constable—one of the few law enforcement jobs available to Confederate veterans.[86] He was still an active member of Mt. Hermon Church, where he taught in the Sunday School and served as clerk. At twenty-five years of age, he was in many ways the man he would permanently be: systematic, thrifty, optimistic, and religious.[87] In spite of his limited education, he was financially successful and, in those days of hardship throughout the South, that condition did not go unnoticed. In December 1869 he received an offer from a large wholesale grocery house in Lynchburg, Virginia. Seeing opportunity again presenting itself, he accepted the offer, bade a reluctant farewell to Bedford County, and moved the short distance to Lynchburg.[88]

The new position, Walker wrote, "meant plenty of work and opportunity to climb."[89] He became the firm's leading salesman within one year and was appointed managing salesman—with a corresponding salary increase—in 1871. As he had done all his life, he linked financial advancement with community activity. He joined the First Baptist Church of Lynchburg where he would serve as a deacon and superintendent of Sunday School. He was a city alderman, acted as a police justice, and was instrumental in the organization of a YMCA.[90] It was not surprising that such a successful and eligible bachelor should attract his share of romances. He seems to have been engaged on at least three occasions, "once as the unfortunate result of some joke; again with a half-heart, and once in earnest ere he met mother."[91] One day in early 1872, his roving eye caught the figure of one Miss Bettie Allen Hamner. "She was extremely handsome," Walker remembered, "tall and of faultless figure, with a beaming face, [and] beautiful countenance like an angel."[92] The nineteen-year-old Bettie had come into Walker's store, accompanied by another member of First Baptist, to solicit money for a church event. By his account, and that of family tradition, Walker stumbled through the conversation, gave a contribution, and, as Bettie left the store, remarked to an associate: "I intend to marry that girl if she will have me."[93]

The object of such ardent fervor was the only daughter of James S. Hamner, a farmer and country merchant, and his wife Mary Chambers Hamner. Bettie had been born and reared in Appomattox—indeed she was living four miles away from the surrender site when Walker laid down his arms—and was descended from several well-established Virginia families.[94] As in the case of her admirer, Bettie was something of a flirt and was known to have received eighteen gentlemen callers on a single Sunday afternoon.[95] At least once she was allegedly threatened with a breach of promise suit, but her flirting seems to have been of a teasing harmless nature as no scandal attached to her reputation. "She never wrote a love-letter ere she was married," her son Douglas remembered, and "never wrote to a young man but that her mother read the letter."[96]

Walker moved systematically toward his goal of capturing Bettie Hamner's heart. The Sunday following their introduction, he approached her at church and asked to walk her home. She accepted, and the courtship began in earnest.[97] The two appeared in a church play together, and Walker became a frequent visitor to the Hamner home throughout the spring of 1872.[98] When the Hamners decided to take in a boarder, Walker promptly moved in. His proximity apparently did not scare off Bettie and, after a few months, he proposed, and she accepted.[99]

Success had crowned every effort Walker Freeman had made since the war. The story sounds almost too trite to be true, but his success came as a result of hard work and single-minded determination. Now, facing marriage in a few months, he decided to strike out again for economic advancement. He established his own wholesale house under the name "Freeman & Steptoe" in the fall of 1873. "Our business," he noted, "succeeded very well."[100] Despite this optimistic report, some evidence suggests that, for the first time in his life, Walker experienced a slight business downturn. The primary reason was a false prosperity resulting from the inflated price of tobacco after the war. A more pernicious, but unconfirmed, explanation is traced to the actions of one of Walker's partners in endorsing notes in the firm's name for his own ill-fated land speculations.[101] Whatever the actual status of the company, Walker was his usual optimistic self as 1874 dawned. The main event of his year occurred when he and Bettie married on January 8, 1874. "The Baptist

Church was crowded yesterday afternoon," the *Lynchburg Virginian* reported, as the "interested audience" witnessed the marriage of the "popular young Main Street merchant" to his "beautiful and attractive" bride.[102] On the way to the church, the "beautiful and attractive" Bettie had allowed herself one final act of unwed flirtation. Passing the store of a former suitor, she leaned out of her carriage window, waved a handkerchief, and sweetly chirped "good-bye."[103]

The newlyweds set up their home in the City Hotel in Lynchburg. In September 1874, Bettie gave birth to their first child, a boy originally named John Hamner Garland and later shortened to Hamner Garland. A second boy, Walker Burford, Jr., was born about a year later in October 1875.[104] As the most prosperous and prominent member of the Freeman/Hamner family, Walker found himself tasked with providing for the "poor kin" of the family.[105] While the Freeman side of the family accepted no more than an occasional night at Walker's home, the Hamners were delighted to partake of Walker's bounty—and to do so with increasing frequency. One family member even took to having his bills forwarded to Walker for payment.[106] If Walker Freeman objected to providing this extensive family security, no comments of his have survived. He is known to have made it clear that no alcohol would be consumed in his home during any of these consanguineous visits.[107]

In 1876, Freeman & Steptoe expanded by buying out an older firm and taking on another partner. With the end of the Reconstruction era, Freeman ran for justice of the peace and was easily elected.[108] His new partnership prospered until the parties amicably dissolved it in 1880. Having made a career in the wholesale business, Walker now turned to retail, which he believed would show a wider margin of profit.[109] Shortly after opening the new store, Walker added a shoe department that was soon "paying nicely."[110] His family continued to expand with his business. In 1881, Bettie gave birth to their third son, Allen Weir Freeman, in the family's new home at 416 Main Street in Lynchburg. Walker had moved his family into the two-story brick house in 1879. Located toward the western end of Main Street, it was only a short distance from a steep bluff leading down to Blackwater Creek. The newly laid Belgian blocks on the street in front of the house bespoke of the progress of both the town and its residents.[111] It was in this comfortable house, on May 16, 1886, that Bettie delivered her fourth—and final—child. Another boy, he was named Douglas Southall Freeman.

Walker Burford Freeman, c. 1879. (Image courtesy of Mary Tyler McClenahan.)

CHAPTER 2

"Heroes Held First Place"

Walker Jr., Hamner, and Allen Freeman were in Sunday School at the First Baptist Church in Lynchburg on the morning their new brother was born. Allen's recollections provide the only surviving description of the event. "The sight of the new member of the family," Allen recalled, "aroused no great enthusiasm in the three little boys who stood around him."[1] Babies "were no rarity" in the growing community, and this particular "red-faced youngster" sparked a resigned concern in Allen. "With two older brothers" he had "already too often to give way to them because they were older." Now he "would have to give way to an infant brother because he was younger."[2] There seemed to be, the youngster glumly concluded, "no privileges attaching to the one in between."

As the newborn lay in a roll of blankets in his mother's room, Bettie Freeman had already made her mind up as to his future.[3] The former flirt of Bedford County had, in marriage and maturity, developed into a deeply religious woman. During her pregnancy with Douglas, she attended a revival meeting conducted by the famous evangelist Dwight L. Moody. Her "condition" required that special arrangements be made so she could sit unobserved in a box at the rear of the theater.[4] Stirred by Moody's eloquence, and prompted by her own beliefs, she resolved that the child she was carrying would become a minister of the gospel.[5] She confided her dream to the family housekeeper "Aunt Mary" Harrison, a former slave in the Hamner household who had remained with Bettie after the war. As religious as her mistress, "Aunt Mary" had also attended the Moody revival and became a willing collaborator in the plan for Douglas's future.[6] Whether Walker Freeman knew of his wife's plan for their son is unknown. In 1886, he was concerned about only one career—his own.

For the first time in his life, Walker was experiencing serious business problems. The success of the dual business he had opened—a dry goods store with a shoe department—began to slow. Upon examination of the

33

business records, he discovered the dry goods store was losing money while the shoe business was prospering.[7] Displaying the same aggressive ingenuity that marked his steady rise in business, Walker decided to sell the dry goods store and operate only a shoe store. He had no difficulty finding a purchaser for the store and, with that contingency met, he rented new business space and placed an order for a sizable stock of shoes.[8] At this point, disaster ensued. The purchaser of the dry goods business could not complete the settlement of the sale, leaving Walker with no money to cover his new business expenses. What happened to the purchaser of the store is unclear. Walker recounted in his *Memoirs* that "the men who bought me out fell down in their plan to raise the cash payment (no fault of their own), and left me suspended in the air."[9] Allen Freeman remembered that the purchaser "suffered such losses" from the dry goods business "that he could not pay for it."[10] Whatever the reason—lack of funds prior to settlement or loses incurred in operating the business that prevented performance—Walker was unable to pay for his shoe order and the expenses of his new business. He was financially wiped out.[11]

Walker's predicament mirrored the lot of many Confederate veterans building new lives in the wake of the war. Their lives, Douglas Freeman would write, consisted "of burned homes and fenceless farms, of a planting season without teams, or of a hungry urban family and no wages with which to feed wife and children."[12] Yet present also with many of those veterans was the indomitable spirit of Lee and of the four-year struggle in which they had fought. Having faced destitution, starvation, disaster, and despair, new assaults no longer held the fear of finality. The Confederate veteran simply started again. Walker Freeman had walked from Appomattox Court House to his father's farm in Bedford County to begin again. Now, twenty-one years later, he would walk away from business failure to begin again.

Making an assignment to his creditors, Walker found work as a bookkeeper with a wholesale shoe company.[13] He moved his family from their comfortable home on Main Street to board with a widowed friend on Harrison Street. Hard work, tough choices, and family economy soon found their reward. Walker's business reputation and community standing remained high and, in February 1887, the New York Life Insurance Company offered him an agency.[14] Although inexperienced in the particulars of the insurance business, Walker knew he would bring to the job extensive sales experience and a reputation in the community that would provide a strong basis for the new venture. He accepted the offer and set to work. It did not take long before Walker reported the agency "was a success from the start beyond my expectations."[15] Within one year of accepting the agency, he paid all his debts from the failed dry goods sale and moved his family back to Main Street, across from the family's previous residence.[16] New York Life was pleased with his success and elevated him to general agent in 1888. Walker responded with a record-setting year—writing almost $500,000 of insurance.[17] It was quite a turnaround in a little more than two years, and the experience left its mark. The events of 1886-88 formed almost as great an influence on Walker Freeman and his youngest son as did the War Between the States. Almost sixty-five years later, Douglas Freeman would still point with pride to his father's recovery from economic disaster. "Any man is apt to lose his way," he wrote of those days. "The test of his manhood and of his intelligence is to find a new way."[18]

The financial recovery of 1887 for the Freeman family was nearly offset by personal tragedy. Douglas, just past his first birthday, was struck with an ailment dubbed "summer diarrhea."[19] When all attempted remedies failed to relieve his suffering, Bettie took the child to a relative's farm in Bedford where, it was hoped, the "pure air and fresh milk" would provide relief.[20] As the hot summer dragged on, Douglas showed no signs of improvement. Distraught over the failure of attempted cures and the tenacity of the illness, Bettie returned to Lynchburg and looked to the family physician, Dr. Thornhill, for treatment. In addition to doing all he could for Douglas, Dr. Thornhill called on the local fire department to come and drench the Freeman house with water from the city main.[21] Having done all that medicine could dictate or custom suggest, the family waited. After a few days back in his own bed, Douglas turned the corner, and the crisis passed.

Aside from the family's temporary financial upheaval and his illness, Douglas's early years in Lynchburg were idyllic in many ways. A "cherubic child" with long blond curls, he was sometimes clad in a "Lord Fauntleroy" suit with a plaid kilt, white shirt, and velvet jacket.[22] He was taught the faith of his family and learned of his father's exploits in the war. Bettie Freeman and Aunt Mary worked toward fulfilling the commitment they made at the Moody revival by teaching the young boy to deliver sermons. As early as four years of age, Douglas would mount a kitchen chair, Bible in hand, and declaim against the evils of alcohol and tobacco.[23] Douglas would recall that the sermons of old Virginia—on which his early efforts were no doubt modeled—were "terrible in length, and in context—theological, controversial, and, alas, dogmatic."[24]

Douglas Southall Freeman, c. 1888.
(Image courtesy of Mary Tyler McClenahan.)

Religion in the Freeman home included tolerance for the beliefs of others. One of Douglas's earliest and best friends was Elmer Nathan, a Jewish boy whose home abutted the Freeman house.[25] The two boys played together in their yards and at each other's homes. Douglas had already developed a serious observant nature, and nowhere was it more exhibited than in his interaction with Elmer Nathan and his family. Young as he was at the time, he appreciated what he saw as "the beauty" of "the Jewish character and faith."[26] He was moved by the "solidarity of Jewish home-life," the "parents' unwearied care of children," and the "children's respect of home."[27] All of these observations were formed by a boy not yet six years of age.

Not all of Douglas's remembrances of youth were as solemnly eloquent. Aunt Mary took Douglas on daily walks downtown, and part of the ritual involved Douglas staring into the office of the C&O Railroad at a model engine. The office manager noticed the young boy—and the object of his intense gaze—and gave the engine to Douglas shortly before Christmas 1891. Playing with his prized possession in the backyard of his home, Douglas was confronted by his brother Allen who advised that real engines were not shiny and gleaming, but black and smoky. Douglas agreed with his brother's critique and accepted his proffered remedy. Allen built a fire and held the engine over it to achieve the desired effect. Moments later, after summoning Bettie, a tearful Douglas watched a punished Allen polishing the ruined toy.[28]

Near the head of Main Street, two blocks from the Freeman home, lived "a glowering old man, fiercely chewing tobacco, who was notorious . . . for eating a bad boy every morning at breakfast": Confederate general Jubal A. Early.[29] General Lee's "bad old man," now approaching seventy-five years of age, was often seen hobbling down to the Arlington Hotel amid groups of respectful veterans and frightened boys.[30] His days as one of Lee's most able commanders long since gone, he had spent the post-war years as an unreconstructed writer of Confederate military history. Characterized by a "bitter tongue and rasping wit" during the war,[31] the passing years had not mellowed him. Once a building in which he maintained an office collapsed, and Early was buried beneath the debris. Local rescuers, including Walker Freeman, dug out the old general who surveyed the damage and snapped, "I didn't know there were that many bricks between me and hell."[32] Douglas heard and believed the stories of the general's malevolence and made it a point to sprint by the general's house in order to avoid capture.[33] The two never met.

While Douglas was running from Confederate generals, Walker faced another economic opportunity. New York Life asked him to relocate his growing insurance agency to Richmond. In addition to being more strategically located, Richmond offered the potential of more contacts and more clients.[34] Walker recalled his thoughts about this latest in a series of life-changing momentous decisions:

It was a great trial for us to leave the dear old city. It was here that I had found and married my wife, here that all of my children were born. I had a large acquaintance and knew almost everybody in the town . . . My business, social and church relations had been of the most pleasant nature.[35]

"But," Walker Freeman concluded, "business called." In April 1889, he established his Richmond office and, at the end of March 1892, he was ready to move his family to the Capital City.[36] "On to Richmond" had been the cry of the Union Army during the war. Now the phrase contained the hopes and dreams of the Freeman family as they set out eastward. Lynchburg and Bedford County had made their mark. "It was from this rugged terrain with its strong red soil," Allen Freeman wrote, "that [Walker] had drawn the strength of mind and body that had carried through the civil war, through the hardship of reconstruction, and of the economic chaos which had followed it."[37]

Moving day was an unforgettable one for Douglas. Dressed in his kilt, he accompanied his family to the train station where neighbors and kin were gathered to bid them farewell. While "wondering what it all meant," Douglas professed he was not "half sorry of the prospect which was before me."[38] The family boarded the train, and Bettie Freeman wept quietly until they crossed the "seven-mile" bridge. Once that river was crossed, Bettie symbolically crossed over to her new life and dried her tears.[39] The trip "was a delight" to Douglas who marveled at the James River and remained "big eyed" at each "new wonder" sighted during the day.[40] Ahead of him lay the biggest wonder of all—the city of Richmond.

Richmond in 1892, although twenty-seven years distant from the war, was still the emotional and commemorative capital of the Confederacy. The years of harsh reconstruction were over, and blue-clad troops were nowhere to be found. In the governor's chair sat Confederate veteran Philip McKinney—a large, burly figure who still limped when he walked due to a wound suffered at the battle of Brandy Station. McKinney was the fifth of seven consecutive Confederate veterans elected to the Virginia governorship. Political power reflected the symbolism of the time. "The greatest events in Richmond," Douglas Freeman would one day write, "were the funerals of military heroes, when torches burned at midnight and the Stonewall band came down from Staunton, and all the stalwarts of the city put on gray jackets again."[41] Next to funerals "the great days on the Richmond calendar were those of Confederate reunions . . . and of dedication of monuments."[42] Social etiquette dictated that "if a youngster . . . met a gentleman of appropriate age who had the unmistakable and ineradicable bearing of a former Confederate soldier, it always was proper to address him as Colonel, on the principle that if he had not attained that rank, he should have received it for valor."[43] Richmond was a city where "heroes held first place," and "lost causes and lost homes were daily in the news."[44]

Richmond had not only been the capital of the South, Richmond had been the South: the center of the Confederate nation's hopes.[45] In the aftermath of war, it was the center of the Confederate nation's memory. Heritage and history walked the streets in the form of veterans; shaped social, economic, and political policy; and glimmered from statues honoring spotless heroes. "It was much more a matter of parental duty," Douglas Freeman learned, "to see that a son knew the Southern estimates of casualties in the principal battles than that he remembered with precision the provoking difference between seven times eight and nine times six."[46] It was an inescapable tradition—not that anyone wished to escape it. Life was shaped by memory, and even as the metal industries were being rebuilt, and tobacco factories spurred vitalization and recovery, the economic engine carried with it the indelible stamp of the Confederate Tradition. "None can walk the old streets," Douglas Freeman wrote, "and not feel grateful that in that high tradition the humblest son of Richmond can spiritually keep the company of kings."[47]

It was in this city that Walker and Bettie Freeman and their four boys arrived in March 1892. The family lived in the "Imboden House" facing the state capitol building.[48] As soon as the family unpacked, Walker took Douglas across the street to the capitol grounds and to the equestrian statue of George Washington. "I had never seen such a horse," Douglas recalled, and the figures of Thomas Jefferson, Patrick Henry, and other patriots that surrounded Washington "looked monsters."[49] The next morning at breakfast, Douglas found "an orange, peeled, it seemed to me, in the most wonderful of ways." His introduction to Richmond had been one of wonder in every way.[50]

A little more than a year after arriving in Richmond, Walker took Douglas to the railroad station where a large crowd had gathered. The seven-year-old boy watched in breathless silence as a special L&N train pulled into the station. A hush came over the crowd as the coffin bearing the body of Confederate president Jefferson Davis was removed. Following his death in 1889, Davis had rested for three years in New Orleans; now he was returned to the city in which he had served as president to be interred in Hollywood Cemetery. A full-scale military funeral was given the Confederate president as he was laid to rest in an oval-shaped plot overlooking the James River.[51] Symbolism, heritage, and history had passed in front of Douglas.

Life in Richmond was good for the Freeman family. "W. B. Freeman Life Insurance" was firmly established, and the forty-nine-year-old Walker reached a level of financial stability and prosperity that would last for the remainder of his life. As he had always done, he involved himself in community activities, joining the Second Baptist Church and rising steadily through the ranks of the United Confederate Veterans, achieving the office of commander-in-chief in 1925.[52] During the family's first autumn in Richmond, six-year-old Douglas was enrolled in a preparatory school under the direction of Simonia "Miss Sye" Roberts.[53] "Miss Sye" practiced a "pedagogical methodology" which had the boys and girls of the class sit in opposite sides of the room with the teacher in the middle.[54] The boys were called "busters," the girls "pinkies," and a "stool of repentance" waited in the corner for any unruly student.[55] Little has survived about Douglas's time in "Miss Sye's" school. Family tradition holds that it was merely a place to receive some instruction until he was old enough to enter the premier Richmond school— McGuire's University School for Boys.[56]

On the northeast corner of Belvidere and Main Streets stood an undistinguished two-story brick building which housed, on its first floor, Chasie Trafieri's Bar, Proffitt's Market, and McClintock's Plumbing Shop.[57] The second floor served as the location of McGuire's University School. Unimpressive though its surroundings, the school was in no way ordinary. Its founder, John Peyton McGuire, the "Old Boss," was a graduate of the University of Virginia and trained as a high school instructor. During the Civil War, he joined the ranks as a private, but was soon assigned to the Confederate Naval School as an instructor. By war's end he was a lieutenant in the Confederate Navy. Five months after the surrender at Appomattox, John Peyton McGuire founded his school and, by teaching the sons of prominent Richmond families for the next forty years, "exerted an influence on the Commonwealth of Virginia hardly second to that of any man."[58] In 1894, McGuire's son, also named John Peyton McGuire, joined the school as a member of the faculty.[59] Both McGuires were active during Douglas Freeman's years there.

The curriculum that faced eight-year-old Douglas, when he and ninety-nine other boys entered McGuire's School for the 1892-93 session, was exacting and demanding. A flyer advertising the school outlined a rigorous first-year course of penmanship, geography, arithmetic, English, and Latin. Ahead of the McGuire student lay Thucydides, Euripides, Cicero,

Xenophon, and Homer. The school would offer "a strictly 'practical' education . . . if desired; but it [was] not recommended."[60] "Prominence in school," the boys were taught, "ought to be attainable only through hard work, tested scholarship, and high character."[61] The school's maxim, "Be Earnest, Work Hard and Speak the Truth," was to be the honest ambition of every boy.[62] Douglas enrolled in the Lower School—for ages five to eleven—where, along with academic and character training, he joined the Literary Society and received his first formal instruction in public speaking.[63]

The "Old Boss," John Peyton McGuire, "had for his guiding star the principle that nothing counted so much as character, and that honorable conduct was the *sina qua non* of a gentleman."[64] To that end, he gathered his boys together every Friday afternoon and told them anecdotes with moral applications from the life of General Lee.[65] While some boys encouraged him to continue talking about General Lee in order that they might avoid what they considered more practical work, Douglas was captivated by the stories.[66] McGuire's stories of Lee and the Confederacy did more than just impress Douglas; they confirmed the lessons he had learned at his father's knee. In his formative years of life, Douglas, who was already devoted to his father, came under the influence of another symbol of the Confederacy. All while living in Richmond. Sitting in a row of desks in front of a raised platform, listening to John Peyton McGuire apply the lessons of Lee's life to the present day, Douglas's future began to take shape.[67]

The younger McGuire, "Mr. John Peyton" to the boys, cut a more dashing figure. The students heard he had traveled as far as Panama and that he was descended from the Virginia Founding Father George Mason.[68] He was progressive in his view of educational instruction but as uncompromising as his father in "his adherence to the spiritual ideal of Virginia."[69] He excelled in the teaching of mathematics, French, and English, but his impact was felt most in introducing the boys to "the matchless glories of Shakespeare."[70] To Douglas he "represented everything that was finest in our old educational ideals and in the life of Virginia manhood."[71] "The 'things that are eternal'," he wrote, "always were to him the values of life most to be cherished and most to be inculcated."[72] The McGuire years were ones of growth and confirmation in Douglas, and he gave credit to his teacher. Thousands of boys, he wrote "Mr. John Peyton," will "rise up to call you blessed and benefactor."[73]

It was during these early school years that a writing by Douglas Freeman was first published. His literary effort, a letter to Santa Claus, was deemed worthy—despite its lack of punctuation—to appear on the pages of the December 23, 1894, issue of the *Richmond Dispatch*.

My dear Santa Claus:
I want so many things that I can't tell all but I will tell the good ones I want a football a gun a bysisle a lot of fire-works a lot of roman candles some sky-rockets and some pop crackers I am 8 years old Good by from

Douglas Freeman
No. 11 South 3rd Street.[74]

Religion continued to be a dominant influence in the Freeman home. Walker and Bettie Freeman taught their sons by example and expected them to follow the family faith. The Freemans regularly attended Second Baptist Church, and it was there, in 1896, that Douglas was baptized.[75] Walker and Bettie both taught Sunday School classes, something Douglas would do as he became older. The boys were excused from attending evening services, but playing sports on Sunday was strictly forbidden.[76] It was to be a quiet day of reflection, worship, and meditation.

Along with devotion to faith, the Freeman boys continued to learn tolerance from their parents. "Mother's religious belief was deep and real and was exhibited in everything she did or said," Allen remembered, "but she was not bigoted or intolerant. Her religion was her rule of life rather than the profession of a particular set of beliefs."[77] Walker's experiences in business and war brought him into contact with people of many faiths and produced in him the same attitude. Douglas's friendship with Elmer Nathan confirmed to him the teachings of his parents. He saw no conflict in being devout in his faith while recognizing and respecting different views. A lifelong hatred of bigotry and anti-Semitism was instilled in him from his youth. "No disgrace of our bewildered world gives me more mental anguish day by day," he wrote in 1938, "than the out-cropping of anti-Semitism."[78] In viewing the world around him, he lamented that "we meet hate with more hate, ignorance with prejudice, intolerance with bigotry."[79] Though these are the comments of a grown man, the sentiments that produced them were developed in the ten-year-old Douglas in the home of Walker and Bettie Freeman.

Nor was tolerant behavior to be limited to religious differences. The Freemans lived in a segregated Southern city. Though slavery had ended, social and economic conditions between the races had, in many respects, reverted to the *antebellum* era. Attitudes regarding racial differences were given credence from city hall to the local pulpit. Yet prejudice *de jure* was not necessarily the rule for the average white Southerner. In many instances "truces" developed between whites and blacks, and their lives mingled inside defined borders of conduct. Black servants were often considered family members, and the death of one was genuinely mourned. Walker recalled with sorrow the passing of "Uncle Billy," a family slave, whose "kindness, quiet modesty, transparent honesty, and fidelity to every duty, will ever be before me as an example worthy of emulation."[80] The means of societal advancement were recognized each by the other—the white man by money, education, and connections, the black man by his wits. To recognize this situation is not to confirm its legitimacy or romanticize its inequality, but to present an accurate picture of the society in which Douglas Freeman came of age. That society did not consist of rampant lynchings and masked Klan riders. It did consist of a paternalistic and condescending attitude toward black citizens, who could hardly be called citizens with no right to vote and restrictions on how far they could advance in the world. Douglas witnessed the actions of a father who exhibited a "love for and devotion to the Negro."[81] "I have always regarded slavery as a curse," Walker Freeman wrote, "and I bless the day when they were freed."[82] This attitude sprang not only from religious conviction, but also from the anti-slavery attitude of Walker's western Virginia. Throughout his life, Walker set the example for his family by doing "what he could to better the lot of the Negro."[83] For the time in which he lived, these actions could amount to little more than basic acts of common courtesy, but even those small acts influenced Douglas. Thus as he approached his teenage years, Douglas's character was being shaped by perceived contradictory forces: a devout Baptist faith, yet a tolerant attitude toward different sects; a devotion to the Confederacy and its heroes, yet a heart for justice among the races; a deep and permanent love of a Southern city, yet a disdain for its latent—and overt—prejudices. The coming years would forge these sentiments—as complex as the time in which they were developed—into the character of Douglas Southall Freeman.

The turn of the century saw fourteen-year-old Douglas grow into a handsome, serious-looking, lad. Gone were the blond curls of youth, a thin patch of brown hair—presaging future baldness—topped his head. His nose had been broken playing football at McGuire's, but the break did not disfigure a pleasant face with small, usually tightly pressed together, lips. His 1901 diary lists his weight as 133 pounds and his height slightly over five feet eight inches.[84] His eyes were already, as they

Douglas Southall Freeman, age twelve, 1898. (Image courtesy of Mary Tyler McClenahan.)

would remain, the distinctive characteristic of his appearance: They shone a brilliant blue-gray, and were as yet unadorned by glasses. Though he was his father's son in spirit and character, the Bettie Hamner strain showed from his features. At age ten, he advanced to McGuire's Upper School where Latin and Greek were added to the strenuous curriculum.[85] A popular boy, he ran track—a talent he attributed to his running past General Early's home[86]—and played football. He also paid increasing attention to the opposite sex. In May 1900, he prepared for a date "with my girl" to Jamestown. Showing meticulous care in planning the day, he wrote himself a memorandum.

(1) I shall fix my cuffs

(2) I shall choose a necktie

(3) I shall fix my shirt

(4) I shall wash all over

(5) I shall take care to wash my hands that I may get the marks off

(6) I shall choose a hat

(7) I shall black my shoes

(8) get out my shirt

(9) put tickets and wherewithal in my pocket

(10) I go to bed.[87]

These teenage years saw Douglas following Walker as a church leader, much to the delight, one can assume, of Bettie. His diary for June 1901—written at the age of fifteen—indicates he was to "preach" on June 14. The text was John 15:13: "Greater love hath no man than this, that a man lay down his life for his friends."[88] Douglas noted in his diary that he had "preached" on the scheduled date but gave no details. At sixteen he started a Sunday School class and wrote friends to encourage a regular attendance of "twenty-five boys in class every Sunday."[89] Assuring them that he would teach the class, he implored his friends not to "fail me now for I am counting on you."[90]

The preparatory work at McGuire's School was designed to gain the students admission to the University of Virginia. The textbooks and examination questions for senior classes were those used at UVA.[91] The school conceded that "boys prepared for the University of Virginia are, of course, ready to enter any other academic institution."[92] That second option would be the one Douglas elected. For although Walker Freeman's business success enabled him to provide for his family, it was not quite sufficient to support a son away at college. Douglas prepared to enter Richmond College in the fall of 1901.

The history of Richmond College was deeply entwined with that of the Virginia Baptist church. In 1832 the Virginia Baptist Education Society founded the Virginia Baptist Seminary to train young men for the work of the ministry. By 1840, the school claimed seventy-five enrollees, some of whom were not ministerial students. The school thus sought a new charter from the Virginia legislature and, on March 4, 1840, Richmond College was established. Over the next few years, the school's enrollment and endowment increased, and the first bachelor's degree was conferred in 1849. The Civil War disrupted the school's steady growth, but ninety students enrolled in the wake of war in 1866, and the college set about rebuilding itself. The task proved extremely difficult and, by 1894, Richmond College teetered on the brink of financial collapse. Staffed by only nine faculty members—who governed the school without a president—and hampered by annual income of only $30,000, the college was gripped, its financial secretary reported, by "uncertainty, anxiety, unrest, and paralysis."[93] It was in such a state that the college turned to a twenty-seven-year-old professor of modern languages, Dr. Frederic William Boatwright, to serve as president. Thus began one of the most remarkable stories in American academia as Boatwright, during his fifty-one-year tenure as president, would save the fledgling college and start it on the path to becoming one of the South's finest universities. For now, though, that record was little more than a vision, and Boatwright contended with critics of his youth by growing a beard.[94] On September 16, 1901, Douglas looked ahead to the biggest event of his fifteen years and wrote in his diary: "Just think, College Thursday! Get ready."[95]

"The session of 1901-02 at Richmond College opened with flattering prospects on the 19th of September," the college magazine reported.[96] The *Messenger* went on to detail the reception held for new students with exercises in the chapel of the local YMCA. Presiding over the welcoming ceremonies was the young president, F. W. Boatwright, and Douglas Freeman was in attendance.[97]

Douglas had decided to complete his course of undergraduate study in three years, so he threw himself fully into the activities of a young collegian. He became the campus correspondent for the *Richmond News* and pledged the Phi Gamma Delta fraternity.[98] He joined the staff of *The Messenger*, the campus literary magazine, and made his first attempts at poetry. From his verse to "Madeline" came the line "at thy sobs, the skies incline. And thy tears are honeyed brine, Madeline!"[99] A serious and studious young man, Douglas gave every indication of heading toward the life of ministry his mother wished for him. College, though, offered new vistas of opportunity and experience, and from an unexpected quarter came a new pull on his future.

The Richmond College Dramatic Club announced to the college community that it would present Augustus Thomas's play *Alabama*.[100] The play told the story of "an Alabama blossom" named Cary Preston and contained a cast of characters consisting of "a relic of the Confederacy," "a northern capitalist," and "a widow who thinks twice."[101] Douglas was given top billing in the cast list for the role of "Colonel

Preston, an old planter." When the four-act play was presented, Allen
Freeman found that Douglas, "still in his teens, was really convincing as
the old man."[102] Douglas left the stage with stars in his eyes. He knew he
had done well in the play, and the exhilaration of performing stole over
him. He immediately set about arranging a repeat performance. He persuaded the Director of Summer School for Teachers at the University of
Virginia to grant permission to present the play at that campus. The performance was offered for a "special admittance price" of ten cents, and
Douglas took the stage in front of a good-sized audience to reprise his
role as Colonel Preston. "Ferocious mosquitoes" tormented both actors
and audience, but the second performance was as successful as the first
one. Douglas's love for the theater was deepened.[103] To that love, he now
added purpose. He would leave college and join a traveling stock company. Theater would be his career.[104]

Such a drastic decision on the part of a young man previously not
inclined to such dramatic shifts in attitude is shocking, even if, in reality, the desire was only a youthful fancy. He had moved through life at a
steady pace, inclined, perhaps, to the ministry as his mother wished.
Now, sparked by one successful show, came this decision to embark on
a drastically different life path. History does not reveal the depth of
Douglas's sincerity in planning to leave college, and Allen alone relates
the tale of his brother's thespian leanings.[105] One can only speculate how
the business-like Walker and the devout Bettie would have received this
news from their son. All were to be spared the consequences of this decision. The stock company was unable to raise sufficient funds to go on
the road, and Douglas reluctantly contented himself with acting in college for the balance of his school years. Allen Freeman remained convinced that if the traveling troupe had been able to finance its venture,
Douglas would have left college for a "life on the boards."[106]

Denied a life as a professional actor, Douglas still enthusiastically
continued his theater work. His abilities as a writer and producer were
put to the test during his senior year. During a visit to the Richmond
Female Institute—the forerunner of the University of Richmond's
Westhampton College for Women—a drama teacher asked Douglas if
he knew of a play with a number of female roles. Douglas vividly
described such a play, titled *When the Bugle Sounds*, to the impressed
teacher. She asked for a copy of the play in order that it could be produced. Upon leaving the institute Douglas confided the truth to a
shocked colleague: The play did not exist; he would have to write it.[107]
Enlisting the support of his brother Allen, Douglas spent the Christmas

holiday crafting together the story of a Revolutionary War Navy captain and his old sailor servant, while ensuring a sufficient number of female roles. Allen found the completed project "actually playable,"[108] and the play was staged to the delight of the Richmond Female Institute. The climatic scene would have the wounded captain—played by Douglas— raise himself on his elbow and deliver some stirring patriotic words. The emotional solemnity of the climatic scene was lost, however, when another cast member, also playing a dying soldier, fell across the prone Douglas.

"Get off me, you fool," Douglas said in a stage whisper heard throughout the theater.

"I can't, you damn fool," came the response, "I'm dead."

The audience's laughter continued during Douglas's stirring final words and the curtain came down on the first—and only—performance of the play.[109] "There was," Allen Freeman remembered, "no active demand for it to be repeated."[110]

Acting had greatly influenced Douglas and almost taken him in an unforeseen direction. During his second year at Richmond College, he would meet with another influence, greater than that of the theater, indeed "one of the most profound influences" of his life: Professor of History Samuel Chiles Mitchell.[111]

S. C. Mitchell "was born on the flight." Union forces had commandeered his parents' home in Memphis, Tennessee, so the expectant Mrs. Mitchell fled to Coffeeville, Mississippi. It was there that she delivered her son Samuel on December 24, 1864.[112] The postwar years were difficult ones for the family, and Samuel found himself at age ten working in a stationery store in Galveston, Texas. From that distant outpost he began an improbable journey that carried him—entirely by his own thrift and ingenuity—to Georgetown College in Kentucky where he received his Master of Arts degree in 1888. It was in Kentucky that he also became an ordained Baptist minister and married the daughter of a prominent seminary leader.[113] After teaching history and Greek for seven years at Mississippi and Georgetown Colleges, he was invited by President Boatwright to join the Richmond College faculty as Professor of Latin Language and Literature. He arrived in Richmond in the fall of 1895.[114]

No Department of History existed at Richmond College during Mitchell's first years there. He therefore began an informal, non-credit, history course in conjunction with his Latin class. From this class grew efforts to establish history as an independent discipline at Richmond College. By 1901, Mitchell was acknowledged as "Acting Professor of

History and Political Science" and, the next year, the "School of History" was formally established.[115] Mitchell's reputation and identification with the History Department grew so great that Richmond students were known to remark that "one does not take history, one takes Mitchell."[116] Douglas Freeman soon entered the class of "the man who above all others" would influence his intellectual development.[117]

It was inevitable that Douglas would be drawn to S. C. Mitchell. Mitchell, like Walker Freeman, had come out of a post-war experience of suffering and deprivation to build a successful new life. He was a devout Baptist and such an admirer of General Lee that he was often overcome with emotion when he delivered an address about the general.[118] He was a dedicated and sacrificial worker who repeatedly reminded his students that "the man who wins is the man who hangs on just five minutes longer after everyone else has quit."[119]

The resemblance to Walker did not end there. Mitchell held an outspoken progressive philosophy regarding politics. In his early days as a professor at Mississippi College, he told his students that "the cheeks of the children of the South would yet burn with shame at the recollection of human bondage."[120] In 1899, in the wake of a dual lynching of a black and white man in Emporia, Virginia, Mitchell took to the pulpit of Second Baptist Church and laid the blame at the feet of Virginia governor J. Hoge Tyler. "The Governor took water and washed his hands," Mitchell thundered with biblical analogy, "saying 'I am innocent of the blood of this just man.'"[121] In S. C. Mitchell—as in Walker and Douglas Freeman—respect for General Lee and devotion to the Confederate cause did not equate to racial prejudice. "Slavery had but one iron law: Thou shalt not think," Mitchell wrote, "and the effects of this were pervasive long after it was officially done away with."[122] Still, Mitchell loved both the old and new Virginia. He praised the "Virginia strain" that produced "the temper of the soul" and "the very stuff out of which to make men of character and culture."[123] Where the "strain" bred a fixation on things past, Mitchell would curtly comment that he "prayed that the Lord Almighty in His providence would rain paint on Virginia for two weeks."[124]

While confirming what Douglas had learned from his family and upbringing, Mitchell also opened a new world to the young student. Douglas "sat breathless at his feet" and marveled at his teacher's historical judgments, passion for accuracy, and vigorous intellect.[125] In Mitchell's classroom, he learned "faith in the out-working of man's destiny."[126] The theater had tempted him, but sitting in S. C. Mitchell's class a new reality grew in Douglas Freeman: the "avocation of historical writing."[127]

Mitchell noticed the serious boy sitting there drinking in his words. "From the day that we became associated in Richmond College," he wrote, "I have been bound in affection to him as a brother."[128] His "initiative and mental vigor" so impressed Mitchell that thirty years later he would be able to point to the spot in class where Douglas sat.[129] For Douglas the intellectual experience approached spiritual proportions, and he likened his hours with Mitchell to "the words of the bewildered Simon on the mountain top, Master, it was good for us to be there!"[130]

Douglas's horizons were not expanding solely in S. C. Mitchell's class. Apart from his writing for the *Messenger* and the *Richmond News*, he wrote plays, poems, and a historical novel since lost to history.[131] "The Adventures of a Frat-Pin" told the story of a young college student through the eyes of his fraternity pin; "Caput Primum," the story of an early-American settler in the Roanoke Island expedition; and "The Kiss," an unfinished story about the title subject.[132] Other titles included "Being in the Spirit," "De Ole Plantation," "Nervousness in Children," "For Her Sake," "Lines Written on a Rainy Day," and "The Two Daisies." Many of these tales were love stories. Indeed, romance was creeping more and more into Douglas's writings because it was becoming more a part of his life.[133] "Again the question," he wrote in his diary, "do I love Madge? Yes, I believe I do, at least at times."[134] He set down the story of one of his romances in a story titled "One Week" about a girl "too heavenly to be long of earthly life."[135]

Her complexion is soft, unusually soft and fresh, rather dark, I suppose, but very delicate. The least excitement flushes it. The hair is dark, full black, in fact . . . and the eyes—what color are they? Hazel, I suppose the world would call them, but when I look into them, can only call them heavenly.[136]

On one occasion, the girl adjusted her skirt in Douglas's presence, and he stole a glance at her leg "for only a second, as it was too sacred for my gaze."[137] The captivated suitor seized an opportunity to kiss her for the first time during a huckleberry-picking outing. He did so "softly, calmly, just as I would kiss my mother."

From that moment, I utter no falsehood when I say that there entered a new light into my life. My love for her became instantly purified . . . but how strange it was that by that holy kiss—for such it was—my opinion of her was raised one hundred percent. I know it is foolish to relate even in my own memoirs which none will see ever, but I almost cried as I kissed her. Then was her childish face turned to me—full of gentle light—and I—I was receiving the most magnificent compliment of my life. This pure noble girl was trusting me, fully, completely.[138]

Douglas spent the next day in a "trance." At their next meeting, on a Sunday afternoon, he ventured another kiss. "'Douglas,' she said, 'please don't do that again.'"[139] With that line, the story—and, one can conclude, the relationship—came to an end. "What can be more interesting to watch," Douglas wrote in another essay, "than the awakening of love in a youthful heart?"[140]

In addition to his emotional and intellectual growth, Douglas concentrated on his spiritual life. "The religion of Jesus Christ," he wrote during his college days, "is primarily a religion of young men."[141] Elaborating on the application of faith to the life of a college student, he wrote:

Who knows the essential difference between Episcopalian and Presbyterian—who cares? But religion, manliness—the two are Brothers—is based on something deeper than dogma. They go back to the fundamental man—to man's better man—and there is where the college man's religion comes in. And, after all, Religion is based on no elaborate rules; it was made for man, not for gods. Religion calls for heart, not form; for belief, not cant. The great laws of religion—of all religions—is unselfishness, and unselfishness is the ideal of every true man's heart.[142]

"A hundred years will see a crisis," Douglas judged, "belief pitted against blasphemy, spirit against skepticism. Oh, for men who believe, and are not ashamed of this belief!"[143] To build such men, Douglas taught a Sunday School class at Second Baptist and pushed for the creation of a "boys' society" to reach out to area young men.[144] It was this dedication to faith that took him to Northfield, Massachusetts, in late June 1902 to attend a Christian summer conference for young men. Allen Freeman had attended the conference the year before and was so affected by it that he was considering entering the missionary field. The trip turned out to be a fateful one for Douglas, but in an unexpected way. He was attacked by an acute case of appendicitis and was forced to undergo emergency surgery in Northfield.[145] While the operation succeeded in removing the ruptured appendix, it caused a hernia that would plague him for many years. On July 3, he began to take solid food and dashed off a post-operative letter to his mother to assure her of his recovery.[146] The illness kept him in bed throughout the conference, leading one to wonder what might have been the impact on the religious Douglas had he attended the meetings.

As he approached the age of seventeen, his articles appeared more frequently in the college literary magazine, *The Messenger*. These writings—composed during his last two years at Richmond College—provide the largest surviving collection of his early works. His stories were generally romances, usually with a touch of mystery or surprising endings, sometimes stamped with autobiographical snippets. An early work, a two-part story titled "Marguerita," tells of the mysterious ending to an unrequited romance. As the hero dies, his doctor—the narrator of the story—finds a letter that will tie together all loose ends. As he draws near to the fireplace to read the letter, the sheet slips from his hand, is burned, and "the mystery remains unfathomed."[147] Douglas followed his article with "The Mystery of Bill Bailey," a tragedy in one act, written in blank verse, that consists mostly of the characters reacting to moans and screams throughout a house. The play ends with one character asking "Who killed Bill Bailey?"[148] It is uncertain whether Douglas meant this play to be a serious mystery or a satirical comedy.

By the spring semester of his second year in college, Douglas was named an associate editor of the *Messenger* and wrote the "On the Campus" segment in addition to his short stories. "On the Campus" was a newsy column passing along tidbits of life at college. Douglas reported on Dr. Foushee's new "Van Dyke" beard, the opening exercises at the YMCA, and the necessity for all students to join the Athletic Association.[149] "All those fair dreams we have been cherishing for years about a Biology course have at last come true," Douglas wrote in describing Prof. A. C. Wightman's new class. He also noted with satisfaction the beginning of "the catalogue on the library."[150]

Douglas's best work for the *Messenger* was his four-part "Stories of the Opera." Told by "Henry Millar," the four short stories center in "Madame Beaumont's" opera school in New York. Henry is a Virginian, with modest singing ability, who spends most of his time in the chorus or managing productions, all the while observing the trials, triumphs, and romances of other singers. "Rudolph," the first in the series, tells the story of "a tall, graceful Italian," who pines over a distant love even as he is to sing the lead in the coming opera. In the climatic scene, Rudolph, who has merely been going through the motions, begins to sing with "some great emotional awakening" as his love, Beccia, surprisingly appears on the stage to sing the duet "Il Trovatore."[151] Though the story is somewhat pat and veers steadily toward its obvious conclusion, Douglas's love of theater—so recently manifested in his own attempts at an acting career—shines forth in the words of Henry Millar.

> The thrill we always felt before the curtain rises was upon us all. Ten minutes would elapse before the opening chorus; the stage men were busily at work setting the castle yard; from the wings came the laughter of the chorus, while in front could be heard the buzz of conversation and the penetrating tuning of the instruments. Unless you have felt this thrill you can have no idea of its power. I have felt it a thousand times.[152]

The second installment, "Francesca," was a two-part cliff-hanger romance about a "little mezzo-soprano" from Georgia named Frances Smith, who takes the name "Francesca Smizzini" and joins Madame Beaumont's company. Once again a long-lost love, "Tom," appears as the heroine is to make her grand debut. Worried that "when the curtain went up that evening Frances could be his no more," Tom hurries to the theater to demand she choose between him and the opera—"heart or art" as Douglas put it. The last scene shows Henry watching as Frances lifts her hand to the crown on her head. "Did she lay it aside?"[153] The story ends with no answer.

In "Francesca," Douglas again shares his heart for the stage and shows some of the disappointment at the failure of the traveling troupe he had wanted to join. "To those who know it not," he wrote, "or at least know it only over that mystic line of the foot-lights, the stage seems to be only a world of brightness. But . . . just as there are great triumphs, so are there dismal failures; singers and actors make their appearances, have their brief moment of notoriety, and then sink back unknown."[154]

"The Minor Chord" was another romantic tragedy, but, as Douglas wrote—and no doubt believed for his own life—"If youth gives license for anything, it is to love."[155] In the story, Phil the stagehand falls in love with the opera star, Nellie. He never expresses his love, and tragedy strikes. The Iroquois Theatre catches fire during a performance. Phil saves Nellie, who has been elevated to the top of the theater by wires for a dramatic descent, but the two are mortally injured. As he lies dying, Phil speaks only once: "When—I—came, she knew it was me." Nellie smiles at him from the next bed and dies. Both Phil and Nellie, Douglas concludes, "lived to the minor-chord; the minor-chord was their requiem."[156]

In his senior year, Douglas was elected editor-in-chief of the *Messenger*. He wrote one last "Story of the Opera," an uninspired tale called "Triumph by Proxy," and then turned his attention to editorial comments. "A young editor seldom takes up his new honors without a solemn oath of betterment and great ideas of revolution," he wrote in his inaugural editorial. He dismissed any revolutionary ideas and pledged only to try "to preserve the present good name and reputation of *The Messenger*."[157] It was a reputation to which he had significantly contributed during his college years.

Douglas's first two years at Richmond College had been an unqualified success. He finished his first year with a 96.6 average over all his courses with individual averages of 98.4 in math, 97.5 in Latin, 96.4 in Greek, and 94 in physics. His second year was no less impressive with averages of 96.8 in Latin, 96.6 in English Literature, 95.8 in Advanced Literature, and 94.6 in Greek.[158]

During the spring semester of 1904, President Boatwright wrote to Walker Freeman about Douglas. He related that a biology professor had hailed a recent paper of Douglas's as the "best he had ever received from any student anywhere since he has been teaching."[159] Boatwright added his own assessment: "Douglas overflows with energy and seems destined for a larger work."[160] What neither Boatwright nor Walker Freeman knew was that Douglas had already decided what that "larger work" was to be. The decision had been reached three months before on one of his father's battlefields.

On November 6, 1903, survivors of Mahone's brigades gathered in Petersburg for a reunion and reenactment of the Battle of the Crater. The week leading to the "sham battle" had been one of excitement and anticipation for the "old Cockade city." The assembling positions for the parade were printed in the *Petersburg Daily Index-Appeal*, and readers learned that Virginia governor Andrew Jackson Montague would arrive on a special train from Richmond to view the festivities.[161] Patriotic resolutions were adopted urging schools and businesses to close for the day. The Virginia Passenger and Power Company announced it would secure additional streetcars to transport the expected crowd.[162] Displaying a proper balance of patriotic spirit and entrepreneurial assiduity, the local business of Barham, Rogers & Company placed an advertisement guaranteeing their ability to "furnish any quantity" of bunting for the coming review. "Concerns and cares of business life will be laid aside," an *Index-Appeal* editorial intoned, "and the day will be sacredly dedicated to commemoration."[163]

The "sacredly dedicated" day dawned overcast with a slight morning snowfall. By noon, the clouds dispersed, and the sun shone on the veterans of the Battle of the Crater as they formed "on Second Street, with their right resting on Bollingbrook."[164] The veterans marched to the "profusely and tastefully decorated" home of Mrs. William Mahone, there to each receive a badge from their commander's widow. Following that reception, the soldiers "gave a yell," and continued their march. "The old fellows' legs were not so strong as they had been," a reporter observed, but they arrived at the site of their triumph and again formed ranks on the brow of the ravine below the crater.[165]

Twenty thousand spectators looked on as 1st. Lt. John T. West, chaplain of the "Crater Legion," offered a lengthy invocation. Then Lt. Col. William H. Stewart, of the Sixty-First Virginia regiment, mounted the platform to "proclaim the truth in love" in the day's principal address.[166] As afternoon shadows began to cover the field, Stewart recounted the events of July 1864 before concluding his speech with a flight of rhetorical flourish:

Men of the ranks, step proudly to the front;
'twas yours unknown through sheeted flame to wade,
in the red battle's fierce and deadly brunt;
yours be full laurels in Mahone's brigade.[167]

Then came the command to charge. From the hill to the right of the crater the Richmond Howitzers opened up their artillery. They were answered in kind by the Norfolk Light Artillery Blues. Then the formed lines began to move as one.

The aged veterans, many displaying the effects of wounds suffered on that very field, began their charge up the hill to the crest of the crater. As they moved forward, with memories surely washing over them, they once again lifted a vibrant Rebel yell. For thirty minutes they reenacted the bloody contest in which they had been participants. When the smoke of the "sham-battle" cleared, Mahone's men once again held the crater.[168]

Seventeen-year-old Douglas stood with his Confederate veteran father and watched the pageant of history unfold in front of him. Back at the hotel, he saw the veterans from a closer vantage point. They were "feeble, crippled, some of them blind, many of them poor."[169] He was profoundly moved by the events of the day. He had experienced, over the past few months, so many varying emotions as he turned from boy to man: the excitement of college, the thrill of the stage, the breathless

rapture of love realized, the despair of love lost, the intellectual stimulation of S. C. Mitchell, and the deepening revelation of his religious
faith. All these emotions, shaped and colored by his heritage as a son of
the South and of Walker Freeman, had evoked self-examination and
prompted action. Now, he made to himself a solemn commitment, one
that he knew would outlast the zeal of youthful novelties.

"If someone doesn't write the story of these men," Douglas Southall
Freeman resolved, "it will be lost forever."

"I'm going to do it."[170]

CHAPTER 3

"I Aim at Many Things"

"The days of some of us are getting short at Richmond College," Douglas Freeman observed in a *Messenger* editorial.[1] Soon he would bid farewell to "the familiar haunts, the old class-rooms, the sleepy campus." It was, he conceded, "enough to make one grow thoughtful." If the "thoughtful" Douglas paused to reflect on his collegiate career as he began his final semester in January 1904, he had every reason to be satisfied. He had carried a heavy course load and never had a monthly average below 90. In his final year he carried a 95 in biology, a 94.6 in history, a 94 in Greek, and a 90.6 in philosophy.[2] He had won the respect of his peers, his teachers, and President Boatwright. He had laid out an ambitious life's work and was in no wise short of confidence that he could achieve it. He now wrote of life at Richmond College in the past tense. "It's going to take years out in the world before we can understand it," he wrote. "We can't appreciate the haven until we have tried the stormy sea."[3]

The "stormy sea" in which Douglas would set his oar was graduate school. "If you intend to succeed in life," he wrote, "then know that particular field of life in which you hope to work. And the world has never seen the man who could *do* unless he knew. Choose your work; then do your work."[4] Having chosen to write history, he set out to obtain the knowledge necessary to "do" this work. He cast his eye northward, to Johns Hopkins University. His application for admission was supported by letters of enthusiastic recommendation from Richmond College faculty members. W. A. Harris, professor of Greek, hailed Douglas's "originality" and "literary spirit." "His career with us," Harris noted, "has been exceedingly successful."[5] Professor A. C. Wightman, who had praised Douglas's biology paper to President F. W. Boatwright, endorsed his admission "most heartily." "He is a hard worker, having enthusiasm, conscientiousness, and success in his work," Wightman wrote. "In addition to this," he concluded, "Mr. Freeman is a thorough gentleman."[6]

S. C. Mitchell noted that Douglas wielded "kindly influences every-where in the Institution." He "gives promise of large usefulness in life," Mitchell judged, and possessed "admirable abilities and firm character."[7] President Boatwright called Douglas "one of the most capable students in the institution" who had never failed an examination. "He will take high rank in University Studies," Boatwright told the Johns Hopkins Board, "as he has already done at college."[8] Armed with ambition, accolades, and strong support, Douglas was granted admission with a scholarship to the class entering Johns Hopkins in the fall of 1904.

The Johns Hopkins University in Baltimore was not yet thirty years old in 1904. Johns Hopkins, its founder and namesake, was a director of the B&O Railroad, a Quaker, and an unmarried millionaire who, in 1867, arranged for the incorporation of a university and a hospital. At his death in 1873, he left $7 million to be divided equally between the two institutions. The university opened on February 22, 1876, dedicated, its first president Daniel Coit Gilman said, to "the discovery and promulgation of the truth."[9] Gilman sought to build a university "national in scope on a plan radically different from any then in operation in America."[10] Embarking on that task, he searched the scholarly world for teachers of the highest caliber and shaped Hopkins into the first American university based directly on German methods of research and scholarship. "Truth for its own sake" was the philosophy that shaped the university; truth discovered, tested, and applied.[11] Douglas would be entering a school with the highest standards of scholarship, and one that would serve him well for his future work.[12]

The young graduate spent the summer of 1904 writing two manuscripts: a short story titled "Betsy Hansford: The True Story of the Virginia Priscilla," and a novel titled "My Lady's Lord."[13] The "Hansford" article, the draft of which is filed in the Freeman papers, was turned down for publication by the Ladies Home Journal.[14] No copy of the novel has survived, but Douglas noted that its chief characteristics were the "earmarks of haste."[15] Despite any misgivings he may have felt over the novel's quality, Douglas submitted it to four publishing houses: Bobbs Merrill, Harper & Brothers, Lothrop, and Putnam's. Each publisher summarily rejected it.[16] "I learned a lesson in that ill-fated little novel," the aspiring author confided to his mother. "A man cannot do a great work in a summer."[17]

Eighteen-year old Douglas arrived in Baltimore in the fall of 1904. He would live with his brother Allen, who was starting his fourth year

Douglas Southall Freeman, c. 1904.
(Image courtesy of Mary Tyler McClenahan.)

as a medical student at Hopkins. The two brothers, and a recent medical school graduate, found a three-bedroom, one-sitting-room suite on the fourth floor of a building at the corner of Broadway and Orleans Streets in East Baltimore.[18] Dubbed the "Hotel Hopkins," the apartment was closer to the medical school than to the university campus, so Douglas faced a lengthy hike each day to the edge of the business district to reach his classrooms.[19] There he began his work in earnest. In his first month at Hopkins, he wrote three papers—"New Phases of International Law in Chinese-Japanese War, Part I-Naval"; "Evolution of [the] Department of State"; and "Gloucester"—and rewrote parts of

"My Lady's Lord."[20] His class lectures included the subjects of Germanic History, American Diplomatic History to 1801, and the Reformation. He listed ten assigned books and dutifully recorded the pages he read.[21] Already an early riser, he now devised a schedule that required him to stay up two minutes later on each successive night to handle this heavy workload. On the first night of the new schedule, October 15, he worked until 11:02 P.M. The next night, he went until 11:04 P.M. By November 13, the last night on the revised schedule, he reached the target of studying until midnight. At the bottom of the time chart, he wrote "November 14, this schedule observed."[22]

His long hours and heavy schedule notwithstanding, Douglas found time every day to write home. He alternated addressing the letters between Walker and Bettie, knowing that each would share the day's message with the other. Generally two pages in length and typewritten, the letters provide an in-depth look at Douglas's daily life, his studies, and his dreams. They reveal a sensitive, hard-working, and ambitious lad; at times driven by cold logic and at times moved by great passion. Confident to the point of arrogance, yet humble to the point of self-debasement, he viewed his professors and surroundings with a critical eye, but was no less hard on himself. The letters are seldom "chatty"— though they contain sundry mentions of weather, food, and daily activities—and often delve into serious soliloquies on religion, history, and the South. They also appear to be as much self-motivation as they are updates to his parents. Day after day, Douglas Freeman assessed himself and his performance and, as his own harshest judge, wrote not only to his parents, but to himself.

His first year at Hopkins centered around two main activities: "seminary papers" presented to his classes and the approval of a thesis. The thesis came quickly to the boy who wanted to write the story of the war. He would start at the beginning: the secession of Virginia from the Union. Although Walker wondered if "as warm a southerner" as his son could objectively address the issue,[23] Douglas began to collect material and write "a few gentlemen throughout the state" for their recollections—or family recollections—of the Virginia Secession Convention of 1861.[24] His inquiry letter centered on five topics: sentiment created by John Brown's raid at Harper's Ferry; local political activity in the presidential campaign of 1860; candidates and positions during the Secession Convention elections; military preparedness and sentiment for war; and the effect on public opinion of Lincoln's call for troops.[25] He also invited comments on "any other facts you may think interesting." The request was sent to thirty-six prominent Virginians. Douglas soon compiled an extensive index of sources and expressed confidence that he would "have something creditable and complete to present to the Board by the end of May."[26] Viewing this paper as the first step in a long process of writing the history of the War Between the States, he took seriously the responsibility of the historian. He was writing, he felt, for the ages.

> I think sometimes of the great weight that is on the historical student—to portray accurately, to tell the truth in every word. The historian is the prophet of the ages; he digs deeply, this man now, and count on him for the truth. Great is the fault if he should misrepresent any event, or any person; it is truly a crime against the ages . . . If there is one man above all others who must tell the truth, that man is the historian. He carries the scales of justice for the minds of men for all times.[27]

By May, with his topic approved by the faculty, Douglas wrote his father that he thought he could finish the job during the coming summer.[28]

Graduate students at Hopkins were evaluated on a relatively informal basis and did not receive grades for their courses. A student remained in school as long as his academic performance pleased the faculty. This progress was charted by the writing and presentation of "seminary papers."[29] Hardly a week passed without Douglas making mention in letters home of such a paper.[30] While enjoying researching and writing about secession, Douglas called seminary papers "the travail of my soul."[31] He would, however, make each paper "bristle with foot-notes" as a "sign that the work came from somewhere and was meant for something."[32] His dismissive attitude toward these papers notwithstanding, Douglas gave to this work the same effort he gave his thesis and proudly reported that one professor was so interested in his presentation "that he had not put down his points to criticize me."[33]

One of the professors under whom Douglas would work during his first year was Dr. James C. Ballagh, the chairman of the History Department. Ballagh did not make the same favorable impression on Douglas as had S. C. Mitchell. A somewhat blustery figure with a talent for delivering multi-hour lectures, Ballagh approved Douglas's major study and, after reviewing his research, summoned the young student for a conference. "Freeman," he growled, "the research in this paper is excellent, indeed exceptional. But you will never make a writer. Your purple prose is execrable."[34] As none of Douglas's graduate papers have survived, it is impossible to weigh Ballagh's judgment, or Douglas's response to it, against any documentation. What is recorded is his later comment to family members that he left Ballagh's office "determined to prove him wrong."[35] Family tradition interprets this resolve to mean that Douglas changed his writing style "until it became as clear and disciplined as it had once been turgid."[36] That may be too hasty a conclusion given Douglas's confidence in his abilities. It is difficult to look at any of his letters during these years and reach the same conclusion as Ballagh. His letters are often quite eloquent, showing a style that would mark his later work. In one such letter to his father, he describes a trip around the world that they plan one day to take.

I am glad too that we have determined to take it from East to West, and I trust that in our trip we will not forget that we are following the course of civilization. As we gaze on the dull fields of China "where a native is never out of sight," we see the world in its primitive state. Here, before our own particular race began, were a people with an antiquity and a history. Here, before the monuments of Egypt took shape, were a people—in China—who had their philosophy from the mouth of the great Confucius, here the arts developed when we were an ignorant wandering Germanic people. Then, in India, "that Indian vale" which Shelley has painted, we see the cradle of our civilization; among the rugged growths of the lofty Himalayas the Aryan was born; then, passing on we come to Egypt, and see a different and more potent civilization developed; a people of blood and of fame, with monuments to the sky, and aims that knew no bounds. Then comes the country of the Hebrew, where all the composite parts were met, while in Greece the world formulated its views before passing them on to Rome. From the Eternal City, in many channels, it was disseminated; then the Germans took up the Roman, fused it with their own; and in England we saw the combined effects; while back across the Atlantic is the afterthought of the ages, our own country.[37]

Such was the style of a boy not yet nineteen years old. If one can assume his historical writings bore some of the same style—and given his later writings, this is not a large assumption—one can hardly draw the conclusion that Douglas would "never make a writer." His reaction to Ballagh's caustic chiding, his "determination" to prove him wrong, might well have manifested itself not in a changed style, but in a maintenance, with some fine tuning, of his present style. In so doing, he would, indeed, prove Ballagh wrong.

Working alongside Douglas in his department was "a motley, and by no means unpleasant company" of "eleven or twelve men."[38] Douglas reported that two were married and a third held "the distinction of widowerhood." Among them as well were two former college presidents and three preachers.[39] "The men come from every part of the country," Douglas noted, with Virginia and North Carolina duly represented with "Princeton, Columbia, Oxford, and other places." Douglas also kept company with Allen's friends from the medical school. He attended medical lectures with his brother and was "a member in good standing" in the discussion groups that took place at "Hotel Hopkins."[40] Douglas "acquired a body of medical knowledge" from his time spent with medical students that sparked a lifelong interest in health and medicine.[41]

Although the brothers lived together, Allen's schedule as a medical student kept him out of the apartment most days and many nights. Not that Douglas's schedule allowed much time for fraternal camaraderie. The two did attempt to hold Saturday nights for joint trips to the theater. Douglas's love of theater had not lapsed since his college days and, for fifty cents each, the brothers could sit in the "peanut gallery" in the local theater and watch touring shows.[42] Baltimore was enjoying the best of current theater, and Allen recalled seeing "all the great actors and the great plays of the day."[43] Among these "greats" were Joseph Jefferson in *Rip Van Winkle*, Richard Mansfield in *Cyrano*, Maud Adams in *L'Aiglon*, and William Gillette in *Sherlock Holmes*.[44] Douglas admitted that Allen had to "drag" him to "the old Lyric to hear the Boston Symphony Orchestra," but this outing started a lifelong love of classical music.[45] Baltimore's fine restaurants were a bit beyond the budget of the boys, but "there were many cheaper places where the food was superb."[46] The weekend provided time for long walks "full of discussion of the many things two young men of congenial tastes could find to discuss."[47] Douglas greatly enjoyed the company of his older brother. "It is really wonderful," he wrote his father, "the similarity of feeling that is within Allen and myself. In fact, take sire take sons, and in the things we like there is not a hairs' breadth of difference."[48]

On Saturday afternoons, Douglas walked through the "moving panorama" that was the downtown market place. "It is not infrequent," he wrote his mother, "that one hears half a dozen languages in almost as many steps . . . what a country is this. A composite society—powerful in all its aspects."[49] The children of the streets, ill clad and grimy, also made an impression. A child "in the slums," he observed, "knows almost from the moment he draws his first breath that he has to scuffle for himself, and how he does go about it."[50] The boy from Richmond was seeing urban poverty for the first time. His reaction was to put his faith into action. He began working at the "Lawrence House," a type of halfway house for the city poor. "I mingle with them," Douglas wrote his father, "give them a little of what God has given me, and try to give them a better social ideal."[51] That ideal was still found in the religion of his youth.

> The greatest thing about the Great Ideal, Christ, is that he is for all classes and for all. People are wont to think, at least some of them, in this day and time, that the teachings which He presented are but for women and children—a mere emotional teaching, a few scattered thoughts for light minds. But how far is it from the truth. There you will find—from his lips—the greatest philosophy the world has ever seen; a system of morals suited to all peoples and to every nation; ethics supreme, learning with the highest of any time—nothing since can approach, and nothing can ever until the Ideal which he set down shall be attained, until his philosophy shall rule supreme, until his ethics are accepted everywhere, and his example acknowledged forever. And that is what the people call the Kingdom of God.[52]

One March afternoon, Douglas came to his apartment like "a lazy hound dog, come in after a long chase, with mud up to his belly, and his eyes sitting back under his ears."[53] This is as close as he comes during his first year at Hopkins to an admission of fatigue. From the time he arrived on campus, Douglas sought "to live up" to the admonition of "Old Mitch" and "cling on just a few minutes after the other fellow has quit."[54] Adopting Mitchell's maxim as his own (he once prefaced the quote with "I often say"[55]) his single-minded discipline and work ethic gained the respect of even Dr. Ballagh. He "always smiles at my enthusiasm," Douglas reported of the professor, "bidding me to keep at it."[56] To "keep at it," Douglas began a system of "taking a brief of every book" he felt would be "of any further service."[57] "In this way, I have brought before me, and kept before me, a great many things that would otherwise be completely forgotten in a day or so."[58] Adding this new self-imposed duty to his existing load carried another benefit: "[W]hen one is up and doing," he wrote his father, "time flies on rapid pinions."[59] He cast a disdainful eye on those less engaged in vigorous work. "Did you ever notice the way," he wrote, "the present generation has of resting so much?"[60] "People talk about the great amount of work done today . . . [but] they overlook the fact that a man nowadays can never let a year go around without resting at least one twelfth of it." Recalling that he had taken off most of the previous summer, he now asserted the best way "to properly take care of oneself" is "to do the best amount of the best work."[61] Pontification aside, Douglas found great joy in his work and genuinely desired more of it. "Work is the greatest satisfaction I know," he wrote his mother. "Talk about delights, but to [my] mind there is no delight commensurate with that of a good long day's work. If there is a prayer on my lips, it is that, a good day's work, and a long one, an humble heart, and a strong one."[62]

It was not just love of work that propelled him. The vision born at the Battle of the Crater reenactment—to write the history of Lee's army— drove him to master the historian's art. At Johns Hopkins, historical technique and method, reflecting the influence of German scholarship, was taught as a science. The scientific approach rested on three principles: critical examination of sources, the preference of primary to secondary sources, and impartiality.[63] Professor Charles McLean Andrews, who would join the Hopkins history faculty during Douglas's third year, articulated the department's policy by defining the historian's goal "as the attainment of truth."[64] Once the truth was found, the historian, like the scientist, needed to understand the underlying influences and grasp the pattern of historical development.[65] A historian was to be an expert scholar, working according to definite principles "pursuing his experiments just as does the investigator in the scientific laboratory."[66] This approach to the study of history fit perfectly in the overall concept of Johns Hopkins as a research institution. It also fit the predisposition of Douglas Freeman, who believed history was a series of facts to be discovered and who was drawn to the objectivity of scientific testing. "Nothing could be more delightful," he wrote, "than the hope and the outlook of a calm study of the events and men which, in turn and time, have made the world what it is."[67]

Not that the scientific approach drained passion from the study of history. "History you know is more to me than mere education and a means of livelihood," Douglas wrote, "it is life itself, and that I am going to follow."[68]

Everyman must have his work, and that is mine—to labour earnestly, to labour honestly, and bring out something that may be worth men's whiles to read, something that in times to come, may be taken as final—a word said on a subject, and a word apropos. I know that means a long time of labour, a long line of years with but slight remuneration. But for my part, I am willing to starve—as the saying goes—for twenty years, if at the end of that time it can be honestly said that I have done a good piece of work.[69]

"Twenty years," Douglas concluded, "is but a trifle for so great a work." The work would take that long because it would be a sweeping story "of our country, that story of the causes which led up to those four dark years of war, which changed the whole tenor of our nation."[70] It would take that long because no work from his pen would be incomplete. "A man ought not to go over a field and leave something else for the next man who comes along to do," he declared. "When you do a thing, do it thoroughly . . . so that not a new word can be said."[71] In writing, researching, culling facts, testing truths, discarding fables, and reaching objective conclusions, Douglas felt he had found the "certain, definite, fixed line" meant for him to follow.[72]

Even so fixed and dedicated a student could find himself subject to some of the basic emotions of lesser mortals. "If I would let myself ever get homesick, which I don't do," Douglas wrote his mother midway through his second semester, "I think I would be homesick tonight."[73] Sitting at his desk, he had started singing "some of those good old Southern songs," and his mind and heart drifted from Baltimore over the Potomac and home to Richmond and the South.[74] "There's no place like the South," he mused.

There is that innate gentility, that ingenious courtesy which makes the south different from all the rest of the world. Give me the South, for mine, the sunny south; of generous men and noble women, the south of a past, and please God, the South of the future.[75]

Douglas longed for "real fried chicken to eat, with lots of good cream gravy, and corn bread—oh, that corn bread sopped in good gravy, and just hot enough to smoke a little bit."[76] Despite denials of homesickness, Douglas turned again and again in his letters to heartfelt tributes to his hometown: "[T]here is no place like Richmond on the face of the globe"; "surely a jewel in the Southern crown"; and "Richmond is fairer far than Heaven."[77] One rainy Sunday afternoon in May, his mind wandered, and he began to recall a romance of a year before. He pushed aside his work and penned a commemorative poem to "Alice Merritt" and their first kiss.[78] Like the average college student, he received his quota of care packages from home: Peanuts, fruitcakes, and a necktie were some of the gifts acknowledged during his first year.[79] From Richmond came assurance from Walker of his pride in Douglas's "great scholarship, honorable achievements, and noble Christian manhood."[80] Douglas, in turn, praised his father as "model . . . preceptor and . . . keenly interested friend and advisor."[81] Walker Freeman was the standard, his son wrote, against whom he measured all men—as well as himself. "When any test matter comes, be it matter of judgment, matter of logic or matter of morals, I have a strict and safe comparison that never fails me: What would my father do in the premises?"[82]

In June 1905, Douglas received the good news that he had been awarded a scholarship for his second year at Hopkins.[83] This achievement capped a successful start to his graduate studies. He ended his first year a confident man of nineteen, with definite goals already established.

I aim at many things in this world, you know. I want to be a good scholar, one whose name will not be forgotten tomorrow; I want to be a keen thinker, the impress of whose mind will mould the thought of days that come after; I want to be a strong speaker, to carry conviction to the hearts of men in matters that concern their welfare most.[84]

Douglas had hoped to spend the summer working as a librarian in the manuscript department of the Virginia State Library, but the job was filled, so he contented himself with work on his dissertation.[85] He also took time to finish a "little drama" titled "Cartersville—an atmosphere play in three acts."[86] He registered the play with the Library of Congress the following November and submitted it to the Belasco Theatre in New York. It was returned unread.[87]

Back at Hopkins in September 1905, Douglas continued the same level of intense dedication to work that had marked his first year. "I enjoy the solitude of a long day's work, and love to commune with my own spirit," he wrote in October. "It's only from the silent hour of contemplation that a man gets impetus and energy for his day's work."[88] Now into these hours of contemplation and solitude crept an intrusion: a new, and apparently serious, romance. As no complete diary of his days at Johns Hopkins has survived, speculation and conjecture must mark the story of this romance with the unnamed girl. The first surviving mention appears in a letter to his father of October 13, 1905. "The little lady is coming over tomorrow," he relates matter of factly. "I want to see her of course; but, just between you and I, so wrapped up have I been in my work, that I have thought but very little of her coming."[89] One week later he reported to his mother that "the girl" was in town for the entire week. He related nothing of their time together except that she "prevented my doing all the work I might otherwise have completed."[90] If her company was such an intrusion, he could have ended the relationship, but less than one month later he advised his father that he had been engaged in the "gentle art of love-making."[91] Two weeks later he wrote his father that he planned to visit the girl, who apparently lived outside Baltimore, and dubbed the trip the "largest event on the horizon."[92] Nothing is heard from Douglas during the trip, but apparently a serious discussion ensued. Another letter from Baltimore then arrives in Richmond for Walker Freeman. "The engagement," Douglas tersely writes, "has been broken off." He offers no details, "for there are none," and affects relief at the situation. "I don't think she was the one for me after all," he flippantly concludes, but his agitated state is revealed by his omission of a date on the letter—something never done in four years' worth of correspondence.[93]

Both mother and father responded with appropriate parental sympathy, in all likelihood having read between their son's lines. "I am not the least concerned in the matter at all," Douglas wrote his mother. "Things always turn out for the best, and I am not one bit disturbed. There are other girls, and doubtless better elsewhere."[94] In a lengthy letter the next day to his father, in which he makes a rare request for money from home, Douglas relegates the affair to a postscript: "I need no consolation over the loss of the lady; the money is more essential."[95] The last mention of the girl, whose name is lost to history, comes in a letter to his mother. In outlining plans for Christmas, Douglas comments that he will have more money for presents as "the chief item on the programme, to wit, a present for a young lady, will not have to be furnished."[96] "That," he concluded, "is a great consolation to my pocket-book; my heart needs none."

The days passed routinely. Douglas heard Prof. Jacob H. Hollander on the origins of the federal banking system, Prof. John Martin Vincent on the laws of medieval Switzerland, and Prof. Westel W. Willoughby on the "real union" of Norway and Sweden.[97] He enjoyed having "good literature right at his command" and was delighted to find eight biographies of Michelangelo in the library.[98] He regularly put in fourteen-hour workdays preparing seminary papers and writing his dissertation,[99] but while he carried his load with his usual cheerful manner, something serious was on his mind.

Always religious as a boy, Douglas the man now thought and wrote more and more about his faith. "Tomorrow I expect to spend in religious contemplation and service," he wrote in November 1905. The evening would be spent in "the Bible and Shakespeare."[100] He attended two churches in Baltimore, even though the old Baptist admitted he went to the Episcopal service for the "good music."[101] Nor did he find science and education weakening his faith. He welcomed scientific examination of "belief in the Eternal Verity," for the doubt that prompted investigation would lead to experience "and from the dawn of Experience, beautiful and bright, the Truth shines forth, and the Truth shall make you free."[102] Even as he began preparation of his dissertation—"the greatest pleasure"—and continued to write about making "a concrete contribution to the sum of the historical knowledge," he wondered aloud if the "noble end you and mother . . . sought for me, would not be the proper one—to tell the Truth to the world." He was not as yet willing to commit to the ministry, but would say "where I can do the most good, there will I go."[103] He closed this letter of March 10 leaving his parents with the definite impression that he was coming under strong conviction to change his course.

Four days later, he wrote his father and announced he was devoting his life to Christian ministry.[104] The letter starts with an injunction of secrecy. He wanted to speak freely to his parents and, unspoken, perhaps leave an honorable way out should he change his mind. He disclosed that for five years he had been considering studying for the ministry. The thoughts faded, then returned with "greater frequence." That evening, as he reflected on how "the greatest good . . . could come from my life to those with whom I am associated—the Light, as it were, came to me."[105] He did not intend to leave college or to change "the plans and course which I am pursuing," but he would search for "whatever opening there is . . . and do the best I can, by God's help, to uplift the social, moral and intellectual sphere where I am cast." In the meantime, he would enter "a period of chastening, so to speak," so his entry into the ministry would "be no sudden transition, but a gradual and proper change."[106] He ended his letter— "fixed in my resolve"—by asking his parents for their prayers and advice.

Was this another lark similar to the traveling theater group? How could a student so firmly resolved to write history—of General Lee, no less—turn so quickly from that resolve? Was it the result of an apparently traumatic romance and broken engagement? Or was it the natural decision of a thoughtful boy steeped in faith from his youth who, upon coming of age, began to see clearly his future? These must remain rhetorical questions, for Douglas Freeman gave no direct answers to any of them. He touched on the suddenness of the decision in a letter to his brother Allen, assuring him that it was "the result of much thought on the subject."[107] One week after his announcement to his parents, he wrote his father that "every day I become more and more convinced at once of the wisdom of that decision."[108] He followed that letter by asking his father if he should "apply for a license to preach" during the coming summer.[109] His parents raised no objection to this turn of events. They were "delighted and thankful" and knew "many hundreds" would rejoice at the news.[110] His father outlined a course of action to assist him on his way: preach whenever the opportunity presented itself, attend Sunday School and church on a regular basis, and "declare your purpose" when you come home.[111] Walker also reminded his son that their pastor had "always predicted that this will be your work."

Only Douglas Freeman knew his thoughts during this month of decision. Only he could describe the emotions and forces coming to bear in his heart and mind. Did he wrestle with an angel till the break of day? His last lengthy letter on the subject shows the beginnings of hesitation. "You will remember," he wrote his father, "that I thought before my intentions were definitely declared, I should have begun, at least, to make some progress in the Christian life."[112] He had previously attempted to walk out his faith, but he now believed a higher level was required. In taking those steps, "might not then, some evil-disposed person be tempted to criticize my morality and the purity of my intentions." No announcement of his intentions could therefore be made until his "walk" had reached an appropriate level. Unanswered was whether or not he would ever be able to meet that high standard.

"In the next place," Douglas continued, "the effect on my University standing should not be overlooked . . . [and] naturally enough, a minister is not viewed in the fairest light around a place of free thinking."[113] Not that he worried about what others thought ("who cares for opprobrium when sure of the justice of his cause"), but he did care about "the standing given me by the University authorities." Was this a broad hint that his scholarship might be in jeopardy if he pursued the ministry? Also, if he were to attempt to preach during the summer, would that not interfere with his dissertation? "I cannot afford," he argued, "to permit any work, however dear to me, to interfere with my University career."[114]

The letter, while not expressly admitting a change of heart, signified the end of Douglas's ecclesiastic leaning. There would be a few casual mentions in future letters but no further lengthy expositions on religion and no pronouncements on a career in the pulpit. Soon the budding historian was back, writing his mother that he looked forward to a "full summer of untrammeled work, without any entangling alliances."[115] Unwilling to admit he had jumped too quickly to a life-changing decision, he simply allowed the issue to fade away. His parents did as well. No attempt was made to reignite whatever spark had briefly flared on that March night; no criticism was made of such a drastic change of heart. But while Douglas walked away from the ministry, he did not walk away from his faith. Except for one season of doubt yet to come, he would be a lay minister all of his life: in Sunday School classes, from the pulpit, over the radio, and in his writings.[116] He was only unable— or uninspired—to take the step of vocational commitment. If nothing else, the events of March 1906 clearly illuminate one thing: The studious twenty-year-old boy with the serious look and the flashing blue-gray eyes had developed into a man of great passion. The things he loved—be it history, hard work, his parents, or his faith—he loved with a passion and sought greater ways to express that devotion. For a short time, his devout faith prompted him to believe that anything less than a lifetime commitment as a minister was less than adequate. As he reflected further, he awkwardly back-pedaled—too proud or embarrassed to admit he had been rash—and settled into a life of service to that faith while adhering to the career path he had chosen. He was soon back on that course. On June 13, 1906, he was appointed a Fellow in History for the year 1906-07.[117]

Douglas was at work in the state library as soon as he returned to Richmond. There his industrious ways came to the attention of the chief librarian, H. R. McIlwaine, and the reference librarian, Kate Pleasants Minor.[118] When Mrs. Minor decided to take a two-week vacation, she recommended that Douglas be hired as her temporary replacement. Dr. McIlwaine agreed with the suggestion and offered the job to Douglas at the rate of forty dollars for the two weeks.[119] Eager to "pick up a little change," Douglas accepted the offer.[120] McIlwaine was impressed with the performance of his new staff member and soon gave him a new assignment. He was writing an introduction to a book titled *Letters of Old Virginia*,[121] and he asked Douglas to annotate his article. Promptly finishing that job, and with the return of Mrs. Minor, Douglas went back to the stacks and his dissertation. Such were passed two seemingly insignificant weeks in the library. Still, these "fateful two weeks" set in motion events that would place Douglas on his dual career path of historical writing and newspaper editing.[122] Douglas's third year at Johns Hopkins settled into the pace established in his first two years. He continued his flurry of work with single-minded determination. He developed a new system of note taking, utilizing two books, a "bibliography" and "commonplace book," to cross-reference criticisms, subject notes, and "general trends" from topics of study. This precluded the necessity to reread a book when facts were needed.[123] He wrote an article that was published in the Richmond Times-Dispatch on the life of "the first of Virginia man of letters," Dr. George W. Bagby.[124] Every day at Hopkins, Douglas wrote, instilled in him more respect for the system of "discipline, lectures and close attention . . . to which a man can unreservedly give himself over, in the fullness of delight to his own inventions."[125] Despite his appreciation of the method, he found little to praise in his instructors. Douglas encountered no S. C. Mitchell at Hopkins. His letters contain a few positive comments about Prof. J. M. Vincent, but his remarks generally skewer faculty, in particular Dr. Ballagh. "Fortunately," he wrote his mother, "this is Vincent's part of the week, and we will have peace at least until Wednesday evening; for Ballagh fires up on Thursday and then—farewell content."[126] The lack of substance in Ballagh's lectures was a recurring theme. Ballagh "thundered away for two hours in the seminary today, as usual, but without effect" and, one December day, "the records show he was at it from 10:00 sharp until twenty-five minutes to two. That is an unexcelled record."[127] Things brightened somewhat during the spring semester when the "new man in history," Prof. Charles M. Andrews, arrived. Douglas noted his first lecture was "very fine."[128] He would come to rank Andrews on the same level with Vincent and would establish his closest student/teacher relationship of the Hopkins years with Andrews.[129]

On February 21, 1907, Douglas received a letter from Kate Minor, the librarian for whom he had substituted in the state library. Mrs. Minor wrote in her capacity as a member of the Confederate Memorial Literary Society and came directly to her point. "Could you and would you," the letter opened, "undertake to make a calendar of the manuscripts in the Confederate Museum to be published at the earliest possible moment?" She went on to explain that the book was "not primarily a money-making scheme . . . but it is with the intention of advancing the cause of historical accuracy."[130] Douglas would have right of first refusal of this offer and, if he accepted, Mrs. Minor judged, he would have "a chance to strike a blow for honest fame as well as to help the cause of the Confederacy."[131]

There it was. The words jumped from the page he held in his hands. "Historical accuracy," "Confederacy," and "publish." And the opportunity was his, and his alone. Was it not just a month previous that he exulted to his father that in the job of research "one feels that he is making some contribution to human knowledge and learning things that were not known before"?[132] To that joy had been added confirmation from an unexpected source. His mother wrote in mid-January about an address commemorating the birth of Robert E. Lee wherein the speaker expressed the hope that some historian would "write a true history of the war and the causes of it."[133] "In my heart," she wrote Douglas, "I said 'I believe my boy can and will do that very thing'—and I do expect you to do it." All the events and plans of life seemed now to converge in this moment of time. What better way to begin writing the story of the war than by organizing the papers he would no doubt need to write such a history?

What Mrs. Minor was proposing was that Douglas review, organize, and chronicle the more than five thousand miscellaneous letters, manuscripts, documents, reports, and pamphlets strewn about the Confederate Museum in Richmond. Once the material was mastered, Douglas was to record them in a book, with appropriate annotations explaining content and identifying parties. Douglas wasted no time in responding. He "hasten[ed] to answer" Mrs. Minor on the same day.[134] His letter began tentatively, he knew "nothing of the number of papers" nor if "sufficient time" would be allowed to permit "a calendar worthy of the papers." These tepid qualifications aside, he "gladly" accepted the task. "It would be no more than the duty which every Virginian owes to the history of the State, no more than I as a student owe to the Museum for the splendid work they are doing."[135] If the job could be done "in a month," he would require only costs; if longer, he thought "10% of the net profits after the cost of publication . . . would be just remuneration." He would be in Richmond in March and would make a "preliminary examination of the material."[136]

"Today I received a letter from Mrs. Minor," Douglas wrote his father on the same day. "I consider the work proposed here of sufficient importance to warrant the offer I made." If done correctly, he concluded, "it will be a good thing for the museum, and a much better for your son."[137]

In April 1907, Douglas visited the museum to examine the holdings. He found the collection in better order than he had suspected and left

convinced it was a job that needed to be done—and equally convinced
that he was the man to do it. He set about to close the deal with the ladies
of the Confederate Memorial Literary Society. Back at Hopkins, he sat
down at his typewriter and began to write. After complimenting the
ladies on the condition of the documents and confirming that the material should be more readily accessible to students, he put the project in
historical context.

> It is a self-evident fact, and one which I need not impress upon the
> Society, that if the real history of the War between the States is ever
> to be written, much matter now hidden away in private hands and
> in the collection of societies must be brought before students in a
> form which will permit historical accuracy and critical citation. The
> day is past, I trust, when history will be maliciously falsified to suit
> the whims of Northern writers and the taste of Northern readers.[138]

In such circumstances, Douglas wrote, it was essential that "one in
such a position" as the society should provide this needed service. It was
no less than "a solemn duty" to publish "these fast-failing literary memorials of the south."[139]

He then presented the scope of the work. To include all the papers
housed in the museum would require a "large amount of time, editorial
work, and money." A book "of some three or four hundred pages"
emphasizing the major papers, with less important ones "merely noted,"
could be produced at less time and cost, yet still "give students the
resources of your archives."[140] Under this scenario, the cost "could be
repaid the Society in a year" and, "in two or three at the most, the work
would net a profit." To seal the business side of the offer, Douglas withdrew his request for 10 percent of the net profits and offered to do the
job—no matter how long—"for the mere expenses of a stenographer."[141]

After stressing the importance of collecting and preserving papers, lest
"the true history of that war will never be written," Douglas outlined a
plan to establish a committee for the collection of other manuscripts and
publication of a second calendar. "There is no work you could possibly do
as valuable to the cause you represent," Douglas wrote as he neared the
conclusion of his letter. Then the son of a Confederate veteran rolled out
the heavy rhetorical artillery for his closing paragraph.

> They say it was a lost cause: Perhaps it was; but it still lives in the
> hearts of the Southern people. Its career of arms ended these forty

years ago; we only live for its justification. And this is not to be done in any other way than through the careful collection and statement of calm historical fact. This, in turn, demands a knowledge of the facts. Many of them are facts contained in no book, hidden away in private hands, liable to all the vicissitudes of fortune. On you as on no other body rests a responsibility, to you is given, by your position, an opportunity to collect these facts.[142]

Douglas ended the letter with an offer to do anything for this cause, "for it is a cause dear to all in whose veins flows southern blood." The minutes of the Confederate Memorial Literary Society report that Douglas's letter was received and read at the meeting of April 24, 1907. The ladies listened "with breathless attention."[143]

Regaining their collective breath, they voted a resolution of appreciation to Douglas, and Mrs. Minor dispatched another letter requesting some follow-up information, the most important item of which was when he could start.[144] On May 25, he was notified that the society was ready to go forward with the project under his direction. "It is with great pleasure," he wrote, "that I shall undertake to assist them in this good work."[145]

Douglas could hardly be faulted for looking forward to the summer and the start of his first book, but he still had seminary papers and a dissertation demanding his attention. He spent some time delving into the history of diplomatic relations during the Spanish-American War, conducted some research in the Library of Congress in Washington, and heard from S. C. Mitchell that there might be "a place" for him at Richmond College.[146] Another job offer came from an unexpected source: Dr. Ballagh. Douglas reported that Ballagh made "an informal offer of a job" but that he did not consider accepting as it was only for one year.[147] As his third year at Hopkins ended, he celebrated three significant achievements: He finished the first draft of his dissertation, he was elected to Phi Beta Kappa, and he was awarded a scholarship for the 1907-08 year.[148] Major events all, but he accorded them little fanfare. His mind was set on the summer's work. "The world is opening up," Freeman wrote his mother shortly after his twenty-first birthday, "and everything is before the fellow who is willing to work."[149]

He had shown he was willing to work. To that willingness he added the conviction that he would be working in a time that would "mark an epoch in the history of the lost cause—an epoch, not of the 'Bloody Shirt,' but of real appreciation of the meaning of the Confederacy."[150]

Some of these days, God willing, we shall see what was the true significance of that long conflict of opposing interests; someone shall perhaps arise who will be able, as no one thus far has had power, to write the war as it was: to tell the story of two different peoples, with a common blood, but entirely contrasting traditions and spirits; two peoples who engaged in the use of slave labor. How one found it unprofitable, and how it paid for awhile in the other, but was recognized as a curse in itself and baleful in its interests— all this has to be told . . . From that civilization of the South, declared by the northern politicians to be rotten through—there came men of principles unimpeachable, of valor indescribable, of powers vast and devoted. These men led the southern men through struggle and through death, through victory and through defeat.[151]

It was in such spirit that Douglas Freeman spent the summer of 1907 working on the calendar while sitting in the dining room of Jefferson Davis's Confederate White House.[152] His work consisted of abstracting the manuscripts, grouping them in sections under specific titles, and preparing brief statements about the content of each paper.[153] He utilized the calendar-entry model of the American Historical Association and supplied footnotes as needed to explain statements in the text.[154] "I found the work there far more interesting than the experiences of the first few days led me to anticipate," he noted in his diary. "The papers were all of some importance; many of great value."[155] Many people wandered through the mansion during the summer and inevitably stopped to speak with the young historian combing the dusty papers. One visitor was the famous sculptor Edward V. Valentine. The two men struck up a friendship, and Valentine invited Freeman to his studio where he was working on a statue of Robert E. Lee. During the visit, Valentine asked Freeman to don the general's uniform while he made some sketches for his statue.[156]

The majority of the calendar was complete by September, and Freeman carried his work with him on his return to Hopkins. There he would add finishing touches and ask Professor Andrews to inspect the final product. Freeman's respect for Andrews had grown during the previous year, and he rejoiced that the new professor was "making good."[157] On October 15, he "carried over a bag full of my Confederate papers" for Andrews's review.[158] Andrews recommended some minor changes and commended the young scholar for "going into a new field, and one which no person in the South was writing about."[159] By November, the first part of the book was sent to the publisher. The following February, Freeman wrote the introduction to his first book.[160]

The soon-to-be published author now looked forward to receiving his doctorate and ending his days at Johns Hopkins. In October he received the welcome news that the Board of University Studies had accepted him as a candidate for the degree of Doctor of Philosophy.[161] This was followed by an appointment as a "Fellow by Courtesy."[162] He plowed through his dissertation for the last time—by now thoroughly tired of it. "If anybody tells you that writing a University dissertation is an easy job," he wrote his mother, "make no bones of it, but call him a liar outright."[163] Busy as these days were, he accepted an invitation to lecture at Richmond College in April. He spoke on "The Unknown of Virginia History—a Plea for the study of Economic History" and received a favorable review in the *Religious Herald*. "Dr. Freeman is, perhaps, the youngest man ever invited by the faculty to lecture," the review noted. "He is a brilliant scholar, who is held in the highest esteem at the University."[164]

Sometime in mid-1908, Freeman held in his hands an advance copy of his first book: *A Calendar of Confederate Papers*. Six hundred fifteen pages in length, the silk-cloth cover was a deep green with gold lettering. Advance sales had been satisfactory; the Confederate Memorial Literary Society reported subscription sales of 279 for the year ending November 30, 1907.[165] General release of the book would occur in late 1908. Before he received his degree from Johns Hopkins, Freeman was a published author.

He was not as fortunate with his dissertation. Upon completion, he submitted the manuscript, titled "The Attitude of Political Parties in Virginia to Slavery and Secession (1846-1861)," to the library. During the cataloguing process, a fire broke out at the Hopkins Library in September 1908, and destroyed much of Freeman's paper. Professor Vincent conveyed the bad news and expressed his hope that Freeman could reconstruct the text from his first draft.[166] Freeman no doubt had his notes and indices, but made no serious attempt to rewrite the paper for publication.[167]

Final examinations took place in May. His exam in political economy, his first subordinate subject, had him contrast the scientific methods of Adam Smith and David Ricardo, criticize the quantity theory of money, and comment upon the Malthusian argument against socialism, among other questions.[168] His exams in American history, English history, and European history were no less challenging. On the horizon loomed the oral examination. The schedule was issued on May 26, 1908, and Freeman saw he was to appear on June 3, 1908, at 10:00 A.M.[169] For the first time in his graduate school career, he confessed concern. From Walker came words of encouragement: "I am sure you are pulling oars with that same determination and will that always characterize your work."[170] June 3 arrived, and he took his place in front of his instructors. It was, he often said, the most terrifying experience of his life.[171] The hours passed. Late that afternoon, he emerged and promptly wired his father.

"Passed the board and accepted. Will be home tomorrow."[172]

Commencement exercises were held on June 9, 1908. The graduates heard an address by Prof. Henry T. Bovey, dean of the Faculty of Applied Sciences at McGill University, Montreal. Freeman and twenty-five others were awarded the degree of Doctor of Philosophy. His doctorate was in history, with subordinate studies in political science and political economy.[173]

The Hopkins years left mixed marks on Freeman. He entered determined to write a history of the war and left with that purpose still fixed, enhanced by his first publication. The scientific approach to the study of history reinforced beliefs he brought with him. He was not tempted by alternative theories of "New History," with its emphasis on social sciences, or persuaded to use psychological analysis in examining historical figures or events.[174] He developed no long-lasting relationships with faculty members, and, with the exception of Charles Andrews, he judged the staff of the History Department to be "mediocre, uninspiring or scatter-brained."[175] In short, Hopkins filled a well-defined and limited purpose in his life. It exposed him to vast sources of knowledge, from which he gleefully drew; it honed his self-discipline; and it gave him credentials to proceed in his chosen realm. Douglas Freeman was very much the same man upon graduation as he had been upon matriculation. Now he returned home to Richmond to start his career. He would, upon arrival, find his serene life severely jolted and forever changed by two women. One who would enter his life, and one who would leave it.

CHAPTER 4

"A Future Large with Promise"

Bettie Freeman was dying.

She felt the first pangs of pain from breast cancer sometime in late 1907 or early 1908. She said nothing, not wanting to distract Douglas from his critical final days at Johns Hopkins.[1] She shared in the joy of his graduation, and then told the family of the concealed terror. She was immediately examined, and doctors confirmed the cancer. Surgery came too late. She was given only a few months to live.[2]

"The world is opening up" Freeman had written his mother only a year earlier. Now that same world closed down on him with a never before experienced force. He was very much his father's son—in attitudes, in character, and in habits—but his mother was, in many ways, the central figure of his life.[3] "I love to think of the many long years that you and I have spent together," he wrote her from Hopkins.

> Years when I was growing up, and did not play in the streets; years when I was at school, and had my best confidant in you; college years, when even the wonderful change in everything did not draw us apart; and these later University years, so full of meaning, which have shown me, among other things, what a blessing a mother is; and what a particular blessing I have in mine.[4]

"You need not think for an instant that anything can come in between us," he concluded. "We—Father, you and I—must always stay together."[5]

Freeman's shock and sorrow were profound. Hard work and dedicated effort, character and willpower, all the lessons of his twenty-two years were as ashes in the face of the raging disease. Even his faith seemed inadequate. From it he now found only condemnation. He judged himself to be "a wretched, sinful boy" and somehow imputed

Bettie's illness to his own perceived lack of righteousness.[6] Spring 1908 brought with it no renewal of life.

Freeman was obviously experiencing the emotional reactions common to the advent of a devastating and traumatic event. First came the stunning paralysis brought on by revelation, the critical self-analysis, and a period of mourning the inevitable end. Only upon examining the life-changing consequences of the situation did Freeman begin to regain his equilibrium. He was the only son living at home and, with Walker Freeman now sixty-five years old, the primary responsibility of managing the household and tending to Bettie was on his shoulders.[7] Responsibility pushed aside sorrow-induced languor.

Pressing on meant starting his career. The natural path for a newly minted Ph.D. was to join a college faculty. Both President Boatwright and S. C. Mitchell wanted Freeman for the History Department at Richmond College, so it came as something of a surprise when Boatwright advised that a lack of funds prevented the opening of a position. "I assure you," Boatwright wrote, "it will give me great pleasure if I can be of service to you in securing a position elsewhere."[8] Going elsewhere proved problematic. Freeman had made inquiries, through a third party, about a position on the staff at Baylor University, but the word came that "no change along the lines in which Dr. Freeman would be interested" had developed.[9] Waiting for the Richmond College position caused him to move too late in applying for a spot at Mercer University in Georgia. "If I had known of you earlier," President Jamison wrote, "the probability is that we would have reached an agreement."[10] With no college job available, Freeman accepted a faculty position at Miss Virginia Randolph Ellett's School for Young Ladies in Richmond. He would teach history and drama to seniors—many of whom were nearly his age—at "Miss Jennie's" school starting in the fall of 1908.[11] He also accepted part-time work as publicity director with the Virginia Department of Health. The job paid five hundred dollars a year and enabled him to utilize the medical knowledge he acquired at Johns Hopkins and work alongside his brother Allen who served as assistant commissioner of health.[12]

It was a somewhat inauspicious career start for an ambitious man. If he chafed at the prospect of employment considerably below his talents, Freeman made no public expression of disappointment. He settled into his new life; eagerly awaiting the release of the *Calendar*, preparing to assume his duties at "Miss Jennie's," and handling the press responsibilities at the health department. As "one of the city's most scholarly young men" he was often in demand as a speaker.[13] One such request came on a Sunday morning in July 1908. Standing on the portico of the Second Baptist Church, Freeman was approached by James Hinton Goddin, a fellow church member. Mr. Goddin had been a successful sand and gravel contractor who had sold his business and opened a Christian mission in Richmond's "red-light" district. He asked Freeman to come to speak at the mission. Still recovering from battling inner demons in the wake of his mother's illness, Freeman initially refused. He was not certain he was back on sound religious footing. But he was fond of the older gentleman, whom he called "Uncle James" (pronounced in local vernacular as "Uncle Jeems"), and he soon acquiesced to the request.[14]

On the appointed evening, Freeman headed downtown to the Goddin mission, which was housed in an unused theater. "On every corner, as outposts of the houses, stood sentinel bar-rooms," he wrote.

Queer places they were, aflame with lights, yet dark with tobacco smoke . . . at the bars thronged excited, restless men; in the rear-rooms laughed tipsy, painted women. And about men and women alike was the wild, abandoned air of hopeless vice.[15]

"Still worse," he noted, "were the people. Young women in loose-flowing silks fled laughing across the way . . . clerks and sailors, loafers and cadets, old men and boys, drunken bruisers and sober thugs."[16] He entered the mission where he observed "the opera chairs, sadly worn and battered, sloped towards the platform . . . a deserted stage with sagging wings and mouldy drop."[17] He watched as society's castoffs gathered in the mission with the thieves, drunkards, and hoboes. Then the service began, and a remarkable transformation occurred. Instead of ministering to the motley congregation, Freeman found himself being ministered to. One by one they rose to give testimonies. "I saw men as sinful, perhaps as I was," he wrote, "who had been lifted out of themselves."[18] As he listened to the dirty, ragged men with the shining faces, he came under "the witness of the spirit" and rediscovered his own shaken faith.[19] "If it works for them," he reasoned, "it may work for me." The experiences of the night could be dismissed as the overly emotional reaction of a young man during a traumatic stage of life. Yet Freeman would, in years to come, point to this night as one of personal revelation and renewal. He had passed through his own season of doubt and now recommitted himself "to try to lead the Christ-life."[20] The words he spoke to the assembly that night were not remembered; the words they spoke to him were never forgotten.

If personal and spiritual rejuvenation were not enough to make the night memorable, there was an equally significant moment in time. A young girl was seated at the piano on stage. A single light bulb hung from the ceiling above her, casting a nimbus of light on her delicate features. Tall and slim, she had her hair in a pompadour, and it shown gold in the dim theater. Freeman's evening was already full of emotional stirrings that touched his innermost being; now, he added another sentiment. The passionate young man was instantly love struck.[21]

The girl at the piano was the youngest daughter of "Uncle Jeems," seventeen-year-old Inez Virginia Goddin. Born in Richmond on December 18, 1890, Inez was the last of ten children born to the Goddin family and one of only four children to survive to adulthood. Inez could hardly remember a summer passing without a small white coffin resting in the family parlor. Her father was a "courtly gentleman," and from that heritage she developed the warm smile, the solicitous nature, and the dignified bearing of a Southern gentlewoman. One word would come to distinguish her entire life: poise. Inez was not, however, all form and no substance. A gifted musician, she studied piano and was able to recall and play melodies after hearing them but once. She enrolled in the Woman's College of Richmond and was preparing to start her senior year when Freeman saw her in the mission.[22] Playing the piano that night, she was unaware of the tremendous force that was about to enter her life.

The spark of romance, along with the renewal of his faith, lifted Freeman from the depressed lethargy that had marked his recent days in Richmond and set off a flurry of activity. He sought invitations to speak at each of Richmond's sixteen Baptist churches, explored the possibility of rewriting and publishing his Hopkins dissertation, and wrote a biographical sketch titled "Something of the Freeman Family."[23] "It might not be improper," he thought, "to write down a few words regarding the Freeman family for the benefit of those who are to live after us." The story, he conceded, "is not a brilliant one, [but] does show the benefits of good honest blood."[24] He recounted the family traditions about his ancestry—tracing it back to Sussex, England—and offered a summary of his heritage with the statement: "I believe all the Freemans were men; I trust they all were Christians. May our children be like our forefathers."[25]

A Calendar of Confederate Papers was released in the summer of 1908. The first edition, limited to one thousand copies, was printed by

Whittet & Shepperson and heralded by the *Richmond Evening Journal* as "skillfully done" and of "inestimable value to the lover of Southern history." The reviews that followed during the coming months were equally laudatory. The *Virginia Magazine of History and Biography* called the work "clear and intelligible" and "a most important contribution to the literature of Confederate history." Freeman, the review concluded, was the "right man" for this "pioneer work."[26] Historian and author Frederic Bancroft reviewed the *Calendar* for the *American Historical Review* and, upon completion of his article, wrote Freeman a letter of praise. "I don't see how anyone could have performed the task better than you have," he wrote, expressing amazement at Freeman's "breadth of view and accuracy."[27] His review was as flattering as the letter. "Whoever writes Confederate history from the sources will find this orderly and thoroughly modern Calendar, supplemented by careful notes, an indispensable *vade mecum.*" Freeman's *Calendar*, Bancroft held, "is the historian's Baedeker for Richmond's best memorials of the Confederates."[28] By any measure, Freeman's first book was a success. He received favorable notices, his work was recognized as scholarly and authoritative, and he was viewed as a rising scholar of Southern military history. His time in the Virginia State Library during the summer of 1906 had been time well spent.

The newly published author now turned his attention to an ardent courtship of Inez Goddin. He appeared more often at the mission and found ways to walk with her from church. What he did not know was that Inez had been admiring him from afar even before he spotted her at the mission. She had noticed him in church—this young man in a hurry whose reputation preceded him. She learned that he caught the streetcar near her home to go to his office at the health department, so she peered through half-open blinds to catch a glimpse.[29] She must have been thrilled when Freeman began to pay her such attention, but her reserve prevented her from admitting it. Freeman proceeded in the dark as to her sentiments. On Saturday, September 26, 1908, he began a letter to Inez on which he would work until Tuesday, October 6. His daily additions to the letter turn it into a diary of his early pursuit of Inez. "For some time after I first saw you at the mission," he wrote, "I have thought but little of you."

But of late, I have thought of no one else. Gradually, so gradually, you have come to own a place in my heart. First, there would be an occasional thought of dear Uncle James' little girl; then, a feeling of pleasure when I saw you; then, a real delight in walking home with and talking with you; then, a strange thrill of pleasure when I touched you or looked into your eyes; now a sensation, so real and so true that I know it can only be the greatest thing of all, love![30]

While confiding his feelings to his letter, he began to give Inez some glimpse of what was going through his mind and heart. One evening he told her he had "about fixed on the woman" of his choice. Inez chided him for always talking about marriage and said no woman could meet the ideals he had for a wife. "Know yourself," Freeman wrote in response in the September 28 portion of his letter. The subtle circling finally became too much for him and on Tuesday, September 29, he professed his love.[31] Inez still held back her feelings, saying only that the future he painted was "the future [she] wanted to see." That tentative acceptance gave Freeman "very sweet hopes," which he duly recorded in his running narrative.

Oh, girl, love me, and you will find me true and faithful. I can do things in this world, and I am going to do them; but I want you to be with me, and to enjoy with me the fruits of my labor.[32]

Early fall days found the two "rambling across . . . old roads" and sharing walks to the mission. Inez was wary of the intense young man, no matter how she may have wanted to return his love. He was four and one-half years older than she, with two college degrees and a published book. His ardor was so intense; he had but seen her in July and now, in September, was professing lifetime love. Freeman noticed that Inez seemed "almost cold," but attributed it to the differences in their age. "Prove me and try me," he wrote on October 6 as he completed his sixteen-page love letter. "Read it, dear heart, and think over it. As God lives, I am honest, as I am true, I love you."[33]

Freeman began teaching classes that fall at "Miss Jennie's" school. The girls found their twenty-two-year-old teacher "enthralling" and delighted in the plays he staged in the park opposite the school.[34] His acting troupe, dubbed "Mistress Ellett's Players," performed Shakespeare's *As You Like It* during his first year at the school.[35] Freeman enjoyed working for Miss Jennie, whom he ranked with John Peyton McGuire and S. C. Mitchell in a triumvirate of the great teachers he had known.[36] "Education as well as the church has its saints," he said, and "Miss Jennie was surely one."[37] Nor was he neglecting his favorite avocation of history. While conducting some research in the Confederate Museum, he discovered a "tin case" in which he found "the original parchment of the so-called 'permanent' Constitution of the Confederacy, signed by all the members."[38] The *Richmond Evening Journal* headlined the discovery as "Worth $25,000" and paid tribute to the "indefatigable and astute" Dr Freeman.[39] That same month, Freeman returned to his alma mater, Richmond College, to lecture on "Research in Southern History."[40]

Freeman's most significant historical activity in the wake of the *Calendar* was to write a lengthy article for inclusion in *The South in the Building of the Nation*. This multi-volume collection, of which S. C. Mitchell was one of numerous editors, sought "to record the south's part in the making of the American nation" and to portray "the character [and] genius" of the southern people."[41] His fact- and statistic-loaded article, "The Aristocracy of the Northern Neck," left little room for eloquence, but was a thorough and complete study of the domestic, ecclesiastical, and business life of this part of Virginia. It further confirmed his standing among the region's historians and demonstrated the confidence S. C. Mitchell had in his former pupil.

Nor had he been forgotten by Dr. McIlwaine of the Virginia State Library, by whom he had been hired as a substitute librarian during the summer of 1906. Freeman was reading in the library one March afternoon when McIlwaine approached him and asked what subordinate subjects he had studied at Johns Hopkins.

"Political science and economics," Freeman replied.

McIlwaine "nodded with approval" and told Freeman that John Stewart Bryan, publisher of the *Richmond Times-Dispatch*, had asked for a recommendation of someone qualified to write a series of editorials on tax reform.[42] McIlwaine remembered Freeman's talents and, after confirming that his studies fit the editorial topic, recommended him to Bryan. The grateful Freeman immediately visited the *Times-Dispatch* publisher. There he learned that Bryan wanted to begin a campaign for the "removal of inequalities of assessment" in the Virginia tax code. If Freeman was interested in writing at least two editorials per week, the pay would be seven dollars a week, and he could start immediately.[43] Freeman accepted on the spot and added the job of "editorial assistant" to his other occupations.

The newspaper Freeman joined had followed a circuitous route to become the *Richmond Times-Dispatch*. It traced its beginnings to 1850 when James A. Cowardin and W. H. Davis founded the *Richmond Dispatch*. In 1886, a new paper entered circulation, the *Daily Times*, later simply the *Times*, founded by Maj. Lewis Ginter. In the winter of 1888, Ginter, who had grown tired of the business, gave the *Times* outright to Joseph Bryan. That same year saw the creation of another paper—the *Evening Leader*. In 1896, Bryan, already owner of the *Times*, bought the *Leader* as well. The last paper to join the increasingly crowded market was the *News*, founded in 1899. Numerous purchases and mergers followed through the years reducing to two the number of players in the field—Joseph Bryan, who owned the morning *Times* and the *Evening Leader*; and John Williams, who owned the morning *Dispatch* and the evening *News*. Recognizing the drain on resources caused by the competition, Bryan and Williams agreed to a swap—the *Dispatch* going to Bryan and the *Evening Leader* to Williams. The result was the establishment, in January 1903, of the morning *Richmond Times-Dispatch* and the evening *Richmond News Leader*. In 1908 Joseph Bryan bought the *News Leader*, thus consolidating his control of Richmond's major papers. John Stewart Bryan, Joseph's son, served as vice president of the *Times-Dispatch*, and, by 1908, succeeded his father as publisher.[44]

Bryan viewed Virginia's tax structure as "unwieldy and almost unintelligible" and wanted a "systematic and thorough-going" review and revision of the entire system.[45] On March 22, 1909, Freeman began what would become a series of thirty-three editorials, stretching over a three-month period, examining every aspect of Virginia's tax code and offering a plan of reform. The editorials reflect the training of a historian: They are fact filled, unemotional, and logical. He did not adopt a "fire-breathing" editorial style; his method was to systematically outline the shortcomings of the system, bolster his opinion with statistics, and offer practical solutions.

The central problems in the tax code were ones of inequality and undervaluation. Virginia levied a flat tax on all real and personal property; localities had the right to levy a similar tax. The assessment of property, for purposes of both state and local taxation, was in the hands of local authorities. With no consistent equalization system, land was assessed at anywhere from 5 percent to 65 percent of its fair market value, and some localities paid twelve times as much tax on the same type of property as other localities. The amount of real estate taxes collected in the city of Richmond for the year 1907-08, for instance, amounted to more than one-fourth of the reported value of all farmhouses and lands in the entire state.[46] It was possible for a locality to avoid its proper tax burden by making a low assessment of certain property, paying the fixed state tax thereon, and then levying a higher local tax on the same property. The state of Virginia thus found itself with significant revenue shortfalls and haphazardly added additional taxes—such as the license tax, writ tax, and seal tax—to make up the losses.[47] Freeman's first salvo at the tax code was directed to this issue of fair and equal assessment of taxes.

> Either through negligence of the commissioners of the revenue, or else through the false reports of tax-payers, the state is losing much revenue that should be paid into the Treasury. We believe, upon good evidence, that if the principal tax laws now on the books were rigidly enforced, the people of Virginia would not have to keep on their books the many minor tax laws, which are becoming burdensome and onerous. The law requires that taxes be levied equally and at full valuation. Is this being done in Virginia? The figures speak for themselves.[48]

He laid out a solution of a new assessment plan and creation of a state tax commission which would "permit of the least possible maladministration."[49] He called for the abolition of several taxes that produced "double taxation" and for appointment, rather than election, of commissioners of revenue.[50] Tax reform was a dry topic on which to write, and the reader could be forgiven if his eyes glazed over at titles such as "Tax Returns from Virginia Cities: Some Comparisons."[51] Yet Freeman's editorials, rarely over five hundred words and usually within one column, clarified the complicated issue and used repetition to establish basic points in the mind of the reader. He also knew how to turn a phrase when the opportunity presented itself. The state tax on seals was "a tax savoring of ante-Revolutionary Hanoverian times."[52] In prodding the gubernatorial candidates to address the issue of tax reform, Freeman asserted "the people are wearying of seeing the old chaff threshed over again; they delight no longer in the ghosts of dead or might-have-been issues."[53] He also made the politically astute point that the *Times-Dispatch* tax reform plan could be implemented without the imposition of new taxes.[54] Bryan had asked for columns only on tax reform, but the thorough Freeman tacked on a short series on the fees charged by commissioners of revenue, sheriffs, and clerks of court.[55] "The entire matter is now in the hands of the people," Freeman wrote in his final editorial of the series. The people had heard—and read—and the legislature would act on tax reform during its next session, with consequences affecting his career.

Legislative action was in the future; the immediate effect of his editorials was to land him a permanent position on the *Times-Dispatch* editorial staff. John Stewart Bryan and Henry Sydnor Harrison, Freeman's supervisor, were impressed by his talents and writing ability and named him editorial assistant in June 1909. After a shaky start, Freeman's professional career was acquiring steady footing. His personal life was still a work in progress.

His ardent courtship of Inez Goddin was producing mixed results. Sometime between September 1908 and May 1909, Inez professed her love for him. At the same time, her reserve seemed to harden into a permanent distance. Unfortunately, no letters or diaries survive that shed any light on Inez's thoughts during that time. One can imagine the tall girl, with her thick braid of blond hair tied with a bow at the back, always immaculately attired, walking slowly to class or to her father's mission, thinking about the passionate and energetic young doctor-editor-historian-author who had so quickly and so certainly made up his mind that they should spend their lives together. She loved him, she had admitted this much, but still there was reluctance. Was it bred of self-doubt? Or did she suspect that Douglas Freeman, "whose brilliance was on every tongue," might grow weary of her as quickly as he had fallen for her?[56]

Whatever the reason, Inez's behavior sent conflicting signals. As he was wont, Freeman attempted to discuss the issue face to face. The conversation was apparently disappointing, for Freeman stewed on it for twenty-four hours before pouring out his confused emotional state in a letter. "I am going to try, my dear girl, to put on paper some of the thoughts which I so poorly expressed last night."[57]

Never has there been, in my heart, anything that was dishonest, insincere, untrue or partial. I have given you my whole heart, and have loved you, I believe, as much as a man can love a woman. It is this feeling which has made me trust you as I never trusted any woman save my poor dear mother. I ask you tonight, Inez, whether I have kept the faith and whether I have been true to you. Surrounded as I am daily with scores of attractive girls, I can honestly say that I have never, by deed or word, done or said anything with any of them that was disloyal or unfaithful to you.[58]

"Having given you my full love," Freeman reasoned, "it is but natural and proper that I should ask as much of you. I cannot be satisfied with less . . . is that not fair?" He went on to express chagrin over a "half-dozen" small slights, including Inez's "point blank" refusal on several occasions to kiss him good night. "I can only make one plea, one last plea, that you give your heart full play, and that you let your actions show what's in your heart," Freeman warned. "Unless you open your heart to that love, dear girl, the future of our love is gloomy and foreboding."[59]

Three weeks after he wrote to Inez, Bettie Freeman succumbed to cancer. One searches in vain for a sentence from Freeman's pen memorializing his feelings during these days. More than a year had passed since he learned the terrible news of her illness, so there was no shock on this May day. Grief had been a yearlong companion as well, coming in waves of despair before withdrawing into settled resignation. Unspoken, but surely felt, was some degree of release: Bettie from her suffering, Freeman from his vigil of nursing and housekeeping. His had been an emotional life, vividly revealed in letters, notes, poems, and plays. The previous August in his essay on the Freeman family, already knowing his mother's fate, he had written a few short lines:

> Never lived a woman in whom the motherly and wifely instinct was more developed. I who write have known her from the days when first I remembered anyone, and I can say this: never did I know her to do a single selfish act; never have I known her to fail the slightest in her duty as a Christian, a mother and a wife. May God bless her forever, Amen.[60]

Now, in May, at this singular emotional moment in his life, there is only silence.[61]

The day before Bettie died, Inez Goddin was graduated from the Richmond Woman's College with a Bachelor of Letters degree. She performed the "Tree Oration" during the exercises.[62] It is not known if Freeman attended, but it is doubtful given his mother's condition on May 28. The relationship between Freeman and Inez, however, would not have prevented his attendance for it seemed to be on the upswing following his letter of May 9. The two passed a cheerful summer, and Freeman's letters bespeak a confidence and security in their relationship.[63] Inez entered Smithdale-Massie Business College and soon took a secretarial position at the State Department of Health.

Freeman continued to write at a furious pace. In July he wrote eleven biographical sketches for the Southern Publication Society.[64] A larger work was editing and writing the introduction to W. W. Baker's *Memoirs of Service with John Yates Beall, C.S.N.* Beall was a Confederate privateer and special agent who thrilled the South with his daring attempts to free Confederate prisoners. He was caught and hanged as a guerilla and spy in 1865. W. W. Baker served under Beall's command and, at Freeman's urging, wrote down his memories. Freeman edited the text and wrote the introduction. While writing of Beall and Baker, he took the opportunity to write of the veterans of the war and their struggle during Reconstruction. In his words, one can see a tribute to Walker Freeman from the pen of his son.

> Most of the men who came back from Appomattox and from other fields of sorrow were young men. All who were to have a part in making the South were young, for many past thirty who came back from the war to contend alone with a hopeless labor force, a denuded country, and a biting poverty, seldom regained their old position and seldom were able to rise . . . All depended on the boys. To be sure, most of them had been snatched from school or from college . . . but however equipped, their minds were those which must make fortunes for themselves and greatness for the South. How they did it, how they surmounted obstacles and repaired their broken fortunes, how they struggled to make life worth living and home worth having; how they rose and toiled and finally succeeded is no less heroic than the tale of their military prowess.[65]

The young writer took on more community service in 1910 by accepting appointment as executive secretary of the Virginia Anti-Tuberculosis Association. Freeman used the largely voluntary position as an opportunity to travel the state and deliver speeches such as "The Responsibility of the Community to Care for the Individual Consumptive."[66] "The time has now come," he lectured one audience, "when no man can live unto himself alone, but must obey the Biblical injunction of 'bear ye one another's burdens.'"[67] This admonition carried with it a duty to contribute financially to care and prevention programs. "What . . . shall we say of that community, strong and healthy, powerful and wealthy, which will stand by and see its citizens die, when a little care for them could prevent their death?"[68] Always interested in health and medical issues, Freeman would hold this post for three years.[69]

Colonel J. Calvin Hemphill served as editor of the *Richmond*

Times-Dispatch during the years Freeman was an assistant. On June 13, 1910, Hemphill clipped one of Freeman's editorials and mailed it to the president of the United States, William Howard Taft. The president responded the next day, commenting that he "enjoyed the style of your assistant much."[70] Hemphill scrawled on the bottom of Taft's letter: "The assistant here referenced is Douglas Freeman, Ph.D., a very likely [*sic*] fellow of amazing knowledge but vicious temper." The editorial is not included with the letter, and it is impossible to guess which one might have been thought of interest to President Taft.[71] The more interesting aspect of this episode is Hemphill's reference to Freeman's "vicious temper." Intensity is never lacking in Freeman's life or letters during these years, but this is the only surviving contemporary reference to a temper so noticeable as to be termed "vicious." Hemphill's observation might be dismissed as an unsubstantiated oddity were it not for the state of Freeman's romantic life during this time. It was, apparently, again in flux. Freeman's letters to Inez from May to August 1909 are upbeat, light, and full of typical love references. After August 29, the letters abruptly stop—lost, destroyed, or, more ominous, unwritten. At the same time the letters disappear, one Emma Gray White appears. Emma Gray attended Miss Jennie's school and was one of Dr. Freeman's students. Tall and handsome, with large dark eyes, Emma Gray alleged that she and Freeman began "a stormy love affair" about this time.[72] Supposedly an engagement occurred, and marriage was prevented only by the intervention of Emma Gray's father. The only source for this story is Emma Gray White in conversations with Freeman's daughter years after the supposed relationship took place. Her story gains some credibility if the lack of letters between Freeman and Inez Goddin during this period indicates a lull in their relationship. Her use of the term "stormy" to describe the alleged love affair also coincides with Hemphill's description of Freeman's temper. Yet speculation can carry one too far. The lack of letters between Freeman and Inez could mean that they were spending so much time together that letters were unnecessary, or the letters may have been lost through the years.[73] There are also no letters in existence from this period between Emma Gray and Freeman. When a letter to Inez makes an appearance on December 18, 1911, Freeman writes as if nothing out of the ordinary has occurred. In short, no one knows what, if anything, happened between Freeman, Inez Goddin, and Emma Gray White between August 1909 and December 1911. Given the turbulent nature of their relationship, it is not out of the question that Freeman and Inez could have experienced a temporary breakup. If so, it would not have been the first time a boy frustrated over the course of one relationship turned to another. Emma Gray's memory of a "stormy love affair" could be an accurate recollection or an embellishment on a schoolgirl crush. Freeman remained close friends with Emma Gray to the end of his life. If a serious romance had at one time existed, one wonders if Inez would have approved of the two remaining so close. One additional fact, perhaps dispositive of the entire matter, needs to be considered: During the time in which no letters are found between Freeman and Inez, he added two new major projects to his already crowded life—projects that left little time for letter-writing or romantic pursuits.

The first opportunity came as a result of his tax editorials in the *Times-Dispatch*. The 1910 session of the General Assembly, responding to the growing cry for tax reform, established a state tax commission to review Virginia's tax and assessment laws.[74] Freeman celebrated that action, for which he was in no small part responsible, not only as a "victory for tax reform" but also as "a striking instance of the fighting power of the press."[75] The commission consisted of the governor, lieutenant governor, Speaker of the House, chairman of the State Corporation Commission, and two legislators—members who, by the very nature of their offices and duties, would have little time to do any actual work on the commission. The real work would fall on the commission's single "technical member" or expert—the secretary. The commission was given $10,000 to complete its work and file a report with the General Assembly. Freeman became the obvious choice for secretary, and the job was offered to him sometime in June 1910. It had been his practice to hold down a number of jobs at one time, and he apparently thought he could continue writing for the *Times-Dispatch* if he accepted the tax commission job. John Stewart Bryan made it clear that he must choose. "I frankly believe that you can serve Virginia better as tax commissioner," he wrote Freeman, citing his "training . . . judgment and . . . capacity for work." Bryan assured Freeman "a call on the place when you wish to come back" and expressed regret that he could not hold both jobs.[76] Bryan also must have believed that having his former editorial assistant serve as secretary would ensure that the *Times-Dispatch*'s position on tax reform would be written into the final report. With his options thus defined, Freeman signaled the commission that he would accept the appointment and was elected at the organizational meeting on June 28, 1910.[77]

The task before Freeman was in many ways similar to organizing and indexing Confederate papers for his *Calendar*. He was to review the entire tax code—as unorganized as musty war documents—craft revisions and recommendations, and write a coherent report. "Taxation is a subject that is interesting to the average citizen at one time only," Freeman said, "when he goes to pay his bill. At all other seasons, he regards the subject as he would a dose of physic—the very thought is nauseous."[78] Freeman, however, was no "average citizen," and he embarked on his new duties with the same dedicated thoroughness that had marked his entire career. He did not have to start from scratch. His *Times-Dispatch* editorials had identified most of the problems "of that crazy-quilt which covers the financial bed of the Commonwealth" and had proffered solutions.[79] "We wearied our reader, no doubt, by proceeding line upon line . . . but we kept it up until every man . . . knew that there was something rotten in the taxation Denmark."[80]

Having outlined the problems and solutions in his *Times-Dispatch* editorials, Freeman the economist turned to his tested methods of historical research to build the case for tax reform. He sent out lengthy circulars to local assessors and revenue commissioners requiring "specific answers to a large number of questions." What he could not find out through correspondence, he learned in individual meetings throughout the state. He went into the field with land assessors and with commissioners on their rounds. He held conferences with the State Corporation Commission, the comptrollers of railroads, and representatives of numerous banks and insurance companies.[81] He read newspapers from all across Virginia to check reported assessments and land transfers. He prepared digests of the tax laws of all other states and read the reports of every tax commission that had worked in the United States since 1876.[82] He studied the recommendations of the Commission of Ontario regarding railroad taxation and traveled to Milwaukee, Wisconsin, to attend the meeting of the International Tax Association. He wrote his economics professor at Johns Hopkins, Jacob H. Hollander, for advice on "any other reference matter on taxation that you think will be helpful."[83] The editor turned economist seemed to be everywhere at once, holding public hearings and castigating sacred cows. "It is usually the case," he said in Portsmouth, Virginia, "that I will find the people saying that while they want tax reform, there is one particular thing that they want reduced or they do not want touched. Each man has some particular thing on which he thinks that taxes should be lower than on anything else."[84] His rhetoric grew more vehement as he detailed the "palpable frauds" and "gross deceits" of the tax system.[85]

Such a life would be his lot until December 1911, when the commission report would be presented to the General Assembly. It was work enough for one man, but another opportunity—far greater than any he had known—presented itself almost simultaneously with the Tax Commission appointment in the spring of 1910.

One of the collections that Freeman had catalogued in his *Calendar of Confederate Papers* was a set of books and pamphlets presented to the museum by Mary De Renne, a wealthy collector devoted to the memory of Robert E. Lee. Freeman judged the De Renne collection to be "the most valuable of the Library" and paid tribute to the "rare judgment" of Mrs. De Renne.[86] One of the readers of Freeman's *Calendar* was Mrs. De Renne's son, the wealthy bibliophile Wymberley Jones De Renne of Savannah, Georgia.[87] Impressed with Freeman's scholarship—and no doubt appreciative of the compliment paid his mother—De Renne came to Richmond in early June 1910 and sought out the young writer. During their meeting, De Renne told an astonishing tale and made a breathtaking offer. He told Freeman that he owned more than two hundred letters—dispatches from the field—from Gen. Robert E. Lee to President Jefferson Davis—dispatches thought long since destroyed. He was mysteriously silent as to how these dispatches came into his hands, but nonetheless asked Freeman to consider reviewing and editing them for first-time publication. Freeman's response is recorded in the letter he dashed off to De Renne shortly after their meeting. "I assure you," he wrote, "that nothing will give me more pleasure than the co-operation in an undertaking which bespeaks so much patriotism on your part and which will be of such great value to the people of the South."[88] Though newly appointed as secretary of the Tax Commission, Freeman did not qualify his enthusiastic acceptance of this considerable task. "Freed at last from the burden of a newspaper life," he wrote, "my time is my own."[89]

The two men met in October at De Renne's vacation home in New York to discuss the particulars of the project.[90] Several weeks later, De Renne stopped in Richmond on his way to Georgia and handed Freeman two morocco-bound volumes. One can only imagine the quickened breath and tightened muscles as Freeman opened the volumes and saw the dispatches for the first time. De Renne made the formal request and Freeman, no doubt unbelieving the fortune that was his, accepted. Although similar to the work he had done on the *Calendar*, this editing job would be more than simply indexing and cataloging papers. Footnotes would have to be written setting the letters in historical context and identifying the persons and events mentioned in the dispatches. Maneuvers would have to be explained, battles recounted, and personalities dissected. A concise history of Lee's active command of the Army of Northern Virginia would need to be constructed. This was far more than a technical editing job; this was, at last, writing history.

For the next five months, while being knee deep in Tax Commission work, Freeman pored over the letters. He needed to determine how many of the dispatches had been previously printed in other publications. This required a painstaking process of checking each dispatch against the seventy volumes of the *The War of the Rebellion: A Compiliation of the Official Records of the Union and Confederate Armies* and at least five other published collections. This required "many, many long hours" ransacking the often unorganized published sets.[91] In February, Freeman reported to De Renne that 136 of the 242 letters "appear never to have seen print." The letters contained "much new material," but he admitted he had "hoped for better things." He left to De Renne the decision on whether to proceed with publication.[92] The word came from Georgia to proceed. Freeman was soon giving the project up to four hours each night.[93]

His first tasks were to copy each document, so he could return the originals to De Renne, continue his comparison with other published sources, and begin to annotate each dispatch. He found the process to be the most "difficult . . . piece of editorial work in my life."[94]

> The letters are so detailed and refer to so many minor matters that, without copious notes, they are practically a sealed book. On the other hand, to secure the information which will make them easily understood is an enormous task . . . In some cases I have worked every night for a week on a single letter.[95]

Freeman urged De Renne to publish all 242 letters—even the previously published ones—in order to present "an incomparable picture of General Lee's character and strategy."[96] Having doubled the project, Freeman received more work. In mid-June 1911, De Renne brought another bound volume to Richmond, this one containing 295 telegrams, all of which would require the same treatment of transcription and analysis. Only ninety telegrams would ultimately appear in the book, but all had to be checked at this early stage. They were, Freeman judged, "valuable, and a few . . . of very great importance."[97] He spent the rest of 1911—or that portion he had devoted to historical work—copying and organizing the dispatches and telegrams. The writing was still to come.

The *Danville Register* wondered in an editorial of January 20, 1911, why the newspapers of Richmond so "often and so eulogistically" referred to the young Dr. Douglas Southall Freeman.[98] So when Freeman traveled to Danville on work for the Tax Commission, the editorial staff met with him. "Now," the paper confessed, "we understand why." He was a "man of unusual talent and ability and of remarkable erudition when his age is considered." The editorial admitted Freeman was not infallible, but judged him "a man of unusual intelligence, energy and capacity . . . He is all this at the age of twenty-five."[99] "Added years," the editorial concluded, "insure for him a future large with promise." The *Tazewell Republican* viewed the Democrat Freeman as an independent and fair-minded crusader whose tax reform efforts "hit the machine and Democrat Party of the state the heaviest blow that has been delivered lately."[100] From S. C. Mitchell came words of praise for his former student. "[I] rejoice to know that you are forging ahead in your career as a thinker and molder of public opinion," Mitchell wrote. "The views for which you stand are the ones that I wish to prevail—sound thinking on public matters, the training of every child for efficiency, and national conciliation."[101] As Freeman's reputation continued to grow, notoriety came from unexpected sources. In 1911, Henry Syndor Harrison, Freeman's former associate at the *Times-Dispatch*, released a novel titled *Queed*, with characters and settings eerily suggestive of personalities and surroundings of Richmond. In March, he dropped Freeman a line warning him about a certain-to-be-made comparison. "Possibly Richmond readers will look to see old friends behind every bush," Harrison wrote, "and in that case—since the hero of the work begins his newspaper life with a series of highbrowed compositions on tax-reform—look to see yourself pointed out as Dr. Queed himself."[102] Although Harrison assured Freeman that his sketch of Queed was not drawn from his life, it is difficult to imagine how Harrison could have realistically expected his disclaimer to be accepted as the truth. Harrison describes "Dr. Queed" as looking "as if he might have been born in a library" with the "dusty air of premature age," a "bold" nose (Freeman's aquiline nose was a distinguishing figure of his face), "long straight mouth," and "great spectacles."[103] Not only did Dr. Queed write tax editorials, he longed to write a definitive study—of sociology, not history—and kept to an "iron-clad" schedule that parceled out specific minutes to his various responsibilities.[104] Having perhaps drawn Queed too close to life, Harrison built in some distinctly un-Freeman like characteristics. Queed is rude in conversation, delinquent in paying debts, and indifferent—almost hostile—to those around him. He understands nothing of the Confederacy and has a cynical indifference to love and family. Thus Queed is patently different from Freeman, but the initial shadings are so obvious that Harrison, his disavowal notwithstanding, certainly modeled his title character in part on the young assistant editor with whom he worked at the *Times-Dispatch*. Freeman's only comment came in a somewhat defensive editorial on the pages of the *Richmond News Leader* in 1921. Noting that *Queed* was being adapted for the stage, he commented that "much nonsense has been written about this splendid novel."[105]

Efforts have been made to find "local hits" on every page and to identify the characters as living Richmond people. The utter absurdity of all this is proved by nothing so much as by the contrary theories advanced as to the "original" of this character or that. If Mr. Harrison had intended to depict actual persons, he would have been much humiliated to know that men, as antipodal as human beings can be, solemnly were averred to be one and the same person in the book. As a matter of fact, though he borrowed a few incidents here and there from Richmond life, The News Leader has the best of authority for saying that neither intentionally nor unintentionally did Mr. Harrison have as model of any sort, good or bad, any person now living in Richmond.[106]

The fall of 1911 was divided between writing the report of the Tax Commission and reviewing the De Renne documents. The tax report was in its final form on December 16, 1911, and was released to the public on December 28. The 417-page book contained a forty-two-page "report" with recommendations, credited to commission members, and a 369-page, nine-chapter "appendix," credited to Freeman.[107] The twenty-one recommendations did not significantly differ from those outlined two years earlier in Freeman's editorials. They called for the establishment of a permanent tax commission, the equalization of assessments, the removal of revenue commissioners for neglect of duty, the formation of standard assessment rules and regulations, and the alteration—some by increase and some by abolition—of several minor taxes. Freeman's "book" within the report is a detailed treatise on every aspect of tax law in Virginia. The *Times-Dispatch* greeted the release of the report with front-page coverage and editorially hailed Freeman's work as "able and exhaustive."[108] The *Times-Dispatch* had "cordially and unreservedly commended the selection of Dr. Freeman, and it feels that by his report its belief in his capacity and fitness has been abundantly justified."[109] Freeman summarized the commission's work in a speech to the Fifth Annual Conference on State and Local Taxation. "We are at the turning of the ways," he said. "Our thriving younger sisters to the South still look to Virginia for counsel. Our success in tax reform will encourage them to like endeavors; our failure to improve conditions cannot but deter them from the course that establishes justice between citizens and maintains equality among brothers."[110] The governor embraced the recommendations—he was, after all, a member of the commission—and submitted them to the General Assembly for approval.[111] The state legislature did what it usually did with lengthy reports: ignored it. No significant tax reform took place in the 1912 session, and Freeman would find himself writing more tax reform editorials—remarkably similar to those he did in 1909—in years to come. No laws went on the books, but Dr. Freeman placed a second publication on his personal bookshelf.[112]

His work on the Tax Commission completed, Freeman rejoined the editorial staff of the *Times-Dispatch* and accepted the chairmanship of the State Board of Charities and Corrections. The later position was similar to his role with the anti-tuberculosis board and offered him speaking opportunities while keeping him current on developments in health and medicine. His themes were generally the problems of "feeble-mindedness," control of communicable diseases, and the importance of better housing. His customary thoroughness and expertise were noted by one reviewer who wrote of one of his speeches: "In composition and diction and logical arrangement of ideas and progress to conclusion, the paper was nothing sort of brilliant and thoughtful, indicating mature study and intelligent deduction and induction."[113] Freeman's personal life was in similarly satisfactory condition. On Inez's twenty-first birthday, Freeman was his usual effusive romantic self, writing that she was "more beautiful, more womanly, purer, more sincere and more lovable than at any time."[114] The passing years had seen their relationship reach the solid ground on which it would remain for the next forty-two years.

In April 1912, he wrote Wymberley De Renne about the book on Lee's dispatches. "I do not want to alarm you," he warned his patron, but

"I must tell you that neither of us had any idea of the extent of the undertaking when we began."[115] The telegrams had proved to be "a veritable mine of new truth," and Freeman now speculated that the work could be done in no less than two volumes. "I am giving to the work the best scholarship of which I am capable and trust to make the finished task worthy of the writer of the letters and of the distinguished owner of them."[116] It was no doubt true that the process of sorting, indexing, and writing about the dispatches was a major undertaking. What Freeman did not tell De Renne was that he was devoting a considerable amount of his time to another new project. He was writing a novel.

On February 6, 1912, "at 3:00 p.m.," Freeman began to write a novel titled "In the Blood," "a story of pulpit and passion." What caused him to turn to this task is unclear. His friend Henry Sydnor Harrison had done quite well with *Queed*, and this success may have influenced Freeman to try his hand at fiction. It might have been to meet a writer's basic need to write. Whatever the reason, he began in earnest and finished the first of four drafts—approximately 117,000 words—on April 3. "In the Blood" tells the story of Dr. Donald Gordon, an Episcopal rector, who rises in position and authority in the church while falling morally. Trapped in a celibate marriage, he has an affair with a sixteen-year-old mission worker, Maggie, and is ultimately discovered.[117] Various scenes of old Richmond appear in the book, and the conscience of the story is a newspaper reporter named Fitzhugh. The mission—housed in an old theater—is described in such detail that it almost certainly is based on "Uncle Jeems" Goddin's mission. Freeman was seized by enthusiasm for the project. It was another passionate—and somewhat bewildering—swing in a new direction. He had in his hands the unpublished dispatches of his hero, Lee, and the singular opportunity to write an even greater book than the *Calendar*. It was a certain step in fulfilling his life plan. Yet, for unexpressed reasons, he veered off into a fictional soap opera, complete with frank—though not graphic—descriptions of the sexual tension between Gordon and Maggie. He did not abandon the dispatches, but his attention was clearly diverted. "What the deuce do I care about success," he wrote Inez. "I am an artist."[118] Even as he wrote about Dr. Gordon, he was thinking about his next book. "I am very anxious to get at it," he told Inez in the same letter, "for the fever of composition has seized and that means I shall have no consolation until I get the thing done." To do so, he would have to "finish the De Renne business."[119]

His pace was reckless. The burdens and responsibilities he carried, to which he constantly made addition, were incessantly demanding. He accepted new assignments while giving up only one job—teaching at Miss Jennie's. Deadlines came—and were met—with unrelenting consistency. He now wrote editorials for the *News Leader* as well as the *Times-Dispatch*. He was sleeping only four hours a night.[120] It was only a matter of time before the danger of this pace manifested itself. The twenty-six-year-old began to complain of "baffling attacks of rheumatism in his hands."[121] He began to walk with a limp. A slight stiffness at first, then a debilitating pain led to a partial paralysis, and Freeman was walking with a cane.[122] He sought the advice of several doctors, the majority of whom had nothing to offer. One diagnosed an embolism and told Freeman he had but two years to live.[123] Despite their professional training, and Freeman's substantial medical knowledge, none noticed the obvious: He was overworking and not sleeping. It was Walker Freeman who saved his son's life by recommending eight hours of sleep every night. Freeman tried the radical suggestion and, within a month, the limp was gone, and he was fully recovered.[124] He began to cheat a little on his sleeping hours, but never again went without averaging at least six hours of sleep at night.

"In the Blood" was completed on November 3, 1912, and was dedicated to Henry Sydnor Harrison the "kindly companion of many days of toil, whose craftsmanship I admire and whose guidance in our journalistic days, I appreciate."[125] Freeman sent the work off to Houghton-Mifflin Publishers. It was rejected.[126] By that time Freeman was working on his second novel, "Billy Walton, Governor," also titled "His Excellency." This story tells of a machine politician who is elected governor and expected to be a mere rubber stamp for the corrupt organization. Through a series of events—including a citywide plague—the governor is converted to an honest progressive and, though forced to resign his office, gives promise of future usefulness to his state.[127] A cynical, but good-hearted, newspaperman again serves as observer of and commentator on the events of the story. Slightly more than 125,000 words in length, the book was completed on August 10, 1913, dedicated to Inez, and "started on [its] journey" to Houghton-Mifflin.[128] It met the same fate as "In the Blood." "It shows," the publishers wrote, "a marked advance in ability of handling and narrative interest over *In the Blood* . . . [it] just misses that last touch of magnetism, unction in telling, or whatever the quality may be that brings success in the crowded market."[129]

Freeman never again attempted to write fiction. Indeed, as his career began to focus on history, and he undertook more newspaper duties, he so represented the antithesis of a fiction writer that one would never assume he had even attempted such a work. No article written about Freeman mentions this foray into fiction writing—most assuredly because none of the writers knew of it. The original manuscripts were stashed away in a "trunk room." Freeman directed that these "adolescent novels" be "burned unread" after his death. "I think a man is entitled to have his amateurish work destroyed," he wrote, and these two books "are very badly written."[130] The family did not burn the novels at Freeman's death in 1953, but put them in a box where they remained unread. In 2000, forty-seven years after Freeman's death, and eighty-seven years after "Billy Walton" was finished, Dr. Freeman's daughter Mary Tyler still had not read these early works. "Father told me not to," she said, "and I haven't."[131]

"A less genial gentleman," Freeman wrote Wymberley De Renne in September, 1912, "would have been inclined long ago to reject me as a fraud and a delusion."[132] He knew De Renne's patience was wearing thin—it was now two years since he had started the work—but Freeman cited "editorial difficulties" which slowed his progress. A year passed. De Renne broke the silence on September 4, 1913: "Will you kindly let me know definitely when the Lee letters I entrusted to you will be ready for publication."[133] In his answer, Freeman recounted the story of his mystery illness of the previous months, but assured De Renne that he was "engaged on the final notes for the 1865 letters."[134] By October, the end was in sight. Freeman was working on the dispatches for February 1865 and drafting his introduction. "I cannot tell you how much I have enjoyed the task so nearing its end," he wrote. "To work with Lee papers is always a joy; to work with Lee papers belonging to a Mycaenas like yourself is about the Paradise of the historical student."[135] With fiction writing permanently set aside, Freeman was now positioned to deliver on his promises to De Renne.

On December 4, 1913, Douglas Freeman asked Inez Goddin to marry him.[136] He went into the Goddin sitting room "whistling a gay tune, [his] eyes brilliant with the love reflected," apparently confident of the answer he was to receive. "Sweet and wonderful words" were spoken, the question asked and answered.[137] Reserved in the past, Inez Goddin now allowed the joy of her deepest emotions to surface. "From that night," she wrote, "I began to really live; up to that time I had existed upon dreams."[138]

The wedding was set for February 5, 1914. Freeman began to take a number of steps to prepare to welcome a partner into his life. He resigned his positions with the Department of Health and the Anti-Tuberculosis Association, and began discussions with John Stewart Bryan about limiting his editorial work to one of the two Bryan news-papers.[139] His only pending historical work was *Lee's Dispatches*, his health was excellent, and he had four hundred dollars in the bank.[140] The wedding ceremony was to be simple; "Uncle Jeems" had passed away, and Mrs. Goddin was suffering from a goiter that was soon to take her life. Reminiscent of the note he wrote in 1900 in preparation for tak-ing his girl to Jamestown, Freeman wrote a memo reminding himself to get the rings on Tuesday, the flowers on Wednesday, and the license on Thursday.[141] More than five years had passed since he first noticed Inez in her father's mission. Now, finally, on a cold and rainy February after-noon, Inez Goddin became Mrs. Douglas Southall Freeman. The cou-ple took an overnight steamer to Baltimore, then traveled on by train to New York.

The first months of 1914 were devoted to completing *Lee's Dispatches*. In May he assured De Renne that he would "not let up" on the book until it was complete.[142] The introduction was saved for last. It would be Freeman's first extended writing on Lee and the Army of Northern Virginia. For all he knew, it might be the only opportunity afforded him to keep the pledge he made at the crater reenactment. Accordingly, it must be more than a guide to the printed dispatches. It must be history and tribute, fact and acclaim.

Freeman the student paid tribute to the collection. These dispatches would not be considered critical to the study of the war if they were from a lesser commander, "but in the case of General Lee, whose every writ-ten line was a lesson in war, the world wants all the correspondence."[143] Freeman the historian outlined the new knowledge gained from the dis-patches, including "the most definitive statement yet made of the Confederate commander's calm view of the unfortunate march into Pennsylvania."[144] Freeman the biographer detailed the "new and inspir-ing view of General Lee as a great commander" drawn in the dispatches as they "show the fixed mind and the intrepid fidelity of one whom nei-ther adversity nor success could shake."[145] Freeman the venerative Southerner gave the reader Lee the hero.

One may look over the General's shoulder, so to speak, and see him in these pages as he writes with his own hand to Mr. Davis of the great struggles of his career; one may know something from these reports of the soul that gave God the glory for the Seven Days' Fight; one may see with what confidence in his Maker and his men he wrote of Second Manassas, of Sharpsburg, of Fredericksburg, and of Chancellorsville; one may appreciate the courage that accepted the responsibility for Gettysburg and marched with spirit unafraid from the victorious trenches of Cold Harbor to the blood-stained works of Petersburg; one may bid farewell to him as he makes ready for the last journey to Appomattox and one may end the letters with the belief that Lee the soldier was great but that Lee the man and Christian was greater by far.[146]

"The influence of personality in History cannot be overestimated," he had written while attending Johns Hopkins. "While there are always great events that stir humanity, it will always be found that these events centre around some one man, and in him have their life."[147] The Lee he discovered in the dispatches—whom he judged "the general of the best army America had ever seen"[148]—confirmed this belief. His introduction to *Lee's Dispatches*, with its focus on the influence of one man on history, is a sign of things to come from his pen.

"Perhaps you have despaired of ever receiving this letter," Freeman wrote De Renne on September 7, 1914, "but here it is: the papers are finally and completely done."[149] Freeman followed this letter with another one of six pages in which he detailed his thinking behind the introduction, the citations, the running narrative through the footnotes, and his technique.[150] Freeman wanted to include a lengthy dedication to De Renne, but that idea was rejected. Having been exasperated at the long delay, De Renne now admitted the work had been more than he supposed and sent Freeman an unexpected check for a thousand dollars.[151] Soon Freeman held the maroon-bound, gilt-edged book in his hands.

We have here in Richmond near my house [Freeman wrote De Renne] a very handsome statue of General Lee—it is the Mercie, the best I think. I walk by it almost daily and I confess that for years I have felt like apologizing for never having done anything to perpetuate the fame of that great man. But now, thanks to you, I can walk by the statue and say to myself "I'm not the man he would have Southerners be, but thank God, I've done a little something to keep alive his fame!"[152]

Douglas Southall Freeman's third book, *Lee's Dispatches: Unpublished Letters of General Robert E. Lee, C.S.A., to Jefferson Davis and the War Department of the Confederate States of America, 1862-65*, was released in June 1915. It is, in fact, two books in one. One book is the text of the De Renne letters and telegrams. The second book consists of Freeman's extensive and exhaustive footnotes. The notes often dominate the page; three entire pages, in fact, consist of nothing but one note.[153] If Lee mentions a soldier, a note identifies him and gives a brief biographical sketch. Letters from other sources are cited—and sometimes printed in full—to illuminate a cursory mention in the dispatch. In Dispatch Number 92, Lee mentions to Davis that he has received his letter of May 2, 1864. Freeman notes that Davis's letter is not found, but as this dispatch from Lee "marks the formal opening of the Spotsylvania campaign . . . a brief review of events from the battle of Gettysburg to this date seems necessary."[154] The explanatory note covers the majority of four pages. Though his notes were fact-laden, Freeman did indulge in an occasional sharp rhetorical jab at Lee's opponents. Sherman's march to the sea was "infamous," and Sheridan's raid through the Valley of Virginia was "one of the darkest blots on the military fame of Grant."[155] The printer's estimate for a book projected at 462 pages, consisted of 244 pages of text, printed at 11-point size, and 176 pages of notes, printed at 10-point size.[156] Wymberley de Renne had admitted the work was more than he had anticipated. Now all could view the scope and detail of Freeman's work.

"One of the literary surprises of the season" declared the *New York Times*.[157] "The volume contains many points of interest," the review noted, "and confirms the verdict of history regarding General Lee's character and military genius." Freeman's notes "bear witness to much patient research and are written with a good taste as unfailing as is the admiration they breathe for General Lee."[158] The *American Historical Review* found the book "admirably edited" with notes so complete "that it is not at all necessary to refer to other works for a full understanding." Freeman was mildly chastised for his hyperbole in speaking of "blunders and worse of subordinates," "culpable" lieutenants, and "atrocities" of Union forces.[159] That slight rebuke aside, Freeman had reason to be pleased with the reception and reviews of *Lee's Dispatches*.

"Writers have found [Lee] so splendid a figure when he assumed command," Freeman wrote in his introduction, "that they have not thought that his knighthood could be further exalted by the hardships, the struggles and the anguish of the war."[160] Freeman, however, saw

---

"outward evidences of inward change." The Lee he found in the dispatches was summarized in one phrase: "Noble he was, nobler he became." In the months following the release of *Lee's Dispatches*, Freeman knew not whether he would write again of his "noble" hero, but he could trace the thread of opportunity that had been his. *Lee's Dispatches* had come about because of his work on the *Confederate Calendar*, which had been prompted by his substituting for Mrs. Minor in the state library; where he had turned to write his dissertation; all of which traced back to his pledge at the Battle of the Crater reenactment. Opportunity had begotten further opportunity. Hardly five months would pass before the thread would reappear.

"Dear Sir," the letter from Charles Scribner's Sons Publishing began, "will you consider contributing a life of General Lee?"[161]

CHAPTER 5

"A Lever, Not a Club"

The letter from Charles Scribner's Sons Publishing was signed by Edward Livermore Burlingame and was another instance of opportunity breaking in Freeman's direction. Burlingame had attended a dinner in New York and found himself seated next to Henry Sydnor Harrison, the author of *Queed* and Freeman's former associate at the *Richmond Times-Dispatch*. Burlingame had read the review of *Lee's Dispatches* in the *New York Times* and asked Harrison about the young author. In the ensuing conversation, Burlingame told Harrison that Scribner's was set to publish several biographies for its "American Crisis" series. One of the subjects would be Robert E. Lee. Did Harrison think, Burlingame asked, that Freeman could write the Lee biography? "Most certainly" Harrison replied. Satisfied with that endorsement, Burlingame sent his letter to Freeman.[1]

"There is, I think, a place for such a series of biographies as you describe," Freeman answered on November 24, 1915. "If arrangements can be made," he continued, "I shall be glad to write the volume on Robert E. Lee." His enthusiasm for the project grew with each sentence. "It so happens that since the publication of *Lee's Dispatches* . . . I have gained access to by far the largest collection of Lee material extant—his early, Mexican and family letters—none of which was used by even Captain Lee in his *Recollections*."[2] This material could be used "with especial effectiveness in preparing such a book." Freeman thus, in one paragraph, accepted the assignment, reminded Burlingame of his previous work, and showed why his biography of Lee would be different from any others. Burlingame did not need to be persuaded. The two men quickly agreed on a 75,000-word biography to be completed in two years.

The year 1915 saw not only the start of the Lee biography, but also Freeman's elevation to the position of editor of the *Richmond News*

Leader. He had returned to newspaper work in 1912 following the completion of his work on the Tax Commission. Two years later, the Bryan family sold the *Times-Dispatch* and concentrated solely on the *News Leader.* Freeman had the option of working for either paper.[3] He opted to go with his friend, John Stewart Bryan, and was named an associate editor of the *News Leader* in July 1914. The historian/editor could have hardly chosen a more opportune time to begin chronicling world events.

On June 28, 1914, a Serbian terrorist assassinated Austrian archduke Franz Ferdinand plunging Austria-Hungary into war with Serbia. Germany sided with Austria-Hungary while Russia stood with Serbia, prompting those two nations to join the war on August 1. Four days later, Germany declared war on France. When the Germans swept into Belgium, Great Britain joined the war. The suddenness of the war was intensified by the swiftness with which the military campaigns began. As the only military historian on the editorial staff, Freeman assumed the responsibility of interpreting the news from the battlefields across the Atlantic. His task of explaining and clarifying the often conflicting dispatches and official government statements was remarkably similar to organizing Lee's dispatches. Only now he worked without historical hindsight. "The European war," he wrote, "presents to the press the greatest news problem with which they have ever been confronted."[4] News wires were censored, coded messages were thwarted, and official statements were volubly vague. Rumor often supplanted fact, and public interest in the war was so high that "the fancies of . . . correspondents" were recounted as established facts. At most newspapers, this maze of information was collected and sorted by veteran newsmen. At the *News Leader,* it was examined by a cautious military historian, just past his twenty-ninth birthday, who displayed a knack for being able to bring order from chaos, separate fact from fiction, and anticipate the next move of the combatants. *News Leader* editorials on the war carried a unique tone of authority.

On August 25, 1914, Freeman judged the news "definite enough" to report on the state of the armies. He took the reader to the Franco-German frontier and pointed out the Germans "massed along the entire line" and "moving behind a heavy screen of cavalry." He addressed the "complicated" situation in Belgium and Luxembourg and warned his readers not to expect a "speedily menacing" advance by the Russians. Casting his eye across the entire theater, Freeman predicted "decisive German victories" followed by "a long and bitter campaign on French soil."[5] The "Battles of the Frontier," trench warfare, and the slaughter of

1915 would confirm his somber predictions.[6] Day after day Freeman painstakingly laid out the basics of military strategy, tactics, and fortifications. He described the defenses of Paris, detailed the geography of Russia, and called up historical analogies to Richelieu, Louis XIV, and William of Orange.[7] He then hit upon a technique he would frequently use in reporting the news from Europe. In describing the location of the battle lines of the two armies and predicting an allied advance in the north, Freeman wrote that if the reader considered "the river Meuse as corresponding to the Chickahominy, the parallel between this situation and that which confronted Lee at the beginning of the seven-days fight is most striking."[8] With one sentence, he had made the abstract concrete. Mezieres, Lens, and Ostend were unfamiliar to most Richmonders, but the situation facing Lee upon his assumption of command was manifestly familiar to all. As Lee "planned to take McClellan on the north side of the Chickahominy," Freeman explained, so French marshal Joseph Jacques Césare Joffre "may try to hurl back the Germans on the Lille line and crush them with a sharp assault."[9] Joffre did make a stand near the Marne River east of Paris and, on the day after Freeman's editorial, the Germans withdrew following the First Battle of the Marne.

Freeman liked the technique of reporting the day's news in conjunction with yesterday's history, and he used it whenever the analogy was apt. His editorial of September 8 began with the line "Robert E. Lee commands the allies in front of Paris—in precept if not in person."[10] The editorial, "Defending Richmond and Paris," juxtaposed the German advance on Paris with Grant's movement toward Richmond in May 1864. "The Germans have moved in precisely the same manner as did Grant," Freeman wrote. "The allies have pursued Lee's course to the letter, [and] the twentieth-century Cold Harbor is now being fought."[11] The French eastern army corresponded "to [Confederate general Joseph E.] Johnston's army in 1864" with the only difference being that the French could call up reinforcements "while the Confederates had no more men to call to the colors." Modern generals were judged in light of historical figures. Freeman questioned why a French flanking maneuver failed when the army faced obstacles "[no] greater than those [Stonewall] Jackson met and overcame time and time again."[12] In reciting the ages of the European commanders (most of whom "are old enough to be grandfathers"), Freeman commented that "millions of youths advance or retreat as a little group of gray beards direct; are the commanders too old to grasp the situation or have years merely brought added experience to them?"[13] He suggested an answer by reminding his readers that, in 1863, "Ewell was 46, Jackson was 39, Longstreet was 41, Anderson the same age, Early was 47, A.P. Hill was 38, and John B. Gordon was 31."[14] More and more, through the early months of the war, Freeman sought historical, Confederate, or local analogies to clarify and explain the news from Europe. On September 16, *News Leader* readers saw on page one a map of Virginia on which was transposed a map of the "war zone of Europe." An allied line stretched across the face of Virginia, from Charlottesville to Yorktown.[15]

Freeman's perceptive analysis of the shifting battles, even without Confederate analogies, brought the editorials notice. In "The Tide of Battle" he outlined each possible German attack, with corresponding allied reactions, and alternative French options.[16] "A Greater Battle Ahead" pointed out allied opportunities at St. Quentin and speculated about troops gathering at Ostend.[17] He occasionally turned from analysis to motivation—"The Allies Must Hit Hard"—or prognostication—"The Germans Must Move."[18] Freeman combed every scrap of information, even down to the "yellow journals" of Berlin streets, to determine the "precise situation" for each editorial. When he reached a conclusion and wrote it in an editorial, readers knew they were getting the most accurate possible report, with the bonus of insightful interpretation. Richmond readers were appreciative, and Freeman noticed that his editorials were receiving "modest attention."[19] One impressed reader paid more than just slight attention. President Woodrow Wilson directed that Freeman's editorials on the war be placed on his desk.[20]

One of the reasons Freeman opted to go with the *News Leader* in 1914 was his respect for, and growing friendship with, John Stewart Bryan. The tall urbane Bryan was in many ways more suited to the academic world than to the hurly-burly of news reporting. Born in 1871 of distinguished Virginia stock, he received his Masters of Art degree at the University of Virginia and then entered Harvard Law School. Following his graduation in 1897, he returned to Richmond and opened a law practice.[21] By that time, his father, Joseph Bryan, was consolidating his control of Richmond's major newspapers. The elder Bryan was a straight-talking, no-nonsense Confederate veteran who had turned the money-losing *Richmond Times* into a successful paper. Along the way he faced down union-affiliated pressmen who threatened to strike and shut down the paper. "Before I will yield to any such coercion," Bryan defiantly told the union, "I will take an ax and break that press to pieces and throw it into the James River. And let me tell you one thing. After the

Battle of Spotsylvania, I had no food for two days, and I found a dead Yankee who had some rotten pork in his hand, I took a ramrod and fished it out and ate it, and can do it again. And if you can't do it, don't go to war with me." The strike was averted.[22]

John Stewart Bryan, more restrained than his father, left the practice of law and became a newspaperman in 1900. Following his father's death in 1908, Bryan took over the helm of both the *Times-Dispatch* and the *News Leader*. This burden was eased with the sale of the *Times-Dispatch*, but Bryan had wide-ranging interests that demanded much of his time. He thus began to build and rely upon an efficient and competent newspaper staff. He had three editors work for him between 1903 and 1914. The third editor, Dr. G. Watson James, was a former literary magazine editor and, while an expert in foreign policy, was not a particularly commanding figure.[23] Bryan found himself acting as the paper's nominal editor in addition to his other duties. When Dr. James's health began to decline in 1914, Bryan shifted more editorial responsibility to Freeman. Early in 1915, with no fanfare or announcement, Bryan named Freeman the new editor of the *Richmond News Leader*. Freeman was twenty-nine years old.[24]

Freeman's authority as editor extended beyond the editorial pages. He directed the news department, and he was first among equals with business manager Allen Potts and managing editor Louis A. McMahon. As was his habit, Freeman was determined to master every aspect of the newspaper operation. "Today I had my first extended talk with Mr. Bryan," Freeman wrote Inez, "one of quite a number necessary to bring things up to date."[25] The reporters soon noticed the effect of having a historian as an editor. Under the old filing system, articles were clipped and filed, creating cumbersome overflowing files containing various-sized yellowing clips. Freeman developed and instituted a system modeled closely on his historical research methods. Each day he prepared an index of items from the pages of the Richmond papers and the *New York Times* considered to have value for future reference. On the same sheet were noted magazine articles, pamphlets, and book references from that same day. The entries were then typed on topical file cards. Successive entries, regarding the same subject, were added to the card, and no clippings were made. A reporter could thus find a detailed and chronological summary of a given subject by glancing at the topical subject cards. If more information was needed, he could refer to the bound volume of index sheets or, finally, to the original newspaper or magazine in the library.[26] This was the organization of a historian, not

Douglas Freeman, c. 1916, at age thirty, new editor of the Richmond News Leader. (Image courtesy of Mary Tyler McClenahan.)

a typical city editor, but the system stuck and, during its first ten years of operation, almost 63,000 cards covering 315,000 entries were catalogued in the *News Leader* library.

Freeman also kept tabs on the comings and goings of his reporters. "The big exclusive stories," he told John Stewart Bryan, "are largely the rewards of carefully working over the ground every day."[27] He suggested reporters "make up a list of the offices" they covered and visit each one every day before the noon run of the paper.[28] This was to be followed by a second visit before two o'clock and a call after the rounds. Both news and editorials were to be governed by "Joseph Pulitzer's motto—'facts, damn you, facts.'"[29] The news section was under "solemn obligation to print as far as their news value justifies both sides of every public question."[30]

The editorial page was under no such obligation, but Freeman recognized he must use his power in a responsible manner. "A newspaper is a lever, not a club," he wrote. "It should never criticize without trying to correct."[31] He would take no editorial stands until he had "all the evidence available." He expected to make enemies—"an editor who never did, never did anything"[32]—but they would be enemies made from taking principled stands, not from manipulating or distorting facts. He discussed his philosophy in a speech to the American Medico-Psychological Association in May 1915—less than six months after assuming direction of the *News Leader*. "The average intelligent male citizen has been shown by investigation to spend fifteen minutes the day in reading his newspaper," the new editor stated. "What other agency is there, for good or for evil, that can be said to hold and to inform the average mind for that length of time every day of the week?"[33] Approaching the topic from the view of his audience, Freeman asserted that "psychologically, the aim of the press must be to link the individual with the crowd, and to unify the mind of the reading public."

This is necessary for good government; it is necessary to protect the people from unscrupulous politicians; it is necessary to give expression to that which we call the "will of the people;" it is necessary to safeguard public interests from the indolence of the individual. Were the newspapers to fail in this, we should be an army which had no outposts, a city with no watchmen on the tower. We have left so much to the newspapers and have become so dependent upon them, as our cities have grown, that they are almost as necessary a public utility as a system of transportation, and almost as essential to political health as are water supplies and sewage disposal to public health.[34]

In fulfilling that role, a newspaper must be aware of the emotions and instincts that move the general public: the suggestion of panic, "curious morality waves," the tendency to exaggeration, and the inclination to imitate.[35] Improperly manipulating any one of these emotions, Freeman argued, could turn "a reading public" into a mob. A newspaper must therefore "keep the mind of the crowd from becoming the mind of the mob . . . keep the instincts from overwhelming the sentiments, the reason, and the emotions of the people."[36] This speech tells as much about the mindset of Editor Freeman as it does about the mind of the reading public. His conduct as an editor will mirror his conduct as a historian: He will be cautious, responsible, and scientific.

Newlyweds Inez and Douglas Freeman set up their home together in the Raleigh Apartments. Living with them was Walker Freeman and "Aunt Mary" Harrison. The apartment was large enough to comfortably accommodate all four, and Inez recorded no resentment at having her father-in-law in the home. The apartment was a short walk from Mrs. Goddin's home, and Inez spent considerable time with her dying mother. When she returned from her daily visits, she spent the afternoon playing the piano and waiting for her husband's return from work. Walker Freeman could not understand this sedentary lifestyle and spoke about it to his son. Freeman conveyed his father's concern to Inez who listened politely, thanked her husband, and continued her daily pattern.[37] This is the only recorded bump in the otherwise tranquil early days of marriage. When Inez took a trip with her mother to Waynesboro in September 1915, her husband wrote her daily, showing that marriage had not lessened his passionate devotion to her.

I am lonesome. There's no use trying to conceal the fact and no use dissembling. It may seem a strange confession for a man to make who spent years on years as a bachelor . . . But since a certain girl entered my life and entwined herself in my affections, everything [has] changed. It is a wonderful life we are living, my girl. When you came it seemed as though there could be no room for love in my heart. I was too much absorbed in my work, too intent on my dreams and too confident that the life I was leading was the proper life for a studious man. But lo! No sooner did you come than I saw how dark and gloomy my life had been before.[38]

"I'm never going to let you stay away from me a whole week again," he wrote toward the end of Inez's vacation. "Home without my girl isn't home at all."[39] Not that Freeman spent much time at home. He had accepted an invitation from the Richmond chapter of the American Institute of Banking to conduct a class in economics for a group of young bankers. As the course progressed, he offered to teach a second class, this one on public speaking.[40] Freeman reported "exactly twice as many boys as I can possibly hope to care for" attended the first night of the speaking class.[41] Lectures on the style and technique of public speaking occupied the class for about a year before one member requested the class include a weekly discussion of current events. By 1916 the public speaking lessons had been abandoned, and the class was devoted to a discussion of current events. The class continued to develop through the years and, on September 23, 1918, it was officially organized as the "News Leader Current Events Class." The class soon became one of Richmond's most sought-after memberships, and Freeman would lead the class every week for the next thirty-five years.[42]

The editorial page of the Richmond News Leader, under Freeman's direction, took on the tone and look of his tax editorials and historical writings. The editorials, though often eloquent, were rarely verbose. He favored tact and persuasion—the "lever" he had described to John Stewart Bryan—to the slash-and-burn approach of the crusading editor. There were the usual editorials on matters of city interest such as schools, roads, and local personalities, but he still favored the editorial series and started one in January 1915 on the old familiar theme of tax reform.[43] As the News Leader did not issue a Sunday paper, he wrote an "Evening Sermon" in Saturday's edition to cover the Sabbath. Above all there were the commemorative editorials, where Freeman the editor and Freeman the historian merged to eloquently bring to the readers' collective memory a particular moment in time. One such moment was April 3, 1915, the fiftieth anniversary of the burning of Richmond in the closing days of the Civil War. "We built on valor, not on ruins," Freeman wrote in the column "Fifty Years from the Ashes."[44] "There were traitors to meet ... [and] enemies amid us ... there was want and privation and hunger and night, but we had met them in the trenches and still we had lived. The enemy could overthrow a government, but never a people." The city of Richmond, Freeman judged, could see the hand of God in its "return from the days of our bondage, the rebirth in power and majesty, the fortress of peace on the sepulchre of war."[45] A few days later fell the fiftieth anniversary of Lee's surrender. "Virginia does not say today that Appomattox was for the best," he wrote. "She can only say that she has made the best of Appomattox."[46] The following June, Richmond served as host to a reunion of Confederate soldiers, and Freeman's two-column tribute dominated the editorial page. "It was a parade, they said on the official program, but to the thousands who lined Monument Avenue, it was more a sermon than a pageant."[47] Was it surprising, Freeman wrote, that "men bared their heads and women wept as the soldiers marched through the court of honor? Was it only delusion that made us all shake fifty years from our shoulders and see in these gray lines the bulwark of a newborn nation's honor?"[48] Alongside editorials paying tribute to the past, the present loomed menacingly large. Freeman's war editorials now not only interpreted events, but also offered policy options and began, ever so slowly, to beat the war drum.

Douglas Freeman greatly admired Woodrow Wilson. He was, he later said, "the only one in politics I believed in with my whole soul."[49] The two men shared many traits. Both were native Virginians and educated at Johns Hopkins. Both were trained as historians and held similar moralistic views on public policies. Both were writers and thinkers whose intellect did not freeze them into inaction. Wilson was also the first Democrat elected president in sixteen years and, in a region where the Republican Party was anathema, he was proudly viewed "as an exemplar of the virile statesmanship of the south."[50] Since the outbreak of war in Europe, Wilson had insisted on American neutrality, but this policy was sorely tested during 1915 as the Germans introduced unrestricted submarine warfare. Freeman offered early and vigorous support of American neutrality. It was not a policy of "babbling, dreamy pacifists," but "the firm, but moderate, demands of an administration which knows the rights of the nation whose will it exercises."[51] When a German submarine sank the liner *Lusitania* in May, he counseled "coolness, common sense and united action."[52] He did, however, draw a harsher line than did Wilson.

We owe a higher duty to one hundred million living Americans than to the one hundred victims of this German attack. Yet we owe a still higher duty to the world—to maintain the rights of peace. We cannot continue as we have gone: we must see to it that Germany either respects those rights or else takes her place as the enemy not only of the allies, but of the world.[53]

Two days later Freeman called for an end to "neutrality of sympathy" and for "the firm prayer and the earnest hope that God will strengthen the hands of the allies to crush out a dynasty that threatens the world by its ruthless disregard of civilized warfare."[54] Perhaps fearing that he was stepping out more vigorously than was Wilson—who was engaged at the time in exchanging diplomatic notes with the Germans—Freeman endorsed Wilson as a man who fights "not from passion, but from conviction, and not with the courage of the brute, but with the conscience of the determined patriot."[55] Wilson was no saber-rattling Theodore Roosevelt—"for which fact," he wrote, "the country should thank its God." Throughout the summer and fall, he continued this editorial two-step of praising Wilson while pushing for tougher measures with Germany. In "A Time for Steadiness," Freeman laid out three options for the United States: immediate severance of diplomatic relations with Germany, rejection of Germany's statement of the *Lusitania* case with full reservation of rights, and continuation of diplomatic notes. Rejecting the first and third—"there is a limit to the debate in which we may indulge with a highwayman"—Freeman endorsed the second option, a definite precursor to war. After presenting that position, he concluded with thanks to God "that we have a president who will view these questions in calmness and decide them in justice."[56]

By New Year's 1916, Freeman had lost patience with Wilson's diplomatic efforts in the face of Germany's continued belligerence. "We stopped to argue with a murderer," he thundered. "Instead of standing for plain humanity and recalling our minister and preparing for war, we have let ourselves be led into the technical mazes of diplomatic construction."[57] He would not directly criticize Wilson—"earnest, patriotic, courageous man that he is"—but he called for a return "to a policy genuinely American" and for a spirit "that will write with the sword what we cannot right with the pen."[58]

Twenty-four years later, with Europe involved in another war and America again affecting neutrality, Freeman would recall with "humiliation" his warlike editorials of 1915-16. "I go back in memory to our screaming declarations in the *News Leader* against Germany after the sinking of the *Lusitania* and I think of myself for the three and a half years thereafter as groping blindly while cheering loudly. I knew not what I did."[59] Freeman's retrospective criticism was based on his view that America's involvement in World War I led to nothing except "dislocation of national life . . . inflamed hatreds and . . . spiritual losses."[60] Those outcomes were hardly foreseeable or predictable in 1916, and while his editorials did call for an aggressive American policy, his support of Wilson guaranteed he would always recommend a cautious course.

COMPLIMENTS OF
THE NEWS LEADER

An interesting palm card handed out by the Richmond News Leader *with the profile and autograph of its new editor, Douglas Southall Freeman.* (Image courtesy of Mary Tyler McClenahan.)

Freeman's faultfinding musings of 1940 seem to have more to do with his disappointment in the post-war world of the 1920s, than with the correctness of *News Leader* policy in the prewar days of 1916.

While analyzing one war, Freeman was researching an earlier one in writing his biography of Robert E. Lee. As with all of his earlier projects, he set out to locate all possible pieces of information about his subject. In the case of Lee, he was in for a stunning surprise. The records of the Bureau of Engineers and of the United States Military Academy had never been examined. Lee's military papers were unassembled and many unpublished. Files at Washington and Lee University, covering Lee's post-war years, were practically untouched. He had seen firsthand how documents ended up in private family collections and now wondered how many more Wymberley De Rennes were scattered throughout the nation. Personal narratives had been written by lesser-known Confederate officers, and many of Lee's staff officers were still alive and would need to be interviewed. Before he wrote the first word, he needed to familiarize himself with all the material available and collect as much of it as he could.[61] At some point early in his research, Freeman perceived that writing another brief study was "senseless." He was uncovering so much unused material that to write only a short volume would be a dis-service to history.[62] This commitment to examination of primary sources was the loadstar that directed Freeman's historical method. "You must go to the sources," he wrote. "There and there only, patiently and not always consciously, you get perspective, you grasp the spirit of the times in which your subject lived, and you learn the credibility of the witnesses whose testimony you are to cite in your brief at the last tribunal of time."[63] It was through original sources that the writer transported himself into that era of history—and found his subject as he was. To write of Lincoln, for instance, one "must turn back to the frontier . . . listen to the axe ringing in the wilderness [and] follow the plow in its first contest with the virgin soil."[64] George Washington could never be understood "by looking at Stuart's portraits." The historian must "read a thousand reports . . . [and] sleep supperless by Washington's side when he was a young surveyor."[65] The entire weight of accumulated fact-based material need not be dumped on the reader, but only when it is all gathered can the historian select the relevant accounts. "You are not able fairly to select," Freeman said, "until you have seen all there is from which to select."[66] His course was set; he must see all the Lee material.

He also believed he could write a military biography only with an extensive knowledge of military science. "Professional biographers writing of scientists," he judged, "have shown themselves good artists, perhaps, but have known too little of science to make an understanding presentation."[67] Before writing about a chemist, the biographer should learn "something of science." In this approach, he was well prepared. He had been studying and observing military tactics and strategies not only in his coverage of the war in Europe, but in his editing of *Lee's Dispatches* and the *Confederate Calendar*. He had grown up surrounded by military men—his father and his Confederate veteran associates—and he had walked every battlefield in Virginia. He was well on his way to developing a vast military acumen.

The combination of exhaustive research, definitive facts, and technical knowledge carried with it the danger of rendering the biography dull and lifeless. Freeman saw this danger and decided to counter it with the "fine brushwork" of "small, illustrative detail." "We need to remember the end from the beginning," he stressed, "the art from the moment we begin to assemble the facts."[68] Here is where the collections of letters and private manuscripts would prove invaluable. For in them would be discovered the details of Lee's life—looks, acts, words, dress—that would enliven a narrative of military tactics and strategy. And it was in the telling of the story that Freeman decided to employ a novel technique. He had long opposed the "Jehovah complex" among historians—the tendency to foretell the outcome of events or actions of characters.[69] This was particularly a danger in writing military biography where the reader knew the outcome of battles before opening the book. How, then, could Freeman sustain interest and suspense in presenting Lee's story? He decided to "maintain a single point of view and to describe the battles on a basis of what Lee knew rather than on a basis of what we now know."[70] This method became known as Freeman's "fog-of-war" technique. The reader would stay with Lee throughout the narrative and learn only those facts that Lee knew as he learned them. The fog was one of the "prime realities" of war, and Lee could only be judged "by the efforts he made to get information, by the nature and extent of the information he collects, and by the skill with which he analyzes it."[71] The technique carried an inherent danger: The fog could become so thick that significant events could occur without the reader learning of them. The solution to that problem was to use detailed footnotes, summaries, and appendices to shed the necessary light. "It seems to me that this is the least confusing way of writing military biography," Freeman wrote.[72] The fog-of-war approach also demanded the meticulous and exhaustive research Freeman was conducting, for if Lee could be judged only by what information he knew, *all* the information he knew must be discovered. With his approach and method thus formed, Freeman continued digging. He did not convey any of these thoughts—which by this time he surely realized meant undertaking the writing of a major biography— to Edward Burlingame at Scribner's.

On the political front, Freeman was writing his first partisan editorials on behalf of Wilson's reelection. Virginia was reliably Democratic; indeed it was in the midst of thirteen consecutive national elections in which the Democrat nominee would carry the state.[73] Wilson had taken 66 percent of the Virginia vote in the election of 1912 and was certain to prevail again in 1916. Freeman, however, left nothing to chance and geared up for the fall election with glowing tributes to President Wilson and slashing denunciations of the Republican Party. "That President Wilson's re-election is sure must be accepted as unassailable, unless intelligence, patriotism and sense of national duty has deserted the overwhelming majority of the thoughtful American voters" he wrote.[74] Wilson's record was "equaled by that of no other executive in the recent history of the United States."[75] He had reformed an "infamous" tariff, revised anti-trust laws, enacted the Federal Reserve System, and accomplished in seventeen months "what Mr. McKinley, Mr. Roosevelt and Mr. Taft failed to accomplish in seventeen years."[76] In foreign policy, he wrote, "Mr. Wilson has learned, Mr. Wilson has mastered. [The] practical experience which he lacked in 1914 he has gained in the combat of mind and spirit with the world's greatest diplomatists."[77] If Wilson's policy had appeared less forceful than it should have been, "the blame is on the party which did not build a navy commensurate with the responsibility it placed upon the executive."[78]

Freeman lashed the Republicans with gusto and turned loose his most vicious attack with a history-laden philippic. "Yes, the country knows" about the Republican Party he wrote.

It knows that during the forty-seven years and more of power of their party since the close of the war between the states the Republicans, in 1876, stole the presidency, and in 1880 bought it with their "blocks of five." It knows that they forced upon the South the reconstruction additions to the constitution in violation of that instrument; it knows that they turned loose upon the South an army of alien cormorants to prey upon what little substance was left us from the wreck of the war. It knows that they made parts of the South political and social infernos, and that in malice and envy they aimed to uproot and destroy the very foundations of Southern civilization. The country also knows that they, the Republicans . . . retarded Southern industrial recuperation and Development . . . bound the nation to a juggernaut of robber protection . . . and perpetuated a banking and currency system that entrenched a currency monopoly.[79]

"What the Republicans would have done and might be expected to do," he concluded, "is not only an issue—but virtually the issue." Freeman tended to be more restrained in his assaults on the Republican nominee for president, former Supreme Court justice Charles Evans Hughes. "We have had in previous years a high respect for Mr. Hughes," he wrote, "and we have believed him a man of courage and capacity."[80] Now that he was the leader of "the party responsible for the most criminal class legislation the United States has ever seen," Freeman dismissed him as a "camp-following wagon-driver."[81] The day before the election, the entire editorial page was given over to one last summary of Wilson's performance titled "The Faith That Is in Us." Only "prejudice or selfishness or a debauched electorate" would fail to endorse Wilson's policy of "restoring to the people the rights and privileges which are theirs" and a vision that "stretches beyond the confines of his own party and his own blood, that the safety, peace and prosperity of our country depend upon our having courage enough and fortitude enough to build justly and without avarice or greed."[82]

The election was a cliff-hanger with early returns showing Hughes piling up majorities in all the Eastern states. By ten o'clock that night, many newspapers were declaring Hughes the victor.[83] Freeman manned the telegraph wire at the *News Leader* office and refused to concede defeat.[84] "Suspense is hard on the nerves," he wrote on the day after the election, "but suspense is better than the gloom that enveloped many of our friends last night."[85] By Friday afternoon, California was confirmed in the Democrat column, and Wilson was reelected. "Saved from the Jaws of Political Death" trumpeted the *News Leader* editorial page.[86]

Freeman ended 1916 "swinging merrily along" on his life of Lee.[87] Inez, who was expecting the couple's first child, took a brief vacation to Cincinnati, staying at the home of Julia and Allen Freeman, leaving her husband alone and complaining about "paying forty-five cents for eggs and thirty cents for a miserable quart of little navy beans."[88] True to his organized nature, Freeman had prepared a memo for Inez covering all the contingencies of train travel. "You can dress and undress more comfortably," he advised, "if after you have buttoned the curtains, you sit on the edge of the berth with your feet to the aisle."[89] The tranquility of these December days soon ended as the tentacles of war in Europe reached across the Atlantic.

Three events knocked the United States and Wilson off the neutrality tightrope. On the last day of January 1917, the Germans renewed unrestricted submarine warfare, reducing to naught all of Wilson's diplomatic efforts. On February 28, the secret Zimmerman Telegram, in which Germany sought an alliance with Mexico in the event the United States entered the war, was made public. Finally, the Germans sank the British liner *Laconia* causing the death of several Americans.[90]"The United States sought world peace," Freeman somberly wrote. "Germany has answered by provoking world war."[91] His patience was exhausted. "We can send no more notes to a nation that has raised the black flag. Unless we are willing to sign away our title as a free nation, we must defend it. The most serious hour in the life of this generation is at hand."[92] He continued to prod the reluctant Wilson—praising his leadership while adopting distinctly un-Wilsonian tones. "Mr. Wilson may be relied upon to pursue in wisdom the course of honor during the next few days—the days that will determine whether this country is to remain an indignant onlooker or an active participant in the war itself."[93] Having thus defined only one "course of honor," Freeman provided *News Leader* readers with "a little catechism" of pro-war doctrine: thirteen questions and answers on the break with Germany, the blockade, and arming merchant vessels.[94] When Wilson addressed a joint session of Congress to finally deliver a war message, Freeman was seated in the press gallery behind the speaker's dais.[95] "Every tick of the clock in the crowded hall of the house," he wrote, "seemed to mark progress in the endless contest for free government." As Wilson asked for a declaration of war, Freeman "could feel the heartbeats of a nation" and noted "the faces of congressmen showed they had cast their vote with the nation's leader."[96] He returned to Richmond to write an editorial in praise of Wilson's address—surprisingly paying no notice to the famous line: "The world must be made safe for democracy"—but hailing "every word of that final vindication" as "a burning blade thrust straight at the heart of autocracy." On Good Friday, April 6, the day Congress declared war, he wrote the most important editorial of his career to date: "To God and to History." Good Friday 1917 was not only the "most solemn anniversary of the church," it may be "the most momentous of the century in the history of the United States."[97] As "lovers of peace," Americans had stayed out of the conflict until it became one "of liberty against autocracy, of humanity against misrule, of all mankind against the destroyers of all."[98] The militant editorialist adopted Wilsonian idealism in outlining America's war aims.

> Our ideal is not to destroy Germany, but to unshackle her and that ideal precludes hate, no matter to what ignoble and futile efforts the enemy may resort . . . Victory is to be won by the multiplication of sacrifice; disaster is to be dreaded only from the non-use, not from the lack, of manhood. With one voice, this great, rich nation will say: Let us endow our children with free seas instead of burdening them with debt; let us pay for this war as we wage it . . . America must enter this war upon her knees, looking to God for the strength she shall need in sustaining the trials of the coming months.[99]

While her husband was expounding the case to God and history, Inez felt the first pangs of labor. She left her home and walked three blocks to Stuart Circle Hospital, named for the Confederate general memorialized by an equestrian statue in the circle in front of the hospital. Learning of his wife's entry into the hospital, Freeman finished his editorial work and hurried to her side. Labor had commenced, but Inez encouraged her husband to go home for dinner. When he returned to the hospital shortly after seven o'clock that evening, he discovered he was a father. The baby girl was named Mary Tyler after Inez's mother.[100] The proud father saw historical significance in the moment of his first child's birth. She was born "in the very hour the old world died."[101]

Though a new father, and just shy of his thirty-second birthday, Freeman set his sights on enlisting in the Army. His appendix operation of 1902, however, had left him with a hernia, and he was classified unfit for duty. Not willing to accept this rejection, he made two more efforts to join and enlisted the help of friends to plead his case. "He will prove invaluable to the Colonel," one such letter on his behalf read, "[he is] a most unusual man of rare military knowledge and ability [and] his influence in the community is commanding."[102] Nothing came of these efforts, and Freeman was destined to serve the war effort on the home front.

While the nation prepared to defend freedom abroad, Freeman found himself defending freedom—of the press—at home. The case sprang from a tragic murder in Charlotte County, Virginia. Two black men, Albert Barrett and his son Aubrey, had been arrested for the murder of William Roach, a farmer, and hurried to trial due to the fear of mob violence.[103] The Barretts were not provided counsel until the day of the trial. Their attorney, William Lancaster, had the elder Barrett plead not guilty and presented his case to the jury. A guilty verdict was returned, and Barrett was sentenced to death. At some point before the trial of seventeen-year-old Aubrey Barrett, Lancaster withdrew as counsel. Aubrey Barrett waived his right to a jury trial and pled guilty—all without advice of counsel. Judge George J. Hundley sentenced the young boy to die in the electric chair on August 30, 1917.[104]

Freeman knew nothing of the case—Charlotte County was not in the Richmond metropolitan area—until a Virginia state senator came to Richmond to plead for clemency for Aubrey Barrett.[105] Once he learned the details, Freeman was immediately struck by the injustice of the penalty on the uneducated and unrepresented minor. "The execution of Aubrey Barrett," he wrote on August 28, "would impugn the justice of Virginia courts."[106] The question of Barrett's guilt or innocence was irrelevant; it was an issue of judicial procedure. "No intelligent, educated man, untrained in law, is capable of conducting his defense against skilled attorneys," he argued. "How can more be expected of a negro boy?"[107] It was not the policy of the *News Leader*, he asserted, "to appeal in the public name against the judgment of our courts" but in this case the paper appealed to the governor to stay the execution. The governor acted the next day and granted a "respite" of thirty days.[108]

Freeman now dug deeper in the case, convinced that "if ever there are cases where the press of the state, as the public pleaders of the weak, should raise their voices, this is one of them."[109] Other voices were raised as well. Judge Hundley dispatched a letter to the *News Leader* asserting that he had "no power to prevent any one from pleading guilty" and condemning "the unwise actions of certain persons, in seeking to have this boy's sentence commuted, by an assault upon the actions of the court."[110] Nonsense, Freeman replied.

> Nobody is attacking the courts . . . [but] guilt is one thing and due process of law is another . . . [The] administration of justice [is] more important than the reputation of any judge or the life of any individual. By pleading guilty to murder in the first degree, and by waiving jury trial, the negro signed his own death warrant . . . [but], it is argued, that is a negro, a bad, dangerous negro. What then? The very fact that he is a negro, unrepresented, friendless, penniless, and ignorant, makes it all the more important that his guilt be established in a court of justice, with every possible safeguard thrown about his rights![111]

Judge Hundley provided more ammunition. He issued a statement claiming he had no discretion regarding the imposition of the death penalty once the defendant pleaded guilty. "With all deference to his superior knowledge of the law," Freeman wrote of the eighty-year-old jurist, "the *News Leader* wishes to state that Judge Hundley did have discretion in this case, that he has unintentionally mistaken his powers, and that he could have imposed a sentence more in keeping with the age and ignorance of the prisoner."[112] Citing numerous Virginia statutes, he argued that the young man should have been committed to "the state board of charities or to a reformatory." The court possessed "the very discretion" it denied it had, Freeman judged, and could not take the position "that the sentence of this negro boy to death was unavoidable."[113]

This editorial brought a howl of protest from the commonwealth's attorney, A. D. Watkins, who demanded equal time in the newspaper for a response.[114] Freeman gave him space on September 11. Watkins made certain the readers knew the case was one "of [an] atrocious murder of . . . a law abiding citizen of the county of Charlotte, by a vicious negro thief" and then defended the actions of Judge Hundley.[115] He further took Freeman to task for "statements derogatory of the court" which "absolutely destroys the usefulness of the Charlotte Court." Freeman responded on the same page—not yielding an inch. "We have said half a dozen times and we reiterate now that neither the details of the murder . . . nor the guilt or innocence of the negroes interest us in the slightest . . . let us not continually dwell upon the horror of the crime and let us not forever stress the fact that the culprits were negroes, when we are discussing neither guilt nor color, but the proper administration of justice."[116] He then dismissed the argument that criticism of a court impairs judicial effectiveness.

The courts of this commonwealth are cloaked with no infallibility or judicial sanctity that entitles them to special rights. They are as properly subject to honest criticism as is the executive department of government, and where they manifestly err or are plainly incompetent, the newspaper that fails to put out the facts is lacking in its proper coverage as the people's advocate.[117]

"Justice," Freeman wrote, "was administered in Charlotte before Judge Hundley's elevation to the bench and will, we trust, still be administered when another is in his place." He ended the editorial by calling for a review of the case by the governor.

The next day Watkins wrote the *News Leader* asking for the name of the editor responsible for the editorials.[118] Freeman could see what was coming, and his fighting dander was up. "If Judge Hundley sees fit to cite us for contempt," he wrote Watkins on September 19, "it would be of great convenience to us if you would notify us immediately."[119] In a separate letter on the same day, he advised Watkins that he and John Stewart Bryan were responsible for editorial comments and seemed to invite service of process. He could, he told Watkins, "be found at the above address by any officer of the court at any time."[120] Two days later, the Supreme Court of Virginia vindicated the position of the *News Leader*. In refusing Barrett's writ and addressing other issues of the trial, the court remarked that Judge Hundley had "all power and discretion vested in the jury by the statutes prescribing the penalties for murder."[121] Freeman seized on the court's decision to call for "a truly Virginia trial"—one by jury. "The blood of this ignorant boy would be on the heads of the people of Virginia if they did not see that he had competent counsel and avails himself fully of his legal rights."[122] That comment was apparently too much for Judge Hundley. Freeman was served with a contempt of court citation, the basis of which was three editorials and one news article.[123]

When news of the contempt proceeding became public, Freeman received numerous letters of support. "It is plain to me that you have ruffled a judge's vanity," one correspondent wrote, "but the Judge of judges looks down upon you and must surely say: this is a son in whom I am well pleased."[124] A former commonwealth's attorney wrote, "[I]t would be a crime for that negro boy to be hung as a result of such a trial," and another letter praised Freeman for "publicly denouncing the cowardly act of this unprincipled wielder of power."[125] For his part, Freeman steadfastly denied any contempt of court and stood "squarely upon . . . our right to comment upon the acts of courts."[126] His lawyers argued the same in the responsive pleading filed in the Charlotte County Circuit Court.[127] The attorneys for both sides met on November 1 during which time Judge Hundley's lawyers admitted the judge "had made a serious mistake, which they hoped we consider as between man and man."[128] On November 7, Freeman's attorneys appeared in Judge Hundley's court, read his answer into the record, and the case was dismissed. Freeman's editorial that day did not gloat over the victory, but merely stated that "if such statements as ours were in contempt of court, the time had come to change the law of contempt."[129] He reiterated his conviction that Aubrey Barrett should not be electrocuted, but should receive executive clemency.

"That would add a very pleasing ending to the chapter." That end was achieved. Aubrey Barrett was not put to death.[130]

The Barrett contempt case displays much more than Freeman's combative spirit and vigorous advocacy for the First Amendment. The tolerance Freeman had learned at the knee of Walker Freeman had become an ingrained part of his character. To champion the cause of a "negro" in a murder trial in 1917 in a rural Virginia county was an act of professional, as well as personal, courage. Freeman steadfastly ignored the issue of whether Aubrey Barrett was guilty or innocent; he was moved by the injustice of an uneducated minor defendant waiving many of his rights and receiving the ultimate penalty, due to the seeming incompetence and indifference of the presiding judge. With the value society then placed on the life of a black man, few would have noticed if Freeman had ignored the entire matter. But to Douglas Freeman justice was color-blind and, when that principle was put to the test, he acted without regard to professional standing or personal safety.

In the midst of war and a new baby and a contempt case, came a voice from New York. "How is the Lee biography coming on?" Edward Burlingame wrote Freeman on January 5, 1918. The editor had "carefully refrained from troubling" him, "although the dates we at first discussed have been for some time passed."[131] Now Scribner's was interested in making a "definite" announcement of the forthcoming biography of Robert E. Lee.

The usually prompt Freeman waited ten days to respond. Then he reported that the "manuscript of the Lee Biography is virtually complete and all the research is done."[132] It needed only some polishing. Scribner's could safely set anytime "after April" for its delivery. Burlingame rejoiced in the good news and told Freeman that delivery in May would be sufficient.[133] On May 10, with no book in hand, Burlingame wrote that he "ought not to put off longer asking you to send us the manuscript."[134] From Richmond came only silence. "I wrote you last month a letter which I hope did not go astray," Burlingame wrote on June 25. "I know you will not think me too urgent under the circumstances if I write again to ask about it."[135] Freeman again waited almost two weeks to answer. "I am having two difficulties with my Lee," he confessed. "The first is to compress it into one hundred thousand words; the second is to keep up with the constant mass of new material I am gathering."[136] Just the previous week, Freeman pointed out, he had discovered reports made by Lee during his days as an engineer. The book was turning into "a military biography" with only brief sketches of Lee's pre-war and post-war life. Asking Burlingame to be "as merciful" as he could, Freeman pushed for more time. Burlingame agreed to wait until August, but objected to a manuscript of 100,000 words. The agreement, he reminded Freeman, was for a 75,000-word book. "I hope that you will do all you can to make it approach that figure."[137] Though Freeman hated to "slaughter" the book to get it to 75,000 words, he pledged to make the effort.[138] August passed with no word. September and October came and went. November brought only silence. Finally, Burlingame again, plaintively, wrote the young author. "You will not think of me, I am sure, as a persecutor in the matter of the Lee biography," he opened his letter of December 18. "I have had a long experience with the difficulty of setting dates for the finishing of an undertaken piece of work, with the unforeseen delays . . . [but] we must make our plans."[139] The announcement of the new Lee book had already been made, based on Freeman's earlier assurances of near completion, and Scribner's wanted it among their next releases.

"I have written it all—most of it twice," Freeman responded. This despite a heavy workload at the newspaper and his work for the "Red Cross, War Work Council, and the [Liberty] Loans." He hoped to deliver the manuscript during the Christmas holidays—six days thence.[140]

Douglas Freeman was not by nature, habit, or practice, a liar. It is impossible to say that he did not have a 100,000-word manuscript on the life of Robert E. Lee nearly complete in December 1918. "I am concluding an extended life of Lee," he wrote in May 1919, and if he had only pieced together the introduction and footnotes from *Lee's Dispatches*, he would have the basis for a substantial manuscript.[141] He had diligently sought for three years to locate letters, manuscripts, and dispatches even tangentially connected to General Lee. He was deploying new techniques in historical method and emphasizing Lee's strategy as opposed to merely reciting facts of battles.[142] He had been working steadily on the biography since the offer came from Scribner's in December 1915. So why does one wonder if he could have produced a manuscript if Edward Burlingame had decided to draw a firm line and demand the manuscript by a date certain or void the contract? It is suspicion born of the curious equivocations in Freeman's letters in which he is clearly putting Burlingame off and buying himself more time. Subsequent information raises more questions as to Freeman's veracity in his exchanges with Edward Burlingame. He wrote in 1936 that he completed the last days of Lee "in 1926 and put it away."[143] He wrote that the "actual composition" of the book started in 1927 after the early years were spent "familiarizing myself with the background and in accumulating material."[144] He told his daughter Anne that he had first written about Lee's post-war years, before writing about Lee's early life or war years.[145] It should be noted that all of these statements were made after Scribner's had authorized a full-scale study of Lee and granted Freeman all the time he needed. It is therefore possible that Freeman's references to when he started writing concern his conduct under the "adjusted" arrangement with Scribner's and not his initial efforts from 1915 to 1918. While some early drafts of the Lee manuscript survive, there are no notes or drafts from the supposedly completed volume of 1918.[146] One is therefore left wondering what, if anything, Freeman could have given Scribner's in 1918. What is clear is that he had decided to do a definitive study and was pushing the patience and goodwill of Scribner's to the limit while busily gathering all possible information.

Denied the use of a sword in the Great War, Freeman used his pen throughout 1917 and 1918 to serve the Allied cause. Gone were the restraints of official neutrality, and his fact-filled editorials were now written as much to uplift the fighting spirit as they were to inform. He was a strong advocate of conscription, encouraged conservation of food, and promoted the sale of Liberty Bonds.[147] No detail of the war effort was too small to merit editorial comment. He paid tribute to an all-black unit—"the colored Selects"—as they marched off to war. "It is a very solemn responsibility that a Southern state assumes in sending to fight the nation's battles men whom grim necessity has forced it to deny the franchise," he wrote, pointing out the obvious contradiction in black soldiers fighting for freedoms they themselves did not enjoy.[148] "*Noblesse oblige,*" he concluded, would "see to it that [such] patriotism is rewarded with justice." Upon hearing a statement by Gen. John J. Pershing that soldiers on leave in Virginia returned to service with a higher rate of sexually related diseases than did soldiers on leave elsewhere, Freeman blasted "the prostitute, the gambler and the panderer" who would defile "the banners of our country . . . by the treacherous lust of the underworld!"[149] "Richmond," he wrote, "shall be clean." A particular telling editorial, given Freeman's disqualification from service, was directed "To the Man Who Cannot Join the Army."

You pass down the street and you envy every boy his uniform . . . You ask yourself, why am I here while they are over there? Sometimes the arguments of friends, the exhortation of wife, the smooth logic of fellow-workers or the stern admonition of your physician drugs the urging of your heart . . . so you come back to that same, pressing, personal problem of duty—[but] if you cannot do the duty you crave, you can maintain your self-respect . . . for savings loaned the country, for old clothes worn, for appetites repressed and for working hours lengthened—all will be honored. For the man who can do no more, a shabby suit long worn to save cloth for uniforms is itself a uniform of honor.[150]

His war editorials continued to outline, and often predict, allied movements with uncanny accuracy. In March 1918, the Germans launched their *Kaiserschlacht*, a massive offensive designed to destroy the Allies before American troops arrived in Europe.[151] Freeman devoted more than two columns to analyze the German move and allay fears that it was "a very serious disaster" for the allies.[152] This was not a successful advance, he argued against logic in the face of retreating Allied forces, "the Germans merely did on a wide front what either side can do at any time, provided it can concentrate its artillery and is willing to pay the price in human life."[153] As the German tide inched forward, Freeman spread a map of the battlefield across the editorial page of March 25 and explained the action sector by sector. The casual reader of news reports would draw the conclusion that the Allies were falling back in defeat; Freeman showed the wisdom of the allied movement and paid particular attention to "the most critical [sector] of the whole fifty miles of fighting." "If the plan of the Germans was to drive a wedge between the British and the French," he wrote, "all the evidence points to a British advantage rather than a reverse."[154] Three days after this analysis, the Germans launched a powerful attack and were repelled with crushing losses. Freeman then predicted "the scene of the next great battle" and fell back on his technique of explaining it in local terms. "Assume the battle line, before the retreat, to follow the course of the James River from Oregon Hill to Libby Hill . . ."[155] The reader learned that the only problems for the British existed on "Fifth and Main" and "Fifth and Franklin" streets. "Altogether," he wrote, "the situation is every whit as good as anyone could expect after so desperate a thrust."[156] The next day, April 5, the German offensive ended in failure.[157]

That Freeman's knowledge of military operations came from a diligent study of war dispatches, tactics, and strategy was apparent, but he believed he had another source for his insight.

When in a historic moment [he wrote] a vision is given to a man and when in consequence he finds that this vision has determined movements of enormous importance in a formidable war, I believe that this vision—and I had it at the Marne, on the Yser and on March 26—comes from a providential power in the hands of which one is the instrument, and I believe that the victorious decision was sent to me from on high by a will supreme and divine.[158]

The summer of 1918 saw the Allies begin to turn the tide against the Germans, and Freeman's editorials pointed the way to victory. "The despised American," he wrote, "has introduced himself to the German army with a vigor and with a military success that will never make it possible for the Germans again to doubt that they are faced by a grim determination of a fighting nation that has never lost a war in which the hearts of the people were involved."[159] In September he noted that "the misgivings of March, the fear of April and the dark doubt of May seem fragments of some dim, half-forgotten nightmare."[160] He predicted the retreating Germans would "soon evacuate the remainder of the Vesle salient" and that the allies would recover all that was lost "in five German offensives."[161] He often ignored the headline stories to concentrate on seemingly insignificant pieces of news. "The occupation by the French today of the village of Essigny le Grand is, in reality, of far greater importance than larger movements."[162] He then explained why that was the case, going into such detail as to describe individual hills around the French village. On October 29, 1918, he reported the movements of Marshal Ferdinand Foch, studied the location of railroads, and analyzed Austrian supply lines. He concluded that "the doom of Germany" was "sealed."[163] Two weeks later, the Armistice was announced ending World War I.

"God's is the victory," Freeman wrote. "His be the praise."[164]

CHAPTER 6

"Above All, Be Clear"

"The war is over," Freeman exulted in his Armistice Day editorial, "in fact, if not in form—over Americans! Ended! Won!" After giving thanks to God, paying homage to the valiant dead, praising the victorious soldiers, and heralding the leadership of Woodrow Wilson, Ferdinand Foch, David Lloyd George, and Georges Clemenceau, Freeman turned his attention to the post-war world.[1] He wasted no time in warning *News Leader* readers that "America's battles are not over." On America's shoulders, he wrote, rested the responsibility to "restore Europe," "to maintain America," "to rebuild," and "to preserve what peace might overthrow at home."[2] Though the editorial set lofty and idealistic goals, it was not as stimulating a topic as war editorials. The world, as well as Freeman's life, was destined in the coming decade to calm down following the frenzy of the previous four years. The nation was growing weary of Wilsonian idealism. It was about to move into an era of Prohibition, Babe Ruth, jazz, and a "return to normalcy."[3] Such topics did not lend themselves to the perceptive analytic editorials Freeman had employed when great issues were contested on distant fields of honor. The news of the twenties would not challenge his intellect or stimulate his creative ability. For that satisfaction, the thirty-two-year-old Freeman had to rely on his biography of Robert E. Lee.

He had so often put off Edward Burlingame of Scribner's that the beleaguered editor could only express his "disappointment" in the continuing saga of the Lee biography. Freeman assured him that he was "more distressed at the delay" than was Burlingame, but that he was still combing records—including private letters held by the family.[4] Burlingame inquired less frequently during the early years of the 1920s, perhaps realizing that Freeman would send the manuscript when he decided it was ready. Burlingame's despair might have been assuaged if he could have seen that the delay did not mask inactivity. Freeman was seemingly everywhere looking for information, no matter how trivial. He located the papers of the military surgeon who attended Lee during part of his illness in 1863, found thirty-nine miscellaneous letters in San Marino, California, and was assisted by a "patriotic lady" in Savannah, Georgia, who forwarded several letters.[5] He discussed technical issues of strategy with Col. Walter Taylor, Lee's assistant adjutant general, studied the papers of Zachary Taylor to better understand the Mexican War, and read the 1829 edition of cadet regulations to complete his picture of life at West Point.[6] Armed with reams of maps and papers, he walked Lee's battlefields to establish facts for himself. He decided to write first of Lee's final campaign and post-war years in order "to find the cords that [made] the fabric of character and to trace them back to the beginning."[7] Preparing to write of the surrender at Appomattox, he turned to a different type of research. He spent "about three weeks" reading Greek tragedies in order to learn "a lesson in simplicity of design."[8] "Brief as the book is, I want to make it as thorough and as good as I can," Freeman wrote Burlingame, still acknowledging, if only for the sake of appearances, that the book would be a short one.[9] Then, suddenly, all things changed.

"You have always been accustomed to correspond with Mr. Burlingame about the life of Robert E. Lee," the letter of January 22, 1923, from Scribner's Publishing began. "I suppose you have heard of his death last month." The letter went on to ask for "some approximate idea" of when the book would be complete. It was signed by Maxwell E. Perkins.[10]

"The whole trouble about my Lee," Freeman responded "is that I have been waiting to have a view of the final cache of Lee papers soon to be deposited . . . in the Confederate Memorial Institute." Once these letters were examined, he could "very quickly reshape" the manuscript.[11] Having provided Perkins with an update, he now made a pitch for an in-depth study. "I sometimes feel that it is a shame to put into this small compass what I think I may say without immodesty is the most extensive study of Lee ever yet made."[12] If Perkins insisted on the small book, he would provide it, but would then offer "a larger, perhaps two volume, life of Lee, that will be as nearly final as existing material permits."[13]

"I was sorry to hear of Mr. Burlingame's death," Freeman concluded. "He was a very patient man in dealing with me. I hope a like mantle covers your shoulders."

On February 3, 1923, Douglas Freeman received the letter one is tempted to say he had long awaited. "We had entertained," Perkins

wrote, "but had rather hesitated at any earlier stage in our correspondence to suggest . . . a life of Lee by you which would be on a much
larger scale than that which we have discussed."[14] Freeman was
"uniquely qualified to do such a book," and, if he agreed to write the
larger work, "the wisdom of publishing any shorter biography" was rendered "questionable." "May we not," Perkins concluded, "look forward to
the idea of publishing a really large and definitive life of Lee by you?"[15]

"Your letter of February third is very kind," Freeman responded. "I
shall go ahead on the theory that I am to finish the biography of Lee in
some detail."[16]

One day at his desk in the *News Leader* office, Freeman typed out a
short quote.

I, Callicles, wrote down from day to day the happenings of our city
and drew thereby on my head the curse of many and the praise of few.
Now with friends and enemies alike I sleep forgotten in the tomb.
Meanwhile new chroniclers record the unchanging circle of events.[17]

He added no comment to the passage, but the quotation fairly summarized his sentiments about newspaper work. "If you had been a newspaper man instead of a railway executive," he wrote a friend, "I believe
you would have risen to the very crest of the calling—not that that
would have been anything of which to be particularly proud."[18] Such
self-deprecating humor belied an intense commitment to make the
News Leader an ever-improving paper. Freeman directed not only the
editorial page but also the "news editors and writers, its feature editors,
its society editors [and] women's page editor."[19] He was quick to
respond when the *News Leader* suffered a "bad beat" and sought to give
his reporters every advantage, even if it meant taking his case to the governor of the state.[20] During the first week of June 1925, Freeman
noticed that on three separate occasions the governor's office issued
press statements too late in the day to make the afternoon papers. He
dashed off a letter to Gov. E. Lee Trinkle "to inquire . . . whether it is
your settled policy to give the important news from your office to the
morning papers of the state in preference to the afternoon papers."[21]
Instead of delegating Freeman's inquiry to a staff member, Governor
Trinkle personally responded. His answer fairly crackled off the paper.

I do not know that there is any reason why I, as Governor of

Virginia, should announce what policy I propose to adopt with reference to giving news to the Richmond papers . . . it is my prerogative to run this office as best I know how . . . I regret to know that
there is so little I can apparently do . . . that meets with the
approval of your paper.[22]

And so on for two and one-half pages.[23] When Trinkle left office in
January 1926, Freeman promptly raised the same issue with his successor. Governor Harry F. Byrd assured him that he would be "careful"
about press releases and hoped Freeman would "not hesitate to call my
attention to the fact if in the future I should release the news to the
morning papers to the disadvantage of the evening papers."[24] For
Freeman it was a mission accomplished for the benefit of his reporters.

Being a historian and an editor meant Freeman often faced the "complications of the ideal and the practical."[25] He wanted the *News Leader* to
perform "a real service in the community," but recognized that to do so
required "reasonable means; [and] to procure the means [a paper] must
have advertising; to get the advertising it must have circulation; to gain
the circulation it must print the news."[26] There was the rub—the type of
news to print. He had discovered the old journalism truth that "the
greater [the] local sensationalism, the greater the interest in the newspaper."[27] The momentous events that had occurred during the past years—
such as the discovery of the North Pole, the sinking of the *Titanic*, and
the First World War—had not marginally affected the circulation of the
News Leader. News of the armistice sold 66,000 copies, but news of the
verdict in a lurid local murder trial sold 72,000 copies.[28] It was a sober
fact, Freeman concluded, "that circulation, which means revenue, never is
stimulated by anything as much as by giving publicity to the . . . sordid
and the criminal."[29] Having to accept this distasteful fact of journalistic
life, Freeman sought to at least utilize it to a higher end. The *News Leader*
"is sometimes forced to win a certain class of reader by sensationalism,"
he admitted, but it would attempt "to hold them by news of a higher
type."[30] As editor, he was "somewhat in the position of a restaurateur who
has to serve a certain amount of fried veal and other indigestibles until he
can train his customers to order better things."[31] While serving "fried
veal," he would attempt "to build up the tastes of its readers by high type,
special articles . . . and thereby to produce a paper that intelligent people
will read."[32] The news section of the paper would attempt to present
"both sides of every public question," while the editorial page would "tell
the truth" with no "pussy-footing on any question."[33]

Freeman believed editorials served three primary functions: "to aid the good and to suppress the evil," to "add to the honest pleasure of a world that has enough of sorrow," and to interpret and complement the news of the day.[34] "Perhaps only those who have been editors of a particular paper for a long term of years," he wrote, "can appreciate what a newspaper really can do through its editorial columns." The voice of the paper could "put the social emphasis where it belongs," carry the "gospel of good cheer," and anticipate and answer the questions of the intelligent reader. "The ideal editor," he judged, "would seem to fulfill ancient Greek's definition of man, 'an animal of large discourse, looking before and after.'"[35] Of one thing he was certain: "[T]he editorial writer must experiment, study the wishes of his public and seek to accommodate his writing to their needs and problems. Otherwise he will become as obsolete as the professional mourner."

Part of building "up the tastes" of the readers was active community involvement. In 1923 Freeman devised the idea of "neighborhood nights" as a venue to spotlight sections of Richmond. On scheduled nights in selected neighborhoods, stores would remain open after hours, a choir would provide a concert, and local leaders would deliver "a few words." The *News Leader* sponsored the events, handled the publicity, and published a "history of the district" prior to the celebratory evening.[36] Music was often the centerpiece of *News Leader* sponsored events. The paper sponsored five public concerts in one year featuring, among other artists, the New York Symphony Orchestra. A series of grand opera by the San Carlo Opera Company brought in attendance of 43,000 during one week.[37] "The new industrial progress of the South," Freeman wrote, "will be in vain if some of the profits arising from it are not devoted to the enrichment of the cultural life of the South."[38] His efforts in 1928 were so successful that he dubbed that year the one that "brought music back to life in Richmond."[39] The paper offered educational classes in sales, writing, and machinery operation, and it was quick to champion popular causes, such as saving trees in Monroe Park from being destroyed.[40]

Freeman's efforts showed signs of success. The *News Leader's* circulation grew from 29,000 in 1914 to 47,000 in 1922.[41] Almost one-third of readers responding to a poll cited Freeman's editorials as the most liked feature in the paper, with current news—that inevitably tended toward the "sensational"—receiving only 9 percent.[42] Though some still accused the paper of being "high brow," Freeman was succeeding in making the *News Leader* "share both the hopes and the problems of the city."[43]

A paper ought never to become impersonal in the sense that those who direct it are detached from the life of the community . . . It should pulse with the people for whose information it is printed. Nothing that pertains to the welfare of the city should be alien to it . . . It should strive, of course, rightly to lead the community, but never in dogmatism and never so far ahead that its effort is wasted . . . Beyond it all should be the ideal that when the reader has finished the paper at the end of the day, he will be better informed, a trifle richer in his education and in his spirit, a bit more nearly able to shape his course as a man and a citizen. That is the spirit in which the *News Leader* seeks to work . . . [44]

Freeman's activist editorship was bound to draw enemies as well as friends. In 1919 two influential members of the Richmond business community tried to persuade John Stewart Bryan to fire Freeman "as a Socialist."[45] A more serious threat grew from Freeman's tilt with the American Civic Association, an organization self-described as dedicated to "the interests of one hundred percent American ideals and institutions."[46] The group had obtained a permit to hold a rally in a local public school. In glancing at a press ticket for the event, Freeman thought he recognized the mailing address. He turned to his trusty indexing system and found that the post office box was the same one used by the state coordinator of the Ku Klux Klan.[47] His suspicion aroused, Freeman passed on his discovery to the superintendent of the Richmond public schools who, after further examination of the issue, revoked the permit issued to the association. Freeman inserted an editorial in the Saturday, July 30, paper asking the association to state whether it had any connections with the Klan. Freeman detailed the events that followed in a letter to John Stewart Bryan.

On Monday we heard rumors of threatened vengeance . . . On Tuesday these threats took form in the report that some of the friends of the American Civic Association prepared to issue 25,000 dodgers making a vigorous attack on me on account of the old Baltimore episode . . . We sent out our scouts but were unable to find that the dodger had been issued. Finally on yesterday we heard that no printer in town had been willing to take it and that consequently that form of attack had been called off.[48]

Freeman was obviously facing some sort of blackmail threat stemming from an "old Baltimore episode." Undaunted by the threat, and whatever repercussions it carried, he met with the event organizer. "I told him that I had nothing to conceal," he recalled, "and that the whole story might come out so far as I was concerned with the single proviso that the whole truth be told."[49] The group's leader denied any knowledge of the intimidation and "denounced it in round terms." Believing a row to be imminent, Freeman went home and told Inez and his father of the evolving situation. "Mrs. Freeman knew, of course, all the details," he wrote Bryan, "because I explained them to her before we were married." Inez's only recorded reaction was concern for her husband's physical safety.[50]

The group held its meeting at a different location, though Freeman's public questioning of the group's affiliation with the Klan held down attendance. "I think the question will hopefully put a quietus on the movement," he wrote Bryan the following Wednesday. "My belief is that it is the Ku Klux Klan," he concluded, and "I thank God that we have had a chance, apparently, to smash an organization that stinks to high Heaven."[51] Though the crisis had passed, Freeman sent his letter to Bryan "in a plain envelope" because he believed the Klan was "way laying" his correspondence as well as tapping his office phone.[52]

Freeman had once again taken a stand at considerable personal risk on an issue with racial overtones. It is impossible, however, to gauge the extent of the risk because the "old Baltimore episode" remains obscured in historical darkness. It apparently was an event significant enough that Freeman felt he needed to discuss it with Inez before they married, and serious enough that it was considered useful fodder for blackmail. If Baltimore was the locale for the "episode," and it took place prior to his marriage, it seems certain to have occurred during Freeman's time at Johns Hopkins. Yet one searches in vain for details of what it could be. His daily letters home to his parents contain no details or clues about any event out of the ordinary. Nor, if the matter was something he would not tell his parents, does one detect any undue stress or concern.

Only two diary entries from the spring and summer of 1907 hint at some problem. Freeman makes reference to a nameless girl by identifying her as "." in his writings. While having dinner in April 1907, a classmate brought him "a letter from . which fixed things all ok [and], I trust, forever. Thank God."[53] In his "summary of summer" entry in the same diary, he wrote the following:

> But the joy of joys came a little earlier in the year. I decided to visit . and to settle once and for all the matter which I had tried to clinch before. Various letters passed between us, and sometime

about the last of July, I received a letter saying I had better not visit her, and informing me of her approaching marriage to E. G. How happy I was!! It was the greatest blessing of the year, the best day since October '05.[54]

If this is the "episode" to which Freeman refers, it is impossible to conclude the nature of the problem; though a breach of promise action suggests itself.

No other mention of the episode appears in any letters to or from Freeman at that time or from the time of the American Civic Association event to his death thirty-two years later. His attitude toward the potential disclosure of the matter—"I had nothing to conceal and . . . the whole story might come out so far as I was concerned"—indicate that he judged the episode was not embarrassing enough to damage his reputation or serious enough to cost him his job. That it was so easily discoverable by the association suggests it was a story fairly well circulated or a matter of some public knowledge. It is also interesting that apparently no printer in Richmond would print the flyer carrying the attack. Finally one must consider that if the event was a serious matter dealing with Freeman's character, integrity, or moral turpitude, it seems it would have been used by any number of enemies during his thirty-four-year tenure as editor of the *News Leader*. Thus the "episode" remains a mystery, in all likelihood worse in speculation than in fact.[55]

A less serious tussle took place between Freeman and Walter Lippmann. *The New Republic* ran an article by Lippmann in which he reviewed the coverage of the Russian Revolution by the *New York Times*. Lippmann drew the conclusion that the *Times* ignored the "real conditions" in Russia and slanted its reporting "because the only people who at that time gave a disquieting picture of Russia were insignificant people like Trotsky or pro-German pacifists."[56] Freeman viewed the article as an attack on the methods of news gathering and editing used by most newspapers, the *News Leader* included, and responded to Lippmann in a blistering editorial. "To have considered technical problems," he wrote, "it would have been thought that the *New Republic* would have chosen men who knew something about those problems."[57] He then unleashed a personal attack on Lippmann who "seems to have spent most of his time [since college] writing for the magazine and weekly reviews. If he ever was a newspaper reporter or editor, he does not mention the fact."[58] Lippmann had offered a thesis that the "*Times* had a definite news policy to which it made reports from Russia conform" and satisfied his own test by showing "that what the *Times* had said would happen . . . did not happen." The natural consequences of Lippmann's analysis, Freeman concluded, was that "the *Times* was a liar, the radical press was vindicated and the time to subscribe to the *New Republic* was at hand."[59]

Freeman's uncharacteristically harsh editorial brought a response from Lippmann. "Opinions will differ as to men's qualifications for dealing with such a problem as that of news gathering," he wrote. "I can say for myself that I am not without practical experience in the subject."[60] He took Freeman to task for implying that he called the *Times* "a liar" and told him he "misunderstood" a major part of the article. "A better press will be made in this country by the willingness of working journalists like yourself to learn the lessons of mistakes in the past," Lippmann lectured, "by a feeling, on their part, that humility and willingness to bear criticism are the roads to wisdom and understanding."[61]

Freeman's three-page response reiterated his criticism of Lippmann's article and delineated the frustrations of a historian in a newspaperman's world.

> I happen to have been a historical investigator before I was a newspaper editor and I trust I am not unconscious of the weakness of my profession. The inaccuracies of the average newspaper grate on anyone who loves truth. The clumsy handling of many stories outrages one's reverence for the accuracy of critical methods. But how much of this is intentional and how much is inevitable? A newspaper, in its very nature, is limited by time. The whole has to be made between eight in the morning and two in the afternoon. And always there is the disheartening knowledge that far more people are interested in Mutt and Jeff than in the most careful analysis of the most important public question.[62]

He offered an apology if "anything I wrote was unfair or struck below the belt," but he still condemned Lippmann's "sweeping charges that brand the honest with the dishonest, the courageous with the corrupt."[63] It was a never-ending frustration for Freeman—a man with the mind of a historian and scholar—to labor in a profession divided "between those who belong to the 'gee-whiz' school and those who are doing their best to improve the standards and the product of an exacting calling."[64]

On July 24, 1924, the *News Leader* moved into its new building at

Fourth and Grace Streets in Richmond. As the staff walked into the newly opened building, Freeman stopped them all in the lobby and asked them to kneel in a prayer of dedication.[65] They did. The *News Leader*, and the people who worked there, moved to his tune. Reporters recognized they had a high standard to meet. One day in 1926, Freeman stepped into the noisy city room, held up the day's paper, and boomed a question at the city editor.

"Who wrote this piece? Is it possible for anyone to write about Edgar Allan Poe and not know how to spell the man's name?"

The culprit was a cub reporter, recently graduated from Washington and Lee University, in his first week with the paper. Upon learning this information, Freeman glared at the young offender.

"And he spells it Edgar A-l-l-e-n Poe?"[66]

It was about this time that Freeman devised "The News Leader's Twenty Fundamental Rules of News Writing." The rules, printed on a card and distributed to reporters, remained in effect until the demise of the *News Leader*, in 1991. One reporter who toiled under the directive remembered the rules as "pretty sound" and used them "faithfully" even after his career at the *News Leader* ended.[67] The rules were the ultimate expression of how a historian writes for a newspaper.

1. Above all, be clear.
2. Therefore, use simple English.
3. To that end, write short sentences.
4. Do not change subject in the middle of a sentence . . .
7. Seek to leave the meaning of the sentence incomplete until the last word. Add nothing after the meaning is complete. Start a new sentence then.
8. Avoid loose construction. Try never to begin sentences with "and" or "but.". . .
12. Avoid successive sentences that begin with the same word, unless emphasis is particularly desired. Especially, in quoting a man, never have one sentence begin "He said" and then have the next sentence start "He stated."
13. In sentences where several nouns, phrases or clauses depend on the same verb, put the longest phrase or clause last . . .
18. Shun the employment of nouns as adjectives; it is the lowest form of careless English . . .
20. Try to end every story with a strong and, if possible, a short sentence.[68]

Freeman's talents as editor were noticed and appreciated outside Richmond. In December 1921, he received a letter from George Lea, a tobacco dealer in Danville, Virginia, inquiring about Freeman's interest in becoming editor and part owner of the two Danville papers, the *Register* and the *Bee*.[69] "I am quite happy in my work, have a good salary and every assurance of permanency," Freeman answered. He was, however, always alert to "the prospect of doing better" for himself and so presented the terms under which he would consider going "to Danville for a confidential conference."[70] He would have to be the majority stockholder, be paid a salary of $12,000 per year, and receive $21,000 in stock as a bonus. He admitted that might be "a stiff price to ask" but told Lea to remind the other investors of the "prestige and experience" he had accumulated at the *News Leader*.[71] "I think I may say without immodesty that no man in Virginia, except Major Allen Potts,[72] has had more experience in more departments of a newspaper than I have had."

"I could not have had a better statement for my preliminary negotiations," Lea enthusiastically responded, but over the course of the month, the opportunity to build a coalition of investors failed, and no formal offer was made.[73] Freeman, who was not "job-hunting or promoting," assured Lea that he considered the offer solely due to his "obligation to [his] family" and expressed no disappointment when the deal fell through.[74]

Freeman wanted the *News Leader* to provide public service to the city, and he set the example by continuing to accept appointments and assignments outside his regimen of editorial work and historical writing. He represented Virginia at the National Conference on Education in 1921, attended the National Conference on State Parks in 1926, and served on the Efficiency Commission investigating the operations of state government.[75] His military acumen was recognized by his appointment in 1925 as a "civilian aide to the Secretary of War in the operation of the citizen's military training corps."[76] He maintained close ties to Richmond business leaders, becoming their confidant as well as their promoter, and could speak with authority on almost any business topic or call on a close friend who could provide the needed expertise.[77] Part of the trust and friendship the business community held for him came from the relationships established in the *News Leader* Current Events Class. The class had grown in size and prestige since its evolution from Freeman's public speaking class. A survey of the forty-nine members in 1927 showed thirteen lawyers, ten investment bankers, seven trust or bank officers, and nineteen others in professions covering real estate, insurance, medicine, railroads, and manufacturing.[78] Twenty-eight members were graduated from the University of Virginia, seven from the University of Richmond, and the remainder scattered among schools from Columbia to Georgia Tech. All who expressed a religious preference were Protestant (five called themselves "free lancers") with Episcopalian being the leading denomination.[79] These seasoned professionals gathered each week at a private Richmond club, shared dinner, and settled down for a generally unstructured discussion of various topics.[80] Freeman led the class discussion, usually beginning with a book review before turning to the week's events. The minutes of the meetings reflect considerable horseplay and gentle tweaking of class members. "Dr. Freeman . . . felt the intellectual pulse of the Class and found it was barely beating," it was reported on February 14, 1921. "He diagnosed the situation and declared the class to be mentally constipated."[81] The members gave as good as they got. "For purposes of brevity," the minutes of May 9, 1921, record, "the Human Encyclopedia, the Human Thesaurus, and the Human Dictionary will hereinafter be referred to as Dr. Freeman."[82] Freeman was, during those days, a heavy user of tobacco, both cigarettes and chewing tobacco. His technique of chewing while lecturing was an inviting target for humorous critique. "The Doctor shifted his quid from right to left," it was reported, "and gave a demonstration of his well known maxim, that the moment of expectoration must synchronize with the completion of a sentence."[83] Other members joined in the habit, and it was duly noted "that for enthusiastic performance and volubility of saliva this feature of our weekly sessions deserves to be recorded in the minutes."[84] The class was more, however, than a fraternity meeting for straight-laced businessmen. Once the meetings were underway, serious discussions occurred on the issues of the day, and Freeman used the class as a sounding board for ideas and editorial opinion. The class was hardly representative of the Richmond community—the members being all successful and prominent white males—but it was certainly representative of the forces that moved the political, economic, cultural, and social life of Richmond. The opinions formed during the meetings spread through the city like the ripple effect of a pebble in water; the consensus of the steady, solid, and responsible leadership of Richmond, of which Freeman was becoming the personification.

His concept of public service extended as well to spiritual growth. He continued to teach a men's Sunday School class and, in early 1920, proposed to a local minister a plan to recruit college students into the ministry.[85] His religious beliefs, not surprisingly, centered on good works and service. He had learned his faith in the home of his parents; he had come to believe it through works.

> I went to work for the Kingdom [he wrote]. Soon, doubts begin to disappear, or at least to lose their importance, because I saw that it really worked with me. Then, little by little, as I saw what the name of Jesus was doing with men, how his power was transforming their lives, I had in my own heart an indefinable conviction that it must be so, this belief that Jesus was God . . . when people come to me with [doubt], I do not attempt to argue with them. I merely tell them to go to work in the service of Jesus, even if they do not believe in Him, to lead His life, even if they do not accept Him as God, and wait until they see what He will do with them.[86]

The "only personal disquietude" he experienced was "over the lack of zeal in the work of the Kingdom of God."[87] It was this work that would "lessen human misery . . . raise the general standard of the race and . . . give as much of happiness as we can to the lot of the average man."[88] Works and service were often the topic in a series of lectures he delivered to his class at Second Baptist Church beginning in November 1924, titled "Parables of the City Streets." These homilies, rare because so few of Freeman's lectures were ever written down, took their themes "from business, from the automobiles, from the life we lead."[89] He applied scripture to lectures on practical aspects of life, such as the value of time, good reading habits, and giving up the use of profanity.[90] Through all of the lectures ran the theme of work. "If, when you turn from evil to doing good," he stated, "if, when you renew your spirit and resolve to dedicate your life to Jesus Christ, if then you do not find a blessed, a sweeter, a richer, a more enjoyable existence, you are being cheated, and you should get that for which you have paid."[91] Through work came faith, and that faith enabled one to do greater work. "A man never 'wastes' the time or money he gives to God: by the very exercise of self-control and by the very sacrifice he makes, he becomes the more capable."[92] He summed up the four treasures of a man's heart as "his reading, his prayer, his experience, [and] his service."[93] These four traits had so marked Freeman's life from his earliest days that it is difficult to judge whether he shaped his life to his beliefs or vice versa. What is clear is that his concept of service included the spiritual as well as the physical or material, things everlasting as well as things fleeting.

Freeman's faith was put to the test in mid-1920 when his daughter Mary Tyler was struck ill. Her physician could only report that he did not "like the look of things." He called in three specialists, and their joint opinion was an attack of meningitis. "I hope you will pray God to take her little life," one of the doctors told Freeman, "because if she is spared, she will live in utter misery with her mind gone all the rest of her life."[94] Freeman rejected that counsel and, as he later described it, "went to the Cross and, like Jacob of old, wrestled with the angel . . . until I got my baby back."[95] Mary Tyler began to recover during the prayer vigil, and a subsequent spinal tap found the fluid normal.[96] His daughter's full recovery was not the only gratifying event in Freeman's family life during these years. A second daughter, Anne Ballard, was born in September 1923, and a son, James Douglas, arrived on April 12, 1925. Freeman's ever-expanding collection of books forced the family to move in 1920 to a large home on Floyd Avenue and, hardly after settling in, to a larger home on Westover Road in 1924. In whatever house the family lived, he set up his study on the third floor. Lined with books and folios, it was spartan in furnishings: a desk, a typewriter, specially cut paper, and a Morris chair bought during his Johns Hopkins days and in which Freeman did all of his historical writing.[97]

In addition to heading his own family, he was becoming *paterfamilias* to the city of Richmond. He was the person to see when any figure of note visited—quite an accomplishment considering his major biography of Lee was not yet published. He spent two days with David Lloyd George during the former British prime minister's visit to America, spoke at a dinner honoring famed aviator Charles Lindbergh, and walked the battlefields of the Seven Days with Winston Churchill.[98] Two meetings among the many during the twenties stand out. The first was with Marshal Ferdinand Foch, general-in-chief of the Allied Forces during World War I. The old general visited Richmond on November 23, 1921, and, following formal ceremonies and a parade, motored out to inspect a section of Lee's outer defensive line at Chickahominy Bluff. Walker Freeman, dressed in the uniform of a general of the United Confederate Veterans, greeted Foch and ushered him on his tour of the field. A map of the Seven Days Battle was spread before Foch, and Douglas Freeman was brought forward to answer "a series of rapid-fire questions" from the general. "Speaking rapidly," Freeman recalled, "[Foch] pointed out the red lines of the old defenses of Richmond and inquired how many troops [Lee] had on the south side of the Chickahominy . . . [and] how many heavy guns . . . In other words, Foch

Inez Freeman with Mary Tyler, c. 1920. (Image courtesy of Mary Tyler McClenahan.)

Douglas Freeman (second from right) escorting David Lloyd George (third from left) and others on a tour of the Richmond battlefields in the mid-1920s. (Image courtesy of Mary Tyler McClenahan.)

sensed immediately the strategy of Lee."[99] The young historian was impressed by this figure from history. "I think," he wrote "the old marshal would gladly have spent the afternoon there talking of the battle."[100] The afternoon was capped by the sight of Foch and Walker Freeman standing side by side "atop the fort with the Confederate flag flapping over [them]."[101]

The other meeting of note was held with a figure not yet known by the general public. In February 1924, Freeman accompanied Col. Allen Potts, business manager of the *News Leader*, on a trip to Washington, D.C. It seems Colonel Potts's son was experiencing some difficulties in the army, and a meeting had been set up in Gen. John J. Pershing's office to discuss the case. Pershing's adjutant met with the two newspapermen and forwarded a report of his findings to Freeman "rather than to mention the details now to Colonel Potts." The disturbing facts of the case are less significant than the impression the soldier made. "Permit me personally, colonel," Freeman wrote Pershing's aide, "to express my deep appreciation of your interest in this matter and my admiration for your instant approach to the crux of the problem. They say you will be general of the armies one of these days. I readily believe it." The letter was sent to Col. George C. Marshall.[102]

In 1925 Freeman ventured into another medium—radio. He was asked by the Chamber of Commerce to broadcast "a little program on Richmond history" from a newly opened station.[103] He delivered his remarks in a small bare room with a microphone suspended from the ceiling.[104] As he left the studio, he heard the announcer tell the listening audience that Freeman would be back on the air the next week.[105] Though he had not agreed to do more than one broadcast, he dutifully returned the next week and soon was broadcasting every Monday night at 9:00 P.M. over station WRVA.[106] The show's original title, "True Virginia Lore," was changed to "The *News Leader* History of Old Virginia."[107] Such was the inauspicious start of what could be deemed Freeman's third career. When the single broadcast expanded to two—on Monday and Wednesday nights at eight-thirty—he devoted one to topics in history and one to current events. Soon the history aspect was dropped as a theme, and the show was one of news and commentary, broadcast twice daily, Monday through Saturday.[108] The response was so positive—it is estimated that he reached 63 percent of the listening audience—that WRVA moved a microphone into Freeman's home study to accommodate his weekend or evening broadcasts. Thus on one sweltering hot summer evening, with Inez and the children away at the beach, the distinguished Dr. Freeman addressed the citizens of Richmond over the air while "in a complete state of nature."[109] When the *News Leader* got into the radio business, he switched from WRVA to station WRNL and continued a pace of thirteen broadcasts a week until his death.[110]

"Few will be the regrets that attend tonight the passing of 1919," Freeman wrote in a New Year's Eve editorial. "It has been a year of industrial progression and of spiritual reaction, a year when business was brisk and men were dull . . . a year of great profits and of great discontent—a combination no thoughtful patriot can relish."[111] He had just completed his first full year as an editor in which a major historical event—the war in Europe—was not a daily news topic. He would still turn out fact-filled, informative, and eloquent editorials, but the sense of commenting on events of historical significance was gone. Editorials in the twenties did not require the perspective of a historian, only the eye of a newsman.

The most significant post-war issue was the ratification of the Treaty of Paris and the creation of the League of Nations. Predictably Freeman followed a pro-Wilson line, though he showed more of an inclination to compromise than did the president. "Wilson's plan is the only one that gives any genuine promise of peace," he wrote, "because it is the only solution, the basis of which is justice."[112] When Sen. Henry Cabot Lodge of Massachusetts introduced a resolution against the League of Nations, Freeman unloaded a vicious attack on the "venom-lean and plunder-hungry Cassius" who opposed the league solely because "a Democratic president inspired it and now supports it."[113] Lodge had launched a "submarine attack"—a stinging analogy to Germany's pre-war policy of unrestricted submarine warfare—"for the sake of his party and regardless of his country." Partisan assaults aside, Freeman counseled compromise when it became clear that an unamended treaty would be defeated in the Senate. "The *News Leader* is of the opinion that while some of the reservations are unnecessary, and some of them are highly undesirable, none of them so far adopted is fatal to the treaty."[114] This position represented a break with Wilson, now incapacitated by a stroke, who directed Senate Democrats to oppose any changes. That directive, Freeman wrote, guaranteed that "both a resolution for ratification without reservations and a resolution for ratifications with the Lodge reservations will be defeated." Freeman's prediction came true that night as the Senate rejected both resolutions. "Today America appears in denial of her own idealism," he wrote the next day, but the fault was not Wilson's. "Upon the head of Lodge, his Republican henchmen, and a few Democrats who disgrace their country rests the responsibility for this."[115] He continued to advocate compromise—"a treaty with mild reservations is far better than no treaty at all"—but Wilson would not bend, and the treaty was a dead letter. Freeman predicted that the Senate's action would "be felt in every European country . . . and will hearten every element of discontent."[116] The League of Nations would "break down utterly," and Europe would be "forced back into old alliances that make another war an absolute certainty."

Despite his slight break with the president over the treaty compromise issue, Freeman continued to be a loyal supporter of Woodrow Wilson, and his staunch partisanship sometimes clouded his objectivity. While stumping for the league in 1919, Wilson was taken ill, most likely with a slight stroke, and rushed back to the White House. On October 2, he suffered a second, far more serious, stroke that left him partially paralyzed. The president became a recluse in the White House, guarded by Mrs. Wilson and his physician. Although the country knew little to nothing about the extent of Wilson's illness, Freeman showed a surprising lack of curiosity about the president's condition and did not make a significant editorial comment until January 1920. "The mental faculties of the president are as acute as they have ever been," he asserted, "and, except for the time he was dazed by his fall, have never been in the slightest degree impaired. Of this the *News Leader* is satisfied."[117] It is unclear from where Freeman received, or how he found credible, such an inaccurate report. While he cannot be faulted for not knowing facts that were being hidden during what Wilson's biographer calls "such a cover-up as American history had not known before," it is clear that Freeman was not applying the critical analysis of a historian or the innate curiosity of a newsman in the examination of a palatably suspicious situation.[118] Another month passed before he mentioned Wilson's condition, this time in connection with the forced resignation of Secretary of State Robert Lansing. "The one consolation" of the entire affair, he wrote, "is that Mr. Wilson must be near recovery and soon can resume his duties in person." He then attempted to seize the advantage of Wilson's illness, while simultaneously minimizing its seriousness. Wilson "would not have shown so much sensitiveness if he had not been sick; he would not have shown so much of fight if he were not nearly well."[119] Freeman, like the Cabinet, the Congress, and the rest of the country, was groping in the dark as to Wilson's condition. In absence of hard facts, Freeman turned to conjecture colored by his devotion to Wilson. If Freeman's finest hour to date as editor had come with his prescient and comprehensive analysis of the battles of the First World War, it can be argued that his lowest point came with his seemingly willing reluctance to question just what was going on with the ill president in the White House. One wonders if he would have been so reticent if the reclusive president had been a Republican.

On the day the nation inaugurated a new president, Freeman devoted the entire editorial page to a tribute to Wilson. "The *News Leader* believed in Wilson when he took office," Freeman wrote, "the *News Leader* believed in him when he asked for a declaration of war, the *News Leader* believed in him when he appealed for the ratification of the treaty in 1919. The *News Leader* believes in Woodrow Wilson now, and by its allegiance to him as president is willing to be judged."[120] While acknowledging that his "performances upon occasion were indifferent," he asserted that the "cold, plain truth" was that Wilson "will appear in his true greatness and to a posterity accustomed to the mediocrity of democratic statesmanship . . . as almost a providential gift to the nation."[121]

Freeman provided dispassionate workmanlike editorials on two other issues of the early twenties—Prohibition and Women's Suffrage. Virginia had adopted statewide prohibition in a 1914 referendum—prior to his editorship—and it was implemented in law on March 11, 1916. The *News Leader* said very little during the legislative stage and warned readers "not to expect too much or too little from the terms and operation of prohibition."[122] After a year in operation, the *News Leader* judged "that the law has done this commonwealth great good."[123] Despite that opinion, Freeman viewed nationwide prohibition with a suspicious eye. "Never before have the people of the United States sought by federal law thus to regulate the habits of people," he wrote. "Advocates of states' rights and inheritors of the old Southern tradition that the least government the better may be permitted serious misgivings as to the future extension of federal control."[124] Once the Volstead Act was the law of the land, Freeman consistently supported the law and encouraged "an educational campaign" against alcohol. "Young men may vote for a return to the saloon," he wrote, "because they never knew it in all its blood-sucking hideousness."[125] His personal beliefs were that "dry laws" were unenforceable and that government "cannot legislate goodness and self-control into men."[126] Freeman's editorials supporting Prohibition seldom reached flights of rhetorical eloquence nor utilized his favorite technique of tying the issue to a great historical event or enshrined principle. He seemed favorably inclined to Prohibition because he noticed that "practically no time had been lost during the past two or three years on account of [his reporters] being unable to attend to business as a result of parties the night before."[127] In short, the *News Leader* supported Prohibition because it was the law, and it effected a general good. Beyond that, the paper was silent.

Suffrage for women brought a number of issues to the fore: voting rights, states' rights, and civil rights. Freeman conceded that women had the inherent right to vote. "Neither biologically, intellectually, socially, or politically," he wrote, "is there any convincing argument against woman's suffrage."[128] That, however, was not the critical issue. The first consideration was that "upon certain questions the people can act more wisely as citizens of particular states than as citizens of the United States." Thus the issue should be decided on a state-by-state basis. He also observed that the men of Virginia were "indifferent" on the subject and would support suffrage "if the women of Virginia want the vote." The issue became complicated when viewed through a racial lens.

> In the nation as a whole [Freeman wrote] the vote of the negro is ten percent . . . but in some Southern states, where the Negroes constitute thirty, forty or even fifty percent of the population, they constitute a problem of which the state must take cognizance . . . If, conceivably, all the negro women qualified to vote were to exercise the franchise and the white women were indifferent, a condition might conceivably arise—we repeat the word purposely—where the negro vote would assume serious proportions.[129]

He went on to discount this concern—white women with the vote would be "conscientious in the discharge of their duty," that is to say they would outvote black women—and lay the issue at the feet of the women of Virginia. He suggested a statewide canvas to determine their wishes. "They can insure action by making their preference known."[130]

His injection of the racial question into the suffrage issue reflects the contradiction between his personal feelings and the era in which he lived. It is no doubt true that he believed the Federal government should not dictate voting procedures to the states—wholly aside from racial considerations. It is likewise true that he took a more liberal position than most Southern editors in arguing that women should decide the issue. Into this mix, however, the segregated society in which he lived dictated that a warning must be issued that "on the control of the election by suffrage majorities in all districts, white government in the South depends. No chances can be taken!"[131] This from the same editor who put to risk his professional career and personal safety in standing by Aubrey Barrett, who defied blackmail threats to thrash a front organization for the Ku Klux Klan, and who believed that black Virginians had a right to "better living conditions, freedom from fear, fair wages, [and] absolute justice under the laws of the Southern states."[132] In Virginia in 1920 the effect of race on an issue of public policy had to be examined before the merits could be addressed. Suffrage would have no possibility of passing unless the racial equation was raised and subsequently dismissed.

With Wilson physically and politically unable to seek a third term, Freeman turned his attention to the field of candidates for the 1920 election. His indifference to the choices manifested itself in a rare mistake. He suggested Massachusetts governor Calvin Coolidge, a

Republican, as a potential Democratic nominee for president.[133] "That was an awful bone I pulled about Coolidge," Freeman wrote his brother. "I remembered only that Wilson had endorsed Coolidge, or at least congratulated him, and forgot he was a Republican."[134] Freeman's forgetfulness could be attributed to his lack of enthusiasm for the uninspiring field of candidates and the ominous feeling that Wilson's sagging popularity and an electorate weary of world concerns made 1920 a Republican year. Freeman still showed a knack for predicting events and, early in the election year, decided on Ohio governor James Cox as his favorite for the nomination. He introduced Cox to *News Leader* readers as a "courageous . . . moderate" who would "arouse the least opposition."[135] He began to push Cox to state Democratic leaders, and by June he wired his brother that the governor was Virginia's second choice behind favorite son Sen. Carter Glass.[136] Cox won the nomination, and Freeman jumped in the electoral fray by heckling Republican nominee Warren G. Harding as a man of "commonplace record" and "narrow views."[137] His rhetorical jabs, however, did not reach the same level as his anti-Republican editorials of 1916, and a sense of pending disaster crept into his editorials during the fall. When Harding was elected in a landslide, Freeman commented: "Never has an American party deserved better of the nation and never has a party received worse."[138]

His editorials tended to treat Harding with bemused condescension. "Intellectually," he reminded readers, Harding "is not in the same class" as Wilson.[139] When Freeman found himself in agreement with a presidential veto message, he seemed shocked to find Harding to be at all literate. "Frankly, the *News Leader* did not believe Mr. Harding capable of this message," he wrote, expressing amazement at the message's "logic, its array of facts and its English."[140] He granted that Harding was "likeable, friendly, clean and sincere" and admitted that "a country that survived Hayes can probably survive Harding."[141] When Harding was struck ill in July 1923, Freeman noted that "Americans should pray for his recovery if for no other reason than that they should wish to be delivered from Calvin Coolidge."[142] When Harding died two days later, Freeman paid brief tribute to the deceased president, but devoted most of a two-column editorial to a scathing critique of Coolidge. The new president was "cold, icy cold, as cold (and as green) as the hills where he was born. He has never led and he never will. He will not be nominated for the presidency, in all human probability."[143] It was, he concluded, "a gloomy day for America and a darker for Europe."

It was, to be sure, a different time for America. Freeman's editorials in the early twenties reflect the paucity of serious issues. He concentrated on international peace, chastised Republicans over the Teapot Dome scandal, and tweaked Calvin Coolidge. "Not since 1876," he wrote, "has any party stood before the country as thoroughly discredited as the Republican party is today."[144] He judged Coolidge's election chances as diminishing daily, but was less than surprised when the president trounced Democrat John W. Davis in the election of 1924. The only hope Freeman saw for the Democratic Party was "through the emergence of a great man or of a magnetizing issue." Until then, the party must keep "the faith of equal rights and honest liberalism."

In 1924, Freeman wrote a lengthy article for *The Nation* titled "Virginia: A Gentle Dominion."[145] In his first extended commentary on life in Virginia, he started not with Jamestown, but at Appomattox; the life story of Walker Freeman apparent in his words.

Virginia buried her beloved at Appomattox, as her sons stood by, very ragged. All that she was, all that she had taken pride she told herself she had interred there. But it was spring for her sons, plowing-season, and they were hungry. They tramped back home and fortunately found in the reclamation of stumpy fields and neglected meadows an outlet for their grief. They thought of the past as seldom as they might and talked of it scarcely at all.[146]

After the war, Virginia retreated "to the second-story bedroom . . . pulled down the blind and through the darkness of reconstruction sat in her mourning."[147] Despite numerous changes to society since that time, "the fundamental characteristic" of the people remained "that quality of consideration for the feelings of other people."[148] It was this "consideration" that guaranteed courteous comments from "a mountaineer on the side of a wretched little clearing or the inheritor of great name chatting over his editions." It was this consideration that explained "the treatment of the Negro."[149] "The Virginia Negro," Freeman wrote, "is the blue-blood of his race . . . [and] has advanced splendidly in many ways." If Virginia were free from the "racial involvements of the north and the trouble of the Gulf states, the two races could live side by side through the centuries and have no strife." The races in Virginia, Freeman asserted, "understood" one another.[150]

Virginians accepted the Democratic Party "as they do their religious affiliation—chiefly by inheritance." The party was a "machine" whose success amounted to "nothing more than defeating the bills the liberals introduce." And here, Freeman judged, was the "skeleton" in Virginia's closet.

In order to exclude the Negro from the polls the framers of the present constitution of Virginia set *chevaux de frise* of qualifications in the voter's way. He must reside in the State two years, in the county or city one year, in the precinct thirty days; he must apply for registration in his own handwriting and must be able to explain a section of the constitution if asked to do so; he must pay a poll tax of $1.50 six months in advance of the election in which he wishes to participate. This last requirement is the stake on which the slow-footed are impaled. Nobody ever seems to remember from year to year when the six months begin or end.[151]

Given these circumstances, Freeman posed the question "is Virginia ever to be great again?" His answer was only if she could make "her superb history dynamic through the new educational movement that is the hope of every progressive Virginian . . . [it] is not enough to say: 'We have Abraham [for] our father.'"[152]

Freeman had not been enthusiastic about writing the article. He did it "rather than take a chance some idiot who lived in Virginia for six months and now resides in Greenwich Village will write thirty-five hundred flippancies."[153] He took the opportunity to pay tribute to the things he loved, but also to lay the shortcomings of Virginia before the nation. In a telling sentence he wrote that blacks had "the moral support of nearly all the whites . . . though the point of contact is . . . the point of friction."[154] As he sought to build a new Virginia—the Gentle Dominion he cherished—Freeman would more and more struggle with this "point of contact."

The major historical effort of his life continued to be the biography of Robert E. Lee. Having received the blessings of Scribner's for a full treatment, he maintained an intensive search for material. He discovered what he believed to be "the only account . . . General Lee ever wrote of his sensations at the time of his marriage."[155] He "unearthed more new material" on Lee's life before 1861.[156] Then he reported "perhaps the greatest" find of his years of research: "not less than twelve unpublished reports by Confederate generals on the Appomattox campaign."[157] Maxwell Perkins received these glad tidings with enthusiasm, but longed for a finished job. He even traveled to Richmond to judge for himself the status of the book. He left with no manuscript, but with an agreement that Freeman would write two articles on Lee for Scribner's magazine.[158] Freeman had committed to paper most of Lee's post-war years—from 1865 to his death—but he was not pleased with his pace. He rose early, having breakfast with Inez and Mary Tyler at six in the morning, but still could not find enough time to consistently work on the "Lee." When the Richmond Rotary Club notified him that he was delinquent in attendance, and his membership was in danger of being revoked, he snapped that he was "very conscious of the delinquency . . . [but it was] one of the handicaps which seem impossible . . . to overcome."[159]

As you know, our paper goes to press at 12:15. This means that during the precise time the midday meetings are held I am compelled to be in my office in case of late developments in the news or complications in the make-up . . . so far as the night meetings are concerned I perhaps can best explain the character of my problem by citing from my notebook my night engagements at the present time. Monday, January 10th, I had my regular . . . News Leader Current Events Class; Tuesday, the 11th, I had to speak at the Classical Study Association of Westhampton College . . . tonight I have a class that meets weekly in English Literature; January 13th I speak at Highland Park . . . Friday night I have open; Saturday I have the annual meeting of my Bible class; Sunday at 11 o'clock I have to preach; Monday . . . I have my class; Tuesday . . . I speak before the Richmond Typothetae; Wednesday . . . I speak in Winchester . . ."[160]

"So," Freeman concluded, "my calendar is crowded week by week." This schedule not only kept him from insignificant Rotary meetings, but also kept him from concentrating on his book. Something had to give, and it most assuredly would not be the Lee biography. He carved out two hours each day—fourteen hours per week—to be devoted to writing.[161] On January 18, 1926, just over eleven years after accepting the assignment from Scribner's, he advised Perkins that he had the life of Lee from January 1865 to the end of the war—just slightly more than three months of the general's life—"in nearly final shape."[162] This seemingly small accomplishment was nonetheless significant—the new schedule was working. He completed Lee's post-war days in Lexington, what would become Chapters 12-22 in Volume Four, during 1927 and on March 20, 1928, he sent that part of the bound manuscript to Max Perkins.[163] "It is 118,000 words," the stunned Perkins replied. "I suppose the whole work will be not less than 500,000 words." Perkins consoled himself by remarking that the completed work "will be *the* Life of Robert E. Lee."[164]

Freeman's organized system of research made the narrative quickly fall into place. He completed the section on Henry "Light Horse Harry" Lee in August 1928 and was writing about Lee's youth by November.[165] By May 1929, the completed portions of the manuscript stood as book-ends to Lee's adult life. Finished was Lee's life from birth to the outbreak of the Mexican War in 1846 and from 1865 to his death. The balance, 1846 to 1865, was complete but "by no means satisfactory."[166] It required a rewrite "in its entirety," but the Mexican War years would take only "two or three months."[167]

Mary Tyler Freeman came home from school one afternoon in late May 1929 and saw a rare sight: her father in bed in the middle of the day. He was suffering intense abdominal pain and heavily perspiring despite the mildness of the weather.[168] Propped up in bed, refusing medical attention, he stubbornly kept at the Lee manuscript. On May 25 he spent another day in agony as the narrative reached a Christmas letter Lee had sent his wife during the Mexican War. "The language," Freeman wrote, "differed little from that which he was to employ in a letter written on a dark Christmas day, with far greater issues at stake, fifteen years thereafter."[169] He could not write the next sentence. The pain had finally dulled his senses, and he reluctantly asked that his physician, Dr. O. O. Ashworth, be summoned. Ashworth diagnosed a strangulated hernia and promptly sent Freeman to the hospital. He was operated on the next day. The operation was successful in treating the malady, but the long incision in Freeman's abdomen would not heal. His busy, but sedentary, life left no time for exercise, and he had little muscle tone. One afternoon he turned over in his bed, and the entire incision opened. A dazed Freeman saw much of his large intestine pour onto the bed. A nurse quickly poured a bottle of saline solution over the abdomen, wrapped the sheet around his midsection, and rushed him to surgery.[170] Freeman's life hung in the balance for several days. While his doctors watched and his family prayed, Freeman had an experience he later described to his family.

I was walking across a white field, on the far side of which was a long white wall. In the wall was a door and I knew that was my destination. The door was closed and I knocked. It was opened by a man of great dignity and sweetness who told me gently that I could not enter; it was not yet time and I must go back. I recognized the man as Christ and I turned with much regret to recross the white field.[171]

Freeman's first recorded account of this out-of-body experience came in a letter written one year later. In responding to a letter from one of his radio listeners, he recounted that "last year, when I was very close to death, I had a special revelation of Jesus so personal and so overwhelming that I have not dared to this day to describe it, even to my own wife."[172] He must have told Inez by 1933 for he makes reference in a letter to her to the "spiritual experience" that had been his during "those dark days."[173] The account recorded by his daughter is the only one in which he provided such detail.

He stayed in the hospital for eight weeks. As he chafed under his confined inactivity, he listened "to some of the terrible Sunday programs" and resolved that he would "undertake to give a program for 'shut-ins' on Sunday, particularly for persons in hospitals."[174] Promptly upon his discharge, he made this request of WRVA, and his new show, *Lessons in Living*, went on the air in the fall of 1929. "I have had much happiness in the result," Freeman commented years later. "Many pleasant associations have been formed and, in the providence of God, perhaps a little good has been done."[175]

Illness had knocked Freeman off his steady pace on *R. E. Lee*, but by the end of 1929 the only part remaining to be written was the period 1858-65. That these years were the most critical portion of the book was reflected in his comment that he would "have to give fully six months" to the Battle of Gettysburg.[176] As the project neared completion, he gave his attention to the structure of the finished product. He projected three volumes. The first one would be called "The Preparation of Robert E. Lee" and would cover his life from birth to the outbreak of war; volume two, titled "The Campaigns of Lee," would cover the war; and volume three, "After Appomattox," would finish the story.[177] He admitted the "possibility that further study of the years of war will disclose so much new material that two volumes, instead of one, will have to be devoted to that period."[178]

"I do not know exactly how to describe the method I have employed," Freeman wrote Perkins in forwarding the manuscript of Lee's pre-war years. "I have tried to keep the light on Lee and to present the man through his writings, and through his acts, great and small . . . I have not presumed to analyze the man's thoughts . . . [and], as far as I know, I have not written a single paragraph of eulogium."[179] He did not include a "terrible first chapter on ancestry that destroys most reader's appetite for a biography." The biographical subject, "a boy of 10," does not "give a hang about his forbears until he gets older," and most readers feel the same way.[180] Freeman therefore wanted to save the reader from "ennui" of biblical-like "begots" and get right to the life of Lee. He estimated that he made reference to "something over 1,200 unpublished letters and reports" in the treatment of Lee's early years. Freeman judged "probably four-fifths of the material in the book is entirely new." It contained the first "full history" of Lee's father's financial tragedy and demonstrated the "dominance of the Carter [rather than of the Lee] influence in his earlier years." Lee's grades at West Point were given for the first time, the only known letters of his mother were included, and all of his duty assignments—"including several previously unknown tours"—and the scope and nature of his duties were described.[181] The Mexican War chapters demonstrated "his debt in strategy" to Winfield Scott and showed "the limited extent of his experience as a soldier in the field." "Most important of all," Freeman stated, "it is demonstrated beyond all doubt that before Lee left Texas in 1861, he had decided he would remain with Virginia" in case of secession. This finding refuted previous accounts of Lee's struggle over whether to accept the command of Union forces.[182] "Lee is presented as 'more human' than he has heretofore been portrayed," Freeman concluded. "His reserve of manner did not come till the eve of the war." Thus were presented the partial results of fifteen years of research and work—and this section would ultimately comprise only twenty-five chapters of a four-volume work.

There was "no considerable collection of Lee material" that Freeman had not examined—except one: several unpublished letters from Lee to his older brother Charles.[183] The letters were held in trust by several members of the Lee family, and use of them was zealously guarded by the formidable Mary Custis Lee deButts—granddaughter of Robert E. Lee. Freeman's first letter requesting permission to see the letters was rebuffed by Mrs. deButts with the explanation that the family would be publishing the letters and did not want them cited in any other book. Freeman reluctantly accepted the excuse—no doubt reasoning that he could use the letters in published form—but the years passed, and no volume was released.[184] So on the day after Christmas, 1929, Freeman wrote a tactful letter in which he inquired about the publication of the letters and offered to delay release of his biography until such time as the collection was made public.[185] Mrs. DeButts advised that the letters were "too personal" to be published and that "the few that would be of interest to the general public have been partially (and some entirely) published." She wished Freeman well, but did not offer to let him examine the letters.[186]

"I certainly do not want to be a nuisance to you," Freeman replied, "but you can understand, I know, how a man who has devoted his leisure time for ten years to a great enterprise of this sort would want to be as accurate as possible." Not wishing to alienate Mrs. deButts, Freeman proposed that he "occasionally" forward questions that she could answer by referring to the letters and, hopefully, she could see the context in which he wished to cite certain letters.[187] This approach produced further disappointing results.[188] Mrs. deButts allowed Freeman to examine Lee papers held in the Library of Congress, but these letters had been previously published and provided no new information. He now pleaded his case to other family members and friends, and, while he found sympathetic ears, these efforts were likewise futile.[189] Freeman's frustration was palpable. "After ten years of work," he wrote a friend, "I shall be compelled in my four volume biography to say that I have been denied the privilege of examining papers in the hands of the heirs of the man to perpetuate whose fame I have given the best scholarship of which I am capable and the most productive years of my life."[190] When Mrs. deButts had the audacity to ask Freeman if he would comment on the abilities of a prospective editor for the letters, he seized the opportunity to offer himself for the job and "to meet and better any offer" for use of the letters.[191] That effort as well went nowhere. *R. E. Lee* went to press without Freeman having seen the first letter from the collection. Always the gentleman, Freeman presented Mrs. deButts with a complimentary four-volume set and tactfully skirted the issue of her obstinacy in his "Foreword" and "Acknowledgements."[192]

This minor disappointment could not obscure the great accomplishment soon to be complete. He had a draft of Lee's war years before him and would now bring to bear the light of his extensive knowledge, the fruits of his exhaustive research, the resources of his indefatigable energy, and the eloquence of his rhythmical prose to finish the job. The words he wrote flowed from rivers of life deep within him. The words were the fortitude of Walker Freeman and the compassion of Bettie Freeman. They were the inspiration of S. C. Mitchell and the enlightenment of Johns Hopkins. They had been tested in the crucible of daily commentary and refined on the lathe of historical analysis. The words were a tribute to the love of Inez and a testament to his children.

His words followed the trail that Lee's campaign traced red across the face of Virginia. During the chill of February, he wrote of June 1862 and Gaines's Mill: "It was a night of groaning and of misery for the thousands of wounded, a night of sorrow and of expectancy for the man who issued late orders to his lieutenants and then gave humble thanks to the God of Battles that the grip of the enemy on Richmond had been loosened."[193] As spring swept along the James River and the old city renewed itself, he completed the stories of Savage Station, Frayser's Farm, and Malvern Hill. It was difficult for him to conceal his abhorrence of war as he surveyed the dead from Mechanicsville to Malvern Hill.[194] "Eleven thousand men . . . lost to the Confederacy for all time . . . [the] leading men in every community, the trained, the intelligent and the martial-minded . . . slain by scores." In June he wrote Inez that he "was at Lee's headquarters figuring out what to do about General Pope."[195] He did, and soon Lee's "troops were making the most triumphant advance these banners had ever shone upon."[196] His summer of recording victory passed into an autumn of chronicling the battles of Sharpsburg and Fredericksburg. Then in November came the simple stirring dialogue between the Southern demigods.

"General Jackson," said [Lee], "what do you propose to do?"
"Go around here," Jackson said, and traced the route that Hotchkins had marked.
"What do you propose to make this movement with?"
"With my whole corps," Jackson answered . . .
"Well," said [Lee] calmly, "go on."[197]

It was a Sunday morning in November when he wrote of Lee's torment of losing his "right arm"—"Stonewall" Jackson—in May 1863. As Christmas was celebrated in Richmond, Freeman wrote of the army in Gettysburg. The bleakness of the winter weather mirrored the forlornness of the chapters: "The Spirit that Inhibits Victory," "What Can Detain Longstreet?," and "It is All My Fault." His emotions were "so stirred in writing" of Pickett's charge that the composition became "a frightful strain."[198] He briefly abandoned the fog-of-war approach and took the reader across the field and up Cemetery Ridge.

The grimy faces of the Federal infantry can be seen where the smoke lifts for an instant in front of the wall . . . still the dauntless men rush upward . . . Armistead is up now, at the low barrier, his sword is high, and his hat, pierced by the point of his sword, is down to the hilt of his blade . . . The enemy is all around them. Where are the thousands who marched in that proud line from the woods . . . No support; no succor! . . . The assault has failed. Men could do no more![199]

The army was reorganized and headed back into the Wilderness. Freeman outlined the thrusts and parries, explained the maneuvers and marches, as Lee battled the onslaught of Grant's juggernaut. His painstaking dissection of the army's movements from "Rapidan to Petersburg" reflected skills honed in describing the action from Meuse-Argonne to St. Quentin. And when the last December sun of 1932 set over Richmond, he wrote of "the last December sun of 1864." It was the eighteenth New Year he had celebrated since Mr. Burlingame's first letter asking for a 75,000-word biography.

"I am vain enough to believe that you will rejoice with me," Freeman wired Maxwell Perkins, "when I tell you I yesterday completed the text of Lee."[200]

It was January 19, 1933—the 126th anniversary of the birth of Robert E. Lee.

CHAPTER 7

"Lee Come to Life Again"

As closely as he could calculate, since 1926 Freeman had devoted 6,100 hours to writing the Lee biography.[1] He had invested thousands of his own dollars into the project.[2] He had written more than one million words. The words covered more than two thousand printed pages filing four volumes. The bibliography consisted of twenty-six pages of sources. Maps were inserted for reference and appendices added for clarification. He dedicated the work to Inez, "who never doubted," but *R. E. Lee* was a monument both to its subject and to the labor of its author.

"I don't think there is a statement in these pages," he wrote, "even to the mud on a man's breeches or the parched corn in his stomach, that I cannot document."[3] The book was written "in plain terms" in order that the average reader could appreciate it, but on a level designed to appeal to the "serious student." This tightrope of presentation carried the risk of rendering the book "insufferably dull," so Freeman "tried to put into the narrative some of the thrill of the events, and . . . to give a literary finish as nearly worthy of the subject as I could."[4] Even the "literary finish," however, was checked by a "restrained style."

Reared in the South, I had listened all my life to the extravagances of rhetorical apostrophe on all that pertained to the Confederacy, and I had felt that we were actually lowering our Southern leaders in the eyes of thoughtful persons by attempting to exalt them into demigods. General Lee himself detested these absurdities of panegyric; I determined to write in his spirit, as I interpreted it, and not to permit myself a single laudatory adjective in describing him. He did not need them.[5]

"I do not see any reason," he wrote to Max Perkins, "why Lee should be presented as the idol of the south."[6] To that end, he followed two threads throughout the narrative: "the military history that . . . escaped the earlier biographers and . . . Lee as essentially human."

Freeman presented the military history over many chapters, but saved his assessment for one chapter: "The Sword of Robert E. Lee." He painted in vivid colors the panorama of obstacles that faced Lee the commander: the odds of troop strength against him, guns outranged by superior artillery, lack of food, and a decrepit railroad system. Lee fought these obstacles in the "apex of a triangle," exposed to naval attack on one side and a "dispersion of forces that weakened his front." All while tasked with protecting the Confederate capital. "With poverty he had faced abundance," Freeman observed, "with individualism his people had opposed nationalism."[7]

To these difficulties were added mistakes, errors, and miscalculations. Freeman outlined at least twelve specific errors that "together . . . exacted of the South some of its bravest blood."[8] More serious than these specific mistakes in the field was Lee's "excessive amiability" to his subordinate officers. "Humble in spirit," he wrote, "he had sometimes submitted to mental bullying." This consideration led him to concede too much to the excuses of commanders or scrap his own battle plans in favor of another's "second best."[9] To this defect was added "a mistaken theory of the function of high command." Lee believed that the function of the general-in-chief was to bring his troops together at the proper time and place, and leave combat to his generals. "Who may say whether when his campaigns are viewed as a whole," Freeman speculated, "[that] adherence to this theory of his function cost the army more than it won for the South?"[10]

He weighed these shortcomings on the scale of historical analysis and then offered his perspective on Lee the commander.

When Lee's inordinate consideration for his subordinates is given its gloomiest appraisal, when his theory of command is disputed, when his mistakes are written red, when the remorseless audit of history discounts the odds he faced in men and resources, and when the court of time writes up the advantage he enjoyed in fighting on inner lines in his own country, the balance to the credit of his generalship is clear and absolute.[11]

Freeman listed the credit side of the ledger. In his first two years as commander of the Army of Northern Virginia, Lee fought ten battles and "indisputably won" six of them while meeting "definite defeat" in only one.[12] When he was free to maneuver in the field, he inflicted 145,000 casualties on the enemy while sustaining 103,000. He occupied so much of the thoughts and attention of the Northern war effort that "he prevented the hosts of the Union" from achieving more success elsewhere. He was superb on both the offensive and defensive. Freeman cited "five qualities" that gave eminence to Lee's abilities as a strategist: "his interpretation of military intelligence, his wise devotion to the offensive, his careful choice of position, the exactness of his logistics, and his well-considered daring."[13] No detail was too small if it concerned the morale or welfare of his soldiers. He maintained the esteem of Jefferson Davis, encountered no friction with the War Department, and welded lieutenants of varying abilities and temperament "into an efficient instrument of command."[14] He kept alive "the hope and the fighting spirit of the South . . . [and] as long as he could keep the field, the South could keep its heart."[15]

He would not compare Lee's record with those of other generals. "Circumstance is incommensurable," he wrote. "Lee's record is written in positive terms; why invoke comparisons?[16]

Freeman waited until he had finished the entire book to assess Lee the man.[17] He had on several earlier occasions offered thoughts about Lee's character. "Remember," he wrote in 1923, "that Lee was dignity, grace and courtesy personified without a touch of surliness."[18] Lee's true character, he wrote three years later, consisted of "his consideration for others, his simplicity, his prayerfulness, his military daring."[19] The years of study had established a bond across the ages between the general and his biographer. Lee had become to Freeman not only a biographical subject, but also someone with whom he shared "spiritual companionship" as he spent hour upon hour, day after day, in the general's "company."[20] Freeman felt he knew Lee—knew him better than anyone else. Knew him as only a man who had read the vast amount of letters, documents, reports, and dispatches could know him. The challenge of the final chapter was to present to the public the man he had discovered; to "look at him for the last time and read from his countenance the pattern of his life."[21] He did so in perhaps the most eloquent paragraph in the entire four volumes.

Because he was calm when others were frenzied, loving when they hated, and silent when they spoke with bitter tongue, they shook their heads and said he was a superman or a mysterious man. Beneath that untroubled exterior, they said, deep storms must rage;

his dignity, his reserve, and his few words concealed sombre thoughts, repressed ambitions, livid resentments. They were mistaken. Robert Lee was one of the small company of great men in whom there is no inconsistency to be explained, no enigma to be solved. What he seemed, he was—a wholly human gentleman, the essential elements of whose positive character were two and only two, simplicity and spirituality.[22]

For thirteen pages Freeman summarized the attributes of the man he knew. A man inculcated with the principles of self-control, possessed of natural dignity, and whose clear conscience resolved every problem into right and wrong. And always there was allegiance to duty and a spirit of self-denial.[23] How many thousands of anecdotes had Freeman read over the years? Yet there was only one that to him typified the message of the man.

It occurred in Northern Virginia, probably on his last visit there. A young mother brought her baby to him to be blessed. He took the infant in his arms and looked at it and then at her and slowly said, "Teach him he must deny himself."[24]

He had come finally, after so many years, to the final sentence. It was early Sunday morning, November 19, 1933, "just as the East was glowing to the sunrise," and he was editing the final draft of Volume IV, Chapter 28. The last sentence read: "Let us leave that simple, spiritual gentleman to his sleep, as we go back to our daily work, heartened by our heritage."[25] Freeman took his pen and lined out that sentence, leaving the first two lines of the paragraph as the final words he would leave to readers throughout the ages.

"That is all. There is no mystery in the coffin there in front of the windows that look to the sunrise."[26]

Scribner's released Volumes One and Two of *R. E. Lee* in October 1934, and the final two volumes six months later. The superlatives began immediately. "It looks as if at last the final and definitive biography of Lee [has] been written," began the review in the *New York Times*.[27] The *Times* heralded the "vitality and color" of the narrative and the "firm and never tedious" prose. The reader followed Lee "minute by minute, often gesture by gesture" through a book with a "finality and conclusiveness" such as "no other life of Lee has ever shown."[28] When the final two volumes were released, the *Times* assessed the entire work as "Lee Complete for All Time."[29] Stephen Vincent Benet, author of *John Brown's Body*, wrote the review for the *New York Herald Tribune* and was no less enthusiastic. "This is a complete portrait—solid, vivid, authoritative, and compelling."[30] Freeman held together a "vast tapestry . . . by a clear and single thread" and "in his frankness, his judiciousness, his skill and, above all, in his true comprehension, [he] deserves all the praise that will be given him."[31] When Benet finished writing his review, he dashed a letter off to Freeman congratulating him for "the best life of Lee that has ever been written and one of the finest American biographies we have ever seen."[32]

Scholarly reviews followed the same pattern. Poet and biographer Allen Tate wrote the reviews for *The New Republic* and concluded that "here, at last, is the definitive Lee."[33] "Where we had glimpses before," Tate wrote, "we now have an unprecedented richness of material; where we had divined the springs of Lee's actions, we are now at the source." Tate's only reservation was that the fog-of-war method would require that readers have a somewhat "detailed knowledge" of the war, which would prevent *Lee* from "being a popular book."[34] Historian Henry Steele Commager wrote in *The Yale Review* that Freeman had "so combined scholarship and art that every line is fact and every page interpretation, and from this fusion has come a figure of indubitable authority and of moving beauty."[35] The *American Historical Review* assigned its two reviews to Dumas Malone, a future Pulitzer Prize winner for his six-volume life of Thomas Jefferson. Malone found that the work revealed Freeman's "intelligent and painstaking investigation, his power of analysis, and his literary skill." Though Malone noticed "a certain flavor of the Confederacy" sprinkled throughout the volumes, he still judged it to be "distinctly objective."[36] Freeman's judgments, Malone concluded, were "likely to be accepted without serious question."[37] Twenty years later, Malone recalled his first impression of *R. E. Lee*. "Great as my personal expectations were," he wrote, "the realization far surpassed them and never did I devour a major historical work with such insatiable appetite and more unalloyed satisfaction."[38] Malone's reaction was typical. Freeman kept a short list of comments made about *Lee* from various reviews around the world. The comments are repetitious in their unqualified praise.[39]

There was one major dissenting opinion. Captain Basil Liddell Hart, a British military analyst and author, wrote two negative reviews in the *Saturday Review of Literature*. While crediting Freeman with writing a military history "almost in a class by itself," he devoted most of his review to an attack on Lee.[40] He found that the character of the young Lee promised only "every prospect of admirable mediocrity" and there existed "several points in [his] career which a student of psychology might find ominous."[41] A "model boy rarely goes far," he sniffed, "and, even when he does, is apt to falter when severely tested." Lee's career was characterized by failure, and while "the man is always lovable . . . the general is almost laughable."[42] The review continued in that vein, more as an appraisal of Lee than a review of Freeman's book. When he did address the attributes of the book, Liddell Hart paid tribute to the presentation, finding it "refreshing" to read a biography "where the hero's failings and failures are recognized when setting forth his qualities and achievements." In his second review, "Why Lee Lost Gettysburg," Liddell Hart concludes that both Lee and Freeman missed "the fundamental reality" that the Civil War was the first modern war and could not be fought according to Lee's methods. "No great commander," Liddell Hart stated, "has been guilty of a madder act" than was Lee in ordering Pickett's charge; and Freeman "stumbled over the same rock in the path as his hero did."[43] Though Liddell Hart's views represented a minority among contemporary reviews of *R. E. Lee*, they left an echo that would be heard in years to come.

While public accolades mounted, Freeman received the praise of friends and prominent figures. Winston Churchill found it "a work of absorbing interest" and fondly remembered his tour with Freeman of local battlefields. "I hope we shall meet again" he added.[44] A former British prime minister, David Lloyd George, wrote Freeman that same week. "I look forward to the joy of reading [the volumes]," he commented. "That joy will be greater because of my personal acquaintance with the author."[45] Lloyd George had likewise been the beneficiary of a Freeman-guided battlefield tour.

From close by in Richmond came the plaudits of a fellow writer, novelist Ellen Glasgow.

Military students are more competent to praise your handling of battles; but as a writer I may tell you how much I admire your treatment of the scenes at Appomattox. This is dangerous ground because the faintest rhetorical accent, the slightest straining for dramatic effect in a tragedy that was beyond drama, would have been fatal. But you have achieved in this chapter, and indeed through all the volumes, that perfect simplicity which makes one feel as one reads, "This is not writing about Lee; it is Lee come to life again."[46]

From Atlanta came praise from Margaret Mitchell, author of *Gone with the Wind*. "Your *Lee* was the very first thing I purchased with my very first royalty check," she wrote. "I had refused to read it until I could have it for my own and it is impossible for me to tell you of the pleasure it gave me and of the great admiration I conceived for you."[47] Freeman wrote Mitchell a note of thanks and invited her and her husband to Richmond. "We could spend a long evening in high converse about the Confederacy."[48]

Next to hearing from fellow writers, Freeman most appreciated "the reception accorded" the book by "professional soldiers."[49] Colonel Wilson Burtt, assistant commandant of the Command and General Staff School, canvassed his faculty for their opinions and sent two pages of comments to Freeman. "It is the simple truth to say," Burtt wrote, "that the faculty . . . is selected from the highest level of professional military intellect in our service." The selected comments included one by an instructor who said the book contained "so many expositions of the imponderables and intangibles . . . that it should be studied by all students of the art of command." Another called it "a model for the student of methodology." All agreed it was of critical importance and value to the professional soldier. "You have taken the faculty by storm," Burtt concluded.[50] From Washington, D.C., came the opinion of another professional soldier. "Measured by the highest standards of biographical writing," Gen. Douglas MacArthur wrote, "it is, in my opinion, an outstanding work and one that will have an enduring place in our country's historical literature."[51] MacArthur was particularly impressed with the fog-of-war method, judging it "so effective" that he expected "to see it copied by military biographers of the future." "I congratulate you," MacArthur concluded, "on the production of a masterpiece."[52] Freeman promptly answered the general. "I had rather have your judgment of my book from the military point of view," he wrote, "than that of any other person now alive."[53] Freeman had a budding reputation as a military expert due to his previous writings and his editorials on World War I. Publication of this book forever sealed that reputation. In June 1935 he received an invitation from the Army War College to present a lecture on Lee. This one speech turned into a series of lectures with Freeman appearing twice a year—in October and February of each term—until the spring session of 1940.[54]

By every standard of measurement, Freeman's *R. E. Lee* was an unqualified success. Scholarly journals and popular magazines praised it; professional soldiers, writers, and historians gave it their highest approbation. The general public showed its support by purchasing a sizable number of copies. By 1963, ten years after Freeman's death, 87,735 four-volume sets and 72,786 single volumes had been purchased.[55] The book so ingrained itself into the public culture that there soon appeared a cartoon in *The New Yorker*. A "Hokinson" girl stands in a library and hands the volumes to the librarian. "I'm afraid," she sheepishly admits, "I bit off more 'Robert E. Lee' than I could chew."

Talk of a Pulitzer Prize for Freeman began almost simultaneously with the release of *R. E. Lee*. Stephen Vincent Benet demanded that the book and its author be awarded "at least ten Pulitzers." Freeman was more skeptical of the process and confided his thoughts to his daughter Mary Tyler.

The reception of the third and fourth volumes of a certain book has been even more cordial than that with which the first and second were received. I have no idea it will affect the Pulitzer award in any way, for—in the strictest confidence—publishers' politics play too large a part for me to swing it; but every time I read a new favorable review in which it is confidently asserted that I will get the prize, I laugh to myself. The literary gangsters will have their way and will award the prize to the book that was picked out months and months ago.[56]

The "literary gangsters" spoke in May and awarded him the "Pulitzer Biography Prize."[57] Freeman was at his current events class meeting when he was informed of the news, and drafted a brief statement for the press.[58] He was surprised and grateful, but felt the award was directed more to the "patriotism and unselfish services" exemplified by General Lee.[59] He had been more than rewarded by "being privileged to live, so to speak, in [Lee's] company for many years." He concluded his statement by comparing the time in which he had figuratively lived, with the Depression days in which he actually lived. "I shall be very happy," he wrote, "if in this day of false fear, doubtful counsel, and whining attempts to escape the consequences of our own acts, this award brings again to public emulation a man who embodied courage, decision, and a willingness to pay the price of loyalty to his convictions."[60]

The *Richmond Times-Dispatch* carried the news of the award, complete with a prominent picture of Freeman, on its front page. Freeman buried the news of his accomplishment on page ten of the *News Leader*.[61]

"A man lives for ten years on bread and no butter," Freeman had written during his days at Johns Hopkins, "ten years with bread and butter, and after that ten years with cake and ale."[62] The twenties and early thirties, dominated by the figure of Robert E. Lee, were also bread and butter years for Freeman.

On March 27, 1926, he realized a lifelong dream as he departed with Inez on a trip to Europe. The month-long vacation, part of an "All Virginia Tour" of Richmond's most noted businessmen, was to be equal portion business and pleasure.[63] He was to study first hand "the labor situation in England and the fiscal status of France," but he would have sufficient time to see the splendor of much of Europe.[64] The couple set sail on the *Minnetonka* with an itinerary calling for stops in London, Paris, Florence, Rome, and Naples.[65] Though he was his usual buoyant self, Inez was more subdued as she left behind her three children—aged eight, two and one half, and eleven months. Unbeknown to her husband, she kept a calendar in the top pocket of her suitcase and marked off the days until she was back home.[66] In England, Freeman found the general atmosphere "one of depression" reflected "by the type of clothes, automobiles and food used."[67] The railroads were dilapidated, building was at a standstill, and "the shabby genteel class dominates." "The whole color scheme," he said, "is blue and the people are serious and watchful." Across the channel, he observed the opposite. "High class automobiles are prevalent," he said upon reaching France. "The people are gaily dressed and are spending money." He found the attitude of the French "not indicative of care or concern." These sharp contrasts meant little to Freeman. He concentrated on only one difference: The Franc was at its lowest point while the British pound sterling was "carefully guarded." He interpreted this as meaning that England had bottomed out and was set for recovery, while France was on the brink of a financial downturn.[68] While in England, the Freemans spent one day under the "hospitable roof" of former British prime minister David Lloyd George. The two men discussed current events—including Winston Churchill's recent defection from the Liberal to the Tory party—but also strayed onto the subjects of *Huckleberry Finn* and Smithfield hams.[69] Promptly upon his return to Virginia, Freeman sent a ham off to Lloyd George with the reminder that he should "watch the boiling as the ham will come to pieces if boiled too long."[70]

The trip was a singular experience for Freeman. Always an art lover, his exposure to the original works of the masters touched his soul. His luggage was significantly increased for the return trip by the numerous reproductions he purchased. For the children, it was Gainsborough's *Baby Stuart* and Reynolds's *Little Girl with a Ball*.[71] For himself it was several Rembrandts and, the prize of the trip, a full-size copy of Vermeer's *The Distant View of Delft*. The painting was promptly mounted on the dining room wall and so remained for the rest of Freeman's life.[72] The trip expanded Freeman's already extensive knowledge of political and economic conditions in Europe. When he reported his findings to the current events class, the secretary noted that the members "marveled" at the "memory, understanding, and comprehension" Freeman displayed in recounting "these intricate matters."[73] He warned the class that the rise of Fascism in Italy "boded no good to the peace of the world" and spoke of the "amazing lack of militarism apparent in France." He made no grandiose predictions to his class, but his observations show he was thinking about the fateful combination of economic instability and militaristic tyrannies. Three years later Freeman would take another trip to Europe, this time adding stops in Germany and Spain.[74]

The presidential election of 1928 was unlike any election Freeman had covered. The Democratic candidate for president, New York governor Alfred E. Smith, faced almost insurmountable odds in the South. He was a Tammany Hall politician who clung to his Lower East Side style of speech; he had called for repeal of Prohibition; and he was a Catholic. These facts, when combined with the general prosperity of the nation and the strength of Smith's opponent, Herbert Hoover, made the Republican Party competitive in the South for the first time in its history. Freeman had been an early supporter of Smith, though he was "wholly opposed to a return of the saloon in any guise."[75] He addressed this issue with the candidate, asking him to moderate his Prohibition stand. Absent a change, Freeman said he could "not answer for the outcome of any Southern states except Florida and Louisiana."[76] The situation quickly turned bleak for Smith in the South. At the current events class meeting of September 24, 1928, "the doors . . . were ordered closed . . . and the silence was dramatically intense as Dr. Freeman began his first review of the political situation."[77] He analyzed each state and commented "that the situation is badly complicated" in Virginia. "Women," he noted, "are the worst element . . . and the preachers are playing the devil with Smith." Freeman confessed he was "alarmed" at the "diversity of the attacks" and surprised at the blatant prejudice in numerous publications.[78] One Hoover supporter asked what would be the consequences to Virginia of a Republican victory. Freeman answered that it would put patronage into the hands of Republicans, be seen as a "distinct discouragement" to the "progressive administration" of Virginia governor Harry Byrd, and would empower "the same old slimy, hypocritical crowd which has run the Virginia legislature for years." The class was not united behind Freeman's view. Eight of the thirty-eight members present, including Freeman's close friend Allen Saville, stated that they were going to vote for Hoover. "I do not see how a man like you can do such a thing as that," Freeman wrote Saville.[79]

Faced with such a deteriorating situation, Freeman adopted a three-pronged editorial policy to advance Smith's candidacy. He would attempt to discredit the anti-Catholic arguments, attack the Republican Party, and remind his readers of the historic tie between the South and the Democratic Party. He told his current events class he would "rather join hands with Tammany and the wild men of Wisconsin for liberalism than be a geographic conservative."[80]

"We are having a real fight in the South," Freeman wrote a friend, "and there is no concealing the fact that the main issue is one of religious intolerance. I think that eighty percent of the opposition to Smith has its origins in religious prejudice."[81] Freeman attempted to approach the issue logically on the editorial page. The "anti-Catholic arguments," he wrote, "are not put out to protect America against some mythical onslaught by non-existent papal legions, but to keep America under the political control of the party that" brought about the Teapot Dome scandal.[82] He heralded Smith as a man who had "humbly held to the church in which he was born," a trait tradition-bound Southerners were bound to respect. He called on the electorate to rise above "the whispering campaign" and become a "south that never again can be imposed upon by hoary and hideous old lies about a church of Christ."[83] Richmond, he wrote, had "suffered from fire, from war, and from pestilence: it must be that she has intelligence enough to disdain religious hatred that is worse than any of these."[84] Freeman argued that the election was a solemn referendum on whether "the precious doctrine of equal opportunity [is] to remain a fact of American life or . . . a fiction."[85]

Opposition [to Smith] on this ground is a negation of everything that has distinguished America among the nations of the earth. It is a challenge of fair play, and a denial of equal opportunity. If nothing else were involved in the election, this discrimination against a qualified man because of his religion ought to rally to him all those who respect that larger liberty, that finer respect for individual right and free choice that America showed in the days of Washington and Jefferson, Henry and [Mason]. How can men of all faiths be asked to upbuild America and to sustain her laws, if they be denied the right to aspire to office because they have exercised the freedom of conscience guaranteed them under the very first amendment to the Constitution?[86]

Freeman made every analogy designed to stir the Confederate heart. He recalled how Tammany Hall had stood by the South after the war and "supplied Jefferson Davis' chief counsel in the threatened treason trial."[87] A vote for Hoover, he wrote, "is not a vote against Smith, but a vote against Virginia, a vote that many a son and daughter of this state will live to regret in tears and anguish. It is not only loyalty to the liberal party and to the principle of equal rights that is at issue: It is loyalty to Mother Virginia as well."[88] On the day before the election, Freeman rolled out one of his biggest guns. Across the head of a two-column editorial was a pro-Smith quotation from the late Woodrow Wilson. Freeman captioned the quote: "He, being dead, yet speaketh."[89]

Smith lost the election in a landslide to Hoover. Virginia went Republican for the first time since Reconstruction, giving 54 percent of its vote to Hoover. "I am bewildered," Freeman wrote a friend, "but somewhere in the ranks of those who fought for and against Smith there are a common tradition and a code of honor by which Virginia can be redeemed. We must wait."[90]

"I am not going to fool with teaching," Freeman had written his mother years earlier. "I am for research, and research as long as I live."[91] Despite this expressed aversion, repeated many times through the years, Freeman found himself frequently sought as a teacher. "He could no more avoid [teaching] than he could breathing," his daughter wrote. "He had a memory that retained almost everything he read or heard, a gift for organizing the most complex ideas and presenting them with clarity and simplicity, and he had an inborn enthusiasm about any subject which he could not help sharing."[92] By 1927, Freeman was teaching in three venues: the current events class, radio broadcasts, and a men's

Sunday School class. To these responsibilities he added one more: instructor at the Richmond Extension Division of the College of William and Mary. Freeman delivered a one-hour lecture on current events once a week at 8:00 P.M.[93] Nor did the solicitations for Freeman's educational services stop at the instructor level. In March 1928, he received a letter asking if he would be interested in the presidency of the Alabama Policy Institute in Auburn.[94] He did not dismiss the offer out of hand, and advised that "my heart lies in that work very much."[95] When another was selected for the position, Freeman expressed no disappointment as he was "so deeply rooted here in Richmond that I hope I will never feel it my duty to move."[96] Before the year was out, he found himself among those mentioned for the presidency of Washington and Lee University. "I devoutly hope," he wrote Prof. William Brown, "that 'mention' will be all there is to it."[97] Freeman's reputation as a historian, his standing in the academic community, his administrative talents as editor, and his far-ranging business connections, guaranteed that he would be a perennial candidate for any vacancy at prominent colleges. In 1933 he was again at the forefront of speculation for a college presidency, this time of the University of Virginia. "I do not know whether I want the place if it were offered me," he wrote his friend Frank Gaines, president of Washington and Lee.[98] He was spared facing the decision when the job went to another. There is no evidence that Freeman ever lobbied for a college job, and his reaction upon hearing of potential offers, or receiving actual offers, was always the same. He would express appreciation, leave his options open, but take no steps to encourage his selection or advertise his availability. If he had ever wanted to be a college president, he could have unleashed considerable support and influence on his behalf. That he never took any such steps, and that he received the news of each new rumor with indifference, signals his true feelings about going any further into the academic world.[99]

Freeman was at his desk at the *News Leader* one April day in 1924, when he pulled out a small envelope and wrote on the back: "Memo of assets this date." He listed his assets in the amount of $98,150—the majority of which consisted of $60,000 worth of shares in the *News Leader*.[100] Freeman paid close attention to his finances, and the 1920s were years of prosperity and expansion for his family. His health was excellent—the hernia being the only significant problem—despite the fact that he was a heavy smoker and complained of occasional attacks of "grippe."[101] Home was full of the bustle and activity of any home occupied by two active parents and three growing children. The family had moved into a derivative Georgian house at 806 Westover Road in the spring of 1924 when Mary Tyler was seven years old and Anne not quite one. The house sat on a single street running through Richmond's Byrd Park and overlooked wide vistas of grass bordered by oak trees and two lakes. It was "a paradise" for the few families who lived on Westover Road, and Freeman took it upon himself to maintain the peaceful atmosphere.[102] "It was all I could do," he wrote the chief of police, "to keep from thrashing two or three boys of eighteen who kept stopping their car to call to girls of fourteen or fifteen."[103] He felt a word to the chief would be sufficient to solve the problem, subtly mentioning that he did not wish to "raise a big stir in the newspaper." Mary Tyler was growing up to be very much her father's daughter. She sat "glued lovingly to his side" as he read the paper, shared his love of music, and showed an early aptitude for writing the same type of thoughtful letters that Freeman wrote in his early age.[104] In September 1923, she had been joined in the family by a sister, Anne. Freeman assured Inez he was not "in any wise or to any extent disappointed" that their second child was not a boy, but he could hardly conceal his joy when James Douglas Freeman arrived in April 1925. The boy was, by all recollections, a beautiful child with "a head of flaxen curls, hazel eyes, and fair, rosy skin."[105] He was soon the prince of the family.

Freeman had developed four rules "by which I try to shape my course. (1) The first law of life is self-control. (2) The great end of life is to find a way of living by which one's aptitudes can be used to make some contribution, however small, to the well being of mankind and to the advancement of knowledge. (3) In this process, life 'is not being, but becoming.' (4) Seek to make each day a thing of beauty in itself—of beauty, not of studied art—as if each day were a lifetime."[106] He wanted to teach these rules to his children, but this lengthy statement was somewhat cumbersome. He therefore developed a short "catechism" through which he would lead the children.

"What is the first law of life?" he would ask.

"Self-control," was the answer.

"The second law?"

"Tell the truth no matter what happens."

"The third?"

"Don't be afraid of anything except doing wrong."

"And the fourth?"

"Don't waste today what you may need tomorrow."[107]

During hot Richmond summers, the family vacationed at

Willoughby Spit— a string of land that jutted into the Chesapeake Bay at the entrance of Hampton Roads. Freeman stocked the getaway with an eighteen-foot sailboat, a thirty-six-foot Newfoundland fishing boat, a canoe, and a dinghy.[108] Inez and the children would head down to Willoughby in June and stay until September, with Freeman joining them on weekends. During the week, he started each day with a letter to Inez—averaging one a day, sometimes two, during all the summers they were apart. The letters were usually one typed page in length and filled with the details of the previous day. He tried to open each letter with a different salutation than he used in the previous letter, so in addition to greeting Inez as "my sweet love," "my darling," "blessed girl," "my sweetie," and "loveliest and best of women," he also opened with "Queen of all the queens," "Woman of all women," "Sister Freeman," and "Dearest matron of the maidens' refuge and seamen's rest."[109] The summers were peaceful and uneventful—except for the summer of 1933 when a hurricane ripped through eastern Virginia. Mary Tyler's boyfriend, Jere Baxter, was staying with the family and woke at five o'clock one morning to find the spit engulfed by a flood and the house already surrounded by two feet of water. He roused the family and all escaped unharmed. The beach house was destroyed.[110] Freeman, who was at his office in Richmond, pulled the Associated Press wire account and read that twelve deaths had occurred on Willoughby Spit.[111] Later the report moved the death toll to one hundred. Through newspaper associates in Norfolk, he learned that no one had been lost, and he soon established contact with Inez. It was, he later related, "an agonizing day."[112]

Freeman was a loving and watchful father, but his increasingly busy life limited the amount of time he could—or would—spend with his children. Mary Tyler came of age when demands on her father's time were fewer than they one day would become. She saw far more of him at leisure and spent more time in his company, though this required having breakfast with him at 6:00 A.M. The two developed a closeness and intimacy that grew deeper through the years, and it can be asserted that no one—even Inez—understood Freeman better than his eldest daughter. The two younger children faced different times. A family member recalls Anne saying that Freeman was "a great father" during her youth, but then "got famous and disappeared."[113] James Douglas was nine years old when *R. E. Lee* vaulted his father to international fame. His abiding image is of a man who was "always gone" or tucked away in his "sanctified" third-floor study, where admittance was only "by invitation or demand."[114] Recollections about Freeman's physical presence differ, but his letters indisputably show an actively involved father. He wrote his children almost daily when they began to spend summers away at camp. "You have been the most glorious daughter a man ever had," he wrote Mary Tyler, "and I am so pleased that you are up there in Vermont where you can meet a lot of interesting people and succeed by standing on your own feet, without relying on who your father is."[115] He teased Anne for staying up until two o'clock in the morning—close to the hour he would be rising to start a new day. "I would not sit up after nine o'clock unless I had to," he wrote, "for St. Paul or any other saint."[116] He offered encouragement and support as each obstacle of childhood was overcome. "You have done many things in your nine years to make me proud of you," he wrote James Douglas, "for you have learned to study and to swim and to ride a bicycle and to throw a baseball and to play first-class football, but you never did anything that made me prouder of you than when you denied yourself the things you wanted."[117] While the children were in one school, he was looking ahead to the next phase of education. "Assuming [James Douglas] is preparing for a first class college," he wrote Dean Herbert Hawkes of Columbia University, "to what prep school above all others should he be sent?"[118] When he heard that St. Catherine's, Mary Tyler's school, might be dropped from the list of accredited Southern prep schools, he immediately wrote the headmistress demanding a full explanation. "We cannot afford," he wrote, "to have Mary Tyler endanger her college entrance, under any circumstances."[119] Education was a frequent topic of his letters to the children. "Getting this report has made me very happy," he told James Douglas upon receiving his report card. "You are doing for your age something that is just as fine as if you made some great discovery or wrote a great book. God bless you, my precious boy! More of my life is bound up in you than you will ever know."[120] When Anne's grades slipped, she wrote her father apologizing that she had added "another worry to [your] busy life" and caused him "bitter . . . disappointment."[121] Freeman did not waste time writing a reply, but immediately telegraphed: "You can overcome it easily. Our faith in you is stronger than ever. Our love is deeper."[122] He had definite ideals that he imparted to his children; not surprisingly they were the same ones by which he lived. "I am happiest," he wrote his son, "when I see you and Anne and Mary Tyler exhibit more real character and self control."[123] His advice to Mary Tyler carried echoes of his advice to himself during his days at Johns Hopkins. "Always do more than your part," he wrote, "and you'll get more than your part."[124] The three Freeman children passed through their child-hood with the usual assortment of adventures, disappointments, and achievements. All three did well in school and were admitted to presti-gious colleges—the girls to Vassar and James Douglas to Princeton. All reacted differently to their father's close, yet distant, watchful eye and loving heart.

Increasing family responsibilities did not limit Freeman's community activities, even those somewhat out of keeping with a serious newsman. On March 24, 1927, he donned a red wig, knee britches, and colonial attire, and delivered Patrick Henry's famous "Liberty or Death" speech at St. John's Church. Freeman stood in the same pew as Henry and "repeated the ringing speech in full with highly dramatic effect."[125] *National Geographic* magazine carried a picture of Freeman, "the silver-tongued orator of the Old Dominion today," surrounded by other suit-ably bewigged Richmonders.[126] He was not only available for public acts of service, but found his advice being sought by strangers who knew him only by reputation. "I am writing to make what I am sure is a very unusual request," R. B. White of Scottsville wrote. "A friend of mine died . . . and I want to write his widow a letter of sympathy, from what I have read of your editorials I am sure you can fix it nearer like I want it."[127] Mr. White enclosed some pertinent facts about his late friend and asked Freeman to write the letter and "enclose [a] bill for your service." Freeman answered the next day with a draft sympathy letter.[128] Though the idea of writing a form sympathy letter for another party is slightly amusing, Freeman's moving letter demonstrates not only his ability to write an eloquent piece in a short time frame, but also his heart for service to others in need.

My dear Mrs. ———:
Ever since (give his name) went away from us, I have been trying to write to you. Every morning I said to myself, "I must do it today," but when the time came, I had to admit to myself that my grief was still too fresh, my wound too deep, for me to attempt it. Even now, when I have resolved to undertake it, my pen runs off after a hundred fancies, and I find myself so crowded with memo-ries that I cannot believe he has gone.
I sit here and think back over the twenty years of my friendship with him. What a princely man! What a friend! What a husband! What a citizen! Can I not recall scores of instances, unknown even to you, perhaps, where he gave of his substance and, what was more,

of himself, to alleviate the distress of others and to promote the welfare of this town? Can I not see before me a multitude of people to whom life will never be quite the same, now that his counsel, his unfailing help, his warm sympathy are taken from them? I feel like crying out with Hamlet: He was a man, take him for all in all, I shall not look upon his like again.

And dead at 45, so young, so full of vigor and of promise, with his greatest achievements yet ahead! Somehow, at the first, that hit me hardest, but now that the days have passed, I no longer rebel against that. It was cruel that he had to go when there was so much work to be done that none could do as well as he, but if the Host said, "Friend, come up higher," there is something inspiring to me in the thought that he went in in the full panoply of manhood, with his shoulders unbowed and with intelligence untouched by destroying time. He lived long enough to see a home perfected by an ideal wife, and two lovely daughters reared to glowing womanhood. He lived to win his place and to show the true steel of his soul: What man can ask for more than that?

It has been a time of sorrow at my house ever since the news came. We live still under the shadow of it, conscious of our dire loss and your irreparable calamity. My wife, my daughter and I have talked often of you in your bewildered affliction. As for him, we have thought of him as going from glory to glory, and we feel that when he, like Mr. Greatheart in Pilgrim's Progress, came down to the river, "all the trumpets sounded for him on the other side." God comfort you with that vision of his entry into that kingdom where for a season, and only a season, he awaits our coming.[129]

"There will be no charge for this," Freeman wrote in forwarding the draft. "I am glad to serve you."

Confederate reunions had been as much a part of Freeman's life as had been writing history. Never was he left unmoved by the sight of Lee's men marching in their gray and butternut uniforms under the Confederate battle flag. It was such a reunion at the crater that had pointed him to his life's work. He always devoted space on the editorial page to these celebrations. It provided him an opportunity to pay tribute to the soldiers of Lee, the companions of his father, and the heroes of his youth. In June 1932, a small handful of surviving Confederate veterans gathered in Richmond for the forty-second annual reunion of the United

Confederate Veterans. Due to the age and physical condition of the boys of 1861-65, this would be, in all likelihood, their last parade.[130] Freeman recognized the significance of this particular reunion, and took special pains to make this commemorative editorial "a labor of love."[131]

The editorial, written in blank verse, recounted parades of the past: "when Bonham brought his volunteers with their Palmetto flag in 1861"; when "Lee was welcomed as the savior of the South"; when the "mourning drums" accompanied the dead Jackson; and when Pickett's soldiers told "how hell itself had opened on that hill at Gettysburg." Other marches followed in the final days of the Confederacy bringing "the clatter of horses' hoofs, the rumble of the trains, the drum at dawn, and the bugle on the midnight air." Then darkness, poverty, and pain, before "the fallen walls were raised again."[132]

Today the city has its last review. The armies of the South will march our streets no more. It is the rearguard, engaged with death, that passes now. Who that remembers other days can face that truth and still withhold his tears? The dreams of youth have faded in the twilight of the years. The deeds that shook a continent belong to history. Farewell; sound taps! And then a generation new must face its battles in its turn, forever heartened by that heritage.

Freeman titled the piece "The Last Parade" and placed it in the paper on the final day of the reunion. It unexpectantly became his fourth published work. The Richmond publishing firm of Whittet & Shepperson printed the editorial in a handsomely crafted book, complete with pictures of Confederate statues on Monument Avenue. Only five hundred copies were printed and, after they were on the market for a short time, Freeman bought the remaining copies and presented them through the years as gifts to friends and associates.[133]

A little more than two years after the last parade, one of the last veterans died: Walker Burford Freeman. "The Colonel" had been in failing health for several years, though his overall physical condition was good almost to the end. He was ninety-one when the end came. "Your grandfather finished his long and honorable life this morning and entered into a happy rest," Freeman wired Mary Tyler, away at Vassar. "You can rejoice always that he left you an unblemished name."[134] The eighteen-year-old Mary Tyler understood what her father felt about his father.

If Grandfather had not had a fine mind and strength of character and courage, and if he had not worked to give his own children the very finest educational equipment for life, then Anne and Freeman and I would never have had you. It is because of what he built, and made it possible for you to build . . . that we three are able to start life far higher up on the ascent than most children . . . Grandfather has always meant to me a life well lived. That is, to me, the highest praise that any person could ever receive.[135]

Freeman never forgot the tall thin man from Liberty and paid tribute to him through the years in speeches and letters. To his diary he confided the simplest eulogy: "Nobody will ever know how much of my best self I owe him."[136]

The academic world reached out again for Freeman on Saturday February 3, 1934. Carl Ackerman, dean of the Columbia University School of Journalism, offered him a full professorship at an annual salary of $7,500. As was his habit, Freeman did not commit, but promised Ackerman he would give the matter "serious thought." He turned immediately to his brother Allen for advice. The salary, he wrote, was "so much below" his current income that he could not see a way to accept. In addition he shuddered "to think of living in or anywhere around New York."[137] Still the idea of having "four months' vacation" and more time for "worth-while historical endeavor" was appealing. Freeman kept the offer alive for a short time.

Less than one week later, he decided that it was "financially impossible" to take the position.[138] He confided to Mary Tyler that other considerations as well entered into his decision. "We are too deeply rooted in the soil of Old Virginia to pull up," he wrote. "I want to live here to the end and die, if I may, while the mocking bird is singing and the tide is swishing on the sands. I think the American people lose a large part of the joy of life because they do not live for generations in the same place."[139] He was less eloquent in his letter to Allen, concurring with his brother's judgment that "Columbia is Babel and New York a Babylon."[140]

The matter might have ended there had not Dean Ackerman continued to press the issue. He told Freeman to "keep an open mind" and asked in March for another meeting.[141] The two men began to discuss "occasional lectures," and that conversation grew into talks about a weekly class.[142] On March 27, 1934, Ackerman and Freeman had "a long conversation" during which an agreement was worked out. Freeman would be appointed a full professor at a salary of $1,500 and would teach one daylong class each Friday during the 1934 fall semester. He would continue as editor of the *News Leader*, and Columbia would cover his weekly travel expenses to New York.[143] John Stewart Bryan approved the extracurricular plans of his editor, and Freeman was formally appointed on May 7, 1934.[144]

His first task was to figure out the logistics of traveling to New York while still meeting his editorial responsibilities. As his class was scheduled for Fridays from 10:00 A.M. to 4:00 P.M., Freeman would write his editorials for Friday's paper on Thursday. Upon completing his day at the paper, and after dinner and writing at home, he would board a sleeper car bound for New York, arriving there early in the morning. He would take his breakfast at the Hotel Pennsylvania across from the station and then ride the subway to Columbia.[145] He would teach his class, have dinner at a Manhattan restaurant, and catch another sleeper to Richmond. The train would pull into the station at the approximate hour that Freeman would be getting out of bed, so he would go straight to the *News Leader* office and have Saturday's editorials prepared on time.[146]

Building the structure of the class proved less cumbersome. "We are to analyze the news of the week," he wrote Mary Tyler, "decide which are important developments, and then are to see where we can get material to explain and interpret these happenings. Having done all this, the members are to spend the afternoon in preparing a feature similar to my 'Week.'"[147] Thus Freeman would teach the class both as a newspaperman and a historian. In preparing his lectures, he wrote a lengthy letter to Dean Ackerman soliciting information on his students. "How much recent American and European history is it safe to assume that [they] know?" he asked. Could he assign parallel reading—"to cover the background of Europe since 1870 and of the United States since the War Between the States"—or require the students to keep "a file of *The New York Times*"? He wondered if any of his students could speak a foreign language and if Columbia would supply "current British and American reviews . . . [and] the Readers Guide to Periodical Literature."[148] Ackerman was somewhat taken aback by the "stimulating questions," but provided detailed answers and assured Freeman of his complete freedom of operation in his class.[149] In September 1934, he settled into his office in Room 513 in the School of Journalism at 116th and Broadway and began a seven-year tenure as a professor at Columbia.[150]

More than sixty years have passed since Freeman delivered his last lecture at the Columbia School of Journalism, yet the memories and impact of those days are still vivid to his surviving students. His reputation preceded him, and the class was intrigued by the thought of his traveling from Richmond to New York just to teach them.[151] He brought with him a few crotchets: His references to "Christian ladies and gentlemen" was humorously noted by his Jewish students, and he took latecomers to task by stopping his lectures in mid-sentence while the offender walked to his seat.[152] He would break the uneasy silence with inquiry about the late edition of that morning's paper or with a comment about "sleeping Lazarus." These minor eccentricities aside, Freeman, who was dubbed "Pappy" by his class, quickly became "the most popular by far" of the faculty members.[153] "He was an imposing figure in delivery and presence," Leonard Sussman, Class of 1941, remembers, "but quite approachable as a friendly mentor."[154] His classes—which started at 8:15 A.M. and continued until 5:00 P.M.—"never seemed dull or over-extended" to John Mayer of the Class of 1936. "Everything he taught us about the newspaper business," Mayer writes, "was always laced with pertinent and interesting observations concerning life itself."[155] Freeman had long since

Freeman lecturing at Columbia University, October 1936. (Image courtesy of Mary Tyler McClenahan.)

mastered the art of public speaking, and his talents were appreciated. His students, most of whom are today in their eighties and nineties, still speak of his "powerful voice," his "charismatic" personality, and his "stately bearing."[156] "He conducted class with lectures that were priceless to us novice journalists," George Larson recalls. "We were spellbound."[157] Robert Schulman found Freeman's "absorption in world news was so compellingly evangelistic—in an historian's as well as a biblical sense—that . . . the week-by-week course of the Spanish Civil War became as alive and pressing to us as anything going on in New York."[158] Daniel Button entered the School of Journalism in September 1938 and discovered "a trove of editorial philosophy and realistic outlook" in Freeman's lectures.[159] He was also impressed by the man.

> He was formal in his informality, courtly beyond measure, personable without being deliberately humorous or clever, intent on seriously delivering his understanding of the craft of the editorial writer, together with much accumulated wisdom. Exhaustive in scope and both extensive and intensive in delivery, but never stupefying.[160]

Freeman's classes were more than just students basking in reflected glory. "He made us work and write a lot," one student recalls.[161] Another student, upon receiving from Freeman a marked-up copy of his news summary, became "convinced that I should give up journalism and maybe dig ditches."[162] His "forceful and firm-handed" technique, however, bore results. "I acquired work habits that have stayed with me all the years," Hope McCroskey writes. Leonard Sussman admits that "even today, in preparing policy papers, I think of him when I'm tempted to write that something is 'over' a certain number, rather than 'more than.'"[163] Dave Hellyer not only adapted a Freeman saying in his own teaching experiences—"If you don't like something, say so!"—he also took on Freeman's accented way of pronouncing "say so" as "sesso."[164] Robert Schulman remembers having to go to "the research volumes for every major news story involving a complex issue . . . [just] to compose a background insert of a few paragraphs."[165] Freeman would demonstrate the use of such knowledge by asking his students to suggest any news topic and then give him three minutes to think about it. "Whereupon," Elwood Thompson recalls, "he would address that subject with relevant information and well-turned phrases for three to five minutes."[166]

Most of Freeman's students went on to long and productive careers in journalism, but their awe of their professor was not dimmed by the passage of years. Philip Hamburger, Class of 1938, joined *The New Yorker* in 1939 and authored eight books in a distinguished career, but still has memories of Freeman the professor that "stand out."

His wide knowledge of world affairs—war, of course, was on the horizon—made his weekly classes utterly fascinating. He taught editorial writing and stressed clarity, simplicity, humility, and, above all else, telling the truth as we saw it. Fancy prose did not appeal to him. He made the forceful point—and one that I have never forgotten—[that] one of the greatest dangers . . . to freedom in the world was propaganda.[167]

"We had sense enough," Hamburger writes, "to know that we were in a True Presence." His fellow students concur. "He was the jewel in the journalism faculty crown" is Hope McCroskey's assessment. "He really did teach us how to solve the mysteries of writing a good editorial," Dan Edelman comments. "I will never forget him."[168]

Freeman returned the affection of his students—"I love them," he confided to his diary—although he found one, "a bolshevist newspaper woman," to be "as crazy as if she were in a ward at Williamsburg."[169] He judged most of his students to be "on the whole, an excellent company of youngsters" whose "most pressing need" was "more facility in writing decent English."[170] His courses were "News of the Week," taught in the fall, and "Editorial Method," taught in the spring.[171] He split his day-long classes into morning sessions—devoted to background development—and afternoon sessions of lectures. Freeman's lectures for the second semester of the 1935-36 year included ones on newspaper organization, the "flow of copy," newspaper crusades—"when they should be undertaken, how they should be organized"—newspaper ethics, and tips on obtaining employment.[172] As war spread in Europe, he added lectures on basic principles of international law, the interpretation of communiqués and war propaganda, and "a brief course in map reading."[173] Dean Ackerman and Columbia realized what they had in a Freeman professorship and in 1935 raised his salary to the originally offered $7,500 even though he taught but one day.[174] Freeman taught at Columbia one day a week, every week during the academic year, for seven years. During that time, he made the Richmond to New York round trip 376 times, traveling a total of 225,000 miles.

When the Democratic Party suffered its second consecutive presidential election defeat in 1924, Freeman wrote that comeback hopes rested on "the emergence of a great man or of a magnetizing issue." By 1932, the Democrats had both: Franklin D. Roosevelt and the Great Depression. Freeman's response to the onset of the Depression in 1929 had been mild. He wrote that the stock market crash was a necessary adjustment needed to end speculative fever.[175] When President Herbert Hoover suggested some form of public works to reduce unemployment, Freeman opposed the notion. He believed all relief should be handled locally—by families, friends, churches, and charitable organizations—before any government action.[176] There was, he argued, no quick fix to a depression. "Work (and plenty of it), Brains (and the hard use of them), Fair Play (and no dodging it for an extra dollar) always have and always will bring happiness and as much prosperity as is good for any of us."[177]

With no improvement in the economy after three years, it was clear that 1932 would be a Democrat year. Freeman supported Wilson's secretary of war Newton Baker for president, but endorsed Roosevelt upon his nomination.[178] His editorials in support of Roosevelt were calm, subdued, and confident. "He faced the pitfalls of a radical appeal and the rocks of extravagant promises," he wrote late in the campaign, "and he avoided all of them."[179] He judged the election to be "an inquest" in which "the American people will sit as a coroner's jury, and . . . bring in their verdict against Herbert Hoover."[180] Roosevelt's landslide election, Freeman wrote, was "a peaceful political revolution" that "returned [government] to the people."[181] He gave the new president almost unqualified support. He endorsed banking reform, the securities act, the Agricultural Adjustment Act, and the granting of additional powers to the president to fight the depression.[182] "Desperate situations," he wrote, "call for desperate remedy." He wrote a worried friend that "we have been in personal contact with Mr. Roosevelt during the last week and feel we can count on him to proceed with as great conservatism as is consistent with the achievement of real results."[183] Freeman even backed the National Recovery Act, the "NRA," which devised a code of fair competition and fair practices for industry and guaranteed labor's right to bargain collectively. While John Stewart Bryan worked to keep newspapers from coming under NRA regulations, Freeman nonchalantly remarked to Inez that "we shall have to conform . . . public sentiment and common conception will demand no less."[184] His support of the NRA was less an endorsement of the idea than a belief that it would keep Roosevelt from adopting a monetary policy of devaluing the dollar.[185]

"We are passing in America through a most notable period of experimentation," he wrote in August 1933. "The atmosphere is much like that of war."[186] It could have been the patriotism inspired by the warlike time that caused him to endorse much of the New Deal, or it could have been loyalty to a Democratic president. Whatever the reason, by the end of 1933 Freeman's innate economic conservatism began to pull him away from Roosevelt. In October 1933, Roosevelt decided to institute direct relief payments. "We cannot believe," Freeman wrote, "that the president will be guilty of such a blunder."[187] Three weeks later, Roosevelt began to tinker with the currency by authorizing gold purchases to raise commodity prices. Freeman wrote several editorials in opposition and dashed off a telegram to U. S. senator Carter Glass. "It looks," he wired, "as if our friend is determined to drive all sound money men from the treasury."[188] Glass agreed and added that "this nation is fast on its way" to hell.[189] Freeman still avoided a direct break with Roosevelt, but hammered his monetary policy so often that it became part of his daily speech. "You are as wrong as Mr. Roosevelt's gold policy," he told Mary Tyler in discussing a non-political matter.[190]

The break came after the 1934 mid-term elections. The Democrats made unprecedented gains in Congress that year, and Roosevelt felt emboldened to veer to the far left. He proposed an increase in surtaxes on individual incomes of fifty thousand dollars or more and on estates valued at more than forty thousand dollars. To Freeman this was not only bad policy, it struck at the heart of what a man should be able to do for his family—earn a good living and pass it on. "We must never make success culpable in itself," he wrote, "or take from any man the incentive to hard labor in order that he may pass on to his children enough to keep his family name alive in honor and dignity. The desire to do that is physiological, not capitalistic."[191] He expanded on this thought in a letter to John Stewart Bryan.

That demagogic message [of Roosevelt's] in which he tried to steal the thunder of Huey Long was a little more than I could stand. The President seems to have given himself over to the left-wing New Dealers . . . he would carry this business of confiscatory taxation to the point where he would make it a crime for anyone to be thrifty enough to bequeath to the next generation enough money to maintain a family tradition. When he does that, it seems to me he destroys one of the great incentives to initiative and to business conservatism. Perhaps that is exactly what he wants to do . . . He is, therefore, not merely destroying family life, but he is taking from democracy one of its few stabilizing and intelligent elements. It is a dark situation.[192]

Freeman viewed Social Security in much the same manner. Not only was it a raid on the treasury and the incomes of Americans, it was an assault on the duty of families to care for the elderly. It was reckless, he judged, to replace "security by thrift" with "security by taxation."[193]

It was in such a frame of mind that Freeman traveled to New York to address a luncheon of the Virginia Press Association. He began his remarks by explaining why Virginia's two U. S. senators were unable to attend the lunch. "Senator Glass is in Washington fighting to prevent the Treasury Department from taking charge of all the banks in the country," he said, and "Senator Byrd is in Washington fighting to prevent the enslavement of private initiative, especially that of agriculture."[194] As he warmed to his subject, New York mayor Fiorello H. LaGuardia, noticeably irritated by Freeman's shot across the New Deal's bow, began furiously scribbling notes. "The best service Congress could render," Freeman continued, "would be to adjourn on its own initiative and not wait on orders from the White House."[195] He then defined his philosophy of political liberalism and fiscal conservatism. "To be a political liberal does not mean to be liberal with other people's money. That is a lesson that might well be taught in the nation's capital." Making the argument that a proper division of authority between the Federal government and the states needed to be restored, he said Virginia was "ready now to do battle on the floors of Congress for States' Rights just as on the battlefields in times past."[196] Freeman sat down to sizable applause as LaGuardia rose. Shaking his fist at the audience, but looking directly at Freeman, LaGuardia snapped: "It is difficult for anyone to talk political liberalism with a man who is hungry."[197] Disdaining the microphone, LaGuardia condemned the "whining, complaining [and] stabbing in the back" promoted under the guise of conservatism. "Some of us," he concluded, "knew you couldn't feed a baby on ticker tape."[198] LaGuardia sat down and John Stewart Bryan injected some needed relief into the awkward moment by telling the audience they had seen "a show today." Freeman and LaGuardia were photographed together, smiling broadly at one another and shaking hands, but it was clear that Freeman had crossed the Rubicon. He was now a nationally recognized opponent of the New Deal.

CHAPTER 8

"Separation Is Better Than Deception"

Political labels, as applied in the South during Freeman's day, took on different shades and hues from those applied in other regions. Though his editorials and comments placed him squarely in the conservative camp on fiscal issues, Freeman considered himself to be a liberal. As he saw it:

A true liberal is a scientific realist who neither is disdainful of the past nor enslaved to it, neither contemptuous of the present nor afraid of the future. He regards yesterday and today as the fixed points by which to project tomorrow. Never does he experiment in order to destroy, but always in an effort to improve. The axe is never wielded when the scalpel suffices.[1]

A liberal was "conscious of his limitations and of the certainty of error [and] tolerant ever of intolerance." Liberalism to Freeman was "not a program but an approach."[2]

In no area did he find that approach so difficult and delicate to apply than in the area of racial relations. In no other area of public policy—or personal ethics—do Freeman's attitudes and efforts appear in such stark contrast: both admirable and inept, noble and shameful, advanced and retarded. He expressed himself on the subject many times through the years—both as an editor in the pages of the *News Leader* and as a private citizen in numerous letters—and from these writings a detailed philosophy takes shape.[3] "The South," he wrote Virginia governor Colgate Darden, "needs to strike the balance between those who see no light ahead and those who are dazzled by it."[4]

"Balance." No other word so aptly describes Freeman's views on race. He was a man of his era—an era of segregation and discrimination—and yet he was ahead of his time. He balanced both eras. He clung to social and cultural traditions, yet believed the South had to change. He balanced both sentiments. He opposed active government intervention, but worked for equality in education, justice, and employment. He balanced both philosophies. He supported segregation, yet he did not accept stereotypical views of blacks. He balanced both beliefs. He promoted economic development and self-improvement regardless of race, yet opposed social intimacy among the races. He balanced both attitudes.

He was not among those who saw "no light ahead"; nor was he "dazzled" by the light. He saw the light. But it blinded as often as it illumined.

Several themes run consistently through Freeman's thoughts on racial matters. From his earliest days as editor, he was an advocate for "decent living conditions, educational facilities, and absolute justice in the courts of law" for black Virginians.[5] He judged that the "South has suffered from the divisions born of racial prejudice"[6] and responded to that conclusion by encouraging whites to do their "civic duty" to "the most intelligent, most law-abiding colored population of any city in the United States."[7] He sought to encourage a "spirit" whereby blacks would "look to the city's sense of justice" to correct grievances, while whites would, in turn, support "better housing, better home life . . . better streets, better sanitation, better schools and adequate hospital facilities."[8] This paternalistic view dominated Freeman's views through the years. His editorials often boasted that Richmond *had* "the best Negroes in America."[9] With the relationship thus defined—with the implicit, even if benign, notion of "ownership"—respective roles would follow. The blacks were to obey the law, respect custom, and improve themselves; whites were to be benevolent and ensure basic needs. Control was the stay in the white community. "The great body of the Negroes in the South," Freeman wrote, "seem to me to be firm and sane and patriotic . . . We must be just. If we follow the economic as well as the judicial implications of that term, the Negro can take care of himself."[10] Above all, everyone should stay calm and collected no matter what the crisis or problem. Nothing aroused Freeman's suspicion and scorn more than agitation of either race.[11]

As foreign as these views seem today, they represent a fairly progressive view for Freeman's day. Indeed, he was often out of the mainstream of conventional thought in his battle to quench "the fires of intolerance and bigotry."[12] He believed the South must change, not a popular sentiment at the time. Part of this belief sprang from necessity—"unless we make some concessions to the Negroes," he wrote, "we are going to have more trouble rather than less"[13]—but much of it was the product of the tolerance he learned as a boy. "Prejudice has to be outgrown rather than outlawed," he wrote, and he believed he had outgrown it. His private relationships with black leaders showed none of the condescension of his editorials, and he genuinely respected Charles Houston, dean of Howard University Law School; Walter White, executive secretary of the NAACP; and John Gandy, president of Virginia State College for Negroes.[14] Houston even requested an autographed copy of *R. E. Lee*.[15] Freeman employed many blacks through the years on his household staff and developed friendly, even close, relationships with many of them. When his chauffeur, Howard Carter, was killed in an auto accident in which Freeman and his daughter Mary Tyler were both injured, Freeman gave his insurance settlement to Carter's widow in the form of a weekly wage. "I grieve for him daily," Freeman wrote of Carter, and he no doubt did.[16]

Nor did he display any of the traits common to racial prejudice. In nearly 100,000 letters, memoranda, and notes housed in the Library of Congress and other depositories, one finds only two letters in which Freeman makes racially insensitive remarks—and one was intended as a compliment. "You know," he wrote his daughter Anne, "a true born Southern Negro will never admit that he knows how to do anything until he finds that he cannot escape doing it. Then, as a rule, he or she does it quite well."[17] The second instance came in a letter written during World War II to Lt. Col. Frank McCarthy, aide to Gen. George Marshall. Freeman used the term "nigger in the woodpile" to describe the conduct of a white member of Marshall's staff. Thus the racial epithet was not directed at a specific individual, but was used as an old, albeit noxious, expression. It is a matter of degree, but given the common usage of derogatory racial terms during this era, Freeman's disdain for their use speaks to his mature racial views.

Thus the currents that flowed in the mind and soul of Douglas Freeman. They settled into an attitude that he expressed most fully in a letter to Agnes Meyer, wife of Eugene Meyer, publisher of the *Washington Post*. "Negroes in America," he wrote, "have made in eighty years from slavery a most amazing advance. I doubt if even the Russian serfs had a much larger percentage of their representation register such gains in two generations."[18] The problem, Freeman judged, arose from the fact "that they are not content to remain Negroes."

Most of the leaders are doing nothing to make their own people satisfied with being Negroes . . . They leave the South because of segregation; they are wretched in the North because segregation [there] is not shaped in terms of law. Often in the North the Negro gets much closer to his goal . . . He sits with the whites in theatres and on the street cars. Some hotels . . . will admit him too. On rare occasions he is invited to dine with white people . . . The moment he attempted to go beyond that and to pay a social call on the daughter of the people who have entertained him, he finds the door slammed in his face.[19]

"Why," Freeman asked, "is this done?" He answered his own question. "North and South, white men recognize the fine achievements, the admirable character, and the mental capacity of individual Negroes; but, in the end, no matter how the issue may be phrased or may be evaded, a white man is guided by the same impulse that keeps the robin from mating with the starling."[20] What some judged to be racial prejudice, Freeman stated, was actually "biological caution." Thus intelligent Southerners, who had close contact with blacks, took what Freeman declared to be "the Southern point of view."

You must have justice and we shall help you get it; we have a common economic stake in this land of sunshine; we must work together to conquer the soil, to develop the mines; and to harness the waterfall; we whites must see to it that you get your part of the profits in generous proportion to the contributions you make; ours is the duty also of seeing that you are not humiliated; but biologically and therefore socially we are different; we are not going to amalgamate; because that is so, you simply are made miserable when you are brought so close to the whites that passion or ambition fires you to seek the unattainable—a white wife; for this reason we believe you should stay apart, build your own society, improve it, strengthen your family life, combat innate promiscuity, and build up race pride; we do not believe it fair to pretend to equality we have no intention of recognizing.[21]

"Separation," Freeman concluded, "is better than deception."

In no other letter did he ever reduce the racial issue to such terms. As such, it cannot be stated definitively that Freeman adopted the entire "Southern view" as his own. In a much milder letter two years earlier he had laid out his familiar refrain of "equal justice and equal opportunity"

194 DOUGLAS SOUTHALL FREEMAN

but "without establishing contacts which are bound to create friction."[22] This seems to be a veiled reference to amalgamation. One draws the conclusion from Freeman's editorials and letters that while he was sincerely committed to equality in many areas, it was most assuredly a separate equality. "Virginia has not receded one step in all her history from her stand on the integrity of the white race," he wrote in 1926. "There should not be the slightest hesitation in the frank discussion of the best means of having the white and the colored people live harmoniously, but separately."[23] Thus Freeman's views on race were as complex, and tragic, as the time in which he lived. Yet unlike the times in which he lived, his actions were more uplifting than his words.

He made small, seemingly insignificant, policy decisions at the *News Leader* with an eye toward improving race relations. In November 1926, he sent a memorandum to John Stewart Bryan suggesting that "all members of the news and editorial staff . . . avoid playing up the fact that any delinquent is a negro, unless his race is an essential fact in the story."[24] This policy would avoid inflammatory headlines such as "Negro attacks Woman." Bryan "heartily approved" the suggestion. This was the first step in what Freeman later described as a "policy of reporting men according to their acts, be they good or bad, and not according to their skin, be it white or colored."[25] Freeman ended the practice of reporting the sports scores of black colleges in a separate column from results from white schools, established a *News Leader* scholarship for students attending Richmond's black college, Virginia Union University, and began to capitalize the word "Negro" in news columns.[26] Freeman's acts were noticed by contemporaries. President J. M. Ellison of Virginia Union called the *News Leader* "one of the great southern dailies" and Freeman one of the college's "good friends."[27] The combining of sports scores was proof to one black high school counselor that the *News Leader* was "becoming an instrument for fostering rather than retarding good will."[28] Freeman acted in conjunction with Agnes Meyer to establish the "Wendell Willkie awards" to honor black newspapermen. He served as chairman of the awards committee, presided over the dinner, and was commended by the president of the Negro Newspaper Publishers Association for his "broad views in regard to segments of the American Press."[29] In 1947 Freeman defied convention by running a photograph of Civil Rights attorney Oliver Hill, a candidate for the school board, on the front page of the *News Leader*. "It never occurred to us," he wrote, "to discriminate in the circumstances that existed."[30] He had long recognized the power of the press for good and evil, and he carefully guarded the words and acts of the *News Leader* in matters of race. He knew how quickly a newspaper could inflame passions in an area where emotions were already tinderbox dry. "Four-fifths of the things that should be done for the betterment of race relationship in the South," he commented, "are things that ought never to get into the newspaper one way or the other."[31] His expressed goal was to reach the "grand day . . . when there is no color line in the newspapers."[32]

Freeman also used his other medium—radio—to reach a large audience with his views. Here one works at a disadvantage, for only a handful of his radio broadcasts or transcriptions survive—and none deal with race. He did, however, devote some broadcasts to the topic, and the gist of his comments can be reconstructed from the letters he received from black listeners. "I am sure that I am correct in saying that every Negro is grateful for your logic and deeply appreciative of you for so courageously expressing it," Amaza Meredith wrote about Freeman's broadcast of October 4, 1942.[33] Her letter does not make it clear what racial issue Freeman addressed, but he received another letter praising the same broadcast. It was "gratifying," Cpl. Alfred H. Neal wrote, "to know that there are people who understand the problems that we as a minority group face, and has brought the true facts of the complex problem to thousands of homes."[34] Freeman responded with thanks to both letters, telling Meredith "we are fighting for God's own truth when we fight for racial understanding."[35] Another broadcast, on May 29, 1942, brought praise from William Cooper of Hampton Institute. "It is going to take a number of expressions like this in many places," Cooper wrote, "to redirect the thinking of many fine people in America who just have not analyzed this attitude and still hold to points of view based upon conditions which have long since passed away."[36] It is a pity that none of the referenced broadcasts survived. Freeman spoke without notes on the radio, so his messages came from the heart. One message in April 1943 apparently went to the heart of a young black soldier, Robert Tolliver, who wrote Freeman a lengthy letter of appreciation—and anguish.

My dearest friend: just a few lines to let you hear from me, sir. I have been listening to your speaking on Sunday . . . Virginia white people don't seem to think that the Negroes are going over there to die and do without food and crawl on their stomach . . . This is America and we will fight for all that we have sir. Why do a white hate a Negro so? What have we done to them [that] they hate us worse than they do Japanese? You're the only one I ever heard

speak like you did Sunday . . . no other man in the world would
have ever spoken plainly like you last Sunday sir and you have
made me feel so much better sir. May God bless you and when I
go over I will be thinking [about] what you have said today. You
are a man. I want to fight more for my country sir than anyone in
the world.[37]

"I can understand how a Negro soldier feels that he ought not to fight
for a democracy that discriminates against him," Freeman replied, "but
I think if he fights he will shame the people who are discriminating
against him. If you have any problems I can help you work out, please
call on me. Every soldier in the American army is dear to me."[38]

Freeman was willing to lend his name and counsel to numerous
groups seeking to improve race relations. At the request of Civil Rights
leader Robert R. Moton, he joined the Commission on Interracial
Cooperation.[39] He helped coordinate a "fair play" conference on race so
"that the liberal South [could] be heard by the nation."[40] The president
of the North Carolina College for Negroes asked for his opinion
"because I know of your friendly interest in the work I represent." The
"work" in this instance was a conference to discuss changes in voting
rights laws and segregation. Freeman saw "many reasons" to hold the
conference. "If we can get the white South to distinguish among
Negroes and not to use the inclusive term opprobriously, we shall have
achieved much."[41] His advice was not always solicited for such noble
purposes. The chairman of an awards dinner noticed his guest list
included the president of Virginia Union University. He wrote for
advice on whether the president should be invited. "I regret to say,"
Freeman responded, "that with all my admiration and respect for the
President . . . I do not feel that we ought to embarrass anyone or raise
any questions by having a colored man at a dinner . . . We had better
avoid the difficulty."[42] Agnes Meyer wrote about her dilemma in host-
ing a biracial dinner at a Washington D.C. club, at which time photographs would be taken during an awards presentation. Some white
guests, she realized, would not want to be in such photographs. While
chuckling at the hypocrisy of "a town, the governmental side of which
boasts much of racial equality and never displays it," Freeman advised
Mrs. Meyer to be "wise as a serpent and as harmless as a dove" and take
the pictures before the dinner.[43]

His record on specific civil rights issues is again complex, but generally positive. He was a vigorous foe of the Ku Klux Klan, and his

opposition was noted by the "Invisible Empire." On Christmas Eve 1922, five-year-old Mary Tyler was hanging an ornament on the tree when she looked out the window and saw "a man on a white horse dressed in a long white robe with a white hood over his head."[44] Inez quickly scurried Mary Tyler away from the window and off to bed, and Freeman faced down the Klansman who had been sent to deliver a warning about anti-lynching editorials in the *News Leader*. His rhetoric never cooled despite the Klan's threats. Virginia had seen no lynchings from 1902 to 1918. Then in 1918, one occurred in Culpeper, Virginia, followed two years later by another in Wise County. "It was not," he asserted, "the 'Virginia way' to put on masks, to hide identity in a mob, to hang some wretch in the dark of the moon, and then to shrink away in blood guiltiness."[45] He advocated the use of deadly force to stop a mob intent on lynching and the swift prosecution of anyone involved. Freeman's editorials, and those of Louis Jaffee of the Norfolk *Virginian-Pilot*, led to the passage in 1929 of one of the strongest anti-lynching laws in the nation.[46] "Stiff state legislation," he wrote, "courageously enforced . . . will prevent the creation of the mob-mind."[47] So strongly did he view this "dark disgrace," that he even supported federal anti-lynching legislation as "essential to protect human life in the south."[48]

Freeman consistently supported improvement in housing, sanitation, education, and medical care for Richmond's black populace. "Richmond should not weary in well-doing," he wrote, "for already in peace she is reaping her reward . . . Justice yields larger dividends than anything in the world, for justice is righteousness."[49] His advocacy of this issue grew from a combination of differing attitudes: his Christian beliefs, his sense of *noblesse oblige*, and his realization that "good will" could not be generated among "people who are herded into crowded, insanitary quarters, devoid, in many instances, of the very fundamentals of reasonable comfort."[50] Thus he appealed not only to the sense of justice he believed most Richmonders possessed, but also to their highly defined sense of self-interest and preservation. He took this approach on the issue of road improvement. Most of the streets running through the black sections of Richmond were unpaved; creating either choking dust or impassible mud. "Is it not the duty of a thriving, wealthy city, a believer in justice," Freeman asked, "to improve this condition?"[51] He reminded his readers that "Negroes are taxpayers," even though they had no vote, and so "justice . . . compounded now with energy" dictated the paving of the streets. He maintained the same mode of analysis on the issue of education. "What right have we to demand a high standard of citizenship of the Negro," he wrote Charles Houston, "when we deny them decent schooling?"[52] To that end he argued for equal—albeit separate—facilities, the appointment of black principals, and some black membership on the city school board.[53] He also used his membership on the Rockefeller Foundation to advise its General Education Board on how it might spend funds to improve education. Freeman told board members that "the most serious defect in the whole structure in Southern education is in the field of elementary education for Negroes, and especially rural elementary education."[54] Education of black children was often "meaningless and futile" due to lack of teachers and supplies and an "economy to provide the necessary support."[55] He often linked educational improvement with expanding economic opportunities for blacks. "Richmond professes to believe that here, if anywhere in the South, the Negro gets good treatment and progress," he wrote, yet "statistics . . . show that in the essentials of housing and employment, Richmond is lamentably backward."[56] Normally no friend of organized labor, Freeman nonetheless credited the union movement for touching "a situation that has long caused concern among the friends of better racial understanding: the Negro must choose, under present circumstances, between manual labor and a profession. There is no middle ground."[57] The union movement, he judged, might create more opportunity for blacks to work as skilled laborers. Better jobs in a wider market fit in his view of "a common economic stake in this land of sunshine."

It was in the area of equal justice in Virginia's courts that Freeman provided his finest, and most significant, leadership. He had staked out his position in the Barrett case in 1918, and he clung to it throughout his life: "The very fact that he is a Negro, unrepresented, friendless, penniless, and ignorant, makes it all the more important that his guilt be established in a court of justice with every possible safeguard thrown about his rights."[58] He championed this philosophy both on the editorial page and by active involvement in cases where justice was not being done. In January 1926, Susie Boyd, a black woman unrepresented by counsel, was sentenced to thirty years for forging three checks in the aggregate amount of twenty-nine dollars.[59] Freeman viewed the case with horror, believing, quite correctly, that "instances of discrimination against defenseless Negroes [threaten] all that we have tried to do for better racial relationship."[60] The court's decision became even more dangerously suspect when a white defendant, on the same day's docket, was found guilty of shoplifting thirteen thousand dollars' worth of merchandise and was given a two-year suspended sentence.[61] Freeman wasted no time in condemning the action. "Nothing quite so damaging to good racial relationship has been done in Richmond in years," he wrote. "Nothing so discourages those who have been trying to convince the Negro that he can live safely and happily in the South."[62] While attempting to sway public opinion on the issue, he brought up the matter before the current events class. He laid out three concerns to the members: that the judge might not possess the "proper temperament to hold the office"; that such sentences would prompt defendants to demand jury trials, thereby crowding the dockets; and the obvious negative effect on racial relations. Freeman hesitated "to say now what can be done in the premises."[63] His subdued argument to his class, along with his reticence to make any suggestions, was intentional. By shifting the emphasis to the administration of justice and the competency of the judge—before a membership predominantly made up of lawyers—he subtly engendered support for his position without making it a racial crusade. In the meantime, the presiding judge reversed himself and reduced Boyd's sentence to six years. Freeman gave the judge credit, stating that the *News Leader* "never assumed for a moment that Judge Mathews intended to let the sentence of thirty years stand."[64] He took the opportunity, however, to warn the judiciary of Virginia of its duty in administering justice in a segregated society. "It is as much a disgrace to justice to show harshness to the weak as it is to be subservient to the strong," he wrote. "The color line ought to end at the bar."[65] Freeman's subtle nudge at lawyer members of the current events class also paid dividends. When Judge Mathews came up for reelection two years later, the Richmond Bar Association recommended another candidate for appointment. The General Assembly acted on the bar's suggestion and appointed John L. Ingram as the new judge. Ingram addressed a thank-you letter to Freeman. "I feel that my election . . . was as much due to your efforts as to any one person in the city," he wrote. "Your editorials were most helpful and your sympathetic interest . . . guided the reporters in handling the news items."[66] Freeman saw Ingram's appointment as proof "that in another year we shall have this great court on such a footing that there will be no discrimination against the poor or against the black."[67] Whatever his other shortcomings on racial matters, Douglas Freeman believed in equal—and colorblind—justice.

He also played a major role in the 1933 trial of George Crawford, a black defendant accused of murdering two white women in Loudoun County, Virginia. The case was fraught with powder kegs. The threat of mob violence simmered due to the race and sex of the victims. Suspicion of guilt was aroused when Crawford fought extradition from Massachusetts. National attention was turned to the case when the NAACP became involved on Crawford's behalf, and it was announced that Charles Houston, dean of the Howard University School of Law, would serve as chief defense counsel. Finally, the Crawford defense team moved to quash the murder indictments on the grounds that blacks had been excluded from jury service in Loudoun County.

Freeman's immediate actions were focused on keeping all parties calm and avoiding any mob action. "The case presents more than an obligation to do justice," he wrote in an editorial of November 1, 1933, "it presents an opportunity to advertise that fact to those who in some instances have had only too good reason to doubt the fairness of Southern juries. Every Virginian must be determined that when the case is ended, nobody, North or South, white or Negro, should say that Crawford has not had absolute justice."[68] While the populace seemed calm, the prosecuting attorney created a problem by refusing to allow defense co-counsel to see Crawford. Dean Houston sent a telegram asking for help, and Freeman took the matter directly to Virginia governor John Garland Pollard.[69] The matter of counsel seeing Crawford was quickly resolved, but Freeman used the opportunity of having the governor's ear to bring up the matter of potential mob violence. Following this discussion, the governor sent ten "undercover men" to the site of the trial in Leesburg, Virginia.[70] That same day, Governor Pollard named Judge James L. McLemore to preside over the case following the withdrawal of the Loudoun judge due to a potential conflict of interest. Freeman immediately dashed a letter off to the newly appointed judge advising that he had "told the Negroes . . . that we are determined, as a people, that when this case is ended . . . they will have to say that the man had a fair trial in every particular."[71] He ended this busy day by writing to Walter White, executive secretary of the NAACP, and reporting on his meeting with the governor and providing his assessment of Judge McLemore.[72]

On the day the motion to quash the indictments was argued, Freeman confidently predicted that "the actual trial of Crawford, whether under the present indictment or under a new one drawn with a Negro on the grand jury, will be a test of Virginia justice that nobody dreads."[73] He reminded his readers that the city of Richmond had already named "Negro grand jurymen," perhaps preparing them for a ruling in Crawford's favor by showing that it would create no radical departure from the administration of justice. Judge McLemore over-ruled the motion to quash, and trial was set for December 12, 1933.[74] Both Houston and McLemore wrote Freeman about the hearing. Houston expressed disappointment in the ruling, but judged the pro-ceedings as "just the same as they would have been in any other court anywhere in the United States." He held out cautious hopes that the trial would "serve as a model for future criminal trials in the South."[75] McLemore said that the hearing was "conducted in perfect order" and that Houston was "a most astute and accomplished lawyer."[76]

In the month leading up to the trial, Freeman served as an unofficial advisor to Houston and White. He told Houston that he "had better be prepared to meet every technicality that may arise" due to McLemore's "essentially legalistic" mind.[77] He passed on—"in the strictest confi-dence"—McLemore's compliment regarding Houston and cautioned White about NAACP news releases on the case.[78] In one letter to Houston, he mentioned the idea of hiring white associate counsel for Crawford. Houston responded that it would be "impossible for [him] to explain to the Negro bar" bringing in white co-counsel.[79] While main-taining that Crawford's interests were paramount, Houston admitted that having "Negro counsel . . . in complete charge of a case in the South . . . [would] do more for the School and the Negro lawyer than any sin-gle thing which I can imagine." Houston admitted that he was "enmeshed in [his] own propaganda," but felt that Crawford stood as good a chance with him as he did with white counsel.[80] Freeman was still concerned that having all black counsel would prejudice the case against Crawford. He solicited the advice of Governor Pollard—a for-mer Virginia attorney general—who advised that he did not think Crawford's "interests will be prejudiced if the case is conducted by Negro counsel."[81] Satisfied with Houston's and Pollard's views, he found him-self a few weeks later giving advice on the flip side of that question. He explained the new dilemma in a letter to Walter White.

> This is the most singular suggestion I have had to make to you: it has come to my attention that some foolish people in Leesburg are con-cerned because they believe you are a white man dealing on terms of 'equality' with Negroes. Of course whether white or colored, you would have a right to deal as you please . . . but in a case of this sort, when we are seeking justice, we want to make no blunder.[82]

Freeman proposed a solution: He would "let it be known through a brief article in the Leesburg paper that you have colored blood." The projected explanatory sentence would report "the fact that you were one of the few known persons of colored blood who has blue eyes."[83]

"Amusing isn't it?" White wired. He authorized him to "arrange" the story.[84]

The trial took place as scheduled in mid-December. Immediately prior to the start of the trial, Crawford admitted his guilt to his attorneys. White reported to Freeman that he was "shocked" at the confession, and Houston had to quickly change his strategy and attempt to gain a life sentence, rather than the death penalty, for his client.[85] The case concluded on December 16. While the prosecuting attorney presented his closing argument, Walter White wrote a longhand note to Douglas Freeman.

> Within an hour the jury will have Crawford's case. In this moment, before we know for certain just what his punishment will be, I want to say something. You were 100% correct in your assurance of an absolutely fair trial. Judge McLemore, [the prosecutors], and everyone else including the press—except the Washington Herald—have been scrupulously fair and more than fair. Virginia has established a record for the whole country to shoot at for a long time . . . My profound thanks for all you and the News Leader have done to bring this about.[86]

Freeman had achieved his goal. Houston did as well when Crawford was sentenced to life in prison. Freeman wrote a final editorial praising the people of Loudoun County and paying tribute to the ability of Charles Houston. He concluded by repeating the theme that ran throughout every word and action he ever took on the issue of equal justice.

> Virginia justice in this instance is vindicated alike by those who doubted it and by those who believe in it . . . We have shown what Virginia can do when she tries to avert race feeling in a case that is apt to provoke it. What we must seek hereafter is to have exactly the same spirit displayed when we make no special effort to assure fair play. We must do as well when we don't try as when we do. For the ideal of justice is a condition in which the race of the accused plays no part whatsoever.[87]

The issue of equal justice brought out the finest in Freeman's attitudes and actions regarding race. He was not as progressive when it came to voting rights and segregation. "The Democratic party," he wrote of the South's dominant party, "makes no pretense to be any other than a white man's party."[88] For that reason, why include blacks in the political process or extend them the franchise? On the other hand, "most Democrats, as individual citizens, realize the necessity of racial co-operation, and, as the dominant element in the South, Democrats appreciate the importance of the political education of the negro."[89] This was a restatement of Freeman's often used argument that whites should take care of blacks, but that blacks should have no active political role in determining their own future. "The duty of the Democrats," he wrote, "is to see that the negro has decent living conditions, educational facilities and absolute justice in the courts of law." He expressed this paternalism in a letter to John Stewart Bryan. "I must say," he wrote, "I do not favor any revision of the constitution as respects the electoral franchise, for it seems to me we ought to raise the electorate to the franchise, rather than lower the franchise to the electorate."[90] He offered no suggestions as to how blacks in the electorate were to be "raised" to the franchise, any more than he explained what his editorial meant by "political education of the negro." In both instances, however, it is clear that he regarded the act of raising or educating the electorate within the prerogative of whites, not blacks.

Kept out with blacks under Virginia's voting laws were many whites. The Constitution of 1902 established so many barriers to voting that in 1924 only 14,890 of Richmond's 183,000 population voted. This proved to be too much for Freeman, and he began to soften his stand on franchise restrictions. "The negroes are eliminated—yes," he wrote, "but who is prepared to say the result is worth what it has cost?"[91] He was a loyal Democrat, but he opposed the political machine that was beginning to run Virginia—maintained in office by low voter turnout—so he reversed his earlier opinion and called for a revision of the Virginia constitution. He did not do so to champion the cause of black suffrage, but he did not let the specter of increased black voting prevent him from taking this stand. It took a few more years for him to openly support full participation by blacks. In 1933, with the courts about to strike down Virginia's primary, Freeman argued that "it will be infinitely better to accept the inevitable and to throw open the primary to those Negroes who are Democrats."[92] He then made an appeal to black voters to participate and vote Democrat in order to "assure for themselves . . . decent political consideration."

Even with the franchise extended, barriers still existed, the most notorious of which was the poll tax. Virginia law required the payment of a $1.50 poll tax six months prior to the general election in which the voter desired to participate. Moreover, if a voter missed paying the tax and wanted to renew, he would have to pay for the current and two preceding years, a total of $4.50, and any other levy the local authority deemed appropriate.[93] In its first year of operation, the poll tax reduced the number of qualified black voters from 147,000 to 21,000. In addition to the poll tax, literary tests were aimed not only at blacks but also at Republicans and recognized machine opponents. In order to register, a voter would have to answer obscure questions regarding the state's election laws or write out entire portions of specific Virginia statutes. One college graduate received a letter from the registrar advising that he had failed the literacy test. "Yo hav fald to rechister" read the notice.[94]

Freeman again started with a hard-line stance. "Shall we," he wrote, "extend the franchise in Virginia by abolishing the prepayment of poll-taxes as a prerequisite to voting? No, a thousand times, No!"[95] He again relied on the old argument of an intelligent electorate. "Interest and participation in government are today desirable only when they are intelligent and well-informed." He worried that the uneducated were voting only to "use government to their advantage, or . . . [to] get something from government."[96] The vote, he argued, should not go to those "not capable of exercising some measure of moral self-restraint." In Freeman's defense, he was not using the intelligence argument as a cover for ulterior motives—namely, to prevent blacks from voting. He truly did believe in only an intelligent electorate casting votes. What he continually failed to do was to link this requirement with any plan to improve the education of the electorate, thereby rendering his restriction useless. Again, it took lawsuits to move him off the poll tax. In 1942 he called it "a practical, though an awkward and unsatisfactory substitute for an intelligence qualification which will place the ballot in the hands of all those . . . regardless of race, who can use the ballot with some sense."[97] A few months later, he gave up completely. Congress was about to act to abolish the poll tax in Federal elections, and Freeman confessed he was "losing interest in the maintenance" of the tax and found that it did more to "perpetuate machine rule than to assure . . . [an] intelligent element."[98]

Freeman's lackluster attitude in regard to voting rights is puzzling given his advocacy of equal justice. He consistently held out the hope that all citizens would obtain the proper education or intelligence to cast a sensible ballot. He was appalled by low voter turnout and opposed the machine that bred off voter apathy. Yet he took no steps until lawsuits or Federal action threatened to change the landscape without him. He repeatedly called for the electorate and the franchise to meet—and they finally did.[99] But he had done little to bring about that junction.

So what can be said about Douglas Southall Freeman and race? He clearly was ahead of his time in advocating better conditions and equal justice for blacks; he was also a man of his time in his support of the doctrine of separation. His liberal philosophy and Christian beliefs often combined to make him a model of racial reconciliation, and, once committed, he was courageous in his advocacy. Yet he never pushed his readers beyond where he thought they would go. Segregation was not a defining issue to him; it was merely one issue to be considered and weighed along with political stability, economic prosperity, and law and order. Two months before his death, he made his last written statement on the subject. "Sometimes I fear we are taking exceedingly long chances when we advance Negroes as rapidly as seems to be the practice now. We all, of course, want Negroes to advance, but we want this progress to be steady. It cannot be if we push them further ahead than they are prepared to go."[100]

Freeman no doubt believed that. But steady progress could have come as well, he must have realized, if he had pushed himself further than he was prepared to go.

CHAPTER 9

"Adventure with the Clock"

"In deciding what you're going to do," Douglas Freeman commented about his active life, "your first decision must be what you're not going to do. To do, you must leave undone."[1] As he approached his fiftieth year, his activities were so vast and varied that it is difficult to ascertain exactly what things he was leaving "undone."

He was not a "joiner" in the normal sense of the word; but his reputation and abilities were of such renown that membership offers from prestigious boards and organizations naturally came his way. Columbia dean Carl Ackerman asked Freeman to forward a brief resume for the university's files and received a list that included the following posts: rector of the Board of Trustees of the University of Richmond, member of the General Education Board and of the Rockefeller Foundation, member of the Board of Trustees of the Carnegie Endowment for International Peace, trustee of the Children's Memorial Clinic, president and trustee of the Edgar Allan Poe Foundation, member of the Council of the Washington Cathedral, chairman of the Rhodes Scholarship Committee for Virginia, and president of the Southern Historical society.[2]

His membership on these boards was not perfunctory. He participated in the activities of each organization as fully as his schedule would permit and was always available for advice and counsel on any issue facing a particular board. When he assumed the presidency of the Southern Historical Society in 1926, the organization was in "financially delicate" circumstances, a condition soon made worse when the society's treasury was wiped out in a Depression-era bank failure.[3] Freeman realized that for the society to survive, it would have to concentrate on the thorough presentation of a single topic. This would keep down costs, while enabling the society to provide a worthwhile service. He chose to publish the proceedings of the Confederate Congress. These sessions, never before compiled in one source, gave "fascinating insight into the character of Congress and into the problems of a beleaguered land."[4] He enlisted moral and financial support for the project from John Stewart Bryan and J. Ambler Johnston, a Richmond architect and close friend, and the volumes were soon being published. It was a laborious task—the last volume did not appear until six years after Freeman's death—but without his efforts it is questionable whether any editions would have been published.

He was very active as a trustee of the Rockefeller Foundation, the General Education Board, and the Carnegie Endowment, even though meetings of these boards took place in New York. "Whenever he spoke at a [Rockefeller Foundation] board meeting, and he did not speak too frequently," Dr. Raymond Fosdick wrote, "he seemed to carry everything before him with an eloquence which was as irresistible as it was completely natural."[5] At one meeting of the General Education Board, the topic of humanistic studies was being debated. Freeman took the floor and "so profoundly" moved the board that "Mr. Rockefeller . . . adjourned the meeting . . . knowing that anything said thereafter would be in the nature of an anticlimax."[6] Freeman got on well with his fellow board members, was committed to the goals of each organization, and provided as much service as his schedule allowed. Not all of his activities, however, bore fruit. Since his days of writing editorials on behalf of Woodrow Wilson and the League of Nations, he had a special interest in and a passionate dedication to the cause of world peace. Thus he viewed his membership on the Carnegie Endowment for International Peace as a real opportunity to advance the dream of Wilson. While he had great affection for board president Nicholas Murray Butler, president of Columbia University, he agreed with a fellow board member that "many of the enterprises we have undertaken have no more relation to International Peace than Eleanor Roosevelt's 'My Day.'"[7] He believed that "three-fifths" of the annual budget was wasted and "regretfully" concluded "that a not inconsiderable sum represents patronage dispensed by Dr. Butler to titled persons whose contributions in America to the cause of peace is, to use the kindest word, vague."[8] Specific complaints included spending money distributing *Alice in Wonderland*, hiring foreign professors to lecture on Marlowe, and sending American professors to South America to lecture on minerals and geology.[9] Freeman decided to resign, stating "that we are contributing no more to peace . . . than we are contributing to astronomy or metaphysics."[10] Before he could submit his resignation, several board members urged him to mediate the disagreement on expenditures between the warring sections of the board. He stayed on and was still on the board a few years later when the endowment's director, Alger Hiss, was accused of being a Communist spy. The subsequent imbroglio on that issue inured to the board little benefit and much controversy. Freeman gave his best efforts to the Carnegie Endowment, but it yielded him little satisfaction.

The post to which he gave his most vigorous service was as a trustee of the University of Richmond. He was named to the board of his alma mater in June 1925 and became rector of it in 1934.[11] His appointment represented a reunion not only with president F. W. Boatwright, but also with his mentor S. C. Mitchell, who still reigned in the History Department. Freeman brought to the board a well-defined philosophy of education that he sought to advance throughout his long tenure. He called his philosophy one of "broad sane Christian education," and it found a welcome home at the Baptist-affiliated college.[12] When he became rector he noted that there was no "real difference of opinion between the University, its officers and trustees on the one hand, and the denomination on the other. We have thought alike and have cherished the same ideals."[13] Nor did Freeman believe those ideals, represented by "the lofty spirit of discerning Christian faith," to be in conflict with "scientific research [or] humanistic study."[14] The latter two dealt with the tools of education, the former with a particular worldview. "The tools of technology may change," he wrote, "but they are devised by trained hands. Methods of business may be modified, but they cannot be shaped rightly except by trained minds. Education is the lathe on which the tools are turned . . . [but] where education is not directed by the spirit of true religion, it is misdirected and robbed of its charity, its beauty, its deeper purpose."[15] Freeman stressed that this ideal should "allow the fullest religious liberty and freedom of choice" and "disavow sectarianism," but maintained that "the true excellence of a college is almost in direct proportion to the sane vigor of the religious spirit that pervades the institution."[16]

This "sane vigor" demanded a realistic approach to the management of the university. Though the school was affiliated with Virginia Baptists, the denomination began to show a decreasing interest in providing financial support. Freeman confronted the issue in 1936 at the annual meeting of the Baptist General Association. Standing in the Tabernacle Baptist Church, he declared that perhaps the time had come for the University of Richmond, like "Lazarus of old," to throw off the "grave clothes" of Baptist affiliation and come forth.[17] His salvo served two purposes: It stimulated to action those who desired a closer

relationship between the university and the Baptists; and it was something of a declaration of independence—or, more to Freeman's historical leanings, an ordinance of secession—for those who wanted the
university to become "in a very real and enduring sense a public institution."[18] In any event, it signaled that the university's rector would not let
denominational ties weaken the school's economic wellbeing.

Freeman and Boatwright applied the "sane vigor of the religious
spirit" in dealing with the university's Jewish students. By the end of his
first year as rector, there were fifty-seven Jewish students at Richmond
College, five at the Westhampton College for Women, seven at the Law
School, and seventeen in the Business School. Twenty-four of them
were receiving full or partial scholarships.[19] Freeman suggested Boatwright
appear before "the Men's Association of Beth Ahabah and . . . report on
the work of the Jewish students."[20] This would serve the dual purpose of
enlightening the community about opportunities for Jewish young people at the University of Richmond, and perhaps spur some contributions
or endowments.

His outreach program also included an elaborate plan "for bringing
the city to the University and . . . the University to the city."[21] The plan
was modeled closely on his tried method—used most notably in the current events class—of bringing together people of influence to deal with
specific issues. The work on the problem of the moment would be soon
completed, but the relationships established in the process would
endure, serving both sides. He proposed bringing in "State and City
officials" to lecture to graduating students in a "Virginia Government
class," to entertain the major civic clubs "once a year," to work "as a unit"
on "various civic campaigns," to "provide a technical committee on any
questions of municipal affairs," and "to act as expert advisors for the
Retail Merchants Association."[22] Simultaneous with these steps, the
university should "build up a strong advisory board for the Law School"
and ask several ladies—including Mrs. Boatwright and Mrs. Freeman—
"to assure some general collective responsibility for the social life of our
girls." Thus in his first year as rector, Freeman laid out an intricate plan
that wove the university, its officials, and its students into the political,
cultural, economic, and social life of the city of Richmond. It was, he
admitted, "a long program not easily completed," but it set the tone for
his sixteen years as rector.

Some things he attempted to leave "undone" in his life were the
numerous social events to which he was invited. "I presume I shall have

to escort some unattended female of mature years and self convinced superiority," he complained to the vacationing Inez about an event in the summer of 1933. "I dread the loss of sleep it will entail, because there is little prospect that the guests of honor will leave much before the hour I should be turning over and contemplating the approach of dawn. However, what can't be cured must be endured."[23] When the movie *Gone with the Wind* made its Richmond premiere, Freeman was persuaded to don a Confederate general's uniform and attend a ball preceding the showing of the four-hour film. He performed this duty, but ducked out before the movie started and was home by 9:30 P.M.[24] "How can I go out to dinners or parties when I get up at half-past three?" he exclaimed, and so he dodged as many nights out as possible. Entertainment was far easier at home, for he had no qualms about leaving his guests early and going to bed. His friends understood this habit, and what might have been considered boorish if done by someone else was accepted when done by Freeman. It also helped that social events at the Freeman home were "flawlessly done."[25] Freeman conferred on the menus—often composing them himself—and he always chose the wine. His wine cellar was one of the best in the city, and at a dinner for John Stewart Bryan, he selected a bottle for each course and printed his comments on the menu. The Grand Chablis Vaudesir, 1935, was "too doggone dry," but the Rupertsburg Hofstuck Riesling, 1921, was "so good that notice is given in advance there will be no second bottle." By the time the dessert arrived, he noted that serving a Malmsey Madeira of 1855 would "be a costly mistake because the guests will be too tight to tell how good it is."[26] His taste for good wine was threatened by Prohibition, but instead of dealing with a "reliable bootlegger," he purchased a truckload of blue grapes and, under the direction of his Italian barber, pressed the grapes in a cider mill and bottled them to age.[27] A year later, he premiered his first bottle of "Chianti" at a dinner with his brother Allen. The dean of the Johns Hopkins School of Public Health Administration tasted it and gave a two-word diagnosis: "It's vinegar." Undaunted by his brother's critique, Freeman sent bottles as gifts to friends. One recipient was William Rush, the headwaiter at the Commonwealth Club. "That was the best wine I ever tasted," was Rush's surprising review. "I just put in a lot of lemon and orange juice and sugar and gin—it was delicious."[28] When the remaining bottles in Freeman's cellar exploded, he gave up the experiment. It was a rare instance of total failure.

Home brewing aside, the Freemans were judged to have "no peers as hosts."[29] He occasionally used this talent not just to entertain, but also to serve. He knew of "a fine old gentleman . . . a scholar and a lover of good books" who had fallen on hard times. While Inez and the children were at the beach, he decided to "have him come out Saturday afternoon" and stay until Monday morning. His goal would be to give him "a little of the life he knew in better days."[30] A few years later, he learned that the daughter of a senior reporter at the *News Leader* was to be married, and he knew the reporter was not financially able to provide a costly wedding. He managed to bump into the reporter during the day and, in congratulating him on the happy news, nonchalantly mentioned that he "loved the good times engendered by a wedding" and wondered if the bride would consider holding her wedding at his home. The unsolicited offer was eagerly accepted, and Freeman and Inez hosted the wedding in their spacious gardens.[31]

His one constant social engagement was the weekly meeting of the current events class. "How I love those tested friends!" he confided to his diary.[32] The fifty-two-member roll of 1933 constituted a who's who of Richmond political and business leadership, but Freeman recognized that all were advancing in age and would need "successors."[33] He decided to start another club for young men aged thirteen to train them for future civic leadership. The class, called the "Tomorrow Club," met at Freeman's home on "alternate Saturday evenings when the cotillion is not held."[34] The meeting started at 5:00 P.M. with recreation for an hour followed by dinner outdoors. "We would talk about current events, and he would lecture," son James Douglas remembers, "but most of the guys were taking bets on how long the ash from his cigarette would last before it fell off."[35] The class did not have the staying power of the current events class—probably due to the distractions of youth—and lasted only one year.

In 1928, Freeman began an eighteen-year run as the narrator of Richmond's annual Christmas pageant, "The Nativity." He no doubt accepted the assignment because John Stewart Bryan was the chairman of the Christmas Celebration Committee.[36] The outdoor production took place on the capitol grounds, before moving in later years to the carillon in Byrd Park, and was complete with live animals and a chorus. One year Freeman was reading the familiar scripture when he came to the verse "suddenly there was with the angel a multitude of the heavenly host." No angels appeared. As he continued to read, the pageant director, "a stout local thespian" named Rose Banks, grabbed the backstage microphone and bellowed "Angels! Angels! Where are those damned angels?"[37] Freeman maintained his decorum and continued reading the old, old story as the tardy "angels" fluttered about him.

While researching his biography of Robert E. Lee, Freeman began to take regular Sunday drives to the battlefields around Richmond. His companion on these outings was his friend Ambler Johnston. The two men noticed that none of the battlefields were marked.[38] "I doubt there were more than a dozen people in Richmond," Johnston recalled, "who could have told you where the battles took place."[39] Freeman appeared before the Richmond Rotary Club and presented a plan to place markers at specific locations around the battlefields. On September 5, 1921, a convoy of twenty-one automobiles filled with Rotary members and Confederate veterans made the first "historically planned Richmond battlefield tour" to check out the proposed sites.[40] The Rotarians embraced the plan to mark the fields, and Freeman, Johnston, and two others formed the Battlefield Markers Association to raise the needed money.[41] "Doug furnished the brains," Johnston wrote, "the rest of us did the footwork." Freeman wrote the majority of the inscriptions for the fifty-nine markers that were dedicated in 1925.[42] Fifty-eight of the markers still stand—each one a cast iron plate set horizontally on a large capstone made of concrete. When dedicated, the markers were the first highway markers in Virginia.[43] They are today called "Freeman Markers."

Springtime in Richmond was signaled by the usual changes in temperatures and colors, but spring carried an additional annual occurrence for Freeman: college commencements. The requests for him to serve as graduation speaker began to roll in with the first wave of warm air. He turned down "ninety-five" percent of speaking requests, but still found himself "wandering all over the face of America to address the 'two or three' who are 'gathered together' to take verbal punishment."[44] During a six-day period in June 1936, he spoke at William and Mary, the University of Virginia, the University of Pittsburgh, and Wesleyan College. In addition to colleges, he faced a constant barrage of speaking requests from civic groups, professional associations, and Civil War organizations. He noted in his diary that during 1937 he had delivered eighty-three "lectures and addresses."[45] As he did with teaching, he expressed dislike at making so many speeches, but he continued to accept engagements. "I never make a speech," he wrote, "but that I sit down in humiliation and distress, feeling that I never approximate the standard of performance that public presentation really requires."[46] If he felt that way—despite the nearly universal praise his speeches received—he refused to alter his habit of speaking without notes. "I lead so crowded a life that I am never able to write out speeches and sometimes not even able to jot down any notes."[47] His closest associates noticed the difference between a "Freeman article" and a "Freeman speech." James J. Kilpatrick, who succeeded him as editor of the *News Leader*, summarized the distinction.

> In writing, he was a classical perfectionist whose greatest love was a balanced and perfect sentence. In his extemporaneous lectures, he was inclined to relax, to unbend, to seek some sense of empathy with his audience. He could let a good-natured "Good God!" slip into a speech with a smile that robbed it of offense, but he never on earth would have let the ejaculation remain in a printed work. Similarly, he often used the intensifying "very" in his talks, but he had an ironbound rule against the word in his writing. Aloud, he might speak of 30 or 40 years of "contact" with public education; in print, never.[48]

He may have disdained prepared remarks, but Freeman made a careful study of the art of speechmaking and gave two extensive lectures on the topic to the current events class. He listed "four fundamentals needed in public speaking": Have something to say, know your audience, have self-confidence, and develop a proper speaking voice.[49] He taught the class the technique of modulating by having them practice a number of sentences, including "Thou still-unravish'd bride of quietness!" That sentence, he said, was an "excellent example of an absolute C Major of a man's normal speaking voice."[50]

It is hard to believe that he did not realize how good he was at delivering speeches—with or without a prepared text. He had a dramatic flair that combined with his strong voice to make his speeches stand out. He often employed the "pathetic" style of delivery. Derived from the Greek word *pathos*, this style was defined as "evoking a feeling of compassion or pity."[51] One memorable address took place at the dedication of the Princeton battlefield. It was a cold day with a raw wind, so Freeman assured his chilled audience that his speech would last "exactly fourteen minutes and thirty seconds." Naturally, heads in the crowd bobbed up and down as many checked their watches during the speech. Mary Wells Ashworth, Freeman's historical associate, witnessed the scene and, between glances at her own watch, recorded "the admiring disbelief of those sixteen hundred listeners [as] the last words of a beautifully rounded, never-to-be-forgotten dedication, unhurried in content or delivery, ended precisely fourteen minutes and thirty seconds from the moment he made his opening statement."[52] If that were not dramatic enough, the bells in one of the college towers began to chime as Freeman began his concluding sentences.

Somewhere in this kaleidoscope of activities, duties, and commitments had to come a time set apart. A time not even intruded upon by historic figures. A time devoted to what most would call "hobbies." Freeman was the first to say that his life was satisfaction enough. "It sounds like a rigid, stern sort of life, I suppose," he admitted. "As a matter of fact, I have the best time of anyone you know and I'm one of the few people you know that's doing absolutely what he wants to do."[53] Even though he spent many working hours reading, his hours of relaxation were often passed in that same pursuit. He judged "the reading of a Psalm, a bit of Shakespeare or a passage from Sophocles, to the accompaniment of a Beethoven record and the quiet sipping of fresh, black coffee" to be "a matchless combination."[54] Shakespeare and the Bible had been two staples in his daily reading since his college days. His other favorites were *The Agamemnon of Aeschylus*, *Meditations of Marcus Aurelius*, and Brother Lawrence's *The Practice of the Presence of God*.[55] One searches in vain for a popular novel; he read *Gone with the Wind* only because he thought Margaret Mitchell's thorough research increased the book's authenticity. His non-historical preferences ran to poetry—Tennyson, Browning, Keats, and Shelley.[56] He even wrote some blank verse—usually in the form of birthday greetings to family and friends. In July 1933 he wrote a sonnet, titled "Harbor," as a gift for Inez.

When winds are hostile, wherefore curse the sea?
When winter storms sweep down, why blame the tide?
In all their moods, whatever they may be,
The waves proclaim the truth. They never hide
In bright pretence, life's dark reality,
Nor tell the negligent his bark will glide
Unsteered. No foolish dream is argosy,
Nor foundered hope is haven where they ride.
And ever the ocean tells of storms that cease,
Of far horizons passed, of work well done.

It leads us to the safety and the peace
Of waiting home lights, with the harbor won;
And that is why, my long adventure through,
The sea speaks to my moored heart of you.[57]

Freeman enjoyed baseball and regularly attended games until this pastime became a victim of his work.[58] When he joined the family at Willoughby, he was often at the helm of his sailboat, the *Andomanez.*[59] He went through a phase of interest in photography, developing a knack at using an awkward Graflex camera while snapping hundreds of pictures of family and flowers.[60] The purchase of a telescope turned his attention to astronomy, and he exchanged many letters with Dr. S. H. Sheib, an expert on the topic, discussing the best viewing times for specific sightings.[61] But if he had an abiding hobby to which he devoted substantial time and from which he derived great pleasure, it was gardening. "Troubles," he wrote, "never are so heavy under the open sky as under a roof."[62] No matter how full his day, he made a concerted effort to spend at least a few minutes digging in his gardens. "Tonight I shall go to the class," he wrote Inez in the summer of 1930, "after having given myself to the luxury of a couple of hours with the hoe."[63] He confessed that he "had good luck" in growing vegetables and regularly turned out black-eyed peas, butterbeans, tomatoes, corn, and cucumbers for the family table.[64] Though military men often wrote asking his analysis of certain battles or tactics, he was delighted when a Navy admiral asked for advice on growing asparagus. He responded with a detailed six-point plan, the "most important" point of which was to use stone and gravel "no larger than a potato" in the bottom of the trench.[65]

Freeman also tended flowers and shrubs, and retained Richmond's finest horticulturist for maintenance and advice. As in all his endeavors, he made specific detailed requests based on research and study. One memorandum of "recommendations" to Charles Gillette, his landscape architect, runs two and one-half, single-spaced, typed pages, and includes suggestions on removing "mulberry and privet" to allow bayberry to grow, placing large maple trees in a "crescent line," and using rotten sawdust before planting azaleas.[66] As the work became more extensive and time consuming, Freeman left more of the work to Gillette's crew, but he still donned "a well used pair of coveralls" to clear brush and mulch his roses.[67]

Gardening proved not only a welcome respite from his strenuous schedule and intellectually challenging work, but also a source of spiritual refreshment. "I never see this stage of spring," he told his Sunday School class, "but that I liken it to a man—a man who, having passed through many storms and divers cycles, having known the seasons, the winds and the rains, comes now to a renewal of life."[68] This spirit of renewal prompted him to write a poem, "My Garden and I."

> Deep opened thou thy heart, oh, garden mine,
> When wooed the summer's sun with ardent plea,
> And phlox wove white thy robe, and columbine
> A chaplet gave—deep burned the fire in thee.
> Now that thy face is gray and wet thy gown
> And mocking winter cries thy lover's dead,
> While lowered skies, unsympathizing, frown,
> And searching winds sweep o'er thy snowy bed,
> Thou dost not heed the lie that winter tells,
> Nor shiver in the blast, nor fear the skies.
> For in thy breast, deep down, the warmth still dwells,
> The sun, thy lover, in thy heart survives.
> So I life's passing summer shall not rue
> When love undying I still find in you.[69]

Freeman's gardening space significantly increased when the family moved to a new home in September 1938. "Westbourne" was a three-story brick mansion with twenty-two rooms and approximately eight thousand square feet.[70] A Greek portico with four stately columns graced the front of the house, which sat in the middle of seven acres. The grounds contained "many mature shrubs and a fine grove" but no garden. Gillette was put to work, and the home was soon renowned for its beautiful landscape. To Freeman, Westbourne typified "one of my ideals of what this generation of Southerners should try to do in a way of gracious living."[71] As in his previous two houses, the third floor became the site of his study. Spartan in comparison with the comfortable luxury of the rest of the house, it reflected the man who occupied it. Ringing most of the room were tall metal bookcases—stark in their cold utility—holding whatever books were needed for the current study. The Morris chair, purchased while he was at Johns Hopkins, had wide arms affixed for writing purposes. Next to the chair, always within reach of Freeman's right hand, was a small shelf containing a single volume dictionary, *Bartlett's* and *Oxford Quotations*, his diary, the *Dictionary of American Biography*, and the *Dictionary of American History*—as well as the omnipresent Bible, Shakespeare, and *Marcus Aurelius*. Behind his chair was a revolving bookcase containing materials used to write his books—outlines, chronologies, and notes. He wrote all his books and articles by hand, but a typewriter sat on rolling wheels nearby for use on note cards or letters. A microphone stood in the corner for his Sunday or evening broadcasts. The little free wall space held autographed pictures of Churchill and Lindbergh, portraits of Robert E. Lee, and prints of Grecian, Libyan, and Roman antiquities. Straight ahead from his desk was a large school-size clock with a red sweep second hand. There was no phone—the silence was broken only by the occasional sound of Beethoven or Hadyn coming from a record player.[72]

A step away from the study was a small room with an altar, complete with a cross, two candles, a kneeling bench, and a stained-glass window. "There is no history behind this little altar," he wrote, "except that one needs a place for prayer and meditation—a place apart."[73]

"Dear Douglas Freeman," the letter of September 21, 1938, began. "We should meet as the only two biographers in the Western Hemisphere who have written a million-word portrait." The letter was signed, "with more than esteem," by Carl Sandburg.[74] The biographer of Lincoln and the biographer of Lee did get together and were drawn immediately to one another. Sandburg mentioned an incident of a Kentucky father and his two sons. Both sons lost their lives in the Civil War, one fighting for the Union and the other for the Confederacy. They were buried in a double grave with one headstone. "Under the names of his two sons," Sandburg related, "the father had the inscription: 'God knows which was right.'"

"Both sides were right," Freeman replied.[75]

Sandburg was struck by the comment. "I still cogitate on it," he wrote later.[76]

Robert Frost was another friend who enjoyed the hospitality of Westbourne. During one visit, he appeared with Freeman on the radio and recited "Mending Wall" and "Stopping by Woods on a Snowy Day." It was Frost's first radio broadcast.[77] Richmond was something of a literary center during those days with authors Ellen Glasgow and James Branch Cabell, both friends of Freeman, living in town and Virginius Dabney editing the *Richmond Times-Dispatch*. Along with these established figures were many aspiring writers who sought an audience with Freeman. "I can't say that I have 'developed any writers,'" Freeman commented about his numerous callers, "but I have helped all I could. That, it seems to me, is an obligation that older writers owe younger men."[78]

When he was not entertaining, Freeman's tastes tended toward simple foods. "The best food that ever is put before me," he wrote, "is black-eyed peas boiled with old Virginia meat—that is to say, bacon or shoulder. This is perfect in itself but superlative when it is mixed with fresh corn cut from the cob, is washed down with buttermilk, and has the glorious concomitant of corn pones. If you have this combination of food, you can endure any hardship with ease and any disappointment with poise."[79] He also had a taste for Brunswick stew, "the gift of the gods to the people of the South," and fried hominy cakes with currant jelly.[80] When Charles Scribner and his family visited Westbourne, Freeman served them "a typical Virginia meal" of "Brunswick stew, broiled oysters, Smithfield ham, mashed black-eyed peas, hominy cakes, corn pudding, and candied sweet potatoes." Dessert was pistachio ice cream. "Believe it or not," Freeman wrote Mary Tyler, "nobody in the party had ever tasted Brunswick stew or black-eyed peas, or our kind of hominy."[81] The reaction of the New Yorkers to such fare was not recorded. In his travels around the world, Freeman enjoyed sampling restaurants with "good cuisine and interesting atmosphere." Nor was he above providing detailed criticism if disappointed. The manager of Keen's Chop House in New York received a letter from Freeman complimenting the "English mutton chop" but castigating the "negligent service" of the waiter. "It was an incredible thing to me," he wrote, "that such good food should have been served with the indifference that I have never seen rivaled in many first class restaurants in 15 countries."[82]

If there was one area where Freeman's famed self-discipline seemed to desert him, it was in the area of tobacco use. Virginia was a tobacco state, and Freeman liberally indulged in the product. He chewed tobacco for some time, but gave up the habit after a few years of marriage.[83] He was soon a heavy smoker. An Associated Press reporter noted, "[H]e smokes one cigarette after another in a filter holder."[84] In July 1932, Freeman wrote Inez that he was quitting and had gone to the dentist "to get all the taste and all the stains out of my mouth."[85] His stated reason for quitting was pure Freeman: "It takes too much time."[86] Almost two years later to the day of his July 1932 announcement, he was back to smoking a pack of cigarettes a day.[87] On March 8, 1937, he noted in his diary that he "stopped smoking! It takes too much time!"[88] Nine months later his diary contains the entry: "stopped smoking today."[89] This latest effort was no more successful than the previous ones, but in 1940 he quit for good. He informed his brother of the glad tidings—quitting "always has a fine effect on my state of mind"—and again asserted that his decision was based on the time factor.[90] His son has a different recollection. Freeman, James Douglas recalls, was being examined by his doctor in "the middle room of the second floor" at Westbourne "and [the doctor] said, 'Doc, if you don't quit smoking, you're going to die,' or something really dramatic and . . . [he] reached over, put the cigarette out, didn't take another drag, and that was the last one."[91]

Smoking aside, Freeman's health was generally good. He stood five feet, ten and one-half inches tall, and sported a medium frame, though his sedentary lifestyle sometimes put a few extra pounds on him. His hair steadily receded during his forties on the way to a bald top in his later years. His aquiline nose had been broken in youth, and he had a strong, squared cleft chin. Even his most ardent admirers would not call him "handsome"; but his research assistant recalled that the "mobility of expression, intensity of feeling and perception and the sparkle of good humor gave him a fascination of countenance that was far more magnetic than regularity of feature."[92] His blue-gray eyes were the focal point of his face. They gazed, Jack Kilpatrick wrote, "with judicious equanimity—and now and then with an unexpected twinkle—upon times present and times past."[93]

One of Freeman's primary ways to view "times present and times past" was over the radio. His broadcast schedule had increased from once a week in 1926 to twice daily Monday through Saturday and once on Sunday.[94] He broadcast initially over station WRVA, but on November 14, 1937, he switched to WRNL, a new station owned and operated by the *News Leader*.[95] WRNL was located in a building adjacent to the *News Leader* and connected to it by a catwalk. It took him exactly two minutes to walk from his office to the microphone, so he did not rise from his chair until 7:58 A.M. to head over for the morning broadcast. "At 7:59:59," Jack Kilpatrick remembered, "he would enter the studio."[96] Freeman's nephew, Mallory Freeman, served for many years as the show's announcer and confirmed his uncle's split-second arrivals. "I was facing an empty microphone as I began the phrase 'And here is Dr. Freeman,' and when I looked up, he was there."[97] Another announcer for the show, Andrew Oberg, told a friend he "had to operate on faith that [Freeman] would be there when he finished his announcement. He always was, but never before."[98]

"Good morning, ladies and gentlemen. It is a beautiful morning on the Virginia Riviera."

So began most of his broadcasts.[99] He then spoke for fifteen minutes on the news of the day. If the news was uneventful, he would tell his listeners not to buy a paper or, much to chagrin of the station, to turn off the radio and do something else. Jack Kilpatrick wrote of Freeman's radio speech, "There was never an 'uh' or an 'er.' He spoke as he wrote, in organized paragraphs, absolutely extemporaneously, moving in easy transitions from one study to another."[100] His son witnessed a few of these unscripted performances and watched in amazement. "He would walk into the studio with a piece of paper, with maybe six things written on it . . . and that was the script. He ad-libbed the whole thing . . . then, stand-by, thirty seconds, fifteen, 'Good day.' Off clean."[101] James Douglas, who himself would spend many years in radio and television, still shakes his head over his father's ability. "He was a 'phenom,' they don't do that any more."

Historian Richard Harwell wrote that Freeman's broadcasts were "an essential of a Virginian breakfast," and author Emory Thomas remembered that "only when Dr. Freeman had concluded his remarks at 8:15 A.M. did I leave the house" for school.[102] WRNL was pleased with the public's response to the broadcasts and judged them "not only valuable but . . . a definite service to the public."[103] There were some dissenting voices. Some Richmonders professed "irritation with the man's confusion of himself with God Almighty," and *Time* magazine noted some were "fed up with his sagelike utterances and sweet-talkin' voice."[104] His style did lend itself to good-natured ribbing. *Times-Dispatch* reporter Parker Rouse recalled that Freeman "loved rendering sonorous words like 'Ben—GOZZ—i' or 'Wal—HALL—a' or 'Bee—ZAHR—tay'."[105] He took the jests in stride, but paid attention to the more serious criticisms. They appeared, he wrote John Stewart Bryan, "to sum up into these six: (1) my style is too 'affected.' (2) on occasion I talk too slowly. (3) Sometime I am too violent in my utterance. (4) I lack the 'cold detachment' [of] Elmer Davis. (5) I often mispronounce foreign names in an irritating manner. (6) the broadcasts are too personal to myself."[106] Agreeing with many of these criticisms—though it is highly unlikely that he ever mispronounced a foreign name—he offered to "retire altogether from that difficult field of public presentation." His offer was rejected. Though he tried many times through the years to go off the air, neither his station nor his public would allow it.

Freeman's Sunday show, *Lessons in Living*, was distinctly different from his daily broadcasts. One-half hour in length, the show's genesis came in the wake of his near fatal illness of 1929. The broadcast topics were usually religious in nature, though he inserted lectures that were "essentially practical" such as "the best organization of one's work; the discussion of fear in the heart; the perplexities of children in adolescence; the delights of reading . . . [and] the joy of making each day a thing of beauty in itself."[107] There were again critics—the broadcasts were "a source of amusement for [some] Sunday sophisticates"—but the popularity of the show was indicated by mail from devoted listeners.[108] "Your class," one shut-in wrote, "is what I have been hungering for for more than a year."[109] Another wrote to tell of the "great comfort and pleasure" brought on by the broadcasts "especially to those who are sick or afflicted and can't get out but little if at all."[110] One listener wrote the president of the American Broadcasting System advising him that Freeman was "the re-incarnation of Ralph Waldo Emerson," while another said "it is no longer necessary to see a great man to know what he is . . . [you] hear his voice on the radio and you know him."[111]

Letters of praise were soon followed by letters seeking advice. A "devoted father" wrote about his problems with his children; a "simple housewife" about "living alone, with two children and an old fraction of a plantation."[112] One message came by telegram. "THOUGH AN ORPHAN AND TOTALLY BLIND SINCE AGE OF SIX I WORKED AND EARNED MY WAY THROUGH COLLEGE GRADUATING FROM DEPARTMENT OF LAW UNIVERSITY OF VIRGINIA AND AM MEMBER OF VIRGINIA BAR. I HAVE SPENT SINCE GRADUATION TWO YEARS IN VAIN SEARCH FOR EMPLOYMENT. MY LITTLE FAMILY AND I NOW STAND AT BRINK OF DISASTER. IS THERE NO PLACE IN THIS LAND FOR SUCH AS I."[113] Freeman was moved by the stories these letters contained and offered what advice and assistance he could, but the number of letters, and the inherent difficulty in offering advice to strangers without knowing all the facts or circumstances, ensured that his responses would be measured. "Hard work, faith, and right living will triumph," he advised one listener. "I have never seen them fail yet and they will not fail you now."[114] His broadcasts also prompted more theological or esoteric queries. One letter alleged he "deliberately [omitted] any references to the Christ," and one opened with the comment: "I gather you feel sex either to be a necessary (though enjoyable on a short range basis) evil or one of man's baser desires."[115] Freeman deftly deflected such letters—he assured the one that he was not "conscious of any" avoidance of Christ, and he told the other the issue was "too complicated for me to answer . . . in as brief a letter as I must make this one"—and concentrated on answering as many questions as he could, in a general manner, over the air.[116] The great majority of letters were positive, though one particularly vicious one stands out. Freeman suggested in one broadcast that eighteen- and nineteen-year-olds should be drafted into military service as opposed to married men with children. "If ever a person's blood boiled," a listener wrote, "mine did when you made that statement . . . I have never yet asked God to curse anyone yet, but in my prayers I shall daily ask God to curse the tongue that made the statement you did this morning."[117] Freeman responded: "That part of the Old Book by which I try to shape my faltering steps bids us to pray for those who despitefully use us. Wherefore, in return for your assurance that you will ask God to curse my tongue, I would like to say that I intend to include you and your son or sons among those for whom I shall pray daily."[118]

People who did not read *R. E. Lee* or subscribe to the *News Leader* came to know Freeman through his broadcasts. Though he often spoke of the job as "a burden," he recognized the opportunity for service it provided.[119] "Everything he learns he applies," Mary Wells Ashworth wrote of him, and radio provided one additional avenue to share his "backlog of information and . . . fund of knowledge."[120]

In looking at the duties, responsibilities, avocations, hobbies, and habits that filled his life—beyond those connected with family commitments, historical writing, and editing the *News Leader*—one can ask only a single question: "How did he do it?" The question "Why did he do it?" is secondary to this first hurdle. How could one man fit all these activities into one twenty-four-hour day—assuming some time for sleep. This thought process is further complicated by the fact that he not only did all these things, but did them well. His editorials were widely acclaimed, his biography won a Pulitzer Prize, his advice was sought by men of influence, his radio show was successful, his efforts on behalf of charity produced support and funds, his speeches moved audiences, his health was good, and he was held in esteem by his superiors and his subordinates. One can shake one's head and conclude he was perfect or a genius, except that he was neither. He was not "a paragon of virtue." He did not suffer fools gladly, and he could be cold and indifferent if he felt his time was being wasted. He disliked "loud-talking women, whistling, and barking dogs."[121] The sound of whistling was a particular bane to his existence. One of Anne Freeman's girlfriends, Frances Valentine, worked at the *News Leader* and often began unconsciously whistling while typing. "I didn't even know I was doing it," she recalled, "until I heard his footsteps."[122] She would stop, but it would be too late. "Owl-face," Freeman would bellow, "stop that blessed noise." Once he heard the annoying sound and waited until the offender was close enough for him to pounce. He clapped his hand on the back of the whistling reprobate and discovered it was the Rev. Theodore Adams of the First Baptist Church. "Good God, Ted," Freeman sputtered, "it's you!"[123]

He expected of others the same that he asked of himself—which often set an unreasonably high standard. Even his staunchest admirers would find little justification in his snapping at the teenage copyboy: "Young man, when I want copy, I want it at 3:30, not 3:29 or 3:31—as it now is."[124] The answer to how he did all he did cannot therefore be answered with a dismissive conclusion of perfection or genius. It was simple will. He said, in effect, "These are the things I will do," then he molded his will and life to achieve these ends. And the supreme exercise of his will was his schedule.

Douglas Freeman's schedule has become the stuff of legend. People unable to name his books will say they heard, somewhere, that he got up at two or three or four o'clock in the morning. Once he achieved national stature, with the awarding of the Pulitzer Prize in 1935, almost every article written about him in subsequent years contains a mention of, or a detailed summary of, "the schedule."[125] The natural assumption, given the tales that have attached themselves to this aspect of his life, is that the schedule is apocryphal. Yet contemporary evidence confirms not only the strict schedule, but also his adherence to it. Mary Tyler McClenahan recalls returning home from late dates and hearing her father arise as she went to bed.[126] His son verifies that his father was out of the house well before he started off to school.[127] In later years, James Douglas and a few teenage friends were having a rollicking evening downstairs, and the time slipped by them. At 3:00 A.M., one boy turned around and saw the distinguished Dr. Freeman—fully dressed and ready to begin his day—standing at the top of the stairs. "Boy," Freeman intoned, "go home!"[128] Reporters tried to beat him in to the office, usually failing in their efforts. Jack Kilpatrick was writing a lengthy story for the *News Leader* on Richmond's transit system and once worked the night through. "I was still at my typewriter and desk at four-thirty or five in the morning when he came in." Kilpatrick recalled Freeman was "startled" to find someone in the office ahead of him.[129] When *Life* magazine assigned two reporters to follow Freeman through his day, they were exhausted by lunch. Inez provided them with two Old Fashioneds to steady them.[130] "The schedule" may have achieved legendary status, but it is far from legend. It is fact.

Freeman had always paid close attention to his time. He outlined his days at Johns Hopkins and, in his early career, had worked such long hours and slept so little that he developed serious health problems. With the advent of marriage and children, he settled into a normal routine of rising slightly before six in the morning.[131] In 1926, he realized that if he was ever to complete *R. E. Lee*, he had to put in at least fourteen hours a week on the work. The waking hour thus crept backward. By 1933, he was routinely at his desk at the *News Leader* by 6:00 A.M. In August 1934, he noted that "on the stroke of four I was out of bed and at four-thirty I was on the job, feeling like a young rooster."[132] Four in the morning became his standard wake-up time, until 1945 when he started his day at 3:55 A.M., "a new early."[133] By 1946, he was arriving at the *News Leader* at 3:50 A.M., meaning he had to wake around 3:15.[134] One year later, the hour was 2:40 A.M., and then, finally, 2:30 A.M. There he stopped the backward movement.[135] That hour remained his rising time until the day he died.

"You and your mother sometimes have laughed," he wrote Mary Tyler, "to reflect that I could tell you on Sunday what I would be doing the following Friday at any given hour, but when I look across the room at the high-piled manuscript of my 'Lee,' I know that I could never have written it had I not husbanded every hour."[136] To husband every hour, Freeman had to master every minute. At the office he developed a method of deftly escorting "loquacious visitors" to the door fifteen minutes after they entered his office. He would rise from his chair during the fifteenth minute of the meeting, extend his hand, and, with a hearty "so good of you to come," walk his visitor to the door.[137] He kept his staff meetings at exactly the same length and practiced "the skillful use of the telephone," though this latter distraction defied easy remedy. "The most difficult part of the telephone call is the goodbye," he mused. "I never have heard anyone describe what seemed to me to be a suave, sure-fire way of getting the conversation ended without running the risk of having the party of the second part recapitulate."[138] He kept down the length of his editorials by typing on short sheets of paper. "When I get to the end of the sheet, I stop."[139] He delighted in saving "at least a thousand minutes" a year by using a ready-knotted bow tie he purchased in New York at Gimbel's, instead of the "four-in-hands" he previously wore.[140] He even worked on making his sleep more efficient; to develop the "ability to stop the flow of thought as if he were turning off a faucet."[141] Freeman averaged between six and seven hours of sleep per night and, by his accounts, he slept almost the entire time. "I am all the seven sleepers of Antioch rolled into one," he wrote a Richmond physician, "and never know what weariness is."[142] The flip side of going to sleep was waking up. Here he was forced to rely on an alarm clock, but he gave considerable thought to "time-keeping in the mind." One morning, he wrote, "I waked myself up while I was counting 'fourteen, sixteen, eighteen.' I switched on the light: the time was eighteen minutes of two. Now, if my mind was 'keeping time' which my foremind 'overheard,' why was the count fourteen-sixteen-eighteen ahead of the hour, instead of thirty-eight, forty, forty-two after the hour? I give up, but I know time seldom runs away if the mind holds a check rein on it."[143] Scraps of time, he said, "may seem so trivial they are not worth saving but the wise use of them may make all the difference between drudgery and happiness, between existence and a career."[144]

Whether he rose at four, three, or two-thirty in the morning, the schedule was set for the subsequent hours. He cooked his own breakfast—usually a poached egg, toast, and coffee—and was at his desk at the *News Leader* within one hour. He sat down at his typewriter and began to write copy. On the wall over his right shoulder was a large clock. Perched on the clock was a sign on which was emblazoned the slogan: "Time alone is irreplacable, waste it not." The word "irreplaceable" was misspelled; unusual for such a precise man. Those who noticed the sign ventured several guesses as to why he did not have the sign replaced. Some say Freeman did not want to pay for a new one, while others said he did not want to hurt the feelings of the man who prepared the placard. Both of these explanations miss the message of both the sign and the man. It would be a waste of time to correct the sign; the message was clear despite the misspelled word.

His schedule had so many changes through the years that it is impossible to present one as the "official" record of any given day. It can be said that he followed four main schedules through the years. From 1915 to 1930, he started his day at 5:00 A.M.; from 1931 to 1945, at 4:00 A.M.; 1945 to 1947, between 2:45 and 4:00 A.M.; and from 1948 until 1953, 2:30 A.M. Sometimes the alarm clock did not sound on time, and sometimes he might "sneak" up a few minutes earlier, but generally he kept to these starting times during the respective years. Sleep, office hours, and historical research and writing accounted for approximately eighteen of the day's twenty-four hours. All the other things he undertook to do would be allotted a specific place in the remaining time.

A capsulation, then, of his "adventure with the clock" is all that can be offered, but while it represents only a snapshot in time, it reflects the spirit that dominated his life.[145]

2:30 A.M.	Awake.
2:30-2:44	Dress, shave, devotional.
2:45	Downstairs to kitchen.
2:45-3:08	Prepare and eat breakfast, walk to car.
3:08-3:25	Drive to *Richmond News Leader* office.
3:25-3:29	Park, walk into building, up to office.
3:30	At desk, Associated Press wires in hand.
3:31-7:58	Read wire dispatches and morning paper, write editorials, mark items for index.
7:58-8:00	Walk to WRNL studio.
8:00-8:15	Broadcast.
8:15-8:17	Walk back to office.
8:17-8:32	Morning staff meeting.
8:32-11:58	Attend to duties of editor. Answer mail, receive visitors, attend meetings, check first edition of paper, block and set editorials. (In later years, Freeman sometimes took a brief nap at 11:00 A.M.)
11:58-12:00	Walk to WRNL studio.
12:00-12:15	Broadcast.
12:15-12:17	Walk back to office.
12:17-12:30	Complete last details of day and prepare for next day. Walk to car.
12:30-12:47	Drive home.
12:48-2:00	Lunch with Inez, work in the garden, walk the grounds. A less structured time.
2:00-2:30	Nap. (Sometimes the nap would last only fifteen minutes.)
2:30-6:30	Work in study on historical projects.
6:30-8:45	Dinner; evening with family.
8:45	Retire for the evening.

This schedule had alterations. His radio program had different times through the years: 8:30 A.M., 1:00 P.M., and 5:45 P.M. During his years at the Columbia School of Journalism, his day at the *News Leader* was lengthened by his having to write two days' worth of editorial. He spent only two hours a day on *R. E. Lee*; it was on his subsequent writings that he increased the time to four hours. Time for speaking engagements or meetings was earned in advance by working longer on writing or rising earlier. These stored hours were noted in his diary as "s.c.o."—"special carry over" hours—or time credits given himself for extra work on his writing. The gasoline rationing of the war years complicated the schedule. Freeman found that he could not operate on the minimum gasoline ration, and the closest streetcar did not pass until almost 7:00 A.M.—far too late in the day.[146] He decided to make a general appeal for help. "Worker leaving Hampton Gardens," the classified ad read, "4:15 weekday mornings, will pay for lift to Fourth Street, or will alternate using car. Call Douglas Freeman, 3-4242."[147] Alfred W. Kenny, a bakery supervisor with a "B" ration card, was one of the few workers up at that hour. He became Freeman's "lift" into town for some time.[148]

Inez did not keep the same schedule, rising at a more typical hour. It was therefore necessary for Freeman to leave little notes if he wanted to communicate with her prior to lunch. "Will the Queen please purchase today," one note began, "at the expense of the undersigned, who hands her $2 herewith: 2 cans of Mansion House Coffee and 3 cans of Old Dutch Cleanser."[149] The notes carried his usual affectionate salutations, such as "For My Matchless!" or "In continuing association of her who always is first in heart and in home!"[150] A request to pick up a repaired Parker pen was accompanied by the promise that "by so doing you have the greater admiration of your adoring spouse—if it is possible for that admiration to exceed what he now cherishes."

"Sometimes I ask myself," he wrote Inez in a more serious letter, "if, after all, I have chosen the wiser alternative in life. Is it better to work, work, work ceaselessly, simply snatching such moments of leisure as I can find, in order to give our children a better financial backing in life and a well-rounded education; or would the life of the family, as considered apart from the life of any individual member of it, be richer if we lived together more in simpler surroundings and with larger leisure."[151] Inez answered the same day.

Your letter today was sad, but it expressed what I have so often thought, and what we have talked about—our separation, and the separation of the children from you. In their association with you they gain a richness and a beautiful understanding of life, along with every educational advantage. There isn't anything that schools can give them that will make up for the loss of their being with you . . . About . . . your devoting your life to so much hard

work—let us talk of that when we are together again, as it is hard
to discuss fully in a letter.[152]

Inez may have been referring to the separation of the family during
the summer, but her tone indicates a broader subject. If the two had a
subsequent conversation on the issue of his work schedule, no details of
it appear in any letters. The couple apparently resolved the issue, for
Freeman's work ethic remained unchanged.

"Most of a man's activity," Freeman told his Sunday School class, "is
between the ages of twenty-five and sixty. Those thirty-five years give
him slightly less than eleven thousand working days. Those eleven thousand working days give to men something less than 750,000 waking
hours. In those we achieve that which is our end as the night draws on
and the balance of the years is reckoned."[153] If his schedule is the answer
to the question "How did he do it?" the reckoning of the years is the
answer to "Why did he do it?" "I repeat to myself over and over again,"
he wrote Inez, "those lines of St. Luke . . . 'for unto whomsoever much
is given, of him shall be much required' . . . I have promised my God and
my conscience that I never shall think that I am entitled to take my ease
because of what I have won but that, on the contrary, I shall exert myself
the more to be faithful of my trust."[154]

It is an unchallengeable fact that Douglas Southall Freeman's faith-
fulness produced many good works. Time was his ally in these accomplishments. Time would also be his judge in the matter of how this
dedicated, intense, and structured lifestyle affected those closest to
him—Inez, Mary Tyler, Anne, and James Douglas. This effect, for better and worse, would be determined only as time passed.

CHAPTER 10

"Glorious and Fascinating Work"

What would he write next? That was the question of 1934.

Did he need to write anything next? The commitment he made on the battlefield in Petersburg had been met. He had spent twenty years of his life writing about Lee while simultaneously editing a major newspaper. Now with a Pulitzer Prize and nationwide acclaim, did he need to write another book?

The question was never seriously considered. Planning for the next book started before *R. E. Lee* was released. That historical writing would remain a part of Freeman's life after *Lee* was never in doubt. The real dilemma was the topic. With what could he follow a four-volume, one-million-word, tour de force?

Several subjects presented themselves. Maxwell Perkins wrote in 1932 that Scribner's "educational department thinks that a short life of Lee by you, somewhat designed for younger readers, a book of about 90,000 words, would do extremely well."[1] Freeman let the idea drop without comment. When the subject came up again in 1934, he advised that he had decided "to write another book" before he considered "a short *Lee*."[2] His new book idea was a curious choice: He and Inez would write "a combined history and guide book of Virginia."[3] The book would give a sketch of Virginia history and describe historic sites with quotations from early travelers. "I think the idea is fundamentally a good one," he wrote Mary Tyler, "to carry the modern tourist along a present-day road and to describe to him what he is to see, but, at the same time when describing an old house, or an old ferry or what not, to use the language of someone who traveled that same road and saw the same sights back, perhaps, in 1750."[4] He believed the book could be done by the fall of 1935.[5] If Max Perkins made any comment about this idea, it has been lost to history. The subject also disappears from Freeman's correspondence as he spent most of 1934 reading and correcting galleys for *Lee*.

229

No notes or drafts of the travel book are in his papers, so it appears the idea simply faded away.

What Max Perkins, and many others, had in mind was a biography of George Washington on the same scale as *Lee*. Stephen Vincent Benet suggested this idea in his review, but it was a choice of subjects obvious to many. The Father of His Country had not been well served by biographers. Chief Justice John Marshall and Washington Irving had each turned out five-volume works that confirmed Washington's heroic stature and established him as an icon, but did little else. The best-known stories about Washington were the fables memorialized by Parson Mason Locke Weems. Washington needed a professionally written, meticulously researched, readable biography, and many viewed Freeman as the one man who could provide it.

The project was appealing as well for other reasons. Washington was Lee's hero, he was a Virginian, and his military campaigns had never been subjected to expert analysis. Freeman admitted he was pondering the idea. "A 'Washington' is much needed," he wrote Allen, but would it not be "foolish to throw away what little acquaintance I have with the war between the states and start in a field concerning which I have little technical knowledge?"[6] On the other hand, he mused, once he began to handle the material, "it does not matter greatly what period of American history" is being treated.

Two days after writing Allen, he wrote Max Perkins about the subject. "A great many" of his friends, he wrote, had taken up Benet's suggestion. Was Perkins "sufficiently familiar with the Washington literature" to know whether such a book was needed?[7] The idea was growing on him. "Last night," he concluded his letter, "I had a thought that perhaps before my race was run, I might write a 'Washington' and a 'Wilson' and would then have paid tribute to my three greatest Virginian heroes."[8] Perkins "vastly" preferred Washington. "As for Wilson," he wrote, "that has to be done sometime by someone . . . a long way off, and I suppose would have to be as the material may become available gradually."[9] Freeman was not so easily moved off the subject. He wrote Wilson's secretary of war, Newton Baker, and asked if he thought "the time has come when a biography of Mr. Wilson can be written in anything approaching final form."[10] He mentioned that he was considering Washington and a new entry in the field—Thomas Jefferson. Baker discouraged the idea of writing about Wilson. It was too early, and more information would be forthcoming through the years on what Freeman termed "unexplained and perhaps inexplicable incidents" of the administration.[11] Freeman accepted Baker's judgment as "final." It came down to Washington and Jefferson. "I must confess," he told Baker, "my inclination is for the gentleman at Monticello." He would have already started researching Jefferson, but thought Dumas Malone was working on the subject. His next letter went to Malone. After explaining his process of eliminating other topics, he warmed to his subject. "Of the two," he wrote, "I would much rather do a 'Jefferson' though I believe a 'Washington' is equally needed. I know, however, that you have done much work on Jefferson . . . consequently, if you intend to take up the 'Jefferson,' I shall leave it alone, but if you have abandoned the book, would you kindly tell me so."[12] One can only imagine the shock Malone felt upon receiving this letter. A former professor at the University of Virginia, Malone was serving as editor of the *Dictionary of American Biography*. He had been collecting material on Jefferson and had some notes, but was in no way close to producing a major biography.[13] Suddenly a Pulitzer Prize-winning biographer, with a publisher at the ready, was indicating his desire to write the biography of Jefferson. Malone admitted that his job as editor had prevented him from giving any attention to the book.[14] "It has been my expectation," he quickly added, "to resume this task when opportunity is afforded." His plans would be more definite in a year. "I cannot help hoping, therefore, that you will tackle Washington instead of Jefferson," Malone somewhat plaintively concluded. "I have no right to ask any sacrifice, but I do appreciate the opportunity of explaining my own situation."[15]

The idea of Freeman writing about Jefferson is an intriguing one, for the two men were in many ways similar. Both were intellectuals with wide-ranging interests. Both combined a limited view of government with a liberal philosophy that sought to elevate mankind. Both loved Virginia, but were not parochial in their vision or attitudes. Both delighted in tilling the soil, in rising early, and keeping rigorous schedules. "He never sat in idleness an hour," Freeman commented admiringly, and "the sun never caught him in bed."[16] He had found Robert E. Lee to be a simple man with no mysteries about him; it would have been interesting to see what he would have concluded about the complex Jefferson.

It was not to be. "Your letter," he wrote Malone, "will be conclusive with me." He would not enter a field of study staked off by another historian. He confided his tentative decision to Max Perkins. "It looks as if the next travail will be over a 'Washington.'"[17]

With his subject apparently selected, Freeman still hesitated. Part of his reluctance could have come from the knowledge of the cost—monetary, physical, and emotional—of undertaking such a task. He hinted as much in an address to the "Friends of the Princeton Library" given during the time he was considering writing about Washington. "The preparation of a full-length biography of any of the great men of America," he said, "involves the close examination of at least 100,000 folios of manuscript, scattered as widely as the wind blows, and the detailed study of a minimum of one thousand printed books."[18] He had given all his leisure moments for twenty years and thousands of dollars to write *R. E. Lee*, he told the group, and remained convinced that "the writing of a biography and indeed of all larger historical work must keep the character of a pastime, and of an expensive one at that."[19] To write "the much needed life of Jefferson or the long-awaited Washington," he concluded, "would take the uninterrupted labor of five years and the direct outlay of at least $5,000 clerical help."

"I have not made a decision yet concerning the 'Washington,'" he wrote Max Perkins in March 1935, "and have some vague misgivings on the subject, for reasons that I am hardly able to analyze."[20] Freeman had never before been indecisive about writing a book. He had seized the opportunities to write the *Confederate Calendar*, *Lee's Dispatches*, *R. E. Lee*, even the report of the state tax commission. Now he hesitated. He became so uncharacteristically withdrawn and moody that his family thought he was ill. In the midst of pondering his "vague misgivings" about Washington, he wrote a series of lectures to be delivered at Dartmouth College. The three lectures, titled "Adventures in Biography," addressed the principles of the "art of Biography," the problems of suppression or misrepresentation of facts, and the notion of "psychography."[21] The lectures represent Freeman's most extensive commentary on writing biography, but he says little beyond what had guided him to that date: fidelity to facts, measured interpretation, and economy of expression. In the third lecture he laid out his argument against psychography and pointed his listeners to "the true conception of biography": the "faithful portrait of a soul in its adventures through life."[22] The journey for the biographer, he said, was no less gratifying.

We have seen inscriptional biography develop into the portrayal of folk and of national heroes; we have seen it take a new form under the cunning styles of great Greek and Roman authors; we have listened as a dark-haired Jew read in a whisper to huddled slaves from the brown manuscript he had brought to the catacombs under his toga; we have passed a long, black watch; we have seen old lands rediscovered by new mariners who had a different faith and a kindlier sympathy, until now the farther shoals have been charted and the wider depths have been sounded. Shall we not, as we go ashore, have a word for the adventurers, a part of whose voyage we have shared? And whose words can we quote more aptly than those of our faithful Sainte-Beuve found in Leopardi? . . . [His] glorious words are, I think, appropriate to all those who have lived in the company of a great man or have caught his spirit in translation. "Oh," said he, "what a beautiful destiny to be unable to die—except with an immortal."[23]

This excerpt from the Dartmouth lectures comes much closer to describing Freeman's heart for biography than does his Princeton address with its cold figures and gloomy outlook. It also provides a clue as to his state of mind during these days of indecision about what to write next. He had "lived in the company of a great man," and he was finding it difficult to extract himself from the era of Lee. He began to gather materials on Washington, though with none of the aggressive vigor that marked his earlier research.[24] Inez had been observing her husband's lethargy, surliness, and general discontent, and, at length, offered her diagnosis. "You have kept General Lee's company daily for thirty years," she said, "and you miss that peerless companionship."[25] Her insight was right on target. Freeman admitted that "it was not easy to leave the struggle" and began to realize that his next work lay again in the shadow of Lee.[26] Sometime in late May or early June 1936, he met with Whitney Darrow of Scribner's and outlined his new plan. He would write a multiple biography of the generals who fought with Lee; a series of sketches—not only of the well-known Jackson, Longstreet, and Stuart, but of "each officer of promise" or those with "unusually picturesque careers."[27] His lethargy disappeared, as Inez had forecast, and the pace immediately picked up. Max Perkins wrote on June 11 that Scribner's was "extremely enthusiastic" about the idea, and Freeman advised him that he planned to start writing on June 24.[28] He couldn't wait that long. On Sunday, June 14, on a train between New York and Meriden, Connecticut, he outlined the scope of *Lee's Lieutenants*.[29]

He faced two initial procedural matters in preparing the book: which officers to include and how best to present their stories. "To dwell too much on the well-known corps commanders would be to thrash over old straw," he wrote Perkins, "to give an encyclopaedic account of all general officers would be to include too much chaff."[30] He thus established a threshold criterion of "historical importance and personal interest." This process would allow him to write something "about all the divisional commanders" but to vary the length of each portrait.[31] The problem of "treatment" was more difficult. The traditional style of multiple biography was to present a series of separate articles. Gamaliel Bradford, an earlier biographer of Lee, had followed this method in *Confederate Portraits*, but his subjects, in most instances, had different roles in the war. That was not the case here. "It sometimes would be necessary," Freeman wrote, "to write of as many as a dozen soldiers who had a conspicuous part in the same battle. If in separate studies of these men, a reader was confronted with essentially the same details of, say Sharpsburg, he would damn the battle, the soldiers, the method and the writer."[32] He was "determined not to follow [that] deadly traditional style." He began to look for "a thread that would hold the story together."[33] He decided to present the campaigns of the army "as a continuing contest, so to speak, between rising and falling men . . . in short, the story will be one of training and of casualty."

> Take John B. Gordon, for instance. I shall introduce him as one of the young lawyer-colonels who commanded so many of the regiments during the early months of the war. My first mention of him will be . . . at Seven Pines. At the end of that passage, I shall put a foot-note reference to the page where . . . I show him leading a brigade at Malvern Hill . . . another footnote will anticipate . . . Sharpsburg . . . I shall bring Gordon in, again and again, till, at last, he appears, after Lee himself, the finest figure at Appomattox. The narration will tell its tale of trial and failure, of promotion and transfer, of advancement and death—I hope in a manner to keep the reader's interest, for the story is Homeric in its tragedy—but will be so constructed that, if you want a sketch of Gordon, you can run from chapter to chapter and . . . get a picture of his emergence.[34]

The method was taking form, but it still required slight adjustments. Freeman had decided to begin the narrative at the moment Lee assumed command of the Army of Northern Virginia on June 1, 1862. He quickly judged this to be an unsatisfactory starting point. The army Lee inherited had been in existence for more than a year and had been shaped by the decisions and actions of others. That story had to be told as well. "This carried me back to April, 1861," he wrote and made necessary the inclusion of Joseph E. Johnston and P. G. T. Beauregard—who were not lieutenants of Lee. This not only lengthened the book and "brought to light a great deal of material that never had been analyzed," it also extended the time frame beyond the expected publication date of Fall 1939.[35]

He also refined his idea about treatment. He had framed the method as "a continuing contest . . . between rising and falling men." This came close, but was not quite the analysis he wanted to employ. "At length," he wrote, "I remembered a letter General Lee had written John B. Hood." The letter of May 21, 1863, contained Lee's statement that "our Army . . . will go anywhere and do anything if properly led. But there is the difficulty—proper commanders—where can they be obtained?"[36] Freeman seized on that quote and determined "that the connecting thread of this book would be just that—the struggle to create and maintain competent command." This was akin to the "rising and falling men," but the focus was not directed at the individual generals, but to the command structure of the Army and the soldiers "marching and fighting under such leaders."[37] Reinvigorated and enthusiastic, he was soon back in his beloved Confederate documents and again in the "peerless companionship" of Lee and his lieutenants.

And he was back to having two jobs. He was completing his twentieth year as editor of the *News Leader* and, before he won the Pulitzer, his reputation in that profession exceeded that as a historian. His counterpart at the *Richmond Times-Dispatch*, Virginius Dabney—a future Pulitzer Prize-winner in Journalism—wrote in his book, *Liberalism in the South*, published in 1932, that Freeman was an "inveterate foe of meddlesome clerics and demagogic psuedo-statesmen."[38] Few editors in the South, Dabney wrote, "are so consistent in their championship of the Negro, or belabor the patrioteers and the industrial Bourbons with greater regularity."[39] While Dabney saw a liberal course, Freeman tried to avoid extremes on both the editorial page and the front page. He found the "temptation" to "run to extremes" one of the most dangerous traits of newspapermen.[40] He preferred papers that "walked humbly and diligently in the middle of the road" to those that ran "to extremes of restlessness or inactivity, to be fussy or indolent, to scold or to connive, to do too much or too little."[41] He stressed this theory in January 1935 at the ceremony opening a model newsroom at the Columbia School of Journalism. Communication was transforming and revolutionizing civilization, he observed, and newspapers were the most vital link in that system. "It is impossible to exaggerate the utility and the history-making power of the modern newspaper," he said, echoing a theme from his first speech as editor of the *News Leader*.[42] It was therefore incumbent on modern papers, and their editors, to present carefully selected news, "intelligently prepared and wisely interpreted."[43]

"Good morning, Christian warriors," he typically greeted the reporters in the city room, "what the *News Leader* needs is more news and less bull!"[44] He meant it. "To see him edit copy was an education," Jack Kilpatrick wrote, "for he went after awkward sentences as if he were polishing scratches out of a favorite piece of furniture."[45] One reporter handed in a story in which he referred to the "1940 census," thus violating one of Freeman's most sacrosanct rules. "Young man," he said, "you are using a noun as an adjective. That is sloppy writing."[46] The words "hosted," "contracted," and "finalize" did not exist in his vocabulary. He equated the use of the word "however" with "a limp handshake."[47] Reporters gave up the use of the word "claim" due to Freeman's position that "if you mean 'maintain' or 'assert' why not say so?"[48] Freeman was chagrined to spot a headline where "one line ended in 'at' and another line ended in 'to.'" He directed the city editor "that in cases where such heads were written he must not stop to loiter or to tarry, but must forthwith change the heads."[49] Style ran a close second to proper word choice. "Don't gush and don't twitter," he told an associate. "Play it straight." Jack Kilpatrick submitted an article about Robert E. Lee's home on East Franklin Street in Richmond. He began "with a lyric sentence" and finished with a slang expression. "Mr. Kilpatrick," Freeman wrote across the top of the page, "If you start purple, stay purple."[50] Once—only once—did an exasperated associate argue a point. "Doctor," he pleaded over the use of a word, "I looked it up in the dictionary, and it's all right there."

"Son," Freeman calmly responded, "sometimes the dictionary is wrong."[51]

He taught by both direct and indirect methods. John Leard was a young Columbia graduate who joined the *News Leader* in 1940. He assisted Freeman in writing the "Week's End" column that appeared in Saturday's paper. He would hand in his copy on Friday morning and invariably would hear "Miss Crump, ask Mr. *Lee-ard* to step in here." Leard would enter the editor's office and be asked one question about a specific point in his article. He would answer and be excused. A short time later he would hear "Miss Crump, ask Mr. *Lee-ard* to step in here." Again, one question. Leard might be summoned ten times on one article. This

Freeman at his desk at the Richmond News Leader. (Image courtesy of the *Richmond Times-Dispatch*.)

went on week after week until it dawned on Leard that he was being taught the fine art of writing. "He was trying to make me reduce the number of visits to his office," Leard remembered. "If I had to keep getting up and answering a single question, I would sooner or later learn."[52] The young reporter soon reduced his trips to one or two per weekly column. He worked his way through the ranks as copy editor, city editor, and managing editor, before becoming the first executive editor of both the *News Leader* and the *Times-Dispatch*. He gave much credit to his first editor. "He went out of his way to teach me the profession."[53]

Freeman's rules were sometimes reiterated during morning staff meetings, but generally the precisely fifteen-minute meeting was devoted to what reporters dubbed "tidbits." Jack Kilpatrick was one of the reporters who attended these meetings.

We had what the reporters called the great pow-wow with the great sachem . . . and the idea was that every reporter would bring Dr. Freeman a little tidbit off his beat so that the Doc could keep up on what was going on in the city and state, and be well informed. It was always a constant struggle to find some tidbit that we could bring up to Dr. Freeman, something off our beats that had not been in the paper . . . or some little inside story. He greatly relished this and there was a good deal of banter back and forth.[54]

The struggle for interesting topics became so acute that one reporter exclaimed "He stole my tidbit" in the middle of another's report.[55] Kilpatrick realized one morning that he had no tidbit, so he proceeded to talk about Confederate general J. E. B. Stuart's famous ride around McClellan. More experienced staffers saw that Kilpatrick was heading onto dangerous ground, but silently marveled at the sight of a young reporter telling Freeman about the Civil War. Finally, mercifully, Freeman raised his hand and ended the soliloquy. "My dear boy," he intoned, "in some quarters I am considered a modest authority on such issues." "I wanted to go through the floor," Kilpatrick remembered.[56] Freeman serenely presided over the conferences, "his hands clasped comfortably over his broad belly," and, in later years, sporting a mandarin skullcap.[57] After listening to all the reports, he would close with "well, gentlemen, that's all I know today."[58]

At his desk, Freeman typed his own editorials "on an old Royal [typewriter] with an elite type face, and he edited copy in a clear but minute nine-point longhand."[59] He did not dictate editorials. "If you dictate them," he said, "they become speeches." His editorial style was restrained and cautious, not fire-breathing. "My dear boy," he told Kilpatrick, "I believe you will discover as you grow older that you will be more persuasive with the soft line than with the hard line, and if you will just suggest that if they had been better informed or had more time to devote to the topic, they would not have taken this course of action."[60]

He continued to make every effort to position his reporters to do their best work. "I know you are always looking out for us," he wrote the commonwealth's attorney of Richmond, "and will never let us be scooped if you can prevent it."[61] He made certain his reporters were being as diligent. In 1933 he established a rule requiring reporters to submit "daily statements of what they covered." Freeman believed this kept up the "daily drive" of the reporter. "The newspaper bible," he wrote, "has no verse that bids the faithful to take their ease in Zion."[62] When the Depression hit, Freeman and Bryan made every effort to hold jobs for all the *News Leader* staff and to keep salaries in place. As finances tightened, they reduced the general overhead and eliminated many feature columns. It was not until May 1932 that a salary cut had to be implemented. The cut was 10 percent on salaries greater than forty dollars per week and graduated cuts up to 5 percent on salaries less than forty dollars per week.[63] This reduction was followed by another in March 1933—another 10 percent on upper salaries and 5 percent on medium—and more drastic cuts in features. Though these represented sizable cuts during hard times, the *News Leader* avoided layoffs, and by October 1934 Freeman was advocating the "restoration of some at least of the pay cuts."[64]

The deliberative, cautious, and solid leadership of Freeman and the "Big Boss" John Stewart Bryan was entering its third decade. The two men were not only business associates but also close friends. In public, and in their private letters, they addressed one another in formal terms—"Dr. Freeman" and "Mr. Bryan"—but amused bystanders by sometimes lapsing into lengthy conversations in Latin.[65] Their camaraderie was the source of some tweaking. A *News Leader* pamphlet featured a picture of Bryan, his son and future publisher Tennant Bryan, and Freeman. Parker Rouse, an irreverent reporter for the *Times-Dispatch*, scrawled "Father" under John Stewart Bryan, "Son" under Tennant, and "Holy Ghost" under Freeman.[66] Bryan was to Freeman "a man who was what all of us would like to be in service to Virginia and to the nation," but in 1935, the long and successful partnership almost came to an end.[67] On January 3, 1935, Bryan confided that he was considering the publication of a Sunday paper. Freeman was certain such an act would provoke reprisals, perhaps even bringing the *Times-Dispatch* into the afternoon field. "I was raised in a competitive field of journalism," he confided in a memorandum to himself, "and I have no dread of returning to such a field,"[68] but what concerned him was the financial impact such a move would have on the paper. "The greater part of my children's inheritance is in *News Leader* stock . . . [and] I doubt very much if when a Sunday *News Leader* were established [Bryan] would be willing to divorce himself from William & Mary and return to direct in person this new venture. In all probability the direction of the daily strategy . . . would be in my hands."[69] Lacking enthusiasm for the plan, he did not feel he could "take such a risk for my own children or for the children of the other stockholders." He weighed the options and outlined a course of action. He would "fight the idea with every argument" he could muster, but, if Bryan proceeded, he would stay long enough to start the new edition and then "offer my stock for sale and . . . resign as editor."[70] He put the memo in an envelope and filed it away. It remained unopened among Freeman's files as Bryan scrapped the Sunday paper idea.[71]

Another potential break occurred in 1940. On June 20, Eugene Meyer, publisher of the *Washington Post*, paid a visit to Westbourne and broached the subject of Freeman becoming that paper's editor.[72] Freeman did not reject the offer outright and, three weeks later, Meyer came again. "I do not think he can get anywhere with me," Freeman wrote Inez, "but I shall have to hear him through."[73] The two men spent six hours in conference—an incredible amount of time given Freeman's schedule. "We covered much ground today," he reported to Inez, "but did not get down to final terms. I still do not think it will attract me, but the seriousness of his attitude leads me to fear he is going to make an elaborate proposition."[74] Inez's sole comment was that it was "nice to have these things come along, even if they aren't accepted."[75] The talks continued through the month, with Meyer making his third trip to Westbourne on July 31. "I like him," Freeman confided to his diary, "but I can't bring myself even seriously to consider his generous offer."[76] He ended Meyer's hopes on August 6, 1940. "Much as I admire you," he wrote, "much as I appreciate the opportunity you would open to me, I cannot come. The reasons are numerous, but as they concern my way of living, my writing of books, my contacts and the sweetest associations of life, they are essentially so personal that they ought not to be written down even for your friendly eyes."[77] In short, his life was established, forever, in Richmond.

In addition to managing his own newspaper, Freeman kept a close eye on the *Times-Dispatch*. The morning paper merited a set of its own cards in his index on which were recorded the slightest mistakes.

"On Monday, June 30, missed the story of suicide . . ."

"Used fake picture, probably of USS Trenton . . ."

"Reported death of 'father' of Mrs. Trinkle, when dead man was her uncle."

"Pulled a boner May 24 in saying that no Confederate parade in Washington had been held."

"Printed picture of Dr. S. C. Mitchell for Dr. S. A. Mitchell."[78]

The cards are sprinkled with expressions such as "nasty attacks," "lame explanation," and "backtracked editorially." Freeman even noted that on August 8, 1927, the *Times-Dispatch* "changed to 7 point ionic no. 5 body type."[79] Competition between the two papers was fierce and once exploded into a $500,000 lawsuit filed by John Stewart Bryan against the *Times-Dispatch* over a story about his purchase of three other newspapers.[80] There may have been no love lost between the papers, but in 1939 merger talks began. Freeman was part of the negotiating team along with John Stewart and Tennant Bryan. On May 18, 1940, the three signed off on what Freeman dubbed a "historic" merger creating Richmond Newspapers, Inc. He noted in his diary that the merger represented "the fulfillment of thirteen years persuasion on my part to correct an absurd situation."[81] Publicly, he was more sardonic. At the announcement of the merger, he turned to managing editor Charles Hamilton and growled: "The day of the *News Leader* is over."[82]

On May 24, 1938, Freeman delivered the commencement address at Charleston College in South Carolina. Traveling with him was twenty-one-year-old Mary Tyler and Howard Carter, a member of the household staff and chauffeur. On the second day of the return trip, the trio set out at 6:00 A.M. in a drenching rain. Six miles north of Fayetteville, North Carolina, their car went around a curve on Dunn Highway, and a Chevrolet truck, two feet in their lane, plowed into the front of the vehicle.[83] Carter was pinned beneath the steering wheel with numerous injuries, Mary Tyler suffered a broken leg, and Freeman had a four-inch gash to the skull on the top of his head, a cut on his left jaw, and a broken little finger on the left hand. All three were dazed and semi-conscious.[84] Freeman vaguely recalled speaking to Carter, but he had no clear recollection of anything that happened following the impact.[85]

When Freeman began to comprehend clearly, he was in R. L. Pittman Hospital in Fayetteville. Unaware that he had been given a dose of morphine, he immediately began to tend to Mary Tyler and summon his friend and doctor, O. O. Ashworth, from Richmond. At some point during this trying time, doctors advised Freeman that Howard Carter had died five minutes after arriving at the hospital.[86] Dazed, stunned, and now saddened by the death of "my faithful Howard," he finally allowed himself to be treated. He and Mary Tyler passed a quiet night.

Dr. Ashworth arrived and took charge of the case. He reported to Freeman that all was well. Mary Tyler had a brief scare when an embolism developed in her right lung, but the worst passed over the weekend. Inez arrived, as did John Stewart Bryan and "kind friends by scores," and Freeman was ready to leave for Richmond by Friday June 4, eight days after the accident.[87]

His first concern, after Mary Tyler's recovery, was for Howard Carter's widow and family. "He had been with us for thirteen years," he wrote Allen, "and was distinctly a member of the household. I grieve for him daily."[88] He was determined to "get something" in settlement for the family. He advised his insurance company that he "had no intention of suing for personal damages" but that "what I most desire in this matter was something for Howard's widow."[89] Freeman ultimately received $3,500, all of which he paid to Mrs. Carter in the form of weekly checks.[90] All that was left to close the book on this tragic incident was to find something noble from what the family had suffered. "Since you came to adolescence," he wrote Mary Tyler, "you have had no test comparable to this . . . now you realize that you have the inestimable blessing of character, courage and fortitude, which will sustain you through life. It's an odd experience, is it not, to be introduced to our real selves when we are in the 'Valley of the Shadow'? . . . *Ex malo bonum* . . . You have lost part of a summer—and have enriched the remainder of your life."[91]

In the same letter to Mary Tyler, he expressed some thoughts about Inez. "God alone knows how I reverence her," he wrote. "After twenty-four years, she charms me even more than she did as a girl of 22, before we were married. When it comes to her influence on me—her inspiring, noble influence—it never was so great as now. Daily, yes hourly, I thank God for such a wife."[92] The passion that was sparked in "Uncle Jeems's" mission thirty summers previous remained unabated through the years. Though Victorian in his attitudes and in public displays of affection, Freeman poured his thoughts into letters to Inez throughout their married life. Whenever they were separated, he wrote her daily. "As the years go on," he wrote during one summer vacation, "love takes on new meaning. Each separation somehow arouses reflection on the beauty and the holiness of love between a man and a woman who have fused all their interests, all their hopes, all their ideals in a perfect understanding."[93] He understood the indispensable role she played in his success. "People sometimes ask me how I continue to keep my nerves intact in the midst of the life I lead. I put off some of them with evasions and some with pleasantries, and to none do I confess the whole sweet truth, which is you."[94] Her contribution was both practical and spiritual. "You circumscribe your worries," he wrote, "even when you indulge them, and you see to it that order and quiet reign in the house."[95] She also provided "that beautiful companionship of spirit that has made our married life perfect."[96] "I do not believe I could live without the holy inspiration of her presence," Freeman confided to his diary, "and I know I should not want to live without her. When she dies, may God call me!"[97]

Inez's letters to her husband are less revealing, though no less a testament to their love. She too emphasized their spiritual connection that made their separations endurable. "Wherever you are, my darling man," she wrote in August, 1933, "I am right with you in spirit—and can you not feel the answering throbs to your heartbeats? You are dearer and sweeter every day and my soul is rich because of your priceless love."[98] She was a full partner in the ambitious plan of his life and appreciated his efforts. "I think you are the finest, best and smartest man that was ever born. I rejoice continuously over your achievements and am proud of you every hour in the twenty-four."[99] Her devotion to him was as complete as his was to her, but one senses that she did not always gladly bear his intense devotion to work. One catches a glimpse of this sentiment in some poems she wrote during the twenties.

When I am with you there's so much to say
   Of all I've thought and felt and longed to tell.
But little flying minutes race away,
   And I've been saying that the car runs well.
Yet even these small words are ecstasies—
   The cosmic thoughts may well remain untold,
For on the brink of immortalities
   I'll pluck a pansy and a marigold![100]

One poem, titled "Reality," conveyed a darker mood.

Once in a year or so
   We meet each other's eyes
Over teacups full
   Of platitudes and lies.
But when the tide creeps silver
   Along the shore of dreams,
A thousand times more real
   To me your shadow seems![101]

Whatever misgivings she may have harbored, the numerous letters between the two give ample evidence of a strong marriage based on deep love and abiding respect. There is no hint among thousands of letters or in the recollections of family and friends of any marital problems. Inez manifested her devotion by making certain the house was efficiently managed, handling the discipline of the children ("She wasn't very good at it," James Douglas remembers), and carrying a load of civic obligations similar to Freeman's. She served as president of the Association for the Preservation of Virginia Antiquities, the Virginia Home for

Incurables, the Woman's Club, and the James River Garden Club. "In her appearance, in her voice, and in her calm manner and dignity," a fellow club member wrote, "one felt that she was always in command of whatever she was doing."[102] The word "poise" is the most frequently used word to describe Inez Freeman. "Tall, poised, and gracious," *Time* magazine reported, "[she] feels that her big job is to 'keep the house quiet for him.'"[103] The reserve of a Southern gentlewoman precluded any public comments regarding her relationship with her husband. "It's a great privilege," she told *Time*, "to be associated with him."[104]

Another trip to a college resulted in unforeseen consequences, though not as tragic as those following the Charleston College appearance. In November 1938, Freeman was invited to deliver the inaugural Dancy lectures at the Alabama State College for Women.[105] The program called for three lectures to be delivered over two days at the school's campus in Montevallo, Alabama. Freeman accepted the invitation and, to this point, the affair was little different from the hundreds of other speaking engagements scheduled through the years. A snag then developed. Professor A. W. Vaughan advised that the committee appreciated Freeman's "cooperative spirit" in agreeing to publish the lectures and that they would be making the appropriate "arrangements" with Scribner's.[106] On the heels of this letter came one from Max Perkins. "We understand from [Vaughan] that your decision about publishing the lectures . . . has been favorable." Perkins laid out the terms for a small book of 30,000 words.[107]

Freeman was befuddled by this turn of events. "If I had understood at the time that the lectures were to appear in book form," he wrote Perkins, "I would not have agreed to accept the invitation to deliver them."[108] It is unclear from his files if the matter of publication had been brought up with him prior to his acceptance.[109] Given his usual thoroughness in matters of time and business, it would be highly unusual for Freeman to miss such a detail. Now that he was caught in some agreement, he saw no polite way out. "Inasmuch as the Alabama people seem intent on publishing the lectures," he fumed, "I shall of course have to devote to them considerable research—much more than otherwise I would have put on them."[110] A week did not improve his mood. "Confound them," he spat out in writing to Perkins about the lectures.[111]

Freeman's annoyance over being forced to write another book stemmed from this excitement over the progress of *Lee's Lieutenants*.

"The material expands," he wrote, "as the study progresses." He had "uncovered all the unused maps" of Stonewall Jackson, "two collections of his papers and tens of thousands of folios of his Topographical Engineer." On top of that discovery, the heirs of Gen. Dorsey Pender had given him "two hundred fascinating wartime letters."[112] He resented every interruption that took him from his work. "To my grief of spirit," he wrote in his diary on March 11, "I had to give the afternoon to writing the Introduction to a biography of Carter Glass."[113] Now he would have to give up much more time than a single afternoon. "Confound them."

The lectures were scheduled for April 27 and 28, a little less than three months away. Freeman decided he would "make [them] a study of the manner in which, having lost the war, the Southerners won the peace by their portrayal of history."[114] He titled the lectures: "The South to Posterity: A Review of Southern Historical Literature and Memoirs since 1865." He started writing on Saturday, April 1, and finished the first lecture on April 12. The second lecture was complete by April 17, and he then "put my tummy against the typewriter all day" and wrapped up the series on April 23.[115]

The lecture may have been routine for Freeman, but it was a major event for the college town of Montevallo. The program of the lecture appeared on the front page of the *Montevallo Times*, and Freeman's time was filled from the moment he arrived in town.[116] The night of the first lecture, he was the guest of honor at a dinner given by the college's president. "The occasion," the *Times* reported, "afforded a never-to-be-forgotten opportunity for the visitors to enjoy the superb personality of Dr. Freeman who is at his best when he talks, laughs, jokes, and philosophizes in the mien of freedom and informality of conversational groups."[117] It was, the article concluded, "one of the richest hours of life." The *Times* editorial page quoted one lecture attendee as saying the exchanges of ideas were "elevated in worship at the feet of the great Dr. Freeman."[118]

In the opening lecture, "Writing in the Ashes," he declared that the "appeal of the South to posterity has not been futile" in that time had created an appreciation for and "tolerance of" Southern history. The struggle had produced "a number of men whose personality appealed to historical imagination," and public acceptance of them allowed Southern literature on the war to be "persuasive without intending to be so."[119] He cited the sale of more than a million copies of Margaret Mitchell's *Gone with the Wind* as proof of the inclination of non-Southerners to read pro-Southern literature. His second lecture, "The

Appeal to the Records," dealt with *The War of the Rebellion: A Compilation of the Official Records of the Union and Confederate Armies,* and his third, "Apotheosis and Realism," with dispelling illusions about the romanticism of war.[120] Freeman noted that he lectured "to a full house, about 1200" and left Alabama the morning after the final lecture.[121]

Back in Richmond, he happily resumed his work on *Lee's Lieutenants.* He spent May and June writing about Jackson's Valley campaign. "It is interesting to write," he noted, "however dull it may be in the reading."[122] On July 9, he began his research into the Seven Days Battle around Richmond.[123] A gentle reminder from Max Perkins about the small book intruded on his bliss. "I have been stalling on the Dancy lectures," Freeman confessed, "but assume I might as well get them behind me." In an uncharacteristic tone of self-pity, he asked if he understood correctly "that we ought to have about 30,000 words of text? That will mean considerable extension of the lectures as they stand, but I have the material. Of course I will erase all references to lecture form."[124] Receiving no reprieve from Perkins, he counted the words of his lectures—finding some relief in the fact that they amounted to 26,000 words—and titled the book *The South to Posterity: An Introduction to Confederate Historiography.*[125] He started writing July 18.

Exactly one month was given to writing and revising *The South to Posterity.* Though committed to the project, Freeman still seemed troubled by its genesis and summarized his complaints in a letter to Charles Scribner. "To make it effective as a series of lectures I had to pitch it rather low . . . when the time came to revise the lectures so that they would escape the stigma of lectures, I had, in effect, to write the whole book."[126] On August 6, "at 6:03," he finished the first draft of the book. "It is readable now," he wrote, "and, I think, will have some sale, but I shall not regard it as a major work." On August 18, "at 4:50," he put the book in the mail bound for Scribner's.[127]

"Here is *The South to Posterity,*" he wrote Max Perkins, "the short unofficial title of which will be 'Audrey' because it is 'a poor thing but mine own.'" He gave Perkins carte blanche in editing. "Do not take the time or trouble to write me about any changes in style or form that seem necessary or desirable," he wrote. Any corrections could be made without "a by-your-leave or even a memorandum of the change."[128] He registered one more complaint about the entire episode—"I kick myself for ever agreeing to publish"—but it was not so much the misunderstanding about the contract or the difficulty in transposing lectures to book form that so disturbed him. It was that it "took more *time* from *Lee's Lieutenants* than I cared to give."[129]

Freeman may have not regarded *The South to Posterity* as a "major work," but it is nonetheless a highly readable book review of the literature of the Confederacy. From the diaries of private soldiers and the memoirs of Confederate chieftains to the publications of the Southern Historical Society and the memorialization of the "lost cause," he recorded not only the works of the post-war years, but evaluated each important book. The abilities of authors were critically examined, regardless of their heroics in other fields. He judged Jefferson Davis's *Rise and Fall of the Confederate Government* to be "not particularly readable" and remarked "perhaps it was well that General Lee did not write his memorial of his Army." Freeman found that his hero "had no aptitude" for "sustained historical narrative."[130] He outlined the beginning of the Southern Historical Society Papers, touched on the controversies between Jubal Early and James Longstreet, and described what books were left to be written. In the final chapter, Freeman summarized "the case the South has presented to the judgment of posterity." Though he wrapped this "petition to the court of time" in the cloak of what Southern literature would argue, it is a restatement of what Freeman believed justified the "misery, anguish, social revolution, [and] waste of the South's best blood."[131]

That there was historical logic in the right of secession, though rising nationalism might challenge; that the right was maintained with conviction; that the South fought its fight gallantly and, so far as war ever permits, with fairness and decency; that it endured its hardships with fortitude; that it wrought its hard recovery through uncomplaining toil, and that it gave to the nation the inspiration of personalities, humble and exalted, who met a supreme test and did not falter. If, again, on the crowded order-book of time, this be too long an entry, then the South amends its petition . . . and [writes] across the record, Character is Confirmed.[132]

"Dr. Freeman can write," Stephen Vincent Benet wrote in his review of *The South to Posterity* for the *Saturday Review*. "[He] can tell the truth so you keep on wanting more of it."[133] The *New York Times* found that in "going through the green room with Douglas Freeman on a tour of the shelves that contain the literary estate of the Confederacy, one may reach more definitive conclusions than might have been possible after first-hand interviews with Confederate generals."[134] Gerald Johnson, in his review for the *New York Herald-Tribune*, agreed that "for anyone who wishes to know what the Confederacy really was like, [Freeman] has furnished unquestionably the most reliable road map extant," but questioned the assumption that this is what the "South," as opposed to the "Confederacy," had to say to posterity. The South, he noted, spoke not only from battlefields, but also "from Mount Vernon, from Monticello, from Ashland, from the Hermitage."[135] Another impressed reader was Gen. George Marshall. He noticed the book on a table in the Red Room in the White House and picked it up while waiting to see the president. He found it so "delightfully interesting . . . [and] instructive" that he walked off with it in his dispatch case. "The only trouble now," the chief of staff confessed, "is to restore the book to the White House without being discovered in the process."[136]

The years 1935 to 1940 had been unsettling for Freeman in many ways. Wars and rumors of wars had occupied his mind, domestic changes—both good and tragic—had come in rapid succession, the *News Leader* had passed through economic hardship and now entered a new era merged with the rival *Times-Dispatch*, and he had written his sixth book under conditions not of his choosing. The steadying source in these years of upheaval, apart from the "blessed influence" of Inez, was the writing of *Lee's Lieutenants*. It was "the most difficult" writing he had ever undertaken, but the challenge of presenting multiple biography and military strategy in a compelling narrative stimulated his creativity. His enthusiastic entries in his diary reflect both the progress of the work and his delight in it.

June 30, 1936: "Glorious and fascinating work."
July 20, 1936: "Worked on First Manassas. I think I have it now."
September 10, 1936: "What a jackass Benjamin was!"[137]
October 21, 1936: "D. H. Hill is an enigma."
December 25, 1936: "Christmas Day. Good heavy work on Chancellorsville."
September 20, 1937: "Am clearing up 1st Manassas, but what a fool it makes of Beauregard."
June 14, 1939: "No composition, but much reflection on Valley campaign."[138]
August 31, 1939: "Thought much of a new style for the book, to avoid repetition. Must experiment."

December 8, 1939: "Worked on that pompously—pathetic old fraud, Pendleton."[139]

"At home alone," Freeman wrote on Sunday, July 25, 1937, "and for the first time that I can remember—barring, of course, when I was sick abed—I did not put on my trousers all day. I spoke to only one person, the substitute cook, and did I kill work!" He recorded thirteen hours of writing that day.[140] "Leap year day!" he noted on February 29, 1940. "It does not lengthen life, but it adds a work day to this year."[141] He recorded with disgust a meeting that took "six mortal hours . . . when diligence would have ended it in half," and, upon his return to work after the near-fatal accident in Fayetteville, he wrote, "[G]ot back on the Williamsburg narrative. Thank God the interruption was no longer."[142] He did take one day away from his writing. On Friday, April 30, 1937, he attended a reenactment of the Battle of the Crater—thirty-four years after he had done the same with his father. He noted the significance of the day and the event. "How different from the scene of 1903 when I first conceived the idea of writing a history of the Army of Northern Virginia."[143]

He had found no enigma in Robert E. Lee; he found the men by Lee's side to be more complex. He approached P. G. T. Beauregard with "sympathetic preconceptions" because Walker Freeman fought for a time under his command. "I was reared," he wrote, "to respect his memory."[144] Familiarity with the general altered that view. After the Battle of First Manassas, Beauregard "shriveled into an ambitious, theatrical poseur who perpetually advanced preposterous strategic plans and blundered incredibly in his tactical dispositions."[145] Freeman decided against using such a frank assessment in the book, but would "merely state the facts as they indisputably appear from the record and . . . leave the reader to draw his own conclusions." He wondered if he showed "too much or two little strophe in my role as Chorus" in judging that Gen. Gustavus W. Smith "cracked nervously" on May 31 at Seven Pines; and worried if he "laughed at" the "fussy and insistent" John B. Magruder.[146]

"Should I attempt," he asked Max Perkins and his other advisors, "to solve the enigma of Joseph E. Johnston?" The first commander of the Army of Northern Virginia carried on a running feud with President Jefferson Davis, primarily on the issue of Johnston's seniority among general officers. "Again and again," Freeman wrote, "when he seemed to have all the equities on his side, Johnston would throw them away by some petulant statement or jealous act. In exactly the same way, when

A close-up view of Freeman's hands as he writes Lee's Lieutenants. (Image courtesy of Mary Tyler McClenahan.)

Davis clearly had Johnston in the wrong, he would pursue his advantage to the point where he creates sympathy for the badgered commander."[147] Freeman decided again to avoid presenting conclusions but to present Johnston as "a loyal friend and an unpredictable adversary, now reasonable and now sensitive and jealous." That, he concluded, "is about as much as I can do with him."

He relished painting historical portraits with such vivid colors. He would never have conceded that Robert E. Lee was a "marble man," but his enthusiasm about this project could have come, in part, from the fact that he was dealing with complex men of flesh and blood. The more difficult a man's story, the more enjoyment he seemed to derive from the telling. He was at once both shocked and delighted that there was so much "distortion, evasion, bluster, omission, and actual suppression of fact" about the Battle of First Manassas. Shocked, because as a historian he had a respect for truth and accurate writing; delighted, because he would be the historian to clear up the mess.

"The light is beginning to fade on the horizon of seventy-five years," he wrote about the Confederates he was studying. "Some gallant men have ridden into the darkness. Jackson and Longstreet and Early still are discernible, but the figure of A. P. Hill is difficult to distinguish and that of R. H. Anderson so far in the twilight that I doubt if I can depict it." Still he would press on toward the fading light. "We lost the war in the field; we still have a chance of winning it in the domain of history."[148]

War and history. Two subjects that would dominate Freeman's life more than ever as America entered 1941.

CHAPTER 11

"The Sanest and Soundest Observer"

"For more than twenty years," Douglas Freeman wrote in the foreword to *R. E. Lee*, "the study of military history has been my chief avocation."[1] It was an avocation that had made him America's foremost military historian. He could discuss the most intricate complexities of strategy, logistics, armaments, and morale with the nation's highest-ranking military officers. He understood the essentials of leadership and the psychology of the combat soldier. He had studied the campaigns of the great chieftains of history and had analyzed contemporary military movements with perception and foresight. The avocation of military history had provided him with the inspiration of noble heroes, epic battles, and courageous acts. His impact on military science extended both to times past and times present. One of the first letters written by Gen. George C. Marshall, upon his assumption of the office of chief of staff, was to Freeman. Marshall told him that his military views "rank in the uppermost strata of importance" and hoped to meet with him in Washington or Richmond "in the near future."[2] A few months later Marshall asked Freeman to be his "guide and lecturer" on a tour of the Civil War battlefields of "Gettysburg, South Mountain and Antietam; the vicinity of Winchester, particularly Bull Run."[3] Few civilians who had never donned a uniform wielded such influence over military matters.

Yet this genius for the art of war did not breed in him a discontentment with peace. He did not long for another war in order to have more campaigns to analyze or heroes to memorialize. "Each new inquiry," he wrote, "has made the monstrous horror of war more unintelligible to me. It has seemed incredible that human beings, endowed with any of the powers of reason, should hypnotize themselves with doctrines of 'national honor' or 'sacred right' and pursue mass murder to exhaustion or ruin."[4] He believed he had been swept up in such a "psychosis of war" during the war hysteria of 1917.[5] Now as another war was waged in

Europe, he was determined "not to permit propaganda, emotion, hate, short-sighted argument and misbranded patriotism" to stampede him into beating the war drum. "All my time will have to be given to editorial critiques," he wrote in his diary ten days before Great Britain declared war on Germany, "and, what will be far more important, to work to keep our land out of war!"[6]

Freeman's devotion to the cause of world peace sprang from his days writing editorials in support of Woodrow Wilson and the League of Nations. As the league faltered without American participation, he kept an eye on the unrest in Europe, sensing the makings of another world war. He called Adolph Hitler, Hermann Goering, and Joseph Goebbels "a trio of neurotics" who "deluded a nation with false promises, seized the mechanical weapons of modern warfare and . . . have the German people completely at their mercy."[7] It was "entirely within the realm of possibility," he judged, "that Hitler or Goering will prove another Ivan the Terrible." While warning his readers about militaristic tyrants, he reminded them about the cost of waging war against them. The *News Leader* ran a three-week pictorial series on the First World War with Freeman providing the historical commentary. Day after day, the pictures brought back the memory of the horrors of trench warfare and the mass destruction that sweep Europe like a scythe. "Can the statesmen of 1914," he wrote, "ever be forgiven for making corpses of such magnificent youth?" Would the world "be mad enough," he asked, "to complete the ruin by another war?"[8] As Germany began to arm, and Europe grew uneasy, Freeman hammered away at the lessons of 1918. "If Europe is determined to destroy its civilization, we cannot protect it," he wrote in 1935, "but we can and we must revise our doctrine of neutral rights and determine . . . to have no part in completing the ruin of the world."[9] He repeated this sentiment several years later in a diary entry. "I have to steel myself always to maintain the principles of American neutrality," he wrote, "while I grieve at the certain death, in a long war, of a British and a French social order that were, in their way, beautiful. What can we do about it? Why should we rush into a burning building that may be doomed? Thank God for the Atlantic Ocean."[10]

He was not an isolationist, but he held to a hard line of neutrality throughout the late thirties. Always he harkened back to the days leading up to the First World War. "Stampede and hasty action are to be avoided at any price," he wrote in August 1938.[11] That theme dominated his editorials into 1939. "What ought one to say about the Czechoslovakian problem," he wrote Nicholas Butler, president of the

Carnegie Endowment for International Peace. "Under God, I want to keep this newspaper from contributing in any way to another and perhaps a final catastrophe in Europe."[12] He decided that Czechoslovakia was not worth risking American lives. "For its part," he wrote as the Czech crisis escalated, "this newspaper has to say frankly that it had rather see Czechoslovakia partitioned in this manner and neutralized than to have the world thrown into another war. The lives of perhaps 10,000,000 boys and what is left of the wealth of the world mean more than property rights in the German districts of Czechoslovakia."[13]

In the wake of the Munich conference, Freeman focused on steering American policy toward neutrality. "Effective neutrality, whether in the present or traditional form," he wrote, "will mean that this nation must maintain, in effect, an embargo on all shipments that belligerents cannot make in their own bottoms from their own resources."[14] He warned that neutrality would carry an economic price, but it was "a price second only to that of participating in the war." As events in Europe began to move with blitzkrieg speed, he outlined the "essentials" of American foreign policy. "We draw a line from Alaska to Hawaii and thence to the approaches of Panama," he wrote. "West of that line, we assume no responsibility."[15] To the east, he granted that the American Neutrality Act should be amended to allow the sale of "munitions of war on the basis of cash and carry." He recognized the moral requirement for the United States to "side with and support the assailed democracies," but "not intervene in their behalf."[16] He was advocating a tightrope neutrality; one that so closely approached the line of involvement that he found it necessary again and again to explain it. "It does not follow that the United States should remain idle in the face of the coming conflict," he wrote in April 1939, "or should accept without qualification the view of the isolationists . . . We must not tie our hands—any more than we should commit ourselves to Britain and to France."[17] He counseled patience, almost as if he expected that clear heads would prevail if only given time. "Patience," he thundered in August 1939 as the Nazi threat loomed over Poland, "patience when violence seems more logical; patience when it is denounced by the unthinking as cowardice! Let time do its work . . . one truth is written across the blood-stained map of Europe: no despot ever survives for long."[18] In a lengthy editorial titled "Be Neutral in Fact" he resurrected the words of Woodrow Wilson and then added his own interpretation. "In 1914 we were unwilling to be neutral in spirit," he wrote. "For that reason we were at war in 1917 and, to this day, are paying the dreadful price of that conflict."[19] Three days later the Germans and the Russians signed a non-aggression pact. "Bleak outlook!" he wrote in his diary.[20] Within the week, Germany invaded Poland, and Great Britain and France entered the war. "This," he wrote gravely, "is not our quarrel."[21]

The outbreak of war saw the return of Freeman the military historian to the editorial page of the *News Leader*. He used the same technique employed during the First World War of placing events in Europe on a map of Virginia.

Perhaps the simplest way of understanding what is happening on the Western front is to assume that Rockbridge county is the Ardennes and that Lexington [Sedan] is close to the point where the James River breaks through the Blue Ridge . . . Richmond [is] fortress Eben Emael . . . Washington would be Antwerp . . . At zero hour last Friday, the fateful 10th of May, the Germans crossed the Appomattox River and moved northward toward the James.[22]

In another analogy Richmond served as Oslo for Freeman to explain how the Germans planned to "sever communications between Doswell and Fredericksburg" and to "envelop the British force around Fredericksburg."[23] He asked his readers what they would suspect if "the Germans were crowding . . . hundreds of planes into the western corner of Henrico?"[24] In addition to geographic analogies, he reached back for historical examples. "Can the voice of experience be heard above the clamor?" he asked in March 1940. "Will the dead be given leave to speak from the grave? They have but one answer to all the insistence upon rash offensive . . . *Do not attack until you are ready.*"[25] While most people were looking across the Atlantic to Europe, he inserted reminders about American policy toward Japan. "Denied American oil, iron and cotton," he wrote, "Japan will be in a desperate plight . . . [a] desperate people might pursue desperate methods."[26] His editorials gained national attention. *Life* magazine reported that Freeman was "probably the sanest and soundest observer of the European war in the U.S. today."[27]

When Germany invaded France in May 1940, he recognized that "sentimentally, the war is brought even nearer to us." Still his message supported preparedness and neutrality. "Are we Americans to undertake to redeem with the blood of our sons the mistakes France and Britain have been making almost from the hour the Treaty of Versailles was signed in 1919?" he asked. "No, a thousand times no . . . Arm to the

teeth, America, and attend to your own business!"28 He took this message to several college commencements in the spring of 1940. His
speech, "Barbed-wire Horizons," sought to place the events in Europe in
their historical context. "The surrender at Yorktown, " he noted, "was a
bitter blow to Britain . . . but in thirty-four years Britain was victorious
at Waterloo and began a full century of world hegemony . . . It is easy to
let the projection of history be written in fear rather than in probability.
An exaggerated appraisal of its own importance leads almost every generation to assume that civilization is being destroyed whenever the social
order changes with balance of power shifts."29 It was the duty of the
scholar, Freeman asserted, to continue intellectual pursuits during time
of war. "The singer must not quench his song; the painter must not put
away his easel or scrape his palette. If we do nothing to exalt beauty and
to replace that which is lost, the ugliness not less than the chains of Mars
will be our lot."30 This was a modified Wilsonian doctrine; instead of
making the world safe for democracy, he was advocating making the
world safe for scholarship and artistic freedom. Some of the students he
was addressing, he admitted, "may be compelled to face barbed-wire
entanglements, but they need not live with barbed-wire horizons." He
asked the audience to look beyond "attacking Messerschmitts and
defending Spitfires" to the contest "between the creation of beauty and
its destruction, between understanding and hate, between barbed-wire
horizons and the concept of the illimitable soul."31

"Barbed-wire Horizons" was Freeman's most pacific—bordering
naïve—policy statement in the years before World War II; though, to
be fair, he was articulating a sentiment felt by many Americans. His
desire to save American lives and avoid another world war had clouded
his judgment. To dismiss the Nazis and Fascists as mere regrettable
regimes that must be outlasted is an assessment staggering in its mis-
conception. He came close to saying that even if the world were
engulfed in war, all would be well if scholars continued to pursue art,
literature, and beauty. His rhetoric was more restrained in the "program
for the crisis" he outlined in June 1940. He presented nine "maxims" to
guide U.S. policy, including arming "to the widest margin of conceiv-
able need," preparing "for the widest selective service," a "benevolent
neutrality" toward Great Britain, and a "higher standard of individual
and of national discipline."32

Three months later, President Franklin D. Roosevelt authorized the
sale of decommissioned American destroyers to Great Britain. "It's the
only time in my life," Freeman wrote in his diary, "where I wished I were

in Congress. If I were, I'd move his impeachment before night."[33] It was in this frame of mind, and with bombs falling on London, that he met with John Stewart Bryan to discuss *News Leader* editorial policy on the war. The two men, he recorded, had an "unpleasant clash."[34] The next day, he typed a seven-page "appraisal of the situation." It is unclear whether or not he gave the memorandum to Bryan. The only copy in Freeman's papers is heavily corrected in pencil and no clean copy or cover letter is found. Whether he sent it to Bryan or merely used the opportunity to vent his feelings, the "appraisal" provides the most detailed statement of his attitude toward the war—and explains his zealous neutrality.

"I find myself," he wrote, "approaching the crisis, which hourly is more serious, from three points of view besides the paramount one of the preservation of national life and independence."[35] The first consideration was a "detestation of everything (save discipline)" for which the Nazis stood, and a sympathy for Great Britain. The second, and perhaps more dominating, consideration was "the memory of the World War . . . [and] all the dislocation of national life, of all the inflamed hatreds and of all the spiritual losses that attended our participation in that overseas war."[36] Freeman took a pencil and replaced "overseas war" with "that futile struggle."

I go back in memory to our screaming declarations in the *News Leader* against Germany after the sinking of the *Lusitania* and I think of myself for the three and a half years thereafter as groping blindly while cheering loudly. I knew not what I did. Judged by the standards that then prevailed, I did my duty. Thrice rejected for military service, I tried to give my utmost to the cause Mr. Wilson represented. I look back on that period with infinitely more of humiliation than of satisfaction. The war and the reconstruction left scars in my soul, but left, still more, a sense of frustration and stultification. Be the price what it may, I am determined not to permit propaganda, emotion, hate, short-sighted argument and misbranded patriotism to bring me again to the psychosis of war I shared with millions of other stampeded Americans. A stampeded editor is worse than a blind leader of the blind.[37]

"Besides," he penciled in above that last line, "I have to live with my mind and my conscience after the war." His third consideration was his knowledge of military history, which might have been one source of conflict between him and Bryan. Almost every event or issue that arose prompted "at least half-a-dozen warnings from old wars and past preparation for war . . . I no more can throw away what I have learned of war than you can throw away your inheritance of noblesse oblige."[38] Bryan apparently believed Freeman's habit of looking back while analyzing current events gave "an uncertain sound" to the editorial page. "I can say in answer only," Freeman responded, "that I unhappily know too much about war to be certain of anything about war except that it is uncertain. Behind the most blaring confident trumpets today may be more of wind than of wisdom."[39]

This remarkable letter seems to trace Freeman's commitment to neutrality to a combination of despair and disappointment over America's participation in World War I. The changes to society wrought by the war—negative changes to his mind—made the slaughter of the war worthless. Its end brought none of the redeeming aspects that followed, and justified, the Civil War. His father had come home after the war and saved the family farm. He built several businesses, reared a family, and set an example his son continued to emulate. This could be said for Lee's life as well. Apparently Freeman believed most soldiers returned from World War I and gave themselves over to the decadence of speak-easies, stock speculation, jazz, and loose women. The literature was that of a lost generation; the leaders were machine politicians. Wilson's League of Nations was in shambles. There was nothing noble to justify the killing fields of France. As such, his advocacy to enter the war was misguided. Now, with the benefit of hindsight, he would do all he could to preserve America's peace and prevent the calamity of another lost post-war generation.

Having laid out the reasons for his position, he listed what he believed should be the editorial policy of the News Leader. First, Britain should be supported with "a well-balanced program of fighters, interceptors, and bombing planes." He believed that if Britain could "hold out another year," they would prevail with air superiority. Second, the United States needed to maintain "friendly—or at least non-belligerent" relations with Japan. "I cannot too strongly state my conviction that the semblance of peace with Japan, if it possibly can be assured, is essential to the proper support of the British communities of nations."[40] It was not too late, he judged, "to reach a modus vivendi with Japan."[41] Third, he warned about uprisings against the United States in Latin America, and, fourth, he noted that the American army "scarcely now has enough modern equipment to put down scattered riots."[42] These observations show that Freeman's strategic mind had not been dulled by his near pacifist attitude. His prediction about England surviving Nazi bombers was born out by British victory in the Battle of Britain, his analysis of lack of military preparedness for war was dangerously accurate, and he recognized the potential threat looming across the Pacific Ocean.

Despite his views on neutrality, Freeman's military acumen was never in doubt, and in May 1940 he was named chairman of the Virginia Defense Council. Governor James Price established the agency to prepare the state to "fully and effectively . . . exert her maximum military and industrial, as well as moral, effort for National Defense."[43] The council was charged with surveying and estimating the state's preparedness and formulating a plan for the "prompt and efficient mobilization and use of the industrial facilities, natural resources, and man-power of the Commonwealth."[44] Freeman began his usual meticulous gathering of facts—he asked the Library of Virginia for information regarding "home guard troops" during World War I—and soon found himself addressing problems related to production, construction, transportation, health, welfare, and morale.[45] In his systematic way, he divided Virginia into four districts, each with a mobilization coordinator, and established district areas of authority and responsibility for civil defense.[46] He studied plans for the evacuation of Virginia's coastal cities, made note of areas more susceptible to "subversive elements," worked with labor and management to prevent strikes, and reported instances of "German propaganda" to J. Edgar Hoover.[47] After a year on the job, he was able to report that the council had performed "a definite service."[48]

Freeman took two additional steps as he saw America drifting toward war. The first was to offer himself for duty. "There is no fool like an old civilian fool," he wrote Gen. George Marshall, "but the blood of an old Confederate will not down. Wherefore, please remember that I am fifty-four, but in good health and that if the worse comes to worst, and you need any one who could recall the experiences of the Union and Confederate Armies in planning or administration, you need only to call on me."[49] Marshall suggested some radio addresses on Selective Service, but that was not what Freeman had in mind, and he deftly avoided the speaking tour.[50] The second step was more practical. "Have decided," he wrote in his diary, "that I will press the writing of [*Lee's Lieutenants*] to the limit of my capacity in the hope that I can get it out in the autumn of 1942 when it may be of help to our army-officers."[51] This necessitated releasing the three volumes one at a time instead of in a complete set.

He thought the need justified that course. "I think practically every error a soldier might make," he wrote Max Perkins, "and most of the wise strikes he might deliver in combat and campaign are set forth in this book."[52] He had written 430,000 words and calculated that the manuscript "could be divided, as it now stands, into two volumes."[53] The first volume would thus run about 550 pages, and he would have "no difficulty" in adding another 43,000 words to the second volume to get it to the same length. He told Perkins he would "press on to the end of Volume II while the heat of the contest is on me" and then revise and submit Volume I. "It's a more exciting book than *Lee*," he commented, "the principal characters whom we try to develop as they come forward in the war do not number more than twenty, but incidents are included about scores of others—from gallant privates in their teens to old Generals."[54] Freeman rapidly whipped the first two volumes into shape. His pace did not affect his eye for detail, and he took time to investigate the specific type of chloroform administered to "Stonewall" Jackson during the amputation of his arm, the exact color of D. H. Hill's hair, and the precise opinion of General McClellan held by Generals Lee and Jackson.[55]

While writing about the trials of earlier commanders, Freeman turned his thoughts to a consideration of Franklin Roosevelt as commander-in-chief. "Some of us who study military history and try at the same time to keep our eyes on current developments," he wrote Edward Weeks of *The Atlantic Monthly*, "are becoming a little anxious about the President's attitude. He seems too much disposed to exercise his prerogative as Commander-in-Chief . . . As he reads practically no historical works, we are afraid he has not learned the great lessons taught by the mistakes of President Lincoln and President Davis during the war of 1861-65."[56] He took up this concern with several Army Intelligence officers, and they suggested he write "an article in which the mistakes of the wartime executives and the clear policy of Mr. Wilson in 1917-18 would be contrasted."[57] His friends assured him that the article would be given to Maj. Gen. Edwin "Pa" Watson, a close aide to the president, to ensure that Roosevelt read it. Freeman wrote the article in the belief that he was writing directly to Franklin Roosevelt.[58]

The article, titled "Who's In Command," posed the question of "will the next President have a proper conception of his duties as Commander-in-Chief of the Army and Navy?"[59] The subtle casting of the question, with its assumption that FDR would not seek a third term, allowed Freeman to be critical of an overreaching president while not casting aspersions on Roosevelt. Indeed, he dismissed consideration of Roosevelt early in the article by stating "the general opinion . . . that Mr. Roosevelt probably would be a vigorous war President but that he would not interfere in operations."[60] The article, then, was addressed to "Mr. Roosevelt's successor," who, as he knew, might very well be Franklin Roosevelt.

"An incompetent, officious war President," Freeman wrote, "is more dangerous to his country than an incompetent General-in-Chief, because he cannot be removed so readily."[61] It was the duty of a competent president to "define the war aims of his country," "muster in support of them the national resources," "insist that the larger strategy of military and naval operations . . . conform to the war aims," "select the best men he can find to develop and execute a sound strategic plan," support his generals and admirals, and "sustain the morale of the nation."[62] This, he asserted, was the "blueprint of ideal relationship . . . [but] the difficulty is that actual conditions seldom conform to theoretical design." He recited the history of previous presidents, their war conduct, and their search for leaders. Polk had Winfield Scott, and Wilson had Pershing, but Lincoln went through six generals before appointing Grant, and Jefferson Davis could not match his selection of Lee with a corresponding quality appointment in the Western Theater. "The whole story," he wrote, "is full of instruction for every soldier and every executive."[63] Freeman was advocating a hands-off style that left the military decisions to the commanders. "I remember asking Newton Baker in 1921," he reflected, "whether President Wilson ever had given him or General Pershing a direct order for a military operation. 'Never' Mr. Baker said."[64] He reminded Roosevelt, who served as assistant secretary of the navy in Wilson's administration, that he had worked for a president "who did not dabble endlessly in departmental affairs." In the event America joined the war before he left office, Roosevelt, he wrote, "would disappoint those who expect him to be President and General-in-Chief and Admiral of the fleet. That is not his method . . . He would state war aims, but he scarcely would dictate strategy."[65] Having thus praised Roosevelt for prospectively following his formula of command, Freeman ended the article by reminding readers that it was the "aptitude" of Roosevelt's successor that would either "add incredibly to the efficiency of [the] national defense" or "butcher their boys."[66]

He had done all he could to address the "cowardly war-hysteria" while at the same time attempting to prepare Virginia, the nation, and the president for war. By July 1941 he had come to the conclusion that

America would soon be involved in the war. "That we have to fight, and soon," he wrote Congressman A. Willis Robertson, "is, I think, inevitable, though I long have hesitated to use that dread word 'inevitable.'"[67] He was pushing himself to stay on top of war news and complete the first volume of *Lee's Lieutenants*. It caught up to him one Saturday morning outside his office at the *News Leader*. He collapsed and was taken to the hospital, but the diagnosis was nothing more serious than "heat and overwork."[68] "I came down on my face," Freeman wrote his brother, "and made a grand mess of it."[69] The incident caused "much excitement among my friends—much humiliation to me."[70]

On December 7, 1941, Freeman put in a "good day's work" on *Lee's Lieutenants* and began to make preparations to depart for New York for a meeting of the Carnegie Endowment for International Peace. At 3:00 P.M. he received word of the Japanese attack on Pearl Harbor. He left Westbourne and went on the air almost immediately upon his arrival at WRNL. "Well," he intoned, "it finally happened."[71] *News Leader* staffers began to gather in the office to cover the historic news. John Leard, remembered Freeman scrutinizing every report off the Associated Press wire and admonishing everyone to "be calm."[72] He was home by 8:00 P.M., all thoughts of neutrality and peace vanished. "The great break has come," he wrote a friend. "For it, praise God, the American people spiritually are prepared. Materially, therefore, they can be. Were the situation reversed, we could not be sure of victory."[73]

With the onset of war, Freeman again sought out active military service. No record exists to show that he ever appreciated the improbability of such a quest, but he must have regarded the odds. He was fifty-four years old and had been excluded from service in World War I due to a hernia, but, undaunted by the odds against him, he pressed on. "This is another letter from a restless old fool," he wrote Marshall, volunteering to "quit all my jobs at any time for military service in any capacity."[74] Marshall gently assured him that he would call "when there is available an appropriate assignment commensurate with your superior qualifications."[75] He mentioned the idea of establishing a corps of civilian specialists, and Freeman seized on that slim chance. "Got a fine and personally exciting letter today from General George C. Marshall," he wrote in his diary. "I hope my son sees it someday."[76] When nothing came of the civilian corps, he appealed to Marshall's aide, Frank McCarthy. "I have been trying mighty hard to fit somewhere," he wrote, because "the point of view of military history ought not to be disregarded entirely."[77] McCarthy sought to reassure the anxious historian. "The matter is constantly in General Marshall's mind," he wrote. "He never forgets anything, and he is looking forward to a time when the proper project will appear."[78] As the months passed, and no appointment was forthcoming, Freeman decided on another approach. "For two weeks," he confided to his diary, "I shall put myself in training to see if I can pass the physical for active duty. Should I be able to pass, I shall try to get permission to enlist as a private soldier."[79] His efforts to join the service, though somewhat quixotic, sprang from sincere patriotic motivations. "As my days shorten," he wrote Mary Tyler, "I want what I do to be done with purpose."[80] He wanted to be a part of the war he had fought so hard to prevent, and he judged that his considerable influence as a writer, editor, broadcaster, and historian was not a significant enough contribution. "I sometimes eat out my heart," he confided to Gen. J. L. DeWitt, "as I reflect that in the greatest struggle of our nation's history I have to stand behind the lines."[81]

Unable to wield a sword, Freeman turned to his pen and microphone. "I talk about you and MacArthur almost daily in my broadcasts," he wrote Marshall, "and I think I have Virginia people in the state of mind where they realize we must not expect miracles even of ablest men."[82] On the *News Leader* editorial page, he fought "more of General Marshall's battles than ever he knows"[83] and heralded Marshall's "great intellect, sound judgment, and magnificent character."[84] He saw progress in his editorial effort. "I think I have built up through the *News Leader* so thorough an understanding in Virginia of what [Marshall] is doing," he wrote Frank McCarthy, "that nobody of any consequence will dare cast aspersions on him."[85] Freeman's greatest fear during the early months of the war was that mistakes would be made through lack of historical perspective. "Every day, it seems to me," he wrote Marshall, "I see some historical analogy of the War Between the States, the Napoleonic Wars, the wars of Frederick the Great or the struggle of 1914-18."[86] It was frustrating, he confided, "to stand reluctantly aside and to see history enacted all over again."[87] He submitted recommendations on a host of issues to the War Department. He wrote memoranda detailing procedures for promotion of officers, recounting General Lee's efforts to combat troop fatigue, and outlining a plan to construct "fake landing craft."[88] Looking to the future, he wrote Under Secretary of War Robert Patterson in October 1942 suggesting the formation of a committee "to study methods of assisting [returning servicemen] in resuming their college work when hostilities end."[89] Patterson responded that he had "passed the suggestion on" to President Roosevelt and later wrote that a committee had been named to "work out a sound plan to carry out the thought you had in mind."[90] The committee would ultimately provide the impetus for the G.I. Bill of Rights.

The reluctant warrior was now all out for Allied victory. He took to the national airwaves in September 1942, participating in a debate over the "Town Meeting of the Air," on the topic "Is America All Out for War." Freeman argued the affirmative position against the negative team of Eric Sevareid, CBS news correspondent, and Walter Wagner, a motion picture producer.[91] In March he had an "incredibly frank" conversation with General Marshall "about past operations," the first of many conferences the two men would have during the course of the war. He also kept an eye on security on the home front. "Some one came in yesterday to complain that a naturalized German who is very outspoken in his sympathy with Hitlerism is at work at the Byrd Airport," he wrote the FBI. "I know nothing of the circumstances or of the man, but pass on the report to you."[92] Freeman waged war as best he knew how—by the written and spoken word. "The ordeal through which the country will pass," he wrote a friend, "is one that cannot be sustained with mere physical strength. There must be well springs of spirit."[93]

Lee's Lieutenants: A Study in Command, Volume One, *Manassas to Malvern Hill* was released in October 1942. In the foreword, Freeman recounted the decision process that led him to abandon the biography of Washington and sketch the lives of Lee's comrades in arms, and explained his method of focusing on the command structure of the army. He reported "four surprises": the disregard of officers' training, the inflated reputation of several Confederates, the close relationship between skillful administration and morale, and the lack of quality officers to replace those leaders killed or wounded in action.[94] He then made the analogy of the trials of the Army of Northern Virginia in 1862 and those of the United States Armed Forces in 1942. "The disadvantages of issuing a three-volume work as if it were a serial story are manifest," he wrote, "but something, perhaps, may be gained by printing in the first year of this nation's greatest war, the story of the difficulties that had to be overcome in an earlier struggle before the command of the army became measurably qualified for the task assigned it."[95] He expressed the same thought in a letter to General Marshall. "You are of course much too busy to read so long a book," he wrote, "but some of the experiences it cites . . . so closely parallel what now we are doing that you might find it worth while to have some less busy man dig out a few of the facts."[96] Marshall read the book himself and wrote that it "made the following reaction on me: that my griefs over the personal feelings of leaders and subordinate leaders these days shrank into insignificance beside those of Lee." Marshall found the account of the Seven Days Battle "one of the most astonishing and instructive revelations of Civil War matters that I have seen."[97]

Freeman may have intended *Lee's Lieutenants* to be of practical use in military science, but it was first of all history and biography, and it was at that level that it was received and reviewed by the public. "In a class by itself," Stephen Vincent Benet wrote of Volume One in the *New York Times*. The "campaigns and the men who made them pass before the eyes of the reader as freshly, vividly and livingly as if they had never been written of before. It is a triumph both of scholarship and of style."[98] The *Saturday Review* called the book "dispassionate in judgment, obviously authoritative, alive and enthusiastic."[99] The scholarly reviews were no less laudatory. "The essential contribution of Dr. Freeman in this study," *The Journal of Southern History* commented, "is his account of the evolution of the successful field commanders in Lee's army from unknown subalterns to dynamic and forceful leaders of men."[100] The *American Historical Review* agreed that the book would prove valuable during the current war effort. "Widely read and heeded," the review noted, "the book would do the nation great good."[101]

While the accolades rolled in, Freeman granted an interview to his friend Frank Fuller of the Associated Press. He returned to the theme of the relevancy of *Lee's Lieutenants* to the American war effort. "The history of command in all American wars is so similar that it scares and then reassures you," he said. "We are passing now through a period analogous to that of 1861-62, and we have many surprises and some disappointments ahead of us." The encouragement to be derived from *Lee's Lieutenants* was that "if a man has the 'military sense' he will rise; if he lacks it, he will fall, no matter how exalted his rank at the beginning of a war."[102] By the end of the first year of fighting, he predicted, "America . . . will have leaders who can be trusted with the lives of our boys."

Freeman completed Volume Two, *Cedar Mountain to Chancellorsville*, on October 4, 1942, while the reviews for Volume One were still coming in. "I think," Max Perkins wrote, "you have written a masterpiece."[103] The second volume had one particularly challenging section—the death of Stonewall Jackson. "I do not believe," Freeman confided to Margaret Mitchell, "I ever had quite so difficult a problem where literature and history came together."[104]

It would have been so easy to slush and, on the other hand, so easy to underwrite the scene. I had to rein myself in at the same time that I applied the spur. The toughest part of it all, perhaps, was the little scene of Jackson's leave-taking the morning the campaign began. The facts were well authenticated but the treatment of them was a problem. How could I get the dramatic effect without anticipating the tragedy. As your discerning eye quickly saw, I tried to do it by a simple statement of the facts and the mere addition of the words "good-bye, good-bye." You were the first person, I think, who has seen what I was trying to do in that exceedingly difficult passage.[105]

Freeman thought Volume Two was "more interesting" than the first, but not as challenging to write. "It was exceedingly difficult to put together the thousands of scattered notes concerning the organization of the Army in '61," he wrote. "When I got to Jackson in '63, of course, the road was fairly smooth."[106] How he presented the facts was almost as important as the facts he presented. "I have tried to eliminate what I thought were pendent participial clauses," he noted. "I know one thing: there is not a transitional 'however' in the book; I despise that word."[107] The second volume met with the same critical acclaim as did the first. "The high standard of scholarship and style set by Dr. Freeman in his *R. E. Lee* has been maintained throughout the present work," H. A. DeWeerd wrote in the *American Historical Review*. "These two works will not only constitute a major contribution to the history of the period, but will set a standard for American military biography."[108] "If his pen still dips occasionally in the rhetoric of reverence and formal emotion," the *Saturday Review* said, "[he] remains altogether objective throughout. His is certainly the soundest and most usable treatment of these actions ever written."[109]

The third volume brought Freeman once again to the field at Gettysburg and to Gen. James Longstreet. His assessment of Longstreet in *R. E. Lee* had been highly critical. In preparing to write again of those July days in 1863, he allowed himself "to look a little over the edge of the hill to see what the enemy is doing" in order to reexamine his critique of Longstreet.[110] "Needless to say," he wrote, "I want to do complete justice to Longstreet and I may have relied too much upon early statements in the Southern Historical Society Papers. The old man was a bitter partisan and did not hesitate to indulge special pleading when it was to his advantage."[111] Freeman spent most of the spring of 1943 working on Gettysburg. He reached the conclusion that he had been "misled by Jubal Early and the parties to the Gettysburg controversy." He was prepared to say that the "condition on the Federal left was far different from what the Confederates thought it was."[112] He accordingly altered his judgment of Longstreet and wrote that "the traditional picture of an unoccupied ridge, waiting seizure while Longstreet loitered, is entirely false. Cemetery Ridge on the 2nd of July, all the way from Cemetery Hill to Little Round Top, was adequately defended from the earliest moment, 9 A.M., at which the Confederates could have launched a strong attack."[113] He still said that Longstreet "sulked" at critical moments during the battle, but was willing to admit that "Old Pete" had been made a scapegoat for Confederate defeat.[114]

Apart from the partial rehabilitation of Longstreet, Freeman was most surprised "that the Confederate Army Command virtually collapsed eleven months" before Appomattox. "Lee carried the whole army on his shoulders after the fall of Longstreet on May 6th, 1864," he wrote Max Perkins. "I did not realize this when I wrote *R. E. Lee* but I see it plainly now."[115] He also selected his own personal favorites among the officers: "Jackson undoubtedly was the first of all Lee's soldiers . . . For a stubborn defensive, Lee had none better than Longstreet. In a dashing infantry advance, when audacity counted most, John B. Gordon was unexcelled. In the cavalry . . . Stuart was supreme, though Hampton and Rosser were not far below him."[116]

On January 9, 1944, Freeman noted that he had spent 6,737 hours of work on *Lee's Lieutenants*. At 11:21 that morning, he was working on Chapter Thirty-five of Volume Three. It was almost thirty-seven years to the time Mrs. Kate Minor had written him about making a calendar of the manuscripts in the Confederate Museum. He thought briefly about writing some more in Chapter Thirty-five about the post-war years of Lee's generals. Then he changed his mind and wrote "The End."[117] He spent the next four months revising the draft, adding another 384 hours to his work total. Then in May came the moment he had envisioned at the crater reenactment in 1903.

At 6:05 P.M., in the presence of dear friends, I finished *Lee's Lieutenants* and concluded 29 years to preserve the record of our fathers of the Army of Northern Virginia.[118]

He invited John Stewart Bryan and several others to join him as he wrote the final words. A photographer recorded the moment. "I was pleased that by pure chance the conclusion came on Memorial Day," he wrote Mary Tyler. "My eyes almost dimmed as I made the entry in my diary because I was thinking of your grandfather and of all the other men whose fame I have been trying to preserve from the canker of time."[119]

The men he preserved from the immolation of time were men "consistently themselves."[120] Each portrait complete in itself, yet integrated into the grand mural of personalities. There was "Beauregard, with a Napoleonic complex . . . 'Joe' Johnston, who had a grievance . . . and an amazing ability to make men believe in him; Magruder, the ever galloping giant . . . Harvey Hill, whom combat stimulated and routine paralyzed."[121]

As Beauregard looked anxiously to the Southwest, he saw a marching column. At its head was its flag. Eagerly Beauregard turned his glass on the standard: was it the flag of the Union or of the South?[122]

"Powell Hill, who was full of contradictions . . . 'Old Pete' Longstreet, brusque, self-controlled, always at his best in battle . . . 'Jeb' Stuart . . . as colorful as his uniform."[123]

"I tell you, sir," Ewell stormed, "[Jackson] is as crazy as a March hare. He has gone away. I don't know where, and left me here with instructions to stay until he returns. But Banks's whole army is advancing on me and I have not the most remote idea where to communicate with General Jackson. I tell you, sir, he is crazy" . . . With that Ewell furiously began to pace the yard.[124]

"Wade Hampton, the Grand Seigneur and huntsman . . . the ramrod John B. Gordon . . . diminutive 'Billy' Mahone."[125]

It was not war; it was mass murder. As in every action of the campaign, the men in the ranks did all they could to make good the blunders and delays of their leaders; but this time they were sent to achieve the impossible. Valor could not conquer those perfectly served batteries on the crest . . .[126]

"John B. Hood, with capacities as a combat officer that was matched by the valor of his troops . . . Fitz Lee, the laughing cavalier, and Tom Rosser, the daring Lochinvar."[127]

Disaster should have been in the air, and with it the first sign of stampede. It was not so. The thrilling news had spread that A. P. Hill was coming. For fate or fame, his was to be the last scene . . . The impetuosity that had been his vice was now his spur . . . Every sound of fire was a summons. Speed the march, close up, close up! The life of the Confederacy might depend on the pace of that one Division. Hill had on his red battle shirt . . .[128]

"Pelham and Pegram, seldom together but always in spirit the Castor and Pollux of the guns; Heth the ill-fortuned and Wilcox the observant."[129]

More there was in the same mutter . . . and then a long, long silence, such a silence as might have come that May night the previous year when he had pushed the Stonewall Brigade forward toward Winchester . . . Long marches and hard battles and wide streams had been ahead. Now . . . the clock was striking three, the spring sunshine in the room, the rustle of new leaves in the breeze, peace and the end of a Sabbath Day's journey . . . and then from the bed, clearly, quietly, cheerfully: "Let us cross over the river, and rest under the shade of the trees."[130]

"Pender the diligent and Ramseur the hard-hitting; the caustic Early and the Nordic Rodes."[131]

The gaunt, desperate men in their Southern ranks are grappling unseen with the Federals beyond the stone wall. All the might of the enemy is now thrown against them. They struggle, they stab, they use the butt end of muskets they cannot load. It is hell, it is death for the bravest of them. A mat of fallen red flags lies under trees. Longstreet strains eyes and ears and knows who the victor in that unequal struggle will be.[132]

And, finally, "two of them, if only two . . . by whom one's personal philosophy of life is shaped beyond understanding": Lee, "the captain of the host, and his right arm, Jackson."[133]

For the first day after the surrender, and for many another day, long and weary roads were theirs, and strange and sometimes winding; but the words of their leader they kept fresh in their hearts:

"Consciousness of duty faithfully performed"—that was the consolation which became their reward, their pride, their bequest.[134]

"If the Confederate sword in the field," one reviewer wrote, "had been as mighty as Freeman's pen in the study . . ." He left the sentence unfinished.[135]

"I am wondering," Freeman wrote George Marshall in May 1942, "if you are putting away anywhere any memoranda of these tremendous days."[136] That inquiry, he admitted, was "not altogether unselfish, because I have made up my mind that . . . I am going to write a memoir of you when this thing is over." It was natural that the idea of writing about the battles and leaders of the Second World War would occur to him. He was not only a witness to history, but also a close acquaintance of most of the war's leaders. His admiration for Marshall extended back almost twenty years to their first meeting in 1924. "I hope sometime you will meet Marshall," he wrote a friend. "He is one of the great Americans of our generation. For my part, I think he is a greater man by every test than is our President, whose many virtues are weakened by some shortcomings as an administrator."[137] Freeman also observed and recorded his impressions of other generals. "I am not so sure about Eisenhower," he wrote his brother in March 1943, "he may be too much of a smoothie."[138] A year later, after Eisenhower's successful North African campaign and his elevation to supreme allied commander, Freeman offered a reassessment. "I believe I can ease your mind a little better concerning General Eisenhower," he wrote. "He does not create, on first impression, as favorable a view as one has of General Marshall, but he is a much more capable man than one would conclude from his photograph. All his years with MacArthur were full of instruction and training."[139] Navy admiral Chester Nimitz was a self-described "avid reader" of Freeman's works. The two men exchanged occasional letters during the war, and it was to Freeman that Nimitz turned on the eve of the battle for Iwo Jima to explain his strategy and express his concerns.

The operations on Iwo Jima are proceeding as satisfactorily as can be expected. It is reported that there are in excess of twenty thousand Japanese on that tiny island . . . To be captured at all, it must be taken by frontal assault, and the Japanese will have no place to retreat. Therefore, they will fight to the last ditch; and our casualties will be heavy . . . I give you the above explanation because I know that before long we will be subject to criticism because our casualties will compare unfavorably with the casualties sustained by Army troops operating in Luzon and Leyte. There is no comparison between these three objectives. The Japanese will retreat if a way to retreat is left open. This is not possible on Iwo Jima. Now comes the obvious question: "Is Iwo Jima worth the cost in lives and is it necessary for the accomplishment of our over-all plan to defeat Japan?" The answer to both is unqualifiedly "yes."[140]

One of Freeman's most interesting relationships was with Gen. Douglas MacArthur. He had known MacArthur for slightly more than ten years and had asked his advice on military matters during the writing of *R. E. Lee*. He admired the general's great military skill, but disapproved of his grandiloquent style. "His temper changes so much from day to day," he wrote his brother, "that one never knows what to expect from him. I am afraid there is something symbolic in the fact that the old cock is getting very bald but wishes to keep the appearance of youth . . . a man who fools himself to that extent may be fooling himself in other respects."[141] He put aside this concern as MacArthur pushed his way north from Australia to the Philippine Islands. "Your campaign from New Guinea to Mindoro," he wrote MacArthur, "is in the strategic spirit of Lee, and is worthy of comparison in spirit, strategy, and in result with anything ever done by an American commander. Every morning, as I come down Monument Avenue in the dark, I salute the monument of General Lee . . . I think if he were in the flesh, he daily would salute you."[142] As news arrived the next day of MacArthur's victory at Leyte, Freeman wrote again. "General Lee would be proud of you," he reiterated. "No campaigns by an Army officer reminded me so strongly of him as your campaigns do."[143] Not one to miss a historical analogy, MacArthur responded in kind. "I am of Virginia," he wrote, "and all my professional life I have studied of Lee and Jackson . . . In some of my lonely vigils at night with momentous decisions impending, when even the most faithful of staff officers will sleep, it has seemed to me almost as though those great Chieftains of the Grey were there to comfort and sustain me."[144]

With such intimate relationships with contemporary leaders, and with his reputation as a military historian at its zenith, it was inevitable that Freeman would consider writing a history of the war. As he thought about such a work, he reminded Marshall, MacArthur, Eisenhower, and others to save their papers and memoranda of the war.[145] The reaction of the potential subjects reflected their personalities. "I have not made a practice of keeping memoranda regarding my work," Marshall responded. "Such a practice tends to cultivate a state of mind unduly concerned with possible investigation, rather than a complete concentration on the business of victory."[146] Eisenhower, still new to high command, wrote that "once in a while a member of the staff comes in and insists that I give him a resume of reasons more or less along the lines suggested in your letter."[147] He was unable to say if any other records were being kept, but expressed pleasure that someone of Freeman's "distinguished standing" was considering writing about the war.[148] Nimitz brusquely wrote that he hoped Freeman lived long enough to write the history and suggested he visit Adm. Ernest King in Washington to discuss details.[149]

The most effusive response to this potential study of World War II came from MacArthur. "My idea," he wrote, "would be to have you join me immediately on the completion of operations and go with me and the appropriate commanders and staffs over the entire battle areas just as the campaign flowed. I have preserved the fullest documentation and I believe the material would be at hand with little or no necessity for research."[150] No other historian, MacArthur concluded, "has the divine gift like yourself. It would be a contribution to military science beyond compare."[151]

It is interesting to speculate about a history of World War II by Freeman. It would undoubtedly have been written on the same grand scale as *R. E. Lee* and *Lee's Lieutenants*. What he would have said of the war's leaders is a matter of conjecture, though he did express some tentative conclusions. In May 1945, he assessed MacArthur's performance in an article for *Reader's Digest*. MacArthur, he wrote, "had to overcome inferiority of force, lack of equipment and shipping, division of authority, inexperience of unacclimatized troops, and the complexities of directing from a remote country troops of different nationalities."[152] Freeman heralded his use of "the supreme art of the soldier—strategy." MacArthur had "to make every American soldier serve as three" while masking vast islands. In so doing, he "neutralized more troops" than he had to fight—"a most amazing feat of war."[153] His assessment of Nimitz was equally approving. Nimitz "effected the coordination of air, land and naval forces as no commander ever was required to do" he said in a 1946 speech at the University of Richmond.[154] It was Nimitz who created "an elastic naval force" to accomplish tasks of "immense tactical complexity." Recalling Nimitz's concern over Iwo Jima, Freeman reminded his audience that the "bloody little island . . . [saved] more lives than were spent to take it."[155]

Eisenhower, he wrote, was "just, chivalrous, resourceful, energetic, decisive."[156] He "encountered no new weapon, no new tactic, no new defenses" that he was not prepared to meet and contributed significantly to strategic thinking by originating the "equivalent of an impassable river line" by "creating in the rear of the enemy a zone of destroyed culverts, wrecked roads and bombed bridges."[157] In this way, and in his management of a coalition army, Freeman concluded, Eisenhower was able to "achieve what Foch did not" and "what Napoleon accomplished only in part."[158]

His enthusiasm for writing a history of the Second World War was tempered by his knowledge of historical method. He realized his relations with the war's principal leaders, while providing unprecedented access, could call his objectivity into question. In late 1945 he concluded that any study of the war must probably wait "until MacArthur and Marshall both are dead."[159] He later wrote Adm. Ernest King that only with "the perspective of time" could a "detached and scientific study" be done.[160] The passing years did not alter his outlook. "The time to write of 1939-1945," he wrote in April, 1949, "has not arrived yet."[161]

The time had arrived, however, to write something. With the final installment of *Lee's Lieutenants* complete, Freeman prepared for his next work. "I have four in the pot," he wrote James Douglas, "but the one we intend to cook is a long-planned brief life of General Lee, in a hundred thousand words, for the use of young people."[162] Max Perkins had mentioned this idea in 1932, but work first on *George Washington* and then *Lee's Lieutenants* prevented any serious consideration of the project. Now it appeared to be time to do it. "It is a curious thing," Freeman wrote, "that I should have started out to write such a book in 1915 and . . . [now] after thirty years . . . come back."[163] It reminded him of the line by Browning: "After last, returns to first." Charles Scribner paid a visit to Westbourne, and he and Freeman agreed on the idea of a "Lee for schools."[164] As was his habit, Freeman was pondering several other projects at the same time. He told Douglas MacArthur that he wanted to "write a study of the Command of the Army of the Potomac" and then "undertake a detailed study of American command in this [World War II] conflict."[165] The thought of the preeminent authority on Robert E. Lee and the Army of Northern Virginia writing about the Union army is slightly suspect, but it was not the first time he considered this topic.

"To uncover the true story of discontent in the Army of the Potomac," he wrote in 1940, "is worthy of the most careful study. It is full of meaning to every man."[166] He actually drafted an outline for the book, but abandoned it, he wrote, "because I could not bring myself to tell the same story over for the third time."[167] He later told *Time* magazine that he had rejected the idea of writing about the opposing side because "there is so much ugliness in the history of the Army of the Potomac that it should not be shown up by a Southerner."[168] Hovering above all considerations of new books was the previously abandoned *George Washington*. "The challenge of Washington appeals to me," he wrote Raymond Fosdick of the Rockefeller Foundation, ". . . I think I have the health and the vigor and I hope I shall not begin to decay mentally within the [eight years] required for the work."[169] His concerns about undertaking such a work were primarily financial. He projected start-up costs of $12,000, "a larger sum than I would care to attempt to provide from my own income." He asked Fosdick for suggestions on any "foundations with which I have no sort of ties [that] would be interested."[170] Fosdick assured him that "there will be no failure to procure the $12,000" and, shortly thereafter, telephoned with the news that the Carnegie Corporation would provide the funding.[171] Freeman tried to concentrate on "Little Lee," as he had dubbed the short biography of Lee, but found himself "increasingly attracted" to the study of Washington. On June 21, 1944, he pulled together some of his prior work on Washington and did some "probing."[172] He spent most of June and July thinking and planning.[173] Movement started in the middle of July. "I am working now on 'Little Lee' for young people," he wrote Mary Tyler, "and expect in a few days to reach a decision, one way or another, about the Washington."[174] Though he did not announce a decision that month, he was busily recruiting research assistants, locating and purchasing books, and retaining Johns Hopkins University to handle the Carnegie Corporation funds. On August 1, 1944, he made up his mind. "I want you to be the first to know," he wrote John Stewart Bryan, "that I have decided, definitely, to write the Washington and shall begin it very soon."[175] With decision came the usual flurry of activity. By August he had "Little Lee" complete to the beginning of the war in 1861 and the "Washington collection in its place."[176] The path ahead was clear. "Now," he wrote in September, figuratively rubbing his hands together, "to finish 'Little Lee' and then into the *Washington*."[177] A sad event intruded and altered Freeman's plans.

On October 16, 1944, John Stewart Bryan died at the age of seventy-two. The *News Leader* publisher had been in declining health for about two years, but his death was still a staggering blow to Freeman.[178] The two men had been business associates, Confederate compatriots, confidants, and close friends for more than forty years. There was no man Freeman admired more—outside of his father and General Lee—and his death was a "loss irreparable."[179] Tennant Bryan understood the relationship between the two men. "Your loss," he wrote, "was as great as ours—and in some ways greater because of the daily contacts that meant so much to both of you."[180] Freeman wrote Bryan's obituary for the *Richmond Times-Dispatch* and then, "in anguish of soul," wrote his editorial for the *News Leader*.[181] His words were remarkably similar to those he had used in the final chapter of *R. E. Lee*.

As he lies today in the library of Laburnum . . . there are no secrets to hide, no vices to ignore, no basic weakness of character to gloss over with a varnish of shining words. Those of us who were awed in his living presence can look at him in triumphant death and we need not apologize for anything he did, or for aught that he was . . . John Stewart Bryan was a shining, triumphant soul because he courageously adhered to ideals of life that were in part inherited and in part developed from his own devoted service and from his communion with Almighty God. This is no oversimplification. His was a transparent soul.[182]

"We laid our chief to rest," Freeman wrote in his diary on October 18. "I can say no more."[183]

In fact, he had much more to say, and two weeks later he began a biography of John Stewart Bryan. He had completed the first draft of "Little Lee" in late September, but it was not yet in acceptable form, and he planned to "rewrite the book in its entirety."[184] Now he decided to pay tribute to his friend with an "intimate" biography "for private circulation, not for general publication."[185]

Balancing two minor works with his major study of Washington proved difficult. "Little Lee" was the first to go. He named the book "Robert E. Lee and American Youth" but set it aside in January 1945 and did not return to it during that year.[186] In February 1946, he asked his brother for help. "I am sending you today," he wrote Allen, "the manuscript of the 'Little Lee' . . . if you could get it in successful, printable form, it will be a great joy to share with you the royalties for it on

Douglas Freeman with his friend and mentor John Stewart Bryan, publisher of the Richmond News Leader. (Image courtesy of Mary Tyler McClenahan.)

a fifty-fifty basis."[187] Allen revised three chapters by April and appears to have sent back the entire manuscript by May 1947. Freeman changed "a few passages" but noted that he retained Allen's "style in all essentials."[188] It is unclear how long he spent with the manuscript upon its return, but it is obvious that he had lost interest. In January 1948, he told Scribner's he was "too busy" to work on the book and permanently dropped the project.[189]

After Freeman's death, the complete manuscript of "Little Lee" was found among his papers. The family sent it to Scribner's, and it was released in 1958 under the title *Lee of Virginia*.[190] At 236 pages, it is a readable and professional study, but contains some ragged sections that Freeman would have no doubt revised before allowing the book's release. It is also unclear how much, if any, of the book is the work of Allen Freeman. The book, rare and difficult to find, adds little to Freeman's stature as a historian. One wonders if he would have released the book in the form in which it was published.

The Bryan biography suffered a better fate. Freeman pursued writing the biography "with a good deal of fierceness," though he tended to work on it only during lapses of time in the *Washington*.[191] He then hit upon the notion of taking the Bryan material to his *News Leader* office to "work on it there in odd moments."[192] This shift in locale did the trick, and he completed "John Stewart Bryan" on December 30, 1946. He sent the manuscript to the Bryan children, assigning all his rights in it to them. It was, he wrote, "a somber pleasure to write this biography of a man who was what all of us would like to be in service to Virginia and to the nation."[193] The eighteen-chapter book was never published and is today housed among the Bryan papers in the Virginia Historical Society. As a biography, it suffers from the obvious affection Freeman holds for his friend. He refers to him throughout the book as "Mr. Bryan," not the usual posture assumed by a biographer in regard to his subject. He also does not make a complete presentation of various events because he leaves himself entirely out of the book. The closest he comes is to use the phrase "Mr. Bryan's staff." Reading the biography, one would never know that Douglas Freeman was the editor of the *News Leader* and Bryan's closest advisor. As such, the work is incomplete. The real value of the book lies in its detailed comments on the political, economic, social, and cultural life of the city of Richmond during the first half of the twentieth century. It should be noted, however, that "Bryan" was never intended to be an objective, definitive biography. It was the one unique gift Freeman alone could offer to the memory of his mentor and friend. It was confirmation of a life well lived, and a tribute to the values of a generation from which Freeman derived his own character.

These minor writings were but detours from the new work that dominated his historical efforts—the life of George Washington. "I have undertaken this with a great deal of hesitation," he wrote, "but I was prompted by three considerations. First . . . a good life of Washington is much needed. Second, after working regularly at biography for so many years, I had to keep at it. And third . . . I had been so spoiled by the study of Lee that I could not write of any other than a great man . . . [W]hen one has kept the company of gentlemen, one cannot descend to the muck heap of literary endeavor."[194]

CHAPTER 12

"The Thing Is Well Done"

Freeman opened "a new account" with himself on November 26, 1944. He dusted off his cards on George Washington and spent his first day on the new book.[1] His preliminary bibliography of Washington material contained more than three thousand titles, and he had stacked his shelves with approximately five hundred volumes. The funds from the Carnegie Corporation enabled him to hire his first full-time research assistant. He settled on Dr. Gertrude R. B. Richards, a native of Loudoun County, Virginia, the daughter of a Confederate veteran, a graduate of Cornell University, and a former associate professor at Harvard and Wellesley Universities.[2] He was characteristically organized as he began this new project, but displayed a new sense of single-minded purposefulness. He had a few years earlier resigned his professorship at Columbia and was accepting fewer speaking engagements.[3] At fifty-eight years of age, "conscious of the many difficulties in the way of writing a life of Washington," he would lift his ever-high standards of dedicated effort to a new level. His new account called for fourteen hours of writing a week on the Washington biography.[4]

Freeman had spent his entire "historical life" writing about a four-year period in the nineteenth century. Now he was stepping back more than one hundred years to the early eighteenth century. Its terrain was unfamiliar, its accents unintelligible, its customs and habits dimmed by non-acquaintance. His first task was to gain control over the era in which Washington came of age. The source material was as diverse as it was plentiful. "These I have likened to stones of a mosaic," he wrote Robert Lester of the Carnegie Corporation. "They have to be put together with a great deal of patience."[5] The mosaic was dominated by the "Fairfax proprietary," the grant system under which patents of land were acquired. No history of the proprietary existed, so Freeman devoted the first six months of his research to pulling together the facts of this arcane system. In addition to firmly grounding him in the law and society of the eighteenth century, this study offered unexpected insight into the attitude and character of young Washington. It was through the Fairfax proprietary, he wrote, that Washington "got his first conception of royal whim and of America's west."[6] It prepared him for "the duties he had to perform during the French and Indian Wars" and taught him the views "of the class that had the advantage, economically, in colonial life."[7] Next to the practice and politics of land acquisition, Washington was influenced by a unique colonial life with "its classes, its institutions, its usages, and its distinctive government."[8] Freeman again had the "uncomfortable feeling" that he was on "unfamiliar ground." He could, he decided, remain uneasy or study and write a detailed profile of "the Virginia of Washington's youth." Not surprisingly, he chose the latter course. Before he put to paper the first word about the life of George Washington, he wrote a 20,000-word narrative on the Fairfax proprietary and a 116-page study of Virginia in the years 1745-50.[9] "Although a hurried reader may not have patience for the minutiae there set down," he wrote, "one has to confess that only when one had finished that study did one feel 'at home' in the society and among the inhabitants that shaped Washington's life."[10]

While "at home" in one era, Freeman was still an active participant in his own historical present. His editorials and broadcasts traced the campaigns of two theaters of war, and he was still able to predict the turn of events with remarkable accuracy. "If we can start the new year with the North African coast ours," he wrote a friend in December 1942, "we ought to be able to knock Italy out of the war in six months."[11] Allied victory in Northern Africa did not occur until May 1943, but Mussolini fell in July, Sicily was conquered in August, and the Italian mainland was invaded in September. "I think it is only a matter of four months—perhaps only a matter of six weeks," he wrote in July 1944, "before we are going to read that a big American force has gone to Davao and has made its landing on the island of Mindanao."[12] Less than one month later, the U.S. Navy made its first attack against Mindanao, and in September landings began on the Palau Island group, three hundred miles south of the Philippines. Freeman was assisted in his analysis of the war, and in his predictions, by detailed and classified maps "supplied . . . confidentially" to him by the Department of War.[13] He had asked for the maps as compensation for his work as a lecturer at the Army War College, and General Marshall was pleased to authorize their release to him.[14] "I doubt that anyone ever really suspected how close he was to Washington

Freeman in his study at Westbourne, checking war maps. (Image courtesy of Mary Tyler McClenahan.)

and the State Department," Mary Wells Ashworth wrote. "Certainly none of us who worked for him knew, for he kept his counsel completely to himself."[15] Many suspected Freeman knew far more about the war than he was able to say, and many worried parents turned to him with questions about their sons in the military. "I want to have the privilege," he wrote an anxious mother, "to say that you need not be concerned about the failure to receive letters from your boy. Since the middle of May there has been good reason for holding the mail. Many of the soldiers in England could see what was planned to be done . . . [and] along with some fine men like your boy, there might be some traitors in the army . . . [Keep] writing and be sure you will hear from your boy before long."[16] One family reported the disappearance of their son, so Freeman pulled the communiqués from the operations and located the boy's unit. "I think," he wrote, "it is possible to say that he came down somewhere in the region between Antwerp and Arnhem."[17] He noted the enemy opposition was "stiff" and made no predictions about the boy's safety. He performed a similar task for his long-time friend Emma Grey Trigg, whose son was reported missing in action. He gathered his maps and communiqués and went to Mrs. Trigg's home. Because of the terrain of the area in which Bill Trigg had been reported missing, and the position of enemy troops during that week, Freeman reasoned that he had only been separated from his engineer unit while in reconnaissance and would soon find his way back. Thirteen long days passed before his words were confirmed, and Emma Trigg's boy was back with his unit.[18] Not all friends were so fortunate, and Freeman wrote many condolence letters during the war. "You have lost a fine boy that was the light of your life," he wrote a grieving father, "and you and your dear wife must feel now that nothing remains except the twilight. I would be a liar and a fool if I pretended that you would get over this loss, but I do know this much: you have given your boy to the greatest cause that ever was championed by our nation."[19]

On May 2, 1944, Freeman wrote an editorial assessing Allied chances for success in an invasion of Europe. At the conclusion of the column, he made an announcement about his choice of words.

> The preceding article . . . is the last time we shall use that word "invasion" in these columns. The mighty drama on which the curtain soon is to rise in Northwestern Europe is not compassed by "invasion." Some of the implications of that term are predatory. "Invasion" suggests going where an army should not go. The correct word, we take it, is "liberation." We shall use it.[20]

President Roosevelt noticed this editorial recommendation and endorsed it at a press conference. "Our friend, Eugene Meyer of the Washington Post," Roosevelt wrote Freeman, "tells me you originated the suggestion that the word 'invasion' be discarded in favor of the word 'liberation' whenever certain expected military operations in Europe are publicly referred to . . . I am writing this note to offer hearty congratulations and thanks."[21] Six days after Roosevelt's letter, the "liberation" of Europe began.

"This morning at 3:32," Freeman noted in his diary of June 6, 1944, "the telephone rang to announce the 'big landing' in France. I broadcast details at 5:00, 7:00, 8:30, 10:15, 12 M, and 4 PM."[22] As events accelerated, Freeman spent more and more time on the radio and at his office.

"I do not believe that even in 1918 we had climax follow climax the way they are today," he wrote Allen.[23] By early 1945 he could sense the end was near. "The war news is simply amazing," he wrote. "I can't begin to express my admiration of the strategy that has been employed."[24] While studying the movements of the Ninth Army as it crossed the Elbe, he was "overwhelmed" by the news of the death of President Franklin D. Roosevelt. "We of the conservative South disagreed often with him in peace," he wrote, "but we admired beyond our powers of praise the leadership he gave us in war."[25] Roosevelt, he judged, "did more than any other single man, save Churchill alone, to save Britain. In doing so, Roosevelt saved America and civilization from enslavement."

"The big news of the Japanese surrender came yesterday morning at 7:50," Freeman wrote Inez on August 11, 1945. "I went on the air immediately and continued to talk until 8:45 . . . about 3 o'clock, announcement came from the White House that no decision would be made public yesterday or last night."[26] While the respective governments exchanged notes, he was on the air almost every hour, both from the studio and from his third-floor study. "I suspect we are at the end of the war now," he wrote Allen in the midst of broadcasting. "If we are not, the Japanese deserve the immolation that will almost certainly be theirs."[27] On August 14, 1945, Freeman was eating dinner when he was alerted that President Harry Truman would be making a statement at 7:00 P.M. He went up to his study and began to prepare for a broadcast. At the studio, an alert assistant decided to record the station's broadcast on that historic evening; thus making one of the few surviving recordings of Freeman on the air. He started at approximately 7:12 P.M.

Well, it's over. Almighty God, we give thee first of all the thanks. It's over. They've been beaten, beaten to their knees. Beaten into absolute and abject surrender, and compelled for the first time in two thousand years of Japanese history to say: you can come on our shores and we shall not dare to strike a blow against you.[28]

In the midst of his peroration, he paused and spoke off microphone on the telephone to the Associated Press; the audience hearing "Yeah, 'scuse me, I had to call the AP." He picked up in mid-sentence after the interruption. "Victory was achieved," he said, "by the unity of America; it could not have been achieved in any other manner." Freeman the newsman then gave way to Freeman the historian. "I propose now to give you the parade of all those great armies that have fought for victory." He took his listeners back to September 1938 and traced the early moves of Hitler and the invasion of Poland. As he spoke, the station provided background music of Polish, French, British, and Russian anthems as befitting the point of the narrative. He defended the Russians' early alliance with Hitler. "We did not then realize," he said, "what we now know: that Russia was preparing, even at this bloody cost, to put between her and Germany, a barrier, a buffer, while Stalin prepared his men for the inevitable conflict, the decisive conflict, of the war."[29] Affecting the "pathetic" style he taught the members of the current events class, and with the "Marseillaise" playing in the background, he described the Nazi attack on France. "Oh God, Paris is lost . . . the beautiful music of the Marseillaise, lost, lost, lost . . . Britain stood alone."

"In that hour," he continued, "there was in Washington a man who realized the risks that were being faced by this country, a man who saw that the struggle was not Britain's alone, but ours, and civilization's, and humanity's. And in that dark hour, to the immortal glory of his country and to his own eternal fame, Franklin Roosevelt turned over to the British all that we had in the way of light reserve artillery . . . small arms . . . [and] high explosives." This tribute to the president differed sharply from his diary entry of September 3, 1940, in which he expressed his opinion that FDR should have been impeached for his actions in support of Great Britain.[30] "Alone Britain stood," he now said, "but not alone; blood was thicker than water and . . . we were making ready."

Freeman quickly reviewed Germany's attack on Russia—"the most incredible day of the war, save this"—and highlighted the island-hopping strategy and "genius of that magnificent man—Douglas MacArthur." He did not have time on this broadcast to cover events in Europe, so he concluded with more thanks to God and with the playing of the National Anthem. He recounted the events of that dramatic evening in a letter to the vacationing Inez, providing posterity with a behind-the-scenes glimpse of the solemn broadcast. "As it happened," he wrote, "I had shut the windows in my study before I came down and I did not think to open them after I got upstairs. Consequently I had to go through my familiar process of shucking while I talked. I concluded in my BVDs."[31]

A little more than a month after the end of the war, Freeman was invited by Assistant Secretary of War John McCloy to accompany him on a trip around the world to inspect U.S. military installations and study "the problems of civil versus military occupation."[32] The month-long trip would start in London and continue with stops in Paris, Frankfurt, Vienna, Cairo, New Delhi, Peking, and Tokyo. Freeman would serve as an advisor to McCloy and assist in the preparation of the commission's final report. It was an incomparable educational opportunity, and he eagerly accepted the invitation. *George Washington* would go on a brief, but complete, hold.

The McCloy commission departed America on September 28, 1945. Even on a transcontinental flight, Freeman followed his schedule. Waking in his berth, he "gasped in awe" at "a gorgeous pink sunrise." "After drinking my full of it," he wrote, "I looked at my watch. It stood at 3:30 Richmond time. Dame Nature had not failed to set off her alarm-clock."[33] Arriving in London on September 29, he set off for a walking tour of the city. "The overwhelming sensation," he wrote, was "one of relief, immense relief. The destruction has been vast . . . but the 'old' city is itself."[34] During his two days in London, he went to Westminster, the National Gallery, and Piccadilly. He also learned the objective of the mission. "In strictest confidence," he wrote Inez, "our mission is to Tokyo to see what can be done to straighten out the lines of authority and administration there. We came the 'long way' round in order not to create the impression on MacArthur that he was being scrutinized so soon . . . this must be regarded as strictly our own secret."[35] He spent most of his time in Paris writing an account of the first leg of the trip for McCloy's report.[36] He did take in some sightseeing, but was more observant of the effect of the war. "Gone is the old chanticleer spirit, the old irrepressible gay spirit," he wrote. "Paris looks humiliated, not conquered . . . Germans were ignored and hated; the Americans are greeted and tolerated—no more than that."[37]

Freeman spent his first afternoon in Frankfurt touring the vicinity in a Mercedes convertible once owned by Hermann Goering.[38] On October 5, while the rest of the party went to Berlin, he spent more than an hour alone with General Eisenhower. He noted in his journal that Eisenhower seemed nervous, but he reported to Inez that "[he] told me an immense quantity of top-fact."[39] Then he was off to lunch with U.S. envoy Averill Harriman and Gen. W. Beedle Smith. Harriman "was as completely confidential as Eisenhower had been."[40] It had been a heady day. He spent his last days in Germany writing a report about a local displaced persons camp and having the "unspeakable thrill of reading the German Generals' statements of what happened in Normandy and during the Battle of the Bulge."[41]

Vienna served as a jumping-off point for a side trip to Budapest.

There Freeman was sought out by Soviet marshal Kliment Voroshilov. The two men clinked wine glasses and discussed the intricacies of the Red Army's final campaign.[42] Back in Vienna, Freeman had another lengthy conversation with an American commander, this time Gen. Mark Clark. The general "opened up completely" about his Italian campaign and made Freeman blush when he told him: "Doctor, at least twenty times during my campaign I wished you were there to give me your slant of the situation."[43]

He viewed the relics of Tutankhamen in Cairo—"indescribable"— and saw Bethlehem—"a little, huddled town"—from the sky. "I stop and marvel," he wrote, "when I think that in four days I have seen three of the great glories of the world—the Parthenon, the tomb of Tutankhamen, and the Taj Mahal."[44] In Calcutta, "the most incredible Babylon I ever have seen," Freeman and McCloy spent the evening together speaking "freely of Stimson, Marshall, F.D.R., King" and others.[45] He dined with Chiang Kai-Shek in Chungking, and then tended to some personal business, spending an entire day with his nephew Hamner who served as the agent in China for an American tobacco company. Hamner was not only a business success, but also had set up "an elaborate system of espionage" during the war. He had placed so many spies over such a wide territory that he was able to monitor the movements of more than 150,000 Japanese troops in the vicinity of Hong Kong. He was hunted by the Japanese and was the target of an unsuccessful ambush.[46] Freeman was justifiably proud of his nephew and, at their parting, "took him in my arms . . . and told him that when I passed on I expected him to be the head of the family, and to maintain the Freeman ideals." Also during this day away from the McCloy commission, he purchased a Mandarin skullcap that would one day become the topic of much bemused conversation in the *News Leader* office. Before leaving for Tokyo, he saw the Great Wall, the Winter Palace, and Peking—sites seen by few Americans of that day and for many years thereafter.[47]

As the plane circled Atsugi airfield in Tokyo, Freeman looked out the window and saw Douglas MacArthur waiting. The two men had exchanged many letters through the years, but this was their first meeting. "[He] is just as captivating," Freeman wrote, "as he is made out to be."[48] The two men spent much time together, discussing military history, tactics, and strategy. During one private meeting, Freeman and McCloy urged MacArthur to watch his public statements.[49] "For a while it looked as if he was heeding our counsel," Freeman later wrote of this conversation, "but afterward he got the bug again."[50] Freeman found Mrs. MacArthur to be "gracious, simple, considerate." He spent more than an hour with the general on his last day in Tokyo, but made no comment in his diary or in any letters about the subject matter. "The main part of the flight," he noted upon completion of McCloy's objective of the trip, "is behind us."[51] He was eager to go home.

Several more stops followed. He stood at the top of Mount Suribachi on Iwo Jima, wrote most of the commission's report while laying over in Guam, experienced two October 30s when crossing the International Date Line, and spent two days with Adm. Chester Nimitz at Pearl Harbor.[52] He gave a press conference in Hawaii, warning that if American forces were brought home too soon, they might be compelled to return to the war zones. "If we reduce our occupation force too fast and too low," he said, "we cannot discharge our responsibilities in Europe and in Asia. Personally, I believe we shall be forced to continue compulsory service so as to provide sufficient troops for occupation needs."[53] Shortly after the press conference, he was approached by a young flyer carrying a charred copy of Volume Three of *Lee's Lieutenants*. "[He] was reading this on a bombing run from Guam to Tokyo," Freeman noted, "and had it at hand when flak struck the plane and set it afire." The crew put out the fire and landed safely, but the cover of the book bore the sign of the fight.[54] Freeman was intrigued by the story and traded the flyer an entire three-volume set of *Lee's Lieutenants* for the one burned book. At 11:05 P.M. on October 31, 1945, the McCloy party set off from Hawaii bound for San Francisco. Freeman arrived in Washington, D.C., on November 3. He calculated that he had traveled 27,000 miles through the air.[55] It is hard to imagine a more perfect trip for Freeman. He fed his spirit with the beauties of antiquity and honed his skills with high-level conferences with world leaders. "Nothing that ever happened in my life in like time," he wrote McCloy, "was of comparable educational value. My poor horizon was widened and my knowledge extended . . . I shall never cease to be grateful to you for remembering me when opportunity offered."[56]

More than an educational opportunity, the world tour cemented Freeman's already close relationship with the leaders of America's military establishment. He was trusted by officers at the highest level, and there is no instance of his violating their confidences. In his vast amount of papers, only a few sentences are found that detail his conversations with military leaders. One wonders what Eisenhower told him in Frankfurt or what Marshall confided during their many meetings during the war. What did MacArthur say when Freeman told him to watch his public statements? What did Nimitz say as he and Freeman stood together and gazed out across the water at Pearl Harbor? From Freeman, on these and thousands of other instances, there is only silence. This discretion, he surely knew, was part of his value to these men. It also helped, no doubt, that he was a newspaper editor and a respected historian. These facts could not have been lost on the leaders of the war who knew, consciously or subconsciously, that they might be having their historical picture taken. Because of (or in spite of) these reasons, Freeman's influence continued to grow. McCloy asked for his advice on handling captured German records; he testified before the House Select Committee on Post-War Military Policy; and Secretary of Defense James Forrestal sought his views on the preparation of "a joint history of the British-American part in World War II."[57] So firmly was he established as America's preeminent military historian that his reputation was part of popular culture. The cartoon "Steve Canyon" showed the comic-strip hero lecturing to a class at the Air Force Academy. "Is it worth all the sweat of this tough grind?" he asks in one panel. "Someone asked Douglas Southall Freeman . . . this question . . . and Dr. Freeman replied 'There never was a great general who had not been a great major!'"[58]

One intriguing part of Freeman's relationship with the War Department was in the area of intelligence. Here one cannot be too certain of his involvement in such matters, but a few surviving comments give some hints. In 1953, he wrote Richmond attorney, and future U.S. Supreme Court justice, Lewis F. Powell Jr., and mentioned that he had been asked, in 1941, to "advise" on counter-espionage. "I shall never forget my depression of spirit," he wrote. "We had no more of the technique of spying on spies than the babes in the woods would have possessed."[59] In July 1948, Freeman sent an interesting letter to Richard S. Reynolds, president of Reynolds Metals Company.

We who are responsible for it do not feel that there is as close cooperation between the Richmond office of the Central Intelligence Agency and the Reynolds Metals Company as we think ought to be . . . [Commander Chandler] and I both feel that your company is the most important one in this area for the information it can give our government regarding certain very important activities abroad . . . May I, therefore, ask that Commander Chandler have the privilege of a personal interview with you, to explain to you exactly what types of information we need and what gaps we have that he thinks your

2

89

company can supply. I need not add that I write to you in absolute candor and confidence, because my own connection with C.I.A. is, of course, unknown to the public, and must so remain.[60]

No other letter or memorandum has been discovered to shed any light on Freeman's apparent relationship with the Central Intelligence Agency. He knew Allen Dulles of the OSS—the future director of the CIA—and, given his connection to business, social, political, and military leaders, it is not beyond reason to conclude that he kept an eye out for any suspicious activity during the war and its aftermath. As with his military involvement, Freeman kept the matter quiet, leaving only an occasional clue of his multi-layered service to his country.

In February 1946, the University of Richmond invited Gen. Dwight Eisenhower and Adm. Chester Nimitz to be awarded the honorary degree of Doctor of Letters. Freeman wrote both men, urging them to accept the degree and come to Richmond for the ceremony. "I felt that it was proper," he wrote Eisenhower, "for the University of the battle-scarred capital of the Confederacy to recognize the great service performed by you and by Admiral Nimitz in accordance with the loftiest tradition of our state."[61] Both Nimitz and Eisenhower accepted. "I am such an admirer of Doctor Freeman," Eisenhower wrote President Boatwright, "that I am always disposed to conform instantly to any suggestion he makes."[62] The event took place on March 28, 1946, in the university's Cannon Memorial Chapel. Freeman delivered the principal address, with Eisenhower and Nimitz speaking briefly. Following the ceremony, a luncheon was held at Westbourne. The two five-starred warriors stood in a receiving line and greeted Congressional Medal of Honor winners, former governors, and the leaders of Richmond society.[63] The *Richmond Times-Dispatch* gave the event front-page coverage and included many photographs. Some showed the guests at Westbourne drinking mint juleps or other alcoholic beverages. A furor immediately arose over the use of alcohol at a function associated with the Baptist-affiliated University of Richmond. "It is a matter of some concern and deep regret to me," one pastor wrote Freeman, "and I am sure to many other Baptists . . . that you provided these intoxicating drinks, or permitted them to be provided and served, to guests in your home . . . This is indeed strange procedure for a Christian school."[64]

"I did not know," Freeman answered, "that it was customary for persons to be called upon to specify the menu they served at private luncheons in

In March 1946, Douglas Southall Freeman entertaining at his home in Richmond Adm. Chester W. Nimitz, Chief of Naval Operations, and Gen. Dwight D. Eisenhower, Army Chief of Staff. (Image courtesy of the Richmond Times-Dispatch.)

their own home; but as you mistakenly associate the University of Richmond with this luncheon, I beg to say that so far as the University was concerned, the ceremonies ended when the academic procession was dismissed . . ."[65] He went on to explain that Nimitz and Eisenhower were his "personal friends" and were being entertained as such. Despite his defiant attitude, the criticism swelled, and, on the same day he answered Pastor Cummins's letter, he submitted his resignation as rector. He cited the "major changes of staff" and the need for "a new point of view," but did not refer to the "mint-julep" controversy.[66] Privately he expressed concerns that the incident "would give the enemies of the institution an opportunity of assailing it." All the while he fumed at having to "waste time now in dealing with fools and bigots."[67] President Boatwright and the board rallied to his defense. "For you to resign now," Boatwright wrote, "would encourage every reactionary and extreme fundamentalist among us . . . [Y]ou would place a club in the hands of the enemies of all you represent . . . [D]on't you owe it to yourself as well as to the University of Richmond to stand fast?"[68] Pastor Theodore F. Adams of the First Baptist Church of Richmond, and one of the leading Baptist ministers in the nation, echoed those sentiments. "To lose you," he wrote, "would be a real catastrophe. Please, sir, do stand by until we can get this thing cleared up. We need you very much."[69] The Board of Trustees appointed a committee to express its "unanimous desire" that Freeman should stay on as rector.[70] Freeman agreed to stay on the board, though the issue continued to nag him as letters kept coming from outraged Baptists.[71]

Dwight Eisenhower had said he was inclined to "conform instantly" to any suggestion of Freeman. A few months after the University of Richmond ceremony, Freeman suggested a new idea to his general-friend. "It is important for the country's sake that I see you," he wrote, and "Ike" responded with an invitation to lunch at the Pentagon.[72] Freeman confided his plan to Mary Tyler. "Strictly between you, Leslie and myself," he wrote, "I am going to try to persuade General Eisenhower to let himself be considered for the Presidency of the United States."[73] He assumed it would be on the Democratic ticket and that the popular Ike could defeat Harry Truman at the 1948 convention.[74] The meeting took place in early November 1946. Freeman began in dramatic fashion: "I believe the hand of the Lord is upon you and that you must accept the presidency and clean up this mess here in Washington."[75] He recalled that Eisenhower snapped, "God forbid." The general explained that "the Army may suffer and the national defense be impaired if he [went] before Congress under any imputation that he is a potential candidate or, as he put it, a partisan."[76] He did concede that he would consider the presidency if "a situation developed in which [he] would be the man to whom the country would turn with the statement that [he] alone could do what had to be done."[77] That ended the discussion of that topic—for the moment. "I think I made a dent in him," Freeman noted, "and I shall follow it up."[78] He was right; Eisenhower later recalled that the conversation "made a deeper and more lasting impression on me than anything else I have yet heard on that subject."[79] The general still declined to run. "I need not tell you," Freeman wrote him, "I am sorry you did not let yourself be a candidate in this election, because you would have been elected and would have been, in the mercy of God, able to render immense service; but you did what you thought you should have done and you were, of course, right in standing squarely to it."[80] Freeman also believed himself to be right, and he would stand "squarely" for Eisenhower for president during the coming years.

His enthusiastic and active support for Eisenhower represented a political break with his friend, President Harry Truman. The two men met in March 1944 while viewing military maneuvers in North Carolina. They struck up a conversation about Truman's Committee on Military Affairs and proper training of officers.[81] Upon his return to Washington, Truman invited Freeman to address his committee on the topic of "the old Committee on the Conduct of the [Civil] War." Truman brought together not only his committee for dinner, but also Gen. George Marshall, Adm. Ernest King, Secretary of War Frank Knox, and Under Secretaries of War Robert Patterson and James Forrestal.[82] "What you said was exactly to the point," Truman wrote in appreciation, "and will have a tremendous effect on our being able to function during this Presidential year, and function correctly."[83] It was natural that the senator from Missouri and the historian from Virginia would hit it off. Truman had an almost as vast and detailed knowledge of history as did Freeman, and the two men could speak as well on military affairs. Freeman began to examine the work of the Committee on Military Affairs, and his estimation of Truman grew daily. "I have found him one of the wisest, most modest men I know," he wrote. "His abilities are high, but he does not trust his own judgment in matters concerning which he has no information. He seeks the best counsel he can get, and follows it."[84] He began to talk of Truman for higher office. "There is no chance of a southerner getting a second place on the ticket," he wrote a friend as the 1944 Democratic Convention approached, "but I am not without hope that my friend, Harry Truman, will land the Vice Presidential nomination."[85] He expressed the same hope to Truman. "I hope I may see you again soon," he wrote, "and I could wish nothing better for the Democratic Party than that you should be Mr. Roosevelt's running-mate."[86] Freeman recognized the stakes in the election of 1944 with the war-weary and ill FDR at the head of the ticket. "I am perfectly willing," he wrote in October of the election year, "to trust [Truman] as Vice President and I would trust him if Mr. Roosevelt died during his Fourth Term."[87] He expressed the same sentiment to Truman after the election. "I made the long analysis of the incumbent's [Henry Wallace's] record and decided that however fine his theories, and however noble his character, his judgment did not justify Democrats in renominating him in a year when he might succeed to the Presidency."[88] He was all but telling Truman that he would shortly become president. "I have great confidence in your judgment and analysis of public officials and commanding generals as they are," Vice President Truman responded. "I hope some time we can have another visit."[89] Two months later, upon the death of FDR, Truman was president. "He will not dazzle with brilliance," Freeman wrote in the *News Leader*, "but if one condition is met, he will satisfy by his honest diligence, courage and thoroughness. The one condition is that he have the support of right-minded patriots."[90] Freeman's admiration and support for Truman had quickly risen. It would fall almost as fast.

Freeman's fiscal conservatism set him on a collision course with the Truman administration. "The historian will be puzzled to understand our day," he wrote Congressman A. Willis Robertson, "unless he realizes that we have above everything else a Labor government in Washington."[91] He believed Truman conceded too much ground to John L. Lewis and striking coal miners. "We are facing," he wrote in June 1946, "a succession of related strikes that seek nothing less than a labor dictatorship."[92] His contempt for Lewis—whom he dubbed "the most dangerous man in the United States"—led him to make a rare personally vicious statement.[93] His brother Allen had suggested that Lewis might be the victim of "a merciful coronary occlusion" and thus be removed from the political scene. "I hope you are right," Freeman snapped somewhat less humorously. "The sooner he dies, the better for America."[94]

Truman's seeming ineptitude in handling post-war labor and inflationary problems caused Freeman to become "heartily disgusted . . . with our distinguished President."[95] He judged the men around Truman to be "common." "The worst of them is scarcely inferior," he wrote, "if inferior at all, to the average of Congress . . . and I never knew [Congress] to be more vacillating or cowardly than it is now. God help us!"[96] He bemoaned "the lack of leadership" that rivaled a "lack of courage." His break with Truman became final over post-war foreign policy. "I think he is being misled into one of the most dangerous adventures in the history of American Foreign Policy," he wrote in March 1947. "This newspaper will oppose him to the last and to the limit."[97] He opposed the Greek relief bill, arguing that "America will bankrupt herself in trying to save bankrupts," and took an even harsher stand against the Marshall Plan.[98] "We are being led astray," he wrote Sen. Harry Byrd, "by men who have never had any conception of what is represented in blood and sweat by the taxpayers of the country. Between you and me, also, I am sorely disappointed in General Marshall as Secretary of State. I do not feel that he has achieved one single success in that capacity."[99] His opposition to the Marshall Plan drove him into an alliance with Republican senator Robert Taft—a man Freeman felt was "a political trickster."[100] The Wilsonian idealism he had touted as a young editor was now firmly subordinate to fiscal conservatism. "The American business man," he wrote Taft, "would not buy a second-hand motor car with as little information as the State Department offers to support the appeal for at least Twenty Billion Dollars."[101] He detailed the crux of his opposition in a letter to Harry Byrd.

> I think some of our legislators have gone crazy, both in Washington and here. They seem to think there is no limit to the taxes the American people will pay. Our public men are very much mistaken. The worm will turn . . . As for the Marshall Plan, if Congress passes it in anything like the form prepared by General Marshall, results are going to be politically calamitous to the party responsible . . . if we make the commitment and do not fulfill it, we shall have a renewal of the discredit that was ours after the First World War. As you well know, there is no surer way of making an enemy than to lend someone money or to do someone a favor that does not accomplish all that the beneficiary expected.[102]

"The more I study the Marshall Plan," he wrote in another letter to Byrd, "the more do I feel myself compelled regretfully to believe that it is half-baked."[103] To Byrd he quoted "the ancient maxim, whom the gods destroy, they first make mad" and stated that evidence "of that madness appears in the policy of our executive branch."[104] To his brother, he was more blunt. "Truman," he judged his old friend, "is a flop."[105]

In the midst of his opposition to the Truman administration and its foreign policy came the distinct possibility that Freeman might become part of it. Virginia senator A. Willis Robertson, a long-time friend, suggested Freeman be nominated as ambassador to Great Britain. "Few Americans," he wrote Truman, "are better known or more greatly admired by the British leaders."[106] Senator Byrd promptly joined his colleague in urging the appointment. "You probably have seen or will hear of the talk that I may be appointed American Ambassador to England," Freeman wrote his brother. "I think this is a piece of 'hooey' and I beg you not to take it seriously."[107] He apparently did take it seriously. "I have no idea the President will call me to the Ambassadorship," he wrote Senator Byrd, "and, frankly, I hope he does not because I don't like to think of making a change to a life that others covet and I don't. Of course, if the President should decide that I had the particular qualities he desires at this time, I would have a serious question to answer."[108] As with offers of college presidencies, he allowed himself to be considered, expressed gratitude, but never pushed for the appointment or admitted any desire for it. The matter faded away by the end of February 1947, and Truman ultimately named another to the post.

In the same year that Freeman became editor of the *News Leader*, another newspaperman arrived in Richmond to start a new career. Harry Flood Byrd was editor of the *Winchester Evening Star*, son of the former Speaker of the Virginia House of Delegates, and the self-made owner of what would become one of the world's largest and most productive apple orchards. One year younger than Freeman, he was elected to the Virginia state senate in 1915 and to the governorship in 1925.[109] In the course of his career, both as governor and U.S. senator, he built a political organization—machine to many observers—that dominated Virginia for more than forty years. The keys to the organization were the county courthouse system, where Byrd loyalists held local offices, and a restricted electorate that kept down the number of voting blacks and Republicans. The organization was not corrupt—indeed it was unique in its honesty—and it did reflect the political philosophy of the great majority of politically active citizens. A candidate for office stood no chance of being elected if he was not a Democrat, and little to no chance of being elected if he was not a supporter or ally of the organization.

Freeman became Byrd's friend, his sometime confidant, and his frequent critic. He generally agreed with the philosophy of Byrd and his lieutenants, but opposed what he saw as the "invisible government" established by the machine. Thus for more than twenty-five years, he conducted a diplomatic two-step with Virginia's most powerful politician: supporting his conservative views on finance, the role of government, and racial matters, while at the same time becoming a recognized anti-machine man.

"Your father is a man whose political star I always followed with enthusiasm," Freeman wrote Byrd in October 1924, "and while I do not think I have ever had the pleasure of meeting you, I have watched your course with the profoundest interest and admiration."[110] A little more than two weeks later, he pledged his support to Byrd in his race for governor. "We afternoon newspaper men" he wrote, "have to stand together."[111] He assured *News Leader* readers that "Mr. Byrd will do his utmost to meet the expectations of his supporters . . . He is young. He is ambitious . . . He has a sense of organization and of method." His administration, he predicted, would "be rich in wisdom, rare in leadership, full in service."[112]

Byrd was easily elected and outlined a progressive program, calling for reorganization of state government into a corporate structure, a "pay-as-you-go" highway system, tax reform, and an anti-lynching law. He also moved to consolidate his gains so that his leadership and philosophy would last beyond his single term.[113] Freeman was an enthusiastic supporter of this agenda, and the friendship between the two men grew closer. Freeman often served as a surrogate speaker for the governor.[114] There were occasional disagreements—"It is always exceedingly distasteful to dissent from anything you do" Freeman once wrote—but at the end of the administration, he stated, "[I]f he has not been Virginia's greatest governor since the days of Henry and of Jefferson, *The News Leader* confesses that it does not know to whom to award that distinction."[115] Though he noticed the makings of a political machine, Freeman was not as yet alarmed by its increasing control of state politics. "The memory of the Byrd Administration," he wrote, "will always be a brilliant chapter in the history of Virginia."[116]

While the Byrd administration was a memory, the Byrd organization was a reality with which Freeman found himself more and more at odds. Byrd's immediate two successors, John Garland Pollard and George C. Peery, were organization "regulars" who continued the policies of their predecessor and sealed his unquestioned control over the Democratic Party and thus over the state. Byrd became a U.S. senator in 1933 and was soon a nationally recognized opponent of Roosevelt's New Deal—a role in which he was fully supported by Freeman. "If we get together a few of the Senators who are really interested in the southern tradition," he wrote the senator in 1935, "we might awaken in them some vague sense of their duty to support the constitutional division of power between the states and the federal government. If you and I together could do that, I think we might be performing a service worth-while."[117] Byrd set up a lunch with "ten or twelve of your admirers in the Senate," but the unity the two men felt regarding national issues did not transcend to state issues.[118]

The split began during the administration of Gov. James H. Price. Elected in 1937, Price was an anomaly in this era: He became governor without Byrd's support and pursued a moderately liberal program that directed government "toward humanitarian ideals."[119] Price's program was enough to cause disquiet among the organization, but his removal of Byrd regulars from state positions caused a significant rupture. Freeman was a strong backer of Price's political and personnel decisions. He had long distrusted the machine regulars—in particular, state compensation commission chairman and top Byrd lieutenant E. R. Combs—and embraced the appointment of non-partisan professionals to state jobs. Price's independence, however, solidified the machine into unyielding opposition to the governor's program. Freeman backed Price editorially and appealed to Byrd to call off his machine. The senator disclaimed responsibility. "I have done nothing directly or indirectly to obstruct a single reform advocated by Governor Price," he wrote. "To the contrary, I have done what I could to prevent factionalism, which has been increasing in Virginia for the past several years."[120] Freeman responded, somewhat disingenuously, that he "never believed for a moment" that Byrd had sabotaged the governor's program, but outlined the reason why he could have drawn such an obvious conclusion.

There is no denying the fact that many of the "old boys" got together with amazing speed when any law that seemed to impair this organization was before the assembly. When the session ended I thought of you and of the famous admonition that we need sometime to be saved from our friends.[121]

Price's legislative program was demolished, and he limped through the remainder of his term. A more accommodating governor, Colgate Darden, was elected in 1941, and organization regulars were soon back in their old positions of authority. "I feel that the state has lost a part of the finest work ever done in my lifetime," Freeman wrote one fired official, "and I pray that somebody will have sense enough in the future to realize this."[122] He stepped up his attacks on Governor Darden and the organization, while continuing to write letters to Byrd under the façade that the senator was not directing events in Richmond. "Many things are being done in your name," he wrote, "and ostensibly under your influence that are not in the spirit you always have displayed for the advancement of Virginia."[123] And again: "I know you have admirable sources of information but sometimes am perplexed to know if you realize fully what some of the men are doing in the name of the 'organization.'"[124] In January 1945, Freeman admitted to Byrd that he was a friend, but one "outside the organization."[125] Byrd sought to reassure him. "I have bitter and relentless enemies who will misrepresent me on every occasion," he wrote. "I can only hope that my true friends will inform themselves of the real facts."[126]

Freeman's activities as an anti-machine man led to some calls for him to increase his political activity. "Certainly no man in Virginia is better qualified to serve as Governor than are you," one admirer wrote.[127] The suggestion was dismissed. "After having aroused, inevitably, thirty years of animosities as a newspaper editor," Freeman wrote, "I would be a fool if I invited these animosities to be returned on my own head."[128] Though he would not seek office, he urged the formation of a "Taxpayers' Association" to counter the machine. This suggestion brought shrieks from the legislature. One House member invited him to stand for office in order that he could "delight in licking the pants off" him, and a senator attributed Freeman's attitude to his "failure to be accepted by the government."[129] More alarming than the rhetoric was a suggested resolution that the monopoly of the Richmond newspapers be investigated. "I have been in the newspaper business upwards of forty years," Freeman wrote, "and would have assumed that I had seen about all that could happen in the way of legislative folly . . . [This] final action . . . goes beyond anything any of us ever have known."[130] His Virginia— the Virginia of Lee and of Washington—"never was in such great danger of begin subjected to machine rule and more suppression of essential rights."[131]

"You must remember," Harry Byrd once wrote an associate, "that Douglas Freeman will never lose an opportunity to discredit you."[132] Freeman did want to strike "one more good blow against those who want Virginia to be in bondage to the invisible government," but he judged he could effect the most change through cultivating relations with other elected officials. Though initially an opponent of Governor Darden, he grew to respect the urbane governor's "scientific approach" and his "character, aptitudes, and equipment."[133] He gave much behind-the-scenes advice to Congressman A. Willis Robertson, an ally of the organization but not a "regular," in his successful bid to become U.S. senator, and he engaged in cordial correspondence with Col. Francis P. Miller, the leading anti-machine Democrat.[134] He even preferred electing "a good machine man" to office rather than risk "a gross reactionary of the same political stripe."[135] Most of all, however, he attempted to influence policy by remaining friends with Harry Byrd. He never ceased chastising him for the actions of his organization, but remained a vigorous supporter of the positions he took in the Senate. He adopted a "federalist" view, "drawing the sharpest line . . . between State and Federal policies," supporting Byrd in the latter, often opposing him in the former. It was an accommodation with which both men felt at ease. "I want to have a long talk with you," Byrd wrote in 1946. "I realize, of course, that I have made many errors of judgment, but I believe it would be rare for any two informed citizens to agree exactly on the momentous questions that have confronted the United States Senate in the past thirteen years."[136] As national politics veered more to the left, Freeman found more reason to support Byrd. "You will be called upon boldly to challenge the extravagances of a leftist administration that seeks to buy the votes of every group foolish enough to listen to its bids," he wrote. "As the years pass, we must never let minor differences of opinion on political questions keep friends from close and unrestrained communication."[137] So Freeman maintained his complex relationship with Byrd. Supporter and critic, friend and opponent, he encapsulated his position in a letter in June 1945. "I oppose many things that are done by men who profess to be your lieutenants," he wrote, "but I know at the same time the invaluable character of the work you are doing in the Senate. I beseech you, do not make it hard for your friends outside the organization to give you full support."[138]

With war and politicians and a world tour bidding for his time and attention, it was Freeman's schedule that kept *George Washington* from falling by the wayside. "He is proving the most interesting and certainly the most misunderstood figure with whom I ever had to deal," he wrote. "It is incredible how very wrong the records prove the popular presentation of Washington to have been for the period prior to the Revolution."[139] He was not a toga-clad Cincinnatus or patriot from the cradle. "From the time he was fifteen and a half years of age," Freeman reported to Robert Lester, "he was making money and was keeping books. By the time he was 19 he was the creditor of the family, the one member who always had ready cash. [To] 1753, it may surprise you to know, there is not a single line of evidence to show any revolutionary impulse of any sort in Washington."[140] While Gertrude Richards plowed through libraries and archives, Freeman conducted his usual thorough examination of any aspect slightly related to Washington's life. He asked for a soil survey of Westmoreland County to explain Washington's shift from growing tobacco to growing wheat; he asked the superintendent of Mount Vernon how far one could see upstream while standing on the front lawn; he sought to determine at what exact time Washington's spring flowers bloomed; and he almost daily discounted some old Washington fable.[141] "Research for feature story indicates George Washington embalmed by pickling process," a telegram from a Columbia journalism student read. "No foundation whatsoever for the story," Freeman wired back.[142]

When he discovered what appeared to be an Italian term of art for a specific military maneuver, he put the question of translation to the military attaché in the Italian embassy.[143] When he needed a legal interpretation of a chancery case in 1759, he wrote Supreme Court justice Felix Frankfurter.[144] The justice was more than happy to oblige; suggesting Freeman consult *Acts of the Privy Council of England*, Volume Four, *1745-66*. "See if it doesn't shed some light on your inquiry," Frankfurter wrote, adding that he marveled at Freeman's progress on the biography.[145] Freeman located the first dated survey prepared by Washington and obtained more money from the Carnegie Corporation to send Miss Richards to Europe to search libraries in England and France.[146] "I think," he wrote, "we can look forward to the time when we can say that no known source or probable source of Washington material has not been explored, to the limit. This may prolong the work for a year or two, but I think it would be justified."[147]

One major source of material was the so-called Havemeyer Collection. The papers consisted of letters written by members of the Washington family during George's youth. Freeman looked for these papers with no success. Then he heard of an eccentric collector in New Jersey who owned a "sizeable collection of Washington material" but had never permitted historians to examine it.[148] Freeman—no doubt remembering the trouble he had with the batch of Lee letters owned by Mrs. deButts—wrote the collector a letter requesting to look at the papers. Much to his delight and surprise, he was granted permission. "When we went into his vaults," he wrote Robert Lester, "we were astounded."[149]

> Nowhere in any private collection could there possibly be such a wealth of Washington and Revolutionary material. All the Havemeyer papers were there . . . In addition, there were about 200 revolutionary letters, several score of unpublished Washington letters, two of Washington's account books and the long vanished cash book (it turned out to be a ledger) that Washington kept as a boy. Some of the autographs of this book, by the way, are the earliest fully authenticated specimens of his

handwriting as a young man. The treasures of this collection are almost past reckoning . . .[150]

Freeman had the entire collection microfilmed and was given unlimited access to the library for any book he could not locate elsewhere. He made other discoveries: those of overlooked material. "I almost hesitate to report," he wrote, "what actually we have found because it may seem to reflect on the diligence and enterprise of men whose scholarship is above challenge. The reality is this: scarcely half the interesting and relevant facts contained in accessible printed materials on 1754 have been used . . . I am unable to account for the superficial treatment of the source material."[151] Privately he was less magnanimous. "The research shows the greatest imaginable neglect on the part of some of the biographers in failing to use even printed sources available to them," he fumed. "It is a human characteristic, is it not, to be 'afraid of that which is high'?"[152] He was still the man who had written from Johns Hopkins that when one does a job, he should leave nothing for those who come behind. "Alas and alas," he observed, "scholars, like other human beings, often are lazy."[153]

He ran into some "blind alleys," but he had enough material to begin writing in earnest. "We now have a picture of some depth."[154]

The figure of young Washington is becoming more rounded. We are, in fact, at the thrilling stage where a figure that has been silent as [a] portrait on the wall suddenly begins to breathe. Washington the diligent young businessman, was determined to equal the older sons in fortune—and he did. He had system, energy, and precocity in business affairs, but he was exceedingly ambitious, almost reckless and most inordinately proud. He learned fast . . . one can see his education almost day by day in the hard school of experience.[155]

He was "by far the most complex young man it ever has been my privilege to study historically." He was no Robert E. Lee. "The transformation of this exceedingly sensitive, ambitious, acquisitive and obstinate young gentleman into the 'Father of his Country' is going to prove the most delightful historical and literary task I could ask."[156] On December 30, 1946, he wrote "End of Volume One" at the bottom of a 210,000-word manuscript.[157] Ten months later, he finished Volume Two. "Something wrong," he noted in his diary. "I'm going too fast. Either I laid it out better than I thought, or else I'm not sufficiently critical of the text."[158]

Try as he might to write only on the *Washington*, Freeman's pen was in demand for other projects. A telegram with a new request arrived at Westbourne on May 15, 1947. "Would you care to read a manuscript by my husband, General Patton, which I have prepared for possible publication?" The telegram was signed by Beatrice Patton, the general's widow, and carried the assurance that her husband considered Freeman "the greatest living military biographer."[159] Freeman advised it would be a "privilege and a pleasure" to look at the manuscript. While he and Patton had not been correspondents during the war, he had observed and made several comments about the flamboyant general. When Patton assumed command from Gen. Lloyd Fredendall, Freeman wrote Allen that "Old Patton is tougher and better in every way."[160] While perceptive in that regard, he made a rare misanalysis when Patton was relieved of command of the II Corps in April 1943, prior to assuming command of the Seventh Army. "The relief of General Patton has behind it, I suspect, more than yet appears," he wrote. "He may have been one of those reckless fellows who threw in his men in circumstances that made his casualties mount up. On the other hand, the explanation may be the familiar one that he never had but so much sense, anyway. He had money, he had personality and he had a way with his men, but he was not intellectually powerful. I speak about him in the past tense as if he were dead. I suspect militarily he is. I don't think General Marshall is disposed to give a man a second chance when he makes a big bust."[161] His analysis was wrong in almost every particular. Marshall would give Patton many chances—following the slapping incidents and numerous ill-considered public statements—and Patton was one of the most intelligent commanders in the army, with a knowledge of military history that rivaled Freeman's own. Despite this misjudgment, Freeman came to appreciate Patton as he studied his campaigns and personality. "Few men in our army had studied more carefully the works of the masters of war," he wrote Secretary of War Robert Patterson, three years after his initial misjudgment. "Probably no man was better informed on American military history . . . [and his] personality was singularly suited to the leadership of combat troops."[162]

Knowing of Patton's "picturesque" qualities, he looked forward to assisting Beatrice Patton with the diaries.[163] He was disappointed. "I ought to tell you confidentially," he wrote a friend, "that the manuscript of General Patton turned out to be a watered down version of his diary, one that had lost all the heat and fire of his personality."[164] He was more tactful with Mrs. Patton. "This manuscript represents one of the closest questions of publication on which I ever have been called to pass," he began. He pointed out that "nearly everyone" knew of the existence of Patton's diary, and knew as well of his "immense vigor and initiative." They would be expecting a sparkling narrative with sensational insights and salty commentary. "You have to take into account," he warned, "the virtual certainty that the narrative you sent me will be regarded as 'watered down' and will be received with definite disappointment."[165] Under these circumstances, Freeman "would issue nothing until I could publish the diary in full." If, however, Mrs. Patton wished to proceed, she should retain a "prudent publisher" and announce that it "is not the full diary, that . . . General Patton 'pulled his punches' and that it is published as a contribution to the history of the Third Army . . . not as a final, frank history of the operations as seen through the General's eyes."[166] He advised her to lower expectations and, to assure that was done, he volunteered to write the book's introduction. The memoirs were released in 1947 under the title *War As I Knew It*. Freeman's introduction laid out the case for the book in such a way as to assuage those expecting "Old Blood and Guts" to vividly jump from the pages, while at the same time explaining why the book added to the historiography of World War II. "It is hoped," he wrote near the end of the essay, "that General Patton will be among the first to attract a competent biographer and that others will leave him alone. He was a man to win, to intrigue, and sometimes to enrage . . . He will be an ideal subject for a great biography.[167] Mrs. Patton seized on that line. "I still hope," she wrote, "that you will be his 'great biographer.'"[168]

In September 1948, the "great biographer" was visited by reporters from *Time* magazine. He was to be featured as the cover story in conjunction with the release of the first two volumes of *George Washington*. The article called Freeman "the nation's number one military historian" and "a past master at converting the legendary dead into durable heroes."[169] His works were described as "monumental . . . built block by patient block, soundly based, immense, monochromatic—and toweringly high." The article gave America its first extended look at his lifestyle: His schedule was meticulously recounted, his radio program described, and his life story sketched. Scattered throughout were Freeman's comments on his historical method. "Washington did not himself climb up on a marble pedestal, strike a pose and stay there," he was quoted as saying. "What we're going to do, please God, is to make him a human being. The great big thing stamped across that man is character." The *Time* writer, or his editor, spelled Freeman's words phonetically to highlight his Southern accent; the article is replete with words such as "goin'," "bein'," "cookin'," and "mo'nin'."[170] Freeman did have a Southern accent that became more pronounced in private conversation than in formal addresses, but one wonders if *Time* was not overemphasizing the dropped "g's"—which was one of Freeman's many grammatical pet peeves. One quote became a common point of reference for future articles about Freeman and *George Washington*. He used the phrase "quenchless ambition of an ordered mind" in describing young Washington. The line provided an obvious analogy between Freeman and Washington, and *Time* made the comparison. It soon became such a common line in reviews of *Young Washington* that he regretted making the statement.[171] "Scholars do not make myths knowingly," Mary Wells Ashworth said in recalling Freeman's reaction to the overuse of the quote, "but men do; and when a capsular comment takes hold—especially one that seems on the surface to sum up what need be said—the die is cast and many more words are required to balance a perfectly valid, though limiting, statement."[172] The *Time* cover story, featuring a photograph of Freeman saluting the statue of General Lee, marked the apex of his national reputation.

What the nation came to know about Freeman's abilities and knowledge had been known for years by many scholars. His opinion was regularly sought about historical figures and issues—some topics that remain in controversy to this day. "Slavery played a small part in the attitude and decision in 1861 of the men you mention," he wrote in addressing the causes of the War Between the States. "They had been born to slavery as a 'domestic institution' and were not sensitive to it; they were conscious, as all decent Southerners were, of its responsibilities; in some instances, had they known a way to get rid of it, they would have done so . . . In general, the vehement defenders of slavery were those who found it profitable. In the average Southern family, it was not profitable."[173] Freeman said that it would take a "book" to properly discuss the causes of the war, but he tried to summarize it for one questioner in a single paragraph.

The War Between the States had its origin between old ideals and new. It was fundamentally a struggle between the rural society of the old colonies and the urban society in New England, which had the full support of the white new states of the Middle West. New England wanted a protective tariff. The South did not. When protectionist New England and the states of the Middle West combined, there was a clash inevitably with the conservative, rural South. Slavery was a factor and an important one, but the slavery issue was exaggerated by the politicians. If you said to me "State the cause of the War in one word," I would protest that this could not be done, and then I would say that the word which more nearly covers everything is the one word, "politicians."[174]

Freeman preferred the term "War Between the States" to "Civil War," although his preference was based on custom rather than logic.[175] "I never had any objection to the term 'Civil War,'" he wrote, "nor, for that matter, after I got of age, did I have any complaint because the Federals called us 'rebels.' If the name was a proper one, our fathers certainly dignified it."[176] If pushed for a term, he believed "the War for Southern Independence" to be "the wisest and soundest name" because that was "precisely what the conflict was."[177] He did not equate the Confederate cause to racist beliefs. "I think," he wrote, "there is no nobler tradition in the world than that of the Confederacy."[178] He was disturbed when the Confederate flag was used for inappropriate purposes. "It is not pleasant to see the symbol of a country's war, intimate to the hearts of us all, used lightly as a mere ornament or symbol of defiance. To many of us the flag represents much that we hold sacred in the ideals of self-government."[179]
The topics of his books never provided an extended opportunity to assess the two presidents during the war: Jefferson Davis and Abraham Lincoln. "Opinions regarding Jefferson Davis always, I suspect, will be divided," he wrote in one analysis, "because he had such a complex personality. My own belief is that he was a devoted and earnest man of high ability, though he was handicapped by physical malady and was cursed with a singular sensitiveness to criticism."[180] Davis's presidential counterpart was a man "much maligned and misunderstood."[181] "I have no hesitation," he wrote, "in telling you that, while I admire the simplicity and the determination of Mr. Lincoln's character, I know his early weaknesses, and his part in precipitating the war. I think the South may well study the qualities of any man, friend or enemy, when those qualities are helpful."[182] He listed those qualities in an editorial on the 126th anniversary of Lincoln's birth. "Few men in American history," he wrote, "ever combined so much humility with so much determination."[183] Even

this mild compliment brought heated objections. "For reasons that have not been apparent to me," he wrote after being criticized for one such editorial, "someone has been trying to make a mountain out of [a] molehill and to present me as disloyal to the South because I realize that along with many bad qualities, President Lincoln had some good ones."[184] In such a situation, Freeman reminded his critics of the words of General Lee that "it should be the object of all to avoid controversy, to allay passion, and give full scope to every kindly feeling."[185]

"I wish I had time to tell you about the progress I am making on *George Washington*", he wrote his brother in July 1947. "I certainly believe I can [say] that he is the most misunderstood great man in American history."[186] Freeman delighted in watching Washington's character develop. "The great fact," he wrote, "is that Washington grew. I have been very much surprised to see how substantial was the development in his character and the change in what would appear to have been his 'temperament' between 1759 and 1775."[187] The final proofs of the first two volumes, titled *Young Washington*, were completed in August 1948. The two volumes, consisting of thirty-three chapters and thirteen appendices, took Washington to the age of twenty-seven. The "heart of the two volumes" was the analysis of Washington's character.[188] Here Freeman would separate Washington from the whimsy of Parson Weems and the marble life-mask of John Marshall and Washington Irving. "Washington," he judged, "was a synonym for ambition. If in repose his 'principles' were the dominant of his life, in action ambition was."[189] His ambition prompted the desire to excel, to acquire wealth, to achieve "honor" and military distinction. "Modesty played no part in it, one way or the other: Honest ambition must be served."[190] This was not the noble Father of His Country, but an emotional son of a landed society; not the revolutionary patriot, but an overly sensitive prima donna. Freeman allowed the young man to vent and scheme and complain, then, finally, to mature. A master of self-discipline, Freeman recognized that budding trait in his subject. "Behind the flaps of his own tent," he wrote behind the closed door of his study, "the young commander sought the self-discipline he inculcated. This was not easy for a man of complicated emotional character." Here Freeman spoke not only from the historical record, but also from his experience.

Historian Allan Nevins reviewed *Young Washington* for the *New York Times*. "If the promise of these first thousand pages is sustained," Nevins wrote, "[Freeman] will give us something more important even than a great biography. He will reveal to us, precisely and vividly, a figure whom Americans have never really known."[191] Many reviewers noted that the books were introducing Washington to his countrymen. "We knew what he did but we did not know why he did it," the *Atlantic* stated. "Now . . . we shall have a completed portrait of our greatest man. And for this all Americans should be grateful."[192] The *London Spectator* expressed gratitude that Freeman had done all that "superhuman energy and modern research technique can do to eliminate mythology."[193] Surveying the facts presented about Washington in the two volumes, Prof. Hugh Lefler of the University of North Carolina joyfully concluded: "In other words, he was human."[194]

The reviews disagreed on the issue of the amount of detail included in the work. "One can only praise a narrative and exposition which even in dealing with trivial details and despite copious notation, is never dull, is always agreeable and easy, and is at times lightened by quiet and charming humor," said the *Atlantic*.[195] Others struck a balance. "Mr. Freeman has marshaled his resources like a general planning a great campaign," L. H. Butterfield wrote in the *Saturday Review*, but "the story . . . often plods."[196] The *New Statesman and Nation* found the work "a little portentous in places, a little slow in narrative," and Allan Nevins admitted that it "has the defects of its virtues; exhaustive thoroughness bears its penalty in an occasional stretch of exhausting detail."[197]

The most negative review was by Bernard Knollenberg, author of *Washington and the Revolution: A Reappraisal*, in his review in the *William & Mary Quarterly*. The review says less about Washington than it does about his mother Mary Ball Washington. Freeman, Knollenberg asserted, "has . . . without evidence, defamed a woman, who, during the part covered by his volumes, seems to have had and to have been worthy of her son's affection and respect."[198] Knollenberg looked at the evidence upon which Freeman based his assertion that Mary "was constantly asking for something more" and found that the few cited instances did not equate to "constant" asking.[199] He criticized Freeman for not assuming that Virginia governor Robert Dinwiddie had read a letter Washington wrote to a third party. Thus Knollenberg managed within the same article to criticize Freeman for drawing conclusions based on evidence, and for failing to draw a conclusion based on no evidence.

"I suspect the critics will say that the narrative is unexciting because it covers so much of the background and does not reach into the period when Washington was at his fullest activity," Freeman wrote, "[but] I know the thing is well done and I am willing to stand on it, because the research will speak for itself."[200]

CHAPTER 13

"I Have Lived Sternly"

From the time the girl had recognized his tall form and had associated it with the word "Father," there had been between her and him an understanding that was independent of speech. Each was to the other as two masters sitting at a game of chess; one move meant five. A familiar phrase, a snatch of an anecdote, a reference to a date—and the eyes of both flashed. Their next words had passed far beyond the obvious thing that others, sentence by sentence, ponderously shaped. They were *en rapport*, not as hypnotist and subject, but in a certain mutuality of mind that was uncanny.[1]

Douglas Freeman wrote these words about another man and daughter, but nowhere else does he so precisely describe the relationship that existed between him and his daughter, Mary Tyler. From the moment "she first blinked those dear eyes of hers," she was to him "the most glorious daughter a man ever had."[2] To his daughter, Freeman was "the pattern for all manhood."[3] More than simple filial bonds connected the two. They shared an "understanding," Freeman wrote, that "passed far beyond the obvious." There was "an absolute meeting of minds, intuitive understanding, and the sacred possession of the same ideals."[4] He was "the creative spirit" whose presence "sheds light everywhere"; she was "a shooting-star, the promise of a great tomorrow" with "emanations of goodness and high virtue and integrity."[5] The dimensions of their love for each other were infinite; the depth of their understanding took on spiritual qualities; and the essential elements of their character were each part of the other. "Ever since you came into this troubled world," he wrote Mary Tyler in 1941, "you have looked at me with different eyes. A different place, surely, you have had in my heart, from that which anyone else has occupied or ever will . . . I have lived sternly, and, to an extent that few ever will know . . . I have lived alone. No vision in my hermitage ever has been so bright, my darling, as that of you!"[6] The two were partners for life's journey as surely as they were father and daughter. "The human spirit flowers," Mary Tyler wrote, "in the knowledge that a beloved one wants it happy . . . [and free] to develop its own particular qualities because those particular qualities are respected and loved."[7]

Mary Tyler was born on April 6, 1917, on the day "the old world died"—America's entry into the First World War. She was immediately the pride and center of the family. "Aunt Mary" Harrison, the nurse who helped rear Freeman, began to take walks, down the center of the street, pushing the infant in her perambulator, oblivious to the increasing number of cars in the area. "Nobody," she insisted, "is going to run over Doctor Douglas's baby."[8] Just past her second birthday, Mary Tyler scribbled the first of what would be hundreds of letters to her father: a number of circles and lines translated by Inez as a report on a tea party.[9] At some point during these early years the two began to refer to one another as "partner"—a sobriquet that would remain throughout their lives.[10]

Their first extended separation occurred in the summer of 1930 when Mary Tyler went to the Teela-Wooket Camps in Roxbury, Vermont. Freeman wrote her frequently during her stay, reminding her of "what I told you about how to make a success of this and of any other new adventures in life."[11] He had special stationary printed for her, with the heading "Freeman & Freeman General Partnership" emblazoned across the top. "How about that letterhead, my sweet partner?" he wrote. "Isn't there class to it? And it simply records a fact . . . we are partners. The best thing that life holds out to me is the belief that you are going to develop into fine womanhood. That will be the greatest reward I can have in life—and its one of the few things I know I am certain to get!"[12] Though only thirteen years old, Mary Tyler was displaying budding powers of observation and expression that delighted her father. "Today being Sunday," she reported, "we went to church . . . The preacher was a real funny sour-faced citizen who thought he was a great deal but who used bad English and said 'he don't' in spite of his pompous manner."[13] "Doesn't the little hussy write well?" Freeman wrote Inez.[14] He showed one letter to John Stewart Bryan who remarked it was "something in life to raise a child that will write a letter like that."[15] While Mary Tyler was at camp, her father began writing colleges—three years in advance—for application forms. He told her to consider "Bryn Mawr, Vassar, Wellesley, and Smith" or "any other colleges in which you want to be entered."[16] It was yet another detail of her life in which he took active interest. He wrote the principal of her prep school requesting that any violations of school policy by his daughter be reported to him "because if she knows I am checking up on her, she will be a little more careful."[17] When she wanted to attend a "Ring Dance" with a cadet at the United States Military Academy, Freeman used his connections at West Point to get a report on the boy and the dance chaperonage.[18] He peppered her with letters updating her on neighborhood events, discussing the status of his books, and teasing her about rolling her "R's."[19]

While monitoring her actions, Freeman also showed great deference to his daughter's judgment. In a letter to Inez, he referred to the fifteen-year-old's "good sense" and told his wife to leave a particular problem "entirely in her hands."[20] Later that same month, regarding another matter, he again advised his wife to "talk to [Mary Tyler] quite frankly . . . and let her make the decision for herself."[21] He expressed this confidence in more detail in a letter to Inez written shortly after Mary Tyler's sixteenth birthday.

As you know, a child fairly bursts into adolescence without warning. I think the same sharp transition comes from girlhood to womanhood. Young as she is, Mary Tyler has reached it. I rejoice to see how many of her troublesome little qualities are disappearing and how many of your fine traits are to be seen in her. It was almost like sitting and talking with you, twenty years ago, so much has she grown to be like you in outlook.[22]

In the fall of 1933, Mary Tyler entered Vassar. "This is a very important time in my life," she wrote her father, "but, as usual, the blessing that I receive from you, and the pleasure given you by my doing well, mean more to me than anything else."[23] "The aim of my life," she wrote shortly before matriculating, "is that I shall not disappoint the man who loves me, and whom I love, best in the world."[24] Freeman's messages during her first year at Vassar mirrored his advice to himself at Johns Hopkins. "The whole secret lies in effort," he wrote. "I doubt if any great work was ever written otherwise than in the blood and sweat of the writer."[25] And again: "Brilliant improvisation is no substitute for toil."[26] When Mary Tyler showed an inclination to major in English and concentrate on writing, he wrote an in-depth letter on the art of writing—one of his few sustained comments on the topic. "To write well," he wrote, "one must read well."[27]

The great defect of some of the young writers who rise like a rocket and fall like a stick is that they have no background of knowledge of our literature . . . one of the things for which I am most grateful intellectually is that when I was a little younger than you are now, I started with Chaucer and read virtually the whole corpus of English literature . . . The second suggestion I have to make is that you find . . . the author whose style interests you most and then go to work and dissect his work and see how it is put together . . . Do not forget, however, that a certain amount of history . . . is essential to an understanding of our literature. History is the great lamp that illumines every other study. Without it, we grope in the dark.[28]

Freeman had cards printed to facilitate Mary Tyler's return letters. The preprinted form had sentences with options she could check off to convey news. "I am well. I am very well. I am disgustingly well. I am not so hot" read one line. In addition to having a line for requesting specific items of food, there was also "Tell Daddy please to look up and send the following data" followed by a blank line for research requests. Mary Tyler occasionally used the forms, but was a regular correspondent during her college years. One such letter congratulated her father on the release of Volume One of *R. E. Lee*. "I cannot tell you, Daddy," she wrote, "how proud . . . it made me feel . . . As I read it, the greatness of the feeling you must now have, of having done your best for something . . . That's the feeling I think I'd rather have than any other in the whole world—except the feeling of loving people . . . Love and work—you have them both in your *Lee*—just as in your life."[29] "To know that you understand what the book has entailed in sacrifice and in effort," Freeman wrote in reply, "is greater compensation than royalties would be."[30]

That the father and daughter understood each other—and were every day drawing closer in attitude—is displayed in Mary Tyler's conduct with regard to her first serious romance. During her last year at prep school, she had fallen "seriously in love" with a handsome young senior at St. Christopher's School, Jere Baxter III. The Freemans accepted the boy into the family circle, invited him to vacation with them at Willoughby Spit, and generally let the two youngsters alone. Freeman sprinkled his letters to Mary Tyler with positive comments about Jere: "[H]e is a fine boy," "I like him better than any of all your fine boy friends," and "he is fine and true and earnest."[31] When Jere asked if he could speak to Freeman "on some very important business," father alerted daughter and gave his first extended appraisal of his prospective son-in-law. "I am not yet sure that Jere is going to grow in spirit as fast as you will," he wrote. "Should he do so, well and good; should he fail . . . I have to tell you that

you must not hurry things along. You have lived all your life in a home
where you had constant intellectual stimulation: life would be very drab
to you without it . . . after health and character, nothing means so much
over the long swing of years as intellect."[32] The exchange between father
and daughter that followed this letter shows the spiritual and intellectual level to which they had raised their relationship.

> I love Jere very much [Mary Tyler wrote] and if he continues to
> develop according to my hopes and my faith in him, then I want to
> marry him—if not—then I could not . . . [He] lacks something . . .
> I could never name that thing—but it's one of the best things in
> life—you and mother have it so pronouncedly . . . and I want to have
> it and I want Jere to have it . . . it's a certain fineness of feeling—of
> living—that colors everything . . . It's the thing that's like old silver-
> ware and old, rich, red wine—and fine music— . . . you know,
> Daddy, what I mean, you always do . . . I have a very definite set of
> ideals—which are dearer to me than anything else—and I'm going
> to be true to them, before everything—no matter what happens. All
> my love, Your Partner.[33]

"Never," Freeman responded the next day, "in all my life have I
received a letter, my precious partner, that gave me a satisfaction as deep
and intense as that which I received this morning from you."[34] He
praised her "clear head" and "noble heart" and devoted a paragraph to
the benefits of marrying well. He then addressed the intangible "thing"
to which Mary Tyler made reference.

> What you are feeling after with some perception is that fine combi-
> nation of sensibility, appreciation, consideration, and understanding
> that we rather ineptly style culture . . . It is culture that shapes what
> we do without our knowing why. When we learn to appreciate great
> character . . . when we can sense the meaning of dawn and can drink
> deep of the wine of sunset; when beauty interprets itself and ugliness
> repels . . . when we think first of excellence and unconsciously resent
> indecency—when we have lived this life and, step by step, have
> developed this state of mind, then, somewhere deep in our mind,
> each day leaves a certain residuum. That residuum we call culture.[35]

He held out hope that Jere would develop this trait, and he would try
"not in a half-hearted way" to help him along.

If, after four or five years, Beethoven is food and drink to him, the night-sky stirs his reverence, a great picture means more than a great dinner; if jade is more than a dish, and jonquils more than flowers in it; if he can have sensibility and poise along with it, enthusiasm and reflection; deeper understanding and continued mirth; then he will have grown in stature to the type of manhood with which your soul will be content.[36]

If not, he concluded, "you will know it." The one essential, he judged, was that Mary Tyler would keep "the deepest treasure" of her heart intact, and "trust time and God." The young couple continued to see each other for more than a year before Mary Tyler ended the relationship.

There would, of course, finally come a man who would meet Mary Tyler's—and her father's—standards. On November 24, 1938, Freeman made the first reference in his diary to Leslie Cheek, Jr., of Nashville, Tennessee, a graduate of Harvard and Yale Universities, head of the Department of Fine Arts at the College of William and Mary, and one of the heirs to the Maxwell House Coffee fortune.[37] Mary Tyler had met Cheek on the recommendation of John Stewart Bryan who thought the two would make a fine couple. Bryan's matchmaking worked. "There has never been anything in my life to compare with this," Mary Tyler wrote her parents. "I never dreamed that it could be half so wonderful."[38] She visited the Cheek family estate, Cheekwood, in late 1938, returning on New Year's Day 1939 with the report that she had the best time of her life. "The reasons," Freeman noted in his diary, "were not altogether architectural, I suspect."[39] On January 12, 1939, he wrote "L. C. came and put the expected question regarding M. T. I tried to make it easy for him, but it was hard for me to think of giving her up."[40] His assessment of his prospective son-in-law was that he "filled my specifications for the man I would like M. T. to marry."[41] Freeman assumed responsibility for much of the organization of the wedding, which occurred on June 3, 1939, and the reception at Westborne. He drafted a two-page, twenty-four-point "Instruction for Traffic" plan and co-authored with Mary Tyler the announcement of the engagement.[42] The county sheriff agreed to convert the street leading to Westborne into a one-way road and to divert traffic on the day of the wedding.[43] It was a typically well-organized, thoroughly planned, Freeman event.

"Mary Tyler's wedding was, to my partial eyes, perfect in all its details," he wrote in his diary. "I have to confess we both wept on the way to church, as we exchanged last-minute thanks for what each had

been to the other; but at the church we held up well."[44] Marriage altered
the context, but not the nature, of their relationship. *The South to
Posterity* was released five months after the Cheeks married, and
Freeman decided to "indulge parental pride" and dedicate the book to
Mary Tyler and Leslie. "I asked myself in what two words I could
describe the motive of your gracious, useful lives, the nexus of my little
work with yours."[45] He chose the words: "Who understand." Though he
included Leslie Cheek in the dedication, it was clearly a tribute to the
"partner" who understood him better than almost anyone. Mary Tyler
was not at all sure she merited the distinction.

> I am beginning now . . . to understand a little—and I am amazed—
> and very humble to think that I am your daughter. I can't begin to
> name all the things I have realized were yours—and I discover new
> ones every day . . . the vision and the faith, the courage and the
> high dedication, and above all, the abiding love for human beings
> and for life itself . . . perhaps I do understand a little—just a little.[46]

Her life was soon as busy as her father's. Added to the responsibilities
of being married to the director of the Baltimore Museum of Art and
meeting numerous civic and social obligations, she eventually became
the mother of four children—three boys and one girl—all born between
1940 and 1949. The couple maintained a home in Baltimore and a farm
in North Carolina. Leslie would leave the Baltimore Museum of Art to
serve in the army during World War II. He then became an editor with
the *Architectural Forum* in New York, before being named director of the
Virginia Museum of Fine Arts in 1948. During these hectic years,
daughter and father had to satisfy themselves with snippets of time
together. "Ever since you were here," Freeman wrote in 1941, "my heart
has beaten up at the remembrance of your coming, and my voice has
choked a little at every mention of it."[47] Mary Tyler rejoiced when
Freeman "took the whole day off just to be with me. That is the best gift
that you have given me in many months—those priceless hours of your
company. I don't merit such a tribute."[48] The two exchanged thoughts
on his books, the love of outdoor life, handling domestic help, and the
"continuing adventure" of life. Freeman's letters, Mary Tyler wrote, "are
received by your humble servant like letters from the gods. They are full
of wisdom and inspiration and I read and reread them with the passionate attention of a fanatic."[49] She shared a closeness to her mother as
well, but the relationship, at least as it is documented in letters, did not

reach the same level of that with her father. "To be with you again for such a long time," Mary Tyler wrote Inez after a visit, "has been a real inspiration. You are lovelier in every way, and more beautiful . . . it is hearty and uplifting to see the way in which all your goodness throughout all your life is being rewarded. All things come to you now, and graces crowd around you; you are a great lady, and you are my Mother! How proud I am of you . . . [and] in the midst of your honors and high stature, you are still as simple and natural and as unselfconscious as a very young child. That is the secret of your dignity, and the touchstone of your great appeal to all hearts."[50]

By all accounts, Leslie Cheek was a difficult man. Brilliant, creative, inventive, and talented, he was in many ways similar to Freeman. He was also driven, vain, and cold, with little of Freeman's humility or selflessness. That dark spot of personality began to enshroud the spirit of the man Mary Tyler had judged to be the "most thoroughly clean and strong and fine person I have ever known."[51] The marriage became equal parts challenge and joy, and Mary Tyler's normal reserve about such private matters burst forth in the fall of 1952. Her father had invited her to join him, Inez, and Mary Wells Ashworth on a trip to Europe. To Mary Tyler, the trip "would be very little short of Paradise," but she reluctantly declined. Father and daughter spoke briefly by telephone, and then she poured out her thoughts in a letter.

> I have made a bargain: Leslie supports me and, as he calls them, "my children," and I could not leave unless in his heart he wished me to have the pleasure of a holiday and the joy of your companionship . . . he thinks of me only as one of the heads of his departments. My department is home management, child care and social assistance . . . this sounds very bitter, and some of it is, I must confess.[52]

Four pages into the letter, Mary Tyler regained herself and apologized for writing a "repulsively egotistical" letter, but she concluded by making it clear "that nothing but the heaviest weighting of the scales with duty and emotion and judgment could make me decline to take the trip of my dreams with the man I love most in the world."[53]

Freeman's answer counseled forbearance. "Selfishness a cure for egoism? Callousness the remedy for harshness? Never!" What he had built in her, he promised, would suffice against all struggles. "He who has lived with a great spirit never thereafter lives alone," he wrote, "and never is touched or tainted by the worst he has to encounter."⁵⁴ The disappointment of not making the trip, he stressed, was offset by Mary Tyler's ability to "get more enjoyment from a sunset hour with God than some people get from a day-long walk in pleasant pastures." He held out the promise of restoration for their spirits.

> You and I are to have a week together when next winter begins to wear on the nerves and spring seems far away. We are going to get in a motor car, just you and I, and we are going to wander southward, to meet the sun, and to spend long and lovely days in talk of strange and blessed things . . . We can gain more in a week than some acquire in a lifetime. Then, a little later, we shall go to Europe together and see with common eyes what our hearts already have beat out in common time . . . Yours for that longer journey, your partner.⁵⁵

Through the twists and vicissitudes of life, Mary Tyler was his partner. She did not supplant Inez—no one could do that—but theirs was a communion set apart. "Once, when you were a little girl," Freeman wrote Mary Tyler in 1933, "you had a jumping-rope on which there were many colored bits of wood. I saw you jumping through it one summer's afternoon and it seemed to me that you were in a rainbow. The next day, you were very ill. I did not know whether you would live. But I told myself then 'if she dies, I'll always see her through the rainbow of that jumping rope!' That's a long time behind us now, and I have lost that old fear for your life; but in my mind's eye now I see you still with emanations from you . . ."⁵⁶ The two never ceased to see each other without a rainbow—a great arc containing the colors of life, with an unfathomable beginning or end, signaling renewal of light after darkness, signifying a promise of eternal love.

Anne Ballard Freeman was born September 21, 1923, and named "Anne" after Mrs. John Stewart Bryan and "Ballard" for her great-great-great grandmother.⁵⁷ Freeman's earliest surviving descriptions of his second daughter note that she was "self-contained," "thoughtful," and "good company."⁵⁸ He kept a watchful eye on her weight, her swimming progress, and her numerous suitors. The two were close, but their relationship differed from that which Freeman shared with Mary Tyler. It could be no other way, for Anne Freeman was a different spirit—more fun loving, outgoing, and carefree than her father, with a dry sense of humor. Freeman treasured these traits—perhaps even envied them—and did not attempt to make Anne into anyone else.

"Tonight we are going to the Pennsylvania Hotel and have supper and hear Tommy Dorsey," fifteen-year-old Anne wrote her father during a trip to New York. The love of fun and good times was a marked trait in the young girl. "She loved to laugh," her sister remembers, "had lots of friends, and lots of fun with the boys."[59] A long-time girlfriend concurred: "She liked boys better than books."[60] As she matured, her father often commented on her hectic social schedule. "I think Anne is going to be up three nights in a row until about day," he wrote his brother. "God alone knows why they ever adhere to the asinine schedule that starts a party about eleven o'clock and keeps it up until four."[61] While grumbling about her late nights, Freeman enjoyed his daughter's sense of humor. "I've now firmly made up my mind," one letter from Anne opened, "that I shall become an old maid and raise pigs for defense forever . . . you won't have to worry about supporting me because my pigs will support me."[62] He fed this aptitude by supplying Anne with jokes during her college days. "I wish I had a dime," she wrote, "for every time I passed on the jokes you wrote me, Pappy. At any rate the morale of the college in general has been immeasurably helped by hearing them."[63] When Anne married in June 1950, with the usual pomp and elaborate organization accompanying a Freeman wedding and reception, she opened her first letter to her father following the wedding with a teasing, "Guess what? I'm married!"[64]

Beyond the humor and parties, she displayed other traits that her father admired and sought to build up. "Anne has so much common sense and executive ability," he wrote Inez, "that she will have a busy and useful place in the world, but precisely what that place is, we must be diligent to ascertain."[65] He admonished Anne with the same advice he gave Mary Tyler and encouraged her with professions of support. "You always have been one of the most gracious and affectionate of daughters," he wrote, "and every day grow in my love and esteem."[66] She seemed to fill a needed void in his life—one that he would not admit existed—of simple enjoyment. "You have never brought me anything but pleasure," he wrote "or been anything to me but a source of joy and pride."[67] It was also evident that Anne had adopted some her father's worldview. "I have found out by tough experience," she wrote him in the spring of 1945, "the importance of work and schedule—of responsibility and cheerfulness—of a thousand little things that make it easier to get along with other people . . . If in time I can pass on some measure of the love and strength and gentleness in living that you have given me, you will have the satisfaction of knowing that the things in life for which you struggled will be perpetuated and find continued rebirth in the spring of moral consciousness."[68] Anne, a friend noted, had "the Freeman drive."[69] Her father took favorable notice as well. His second daughter, he commented, "is growing steadily."[70]

She initially struggled academically—going on probation at Vassar— but regained her standing and did well in history and English.[71] She relied heavily on her father for assistance, and it appears Freeman wrote at least three papers for her during her college years.[72] He rejoiced when one of their papers received an "A"—"you had worked so hard and so earnestly" he told her—but was a bit chagrined that Anne's genealogy paper, to which he had devoted much time, merited only a "B." "Does that bird think that we can create historical materials that do not exist?" he wrote. "I would like to know what papers he graded 'B-plus' and what material the girls had who got that rating."[73]

Upon graduation from Vassar, Anne decided to move to New York City. More than one of her surviving family and friends say her move to New York was an "escape." From what she escaped, they say not, nor did Anne. Freeman was hesitant to endorse the decision, but, seeing her determination, supported the move. "Great days," he wrote, "are ahead for all of us."[74] Anne took a job with the National Concert and Artists Corporation and was soon sounding much like her father. "The only way to get the things done that you want to do," she wrote, "is simply do them!"[75] Maturity and distance brought perspective and appreciation. "What is more peerless in this world," she wrote her father, "than to be able to understand, sympathize, and, what's more, encourage someone effectively! But then that sort of thing is no new experience for me regarding you."[76] Anne settled in New York, married Julius Ochs Adler, Jr., son of the general manager of the New York Times, and had three children. "I wonder at you," she wrote her father, "I literally wonder. For never do I see you or talk with you that I am not completely struck with the magnificence of thought and feeling that goes into everything you do."[77] There was wonder in their relationship, and great love, respect, and devotion. There was also distance, both emotionally and geographically. That distance was hinted at by Freeman in a diary entry on the occasion of the death of Mrs. John Stewart Bryan in 1952. "She was one of the five women who have influenced me most," he wrote. "My mother, Inez, Mary Wells Ashworth, Mary Tyler, and Mrs. Bryan. My own Anne, named after her, must take her place in my life."[78] That Freeman wanted Anne to hold that position in his life speaks to the nature of their relationship. That she did not already hold that position in his life does as well.

In writing the biography of John Stewart Bryan, Freeman described the relationship between Bryan and his father, Joseph Bryan. "From the strong love of Joseph Bryan," he wrote, "there was little or none of the drifting away that often occurs with the sons of weak or preoccupied fathers."[79] When he wrote those words in 1944, his nineteen-year-old son, James Douglas Freeman, had almost completely drifted away from him. Freeman never comprehended the depth of his son's estrangement nor did he consider himself a "weak or preoccupied" father. He gave to his son the same strong love he provided his daughters, but somehow the message sent was not the one received. "From the time I can remember," James Douglas recalls, "I was afraid of my father."[80]

"He is a precious boy full of intellectual promise," Freeman wrote Inez about his nine-year-old son. "His physique and his temper must be brought up to par with his mind."[81] They soon were. James Douglas, alternatively called "Joe," "Freeman," or "J. D.," excelled in sports—football and tennis in particular—and was a strikingly handsome young man. He was a leader in school, and Freeman noted that "he takes very heavily his responsibility."[82] His grades in school were good, and his father told him he could "be anything you want to be that's fine and high."[83] Behind the accomplishments of the handsome young man lay a smoldering resentment of the man who kept such a rigid schedule and worked so hard at so many jobs. "To say he was an absentee dad is unfair and untrue," he says, "but I just sort of wondered 'what's the matter with me'?" Signs began to appear during the teenage years that all was not well. An unidentified "school problem" prompted Freeman to write his friend, Columbia dean Herbert Hawkes, asking him to "size [J. D.] up educationally."[84] A shoulder injury effectively ended a promising athletic career, and J. D.'s grades plummeted. He returned from a camping trip and extolled to his father the virtues of the trip's leader and how much he enjoyed his company. "I think the best he could allow his father," Freeman wrote the camp leader, "was that he saw in him some shadowy and feeble outlines of your powerful personality."[85]

J. D. joined the naval pre-officer program and entered Princeton University in February 1943. "As far as I know," Freeman wrote his son's faculty advisor, "he is a perfectly normal boy, capable of excellent work, but of interests so diversified that he sometimes in the past has not concentrated on his studies as he should."[86] Freeman wrote his son almost

An early photograph of Douglas Freeman's three children:(left to right) Mary Tyler, James Douglas, and Anne. (Image courtesy of Mary Tyler McClenahan.)

daily. "Nothing in my life means more than you," he wrote during his freshman year. "Your well-being, your happiness and your advancement mean more to me than another Pulitzer Prize . . ."[87] He wrote him about current events and the war; family news and local gossip; paying bills and keeping down college expenses; and trying to enlist in order to fight alongside his son.[88] All his letters carried encouraging words and promises of a future closeness. "I thank God for you," he wrote, "and look forward to the day when we can have more fun together. I have had to discipline myself pretty hard to get what I have needed to provide for my lovely family but I haven't killed my love of fun."[89] Later he promised that "when this war is over, we shall sniff the salt together, my boy, and have some glorious times as sea-faring men."[90] Low grades and irregular class attendance brought J. D. to the brink of failure at Princeton. In 1944 he left and joined the Navy. "I am persuaded," Freeman wrote his son, "that no matter what turn things take, a man is able to make adjustments to them and to get from them just as much as he will."[91] He then offered an analysis (a defense?) of his role as a parent.

> I have been vexed by this question: How easy ought we to make it for you? We cannot be sure of anything about the future except that we can give you the memory of a loving home and a beautiful youth ... Have we been too indulgent? These have been questions I have asked myself ten thousand times and I have tried to answer these in the fear of God. Perhaps my answer was not the wisest, but it was that we would continue to make your youth beautiful, that we would trust more to example than to discipline, and that we would rely on the development of the character we felt was in you.[92]

Freeman believed that he had set an example of hard work, self-discipline, dedicated study, selfless public service, and love for his wife and children. James Douglas perceived quite another example. "I don't think my father ever came to a [football] game. I don't think he ever came to a graduation. I don't ever remember going fishing with him ... All the things I learned with my hands—how to throw a baseball, how to carry a football, how to fish, how to paint a room, how to change spark plugs—I taught myself."[93] No amount of loving encouragement, no doses of sound advice, no promises of future bonding, no musings on the correctness of past decisions could bridge the gap between father and son. The example Freeman thought he had set, instead of providing the basis for achievement, sowed in his son seeds of discontent.

Wandering years followed. After service in the Navy, James Douglas returned to Princeton where his grades fell, in part due to an increasing fondness for alcohol and an abiding enjoyment of a good time. He was asked to withdraw in the spring of 1947 due to academic failure.[94] "I find," Freeman wrote Mary Tyler, "I am philosophically reconcilable to what I cannot change."95 J. D. married in 1947, fathered a son in 1949, and confided marital problems to his father later that year. "The first obligation," Freeman wrote, "is that of being in the whole affair a gentleman of honor and of conscience . . . [and] you cannot disregard the little boy. You begot him and you have a responsibility for him that you must discharge."96 James Douglas's self-destructive behavior was only beginning. Divorce, alcoholism, and lawsuits mingled with a series of jobs from the *Washington Post*, to radio, to real estate, to department stores. Freeman found himself paying his son's bills, negotiating with the local bank on his behalf, paying child support, and "bailing" him out of a number of financial difficulties.97 All of this was done readily, but with entreaties—soon pleadings—to change course. "The time has come," he wrote in a letter typical of many others, "when you must put these follies behind you and make your career one of achievement and of high character . . . there is a limit to what a man can do without impairing permanently his future. You have reached that limit."98 The nadir was reached on Freeman's sixty-fifth birthday, celebrated by an elaborate party staged by Inez, where J. D. apparently was heavily intoxicated and "conspicuous" in his inappropriate conduct.99 The relationship between the two men in the coming years—the last two of Freeman's life—would provide only additional heartache.

James Douglas Freeman—seventy-five years old at the time he spoke—sitting across the table from the author, was still an impressive-looking man. Distinguished in appearance, with a full head of gray hair, he resembles his mother more than his father. Sober for more than twenty years, he returned to college, received a degree in rehabilitative counseling, and worked as a substance abuse counselor. Public service, he observes, is "part of the [Freeman] tradition."100 He speaks reluctantly, but frankly, about his misspent years, but dismisses it with "that was then, this is now." He speaks with pride about his father's accomplishments and gives him credit for always providing for the family. He accepts his share of responsibility for his mistakes—not laying them entirely at the feet of his father. Once again, he hears the words of his father as he is read a portion of a letter written more than fifty years earlier. "We cannot be sure of anything about the future except that we can give you the memory of a loving home and a beautiful youth."

James Douglas Freeman leans forward and shakes his head at the sound of the words. He grants that may have been his father's intention, but that is not the memory he carries. "He was always gone."

CHAPTER 14

"Life Has Begun"

"Every phase of this study has been a delight," Douglas Freeman wrote in the introduction to *Young Washington*. "In writing of General R. E. Lee and of the Confederate States of America, one felt always the pervasion of tragedy . . . with Washington, the atmosphere is that of dawn. Disaster never is without hope. Battles may be lost but the war will be won. Even when the men themselves grow old, the nation is still young."[1] The delight he found in writing Washington—in looking at times past—compensated for the growing ambivalence with which he viewed the world around him. He voted Republican for the first time in his life in 1948, casting his vote for Thomas E. Dewey over Harry Truman, but he seemed to care less and less about the machinations of public figures.[2] He was not intrigued by the development of a State's Rights Party and offered it no support.[3] "My chief aim is to get character in government," he wrote. "If we have this, it scarcely matters where we stand, to the left or to the right. Character can be trusted."[4]

He also had an increasing uneasiness about the future of newspapers. "The more I reflect on the future of our business," he wrote *News Leader* publisher Tennant Bryan, "the more I become convinced that . . . the afternoon paper is going to be a heavy sufferer from the radio and soon from television. I am depressed frequently when I hear so many persons talk of the programs to which they are listening when they ought to be reading their newspaper after dinner."[5] He believed morning papers were safe, but that afternoon papers faced "tough going." The times were changing. Freeman had, in the past, welcomed change, seizing the opportunity it brought on its wings to inculcate it with timeless principle. Now he showed little inclination to deal with a new era, with its talk of "cold war," hydrogen bombs, and communist spies. The pull of history and writing—always great—became greater.

The thought of a career change entered his mind as early as 1947.

"Unless there is some international crisis in which experience might be of some use," he wrote Allen, "I do not think I can render much service to my day and generation by editing the *News Leader* as I can by devoting my last years to the sure completion of *George Washington* before Father Time begins to stick a tooth in me."[6] He was scheduled to retire from the paper in May 1951—the month of his sixty-fifth birthday—but he began to think of moving up the time. "I continue to wonder," he wrote in March 1949, "whether I am doing the wise thing in staying here at the paper . . . when I have what undoubtedly is the golden opportunity of American biography."[7] He turned for advice to his friend Raymond Fosdick of the Rockefeller Foundation. "Daily I am coming closer to the conviction that I should put aside everything else, lengthen the period during which I intended to complete the work, and make it the supreme endeavor of my life," he wrote.[8] He laid out his economic concerns. His newspaper salary was $25,000 a year. By paying "about $7,000" he could anticipate his retirement salary and begin to draw $4,600 in July 1949. He had a small pension from Columbia University—$1,100 a year—and with his savings, continued royalties, some speaking engagements, and "large domestic economics," he felt he could live on the smaller income.[9] "That," he wrote, "brings me to the x in my equation—the question of financing the research." He projected that he would require $35,000 over five years in addition to the funds from the Carnegie Corporation. "I could think of no employment of my life that will be more useful," he wrote in a follow-up letter to Fosdick, "and I want to use my whole energies in it at a time when I am at the peak of whatever powers I possess."[10]

"Just leave the matter in my hands," Fosdick replied.[11]

On a small note card, Freeman wrote, in his distinct handwriting, "Why do I want to retire?"

1. I am too much engrossed to find time to do all the things I want to do before I am too old to enjoy them or to do them well.
2. I am alone in my age-group and cannot share fully in what is to be done to shape the policy of the papers, which is apt to be more and more reactionary.
3. I face, probably, a dull period of confused public policy during which little is to be accomplished that will be either useful or interesting.
4. I acutely dislike the spirit and the management of the radio station . . .
5. I have the [*George Washington*] to finish . . .

6. I have other books to write . . .
7. I am at my peak . . .[12]

His arguments against early retirement were primarily financial,
though he was concerned that the *News Leader* "may drift into so reactionary a view that the papers will cease to do their measure of public
service."[13] He calculated the figures again and found that with anticipated royalties and different tax consequences, he would suffer a loss of
only $7,000 per year. "I think," he wrote Allen, "the time I spend at the
newspaper is worth more than that to me net."[14] By early April 1949, he
was confident that Fosdick would procure research funds. He had "made
all the mental adjustments." He was ready to retire—after thirty-four
years—as editor of the *Richmond News Leader*.

On May 3, he sat down with publisher Tennant Bryan and general
manager Jack Wise. The two men were completely unaware of what was
about to happen. Freeman opened the meeting by saying that, to save
time, he would like to read a letter to them.[15] He assured Bryan that he
had no grievance or complaint against the paper, but asked to be allowed
to "lay down all editorial and all radio duties as of July 1, 1949."[16] He
based his resignation solely on the desire to write *George Washington*. "I
believe that I best can serve my day and generation if I devote the
remaining years of my life to the completion of my *George Washington*
and of certain other works I have planned . . . There naturally are more
qualified newspaper editors than there are military biographers."[17] He
promised to be available for assistance and offered to remain on the
board of directors. He asked that his decision be kept "a strict secret"
until after he completed his "regular day's work" on June 30, and that he
be allowed to "purchase the chair and desk" he used as editor. "All I
desire to say of the past," he concluded, "is compressed in substantially
those same words: I have done the best I knew how to do."[18] He handed
the letter to Bryan, shook the hands of both men, and left the room.

Freeman's words hit Bryan "like a bolt out of the blue."[19] He found it
impossible . . . to grasp immediately the effect of so extensive a modi-
fication of a business relationship." Concluding that Freeman's mind was
made up, he "reluctantly" accepted his resignation. The terms of his
departure were worked out that week.[20]

"Newspaper writing," Freeman explained in an interview, "is just
writing in the sand."[21] Though he had been a newspaperman for more
than half his life, he showed little regret at leaving the profession. "It will
be a definite relief," he wrote Allen, "not to have to think about my

Freeman broadcasting from his home. (Images courtesy of Mary Tyler McClenahan.)

responsibility for this particular ordinance in City Council or the condition of such and such a street."[22] He would miss the "associations" established through the years, but "scarcely [could] wait" to begin his "new life."[23] While he was able to relinquish all newspaper duties, he was unable to relieve himself of his radio job. He would still give a morning broadcast. "I have been irked beyond expression in so many ways," he seethed, "not so much by the daily routine of broadcasting as by connection with an industry for which I have a fundamental and ineradicable contempt."[24] An Associated Press "main circuit teletypewriter" was soon installed in his office at Westbourne. This slight annoyance aside, Freeman felt a surge of enthusiasm and energy. "Sixty-three today," he wrote on his birthday on May 16, 1949, "and just beginning to live!"[25]

He had given some thought to his successor. James J. Kilpatrick had joined the *News Leader* in March 1941 and had established himself as one of the paper's top reporters. "I covered the Main Street beat, and the General Assembly and the Governor's office, and the Supreme Court, and the Law and Equity courts, [and] the business beat," Kilpatrick recalled. "I was the one-time business editor and another time I was outdoors editor . . . so I had done a pretty wide range of material and I suppose that impressed the Doc."[26] Kilpatrick's supposition was correct. "Simply as a matter of record," Freeman wrote Tennant Bryan in November 1948, "and a comforting thought for the future, I would like to say that as of the present time, much the promising young man around these parts for my assistant and perhaps ultimately for my successor is Kilpatrick."[27] Shortly after writing Bryan, Freeman summoned Kilpatrick to his office and offered him the position of associate editor. Kilpatrick accepted and moved from the city room upstairs to the editorial offices. There he would "fish around for subjects" on which to write until he was elevated to editor of the editorial page.[28]

Despite Freeman's admonition of secrecy, word of his retirement leaked out.[29] He thus authorized the paper to release the story on Saturday, June 25, a slight four days before his final day. "I do not consider that I am 'retiring' in the usual sense of the word," he said in a statement, "but 'changing over' . . . because I think I can serve my day and generation better in my final years of full productivity if I devote myself to writing history and biography . . ."[30] The announcement of Freeman's impending departure, Jack Kilpatrick wrote, "fell upon the city as if an earthquake had found its epicenter at Fourth and Grace."[31] The *Times-Dispatch* carried the story on its front page the following morning, and the *New York Times* and *Atlanta Journal* were among the many papers that gave prominent coverage to the story.[32] From the University of Richmond came approval for the decision. Freeman's friend and mentor, F. W. Boatwright, who had predicted in 1904 that Freeman was "destined for a larger work," perfectly captured the sentiments of his former student. "An editor deals with much that is transient," he wrote. "The historian with ultimate and permanent values . . . I should rather be remembered as Thucydides than as Themistocles."[33] "You understand precisely," Freeman responded.[34]

His last day at the *News Leader* was no different from the previous twelve thousand. He was at his desk by 3:30 A.M. writing editorial. He worked off a battered piece of cardboard on which he had jotted down some ideas. His last editorial page consisted of comments about Albert Schweitzer, public housing, Joe Dimaggio, the Taft-Hartley Act, and the function of the Joint Chiefs of Staff.[35] There was no eloquent farewell, no public thanks, no reflections. There was only a hint in the line from Tennyson he inserted at the top of the page: 'Tis not too late to seek a newer world. He suffered a few photographs, and, at 1:00 P.M., put on his hat, picked up his thermos, and left the building. Surely a historian recognized that a part of Richmond history ended that day. Those who watched him go down the hall to the elevator seemed to feel it more acutely than did Freeman. He had lunch with Inez and went up to his study to work on *Washington*. At some point during the afternoon he made a short diary entry: "Free! Completed morning at 1 P.M. Life has begun! Free, free, free!"[36]

At three o'clock the following morning, July 1, 1949, he was at his desk working on Volume Three of *George Washington*. His diary entries and letters reflect his complete contentment. July 1 was "a most beautiful day"; July 2, "another perfect day"; July 3, "another fine day; flawless in fact."[37] He wrote his brother that he was enjoying "a new heaven and a new earth" and noted that he had not once left the grounds of Westbourne during the first week following his retirement.[38] He "scarcely" read the newspaper and was amazed at his "absolute . . . divorce of interest" from public affairs.[39] On Friday, July 8, he completed Volume Three and noted the accomplishment in his diary. Then he added one further comment: "Life is so beautiful now I'm afraid it is a dream, from which I shall be awakened by a voice that says: 'Get up and go downtown and write two columns of editorial.'"[40]

Raymond Fosdick once asked Freeman for the secret of his success in writing. "First," he replied, "I married a very tolerant girl and, second, I get up early in the morning."[41] Missing in that good-humored, but incomplete, response was an explanation of his historical method; a system as meticulous and methodical as the man who designed it. It was a method developed after "forty years of experimentation" and one that "saved thousands of wasted motions by maintaining uniformity and perfect order."[42] In one of the hundreds of books lining his study wall, or in one of the thousands of letters tucked in a file, or in one of the tens of thousands of note cards covering every aspect of his subject's life, or among the millions of words he had read and pondered over the years, there was, at any given moment, just one fact he might need. His method guaranteed the fact could be authoritatively retrieved in no more than three minutes.[43]

"However complicated the description of Dr. Freeman's historical methods may sound here," Mary Wells Ashworth wrote, "they are, in fact, a system of amazing simplicity in their application."[44] The first step was reading the source material. "He never saw things through the eyes of anybody else," Dumas Malone observed. "No scholar whom I have known was more conscientious about personal examination of source material."[45] In his early years of writing, Freeman not only read the sources, but did his own copying and microfilming as well. Now with the ability to hire assistants, he delegated much of that responsibility—even trusting them to abstract and summarize findings—but he would still read the original document for himself. The historian, he wrote "never knows what he is going to find or where . . . A great file of papers, with impressive signatures, may yield little. Diaries kept by men who lived at the very pivot-point of history may be concerned with nothing more than eating and sleeping and the report of the dull doings of dummies. Then, perhaps suddenly, when the researcher is digging his way through what seem to be endless strata of dull earth, he may turn up a nugget or some treasure that a great man buried or forgot."[46] Once it was determined that a letter, book, or manuscript contained information that might be useful, the next decision was what type of note to make of it. There were three categories of notes: "Now or Never Notes" which contained "absolutely necessary" information; "Maybe Notes" with a brief summary of the information; and "Companion Notes" that gave the pages and citation to a source close at hand.[47] Whatever the category, note taking was done in a consistent form. The cards—called "quarter-sheets"—were 5½ x 4¼ inches. In the upper left corner of the card the date was noted—year, month, day. In the upper right, the source and page citation.[48] The subject was written in the center-top of the card. A brief abstract of the contents of the item was typed across the card. An example from *George Washington* appears as follows:

1781, Sept. 13 ADVANCE J. Trumbull's Diary, 333
Leave Mount Vernon, between Colchester and Dumfries, meet
letters that report action between two fleets. French have left Bay
in pursuit—event not known. "Much agitated."[49]

All notes were to be typed, single spaced, with all "personal movements and opinions" noted. Brevity was stressed. Supplementing the
cards were "long sheets" held in three-ring binders. The long sheets contained more details from the source; often including entire letters or
lengthy extracts.[50] The cards were filed chronologically, the long sheets
by topic. When a particular source had been thoroughly examined, and
notes and long sheets prepared, the cards were numbered with a num-
bering machine. This device was a relatively new addition to Freeman's
technique—he discovered its value in July 1945. He used it because it
passed the supreme test—it saved time.[51] With cards and long sheets
complete, Freeman recorded the information in another notebook, a sort
of working outline. In these entries, key words were capitalized so he
could tell at a glance what his subject was dealing with at a particular
moment.[52] His notebook page for George Washington on August 17,
1775, has two words capitalized: POWDER and QUARTERMASTER.
"When I read over these pages," he told an interviewer, "I'll not only
know where Washington was and what he was doing each day, but I'll
know exactly what problems were most in his mind. I'll know, for example, just here that powder and quartermaster problems were the matters
which came up most this day."[53] The cards, long sheets, and notebooks
were cross-referenced and carried identical numbers if they touched on
the same topic.[54] For a fact to be lost or slip through the cracks would
require failure at four different places.

   With his facts thus arranged, Freeman would prepare a chapter outline. "The interesting thing is to see how much time I save by spending
time in preparing a detailed outline," he wrote Allen. "Quite frequently,
if I spend a couple of weeks preparing to write a chapter, I almost write
it while outlining it, and after am able to complete the text in as little as
a week."[55] The outline referred by number to specific cards or long
sheets. It was painstakingly constructed. The outline for the chapter on
Virginia during Washington's youth took seventy-three hours and cited
1,316 cards; the outline of Washington's first surveying mission took
twenty-five hours to prepare.[56] Freeman was certain this was time well
spent. "Finished notes of Chapter XVII (Braddock's defeat)," he noted
in his diary. "It took about 11 hours and it will save 20 at least."[57]

Footnotes and some topical passages were outlined and written out before the narrative.[58] Only when all these tasks were completed, only when every detail was in its assigned place, only when he had surveyed the vast panoply of facts and pronounced them definitive on a certain topic, would he sit in his Morris chair and begin to write.

He wrote by hand, not with a typewriter. The typewriter, by its speed, encouraged "careless utterance."[59] He wrote neatly and precisely on specially prepared lined paper. The lines were triple spaced to allow for additions or corrections.[60] Everything in his study—from the weights used to keep books open to the Beethoven playing from the phonograph—was there to facilitate his work. He sought to temper his words. "Moderation of statement," he wrote, "and recognition of the honesty of opposing points of view are among the most important things I know."[61] A writer of history needed "complete intellectual humility." The "simplest style is the most effective," he advised another. "Too many good ideas are ruined by being overdressed—much as women are."[62] Writing the narrative was only the beginning. "Nothing that one writes of a historical nature," he told Mary Tyler, "usually is fit to print until it has been revised four or five times."[63] Over and over he studied what he had written. He struck out repetitive words and hunted down his two pet dislikes—"pendant participial clauses" and the word "however."[64] When several chapters were thought to be final, he read them aloud to Inez and Mary Wells Ashworth.

It was an exacting process, but not without sparks of humor to lighten the load. Geneva Snelling served as librarian and one of his research assistants. One day she was preparing a bibliography for *Washington* when she came across a reference, in Freeman's hand, to "O. B. Gordon." She searched for hours for a book by that author and finally appealed to Mary Wells for assistance. She was told that "O. B. Gordon" was, in fact, William Gordon, a contemporary of Washington, whom Freeman had dubbed "Old Bastard Gordon."[65] Snelling did not ask any questions when she found a reference to "B. O. B. Maclay." Another day saw Freeman researching the life of a minor general and reading aloud the subject's biographical sketch in the *Dictionary of American Biography*. "I declare," he said to Snelling and Ashworth, "that's a mighty clear account. Let's see who wrote it." The author was "D. S. Freeman."[66]

The funds from the Carnegie Corporation and the Rockefeller Foundation, and a later grant from the John Simon Guggenheim Foundation, enabled him for the first time to assemble a staff. Gertrude Richards joined in 1944 and served as chief research associate; John Carroll, a graduate student at Georgetown University, was chief researcher

Freeman completes a volume of George Washington *in the company of Mary Wells Ashworth and Gertrude Richards, research assistants, and Inez Freeman.* (Image courtesy of Mary Tyler McClenahan.)

outside Richmond starting in 1952; Snelling was librarian and researcher; and Floretta S. Watts was copyist and typist.[67] First among equals on the staff was Mary Wells Ashworth. A graduate of Hollins College, Mary Wells was the widow of Freeman's close friend and physician, Dr. O. O. Ashworth. She was more than a friend; she was a member of the family—affectionately called "Aunt C" by the Freeman children due to a disastrous episode of preparing chutney. When Dr. Ashworth passed away, the Freemans grew closer to Mary Wells and her two boys. Impressed with her scholastic abilities, Freeman gave her the task of critiquing the first volume of *George Washington*. That assignment grew to a permanent position of secretary, researcher, writer, and confidant—all under the title "Historical Assistant." Freeman was closer to Mary Wells than anyone in his life—save Inez and Mary Tyler—and every major event that occurred during these last years included Mary Wells as a member of the family. She even joined in the tradition of writing poems and sonnets to family members. She penned one about Freeman.

His is the joy of the morning. He knows
How priceless those quiet hours. He works
In the dark, yet mindful of light that glows
Beneath earth's curve. Within, no shadow lurks,
Nor trace of night or gloom. Soft music there,
Wafts across the room, as if in greeting
To first bird songs that break the pre-dawn air.
Spirit and body refreshed, he's meeting
Anew the challenge. Ere the whole world wakes,
His labor's half done. The hours were golden.
He teaches the lesson of time and makes
Us twice, thrice blessed, and to him beholden
    For beauty immortal in patience wrought;
    For the way of life his living has taught.[68]

With a full staff, an interesting subject, and a joyful attitude, Freeman moved forward to Volumes Three and Four, scheduled for release in October 1951. Volume Three covered Washington's life from January 1759, the date of his marriage to Martha Custis, to December 1775, and his assumption of command of the Continental Army. "Washington displayed qualities for which I certainly was not prepared," he wrote. "Nothing in his career as a young Virginia officer or as a Potomac planter and land speculator indicated that he possessed the vision, the judgment, the art of managing men and above all the patience he developed."[69] While this surprised him, Freeman continued to be annoyed by finding readily available material that had been ignored by previous writers. "The stubborn fact stands out," he wrote. "More that is 'unknown' about Washington exists in his papers in the Library of Congress and in printed books and records than in everything else combined. The great 'discoveries' are those of overlooked fact."[70] These "overlooked" facts extended the length of the book. He had planned to complete the revolution by the end of Volume Four; by September 1949, he knew that would be impossible. Volume Four would carry Washington only as far as Spring 1778. The book was also extended by a shift in emphasis.

Instead of watching step by step the development of Washington's strategy . . . I have had to describe how he sought vainly to get shoes for his men, how he tried to prod negligent commissaries and somnolent quartermasters, how he had to rid the Army of incompetent officers and to repeat year by year the disheartening task of rebuilding an army that disbanded in December. I have had to deal with the problem of desertion and, above all, with perplexities of human relationships that involved more arrogance and self-assertiveness on the part of subordinates than was shown in any of the other wars I have studied or witnessed.[71]

Freeman was delighted in this new twist on an old story. Washington, he discovered, "was one-tenth field commander and nine-tenths administrator. His prime duty was not to kill the British but to keep the American army alive . . . the states were falling apart: he was the moral cement of the loose union."[72] It was during the writing of this volume that Washington grew in Freeman's estimation.

More clearly than at the time of my last report, I see that Washington, and probably Washington alone kept the Revolution alive. He was the only man who combined military experience with infinite patience, inflexible determination, a sound sense of organization, absolute integrity, regard for civil rights, and a justice so manifest in every act that even his rivals had to admit his superiority of character . . . I believe that if he had been captured or killed, the Revolution would have collapsed in 1777 . . . It is not popular, of course, to say such a thing, but I believe that in the black year of the Revolution there were not more than 500 intelligent leaders—political and military—who were willing to sacrifice all they had and all they hoped to be, for the triumph of America.[73]

The outside world still managed to intrude into the study at Westbourne. Freeman's biting cynicism about national affairs had not mellowed in retirement. He shared a platform with President Truman in May 1950, at the announcement of the release of the first volume of the writings of Thomas Jefferson. Truman was cordial, but Freeman did not alter his opinion of the president. He snapped to his brother that he disliked to "keep company with a demagogue."[74] He viewed with a wary eye the rise to national prominence of Wisconsin senator Joseph McCarthy. "The interesting, and perhaps the dangerous thing, is the possibility that he may fool the people," he wrote. "Incredible as it seems, in a choice between Truman and McCarthy, I would have to take Truman."[75] He again manned the microphone for a long afternoon of broadcasting when the Korean War broke out. "My broadcasts have been pessimistic," he wrote, "and, therefore, I suspect will not be popular."[76] He frequently found himself at odds with America's cold war policy of "fighting communist aggression everywhere" which he believed was based on "the concept of [national] omnipotence."[77] He thought Korea should be abandoned if "all-out conflict with Red China" threatened. He included this position in a "Ten point program" he drafted on December 1, 1950. It is not clear if he broadcast this plan or merely distributed it among friends. In the plan, he called for negotiations with the Soviet Union, increased armament of Western Europe and the United States, universal military training, wage and price controls to stop inflation, and "a complete political truce in the United States." The plan was both conservative and liberal, naive and insightful, Wilsonian and militaristic. In short, it was uniquely Freeman. It was this frame of mind that led him to overlook his opposition to Truman and to vigorously support the president when he removed his old friend General MacArthur from command in the Far East. "Well done!" he wired Truman. "You have applied courageously a basic constitutional principle asserted and maintained to the nation's benefit by discerning presidents in some of the most critical hours of American military history."[78] The White House was pleased to have the support of the nation's top military historian. "Not all Americans have your wonderful historical sense," Joseph Short, the president's press secretary wrote, "You probably know this, but the President is a great admirer of your historical work and has read—and still re-reads—your books on Lee and his lieutenants."[79]

With the national and international scene in such an unsettled state, Freeman turned again to "the one man who can redeem the evil hour in America": Dwight Eisenhower.[80] "Do you remember what you told me when I came to you in the autumn of 1946 and told you that you must run for President?" he wrote Eisenhower in September 1950. "You said you could not and would not unless a situation developed in which you would be the man to whom the country would turn . . . That hour is near at hand."[81] Freeman warned him that America was in the greatest danger and that Washington was dominated by "the basest, most selfish politicians." Eisenhower was the only man, he argued, who could "speak in clear, exalted tones" in the "most fateful hour in American history." He could carry Virginia, Freeman assured him, and "nearly the whole" South. "Ponder these words."

Eisenhower was gracious, but noncommittal; though he acknowledged the impact of Freeman's words in 1946.[82] Freeman waited a year before he tried again, telling the general that "the demand is increasingly compelling."[83] By this time, his was not the only voice saying the phrase "I like Ike."

The new decade of the fifties saw Freeman end his long association with the University of Richmond. Things had been changing at his alma mater, and he was less inclined to change with them. He had threatened to resign in June 1949 over a break with the executive committee regarding fraternity housing.[84] "Work as Rector," he confided to a friend, "has been a long, thankless task, to which nothing but a sense of duty has held me."[85] His longtime friends were leaving the scene. History professor S. C. Mitchell retired in 1945 and died three years later. President Boatwright closed his remarkable fifty-one year tenure in 1946. In early June 1950, Freeman reviewed the university's budget. He noticed an appropriation to underwrite a substantial amount of athletic scholarships.[86] Upon investigation, he learned, to his "horror," that promises of "free tuition and board and lodging" had been made by unauthorized personnel to incoming athletes. Freeman believed "physical education" had a place, "but no more than its proper place in academic training." The university, he wrote, had decided to "debauch" itself academically in order to have a winning athletic program.[87] Freeman announced his resignation at a meeting of the board of trustees on June 5, 1950, and the next day sent a terse letter confirming his decision to the secretary of the board.[88] Boatwright's successor, George Modlin, asked him to give up only the position of rector and remain on the board. For whatever reason, Freeman was unwilling to compromise. He called the action of the university "the most dangerous and backward step" taken during all his years on the board. He could see no value in increasing expenditures for athletics. "I never have been able, with my feeble mind, to ascertain how every college could have a winning team and nobody have a losing team."[89] He could not bring himself to be a party "to a fiscal policy which I think is dangerously unsound in itself and is fatal to your success as President." It was an unpleasant end to a nearly fifty-year association.[90]

"I am working too long hours," Freeman wrote, making an unusual confession in his diary, "and, for the good of myself and the completion of the work at a high level, I must shorten the week so as to give me time every day for exercise."[91] He committed to writing "eight hours daily and seven on music days." The latter were days on which he took piano lessons. He had long wanted to study piano and now started lessons because he believed part of "every man's needful, daily, discipline" was to attempt "something new and difficult."[92] So, at the age of sixty-four, he started to take piano under the direction of Mrs. Channing Ward.[93] His aptitude for music did not match his skills in other areas.

He had always participated fully in the events around him, but now he drew back. "Visitors, visitors, visitors!" he wrote in his diary. "They will be the death of me yet! Meantime they tore this day to bits."[94] He had other things as well on his mind. "Your mother tells me you are in dire financial distress," he wrote his son, "please write me . . . what is the minimum weekly sum on which you can live decently."[95] Much of June 1951 was given over to dealing with James Douglas's latest crisis. Between June 22 and July 26, Freeman sent five hundred dollars to his son, paid the premium on his government insurance, and exchanged letters with his son's former wife regarding support payments for their son.[96] James Douglas's employment was always changing; he went from working for a chain of radio stations to selling real estate to working at Garfinkel's Department Store.[97] Disappointed and concerned over this situation and distressed over national events, Freeman found himself looking for answers. "Surely," he wrote his brother, "there is more to life than blind groping in the dark. Even if we do not know whence we came or whither we go, we know, or at least think we know, what we are doing here and I maintain, for my part, that we can have a lot of fun doing it."[98] Never before in any of his letters had Freeman confessed any questions over "whence" he came or "whither" he would go. Nor had he ever expressed any doubt over "what" he was doing here. "I do not covet the traditional immortality of the Christian faith," he continued, "and feel that I would be very much bored if I had it . . . Be that as it may, we have an obligation . . . of lessening human misery and adding as best we can to human knowledge and, we hope, to human happiness."[99] It was, despite its upbeat conclusion, an uncharacteristically disturbing letter, indicating Freeman was passing through an uncharacteristically disturbing time. Ten days after writing the letter to Allen, he showed signs of renewed spirit. "Ignorant of the past," he wrote Dr. S. L. Morgan of Wake Forest University, "man thinks his difficulties in every generation are greater than those of the previous generation—greater than those of any generation, perhaps, or of any age or time. This, of course, is not true. As man has overcome difficulties as great as those we now face, what reason is there to assume that he will not continue his unbroken record with triumph over circumstance?"[100] He would continue his efforts to "triumph over circumstance" despite the occasional season of despair. "I sometimes wonder," he wrote, "whether there is any limit to a day's delightsome possibilities if a man only will take the time to find its beauties."[101]

George Washington, Volume Three, *Planter & Patriot*, and Volume Four, *Leader of the Revolution*, was released in October 1951. Freeman judged the work to be at midpoint. "It became manifest," he told the Associated Press, "that it would require six volumes before I finished the second volume, and when I completed the third, I knew it would be eight."[102] He warned that Washington's life from 1759 to 1773 was "undramatic," but he devoted fourteen chapters to that era.[103] Once those years were past, he found himself again a military historian, and the pace of the work picked up. He explained the intricate defensive maneuvers in shifting continental forces from Boston to New York to New Jersey; took the reader in the boats on the Delaware River where the army was carried by "youth and resolution and the patience of Washington"; stood with Washington on the high ground of Trenton as the Hessians broke and surrendered; described defeat at Germantown and courage at Valley Forge. In the midst of battles, marches, and maneuvers, Freeman hurled at the reader the litany of problems plaguing Washington: jealous subordinates, deserting troops, treachery and treason. No food. No powder. No shoes. No clothes. It was not the Revolution of Trumbull's paintings; it was "baffling uncertainty," "pallor, hunger, tatters and foul odors," and defeat after defeat—told "as only" he could tell it.[104] He told also of spring in America, "blessed in memory because it was the season when all the gardens were blooming on the Potomac." The spring that ended Volume Four brought with it a turning point: French recognition of American independence.

The reviews of the latest Washington volumes paid tribute to Freeman's research, his style, and his conclusions. Most found as well that "the often inconsequential detail becomes so tedious that even the student nods."[105] Once one made it through the details, Avery Craven noted, "he becomes conscious of the fact that Freeman is evolving something of a new and clearer picture of this great American."[106] This George Washington "is not on a pedestal," wrote L. H. Butterfield in the *Saturday Review*, but "more nearly as he was."[107] Perry Miller and Bernard Knollenberg, both of whom had been critical of the first two volumes, found fault as well with the new releases. "Freeman must pay the penalty for becoming a classic on the day of publication," Miller snipped. "After we have put by the enchantment of the four volumes . . . [we] still do not know how [Washington] got that way."[108] Knollenberg wrote that any "defects . . . fall into second place" behind the full, fair, and convincing portrayal. He then devoted one paragraph to the book's attributes and eight pages to its "defects."

His "chief disappointment" was "Freeman's indiscriminate use of memoirs, notes of conversations, and letters written years, some of them
dozens of years, after the event."[109] What Freeman was supposed to
base conclusions upon, absent contemporary accounts, if not recollections of credible witnesses—John Adams being one—Knollenberg did
not say.

Freeman read the reviews of his books, but rarely commented on any
criticism. He wrote Perry Miller, following his critical review of the first
two *Washington* volumes, and advised he was "profiting" by what Miller
had said. "You have put a caveat in front of me," he wrote, "I am most
grateful for it." He did find it necessary to put down some thoughts about
criticism following the *New York Times* review of Volumes Three and Four.
The reason was personal; Anne Freeman was married to Julius Ochs
Adler, whose family was part owner of the paper. Anne was apparently
annoyed at the generally negative reviews given her father's work by the
Times, and it made for an awkward family situation. Freeman wrote Anne
a long letter, one that he subsequently decided not to mail, in which he
discussed the *Times* in particular and criticism in general. "The intentions
and ideals of the owners of the *Times* are of the highest," he wrote, "they
simply are the prisoners of the editors and they do not know the vindic-
tiveness, the prejudices or the complacency of [their editors]."[110]

> Deliberately or ignorantly or accidentally the *Times* selected as
> reviewer of the third and fourth volumes of *George Washington*, the
> small-minded jealous former head of the Institute of Early
> American History and Culture at Williamsburg, a man named
> Bridenbaugh to whom it was intolerable that I, instead of he,
> seemed to have first place as a historical writer in the estimate of
> Virginians and even in the opinion of Bridenbaugh's idol, my dear
> friend Sam Morison. No chance has ever been lost by Bridenbaugh
> to smear me—or anyone else. He is the embodiment of jealousy in
> historical writing . . . Truth is, the *Times* never has spoken a kind
> word of me except in reviews that happened, by some fluke, to be
> entrusted to friends of mine . . . such is the situation.[111]

Freeman told Anne not to say anything to her husband or to take
the criticism seriously. "Remember, it does not hurt me as an individual or as a writer." He was far more pleased with the "letters from men
who know the complexities of the task—men like Randall and Nevins
and Rupert Hughes." This unsent letter to Anne is the only extended

comment he made about his critics during the forty-three years following the release of *A Calendar of Confederate Papers*.

The materials, cards, folios, and files on *Washington* filled the drawers of a small steel cabinet in Freeman's study. One drawer held a different annotation: "I've Laughed All My Life." In the drawer were pages of amusing stories that he intended to put together as a small book.[112] He had prepared a list of nine topical headings for the book: Veterans, Church, Negroes, Teachers, Old Ladies, Politicians, County Folks, Newspaper, and Children.[113] Under each heading he listed the stories to be included in the chapter. Unfortunately, he included only two or three words to indicate the content, rendering the list all but useless to those unfamiliar with the stories. Titles such as "Lord not at home," "the dog-fight at King William Court House," and "ain't nobody complained about my being slow" are but three of the more than 150 apparently amusing stories of the Old South. All but one have been lost to another era. The notation "Hell of a git you got" comes from one of his favorite stories:

> [An] emaciated, bone-tired Confederate . . . was pounced on by three Yankees shouting, "Got-chu!" "Yes," the rebel flared back, "and a hell of a git you got."[114]

A typed list of the humorous topics was saved by Mary Wells Ashworth, who noted on the bottom that Freeman had "promised or threatened" to one day treat these subjects.[115] He still mentioned writing a study of World War II, but he made a concerted effort to keep his focus on Washington to the exclusion of all other ideas or projects. "Time is of the essence of the enterprise," he wrote Robert Lester in March 1951. "I shall be 65 in May and have set 1954 for the completion of the work. I am in the best of health, but I do not intend to pursue elaborate research, at the expense of any organization, after I feel my powers waning. The work must be finished by the time I am 68."[116]

Volume Five, *Victory with the Help of France*, was a pure joy to write. It was almost entirely military history, with the added intrigue of Benedict Arnold. "All the traditional talk about Arnold's resentment of the injuries and injustice he had received at the hands of the Congress, and so on, is nothing but misunderstanding," he wrote Allen. "He was out for money and sold himself for British guineas—that is the whole story."[117] He sent Gertrude Richards to Europe in the spring of 1951 to research French comments on the war and on Washington. He also wanted a good picture of Martha Washington. "All that I ever see show her with those damnable headdresses that make her look like a wash-woman."[118] While Richards toiled in Europe, Freeman drove to Yorktown to take a first-hand look at the battlefield that decided the war. He checked to see if the tide ran into the marsh above Moore's Pond, assessed whether American troops were exposed at Wormeley's Creek, and debated whether a particular redoubt was in fact a redan or fleche work.[119] "It probably will be," he wrote, "the last military campaign of which I shall write in detail. I could not ask for one more interesting."[120] He may have thought that, but it hardly seemed possible that America's premier military historian was anywhere near finished writing of war. "His extended narrative-analysis of the Yorktown campaign," his nemesis the *New York Times* stated, "will, no doubt, long remain a standard authority . . . The blending of the dramatic and the commonplace achieves a realistic effect, without deadening the narrative."[121]

"I'm glad you like the *Washington*," he wrote Allen. "It of course was written for posterity and not for the casual reader. That individual will find too much detail, but I hope the prime objective will be achieved, namely, that Washington will emerge as the great man he was in almost every respect and, second, that nobody will have to do the work over again."[122] While writing about one "great man," Freeman renewed his efforts to influence the actions of another "great man." "I saw Eisenhower," he wrote Allen in late 1950, "and found him in good trim, though physically I thought he was a little flabby. There is, I think, no doubt of his willingness to run for president if the crisis gets worse or remains as bad as it is."[123] When the 1952 election year opened, Freeman joined with a number of "prominent Richmonders" and established a "Virginians for Eisenhower Club." The formation of the group—and Freeman's participation—made front-page news in Democratic Virginia.[124] In April, Eisenhower asked to be relieved from his assignment as Supreme Commander of the Allied Forces in Europe and announced he had consented to become a Republican candidate for president.[125] Freeman had promised Eisenhower his full support and, in September, he gave him a hefty boost: a major article in *Life* magazine extolling Ike's qualifications for the presidency. "To a distinguished Democrat," the article was captioned, "the times demand a man of Eisenhower's stature."[126] Freeman recounted the details of their 1946 meeting, when he first broached the subject of an Eisenhower presidency, and of their many other times together. "Always," he wrote, "he was clear, explicit—and shaped every order by the T-square of duty." He praised Eisenhower's "humility of spirit," "uncommonly keen and true sense of values," and "high, practical intelligence."[127] As a military historian, he ranked Eisenhower's European campaign as "one of the half-dozen most magnificent achievements of modern history." As a Southerner, he gave other Southerners the cover they needed to support a nominee of the hated—even in 1952—Republican Party.

> We of the South . . . seldom have attained; we never have ceased to aspire. Few heroes have been ours to worship, but those we have enshrined. The Confederate tradition survives in the South . . . Every Southerner thought better of himself because he belonged to the society that had produced Robert E. Lee and "Stonewall" Jackson . . . To that revered company, Eisenhower may be admitted . . . the more grueling the test, the stronger the man who emerges. When he does appear, there seldom is doubt concerning his worth and dependability . . . Eisenhower is not lacking; he is worthy of the presidency. He can be trusted with its powers.[128]

During the campaign, Eisenhower had a discussion with Julius O. Adler of the *New York Times*, father-in-law to Anne Freeman Adler. He took the opportunity of the family connection to tell Adler that "the first man to tell him he should enter politics" was Douglas Freeman.[129]

Though involved in contemporary politics, Freeman had never written extensively about historical politics. The revolution was over for George Washington, and Volume Six would take him into the presidency. Soldiers would be replaced by politicians; divisions and brigades by Cabinets and Congresses; orders and maps by bills, speeches, and pamphlets. While duty and honor were clear on a battlefield, virtue was not always so apparent in the caucus and the cloakroom. Politics had played a tangential part in Freeman's other writings—Washington the general had to deal with Congress and politicians, as had Lee—but it had never been the featured locale for any of his subjects. Freeman had stood, figuratively and literally, in many councils of war; he had seldom entered a historical council of state. Was he up to the challenge? Would the fog-of-war method work as well in the political arena as it did in a theater of war? Would it be possible to judge Washington the president without knowing something of Hamilton, Jefferson, Jay, and others?

On May 12, 1952, Freeman began to answer these questions.

CHAPTER 15

"That Is My Message"

"Home was contrast and content." So read the first sentence of Volume Six of *George Washington*. Though the phrase was cast to contrast Washington's calm life at Mount Vernon with the tumult of war, it was equally applicable to Freeman's life at Westbourne as 1952 neared its end. There was enthusiasm at the prospect of an Eisenhower presidency, but deepening cynicism with politics in general; there was joy in sharing days with Inez, hearing of Anne's latest adventure, and the ever-satisfying closeness to his partner Mary Tyler, and there was the anguish over the travails of his only son; there was the exacting schedule, but a hint of weariness creeping in on his sixty-six-year-old body; there was acclaim as the nation's preeminent historian, and a gnawing wariness about whether *George Washington* met his own high standards. There was no rocking chair or slowing down as Freeman entered his sunset year, there was only motion—perpetual motion—colored with phrases honed through a life of motion: "I'd rather wear out than rust out," and, "It is history that teaches us to hope."

In September 1952, Freeman, Inez, and Mary Wells Ashworth departed on a trip to Europe. The trip was, naturally, equal parts vacation and work. "I must keep myself up to date on numerous aspects of foreign affairs if I am to do my duty to my auditors," Freeman wrote. "As I have not been to Europe in seven years, I must postpone another visit no longer . . . I hope I may hear plain people express themselves without fear."[1] He planned to cable reports to WRNL to be included in the news reports given in his 8:00 A.M. time slot. The trip was also relaxation and rapture. "This is an ambitious and, undoubtedly, an expensive trip," he wrote Allen shortly before departing, but added, "I am not going to hurry."[2] The trio spent ten days in England and saw King Arthur's Round Table, the Tower of London, Stratford-on-Avon, and many other wonders.[3] Freeman picked up local color, bought a suit, and ate "four kinds of potatoes" at one dinner. "We Americans assume the British want to know all about Eisenhower's speeches and Stevenson's expense account," he cabled WRNL, but he found the average Englishman's interests centered on more basic curiosities, such as "the amount of bone he is apt to get in next week's meat ration."[4] They crossed over to the continent and passed a relaxing month in Florence, Rome, Paris, Naples, and Madrid. He took one excursion on his own, flying to Tripoli for three days before rejoining Inez and Mary Wells in Rome. He was in Madrid when he heard of Eisenhower's election to the presidency.[5] "God be praised for the triumph of American common sense and decency!" he wrote in his diary.[6]

The travelers arrived in New York on November 18. "Two wonderful months to be remembered always," Inez wrote on the final page of her trip diary.[7] Freeman concurred, adding his own unique perspective on the trip's value. "I have made many observations," he wrote Mary Tyler, "that have modified my views on many phases of international relations. In out-of-way towns, such as Tournos and Revello, I have seen architecture and statuary that have explained more clearly the link between Romanesque and Gothic, and the influence of Asia Minor on late Byzantine sculpture—something I never had considered."[8]

During his trip to Tripoli in October 1952, Freeman is entertained by the Libyan minister of defense (to Freeman's left) and the mayor of Sabatha (to his right). (Image courtesy of Mary Tyler McClenahan.)

He returned home to speculation that Eisenhower would soon appoint him to the Cabinet or to an ambassadorship. "I am not saying that I will not accept what has not been offered me," he wrote Allen, "and I know Eisenhower will actively try to give me anything I want, but the point is—again—that under no circumstances would I consider anything permanent or semi-permanent. The completion of *George Washington* means much more than service at some court or other."[9] Freeman confirmed this sentiment in a letter to Eisenhower. He offered him "the detached judgment" of an old friend "who will accept no office and will burden you with no letters of recommendation."[10] The president thanked him for his "typically thoughtful letter" and expressed satisfaction at having his continued "advice and counsel." No government job was offered, nor did Freeman seek an appointment.[11]

"Home was contrast and content." The return to Virginia renewed family worries. His son had "ignored . . . letters and birthday greetings" and had not advised him of his plans or, in many instances, his whereabouts. Freeman saw James Douglas once during the course of ten months. In the early morning of November 26, 1952, he wrote by hand an eleven-page letter into which he poured his frustration, his disappointment, his advice, his hope, and his love. It was, in many ways, the last desperate effort of a father to reach his son.[12] Freeman's words reveal that he never quite understood the gulf between the two men or his part in creating it. Father and son existed on different planes of attitude and viewpoint. It was as if they spoke different languages.

"May God give me the wisdom with which to write this letter!" Freeman began.

> Something is paralyzing your efforts. I have spent long hours of midnight in asking myself, What is it that keeps this magnificent young man from swimming in the flooded stream of his nation's activity when he is strong and vigorous? I have not ever been able to guess at an answer that satisfied my reason and accorded with my good opinion of your character and abilities . . . I have to resort to questions, in the hope that one or another of them may prompt an answer.[13]

He was unable to comprehend that any man—not the least of all his own son—would be content not to develop some life ambition and begin to execute it. It was, to him, the most basic and simplest requirement of life. He thus questioned J. D. as he would have expected to be questioned if similarly situated. "Are you discouraged?" he asked; if so, he told him to "get a job, almost any sort of a job." Was it debt? If so, and if he were willing to do his "full part," Freeman would "get some speaking engagements and maybe write a magazine article that will yield" some money. Did he think something was "wrong with [his] head"? That notion was dismissed as absurd. "Is it women? Is it liquor?" He went through the litany of vices that he deemed detrimental to success; vices that could be overcome with hard work and proper scheduling of one's time. Hoping that J. D. would find one of these to be the source of his difficulties, Freeman offered to make what would be for him the supreme sacrifice.

When you are willing to give me assurance, and will keep up to it, you can come back here and stay as long as is necessary to put you on your feet again. I then will give up everything else I am doing, including all work on my books, to be with you, to work with you on the grounds, to study with you, and to nurse you back to full vigor. The condition of this is that you must promise in advance that you will do absolutely no drinking while here and that you will go to bed at the hour the rest of the household do. Frankly, your mother and I could not stand the strain of having you out at night when we did not know when or in what condition you would come home. A few months of this strain would kill us both.[14]

"Your failure in life," he wrote, "would be my final and fatal frustration." He suggested he consider going back to college and offered him a job doing research on *Washington* at the Library of Congress. "Think over what I have stated here," Freeman concluded, "the hour of opportunity is striking." His son could count, he said, "on the support and best counsel of him who loves you far more than he loves fame or distinction or any reward that man can give."[15]

If Douglas Freeman had received such a letter from his own father—assuming circumstances ever existed to warrant such a letter—the result would have been immediate action. Such was their relationship.

This letter from Douglas Freeman to his son went unanswered. Such was their relationship.

Father and son remained estranged over the last months of Freeman's life. James Douglas wrote one letter, in January 1953; a chatty letter discussing his new bartending job and asking for advice on whether he should accept similar employment in the Virgin Islands. Freeman responded with a detailed analysis, but it was clear he was less than enthusiastic about that job prospect.[16] Soon after this exchange began the familiar cycle of paying debts and keeping his daughter-in-law from taking action to compel support payments.[17] "I have sinned against God and against you in failing to hold you to a rigid standard of the sort of work every man ought to do in the world," Freeman wrote. "Whatever my mistakes in dealing with you in the past, they were mistakes of love and of regard for your sensitive and easily-discouraged spirit."[18] He ultimately believed his son's problems were based solely in laziness. "I am often puzzled," he wrote Allen, "to think that he has done less well than almost any boy with whom he was associated, yet he possesses a mind which is clearer in judgment and more accurate than the mind of any of his comrades. Ability, I must conclude, is not enough; there must be balance and initiative along with it."[19]

Home was contrast and content. "To this day," Freeman wrote, "for one letter that I get about Washington, I receive at least three concerning Confederate leaders. When, therefore, a discerning reader understands what I am trying to do in bringing Washington back into the full light of his immense service to America, I am made very happy and am encouraged to go with the labor which will consume this most productive ten years of my life."[20] He had brought his subject to the presidency; though Washington's first term would cover only 199 pages as compared with 1,348 pages devoted to the revolution. He applied the same meticulous exhaustive research and clear and disciplined prose to tell this nonmilitary story, but he seemed uninspired by this part of Washington's life. Part of this lack of enthusiasm may be attributed to what Freeman described as Washington's "almost monarchical detachment" from many of the actions being taken by Jefferson, Hamilton, Randolph, and others. If Washington's detachment did not limit the story, the fog-of-war method prevented analysis of surrounding political intrigue, such as the Hamilton-Jefferson deal over Federal assumption of state debts, and muted coverage of the raucous debate over Jay's Treaty. Freeman had sought to paint a portrait of Washington different from the stern visage rendered by Gilbert Stuart. In one way, he had succeeded. Washington becomes real as he thinks and plans and governs and leads. In the same way, Washington is set apart from the swirl of activity as the young nation defines itself. "Around him," Freeman wrote, "conflict was rising but he was still apart from it. No influence approached his; he had no rival . . ."21 Volume Six would take the president to the end of his first term. Freeman planned to tie together all the loose pieces and present the final portrait in Volume Seven.

Shortly before he departed on his trip to Europe, Freeman received a letter from his physician. "It might be wise," Dr. William H. Higgins, Jr., wrote, "for you to have in your possession certain information of a medical nature about yourself which would be of help to any physician who might have to see you professionally while overseas."22 The medical report noted that Freeman had "always had excellent health." This report notwithstanding, Freeman began to act as if he knew he had but a short time left to live. On April 20, 1953, he began what would be a twenty-page memorandum "designed to be of assistance to anyone who is called upon after my death to clear out my litter and to dispose of my papers."23 He started in his third-floor study, "southeast corner," and went room by room through the entire house, suggesting the fate of each significant item. While describing personal property, the memorandum also charted the record of a full life of usefulness: "my early volumes of poems learned at school," "original ballot of Jefferson Davis," "my Father's Confederate coat," "set of Sharpsburg maps," "President Roosevelt's letter," "picture Mr. Churchill gave me," "bound manuscript copies of adolescent novels,"24 "my Mother's desk," "the old unpainted electric clock . . . that counted off the minutes during which, whether fresh or weary, I tried to write the history of the South's great men," "the paper placard that stood on top of my clock in the newspaper building: Time Alone is Irreplaceable. Waste It Not."25

"I despair," he wrote, "of ever preparing a bibliography even of the things that appeared between covers. I have no idea how many introductions I have written for books or how many addresses of mine have been put in print. There will be no occasion, I know, to prepare such a bibliography, but this note of discouragement is entered in the bare possibility that somebody might want to follow through with all the titles. It cannot be done."26

A letter to Allen carried the tone of an affectionate farewell. "I have told you many times," he wrote, "and shall say to the last breath, that a younger brother never had wiser guidance from an elder, or sounder counsel, or more helpful love than you have given me. Were my career notable, which it most certainly is not, no small part of the credit would belong to you."27 His friend Ambler Johnston noticed that Freeman seemed thinner than usual, perhaps twenty pounds lighter in weight.

Johnston later asserted he noticed "the fatal mark was on him."[28] He was not the only one who noticed. Jack Kilpatrick was invited to Westbourne for a luncheon given directors of the Southern Railway. "Several of us," Kilpatrick noted, "would remark that he seemed uncharacteristically tired that afternoon."[29] It was May 1953. What the observers did not know was that he had begun experiencing periodic heart pain. One day he rose from the lunch table and immediately sat down on a side chair. He assured Inez it was nothing.[30]

On June 10, 1953, Freeman swirled his chair to face his typewriter and began another memorandum.

Within the last fortnight, I have had two attacks which seem to me to be of angina pectoris or pseudo angina. I have not yet decided whether I shall talk of them with Dr. Higgins, because he may restrict my movements so severely that I had rather be dead.[31]

His will, he wrote in the memorandum, was in the safe-deposit box of the State Planter's Bank. The key was in the middle drawer of his desk. The inventory was complete. He directed that he "be buried from Second Baptist Church at the hour least inconvenient to friends who wish to attend." Pallbearers were to be the senior members of the current events class. The hymns: "The Strife is O'er" and "Welcome Happy Morning." He wanted a fast-paced service "to save my family from the long agonizing haul that racked the nerves of 'mourners' in the days of horse-drawn vehicles." While his body was at Westbourne, he wanted the "third movement of Beethoven's Ninth Symphony to be played over and over again." The gravestone was to carry his name and the "inscription in letters large enough to be seen and read from the road—'Tis not too late to seek a newer world."[32]

"That," he concluded, "is my message to my wife, to Mary Wells, and to my children and grandchildren."

He placed the letter in an envelope titled "Directions for my funeral, etc. To be opened immediately after my death."

The night before he wrote the memorandum, Mary Tyler called. She was busy preparing to leave with Leslie and her four children for their farm in western North Carolina.[33] Unable to stop by Westbourne before she left, she phoned to say good-bye. Was it only in retrospect that he sounded sad? "Good-bye, my darling," he said as the conversation ended. "You are my eyes and my heart—remember that."[34]

Friday, June 12, was a typical workday. Frank McCarthy, a long-time friend and former Chief of Staff to General Marshall, came by for a visit. Freeman went downtown to see the "superb coronation pictures of Elizabeth II," and made plans to visit Anne in New York.[35] "If I do not have the lily in my hand by that time," he wrote, "I shall be in New York Wednesday, the 17th of June . . ."[36]

The alarm sounded at 2:30 A.M. It was Saturday, June 13, 1953. Freeman dressed, had his morning prayer, and fixed his own breakfast. He knew this morning would see the completion of the final chapter of Volume Six of *George Washington*. Into his study he went. The light from his window was the only light shining on the darkened grounds of Westbourne. He spent the hours writing about Washington's desire to retire and his subsequent reelection to the presidency. He faced page sixty-four of his manuscript and began the final paragraph of the chapter and the volume. "He was 61," he wrote of Washington,

and he complained mildly of waning memory and of poor hearing, but few others saw any evidence of decline, and his daily life showed none, unless it was an increasing disposition to spend too much time on trifling matters of farm management. Was he not mounted and ready for four years more on the road of service to his country?[37]

That rhetorical question might have provided a suitable ending, but Freeman decided to answer it.

The multitude of his followers and the handful of envious foes would have admitted that the answer was "yes," but there were some developments to indicate the road would be stony and cloud-covered, and there were voices prophesying strife.[38]

That would be the final sentence, but it appeared to need revision. Departing from his habit of revising at a later time, he lined out most of the sentence and wrote:

The multitude of his followers and the handful of envious foes would have proclaimed the certainty with joy or would reluctantly have admitted the probability, but there were omens the road would be stony and cloud-covered, and there were voices prophesying strife.[39]

There. The sentence was vastly improved. He had finished his sixth volume of *George Washington*; his thirteenth major work, and his nineteenth book overall.[40]

Douglas Southall Freeman laid down his pen for the last time.

The end came suddenly, unfittingly out of place for a man whose life was so unhurriedly ordered. He finished the chapter in *Washington*, delivered his morning broadcast, and drafted the day's mail. One letter placed an order for sixty-four and one-half pounds of ham, and one acknowledged receipt of a new issue of *The Quarterly* magazine.[41] He then set to work, "with the greatest vigor," in his garden.[42] He had on his old clothes and was tamping in fertilizer around his dogwood and magnolia. Inez joined him. "You know," he told her, "I've always been blessed with energy. It's an endowment for which I can't take any credit. But I've felt all my life that laziness is a sin against the Holy Ghost!"[43] After work, the two had lunch. He mounted the steps to his third-floor bedroom and prepared to take a nap. An uneasy feeling began to creep over him, and this time the pain did not subside. It crashed down upon him with a previously unfelt power. He asked Inez to summon help. It was shortly before 3:00 P.M.

Dr. Higgins arrived in the shortest of time. He examined his patient and sent for his father, also a doctor. Freeman joked with both men that they must keep him alive to finish *George Washington*.[44]

"He realized the seriousness of his condition," Inez remembered.[45] As the companion of Lee and Washington, and commentator on world events, Freeman had seen death many times in his sixty-seven years. He had described it at Malvern Hill and Gettysburg; on the Marne and the Somne; at Princeton and Yorktown; at Leningrad and Berlin. If he believed it was now time to receive his final summons, he did not express that thought to his attending friends. Around four o'clock came a more devastating attack. The ambulance was in route. Everything was prepared at Stuart Circle Hospital. The two doctors stepped out of the room to confer. The clock stood at 4:20 P.M.

Douglas Freeman closed his eyes and was gathered unto his fathers.

"I expect," he had written in 1948, "to die with a pen in my hand, with thanks to God on my lips for the opportunity of having led a life where I was permitted to work . . . on the glorious yesterdays adorned by the noble figures whom I have had the privilege of knowing."[46]

Inez drew a dark line across the day on her calendar and wrote "My Beloved."[47]

The house seemed to fill up within minutes, as if to compensate for

Freeman in the garden of his home reviewing galleys of George Washington.
(Image courtesy of Mary Tyler McClenahan.

the spirit and force that had just left it. Tennant Bryan. Jack Kilpatrick. Mary Wells Ashworth. Members of the current events class. The calls went out. Anne was at home in New York and immediately set out for Westbourne. James Douglas was working in a bar in Boynton Beach, Florida. "You Doug Freeman?" a patron asked. "Your daddy's dead."[48] The call to the Cheek residence was taken by Leslie Cheek. Mary Tyler was working in her garden. Her husband rose to the occasion and "gently, with much sadness" broke the devastating news.[49] The family quickly packed and prepared for the long night's journey to Richmond. As the car headed north, Mary Tyler wrote her last letter to her father, "who died thirteen hours ago, at 4:20 P.M."

> You left so suddenly, while we were in the country with the children, that I did not have a chance to say good-bye. You always said you would rather wear out than rust out, and so you did . . . Nobody but God knows how I shall miss you, every hour of every day, but I won't dwell on that. I want to thank you for being the most wonderful Father a girl ever had. You did everything better than everyone else, and you were a better Father, too, particularly to me. Having you for a Father was like carrying a banner; I was so proud of you. I was proud of your achievement, proud of your intellect—the most brilliant I have ever known—and proud of your greatness of spirit . . . Something of you was recreated in me; we were the same so deep down that we had a wordless communion. I gloated over my special place in your life because I knew nothing could touch it or spoil it; it was deeper than personality, it was nature itself . . . You are silent this morning, and I shall never hear your voice again. But you are here in my heart, and in my eyes, and you will go with me wherever I go . . . I shall go to Westbourne and kiss your body good-bye, but yourself I have with me, and we shall go on together.[50]

"Profoundly distressed" the telegram began. "America has lost one of her most distinguished citizens. He was a true friend whom I shall miss greatly. /s/ Dwight D. Eisenhower."[51] Hundreds of telegrams followed the president's. "His work will live long," wired Carl Sandburg. "I loved him so much that my feeling is far far deeper than sympathy," wrote Frank McCarthy. The heartfelt superlatives became redundant: the "greatest son of this era"; "a true friend to all people"; "we will never know the like of him again"; "ability and distinction equaled by few men and surpassed by none."[52] Editorial comment followed on Sunday and Monday in the *Washington Post, New York Times, New York Herald Tribune, Baltimore Sun,* and *Atlanta Journal.* And, of course, Freeman's *Richmond News Leader.* Jack Kilpatrick expressed the frustration felt by many in attempting to reduce the sweep of such a life into words.

> Those who knew the Doc, and loved him for the essential humanness at the core of his genius, have no very adequate way of paying him tribute or expressing their sense of loss and sorrow at his death. There is a numbness now, left by shock and disbelief, and it will be a while before we realize how much has been taken from us by his death.[53]

Kilpatrick knew, though, that "the Doc" had lived precisely the life he had wanted to live. "His satisfactions endlessly outnumbered his irritations," he wrote, "and he found in his books and his music and the serenity of his well-ordered life a world of peace and contentment."[54]

"The strife is o'er," the mourners sang at his funeral.

> The strife is o'er, the battle done;
> The victory of life is won;
> The song of triumph has begun.

Battle. Victory. Triumph. The words that drifted through the Second Baptist Church seemed to speak the lives and names of Lee, Washington, Freeman.

Epilogue

The imposing iron gates bespeak not only a cemetery, but also a landmark. Hollywood Cemetery is of another era. It commands a breathtaking view of the James River and the city of Richmond. In its grounds rest James Monroe, fifth president of the United States; John Tyler, tenth president of the United States; and Jefferson Davis, only president of the Confederate States. The respectful quiet that permeates the ground highlights the rustle of the wind through the trees and whispers volumes of history. Here lies John Randolph of Roanoke, Fitzhugh Lee, Ellen Glasgow, and George Pickett. Only one looking for it would notice the marker of Walker Burford Freeman.

A winding road comes upon a triangular island—set aside from other burial sites. Three large magnolias surround the two markers. Douglas Southall Freeman and Inez Goddin Freeman. One of the roads intersecting at this spot is named "Freeman Road." One need not get out of the car to read the inscription: "'Tis not too late to seek a newer world."

Inez Freeman survived her husband by twenty-one years. They were twenty-one kindly years, full of positive service and constant activity. Westbourne proved too large—and perhaps too lonely—for her, so not long after her husband's death she moved to the fashionable Tuckahoe Apartments in Richmond. On the walls of her softly lighted suite were photographs and memories. Mounted on her bookshelf was a yellowing and well-worn sign: "Time Alone Is Irreplacable. Waste It Not."[1] She was involved in dozens of civic activities, as much for what she could contribute as for carrying on the tradition of her husband. "A man who had visited Assisi told me once how it seemed that when a good man has lived, his influence is felt forevermore," she told a reporter. "My husband lived his life on a high plane of dedication and service to his fellow man—and I have tried to make this my guiding star."[2] She had been a guiding star as well. "I marvel every day at the mercy of God," Freeman wrote Mary Tyler, "which gave me such a woman. You wrote her on Monday, very aptly, that whenever you were in a difficult situation, you always tried to act as you thought she would. Never could you do a wiser thing, for never, I think, will you see such another."[3] The end came on October 30, 1974, and Inez Freeman joined her husband at Hollywood.

Anne Freeman had written her father about her intent to "pass on some measure of the love and strength and gentleness in living that you have given me," and so she did. After her marriage ended in divorce, she began a teaching career by serving as a learning specialist at the Lennox School in New York. She went back to college and received a master's degree from the Teacher's College at Columbia University in 1970. She became Director of Special Learning at St. Bernard's School in New York in 1977, a post she held until her retirement in 1992. The last years were both joy and sorrow; she married a long-time friend, Royall Turpin, but found herself locked in a twilight struggle against cancer. The humor and delight in living, so cherished by her father and that had marked her own life, carried her to the end, which came one month before her seventy-first birthday in August 1994. "I now understand what unconditional love is," her brother remembered. "I've experienced it from Anne."[4]

James Douglas Freeman defeated the demons of his youth. Plagued by alcoholism, divorces, and failed jobs, he turned his life around with a show of discipline his father would have admired. He went back to college, obtained his degree, and spent many years counseling those facing the same destructive forces he overcame. The bitterness he held for his father has faded into a resigned acceptance of the terms under which the two men lived. "Well, Dad," he now says in a figurative conversation, "that's just the way it is."[5]

Mary Wells Ashworth prepared Volume Six of *George Washington* for publication and, with John Carroll, wrote Volume Seven, *First in Peace*. The entire seven-volume set was awarded the Pulitzer Prize in May 1958. Mary Wells never wrote another book. She stayed close to the Freeman family and devoted the remaining years of a life of large usefulness to civic duties and her great love, St. Stephen's Episcopal Church.

The *Richmond News Leader* continued in the hands of the Bryan family. Jack Kilpatrick left his post as editor in 1966. Freeman had predicted difficult times for afternoon newspapers, and in May 1992 the *News Leader* ceased operation. J. Stewart Bryan III continues as president and chief executive officer of Media General Inc., which operates the *Richmond Times-Dispatch*.

Mary Tyler Freeman Cheek McClenahan will someday be the subject of a biography. With the poise of her mother and the disciplined drive of her father, she has filled her life with activities touching every chord of the civic, cultural, political, religious, historical, and economic life of Richmond. Eighty-four years of age at the time of this writing, she maintains a pace equaled only by her father. Her husband, Leslie Cheek, died in 1992, in the fifty-third year of their marriage. She is now the wife of Dr. John L. McClenahan, and the two live happily—always happily due to the laughter that fills their home—in her stately graystone house behind a tall ivy-clad wall. In her home, as in her activities, one senses the presence of the man she still refers to as "Father" as if he were in the next room. Here is his Morris Chair, his desk from the *News Leader*, the books he inscribed to her. Yet Mary Tyler McClenahan does not live in, or long for, the past. The past becomes present in her—much as it did with her father. She is generous with her time and memories, but has not the time to dwell too long on such topics. She has another appointment coming up . . .

Words by which one chooses to be remembered are often not representative of one's life. Having written and read millions of words, Douglas Freeman chose to be remembered with words from Tennyson's *Ulysses*.

I am a part of all that I have met . . .

The influences that shaped his life never left him. Always there was Walker Freeman—wounded veteran, struggling clerk, successful businessman, keeper of the faith; always there was the city of Richmond—its traditions, its heritage, its tragedies, its future; always there was Inez—all poise and support and love; always there was Mary Tyler—the recreation of himself in the lithe form of his eldest child, two bodies with one soul and spirit; always there was Lee—the supreme example of service and sacrifice.

Yet all experience is an arch wherethrough
Gleams that untravelled world, whose margin fades
Forever and forever when I move.

The past captured his heart, it thrilled his soul, it stimulated his mind, it spurred him to action. Yet it also prodded him into the untraveled world of acquiring knowledge unknown, adventure unexperienced, wonders unseen. He would teach at Columbia, he would broadcast, he would plan new books, he would lecture week after week on current events, he would fascinate himself with the sighting of one of Jupiter's moons or the latest technique in growing roses. How often did he say it: "It is history that teaches us to hope."

How dull it is to pause, to make an end,
To rust unburnished, not to shine in use!

He was the only thing shining in use at two-thirty in the morning. The schedule guaranteed he would not "rust unburnished."

This labour, by slow prudence to make mild
A rugged people, and through soft degrees
Subdue them to the useful and the good.

Thirty-four years of editorials. Two to three columns, Monday through Saturday. He pushed "by slow prudence," he argued "through soft degrees," he urged a city and a state to seek a higher standard of "the useful and the good."

Did he too often mirror the faults of his readers? Could he have flown bolder colors? The skeptic in retrospect may smugly sniff that he could have done more, but he was a man both of his time and ahead of his time. Nothing would come of a disastrous social revolution except a charred city and a disengaged people. He would labor—slowly, cautiously, prudently—in the pages of the paper that he, more than any other, came to personify.

> ... *but something ere the end,*
> *Some work of noble note, may yet be done,*
> *Not unbecoming men that strove with Gods.*

He framed these words and placed them on his desk. There was always "something ere the end." *Lee. Lee's Lieutenants. The South to Posterity.* "John Stewart Bryan." *The Calendar of Confederate Papers. Lee's Dispatches. Lee of Virginia. George Washington.* Works of noble note.

> *One equal temper of heroic hearts,*
> *Made weak by time and fate, but strong in will*
> *To strive, to seek, to find, and not to yield.*

He was not as simple as his hero Lee; nor as ambitious as Washington. He was a modest, humble man, but could be forgiven if some vanity, born of the reputation he so carefully crafted, crept into his personality. He was warm and gracious and kind, but not without the ability to be distant and cold. He was brilliant—one is tempted to call him a genius—but did he master himself and his subjects to such an extent that some of his family suffered? He was passionate in his loves, loyal to his dreams, and faithful to his character; but, at times, insufferable in his slavish fidelity to his self-imposed regimen, and annoyingly petty in his judgments about those who failed to meet his incredibly high standards. He gave selflessly of himself to his fellow man, yet only a handful knew him. Those who did know him—who saw him in the study at Westbourne, who caught the gleam of humor in his eye, who felt the warmth of his embrace, who saw the admirable traits and regrettable shortcomings of his entire character—would testify that Tennyson's words found form and being and substance in his daily life. "To strive, to seek, to find, and not to yield."

Then, with shadows creeping in the window at Westbourne, with Lee and Jackson and Stuart and Washington forever enshrined in historical fact by the work of his pen, this man of the past looked to the future and claimed as a testament to his life and as a bequest to the ages, the words of an almost autobiographical poem:

> *'Tis not too late to seek a newer world.*

Appendix 1

The Virginia Tax Commission, on which Freeman served as secretary, made the following recommendations on December 16, 1911, to the General Assembly of Virginia.[1]

1. To create a permanent unpaid Tax Commission of nine existing State officers with a paid executive officer, which Commission shall have power (1) to equalize assessments among the counties and cities of the State by fixing a standard valuation for each class of tangible personal property, an average per acre valuation for each county and average frontal valuations for each city; (2) to remove Commissioners of the Revenue for violation of the law or for neglect of duty; (3) to formulate reasonable rules and regulations for the uniform assessment of improvements and for the general enforcement of the revenue law.

2. To provide proper appeal from the rulings of the Tax Commission, in fixing averages and standard valuations, said appeal to lie to the Circuit Court of the city of Richmond.

3. To require the statement of the exact valuable consideration involved in the transfer of real property in order to form a basis for an average per acre or frontal valuation.

4. To abolish the land Assessors as separate officers of the law and to provide for the assessment of lands and improvements by Commissioners of the Revenue.

5. To reduce the State tax on stocks, bonds, and other evidence of debt to 25 cents on the hundred dollars' valuation and to limit the local tax to the same amount.

6. To make any class of property subject to lien for taxes due on any other class of property.

7. To require local Treasurers to mail tax bills to all tax-payers whose bills exceed $2.50, exclusive of polls.

8. To give Commissioners of the Revenue power to modify, after five days' notice, any tax return which they may believe to be erroneous, giving the tax-payer the right of appeal.

9. To exempt from taxation by any locality the bonds of all other Virginia localities when such bonds are not taxed by the locality issuing them.

10. To place all public service corporations on a gross earnings basis of taxation as soon as the decisions of the Federal Courts will warrant such action.

11. To require an accurate report of the gross earnings of all telephone and telegraph, express and passenger car service companies.

12. To increase the tax of passenger car service companies from $2 the mile to $4 the mile; and to increase the tax on express companies from $6 the mile operated to $7.50 the mile operated, requiring the latter to pay a tax for each line of steamships operated over the same course.

13. To impose a tax on the property of freight car service corporations used in the State.

14. To make the following changes and additions to the specific license taxes:

    a. To increase the license of the dealer in options from $200 to $300.

    b. To increase the stock broker's license from $100 to $150 in small cities and from $250 to $350 in larger cities.

    c. To increase the pawnbroker's license to $500 and to reduce the interest rates chargeable 50 per cent.

    d. To provide a fine of $100 in addition to the penalties already prescribed for violation of the money lenders' act.

    e. To make clear the distinction between eating houses and houses of private entertainment.

    f. To include professional baseball games in those subject to taxation as public performances.

    g. To increase the license of vendors of medicine from $25 to $100.

    h. To impose license registration taxes on certain classes of investment companies.

    i. To extend the license tax on traveling companies of gypsies to each individual clairvoyant, medium, astrologer, etc., and to make this tax $500.

15. To require every firm, corporation, etc., operating in Virginia to report to the Tax Commission the amount of all salaries, fees, etc., paid by such firm, etc., to any citizen of Virginia in excess of $1,000 the year, said reports to be forwarded to the Commissioners of the Revenue and to be *prima facie* evidence of assessment with income in that amount.

16. The amendment of the Mineral Assessment law to provide (a) that the assessment be made in every year by the Mineral Assessor and the Commissioner of the Revenue, (b) that in the case of disagreement between the assessing officers, the opinion of the Mineral Assessor

shall prevail, subject to appeal; (c) that notice of appeal from any assessment be served on the Corporation Commission.

17. To abolish the 10 per cent, offset in the bank tax, now allowed for debts due by shareholders.

18. To increase the tax on the manufacturers of fish oil and manure from one-half of one per cent, to one per cent, on sales.

19. To impose on Commissioners of the Revenue the duties now performed by Examiners of Record and to abolish the latter as officers of government.

20. To prosecute vigorously the examination of the books of local assessing officers and to establish a uniform system of bookkeeping among them, under the general supervision of the Tax Commissioner.

21. To equalize assessments and to bring them to the constitutional valuation, with a view to the ultimate separation of the sources of local and State revenue.

Appendix 2

The "News Leader's Twenty Fundamental Rules of News Writing," were compiled by Freeman in the 1920s. They remained in effect until the demise of the *News Leader* in 1992.[1]

1. Above all, be clear.
2. Therefore, use simple English.
3. To that end, write short sentences.
4. Do not change subject in the middle of a sentence unless there is (a) definite antithesis; or (b) no possible way of avoiding the change of subject. If you must change subject, always insert a comma at the end of the clause that precedes the one in which you make the change.
5. Do not end sentences with participial phrases. Beware such construction as "The mayor refused to discuss the subject, *saying* it was one for the consideration of the council."
6. Do not change the voice of a verb in the middle of a sentence. If you start with an *active* verb, keep it active. It is sloppy to say: "He went to Hopewell and was met by," etc.
7. Seek to leave the meaning of the sentence incomplete until the last word. Add nothing after the meaning is complete. Start a new sentence then.
8. Avoid loose construction. Try never to begin sentences with *"And"* or *"But."*
9. Never use vague or unusual words that divert the reader's attention from what you are reporting.
10. Make every antecedent plain: Never permit "it" or "that" or any similar word to refer to different things in the same sentence.
11. Where you write a clause beginning with *"which,"* do not follow it with one that begins *"and which."* Never write a sentence such as "The ordinance which was considered by the finance committee and which was recommended to the council," etc.
12. Avoid successive sentences that begin with the same word, unless emphasis is particularly desired. Especially, in quoting a man, never

have one sentence begin "*He* said" and then have the next sentence start "*He* stated."

13. In sentences where several nouns, phrases or clauses depend on the same verb, put the longest phrase or clause last. For instance, do not say "He addressed the general assembly, the members of the corporation commission and the governor."

14. If you are compelled, for condensation, to use many long sentences, relieve them by employing very short sentences at intervals.

15. In conditional sentences, seek to put the conditional clause before the principal clause. An "*if*" clause at the beginning of a sentence is better placed than at the end, unless the whole point of the sentence lies in the "*if.*"

16. Be accurate in the use of synonyms and avoid overloading a sentence with a long phrase employed as a synonym. You will do well to buy and keep on your desk a copy of *The Roget Dictionary of Synoms* [sic] *and Antoymns*. If in doubt, consult *March's Thesaurus* in the editor's office.

17. Avoid successive sentences with the same form and conjunction. One of the surest ways to kill interest and to make a story dull is to use a succession of compound sentences, the clauses of which are connected by "*and.*" Change the conjunction and the form of sentences as often as possible.

18. Shun the employment of nouns as adjectives; it is the lowest form of careless English. There always are better ways to condense than to pile up nouns before a noun and to pretend they are adjectives.

19. Avoid successive words that begin or end with the same syllables, for instance "*re*" or "*ex*" at the beginning of words and "*ly*" or "*ing*" as the final syllable.

20. Try to end every story with a strong and, if possible, a short sentence.

Appendix 3

The influence of *R. E. Lee* has continued in the more than sixty-five years since its release. With that influence has come reassessment of its authoritative place in historical literature. While the book's standing and Freeman's reputation remain high, both have come under substantial revisionist criticism.

The most serious charge leveled against Freeman is that he "had such intense regard for Lee that he lacked a certain critical distance and became protective of his subject," or, put another way, "he was a little too worshipful of Lee."[1] This criticism has turned into a standing joke that "Freeman physically assumed an attitude of prayer while writing" about Lee.[2] Thomas L. Connelly makes the most detailed statement of this criticism in his biography of Lee, *The Marble Man.* Connelly devotes almost an entire chapter to an assessment of Freeman's "harmful" study. The faults he finds with Freeman read like an indictment: He "wrapped Lee in an almost impregnable mantle and deterred further examination of his career"[3]; he "deliberately discouraged probing into Lee's personality and scorned those who do so"; and he portrayed Lee "as virtually flawless in physical appearance," with "no equal . . . in character," and possessing psychic and "prophetic talents."[4] In doing these things, Freeman "presented the familiar Lee image" but with more "research, writing skill, and scholarly respectability" than ever before. He thus enshrined an "image" and "generated a new era of paranoia among Civil War writers."[5]

Connelly favorably cited T. Harry Williams, author of *Lincoln and His Generals*, who laid out the "too worshipful" argument in an article based on a speech he delivered in Chicago in December 1953—six months after Freeman's death. "Although on occasion," Williams wrote, "Freeman was capable of pointing out Lee's mistakes and deficiencies, he was more likely to concern himself with making excuses for his hero." Thus "several chapters in the *R. E. Lee* . . . are open to serious question," and "Freeman came close to arguing that whatever Lee did was right because he was Lee."[6] Frank Vandiver commented as well on Freeman's "worshipfulness," although in more restrained terms.

Another criticism of Freeman is that he tended too much toward idolizing Lee. He did. Few biographers can escape the pull of their hero. Generally those who do elude this attraction write debunking books about their subjects for whom they can generate little sympathy. Freeman sympathized with this great Virginian, understood his milieu, shared his values and prejudices; consequently he saw virtue where others perhaps see cant. But a biographer ought not be condemned for achieving rapport with a man in his time.[7]

Contemporary reviewers of *R. E. Lee* did not comment on any worshipfulness. Liddell Hart, in his negative review of the first two volumes, wrote that Freeman chronicled both "the hero's failings and failures."[8] Henry Steele Commager found that Freeman challenged "many cherished theories" and "much inveterate dogma" and "has not attempted to exonerate Lee for his failings."[9] Dumas Malone made similar statements in his reviews regarding Freeman's objectivity.

Similar to the "worshipful charge" is the observation that Freeman's attitude "led him to misjudge altogether" information regarding Lee. This argument was made by Prof. John L. Gignilliat in *The Journal of Southern History*.[10] His article revolves around a letter written by Lee in the summer of 1835 during a surveying mission on Canada's Pelee Island. The letter, bought by Freeman in November 1935 following the release of *R. E. Lee*, contains an intriguing comment. Lee and a companion entered a lighthouse and "discovered the keeper" at the door. "We were warm [and] excited," Lee wrote, "he irascible [and] full of venom. An altercation ensued which resulted in his death."[11] The letter, bantering in tone throughout, seems to implicate Lee in the accidental death of the lighthouse keeper. Freeman referenced the letter in a footnote inserted in a new printing of *R. E. Lee* in 1949. His explanation reads as follows:

> An unhappy incident of Lee's experience on this survey was the accidental death of a Canadian lighthouse keeper "in a scuffle" over the use of his tower for running one of the surveying lines. The only reference to this, so far as is known, is in Lee to G. W. Cullum, July 31, 1835 (Freeman MSS). A search of Canadian records yields no details.[12]

Gignilliat found that "Freeman's protectiveness toward Lee is apparent in his handling of this matter."[13] He relegated Lee's involvement in the death of the lighthouse keeper to a footnote and "almost certainly misinterpreted" the incident. Gignilliat's article solves the mystery with the very likely supposition that the lighthouse keeper "full of venom" was a snake.[14] This would explain Lee's flippant description of its death. Freeman's protectiveness of Lee, therefore, not only caused him to misjudge the matter, but to misjudge it to Lee's detriment— an ironic turn given Freeman's alleged motivation of protecting Lee.

Freeman's actions with regard to the Lee letter do display a protective attitude. He was not, however, lax in investigating the matter. In 1937, less than two years after acquiring the letter, he consulted Prof. Donald Bartlett of

Dartmouth College and asked for his assistance in the matter. Bartlett reported his findings on May 6, 1937. He had searched the Public Archives of Canada at Ottawa, located a statute authorizing the erection of the Point Pelee Island lighthouse, and found a commission report that provided "no money" for a keeper's house.[15] Bartlett proposed seeking out more information "in Detroit concerning the contractor." Freeman thanked him for his work and asked him to keep him informed.[16] He also advised that he was putting "a woman to work in the archives in Washington, and shall ask her to run down all possible leads." In October, Bartlett reported he had researched the life of the contractor of the lighthouse, John Scott. "Scott died in 1846," Bartlett wrote, "which clearly indicates that he was not himself the victim."[17] Bartlett was looking in the Dominion Archives at Ottawa, researching reports made to London, and investigating an unrelated "Caroline Affair of 1837" in the event that some enclosures in that file "could very well be something on our subject."[18] Bartlett said he would pick up the work again during a summer sabbatical. Freeman responded that he was "very grateful" for Bartlett's assistance, but worried that "there is not a great deal . . . that can be learned."[19]

Freeman's action upon his purchase of the Lee letter followed his standard research method. Unable himself to make the trip to Canada or Detroit, he secured the services of a competent historian who followed every lead in a systematic way—by checking letters, reports, contracts, and statutes. Bartlett was even eliminating potential victims by looking up the life of John Scott. It appears Freeman directed a second associate to search the archives in Washington—though no letters of instruction are found. He was stunned at the apparent revelation about Lee and proceeded with even more caution than usual. He would make no rash judgments, despite the *prima facie* evidence of the letter, and at length offered an opinion to Milo Quaife of the Burton Historical Collection of the Detroit Public Library.

> I want to say, also, that the internal evidence seems to suggest that the lighthouse keeper was killed by General Lee's companion. My reason for saying that is that General Lee throughout his life always acknowledged his own responsibilities, but when responsibilities were coupled with someone else, he took pains to use an indirect form of discourse that would not put the blame on the other man though the language was so shaped that he did not, himself, assume the blame.[20]

When *R. E. Lee* was reset for a new printing in 1949, Freeman drafted the new footnote in which he stated only those facts that he knew. He did not go as far as his letter to Quaife, because he could not state the facts of the matter with certainty. He did not know what happened, so he did not speculate. The only thing he knew for certain was that the letter existed. He therefore noted it and offered only what he could say.

Freeman's perspective, or lack thereof, was called into question by Connelly, Williams, and, to a lesser degree, Allen Tate. "It is as though Lee and the Army of Northern Virginia are wrenched out of the context of military history," Williams wrote, "to be presented brilliantly in a kind of historical void."[21] Connelly found this trait "consistent with the picture put forward by Virginia writers during Reconstruction . . . [that] the South centered all its hopes upon both Virginia and the General."[22] This criticism places upon Freeman a task he did not set out to do; namely, write a history of the entire Civil War.[23] It was this lack of perspective, it is argued, that led Freeman to ignore developments in modern warfare—a criticism first leveled by Liddell Hart. "In this regard," Williams wrote, "Freeman was as unmodern-minded as Lee."[24] Here Williams heads into troublesome ground, asking the reader to believe that a man who had studied war for more than thirty years, both as a historian examining the Civil War and as an editor analyzing the war in Europe, did not understand the changes that had occurred in tactics, strategy, and theories of war.

Freeman's treatment of Confederate general James Longstreet has been the subject of much critical analysis. The publication of *R. E. Lee*, according to Longstreet biographer William Garrett Piston, marked the "nadir" of the general's reputation. Freeman's research "was based entirely on works by members of the anti-Longstreet faction," Piston alleged, "or others reflecting a similarly negative view of the General."[25] There is no question that Freeman harshly judged Longstreet. He criticized his actions at Second Manassas—writing that the "seeds . . . of disaster at Gettysburg" were sown there—and laid defeat at Gettysburg primarily on Longstreet "eating his heart away in sullen resentment."[26] Yet Freeman's criticism of Longstreet carried with it an explicit criticism of Lee. "It is scarcely too much to say," he wrote, "that on July 2 [the second day of the Battle of Gettysburg] the Army of Northern Virginia was without a commander."[27] Included with that indictment of Lee is condemnation of the actions during the battle by Confederate generals "Jeb" Stuart and Richard S. Ewell.[28]

Nor did Freeman stubbornly cling to his conclusions in the light of new evidence or further analysis. As he conducted his research for *Lee's Lieutenants*, Freeman concluded, in light of information discovered after the publication of *Lee*, that he "had been a little too severe on Longstreet."[29] He therefore included an appendix in Volume III "concerning the bringing up of the Federal left at Gettysburg" and wrote in the "Introduction" that Longstreet "was correct in maintaining that the position could not be taken by assault."[30] Critics of Freeman have pointed out that he "sought to discredit" Longstreet by making much of the fact that the general wrote three accounts of the events at Gettysburg.[31] Though one wonders why Freeman is at fault for reporting this fact—and the instances in which Longstreet "changed his story as he grew older"—he nonetheless sought new information to supplement or confirm any of the general's accounts. "The great difficulties," he wrote, "[is that] he left no private letters that anyone has ever found and, second, the political controversy . . . prejudiced judgment against him."[32] Freeman also recognized that the troubles with the three accounts did not originate solely with Longstreet. "The man who assisted him was a Northerner who wrote very well but did not know much about the intimacies of the Confederacy," he wrote. "Further, General Longstreet's assistant was a careless man who did not reconcile what General Longstreet said in his latest book with what he had written earlier. The result has been an unjust impairment of the General's reputation."[33]

Thus while being critical of Longstreet, Freeman was not so blinded with contempt that he refused to reexamine the facts and reverse himself where appropriate. This has not silenced his critics who still seize on his treatment of Longstreet as proof of bias. One example demonstrates the difficulty in maintaining that position. On the first day of Gettysburg, Longstreet suggested to Lee that the army disengage and conduct a flank march to the south and east across the Union army's line of communication and set up a defensive position. Freeman dismisses Longstreet's suggestion, citing the absence of the greater part of cavalry, Lee's lack of knowledge as to the Federal army's position, and the stress of a continuous concentration with no chance of foraging for the army.[34] Though these are all sound military reasons for rejecting Longstreet's advice, Gary Gallagher writes that Freeman merely relied on the opinions of "stalwart members of the Lost Cause school of interpretation."[35] Yet Longstreet's most supportive biographer, Jeffrey Wert, judged Longstreet's "proposal of a vague flank movement" to be an "impractical" one "rightly dismissed" by Lee.[36] Did Wert rely as well on the faulty sources of the Lost Cause school?

Gallagher writes that Freeman "even refused to grant Longstreet his full physical stature," shrinking the general "to five feet, ten and a half inches" from his proper six-foot-two-inch frame.[37] The description favorably citied by Gallagher—one by Longstreet aide Moxley Sorrel—is quoted by Freeman in *Lee's Lieutenants* in describing the "powerful figure, nearly six feet tall," but apparently this misstatement of Longstreet's physical height is regarded as proof of a desire to reduce his historical stature as well.[38]

A final criticism is that Freeman "never tried to penetrate the inner Lee personality."[39] This technique, the art of psychography, was not new in historical writing during Freeman's time. It achieved significant attention, and some standing, in the wake of the writings of British writer Lytton Strachey, the author of *Eminent Victorians*, *Queen Victoria*, and *Elizabeth and Essex*. Strachey selected only some facts about his subjects—occasionally sacrificing the truth—and sought to present vivid portraits by delving into their minds and personalities. Thomas Connelly adopted a similar technique in his psychography of Lee and took Freeman to task for his failure to look into Lee's mind, claiming that Lee was "neither serene nor simple."[40] Lee was, Connelly concluded, "a troubled man, convinced he had failed as a prewar career officer, parent and moral individual" who had been "shaped into what others wished him to be, and has become something he never was."[41]

Freeman's attitude toward this method of biography was consistent throughout his career: He detested it. It ran counter to the scientific method he had learned at Johns Hopkins and required the historian to assume facts not in evidence. To make a statement such as Connelly's would have required him to guess at what was in Lee's "troubled" mind, divine his "self-doubt," and discern his "feeling of failure." All that, by necessity, required speculation and assumption. This he would not do. "I know where Lee was and what he did every minute of the Civil War," Freeman said, "but I wouldn't dare presume what he was thinking."[42] He believed that psychography was one of the worse "frauds that ever have been perpetuated on our generation."[43] While he admired Strachey's "literary craftsmanship," he could not accept his method.

> Mr. Strachey devotes five pages to the thoughts of Queen Elizabeth at a moment and in a manner concerning which we have not one line of contemporary historical evidence . . . It is difficult enough for one of us to recall his own thoughts in any given crisis of his life three years ago; it is absurd to pretend to know what another person was thinking about three hundred years ago. We may learn enough about a subject's method of analysis to hazard a reasonably safe guess . . . and we may be confident in our belief that he . . . was not guided by certain considerations. Beyond that we cannot go; at least I cannot.[44]

Freeman's opposition to the method went beyond his commitment to a scientific presentation of facts. If there were no facts to support what the subject was "thinking," the writer "being prodded, quite often unconsciously presents his own counsel when he professes to 'interpret' what a great man would do in circumstances that man never faced."[45]

Other than making general comments on historical method, Freeman never responded publicly, and rarely commented privately, about any of his critics. "It is better simply to state the facts," he wrote, "and to leave the court of time to reach its own decision."[46]

For more than sixty-five years, Freeman's four-volume "brief" has occupied a prominent place in the "court of time." It is not perfect; it is obvious that he greatly admired Lee and that this admiration, at times, colored his judgment. That the work has held up so well in light of new discoveries, old animosities, and revisionary critiques, speaks well of the facts so eloquently and definitively stated therein.

Notes

PROLOGUE

1. Douglas Southall Freeman, "The Fine Art of Saving Time," Douglas Southall Freeman Papers, Manuscript Division, Library of Congress (hereafter referred to as DSF MSS), Container 128, 5. Douglas Southall Freeman is hereafter referred to as "DSF."

2. DSF, Diary, 15 July 1945, DSF MSS, Container 1.

3. "The Virginians," *Time*, 18 October 1948, 109.

4. Mary Wells Ashworth, "Some Questions and Answers Concerning Dr. Douglas Southall Freeman," Mary Tyler Freeman Cheek McClenahan Papers (hereafter MTM MSS), 3-4. Dr. Freeman's eldest child, Mary Tyler, is herein referred to under three surnames: Mary Tyler Freeman from 1917 to 1939; Mary Tyler Cheek from 1939 to 1993; and Mary Tyler McClenahan from 1993 to present.

5. DSF to Mrs. R. L. Chenery, 5 April 1921, DSF MSS, Container 5.

6. DSF to Inez G. Freeman, 7 August 1946, MTM MSS.

7. DSF to Mrs. Perry Evans, 25 March 1937, DSF MSS, Container 29; *see Time*, 18 October 1948, 108.

8. Carl Shires to Mary Tyler Cheek, 9 September 1985, MTM MSS; Carl Shires to DSF, 5 June 1950, DSF MSS, Container 102.

9. DSF to Stephen Early, 8 September 1939, DSF MSS, Container 29.

10. DSF to Mary Tyler Freeman, 22 October 1936, MTM MSS.

11. DSF to John Stewart Bryan, 18 March 1921; 2 November 1926; DSF MSS, Container 5; 17 August 1934, DSF MSS, Container 29; DSF, "The Library of the Richmond News Leader," DSF MSS, Container 15.

12. DSF to Lillian Rixey, 31 May 1940, DSF MSS, Container 39; Page Williams to DSF, 9 January 1937, DSF MSS, Container 34; Winston Churchill to DSF, 3 November 1934, DSF MSS, Container 22.

13. James J. Kilpatrick, Interview with author, March 8, 2001; James J. Kilpatrick, "Douglas Southall Freeman, 1886-1953," a commentary in the pamphlet *Lee: An Abridgment* by Richard Harwell (Birmingham, Alabama: Southern Living Gallery, 1982), 15.

14. DSF to E. R. W. McCabe, 31 July 1926, DSF MSS, Container 7.

15. DSF to Inez G. Freeman, 15 June 1931, MTM MSS.

16. DSF, Diary, 5 February 1945, DSF MSS, Container 1.

17. DSF, "Addenda to Memoranda," 20 April 1953, MTM MSS, 2.

18. DSF to Wallace Meyer, 17 November 1945, DSF MSS, Container 62; DSF, *George Washington*, Vol. 1, *Young Washington* (New York: Charles Scribner's Sons, 1948), xiii-xiv. Allan Nevins, "How a Great Historian Studied a Great American," *American Heritage* (February 1956), 65.

19. Mary Wells Ashworth, "Prefatory Note," *George Washington*, Vol. 6, *Patriot & President*, by Douglas Southall Freeman (New York: Charles Scribner's Sons, 1954), xliv.

20. DSF to Mrs. Eugene Meyer, 25 September 1940, DSF MSS, Container 38.

CHAPTER ONE

1. Walker Burford Freeman, "Memoirs of Walker Burford Freeman: 1843-1935" (privately published, 1935), 25.

2. W. B. Freeman, "Memoirs," 25-26; DSF, "Walker B. Freeman," 1935, DSF MSS, Container 238, 2.

3. Lula Jeter Parker, *Parker's History of Bedford County, Virginia* (Bedford: Hamilton's, 1954), 9.

4. Ibid., 10-11.

5. W. B. Freeman, "Memoirs," 1.

6. DSF, "Something of the Freeman Family," 1908, DSF MSS, Container 238, 3.

7. "Freeman Recalls Pioneer Past of Historic Mt. Hermon Church," undated, unattributed newspaper clipping, MTM MSS. Douglas Freeman wrote that Garland's first wife was named "Sallie Holland." DSF, "Freeman Family," 4.

8. Amherst County records show four different Burfords patenting almost 2,000 acres of land from 1762 to 1780. Garland Evans Hopkins, "Freeman Forbears" (privately published, 1942), 73.

9. W. B. Freeman, "Memoirs," 1.

10. DSF, "Freeman Family," 5; "Walker B. Freeman," 1.

11. DSF, "Introduction" in Rebecca Yancey Williams, *The Vanishing Virginian* (New York: E. P. Dutton & Co., 1940), 8.

12. W. B. Freeman, "Memoirs," 4.

13. Ibid., 11.

14. DSF, "Freeman Family," 4; W. B. Freeman, "Memoirs," 13; Anne Ballard Freeman, "The Bedford Freemans: A Puritan Family in Virginia" (paper presented, Vassar College, March 20, 1944), 17. Though this paper was written by twenty-year-old Anne Freeman, it gains credibility and probative value due to Douglas Freeman's extensive involvement in its production. Freeman spent at least "sixteen hours" writing and revising the paper for his daughter, relying on his own sources of information and personal recollections. *See* DSF to Anne B. Freeman, 5 November 1943, DSF MSS, Container 49; DSF to Anne B. Freeman, 14 March 1944; 20 March 1944, DSF MSS, Container 55.

15. W. Harrison Daniel, *Bedford County, Virginia, 1840–1860* (Bedford: The Print Shop, 1985), 163.

16. Ibid.

17. W. B. Freeman, "Memoirs," 8.

18. Ibid.

19. Ibid., 11.

20. Ibid.

21. Ibid., 14.

22. Ibid., 15-16.

23. Ibid., 14.

24. Anne B. Freeman, "Bedford Freemans," 18; DSF to Ralph Habas, 30 March 1945, DSF MSS, Container 62; Daniel, *Bedford County*, 24.

25. W. B. Freeman, "Memoirs," 6, 9.

26. Ibid., 6; Anne B. Freeman, "Bedford Freemans," 19.

27. Anne B. Freeman, "Bedford Freemans," 19.

28. Mary Tyler McClenahan, "Douglas Southall Freeman, My Father," MTM MSS, 5.

29. W. B. Freeman, "Memoirs," 7-8.

30. Ibid., 8.

31. Ibid., 9.

32. *Religious Herald*, 2 April 1857, quoted in Anne B. Freeman, "Bedford Freemans," 20-23; DSF to Anne B. Freeman, 20 March 1944, DSF MSS, Container 55.

33. W. B. Freeman, "Memoirs," 9.

34. Ibid.

35. Anne B. Freeman, "Bedford Freemans," 23; DSF to E. W. Poindexter, 18 November 1949, DSF MSS, Container 98.

36. W. B. Freeman, "Memoirs," 9-10.

37. Ibid., 10. Walker Freeman reported the rumor, but did not believe it. A search of Brown's life does not indicate that he was in or near Virginia in May 1857.

38. Ibid., 16.

39. Ibid., 17.

40. Parker, *History of Bedford County*, 44.

41. Walker B. Freeman to T. C. Holland, 22 February 1861 (a copy made by W. B. Freeman in 1918), DSF MSS, Container 123. The use of the plural "folks" is curious as Walker's father had passed away.

42. W. B. Freeman, "Memoirs," 17.

43. Ibid., 17-18.

44. Ibid., 20.

45. Ibid., 17.

46. Ibid.

47. Ibid.,17-20.

48. Ibid., 22.

49. Ibid.
50. Ibid., 23.
51. Ibid., 22-23.
52. Ibid., 23-24.
53. Anne B. Freeman, "Bedford Freemans," 36.
54. DSF, *Lee's Lieutenants: A Study in Command*, Vol. I, *Manassas to Malvern Hill* (New York: Charles Scribner's Sons, 1942), 225.
55. W. B. Freeman, "Memoirs," 25.
56. Ibid.
57. Ibid., 26.
58. Ibid.
59. Ibid.
60. Ibid.
61. Ibid., 28.
62. Ibid., 29.
63. Ibid., 29-31.
64. Ibid., 35.
65. Ibid., 35-36.
66. Ibid., 37-39.
67. Ibid., 39.
68. Ibid.
69. Ibid.
70. Ibid., 40.
71. Ibid.
72. Ibid., 42-43; DSF, "Walker Freeman," 2.
73. W. B. Freeman, "Memoirs," 45.
74. Ibid., 44.
75. M. T. McClenahan, "Douglas Freeman and General Lee," *The Quarterly Review of the Lee-Jackson Foundation*, Vol. 13 (Fall-Winter, 1984), 1.
76. W. B. Freeman, "Memoirs," 49.
77. Ibid.
78. DSF, "Address at Appomattox Court House," 16 April 1950, MTM MSS, 4.
79. W. B. Freeman, "Memoirs," 49.
80. Ibid., 52.
81. Ibid., 52-53.
82. Allen W. Freeman, "My Brother Douglas," 1953, DSF MSS, Container 120, 3.
83. Ibid., 54.
84. Ibid.
85. Ibid.
86. Ibid., 55; Anne B. Freeman, "Bedford Freemans," 33.
87. Anne B. Freeman, "Bedford Freemans," 6-7.
88. W. B. Freeman, "Memoirs," 55-56.

89. Ibid., 56.

90. Anne B. Freeman, "Bedford Freemans," 36.

91. DSF, "Freeman Family," 5-6.

92. W. B. Freeman, "Memoirs," 56.

93. Ibid.; DSF, "Freeman Family," 6; Anne B. Freeman, "Bedford Freemans," 34.

94. W. B. Freeman, "Memoirs," 50-51; DSF, "Freeman Family," 6.

95. DSF, "Freeman Family," 7.

96. Ibid.

97. W. B. Freeman, "Memoirs," 56.

98. Ibid.; DSF, "Freeman Family," 7.

99. DSF, "Freeman Family," 7.

100. W. B. Freeman, "Memoirs," 57.

101. A. W. Freeman, "My Brother Douglas," 4.

102. *Lynchburg Virginian*, 9 January 1874, quoted in Anne B. Freeman, "Bedford Freemans," 36.

103. DSF, "Freeman Family," 7.

104. The life of Walker B. Freeman, Jr. is shrouded in mystery. At sixteen he was forced to leave school, and his behavior grew erratic. Douglas Freeman wrote that "he caused his father and mother much grief by his fondness for things which had best be avoided" and died at the age of twenty-two on Christmas Eve, 1897, "under circumstances of peculiar distress." DSF, "Freeman Family," 8. What Freeman did not report in his cryptic comments was that Walker Freeman Jr., apparently distraught over a broken romance, committed suicide. Mary Tyler McClenahan, Interview with author, 4 June, 2001.

105. Anne B. Freeman, "Bedford Freemans," 37.

106. Ibid., 38.

107. Ibid.

108. W. B. Freeman, "Memoirs," 57-58.

109. Anne B. Freeman, "Bedford Freemans," 35.

110. W. B. Freeman, "Memoirs," 58.

111. Ruth H. Blunt, "The Birthplace of Douglas Southall Freeman and Allen Weir Freeman," *Lynchburg Historical Society Museum*, Vol. VI, No. 1, 2-3.

CHAPTER TWO

1. Allen W. Freeman to DSF, 16 May 1948, DSF MSS, Container 121; Allen W. Freeman, "My Brother Douglas," 1.

2. Allen W. Freeman, "My Brother Douglas," 1-2.

3. Ibid., 2.

4. Anne B. Freeman, "Bedford Freemans," 41.

5. M. T. McClenahan, "My Father,"5; M.T. McClenahan, "Untitled Manuscript," MTM MSS, 4-5. Mrs. McClenahan graciously permitted the author to read and quote from her unpublished recollections of her youth and her father.

6. M. T. McClenahan, "My Father," 6; M. T. McClenahan, "Manuscript," 5.

7. W. B. Freeman, "Memoirs," 58.

8. Allen W. Freeman, "My Brother Douglas," 4; Anne B. Freeman, "Bedford Freemans," 35.

9. W. B. Freeman, "Memoirs," 58.

10. Allen W. Freeman, "My Brother Douglas," 4.

11. Anne B. Freeman, "Bedford Freemans," 35.

12. DSF, *Lee's Lieutenants*, Vol. III, *Gettysburg to Appomattox* (New York: Charles Scribner's Sons, 1944), 752.

13. Allen W. Freeman, "My Brother Douglas," 4-5; Anne B. Freeman, "Bedford Freemans," 35; W. B. Freeman, "Memoirs," 58. It is unclear if Walker Freeman declared bankruptcy. Allen Freeman says he was "thrown into bankruptcy" but that may be more an expression of condition than a statement of legal status. Douglas Freeman never mentions any bankruptcy filing in numerous references through the years to his father's financial struggle.

14. Anne B. Freeman, "Bedford Freemans," 35; W. B. Freeman, "Memoirs," 58.

15. W. B. Freeman, "Memoirs," 58.

16. Anne B. Freeman, "Bedford Freeman," 35; DSF to Evelyn Moore, 23 July 1936, DSF MSS, Container 25.

17. Anne B. Freeman, "Bedford Freemans," 35; W. B. Freeman, "Memoirs," 58.

18. DSF to James Douglas Freeman, 26 November 1952, MTM MSS.

19. Allen W. Freeman, "My Brother Douglas," 5.

20. Ibid.

21. Ibid., 6.

22. M. T. McClenahan, "Manuscript," 5; Allen W. Freeman, "My Brother Douglas," 7.

23. Allen W. Freeman, "My Brother Douglas," 7; M. T. McClenahan, "Manuscript," 5; Interview with author, 4 June 2001.

24. DSF to Lt. Col. Norman Beasley, 26 July 1945, DSF MSS, Container 45.

25. DSF to E. N. Calisch, 30 April 1936, DSF MSS, Container 22; DSF to Elmer Nathan, 17 March 1947, DSF MSS, Container 81.

26. DSF to Elmer Nathan, 17 March 1947.

27. DSF to E. N. Calisch, 30 April 1936.

28. M. T. McClenahan, "Manuscript," 5; "My Father," 6.

29. DSF, "Introduction," *Vanishing Virginian*, 9.

30. Ibid.

31. DSF, *Lee's Lieutenants*, Vol. I, xlix.

32. DSF, "Introduction," *Vanishing Virginian*, 8.

33. M. T. McClenahan, "Manuscript," 5; "My Father," 7.

34. W. B. Freeman, "Memoirs," 58.

35. Ibid.

36. Ibid.; Anne B. Freeman, "Bedford Freemans," 35-36; Allen W. Freeman, "My Brother Douglas," 8; DSF to Evelyn Moore, 23 July 1936.

37. Allen W. Freeman, "My Brother Douglas," 16.
38. DSF to Bettie A. Freeman, 8 May 1905, Ms. 19, Douglas Southall Freeman Papers, The Johns Hopkins University (hereafter "DSF JHU"), Box 1.
39. Ibid.
40. Ibid.
41. DSF, "The Lares Praestites of Richmond," DSF MSS, Container 128, 6.
42. DSF, "Richmond: A City That Remembers," DSF MSS, Container 105, 5.
43. Ibid., 4-5.
44. DSF, "The Tonic of Southern Folklore," *American Scholar*, Vol. 19, No. 2 (April 1, 1950); "John Stewart Bryan," Bryan Papers, Virginia Historical Society, 17.
45. DSF, "Lares Praestites," 5.
46. DSF, "Tonic."
47. DSF, "The Confederate Tradition of Richmond," *Civil War History*, Vol. III (December 1957), 369. This is a reprint of the article that earlier appeared in *Richmond Magazine* in 1932.
48. Allen W. Freeman, "My Brother Douglas," 8.
49. DSF to Bettie A. Freeman, 8 May 1905, DSF JHU, Box 1.
50. Ibid.
51. "Governor Battle and Dr. Freeman Pay Tribute to Jefferson Davis at Unveiling of Bust Here," *Richmond Times-Dispatch*, 26 June 1952, 5. Hudson Strode, *Jefferson Davis: Tragic Hero* (New York: Harcourt, Brace & World, Inc., 1964), 529.
52. DSF, "Walker B. Freeman," DSF MSS, Container 22.
53. M. T. McClenahan, "Manuscript," 6; Anne B. Freeman, "Bedford Freemans," 41; Allen W. Freeman, "My Brother Douglas," 9.
54. Virginius Dabney, *Richmond: The Story of a City* (New York: Doubleday & Co., 1976), 231.
55. Ibid.
56. *See* Anne B. Freeman, "Bedford Freemans," 41; M. T. McClenahan, "Manuscript," 6; both mention the school only in perfunctory sentences. Mary Wells Ashworth called Sye Roberts an "outstanding teacher." Mary Wells Ashworth, "The Man and the Making of a Book" in *Douglas Southall Freeman: Reflections by His Daughter, His Research Associate, and a Historian* (Richmond: Friends of the Richmond Public Library, 1986), 15. The author has discovered no letter in which DSF comments on "Miss Sye" or her abilities as a teacher.
57. William Wheeler Jones, *Of Two Virginia Gentlemen and Their McGuire's University School* (Richmond: The McGuire School Alumni Association, 1972), 27.
58. Ibid., 2.
59. Ibid., 3.
60. "McGuire's School Organization and Course of Study," c. 1869-70, McGuire's University School Papers, Virginia Historical Society, Box 2, Folder 6.
61. Jones, *McGuire's*, 48.

62. Ibid., 48, 56.

63. D. Edward Bass, Jr., "Douglas Southall Freeman," a term paper submitted to Professor Samuel Chiles Mitchell, University of Richmond, c. 1934. S. C. Mitchell Papers, Virginia Baptist Historical Society. Ordinarily a term paper written by a college student would not be considered an authoritative source, but DSF granted this student an interview and is quoted in the paper. Freeman noted an interview with another student from Mitchell's class, Jere Baxter III, in a letter to his wife. DSF to Inez G. Freeman, 17 April 1934, MTM MSS.

64. V. Dabney, *Richmond*, 214.

65. M. T. McClenahan, "Manuscript," 6-7; "My Father," 7.

66. DSF, "John Stewart Bryan," 144.

67. Jones, *McGuire's*, 68.

68. *Richmond News Leader*, 15 November 1948, 10.

69. Jones, *McGuire's*, 12.

70. Ibid.

71. DSF to John P. McGuire, Jr., 16 November 1948, DSF MSS, Container 90.

72. *Richmond News Leader*, 15 November 1948, 10.

73. DSF to John Peyton McGuire, 17 October 1942, DSF MSS, Container 44.

74. *Richmond Dispatch*, 23 December 1894; Benjamin W. Brockenbrough to DSF, n/d, DSF MSS, Container 121; M. T. McClenahan, "Manuscript," 7.

75. DSF to the Rev. James Ivey, 12 December 1952, DSF MSS, Container 111.

76. Allen W. Freeman, "My Brother Douglas," 12-13.

77. Ibid., 13.

78. DSF to Edward Calisch, 2 July 1938, DSF MSS, Container 29.

79. DSF to John Jones, 17 June 1925, DSF MSS, Container 6.

80. W. B. Freeman, "Memoirs," 29.

81. Anne B. Freeman, "Bedford Freemans," 2.

82. W. B. Freeman, "Memoirs," 13.

83. Anne B. Freeman, "Bedford Freemans," 5.

84. DSF, Diary, 1901, MTM MSS.

85. Jones, *McGuire's*, 32.

86. M. T. McClenahan, "Manuscript," 7.

87. DSF, "Scrapbook," Freeman Papers, Virginia Historical Society (hereafter DSF VHS).

88. DSF, Diary, 14 June 1901, MTM MSS.

89. DSF, draft letter to Sunday School class, 24 September 1902, MTM MSS.

90. Ibid.

91. Jones, *McGuire's*, 31.

92. Ibid.

93. "Boatwright: Valiant for Truth," *Alumni Bulletin of the University of Richmond*, Vol. XVI, No. 2 (January 1952), 2.

94. V. Dabney, *Richmond*, 252.

95. DSF, Diary, 16 September 1901, MTM MSS.

96. *Richmond College Messenger*, Vol. XXVIII, No. 1 (October 1901), 46.

97. Ibid.
98. M. T. McClenahan, "Manuscript," 8; *Spider Fiji*, 3, DSF MSS, Container 220; Allen W. Freeman, "My Brother Douglas," 20.
99. George F. Scheer, "Plutarch on the James," *The Southern Packet*, Vol. V, No. 2 (February 1949), 2.
100. *Alabama* Playbill, DSF MSS, Container 122.
101. Ibid.
102. Allen W. Freeman, "My Brother Douglas," 22.
103. M. T. McClenahan, "Manuscript," 8; "Tramp Newspaperman" (unpublished manuscript), MTM MSS, 2-3; "Reflections," *The Virginia Magazine of History and Biography*, Vol. 94, No. 1 (January 1986), 26-27.
104. Allen W. Freeman, "My Brother Douglas," 24.
105. Mary Tyler McClenahan remembers her father "joking" about his collegiate acting career, but does not recall his relating the details of this failed effort to join the acting company. Mary Tyler McClenahan, Interview with author, 4 June 2001.
106. Allen W. Freeman, "My Brother Douglas," 24; M. T. McClenahan, "Manuscript," 8. It is difficult to gauge the seriousness of Freeman's fling with an acting career. Allen Freeman is the only one to write a first-hand account of the incident, and no letters have been found from DSF offering any details. There is one surviving diary entry in which Freeman writes about acting. He pronounces one production "a rousing success" that "came out clear financially." DSF, Diary, 9 May 1902, DSF MSS, Container 1.
107. John A. Cutchins, *Memories of Old Richmond:1881-1944* (Richmond: McClure Press, 1973), 101-2.
108. Allen W. Freeman, "My Brother Douglas," 23.
109. Cutchins, *Memories*, 102-3; Allen W. Freeman, "My Brother Douglas," 22-24.
110. Allen W. Freeman, "My Brother Douglas," 22-24. The title page of DSF's copy of *When the Bugle Sounds* lists the playwrights as "Donald O'Connell with the collaboration of Albert Chambers French." Given the recollections of John Cutchins and Allen Freeman, and the lack of other plays by these "writers," these names are most certainly pseudonyms used by DSF and Allen Freeman. *When the Bugle Sounds*, MTM MSS.
111. DSF to Samuel Chiles Mitchell, 7 December 1943, DSF MSS, Container 57.
112. S. C. Mitchell, *An Aftermath of Appomattox* (privately published, 1942), 1.
113. *Richmond News Leader*, 20 August 1948, 15; Nelson Lankford, "Samuel Chiles Mitchell," *An Occasional Bulletin*, The Virginia Historical Society, No. 51 (December 1985), 3-4.
114. W. Harrison Daniel, *History at the University of Richmond* (Richmond: University of Richmond, 1991), 15.
115. Ibid., 17.

116. Mallory Freeman, Interview with author, 8 February 2001.

117. M. T. McClenahan, "Manuscript," 9-10.

118. *Richmond News Leader*, 20 August 1948.

119. Ibid.; M. T. McClenahan, "Manuscript," 9-10.

120. Mitchell, *Aftermath of Appomattox*, 35.

121. Ibid., 74-75.

122. Ibid., 82.

123. Ibid., 51-52.

124. DSF, "Commencement Speech at the College of William & Mary," 11 June 1950, Tape recording, MTM MSS.

125. *Richmond News Leader*, 20 August 1948; M. T. McClenahan, "Reflections," 26; "My Father," 7-8.

126. DSF to S. C. Mitchell, 7 December 1943, DSF MSS, Container 51.

127. Ibid.

128. S. C. Mitchell to Mary Tyler Goddin, 6 February 1914, MTM MSS.

129. S. C. Mitchell to DSF, 25 January 1910, DSF MSS, Container 121; Scheer, "Plutarch on the James," 2.

130. *Richmond News Leader*, 20 August 1948.

131. Allen W. Freeman, "My Brother Douglas," 20.

132. DSF, "The Adventures of a Frat-Pin"; "Caput Primum"; "The Kiss"; MTM MSS.

133. Allen W. Freeman, "My Brother Douglas," 19; Cutchins, *Memories*, 101.

134. DSF, Diary, 26 April 1902, DSF MSS, Container 1.

135. DSF, "One Week," 1, MTM MSS.

136. Ibid., 2.

137. Ibid.

138. Ibid., 3-4.

139. Ibid., 5.

140. DSF, "On Youthful Love," MTM MSS.

141. DSF, "Young Men and the Church," MTM MSS.

142. DSF, "College Religion," *Richmond College Messenger*, Vol. XXXI, No. 1 (October 1904), 29.

143. Ibid., 30.

144. DSF, "The Boys Society in the Church," MTM MSS.

145. DSF to Bettie A. Freeman, 3 July 1902, DSF JHU, Box 1; Allen W. Freeman, "My Brother Douglas," 26; C. A. Cornelson to DSF, 29 April 1905, DSF MSS, Container 4.

146. DSF to Bettie A. Freeman, 3 July 1902, DSF JHU, Box 1; Allen W. Freeman, "My Brother Douglas," 26.

147. DSF, "Marguerita," *Richmond College Messenger*, Vol. XXIX, Nos. 7 & 8 (April-May 1903), 252-59.

148. DSF, "The Mystery of Bill Bailey," *Richmond College Messenger*, Vol. XXIX. Nos. 7 & 8 (April-May 1902), 279-83.

149. DSF, "On the Campus," *Richmond College Messenger*, Vol. XXX, No. 1 (October 1903), 53-55.

150. Ibid., 55-56.

151. DSF, "Rudolph," *Richmond College Messenger*, Vol. XXX, Nos. 2 & 3 (November-December 1903), 75-86.

152. Ibid., 82.

153. DSF, "Francesca," *Richmond College Messenger*, Vol. XXX, No. 4 (January 1904), 136-43 (Part 1); Vol. XXX, Nos. 5-6 (February-March 1904), 184-92 (Part 2).

154. DSF, "Francesca," 136.

155. DSF, "The Minor Chord," *Richmond College Messenger*, Vol. XXX, No. 7 (April 1904), 237.

156. Ibid., 233-34.

157. DSF, "Editorial Comment," *Richmond College Messenger*, Vol. XXX, No. 7 (April 1904), 244.

158. Report Book, Richmond College, 1898-1902; Report Book, 1902-1906; Virginia Baptist Historical Society.

159. F. W. Boatwright to W. B. Freeman, 20 February 1904; DSF, "Scrapbook," DSF VHS.

160. Ibid.

161. *Petersburg Daily Index-Appeal*, 1 November 1903, 8.

162. *Petersburg Daily Index-Appeal*, 4 November 1903, 6.

163. *Petersburg Daily Index-Appeal*, 6 November 1903, 4.

164. *Petersburg Daily Index-Appeal*, 1 November 1903, 8; 7 November 1903, 1.

165. *Petersburg Daily Index-Appeal*, 7 November 1903, 1.

166. Ibid., 6.

167. Ibid.

168. Ibid.

169. DSF to Thomas Fina, 24 October 1940, DSF MSS, Container 36.

170. Ibid.; "The Virginians," *Time*, 18 October 1948, 112; DSF, Diary, 30 April 1937, DSF MSS, Container 1; DSF to Bettie A. Freeman, 25 October 1905, DSF JHU, Box 1; DSF to John H. Devlin, Jr., 20 April 1936, DSF MSS, Container 22.

CHAPTER THREE

1. DSF, "What It All Means," *Richmond College Messenger*, Vol. XXX, Nos. 8-9 (May-June 1904), 299.

2. Record Book, 1902-1906. Proving he possessed some human frailties, Freeman began a class in German but dropped it with an 86.3 average.

3. DSF, "What It All Means," 299.

4. DSF, "After College, Then What?" *Richmond College Messenger*, Vol. XXXI, No. 1 (October 1904), 28.

5. W. A. Harris to Ira Remsen, President, Johns Hopkins, May 1904, DSF MSS, Container 121.

6. A. C. Wightman to the Board of University Studies, May 1904, DSF MSS, Container 121.

7. S. C. Mitchell to the Board of University Studies, May 1904, DSF MSS, Container 121.

8. F. W. Boatwright to the Board of University Studies, May 1904, DSF MSS, Container 121.

9. Hugh Hawkins, *Pioneer: A History of the Johns Hopkins University, 1874-1889* (Ithaca, New York: Cornell University Press, 1960), 22.

10. Ibid., 21-22.

11. Ibid., 293.

12. August Heckscher, *Woodrow Wilson* (New York: Charles Scribner's Sons, 1991), 67.

13. DSF to Bettie A. Freeman, 23 May 1905; DSF to Walker B. Freeman, 8 October 1905, DSF JHU, Box 1.

14. DSF, "Betsy Hansford: The True Story of the Virginia Priscilla"; *Ladies Home Journal* to DSF, 16 November 1904, DSF MSS, Container 4.

15. DSF to Walker B. Freeman, 8 October 1905, DSF JHU, Box 1.

16. Bobbs Merrill to DSF, 17 October 1904; Harper & Brothers to DSF, 18 October 1904; Putnam's to DSF, 15 November 1904; Lothrop Publishing to DSF, 9 January 1905, DSF MSS, Container 4.

17. DSF to Bettie A. Freeman, 23 May 1905, DSF JHU, Box 1.

18. Allen W. Freeman, "My Brother Douglas," 27-28.

19. Ibid.

20. DSF, "Record of Work, 1st Month, JHU," 4 November 1904, DSF MSS, Container 236.

21. Ibid.

22. DSF, "Schedule," 14 November 1904, DSF VHS. His diary in 1907—his third year at Hopkins—consistently records a rising hour of 6:45 A.M. and a bedtime after midnight. DSF, Diary, 1907, DSF MSS, Container 1.

23. Walker B. Freeman to DSF, 21 November 1904, DSF JHU, Box 2.

24. DSF to L. L. Lomax, undated, but probably 30 March 1905; John S. Wise to DSF, 31 March 1905, DSF MSS, Container 4.

25. DSF, "Suggested Form of Statement," DSF MSS, Container 4.

26. DSF to Bettie A. Freeman, 22 January 1905; 7 March 1905; DSF to Walker B. Freeman, 7 April 1905, DSF JHU, Box 1.

27. DSF to Walker B. Freeman, 16 March 1905, DSF JHU, Box 1.

28. DSF to Walker B. Freeman, 28 May 1905, DSF JHU, Box 1.

29. James Stimpert, Archivist, Johns Hopkins University, to author, 15 March 2001.

30. *See* DSF to Walker B. Freeman, 11 January 1905; 23 January 1905; 1 April 1905; DSF to Bettie A. Freeman, 16 January 1905, DSF JHU, Box 1.

31. DSF to Walker B. Freeman, 30 January 1905, DSF JHU, Box 1.

32. Ibid.

33. DSF to Bettie A. Freeman, 6 April 1905, DSF JHU, Box 1.
34. M. T. McClenahan, "Manuscript," 11; "Douglas Southall Freeman, My Father as a Writer," *Richmond Literature and History Quarterly*, Vol. 1 (Spring 1979), 35; "Tramp Newspaperman," 4.
35. M. T. McClenahan, "Tramp Newspaperman," 4.
36. M. T. McClenahan, "My Father as a Writer," 35.
37. DSF to Walker B. Freeman, 5 May 1905, DSF JHU, Box 1.
38. DSF to Bettie A. Freeman, 22 January 1905, DSF, JHU, Box 1.
39. Ibid.
40. DSF to Bettie A. Freeman, 16 January 1905, DSF JHU, Box 1; Allen W. Freeman, "My Brother Douglas," 30.
41. Allen W. Freeman, "My Brother Douglas," 30.
42. Ibid., 29.
43. Ibid.
44. Ibid. Ashworth, "The Man and the Making of a Book," 16.
45. DSF to Allen W. Freeman, 14 April 1952, DSF MSS, Container 111.
46. Allen W. Freeman, "My Brother Douglas," 29.
47. Ibid., 30.
48. DSF to Walker B. Freeman, 24 March 1905, DSF JHU, Box 1.
49. DSF to Bettie A. Freeman, 4 February 1905, DSF JHU, Box 1.
50. Ibid.
51. DSF to Walker B. Freeman, 4 March 1905, DSF JHU, Box 1.
52. DSF to Walker B. Freeman, 1 April 1905, DSF JHU, Box 1.
53. DSF to Walker B. Freeman, 12 March 1905, DSF JHU, Box 1.
54. DSF to Bettie A. Freeman, 16 January 1905, DSF JHU, Box 1.
55. DSF to Bettie A. Freeman, 31 January 1905, DSF JHU, Box 1.
56. DSF to Bettie A. Freeman, 22 January 1905, DSF JHU, Box 1.
57. DSF to Bettie A. Freeman, 4 February 1905, DSF JHU, Box 1.
58. Ibid.
59. DSF to Walker B. Freeman, 16 March 1905, DSF JHU, Box 1.
60. DSF to Walker B. Freeman, 22 March 1905, DSF JHU, Box 1.
61. Ibid.
62. DSF to Bettie A. Freeman, 8 May 1905, DSF JHU, Box 1.
63. John L. Gignilliat, "Douglas Southall Freeman" in Clyde Norman Wilson, ed., *Dictionary of Literary Biography*, Vol. 17 (Detroit: Gale Research Co., 1983), 159; *see also* Acton, *Selected Writings of Lord Acton*, Vol. II, *Essays in the Study and Writing of History* (Indianapolis: Liberty Classics, 1985), 527-31.
64. A. S. Eisenstadt, *Charles McLean Andrews* (New York: Columbia University Press, 1956), 110.
65. Ibid., 111.
66. Ibid., 113-14.
67. DSF to Walker B. Freeman, 5 May 1905, DSF JHU, Box 1.
68. DSF to Walker B. Freeman, 30 January 1905, DSF, JHU, Box 1.

69. Ibid.
70. Ibid.
71. DSF to Walker B. Freeman, 18 March 1905, DSF JHU, Box 1.
72. DSF to Walker B. Freeman, 30 January 1905, DSF JHU, Box 1.
73. DSF to Bettie A. Freeman, 22 March 1905, DSF JHU, Box 1.
74. Baltimore, at the turn of the century, was hardly a "Northern" city, but as Maryland had not been part of the Confederacy, to DSF the "South" began at the Virginia line.
75. DSF to Bettie A. Freeman, 22 March 1905, DSF JHU, Box 1.
76. DSF to Bettie A. Freeman, 9 April 1905, DSF JHU, Box 1.
77. DSF to Walker B. Freeman, 1 April 1905; 29 April 1905; DSF to Bettie A. Freeman, 8 May 1905, DSF JHU, Box 1.
78. DSF, "Notes," DSF MSS, Container 5.
79. DSF to Bettie A. Freeman, 16 January 1905; 4 February 1905, DSF JHU, Box 1.
80. Walker B. Freeman to DSF, 9 November 1904, DSF JHU, Box 2.
81. DSF to Walker B. Freeman, 24 March 1905, DSF JHU, Box 1.
82. Ibid.
83. Ira Remsen to DSF, 10 June 1905, DSF MSS, Container 122.
84. DSF to Walker B. Freeman, 24 March 1905, DSF JHU, Box 1.
85. Library of Virginia to DSF, 3 December 1904, DSF MSS, Container 4.
86. DSF to Bettie A. Freeman, 5 March 1905, DSF JHU, Box 1; "Library of Congress Certificate for 'Cartersville,'" 18 November 1905, DSF VHS.
87. Belasco Theatre to DSF, 2 January 1906, DSF MSS, Container 4.
88. DSF to Bettie A. Freeman, 28 October 1905, DSF JHU, Box 1.
89. DSF to Walker B. Freeman, 13 October 1905, DSF JHU, Box 1.
90. DSF to Bettie A. Freeman, 21 October 1905, DSF JHU, Box 1.
91. DSF to Walker B. Freeman, 15 November 1905, DSF JHU, Box 1.
92. DSF to Walker B. Freeman, 28 November 1905, DSF JHU, Box 1.
93. DSF to Walker B. Freeman, n/d 1905, DSF JHU, Box 1.
94. DSF to Bettie A. Freeman, 4 December 1905, DSF JHU, Box 1.
95. DSF to Walker B. Freeman, 5 December 1905, DSF JHU, Box 1.
96. DSF to Bettie A. Freeman, 12 December 1905, DSF JHU, Box 1.
97. DSF to Walker B. Freeman, 4 January 1906, DSF JHU, Box 2.
98. DSF to Walker B. Freeman, 4 November 1905, DSF JHU, Box 1.
99. DSF to Walker B. Freeman, 16 February 1906, DSF JHU, Box 2.
100. DSF to Walker B. Freeman, 4 November 1905, DSF JHU, Box 1.
101. DSF to Bettie A. Freeman, 16 December 1905, DSF JHU, Box 1.
102. DSF to Walker B. Freeman, 20 February 1906, DSF JHU, Box 2.
103. DSF to Walker B. Freeman, 10 March 1906, DSF JHU, Box 2.
104. DSF to Walker B. Freeman, 14 March 1906, DSF JHU, Box 2.
105. Ibid.
106. Ibid.

107. DSF to Allen W. Freeman, 21 March 1906, DSF JHU, Box 2.
108. DSF to Walker B. Freeman, 19 March 1906, DSF JHU, Box 2.
109. DSF to Walker B. Freeman, 21 March 1906, DSF JHU, Box 2.
110. Walker B. Freeman to DSF, 20 March 1906, DSF JHU, Box 2.
111. Walker B. Freeman to DSF, 22 March 1906, DSF JHU, Box 2.
112. DSF to Walker B. Freeman, 23 March 1906, DSF JHU, Box 2.
113. Ibid.
114. Ibid.
115. DSF to Bettie A. Freeman, 20 May 1906, DSF JHU, Box 2.
116. His abilities and reputation in this area were so respected that several Richmond churches wanted him to serve as pastor. Mary Tyler McClenahan, Interview with author, 4 June 2001.
117. Ira Remsen to DSF, 13 June 1906, DSF VHS.
118. M. T. McClenahan, "Reflections," 27.
119. Ibid.; Ralph A. Habas, "Untitled Manuscript," DSF MSS, Container 97, 9; Anne B. Freeman, "Bedford Freemans," 43.
120. M. T. McClenahan, "Manuscript," 12.
121. Ibid.; Bass, "Term Paper," 3.
122. Habas, "Untitled Manuscript," 9. Habas and Anne Freeman place these events in the summer of 1907. This gives one pause due to DSF's extensive involvement in the production of both of these writings. Subsequent events and letters, however, confirm that these events took place in the summer of 1906 and the Habas/Anne Freeman cites are in error.
123. DSF to Walker B. Freeman, 14 October 1906, DSF JHU, Box 2.
124. DSF, "The Gifted Dr. G. W. Bagby and His Brilliant Literary Work," *Richmond Times-Dispatch*, 21 October 1906, 4.
125. DSF to Walker B. Freeman, 29 October 1906, DSF JHU, Box 2.
126. DSF to Bettie A. Freeman, 21 January 1907, DSF JHU, Box 1.
127. DSF to Walker B. Freeman, 14 November 1906; DSF to Bettie A. Freeman, 6 December 1906, DSF JHU, Box 1.
128. DSF, Diary, 4 February 1907, DSF MSS, Container 1.
129. DSF to Bettie A. Freeman, 4 February 1907, DSF JHU, Box 1; DSF to Walker B. Freeman, 5 February 1907, DSF JHU, Box 2.
130. K. P. Minor to DSF, 19 February 1907, DSF JHU, Box 3.
131. Ibid.
132. DSF to Walker B. Freeman, 12 January 1907, DSF JHU, Box 2.
133. Bettie A. Freeman to DSF, 20 January 1907, DSF JHU, Box 2.
134. DSF to K. P. Minor, 21 February 1907, DSF JHU, Box 3.
135. Ibid.
136. Ibid.
137. DSF to Walker B. Freeman, 21 February 1907, DSF JHU, Box 2. His diary entry mentions only that he "Got informal offer to write Calendar of Confederate Museum MSS." DSF, Diary, 21 February 1907, DSF MSS, Container 1.
138. DSF to Confederate Memorial Literary Society, 15 April 1907, Freeman

Papers, Eleanor S. Brockenbrough Library, The Museum of the Confederacy, Richmond, Virginia (hereafter cited "DSF MOC").

139. Ibid.

140. Ibid.

141. Ibid.

142. Ibid.

143. Minutes, Confederate Memorial Literary Society, 24 April 1907, DSF MOC.

144. Ibid.; DSF to K. P. Minor, 25 April 1907, DSF JHU, Box 3.

145. DSF to M. A. Baughman, 27 May 1907, DSF MOC.

146. DSF to Walker B. Freeman, 28 January 1907, DSF JHU, Box 2; DSF to Bettie A. Freeman, 16 February 1907; 19 February 1907, DSF JHU, Box 1.

147. DSF to Walker B. Freeman, 28 May 1907, DSF JHU, Box 2; DSF, Diary, 28 May 1907, DSF MSS, Container 1.

148. DSF to Bettie A. Freeman, 29 April 1907, DSF JHU, Box 1; DSF to Walker B. Freeman, 26 April 1907, DSF JHU, Box 2; F. R. Ball to DSF, 10 June 1907, DSF VHS.

149. DSF to Bettie A. Freeman, 27 May 1907, DSF JHU, Box 1.

150. DSF to Walker B. Freeman, 23 May 1907, DSF JHU, Box 2.

151. Ibid.

152. DSF, Diary, "Summary of Summer," n/d, contained in 1907 diary starting at page 267, DSF MSS, Container 1. He noted that he worked in the mansion from June 17 to September 28.

153. DSF, Introduction to *A Calendar of Confederate Papers* (Richmond: The Confederate Museum, 1908), 11.

154. Ibid., 12-13.

155. DSF, Diary, "Summary of Summer," 1907, DSF MSS, Container 1.

156. Ibid., 269-70.

157. DSF to Bettie A. Freeman, 11 October 1907, DSF JHU, Box 1.

158. DSF to Bettie A. Freeman, 15 October 1907, DSF JHU, Box 1.

159. DSF to Bettie A. Freeman, 17 October 1907, DSF JHU, Box 1; DSF to M. A. Baughman, 30 October 1907, DSF MOC.

160. DSF to M. A. Baughman, 3 December 1907, DSF MOC; DSF, "Introduction," *Calendar*, 14.

161. F. R. Ball to DSF, 30 October 1907, DSF VHS.

162. F. R. Ball to DSF, 17 January 1908, DSF VHS.

163. DSF to Bettie A. Freeman, 12 February 1908, DSF JHU, Box 1.

164. "Review," *Religious Herald*, 21 April 1908, DSF VHS.

165. *Confederate Memorial Literary Society Year Book, 1907* (Richmond: The Baughman Stationary Co., 1908), 19. DSF MOC.

166. J. M. Vincent to DSF, 1 March 1909, DSF MSS, Container 121.

167. The charred manuscript, with Freeman's notes about the fire, is housed among his papers in the Library of Congress. DSF MSS, Container 126.

168. DSF, "Examination in Political Economy," 19 May 1908, DSF VHS.

169. DSF, "Oral Examination Schedule," 26 May 1908, DSF VHS.
170. Walker B. Freeman to DSF, 28 May 1908, DSF JHU, Box 2.
171. M. T. McClenahan, "Manuscript," 17.
172. DSF to Walker B. Freeman, 3 June 1908, DSF VHS.
173. DSF, "Scrapbook," DSF VHS.
174. Gignilliat, "Freeman," 159.
175. DSF to Mrs. Charles M. Andrews, 25 September 1943, cited in Eisenstadt, *Andrews*, 247. In the same letter, DSF pays a carefully worded tribute to Andrews saying he "exercised more influence over my mind and my style than all the other History Professors at Johns Hopkins combined." It was to Andrews, Freeman wrote, that he owed his "start in historical editing and writing."

CHAPTER FOUR

1. Bettie Freeman underwent an unidentified operation in June 1907. DSF made several diary entries about this event, but gave no indication that it was serious. He reported that his "mother's recovery is little short of wonderful." DSF, Diary, 3, 4, 5, 7, 13 June 1907, DSF MSS, Container 1.
2. Allen W. Freeman, "My Brother Douglas," 40-41; Anne B. Freeman, "Bedford Freemans,"42; M. T. McClenahan, "Manuscript," 17. Allen Freeman, a physician, provides the most details about Bettie Freeman's fatal illness. He states she "concealed the existence of the tumor from her family until Douglas was graduated and back home." He concludes that this delay lost the opportunity "for a complete cure which she might have had if she could have been operated on promptly."
3. Mary Tyler McClenahan once wrote that Bettie Freeman was "the greatest single influence in [Freeman's] life." Mary Tyler Cheek to Ruth H. Blunt, 13 August 1968, MTM MSS.
4. DSF to Bettie Freeman, 17 January 1907, DSF JHU, Box 1.
5. Ibid.
6. DSF to Mrs. R. L. Chernery, 5 April 1921, DSF MSS, Container 5; M. T. McClenahan, "Manuscript," 17.
7. Allen W. Freeman, "My Brother Douglas," 40-41, 44.
8. F. W. Boatwright to DSF, 11 July 1908, DSF MSS, Container 4; M. T. McClenahan, "Manuscript," 17.
9. President Samuel Brooks to William Whitsett, 24 March 1908, DSF MSS, Container 4.
10. S. Jamison to DSF, 3 September 1908, DSF MSS, Container 121. Anne Freeman writes that her father did not seek a college position in order that he could remain at home with Bettie. Freeman's tepid pursuit of a teaching post, so unlike his zealous efforts in any other undertaking, seems to confirm Anne Freeman's speculation. Anne Freeman, "Bedford Freemans," 42.
11. M. T. McClenahan, "Reflections," 27; "My Father," 9; Anne B. Freeman, "Bedford Freemans," 43.
12. Allen W. Freeman, "My Brother Douglas," 43.
13. "Prepares Calendar of Confederate Papers," *Richmond Evening Journal,* September 1908.

14. DSF to Inez G. Freeman, 5 August 1933, MTM MSS; M. T. McClenahan, "Manuscript," 18.

15. DSF, "In the Blood" (unpublished manuscript, 1912), MTM MSS, 100-103. This book by Freeman is discussed at pages 99-100. It is admittedly a risky proposition to cite a work of fiction in relating a factual story. Freeman's descriptions of the red-light district and mission are so detailed, however, that they must have been formed by first-hand observation during his visit to the Goddin mission. They are therefore used here, with this disclaimer, to describe a few features of this important night.

16. Ibid., 103.

17. Ibid., 7-8.

18. DSF to Mrs. Chenery, 5 April 1921, DSF MSS, Container 5.

19. Ibid.; M. T. McClenahan, "Manuscript," 18.

20. DSF to Mrs. Chenery, 5 April 1921, DSF MSS, Container 5.

21. DSF to Inez G. Freeman, 26 September 1908, MTM MSS; M. T. McClenahan, "Manuscript," 18; "A Quality of Love" (unpublished manuscript), MTM MSS, 1. *See also* "In the Blood" where Freeman describes a young girl playing the piano at the mission.

22. M. T. McClenahan, "Quality of Love," 3-6.

23. Allen W. Freeman, "My Brother Douglas," 41; Charles Andrews to DSF, 29 July 1908, DSF MSS, Container 4; DSF, "Freeman Family," DSF MSS, Container 238.

24. DSF, "Freeman Family," DSF MSS, Container 238, 1.

25. Ibid., 1, 10. The genealogy of the Freeman family is not treated in this study. Family tradition is divided over whether the line goes to Edmond Freeman, who emigrated from England to Massachusetts in 1635; or to Bridges Freeman, who emigrated from England to Virginia in 1622.

26. "Book Reviews," *The Virginia Magazine of History and Biography*, Vol. XVII, No. 3 (July 1909), 332-33.

27. Frederic Bancroft to DSF, 16 February 1909, DSF VHS.

28. Frederic Bancroft, "Minor Notices," *American Historical Review*, Vol. XIV, No. 3 (April 1909), 623-24.

29. Mary Tyler McClenahan, Interview with author, 4 June 2001.

30. DSF to Inez Goddin, 26 September 1908, MTM MSS.

31. Ibid.

32. Ibid.

33. Ibid.

34. M. T. McClenahan, "My Father," 9; "Manuscript," 19.

35. "Program—*As You Like It*," 31 May 1909, DSF VHS.

36. "Tribute paid to the memory of Miss Ellett," *Richmond News Leader*, 8 November 1951, 23.

37. Ibid.

38. DSF to Monroe F. Cockrell, 21 July 1950, DSF MSS, Container 100.

39. "Worth $25,000," *Richmond Evening Journal*, 29 December 1908; DSF to

Monroe F. Cockrell, 21 July 1950, DSF MSS, Container 100. The *Evening Journal* story is incorrect in several details. Freeman did not "come across" the copy, but found it during the course of his review of all documents held by the museum. Nor had the constitution been neglected for decades. It had arrived in Richmond only the previous February. The significance of the event—other than furthering Freeman's local reputation—is that it brought Freeman into contact with the De Renne family, the previous owners of the document. Wymberley De Renne took notice of Freeman's abilities during this time and turned to him to publish a collection of Lee's dispatches. See pages 94-96. William Harris Bragg, *De Renne: Three Generations of a Georgia Family* (Athens: University of Georgia Press, 1999), 255-61.

40. Daniel, *History at the University of Richmond*, 36.

41. *The South in the Building of the Nation*, Vol. X, S. C. Mitchell, ed. (Richmond: The Southern Historical Publishing Society, 1909).

42. Habas, "Untitled Manuscript," 9-10.

43. DSF, "John Stewart Bryan," 224; Habas, "Untitled Manuscript," 10; DSF, *"Richmond News Leader* Biography," DSF MSS, Container 30.

44. DSF, "John Stewart Bryan," 69, 124, 175; Earle Dunford, *Richmond Times-Dispatch: The Story of a Newspaper* (Richmond: Cadmus Publishing, 1995), 24-46.

45. *Richmond Times-Dispatch*, 15 March 1909, 4.

46. *Richmond Times-Dispatch*, 22 March 1909, 4.

47. DSF, "Taxation Conditions in Virginia" in *State and Local Taxation* (Columbus, Ohio: The National Tax Association, 1912), 67-71.

48. *Richmond Times-Dispatch*, 22 March 1909, 4.

49. *Richmond Times-Dispatch*, 4 April 1909. *See also* 28, 30 March 1909; 1, 6 April 1909.

50. *Richmond Times-Dispatch*, 22 May 1909. *See also* 8, 10, 12 , 14 , 17 April 1909; 8, 10 May 1909.

51. *Richmond Times-Dispatch*, 26 April 1909.

52. *Richmond Times-Dispatch*, 10 May 1909.

53. *Richmond Times-Dispatch*, 14 April 1909.

54. *Richmond Times-Dispatch*, 20 May 1909.

55. *See Richmond Times-Dispatch*, 13, 15, 17, 19, 21, 24, 26, 28 June 1909.

56. M. T. McClenahan, "Manuscript," 23.

57. DSF to Inez Goddin, 9 May 1909, quoted in M. T. McClenahan, "Manuscript," 24-25.

58. Ibid.

59. Ibid.

60. DSF, "Freeman Family," 6-7.

61. Freeman maintained this reticence throughout his life. He often referred to his mother, always in exalted terms, but rarely expressed his feelings. An exception appears in a letter in 1952. "My mother has been dead more than forty-three

years," he wrote, "but I miss her still." DSF to D. Tennant Bryan, 14 September 1952, DSF MSS, Container 109.

62. "Class Day Exercises," 28 May 1909, MTM MSS.

63. M. T. McClenahan, "Manuscript," 25-26.

64. Southern Publication Society to DSF, 9 July 1909; 12 August 1909, DSF MSS, Container 4. The subjects of the articles are unknown, and it is not clear whether the society ever published them.

65. DSF, "Introduction" in W. W. Baker, *Memoirs of Service with John Yates Beall, CSN* (Richmond: The Richmond Press, 1910), 7-8.

66. *Charleston* (WVA) *Gazette*, 11 April 1911, DSF VHS.

67. Unattributed Winchester, Virginia, news clipping, 10 February 1911, DSF VHS.

68. *Charleston Gazette*, 11 April 1911.

69. In 1953, the Virginia Tuberculosis Associated established the Douglas Southall Freeman Award to honor that person "who has contributed the most to tuberculosis control." *Richmond Times-Dispatch*, 28 October 1953.

70. William Howard Taft to J. C. Hemphill, 14 June 1910, DSF VHS.

71. On June 11, 1910, the *Times-Dispatch* ran an editorial titled "Harrison and Taft" complimenting Taft on his conduct toward a congressman who had accused the president of misleading Congress. This could have been the clip Hemphill sent to Taft, but as the editorial has no by-line, it is impossible to say for certain that Freeman wrote it. *Richmond Times-Dispatch*, 11 June 1910.

72. Mary Tyler McClenahan, statement to author, 13 February 2001. *See also* M. T. Cheek, "Galatea in Richmond: Emma Gray Trigg," *The Richmond Quarterly*, Vol. 5, No. 1 (Summer, 1982), 30. Emma Gray White's married name was Emma Gray Trigg.

73. Although there are no letters between Freeman and Inez during this period, there is a letter in August 1911 from Inez to W. J. De Renne acknowledging receipt of payment for copying "400 folios [of] Lee telegrams." These telegrams were for use in Freeman's book, *Lee's Dispatches to Davis*. So it appears Inez and Freeman were on friendly enough terms in August that Inez was doing copy work for him. Inez Goddin to W. J. De Renne, 16 August 1911, W. J. De Renne Library Correspondence, Hargrett Rare Book & Manuscript Library, University of Georgia Libraries, Athens (hereafter referred to as DeR MSS), Box 38.

74. Acts of the Assembly, Chapter 147, 1910.

75. DSF, "Tax Reform in Virginia: An Address to the Virginia Press Association, July 12, 1911" (Richmond: State Tax Commission, 1911), 4. DSF VHS.

76. John Stewart Bryan to DSF, 28 June 1910, DSF MSS, Container 4.

77. *Richmond Evening Journal*, 28 June 1910, 1; *Richmond Times-Dispatch*, 28 June 1910, 2.

78. DSF, "Tax Reform," 3.

79. Ibid.

80. Ibid., 5.

81. Ibid., 15.

82. Ibid., 16. Although in this speech, Freeman uses the pronoun "we" in describing all these activities, he most certainly is referring only to himself. It is highly unlikely that the other commission members had the time, or inclination, to do the legwork he describes. This sort of attention to detail is typical of any project undertaken by Freeman.

83. DSF to Jacob H. Hollander, 15 July 1910, Ms. 59, Jacob H. Hollander Papers, The Johns Hopkins University, Series 1, Box 3. *See also* DSF to Hollander, 28 July 1910.

84. Unattributed clipping, 8 January 1911, DSF, "Scrapbook," DSF VHS.

85. "Income Tax in Virginia a Farce, says Freeman," *The Virginian Pilot*, 7 January 1911, DSF VHS.

86. DSF, *Calendar*, 501; DSF to John H. Devlin, Jr., 20 April 1936, DSF MSS, Container 22.

87. DSF to John H. Devlin, Jr., 20 April 1936, DSF MSS, Container 22.

88. DSF to W. J. De Renne, 14 June 1910, DeR MSS, Box 38.

89. DSF to W. J. De Renne, 14 September 1910, DeR MSS, Box 38.

90. DSF to W. J. De Renne, 8 October 1910, DeR MSS, Box 38.

91. DSF to W. J. De Renne, 6 February 1911, DeR MSS, Box 38.

92. Ibid.

93. DSF to W. J. De Renne, 11 February 1911; 5 August 1911, DeR MSS, Box 38.

94. DSF to W. J. De Renne, 2 June 1911, DeR MSS, Box 38.

95. Ibid.

96. Ibid.

97. DSF to W. J. De Renne, 26 June 1911, DeR MSS, Box 38.

98. "A Brilliant Virginian," *The Danville Register*, 20 January 1911.

99. Ibid.

100. *The Tazewell Republican*, 27 July 1911.

101. S. C. Mitchell to DSF, 25 January 1910, DSF MSS, Container 121.

102. Henry S. Harrison to DSF, 22 March 1911, DSF VHS.

103. Henry S. Harrison, *Queed* (New York: Grosset & Dunlap, 1911), 27.

104. Ibid., 102-4.

105. *Richmond News Leader*, 30 May 1921, 4.

106. Ibid. Mary Tyler McClenahan believes, Harrison's statement notwithstanding, that Queed is modeled in part on her father. Mary Tyler McClenahan, Interview with author, 4 October 2000.

107. *Report to the General Assembly of Virginia by the Tax Commission* (Richmond: The Richmond Press, Inc., 1911).

108. *Richmond Times-Dispatch*, 29 December 1911, 1, 4.

109. Ibid., 4.

110. DSF, "Taxation Conditions in Virginia," 74.

111. "Mann Urges Revision of Tax Laws of State in Special Message," *Richmond News Leader*, 11 January 1912, 1; "Must Equalize Tax Valuation," *Richmond Times-Dispatch*, 12 January 1912, 1.

112. The recommendations of the Tax Commission are listed in Appendix 1, pages 359-61.

113. *The Danville Bee*, 27 January 1913, DSF VHS.

114. DSF to Inez Goddin, 18 December 1911, quoted in M. T. McClenahan, "Manuscript," 26.

115. DSF to W. J. De Renne, 29 April 1912, DeR MSS, Box 38.

116. Ibid.

117. DSF, "In the Blood."

118. DSF to Inez Goddin, quoted in M. T. McClenahan, "Manuscript," 27.

119. Ibid.

120. Ibid., 28.

121. DSF to W. J. De Renne, 8 September 1913, DeR MSS, Box 38.

122. Ibid.

123. M. T. McClenahan, "Manuscript," 28; Interview with author, 12 August 2000; "My Father as a Writer," 37.

124. Ibid.

125. DSF, "In the Blood," Dedication.

126. Houghton-Mifflin to DSF, 19 August 1913, DSF MSS, Container 4. This letter actually rejects "His Excellency"—the follow-up work to "In the Blood"—but refers to the publisher's earlier rejection of "In the Blood." DSF indicates he submitted the text as well to Harper Brothers, but no letters have been found to verify that statement. *See* DSF to Inez Goddin, 12 October 1912, quoted in M. T. McClenahan, "Manuscript," 27.

127. DSF, "Billy Walton, Governor" (unpublished manuscript), MTM MSS.

128. Ibid., 424.

129. Houghton-Mifflin to DSF, 19 August 1913, DSF MSS, Container 4.

130. DSF, Memorandum, 20 April 1953, 9. MTM MSS.

131. Mary Tyler McClenahan, Interview with author, 2 March 2000. Mrs. McClenahan graciously allowed the author to read the books.

132. DSF to W. J. De Renne, 30 September 1912, DeR MSS, Box 38.

133. W. J. De Renne to DSF, 4 September 1913, DeR MSS, Box 38.

134. DSF to W. J. De Renne, 8 September 1913, DeR MSS, Box 38.

135. DSF to W. J. De Renne, 24 October 1913, DeR MSS, Box 38.

136. DSF to Inez G. Freeman, 4 December 1916, MTM MSS.

137. Inez G. Freeman to DSF, 6 December 1916, MTM MSS.

138. Ibid. It is certain that the two had discussed marriage, and perhaps become engaged, earlier than December 4, 1913. This conversation may have been one merely of confirmation, Freeman having just recovered from his illness and settled in with the newspaper. Both Freeman and Inez, however, point to this date as, next to their marriage date, the most significant one of their relationship.

139. M. T. McClenahan, "Manuscript," 31; DSF to John Stewart Bryan, 25 November 1913, DSF MSS, Container 4.

140. M. T. McClenahan, "Manuscript," 31.

141. DSF, "Note," MTM MSS.

142. DSF to W. J. De Renne, 1 May 1914, DeR MSS, Box 38.

143. DSF, "Introduction," *Lee's Dispatches: Unpublished Letters of General Robert E. Lee to Jefferson Davis and the War Department of the Confederate States of America, 1862-65* (New York: G.P. Putnam's Sons, 1915), v.

144. Ibid., vii.

145. Ibid., xi

146. Ibid., xvii.

147. DSF, "Oliver Cromwell," n/d, Johns Hopkins Scrapbook, DSF MSS, Container 238.

148. Ibid., xviii.

149. DSF to W. J. De Renne, 7 September 1914, DeR MSS, Box 38.

150. DSF to W. J. De Renne, 15 September 1914, DSF MSS, Container 4.

151. DSF to W. J. De Renne, 15 September 1914; W. J. De Renne to DSF, 21 September 1914, DeR MSS, Box 38.

152. DSF to W. J. De Renne, 2 July 1915, cited in William Harris Bragg, "Our Joint Labor: W. J. De Renne, Douglas Southall Freeman, and *Lee's Dispatches*, 1910-1915," *The Virginia Magazine of History and Biography*, Vol. 97, No. 1 (January 1989). This article, written by De Renne's biographer, is the most thorough account of the events surrounding the writing of *Lee's Dispatches*.

153. DSF, *Lee's Dispatches*, 61-64, n.

154. Ibid., 169, n.

155. Ibid., 315, n., 290, n.

156. Bragg, "Our Joint Labor," 23, n66.

157. "Unpublished Dispatches from General Lee," *The New York Times Review of Books*, 27 June 1915, Section 5, 1.

158. Ibid.

159. "Review of Books," *American Historical Review*, Vol. XXI, No. 2 (January 1916), 357, 359.

160. DSF, *Lee's Dispatches*, xix.

161. E. L. Burlingame to DSF, 22 November 1915, Archives of Charles Scribner's Sons, Manuscripts Division, Department of Rare Books and Special Collections, Princeton University Library (hereafter Scribner MS), Box 57, Folder 1. Published with the permission of the Princeton University Library.

CHAPTER FIVE

1. DSF to John H. Devlin, 20 April 1936, DSF, Container 22; E. L. Burlingame to DSF, 22 November 1915, Scribner MS, Box 57, Folder 1; M. T. McClenahan, "A High Calling" in *Douglas Southall Freeman: Reflections by His Daughter, His Research Associate, and a Historian*, 10; "Reflections," 29.

2. DSF to E. L. Burlingame, 24 November 1915, Scribner MS, Box 57, Folder 1.

3. DSF to John Stewart Bryan, 25 November 1913, DSF MSS, Container 4; John Stewart Bryan noted in his diary of July 13, 1914, that "Douglas Freeman came to the News Leader today." M. T. McClenahan, "Manuscript," 31.

4. *Richmond News Leader*, 27 October 1914.

5. *Richmond News Leader*, 25 August 1914.

6. Martin Gilbert, *The First World War* (New York: Henry Holt & Co., 1994), 55-73; John Terraine, *To Win a War: 1918, The Year of Victory* (New York: Doubleday & Company, Inc., 1981), xv.

7. *Richmond News Leader*, 1, 4 September; 2 October 1914.

8. *Richmond News Leader*, 28 August 1914.

9. Ibid.

10. *Richmond News Leader*, 8 September 1914.

11. Ibid.

12. *Richmond News Leader*, 8 October 1914.

13. *Richmond News Leader*, 28 October 1914.

14. Ibid.

15. *Richmond News Leader*, 16 September 1914.

16. *Richmond News Leader*, 11 September 1914.

17. *Richmond News Leader*, 16 September 1914.

18. *Richmond News Leader*, 28, 30, September 1914.

19. DSF to Ralph Habas, 30 March 1945, DSF MSS, Container 62.

20. DSF to Steve Early, 8 September 1939, DSF MSS, Container 29.

21. "John Stewart Bryan, 72, Publisher, William & Mary Chancellor, Is Dead," *Richmond Times-Dispatch*, 17 October 1944, 1, 12; "John Stewart Bryan's Rites Wednesday at 11," *Richmond News Leader*, 17 October 1944, 1, 11.

22. Dunford, *Richmond Times-Dispatch*, 5.

23. "News Leader Served by Four Editors since Consolidation," *Richmond News Leader*, 26 July 1924, 18.

24. It is impossible to fix a certain date for Freeman's appointment. No correspondence has been found in any collections memorializing the event. Freeman wrote in his resignation letter that he "became editor without any public announcement." DSF to D. Tennant Bryan, 3 May 1949, DSF MSS, Container 95. A *News Leader* financial report, printed in the edition of March 1, 1915, contains the first listing of DSF as editor.

25. DSF to Inez G. Freeman, 24 September 1915, MTM MSS.

26. DSF, "The Library of the Richmond News Leader," c. 1932, DSF MSS, Container 15; DSF to Col. W. S. Copeland, 28 July 1927, DSF MSS, Container 10.

27. DSF to John Stewart Bryan, 18 March 1921, DSF MSS, Container 5.

28. Ibid.

29. DSF to John Stewart Bryan, 25 November 1913, DSF MSS, Container 4.

30. DSF to Henry C. Riely, 21 June 1920, DSF MSS, Container 8.

31. DSF to John Stewart Bryan, 25 November 1913, DSF MSS, Container 4.

32. DSF to Ralph Habas, 30 March 1945, DSF MSS, Container 62.

33. DSF, "Publicity and the Public Mind," Address delivered to the Seventy-first Annual Meeting of the American Medico-Psychological Association, *American Journal of Insanity*, Vol. LXXII, No. 1 (July 1915), 18-19.

34. Ibid., 31.

35. Ibid., 20-26.

36. Ibid., 31-32.

37. Mary Tyler McClenahan, Interview with author, 4 June 2001.

38. DSF to Inez G. Freeman, 26 September 1915, MTM MSS.

39. DSF to Inez G. Freeman, 28 September 1915, MTM MSS.

40. DSF to Inez G. Freeman, 27 September 1915, MTM MSS; Minutes, *News Leader* Current Events Class, 24 September 1931, DSF MSS, Container 176; Minutes, *News Leader* Current Events Class, 15 June 1953, MTM MSS.

41. DSF to Inez G. Freeman, 25 September 1915, MTM MSS.

42. Minutes, *News Leader* Current Events Class, 24 September 1931, DSF MSS, Container 176; 23 September 1918, DSF MSS, Container 177. There are conflicting reports of the exact date that the current events class came into existence. The minutes of September 24, 1931, quote Freeman as saying the class developed "soon" after the economics class of 1914. The minutes of June 15, 1953, place the start of the class in 1916. The minutes of September 23, 1918, purport to be the minutes of the organizational meeting. What is clear is that Freeman taught an economics class in late 1914 and early 1915, a class on public speaking concurrent with and subsequent to the economics class, and that the speaking class in turn became the current events class by 1918.

43. See *Richmond News Leader*, 8, 12, 13, 14, 16, 18, 20, 21, 22, 23, 25, 27, 29, 30 January; 1, 2, 3, 5, 8, February 1915.

44. *Richmond News Leader*, 3 April 1915.

45. Ibid.

46. *Richmond News Leader*, 9 April 1915.

47. *Richmond News Leader*, 3 June 1915.

48. Ibid.

49. "Poll by Digest Is Inaccurate, Freeman says," *Richmond News Leader*, 31 October 1936.

50. *Richmond News Leader*, 25 February 1915. See Arthur S. Link, "Woodrow Wilson: The American as Southerner," *The Journal of Southern History*, Vol. XXXVI (February 1970), 3-17.

51. *Richmond News Leader*, 12 February 1915.

52. *Richmond News Leader*, 8 May 1915.

53. Ibid.

54. *Richmond News Leader*, 10 May 1915.

55. *Richmond News Leader*, 13 May 1915.

56. *Richmond News Leader*, 12 July 1915.

57. *Richmond News Leader*, 4 January 1916.

58. Ibid. True to form, this combative editorial was followed the next day with

a tribute to Wilson. *Richmond News Leader*, 5 January 1916.

59. DSF, "An Appraisal for John Stewart Bryan of the Situation, September 28, 1940," DSF MSS, Container 35.

60. Ibid.

61. DSF to Maurice Van Schalshar, 16 February 1937, DSF MSS, Container 34; DSF, "Foreword," *R. E. Lee*, Vol. I (New York: Charles Scribner's Sons, 1934), vii.

62. DSF to Louis V. Naisawald, 2 July 1946, DSF MSS, Container 71; DSF to Charles L. Friend, 4 February 1947, DSF MSS, Container 78; DSF to John H. Devlin, Jr., 20 April 1936, DSF MSS, Container 22. It is impossible to determine exactly when Freeman decided to write a larger biography of Lee. In his letters to Naisawald and Friend, he places the idea as coming almost immediately after starting his research. He wrote Devlin that it occurred to him after "a short time." Future letters with Scribner's Publishing tend to endorse the idea that he had it in his mind to do a large work almost from the beginning of the project.

63. DSF, "Adventures in Biography: The New Horizons," The Gueinsey Moore Lectures at Dartmouth College, 1935-36, DSF MSS, Container 127, 8.

64. Ibid., 9.

65. Ibid.

66. Ibid., 10.

67. Ibid., 21.

68. Ibid., 22-23.

69. Ibid., 23-24.

70. DSF to E. L. Burlingame, 13 June 1919, DSF MSS, Container 5.

71. DSF, "Introduction," *R .E. Lee*, Vol. I, ix.

72. DSF, "Confidential Foreword," DSF MSS, Container 242.

73. The Democratic nominee for president carried Virginia in every election from 1876 to 1948, with the exception of Herbert Hoover in 1928. Virginia did not elect a Republican governor until 1969.

74. *Richmond News Leader*, 8 June 1916.

75. *Richmond News Leader*, 14 June 1916.

76. Ibid.

77. *Richmond News Leader*, 4 November 1916.

78. *Richmond News Leader*, 14 June 1916.

79. *Richmond News Leader*, 14 October 1916.

80. *Richmond News Leader*, 2 August 1916.

81. Ibid.

82. *Richmond News Leader*, 6 November 1916.

83. Heckscher, *Woodrow Wilson*, 415.

84. DSF, "John Stewart Bryan," 286.

85. *Richmond News Leader*, 8 November 1916.

86. *Richmond News Leader*, 10 November 1916. Wilson carried 67 percent of the vote in Virginia in the 1916 election, while carrying just less than 50 percent nationwide.

87. DSF to Inez G. Freeman, 5 December 1916, MTM MSS.
88. Ibid.
89. DSF, "Note to Inez G. Freeman," December 1916, MTM MSS.
90. Heckscher, *Woodrow Wilson*, 426-29.
91. *Richmond News Leader*, 1 February 1917.
92. Ibid.
93. *Richmond News Leader*, 5 February 1917.
94. *Richmond News Leader*, 13 February 1917.
95. *Richmond News Leader*, 3 April 1917; "The old boy doesn't make up his mind rapidly," Allen Freeman wrote his brother about Wilson, "but when he moves, look out." Allen W. Freeman to DSF, 8 April 1917, MTM MSS.
96. *Richmond News Leader*, 3 April 1917.
97. *Richmond News Leader*, 6 April 1917.
98. Ibid.
99. Ibid.
100. M. T. McClenahan, "Manuscript," 36-37.
101. DSF to Mary Tyler Freeman, 5 April 1934, MTM MSS.
102. J. C. Wise to W. E. Dame, 14 May 1917, DSF MSS, Container 121.
103. "Judge Hundley to Cite Editor of *News Leader*," *Richmond News Leader*, 22 September 1917, 1; "Hundley to Cite Richmond Editor," *Richmond Times-Dispatch*, 23 September 1917, 1, 4.
104. Ibid; "More Conflicting Statements Concerning Procedure in the Case of Negro Youth Barrett," *Richmond News Leader*, 29 August 1917, 1; *Richmond News Leader*, 31 August 1917, 4; DSF to S. Gordon Cumming, 1 November 1917, Douglas Southall Freeman Papers (#5220), The Albert H. Small Special Collections Library, University of Virginia Library (hereafter DSF UVA), Box 5.
105. DSF to S. Gordon Cumming, 1 November 1917, DSF UVA, Box 5..
106. *Richmond News Leader*, 28 August 1917.
107. Ibid.
108. *Richmond News Leader*, 29 August 1917, 1.
109. Ibid., 4.
110. "Elder Barrett Pays Death Penalty," *Richmond News Leader*, 31 August 1917, 1.
111. *Richmond News Leader*, 30 August 1917.
112. *Richmond News Leader*, 31 August 1917.
113. Ibid.
114. A. D. Watkins to the *Richmond News Leader*, 7 September 1917, DSF UVA, Box 5; DSF to A. D. Watkins, 10 September 1917, DSF UVA, Box 5. Prosecuting attorneys in Virginia are called "commonwealth's attorneys."
115. "Mr. Watkins Discusses Court's Discretion," *Richmond News Leader*, 11 September 1917, 4.
116. *Richmond News Leader*, 11 September 1917.
117. Ibid.

118. A. D. Watkins to the *Richmond News Leader*, 18 September 1917, DSF UVA, Box 5.

119. DSF to A. D. Watkins, 19 September 1917, DSF UVA, Box 5.

120. Ibid.

121. "Aubrey Barrett Writ Refused by Supreme Court," *Richmond News Leader*, 15 September 1917, 1.

122. *Richmond News Leader*, 15 September 1917, 1.

123. Ibid.

124. M. Milton Tolkin to DSF, 22 September 1917, DSF UVA, Box 5.

125. Algernon B. Chandler to DSF, 24 September 1917; William J. Schiner to DSF, 3 October 1917, DSF UVA, Box 5.

126. DSF to S. Gordon Cumming, 1 November 1917, DSF UVA, Box 5.

127. "Demurrer, Motion to Dismiss, and Answer of Douglas Southall Freeman," 5 November 1917, DSF UVA, Box 5.

128. DSF to R. H. Pitt, 16 November 1917, DSF UVA, Box 5.

129. *Richmond News Leader*, 7 November 1917.

130. Ibid. Judge Hundley persisted in attempting to get the *News Leader* to print his opinion from the case, but Freeman was finished with the matter. Murray M. McGuire to A. D. Watkins, 12 November 1917, DSF UVA, Box 5; George Hundley to the *Richmond News Leader*, 8, 10 November 1917; DSF to George Hundley, 10 November 1917, DSF UVA, Box 5; Records, Virginia Department of Corrections, Greensville Correctional Center.

131. E. L. Burlingame to DSF, 5 January 1918, DSF MSS, Container 5.

132. DSF to E. L. Burlingame, 15 January 1918, DSF MSS, Container 5.

133. E. L. Burlingame to DSF, 19 January 1918, DSF MSS, Container 5.

134. E. L. Burlingame to DSF, 10 May 1918, DSF MSS, Container 5.

135. E. L. Burlingame to DSF, 25 June 1918, DSF MSS, Container 5.

136. DSF to E. L. Burlingame, 8 July 1918, DSF MSS, Container 5.

137. E. L. Burlingame to DSF, 11 July 1918, DSF MSS, Container 5.

138. DSF to E. L. Burlingame, 16 July 1918, DSF MSS, Container 5.

139. E. L. Burlingame to DSF, 18 December 1918, DSF MSS, Container 5.

140. DSF to E. L. Burlingame, 19 December 1918, DSF MSS, Container 5.

141. DSF to Dr. B. S. Warren, 1 May 1919, DSF MSS, Container 8.

142. DSF to E. L. Burlingame, 13 June 1919, DSF MSS, Container 5.

143. DSF to John Devlin, 20 April 1936, DSF MSS, Container 22.

144. DSF to M. Van Schalshar, 16 February 1937, DSF MSS, Container 34.

145. Anne B. Freeman, "Introduction," "Bedford Freemans."

146. Dr. John S. Ashworth, son of Freeman's research associate Mary Wells Ashworth, tells of his being asked by Freeman to burn "a stack of papers." Eager to please Dr. Freeman, young Ashworth did a thorough job and did not take the time to examine what he was burning. He recalled that it took "a week" to burn the papers. Given that so many of Freeman's writings have survived in various collections, it is possible that Freeman was destroying his early writings, perhaps including an early manuscript of *R. E. Lee*. This is pure speculation, but

one wonders what papers could have been so voluminous to take so much time to burn. Dr. John S. Ashworth, Interview with author, 8 February 2001.

147. *Richmond News Leader*, 25, 27 April; 20 June; 18 October 1917.

148. *Richmond News Leader*, 27 October 1917.

149. *Richmond News Leader*, 12 June 1918.

150. *Richmond News Leader*, 24 June 1918.

151. Terraine, *To Win a War*, 43-45; David F. Trask, *The AEF and Coalition War Making, 1917-1918* (Lawrence: University of Kansas Press, 1993), 46-49. *Kaiserschlacht* is translated "emperor battle to end the war."

152. *Richmond News Leader*, 23 March 1918.

153. Ibid.

154. *Richmond News Leader*, 25 March 1918.

155. *Richmond News Leader*, 4 April 1918. The James River runs through the city of Richmond, and Oregon and Libby Hills are located in the city.

156. *Richmond News Leader*, 4 April 1918.

157. Trask, *The AEF and Coalition War Making*, 52; Gilbert, *The First World War*, 412.

158. DSF, "Undated Memo," DSF MSS, Container 238.

159. *Richmond News Leader*, 19 July 1918.

160. *Richmond News Leader*, 7 September 1918.

161. Ibid.

162. *Richmond News Leader*, 20 September 1918.

163. *Richmond News Leader*, 29 October 1918.

164. *Richmond News Leader*, 11 November 1918.

CHAPTER SIX

1. *Richmond News Leader*, 11 November 1918.

2. *Richmond News Leader*, 15 November 1918.

3. David Jacobs, "Warren G. Harding," in *The American Heritage Book of Presidents*, Vol. 9 (New York: Dell Publishing Co., 1967), 774.

4. E. L. Burlingame to DSF, 21 June 1919; DSF to E. L. Burlingame, 22 September 1920, DSF MSS, Container 5.

5. DSF, *R. E. Lee*, Vol. IV, 549-50.

6. Ibid., 533, 552, 556.

7. Anne Freeman, "Introduction," "Bedford Freemans."

8. DSF to Louis Towley, 5 June 1943, DSF MSS, Container 52.

9. DSF to E. L. Burlingame, 13 June 1919, DSF MSS, Container 5.

10. Maxwell E. Perkins to DSF, 22 January 1923, DSF MSS, Container 7.

11. DSF to Maxwell E. Perkins, 1 February 1923, DSF MSS, Container 7.

12. Ibid.

13. Ibid.

14. Maxwell E. Perkins to DSF, 3 February 1923, DSF MSS, Container 7.

15. Ibid. Perkins's biographer, A. Scott Berg, writes that Perkins had developed this plan for a full study of Lee from the beginning of his involvement with the project. He "would postpone the appearance of Dr. Freeman's work for another

decade but might ensure its place for centuries." A. Scott Berg, *Max Perkins: Editor of Genius* (New York: E. P. Dutton, 1978), 76.

16. DSF to Maxwell E. Perkins, 5 February 1923; Maxwell E. Perkins to DSF, 7 February 1923, DSF MSS, Container 7.

17. DSF, "Undated Memo," c. 1927-30, DSF MSS, Container 10.

18. DSF to Fairfax Harrison, 2 December 1927, DSF MSS, Container 11.

19. "Directing Heads of Three Departments," *Richmond News Leader*, 26 July 1924.

20. DSF to John Stewart Bryan, 18 March 1921, DSF MSS, Container 5.

21. DSF to E. Lee Trinkle, 9 January 1925, DSF MSS, Container 8.

22. E. Lee Trinkle to DSF, 10 January 1925, DSF MSS, Container 8.

23. Part of Trinkle's angst stemmed from the *News Leader*'s endorsement of his opponent in the 1921 Democratic primary for governor.

24. DSF to Harry F. Byrd, 28 June 1926; Harry F. Byrd to DSF, 29 June 1926, DSF MSS, Container 5.

25. DSF to Miss Virginia Withers, 15 November 1922, DSF MSS, Container 8.

26. Ibid.

27. Minutes, *News Leader* Current Events Class, 12 February 1923, 5, DSF MSS, Container 177.

28. Ibid.

29. DSF to Virginia Withers, 15 November 1922, DSF MSS, Container 8.

30. Minutes, *News Leader* Current Events Class, 12 February 1923, DSF MSS, Container 177.

31. DSF to Virginia Withers, 15 November 1922, DSF MSS, Container 8.

32. Minutes, *News Leader* Current Events Class, 12 February 1923, DSF MSS, Container 177.

33. DSF to Henry C. Riely, 23 June 1920, DSF MSS, Container 8; DSF to Maj. Richard F. Beirne, 30 March 1928, DSF MSS, Container 9.

34. *Richmond News Leader*, 3 October 1923.

35. Ibid.

36. DSF, "Memorandum to John Stewart Bryan Regarding Neighborhood Nights," 10 May 1923, DSF MSS, Container 5.

37. DSF, "Memorandum on the Public Service of the News Leader in 1928," n/d, DSF MSS, Container 9.

38. Ibid.

39. Ibid.

40. DSF, "Memorandum for the Publisher," 2 December 1922, DSF MSS, Container 5; DSF to John Stewart Bryan, 4 December 1928, DSF MSS, Container 9.

41. "Statement of Ownership," *Richmond News Leader*, 3 October 1922, 4.

42. "Summary of Answers to Questionnaires Returned, July-September 1925," DSF MSS, Container 5. The top finishers in this unscientific poll were as follows: Editorials 31 percent; "All" 9 percent; Current News 9 percent; Dorothy Dix 9 percent; Sports 8 percent.

43. *Richmond News Leader*, 1 January 1923, 4.
44. Ibid.
45. DSF to D. Tennant Bryan, 14 September 1952, DSF MSS, Container 109.
46. *Richmond Times-Dispatch*, 30 July 1921, 2.
47. *Richmond News Leader*, 30 July 1921.
48. DSF to John Stewart Bryan, 5 August 1921, DSF MSS, Container 5.
49. Ibid.
50. Ibid.
51. DSF to John Stewart Bryan, 11 August 1921, DSF MSS, Container 5.
52. Ibid.
53. DSF, Diary, 27 April 1907, DSF MSS, Container 1.
54. Ibid. "Summary of Summer," 270-71. The reference to October 1905 is unclear, but the reader will recall that during that period Freeman was involved in a relationship with the unnamed girl that resulted in an apparent broken engagement.
55. No surviving family member has any idea to what this episode could refer. Mary Tyler McClenahan, Interview with author, 24 March 2001; James Douglas Freeman, Interview with author, 31 January 2001.
56. *Richmond News Leader*, 9 August 1920; Walter Lipmann to DSF, 17 August 1920, DSF MSS, Container 7.
57. *Richmond News Leader*, 17 August 1920.
58. Ibid.
59. Ibid.
60. Walter Lipmann to DSF, 17 August 1920, DSF MSS, Container 7.
61. Ibid.
62. DSF to Walter Lipmann, 26 August 1920, DSF MSS, Container 7. Mutt and Jeff was a popular cartoon strip of the day.
63. Ibid.
64. Ibid. Lipmann still sought a public apology, but Freeman let the matter drop. Walter Lipmann to DSF, 31 August 1920, DSF MSS, Container 7.
65. Parker Rouse, Jr., *We Happy WASPs: Virginia in the Days of Jim Crow and Harry Byrd* (Richmond: Dietz Press, 1996), 155. That day across the top of the editorial page was the verse "Except the Lord build the house, they labor in vain that build it." *Richmond News Leader*, 14 July 1924, 4.
66. Charles Henry Hamilton, "The Most Unforgettable Character I've Met," *Readers Digest*, July 1960, 149. Hamilton, the young reporter who misspelled Poe's name, was to become managing editor of the *News Leader*.
67. James J. Kilpatrick, Interview with author, 8 March 2001.
68. DSF, "The News Leader's Twenty Fundamental Rules of News Writing," DSF MSS, Container 98. For the complete list of rules, see Appendix 2, pages 362-63.
69. George Lea to DSF, 8 December 1921, DSF MSS, Container 7.
70. DSF to George Lea, 11 December 1921, DSF MSS, Container 7.
71. Ibid.
72. The business manager of the *News Leader*.

73. George Lea to DSF, 13 December 1921; 16 December 1921, DSF MSS, Container 7.

74. DSF to George Lea, 14 December 1921, DSF MSS, Container 7.

75. Harry F. Byrd to DSF, 24 May 1926; 11 June 1926; DSF to Harry F. Byrd, 14 June 1926, DSF MSS, Container 5.

76. James Davis to DSF, 6 April 1925, DSF MSS, Container 5.

77. *See* DSF to John Stewart Bryan, 26 July 1927; 22 August 1927, DSF MSS, Container 9.

78. "Poll of Members, 1927," DSF MSS, Container 178.

79. Ibid. Religious affiliations were listed as: twenty-seven Episcopalians, nine Baptists, six Presbyterians, five "free lances," [*sic*] one Unitarian, and one Lutheran. Freeman, of course, was a Baptist newspaperman from the University of Richmond.

80. The Westmoreland Club was the location in the early days of the club; the Commonwealth Club for the majority of years.

81. Minutes, *News Leader* Current Events Class, 14 February 1921, DSF MSS, Container 177.

82. Minutes, *News Leader* Current Events Class, 9 May 1921, DSF MSS, Container 177.

83. Ibid.

84. Minutes, *News Leader* Current Events Class, 7 March 1921, DSF MSS, Container 177.

85. DSF to H. D. C. MacLachlan, 12 March 1920, DSF MSS, Container 7.

86. DSF to Mrs. R. L. Chenery, 5 April 1921, DSF MSS, Container 5.

87. DSF to Mrs. John R. Jones, 17 June 1925, DSF MSS, Container 6.

88. Ibid.

89. DSF, "Parables of the City Streets," 23 November 1924, DSF MSS, Container 126.

90. DSF, "Parables of the City Streets," 30 November 1924; 29 March 1925; 19 April 1925, DSF MSS, Container 126.

91. DSF, "Parables of the City Streets," 19 April 1925, DSF MSS, Container 126.

92. DSF, "Your Pledge to the Lord," c. 1921-23, DSF MSS, Container 6.

93. DSF, "Parables of the City Streets," 29 March 1925, DSF MSS, Container 126.

94. Ibid.

95. Ibid.

96. Ibid. M. T. McClenahan, "Manuscript," 39.

97. M. T. McClenahan, "Manuscript," 41; DSF to Bettie A. Freeman, 26 May 1906, DSF JHU, Box 2.

98. DSF, "Memorandum on Meeting with David Lloyd George," 28 October 1923, DSF MSS, Container 244; Minutes, *News Leader* Current Events Class, 17 October 1927, DSF MSS, Container 178; *R. E. Lee*, Vol. IV, 532; Program, "Dinner Given in Honor of Col. Charles A. Lindbergh," 15 October 1927, MTM MSS.

99. *Richmond News Leader*, 24 November 1921.

100. DSF to Mary Tyler Freeman, 23 November 1921, MTM MSS.

101. Ibid.

102. DSF to George C. Marshall, 29 February 1924; George C. Marshall to DSF, 28 February 1924, DSF MSS, Container 121. Freeman saved Marshall's letter and noted at the top that it showed "how thorough a great soldier was even when Lieutenant Col., ADC."

103. DSF to Ralph Habas, 30 March 1945, DSF MSS, Container 62; DSF to Edward S. Whitlock, 29 May 1951, DSF MSS, Container 108.

104. M. T. McClenahan, "Manuscript," 62.

105. DSF to Ralph Habas, 30 March 1945, DSF MSS, Container 62.

106. DSF to J. O. Freeman, 19 August 1926; DSF to Herbert W. Jackson, 21 January 1926, DSF MSS, Container 6.

107. "WRVA Program Listing," 7 February 1927, DSF papers, Virginia Baptist Historical Society. Harry M. Ward, "Douglas Southall Freeman: A Historian's Overview," in *Douglas Southall Freeman: Reflections by His Daughter, His Research Associate, and a Historian*, 27.

108. DSF to Mrs. A. L. Smith, 25 November 1932, DSF MSS, Container 20; DSF to Herbert Bruckner, 19 January 1942, DSF MSS, Container 41.

109. DSF to Inez G. Freeman, 1 September 1932, MTM MSS.

110. "WRNL Begins Broadcasting This Afternoon," *Richmond Times-Dispatch*, 14 November 1937.

111. *Richmond News Leader*, 31 December 1919.

112. *Richmond News Leader*, 10 January 1919.

113. *Richmond News Leader*, 4 March 1919.

114. *Richmond News Leader*, 18 November 1919; *see also* 17 November 1919.

115. *Richmond News Leader*, 20 November 1919.

116. *Richmond News Leader*, 19 March 1920.

117. *Richmond News Leader*, 8 January 1920.

118. Heckscher, *Woodrow Wilson*, 613.

119. *Richmond News Leader*, 14 February 1920.

120. *Richmond News Leader*, 4 March 1921.

121. Ibid. Time did not alter Freeman's attitude about Wilson. He wrote another full-page editorial on the occasion of Wilson's death in 1924 and, as late as 1945, referred to Wilson as "one of the heroes of my youth." *Richmond News Leader*, 4 February 1924; DSF to Henry D. Gideonse, 6 November 1945, DSF MSS, Container 64.

122. *Richmond News Leader*, 11 March 1916.

123. *Richmond News Leader*, 31 October 1917.

124. *Richmond News Leader*, 16 December 1919.

125. *Richmond News Leader*, 17 June 1921.

126. DSF to Mary Tyler Freeman, 7 October 1933, MTM MSS.

127. Minutes, *News Leader* Current Events Class, 19 February 1923, DSF MSS, Container 177. Freeman enjoyed an occasional drink and was something

of a wine connoisseur, but Prohibition likely had no personal effect on him.

128. *Richmond News Leader*, 10 June 1919.
129. Ibid.
130. Ibid.
131. *Richmond News Leader*, 18 September 1920.
132. *Richmond News Leader*, 4 June 1923.
133. *Richmond News Leader*, 15 April 1920.
134. DSF to Allen W. Freeman, 30 April 1920, DSF MSS, Container 6.
135. *Richmond News Leader*, 13 April 1920.
136. DSF to Allen W. Freeman, 23 June 1920, DSF MSS, Container 6.
137. *Richmond News Leader*, 14 June 1920.
138. *Richmond News Leader*, 3 November 1920.
139. *Richmond News Leader*, 4 March 1922.
140. *Richmond News Leader*, 20 September 1922.
141. *Richmond News Leader*, 3 November 1920; 31 July 1923.
142. *Richmond News Leader*, 31 July 1923.
143. *Richmond News Leader*, 3 August 1923.
144. *Richmond News Leader*, 11 April 1924.
145. DSF, "Virginia: A Gentle Dominion," *The Nation*, Vol. CXIX (July 16, 1924), 68-71. This is an edited version of Freeman's article. Reprined from Douglas Southall Freemann, "Virginia: A Gentle Dominion," in *These United States: Portraits of American from the 1920s*, David H. Borus (ed.) (Ithaca, New York: Cornell University Press, 1992), 374-81.
146. DSF, "A Gentle Dominion," 374.
147. Ibid., 375.
148. Ibid., 378.
149. Ibid., 378-79.
150. Ibid., 379.
151. Ibid., 380.
152. Ibid., 381.
153. DSF to Fairfax Harrison, 20 December 1923, DSF MSS, Container 6.
154. DSF, "A Gentle Dominion," 379.
155. DSF to Maxwell E. Perkins, 18 January 1924, DSF MSS, Container 7.
156. DSF to Maxwell E. Perkins, 15 April 1925, DSF MSS, Container 7.
157. DSF to Maxwell E. Perkins, 12 August 1925, DSF MSS, Container 7.
158. Maxwell E. Perkins to DSF, 5 May 1924; 13 May 1924; 22 May 1924; DSF to Maxwell E. Perkins, 8 May 1924; 19 May 1924; 23 May 1924, DSF MSS, Container 7. The articles, "Lee and the Ladies," were published in successive editions of *Scribner's Magazine*, Vol. LXXVII, No. 4 (October 1925), 339; Vol. XXVII, No. 5 (November 1925), 459.
159. DSF to Howard D. Bryant, 12 January 1921, DSF MSS, Container 5.
160. Ibid.
161. DSF to Maxwell E. Perkins, 25 January 1928, DSF MSS, Container 13; DSF to Inez Freeman, 6 July 1933, MTM MSS.

162. DSF to Maxwell E. Perkins, 18 January 1926, DSF MSS, Container 7.
163. DSF, *R. E. Lee* Drafts, DSF MSS, Container 133; DSF to Maxwell E. Perkins, 20 March 1928, DSF MSS, Container 13.
164. Maxwell E. Perkins to DSF, 23 April 1928, DSF MSS, Container 13. Perkins was off in his prediction; the final manuscript exceeded one million words.
165. DSF to G. T. Lee, 2 August 1928, DSF MSS, Container 12; DSF to Maxwell E. Perkins, 1 November 1928, DSF MSS, Container 13.
166. DSF to Maxwell E. Perkins, 16 May 1929, DSF MSS, Container 13.
167. Ibid.
168. M. T. McClenahan, "Manuscript," 71-72.
169. DSF, *R. E. Lee*, Vol. I, 214. Freeman recorded the precise spot where he finished writing before his illness. In autographing a copy of *R. E. Lee* for Dr. Ashworth, he drew a line across the middle of page 214 in Volume One, following the referenced sentence, and wrote that he "would never have written another" were it not for Dr. Ashworth's diagnosis. Mary Wells Ashworth Papers.
170. M. T. McClenahan, "Manuscript," 72.
171. Mary Tyler McClenahan, Interview with author, 4 June 2001.
172. DSF to Mrs. M. B. Graves, 22 May 1930, DSF MSS, Container 13.
173. DSF to Inez G. Freeman, 11 July 1933, MTM MSS.
174. DSF to Edward S. Whitlock, 29 May 1951, DSF MSS, Container 108.
175. DSF to Brantley Henderson, 11 August 1947, DSF MSS, Container 78.
176. DSF to D. F. Houston, 9 December 1929, DSF MSS, Container 11.
177. DSF, "A Note to Maxwell Perkins," DSF MSS, Container 12; DSF to Maxwell E. Perkins, 15 March 1930, DSF MSS, Container 13.
178. DSF, "Note to Perkins." As it turned out, Lee's war years consumed eleven chapters of Volume One, all of Volumes Two and Three, and the first eleven chapters of Volume Four.
179. Ibid.
180. Ibid.
181. Ibid.
182. Ibid.
183. DSF to Mrs. Hunter deButts, 4 January 1930, DSF MSS, Container 10.
184. DSF to George Bolling Lee, 21 November 1929, DSF MSS, Container 12.
185. DSF to Mrs. Hunter deButts, 26 December 1929, DSF MSS, Container 10.
186. Mrs. Hunter deButts to DSF, 2 January 1930, DSF MSS, Container 10.
187. DSF to Mrs. Hunter deButts, 4 January 1930, DSF MSS, Container 10.
188. DSF to Mrs. Hunter deButts, 18 February 1930; Mrs. Hunter deButts to DSF, 25 February 1930, DSF MSS, Container 10.
189. *See* C. Carter Lee to DSF, 25 July 1930, DSF MSS, Container 12; 30 January 1933; 7 February 1933, Container 18; DSF to Fairfax Harrison, 21 July 1933, Container 17.
190. DSF to Fairfax Harrison, 21 July 1933, DSF MSS, Container 17.

191. Mrs. Hunter deButts to DSF, 27 April 1932; DSF to Mrs. Hunter deButts, 28 April 1932, DSF MSS, Container 16.

192. "I encountered only three individuals . . . possessing Lee papers that did not cheerfully permit their use." DSF, *R. E. Lee*, Vol. I, viii. "Mrs. Hanson Ely and Mrs. Hunter deButts, daughters of Captain Robert E. Lee, permitted the writer to verify references in the Lee Papers at the Library of Congress." *R. E. Lee*, Vol. IV, 533. Mrs. Ely was Mrs. deButts's sister and had ownership interest in the letters as well, but deferred to Mrs. deButts on questions regarding use of the letters. Other family members had supported Freeman's efforts and seemed genuinely embarrassed by Mrs. deButts's actions. "Since reading the first volume," C. Carter Lee wrote Freeman, "I have regretted very much the attitude of some of my relatives in not co-operating with you." C. C. Lee to DSF, 2 October 1934, DSF MSS, Container 24.

193. DSF, *R. E. Lee*, Vol. II, 158.

194. DSF, *R. E. Lee*, Vol. I, xiv; Vol. II, 230-31.

195. DSF to Inez G. Freeman, 26 June 1931, MTM MSS.

196. DSF, *R. E. Lee*, Vol. II, 335.

197. DSF, *R. E. Lee*, Vol. II, 523-24.

198. DSF to J. B. Brown, 6 November 1939, DSF MSS, Container 28.

199. DSF, *R. E. Lee*, Vol. III, 125-28.

200. DSF to Maxwell E. Perkins, 19 January 1933, DSF MSS, Container 19.

CHAPTER SEVEN

1. DSF, Diary, 10 December 1933, DSF MSS, Container 1; Mary Wells Ashworth, "Calendar of DSF Historical Works," DSF MSS, Container 123.

2. DSF to G. T. Lee, 24 September 1928, DSF MSS, Container 12; DSF to Maxwell E. Perkins, 17 October 1933, DSF MSS, Container 19. Freeman estimated he spent $4,000 in cash and "$75,000 in time" on *R. E. Lee*.

3. DSF, "Confidential Foreword," DSF MSS, Container 242.

4. Ibid.

5. DSF to Isabel Patterson, 30 January 1935, DSF MSS, Container 25.

6. DSF to Maxwell E. Perkins, 8 December 1924, DSF MSS, Container 7.

7. DSF, *R. E. Lee*, Vol. IV, 166-67.

8. Ibid., 168.

9. Ibid.

10. Ibid., 168-69.

11. Ibid., 169.

12. Ibid., 169-70. Freeman lists Lee's victories as: Gaines's Mill, Second Manassas, Fredericksburg, Chancellorsville, The Wilderness, and Spotsylvania. Gettysburg is the sole loss, with Frayser's Farm, Malvern Hill, and Sharpsburg indecisive.

13. Ibid., 175.

14. Ibid., 181-82.

15. Ibid., 185.

16. Ibid., 187.
17. DSF to Mrs. W. A. Shepherd, 9 December 1950, DSF MSS, Container 102.
18. DSF to Murdock Pemberton, 31 October 1923, DSF MSS, Container 7.
19. DSF to Dr. N. W. Stephenson, 19 October 1926, DSF MSS, Container 8.
20. DSF to Katharine Johnson, 16 December 1936, DSF MSS, Container 23.
21. DSF, *R. E. Lee*, Vol. IV, 494.
22. Ibid.
23. Ibid., 493-505.
24. Ibid., 505.
25. DSF, "Draft of *R. E. Lee*," 128-21, DSF MSS, Container 38.
26. DSF, *R. E. Lee*, IV, 585; DSF, "Draft of *R. E. Lee*," 128-21.
27. Charles Willis Thompson, "Robert E. Lee: A Final Portrait," *The New York Times Book Review*, 14 October 1934, 1.
28. Ibid., 1, 14.
29. Charles Willis Thompson, "Dr. Freeman Concludes his Monumental Life of Lee," *The New York Times Book Review*, 10 February 1935, 1.
30. Stephen Vincent Benet, "Great General, Greater Man: Robert E. Lee," *New York Herald Tribune*, Books, 10 February 1935, 1.
31. Ibid., 1-2.
32. Stephen Vincent Benet to DSF, September 1934, DSF MSS, Container 21.
33. Allen Tate, "The Definitive Lee," *The New Republic*, 19 December 1934, 171.
34. Ibid. *See also* Allen Tate, "Robert E. Lee Complete," *The New Republic*, 10 April 1935, 225.
35. Henry Steele Commager, "New Books in Review: The Life of Lee," *The Yale Review*, Vol. XXIV, No. 3 (March 1935), 594.
36. Dumas Malone, "Review of *R. E. Lee*," *American Historical Review*, Vol. XL, No. 3 (April 1935), 534.
37. Dumas Malone, "Review of *R. E. Lee*," *American Historical Review*, Vol. XLI, No. 1 (October 1935), 164.
38. Dumas Malone, "The Pen of Douglas Southall Freeman," in *George Washington*, Vol. 6, xviii -xix.
39. "Untitled Document," DSF MSS, Container 24. It is unclear if Freeman prepared this summary or if it was provided to him by Scribner's. It could also have been prepared years later by Mary Wells Ashworth and placed in an earlier file.
40. Basil Liddell Hart, "Lee: a Psychological Problem," *Saturday Review of Literature*, Vol. 1 (15 December 1934), 1. This was nothing new for Liddell Hart, who for many years had criticized professional military men for studying Lee's operations in the Eastern Theater of war at the expense of the Western Theater. His ideal commander was Union general William T. Sherman. Thomas Connelly, *The Marble Man: Robert E. Lee and His Image in American Society* (New York: Alfred Knopf, 1977), 154.

41. Liddell Hart, "Lee: a Psychological Problem," 367.

42. Ibid.

43. Basil Liddell Hart, "Why Lee Lost Gettysburg," *Saturday Review of Literature*, Vol. XI (23 March 1935), 1, 569.

44. Winston Churchill to DSF, 3 November 1934, DSF MSS, Container 22.

45. David Lloyd George to DSF, 8 November 1934, DSF MSS, Container 24.

46. Ellen Glasgow to DSF, 3 February 1935, DSF MSS, Container 23.

47. Margaret Mitchell Marsh to DSF, 13 October 1936, DSF MSS, Container 24.

48. DSF to Margaret Mitchell Marsh, 15 October 1936, DSF MSS, Container 24.

49. DSF to Col. Wilson B. Burtt, 6 June 1935, DSF MSS, Container 21.

50. Col. Wilson B. Burtt to DSF, 3 June 1935, DSF MSS, Container 21.

51. Douglas MacArthur to DSF, 15 November 1934, DSF MSS, Container 24.

52. Ibid.

53. DSF to Douglas MacArthur, 17 November 1934, DSF MSS, Container 24.

54. Stuart W. Smith, ed., *Douglas Southall Freeman: On Leadership* (Shippensburg, PA: White Mane Publishing Co., 1993), 61. Freeman also delivered lectures at the Naval War College. Freeman's relationships with military leaders is discussed on pages 270-73.

55. Gignilliat, "Freeman," 161.

56. DSF to Mary Tyler Freeman, 25 February 1935, MTM MSS. *See also* DSF to Carl W. Ackerman, 23 February 1935, DSF MSS, Container 21, in which Freeman makes a similar observation about the Pulitzer Prize.

57. Philip M. Hayden to DSF, 6 May 1935, DSF MSS, Container 25.

58. "Dr. Freeman's 'R. E. Lee' Awarded Pulitzer Prize," *Richmond Times-Dispatch*, 7 May 1935, 1, 4.

59. DSF, "Draft Statement on Receipt of Pulitzer Prize," DSF MSS, Container 24.

60. Ibid.

61. "Three of Pulitzer Literary Awards Given to Women," *Richmond News Leader*, 7 May 1935, 1, 10.

62. DSF to Bettie A. Freeman, 14 May 1905, DSF JHU, Box 1.

63. Minutes, *News Leader* Current Events Class, 24 May 1926, DSF MSS, Container 176.

64. DSF to Carter Glass, 17 February 1926, DSF MSS, Container 6.

65. "Richmonders Sail for Europe," *Richmond News Leader*, 29 March 1926; "Itinerary," DSF MSS, Container 6.

66. M. T. McClenahan, "Manuscript," 62-63.

67. Minutes, *New Leader* Current Events Class, 24 May 1926, DSF MSS, Container 176.

68. Ibid.

69. DSF to David Lloyd George, 25 May 1926, DSF MSS, Container 7.

70. Ibid.

71. "He was determined that we were going to have good taste," his daughter

recalls about her father's gifts from this trip. Mary Tyler McClenahan, Interview with author, 4 June 2001.

72. M. T. McClenahan, "Manuscript," 63.

73. Minutes, *News Leader* Current Events Class, 24 May 1926, DSF MSS, Container 176.

74. DSF to Inez G. Freeman, 14, 22, 24, 31 March 1929, DSF MSS, Container 121.

75. DSF to Mrs. T. R. Handy, 13 June 1927, DSF MSS, Container 11.

76. DSF to Alfred E. Smith, 11 August 1928, DSF MSS, Container 13.

77. Minutes, *News Leader* Current Events Class, 24 September 1928, DSF MSS, Container 178.

78. Ibid.

79. DSF to Allen J. Saville, 22 September 1928, DSF MSS, Container 13.

80. Minutes, *News Leader* Current Events Class, 8 October 1928, DSF MSS, Container 176.

81. DSF to J. Marshall Vanneman, 7 September 1928, DSF MSS, Container 14.

82. *Richmond News Leader*, 2 August 1928.

83. *Richmond News Leader*, 5 September 1928.

84. *Richmond News Leader*, 1 November 1928.

85. *Richmond News Leader*, 5 November 1928.

86. Ibid.

87. *Richmond News Leader*, 1 September 1928.

88. *Richmond News Leader*, 5 November 1928.

89. Ibid.

90. Fairfax Harrison to DSF, 7 November 1928; DSF to Fairfax Harrison, 8 November 1928, DSF MSS, Container 11.

91. DSF to Bettie A. Freeman, 23 March 1905, DSF JHU, Box 1.

92. M. T. McClenahan, "My Father as a Writer," 36-37.

93. H. H. Hibb, Jr. to DSF, 27 July 1927, DSF MSS, Container 11; DSF, "Arrangement with William & Mary," undated, DSF MSS, Container 11.

94. W. C. Griggs to DSF, 7 March 1928, DSF MSS, Container 11.

95. DSF to W. C. Griggs, 10 March 1928, DSF MSS, Container 11.

96. DSF to W. C. Griggs, 22 March 1928, DSF MSS, Container 11.

97. DSF to William M. Brown, 13 December 1928, DSF MSS, Container 8.

98. DSF to F. P. Gaines, 5 June 1933, DSF MSS, Container 17.

99. While Freeman discouraged offers, John Stewart Bryan accepted the presidency of the College of William and Mary in 1934. He continued to serve as publisher of the *News Leader*.

100. DSF, "Memo of Assets," MTM MSS.

101. DSF to Nannie Jones, 13 March 1926, DSF MSS, Container 6; DSF to G. T. Lee, 23 March 1926, DSF MSS, Container 7.

102. M. T. McClenahan, "Manuscript," 58.

103. DSF to R. B. Jordan, 13 October 1926, DSF MSS, Container 6.
104. M. T. McClenahan, "Manuscript," 40, 42-44, 56.
105. Ibid., 62.
106. DSF to Ralph Habas, 31 March 1945, DSF MSS, Container 62.
107. M. T. McClenahan, "Manuscript," 79-80.
108. Ibid., 74.
109. DSF to Inez G. Freeman, 24 July 1930; 14, 25 August 1930; 13, 14, 27 June 1933; 20 July; 7 August 1934, MTM MSS.
110. M. T. McClenahan, "Manuscript," 92; "Associated Press Report," n/d but c. August 1933, MTM MSS.
111. Ibid.
112. DSF to Inez G. Freeman, 23 August 1933, MTM MSS.
113. Royall Turpin, Interview with author, 27 January 2001.
114. James Douglas Freeman, Interview with author, 31 January 2001.
115. DSF to Mary Tyler Freeman, 3 July 1930, MTM MSS.
116. DSF to Anne B. Freeman, 12 August 1936, DSF MSS, Container 22.
117. DSF to James Douglas Freeman, 10 July 1934, MTM MSS.
118. DSF to Herbert E. Hawkes, 25 July 1939, DSF MSS, Container 31.
119. DSF to Louise Bacot, 8 January 1930, DSF MSS, Container 9.
120. DSF to James Douglas Freeman, 13 July 1933, MTM MSS.
121. Anne B. Freeman to DSF, 21 February 1943, MTN MSS.
122. DSF to Anne B. Freeman, 24 February 1943, DSF MSS, Container 49.
123. DSF to James Douglas Freeman, 13 July 1933, MTM MSS.
124. DSF to Mary Tyler Freeman, 16 July 1930, MTM MSS.
125. "Historical Pageant at Old St. John's Church," *Virginia Journal of Education*, Vol. XX, No. 8 (April 1927), 337.
126. "Virginia—A Commonwealth That Has Come Back," *National Geographic*, Vol. LV (April 1929), 409. "My soul was fired with the ardor of the hour," Freeman joked in recounting his performance to a friend, "when that latest installment of the great epic arrived. I think Henry should have included in his speech: 'And when the kleagle sounds his klarion kall, I'm there with the tar and feathers and all'." DSF to Hamilton Owens, 24 March 1927, DSF MSS, Container 120.
127. R. B. White to DSF, 21 November 1929, DSF MSS, Container 14. Although the letter is dated November 21, Freeman notes it was actually November 20.
128. DSF to R. B. White, 21 November 1929, DSF MSS, Container 14.
129. Ibid.
130. DSF to Newton Wanliss, 10 June 1932, DSF MSS, Container 20.
131. DSF to Robert W. Daniel, 28 June 1932, DSF MSS, Container 16.
132. Ibid.; *Richmond News Leader*, 21 June 1932.
133. DSF, *The Last Parade* (Richmond: Whittet & Shepperson, 1932).
134. DSF to Mary Tyler Freeman, 9 February 1935, MTM MSS.

135. Mary Tyler Freeman to DSF, 10 February 1935, MTM MSS.
136. DSF, Diary, 28 August 1943, DSF MSS, Container 1.
137. DSF to Carl Ackerman, 5 February 1934, DSF MSS, Container 21; DSF to Allen W. Freeman, 5 February 1934, DSF MSS, Container 22.
138. DSF to Allen W. Freeman, 9 February 1934, DSF MSS, Container 22.
139. DSF to Mary Tyler Freeman, 11 February 1934, MTM MSS. Freeman expressed the same sentiment in a letter to his former professor at Hopkins, Charles Andrews. DSF to Charles McLean Andrews, 24 May 1934, DSF MSS, Container 21.
140. DSF to Allen W. Freeman, 20 February 1934, DSF MSS, Container 34.
141. Carl Ackerman to DSF, 23 February 1934; 13 March 1934, DSF MSS, Container 21.
142. DSF to Carl Ackerman, 15 March 1934; DSF to John Stewart Bryan, 2 April 1934, DSF MSS, Container 21.
143. DSF to John Stewart Bryan, 2 April 1934; DSF to Carl Ackerman, 5 April 1934; Carl Ackerman to DSF, 10 April 1934; DSF to Carl Ackerman, 12 April 1934, DSF MSS, Container 21. Frank Fackenthal to DSF, 7 May 1934; DSF to Frank Fackenthal, 10 May 1934, DSF MSS, Container 22; DSF to Mary Tyler Freeman, 17 April 1934, MTM MSS.
144. DSF to Carl Ackerman, 17 April 1934, DSF MSS, Container 21; Frank Fackenthal to DSF, 7 May 1934, DSF MSS, Container 22.
145. DSF to Mary Tyler Freeman, 15 October 1934, MTM MSS.
146. M. T. McClenahan, "My Father as a Writer," 38; "Bulletin of Information—Columbia University School of Journalism," 1934-35, Columbia University Library, New York, 29. Freeman's classes were held on Fridays during his first two years at Columbia. They shifted to Monday for the following two years and to Tuesday during his final three years. His traveling schedule was not altered with the change of days. He continued to write the next day's editorials on the day prior to his departure and to take two sleepers.
147. DSF to Mary Tyler Freeman, 20 May; 17 April 1934, MTM MSS; "Bulletin of Information," 1934-35, 29. "The Week" was a column in the *News Leader* summarizing the news of the week and offering analysis and interpretation.
148. DSF to Carl Ackerman, 23 April 1934, DSF MSS, Container 21.
149. Carl Ackerman to DSF, 25 April 1934, DSF MSS, Container 21.
150. DSF to J. C. Pemberton, undated, DSF MSS, Container 39.
151. John R. Mayer to author, 3 January 2001; David Brown, Conversation with author, 3 January 2001.
152. John Tebbel to author, 15 January 2001; Haynes W. Dugan to author, 2 January 2001; Mayer, 3 January 2001; Brown, 3 January 2001; Daniel J. Edelman to author, 17 January 2001.
153. Philip Hamburger to author, 26 December 2000; George R. Metcalf to author, 20 December 2000; Betty Ryan Wolfe to author, n/d, 2000; Brown, 3 January 2001.

154. Leonard Sussman to author, 19 December 2000.
155. Mayer, 3 January 2001.
156. Tebbel, 15 January 2001; Edelman, 17 January 2001; George H. Larson to author, n/d, 2001.
157. Larson, n/d, 2001.
158. Robert Schulman to author, 24 December 2000.
159. Daniel E. Button to author, n/d, c. April 2001.
160. Ibid.
161. Damon M. Stetson to author, 12 March 2001.
162. Tebbel, 15 January 2001.
163. Hope Kimbrough McCroskey to author, 8 January 2001; Sussman, 19 December 2000.
164. Clement David Hellyer to author, 18 December 2000.
165. Schulman, 24 December 2000.
166. Elwood N. Thompson to author, 5 January 2001.
167. Hamburger, 26 December 2000.
168. McCroskey, 8 January 2001; Edelman, 17 January 2001.
169. DSF to Mary Tyler Freeman, 15 October 1934, MTM MSS. "Williamsburg" refers to Eastern State Mental Hospital located in Williamsburg, Virginia.
170. DSF to Herbert Brucker, 28 December 1935, DSF MSS, Container 21.
171. "Bulletin of Information," 1934-35; 1935-36; 1936-37; 1937-38; 1938-39; 1939-40; 1940-41. During his last two years, Freeman taught Editorial Method in the fall and Editorial Technique in the Spring.
172. Ibid.
173. DSF to Carl Ackerman, 13 September 1939, DSF MSS, Container 28.
174. DSF to Carl Ackerman, 27 December 1934; Carl Ackerman to DSF, 21 January 1935, DSF MSS, Container 21.
175. *Richmond News Leader*, 24 October 1929.
176. *Richmond News Leader*, 2, 10 December 1930.
177. *Richmond News Leader*, 1 January 1931. *See* 18 February 1931.
178. *Richmond News Leader*, 14 September 1931; 3, 7 November 1932.
179. *Richmond News Leader*, 25 October 1932.
180. *Richmond News Leader*, 7 November 1932.
181. *Richmond News Leader*, 9 November 1932.
182. *Richmond News Leader*, 7, 10, 17, 29 March 1933.
183. *Richmond News Leader*, 4 April 1933; DSF to W. S. Rhoads, 12 May 1933, DSF MSS, Container 19.
184. DSF to Inez G. Freeman, 4 August 1933, MTM MSS.
185. *Richmond News Leader*, 7 August 1933; 18 May 1933.
186. DSF to Newton Wanliss, 30 August 1933, DSF MSS, Container 20.
187. *Richmond News Leader*, 2 October 1933.
188. DSF to Carter Glass, 16 November 1933, DSF MSS, Container 17; *Richmond News Leader*, 30 October; 14, 16 November 1933.

189. Carter Glass to DSF, 17 November 1933, DSF MSS, Container 17.
190. DSF to Mary Tyler Freeman, 25 November 1933, MTM MSS.
191. *Richmond News Leader*, 20 June 1935.
192. DSF to John Stewart Bryan, 24 June 1935, DSF MSS, Container 21.
193. *Richmond News Leader*, 20 April 1935; *see* 19, 28, 31 January 1935.
194. "New Deal Attack Stirs Mayor's Ire," *New York Times*, 20 July 1935, 14.
195. "LaGuardia, Freeman Debate New Deal at Press Meeting," *Richmond Times-Dispatch*, 20 July 1935,1.
196. Ibid., 3.
197. *New York Times*, 20 July 1935.
198. *Richmond Times-Dispatch*, 20 July 1935, 3.

CHAPTER EIGHT

1. DSF, "Definition of a Liberal," undated note, MTM MSS. It is not clear when Freeman committed this definition to paper. The note is undated. He used this same language in 1952 when asked to define a liberal. DSF to Henry Preston, 24 November 1952, DSF MSS, Container 112.
2. Ibid.
3. There are more than one hundred letters touching on the issue of race scattered throughout Freeman's papers in the Library of Congress.
4. DSF to Colgate Darden, 28 February 1945, DSF MSS, Container 60.
5. *Richmond News Leader*, 15 July 1921.
6. *Richmond News Leader*, 7 September 1928.
7. *Richmond News Leader*, 22 June 1920.
8. Ibid.
9. *Richmond News Leader*, 24 March 1933; *see also* 22 June 1920; 16 March 1921; 13 January 1930.
10. DSF to Julian R. Harris, 3 October 1942, DSF MSS, Container 43.
11. "The most dangerous influence in the South today," he wrote in 1942, "is beyond question that of Mrs. Roosevelt herself. Wherever she goes to fraternize with Negroes, she leaves behind her a cesspool of strife. If only we could gag her, we could hope to endure successfully the hard strain on sane race relations that the war has brought in the South." DSF to Clifton A. Woodrum, 18 December 1942, DSF MSS, Container 46.
12. DSF to Dr. Archibald Harrison, 19 August 1925, DSF MSS, Container 6.
13. DSF to the Rt. Rev. Beverley D. Tucker, 6 March 1948, DSF MSS, Container 93.
14. DSF to W. C. Jackson, 16 October 1929, DSF MSS, Container 9; DSF to John Gandy, 22 December 1942, DSF MSS, Container 42.
15. Charles Houston to DSF, 10 October 1934, DSF MSS, Container 23.
16. DSF to Allen W. Freeman, 21 June 1938, DSF MSS, Container 30.
17. DSF to Anne B. Freeman, 5 March 1943, DSF MSS, Container 49.
18. DSF to Mrs. Eugene Meyer, 10 May 1944, DSF MSS, Container 57.
19. Ibid.

20. Ibid.
21. Ibid.
22. DSF to Mrs. Mary Rogers Myers, 4 August 1942, DSF MSS, Container 44.
23. *Richmond News Leader*, 8 February 1926.
24. DSF to John Stewart Bryan, 2 November 1926, DSF MSS, Container 5.
25. DSF to J. M. Ellison, 17 May 1945, DSF MSS, Container 61.
26. A. G. Macklin to DSF, 10 October 1946; DSF to A. G. Macklin, 14 October 1946, DSF MSS, Container 70; *Richmond News Leader*, 16 July 1934; John L. Gignilliat, "The Thought of Douglas Southall Freeman," Ph.D. Thesis, University of Wisconsin, 1968, 321.
27. J. M. Ellison to DSF, 16 May 1945, DSF MSS, Container 61.
28. A. G. Macklin to DSF, 10 October 1946, DSF MSS, Container 70.
29. Mrs. Eugene Meyer to DSF, 9 November 1944; DSF to Mrs. Eugene Meyer, 11 November 1944, DSF MSS Container 57; Frank L. Stanley to DSF, 15 March 1947, DSF MSS, Container 83.
30. DSF to the Rev. H. G. Knight, 11 August 1947, DSF MSS, Container 80.
31. DSF to Croswell Bowen, 23 March 1945, DSF MSS, Container 59.
32. DSF to Beatrice Gosford, 11 March 1947, DSF MSS, Container 78.
33. Amaza Meredith to DSF, 5 October 1942, DSF MSS, Container 44.
34. Alfred H. Neal to DSF (letter dated 4 September 1942, but topic suggests 4 October 1942. DSF answered on 7 October 1942 and it is unlikely he would have waited a month to respond), DSF MSS, Container 44.
35. DSF to Amaza Meredith, 7 October 1942, DSF MSS, Container 44.
36. William M. Cooper to DSF, 31 March 1942, DSF MSS, Container 42.
37. Pvt. Robert Tolliver to DSF (undated but c. April 1943), DSF MSS, Container 52.
38. DSF to Pvt. Robert Tolliver, 15 April 1943, DSF MSS, Container 52.
39. R. R. Moton to DSF, 18 January 1930, DSF MSS, Container 12; R. E. Blackwell to DSF, 5 January 1931, DSF MSS, Container 15.
40. DSF to Frank P. Graham, 26 November 1931, DSF MSS, Container 17; *Richmond News Leader*, 8 December 1931.
41. James E. Shepard to DSF, 18 January 1943; DSF to James E. Shepard, 22 January 1943, DSF MSS, Container 52.
42. L. Howard Jenkins to DSF, 1 February 1945; DSF to L. Howard Jenkins, 3 February 1945, DSF MSS, Container 62.
43. DSF to Mrs. Eugene Meyer, 21 February 1946, DSF MSS, Container 171.
44. M. T. McClenahan, "Manuscript," 55.
45. *Richmond News Leader*, 16 August 1926.
46. Ronald L. Heinemann, *Harry Byrd of Virginia* (Charlottesville: University Press of Virginia, 1996), 80.
47. *Richmond News Leader*, 3 December 1934.
48. *Richmond News Leader*, 10 January 1938; DSF to Walter White, 27 January 1940, DSF MSS, Container 40.

49. *Richmond News Leader*, 22 June 1920.
50. *Richmond News Leader*, 1 November 1919.
51. *Richmond News Leader*, 9 April 1928.
52. DSF to Charles Houston, 18 March 1940, DSF MSS, Container 37.
53. *Richmond News Leader*, 24 March 1933; 25 June 1936; 15 September 1942; DSF to Christopher J. Foster, 21 May 1946, DSF MSS, Container 68.
54. A. R. Mann, "Douglas S. Freeman Memo on the Negro Problem," 6 March 1944, DSF MSS, Container 57.
55. Ibid.
56. *Richmond News Leader*, 13 January 1930.
57. *Richmond News Leader*, 7 January 1930.
58. *Richmond News Leader*, 30 August 1918.
59. Boyd had forged twenty-two checks in the total amount of $183, but the court dealt only with three indictments. The sentence was ten years for each act. Minutes, *News Leader* Current Events Class, 14 June 1926, DSF MSS, Container 176; *Richmond News Leader*, 7 July 1926.
60. DSF to John L. Ingram, 19 January 1928, DSF MSS, Container 11. This letter was written two years later but is on the subject of the Boyd case and reflects Freeman's thoughts at the time of the incident.
61. Minutes, *News Leader* Current Events Class, 14 June 1926; *Richmond News Leader*, 7 July 1926.
62. *Richmond News Leader*, 7 July 1926; 6 July 1926.
63. Minutes, *News Leader* Current Events Class, 14 June 1926.
64. *Richmond News Leader*, 7 July 1926.
65. Ibid.
66. John L. Ingram to DSF, 18 January 1928, DSF MSS, Container 11.
67. DSF to John L. Ingram, 19 January 1928, DSF MSS, Container 11.
68. *Richmond News Leader*, 1 November 1933.
69. DSF to Walter White, 2 November 1933, DSF MSS, Container 20.
70. DSF to Walter White, 4 November 1933, DSF MSS, Container 20; DSF to Freda Kirchway, 12 June 1934, DSF MSS, Container 24.
71. DSF to James L. McLemore, 2 November 1933, DSF MSS, Container 18.
72. DSF to Walter White, 2 November 1933, DSF MSS, Container 20.
73. *Richmond News Leader*, 6 November 1933.
74. *Richmond News Leader*, 7 November 1933, 1, 11.
75. Charles H. Houston to DSF, 8 November 1933, DSF MSS, Container 17.
76. James McLemore to DSF, 9 November 1933, DSF MSS, Container 18.
77. DSF to Charles H. Houston, 9 November 1933, DSF MSS, Container 17.
78. DSF to Charles H. Houston, 10 November 1933, DSF MSS, Container 17; DSF to Walter White, 28 November 1933; Walter White to DSF, 29 November 1933, DSF MSS, Container 20.
79. DSF to Charles H. Houston, 10 November 1933; Charles H. Houston to DSF, 11 November 1933, DSF MSS, Container 17.

80. Charles H. Houston to DSF, 11 November 1933, DSF MSS, Container 17.

81. DSF to Walter White, 13 November 1933, DSF MSS, Container 20; DSF to Charles H. Houston, 13 November 1933, DSF MSS, Container 17; DSF to John Garland Pollard, 15 November 1933; John Garland Pollard to DSF, 20 November 1933, DSF MSS, Container 19.

82. DSF to Walter White, 9 December 1933, DSF MSS, Container 20.

83. Ibid.

84. Walter White to DSF, 11 December 1933, DSF MSS, Container 20.

85. *See Richmond News Leader*, 11, 13, 16, December 1933; Walter White to DSF, 18 December 1933, DSF MSS, Container 20; DSF to Freda Kirchway, 12 June 1934, DSF MSS, Container 24.

86. Walter White to DSF, 16 December 1933, DSF MSS, Container 20.

87. *Richmond News Leader*, 18 December 1933.

88. *Richmond News Leader*, 15 July 1921.

89. Ibid.

90. DSF to John Stewart Bryan, 19 September 1921, DSF MSS, Container 5.

91. *Richmond News Leader*, 6 November 1924.

92. *Richmond News Leader*, 13 November 1933.

93. J. Harvie Wilkinson, III, *Harry Byrd and the Changing Face of Virginia Politics* (Charlottesville: University Press of Virginia, 1968), 37-38.

94. Frank B. Atkinson, *The Dynamic Dominion* (Fairfax, VA: George Mason University Press, 1992), 15.

95. *Richmond News Leader*, 29 July 1936.

96. Ibid.

97. *Richmond News Leader*, 14 October 1942.

98. *Richmond News Leader*, 25 May 1943.

99. *See* DSF to J. D. Eggleston, 9 June 1942, DSF MSS, Container 42. "I am willing at anytime to substitute for the poll tax an intelligence requirement, provided only that requirement cannot be made a vehicle of one-party tyranny. I do not feel we are serving the Negro in any way when we enfranchise the ignorant element of his race. The intelligent element we should and, in time, will enfranchise."

100. DSF to Lloyd S. Riddle, 21 April 1953, DSF MSS, Container 118.

CHAPTER NINE

1. "'Tramp Newspaperman' from Dixie," *New York Post*, 11 November 1948.

2. DSF to Carl Ackerman, 16 December 1937, DSF MSS, Container 28.

3. Frank E. Vandiver, "Douglas Southall Freeman," *Southern Historical Society Papers*, No. XIV, Whole No. LII (Richmond: Virginia Historical Society, 1959), v-vi.

4. Ibid., vi.

5. Raymond B. Fosdick to Mary Wells Ashworth, 25 June 1953, Mary Wells Ashworth Papers, MTM MSS.

6. Ibid.

7. William Marshall Bullitt to DSF, 17 February 1942; DSF to William Marshall Bullitt, 20 February 1942, DSF MSS, Container 41. "My Day" was Mrs. Roosevelt's newspaper column.

8. DSF to William Marshall Bullitt, 20 February 1942.

9. William Marshall Bullitt to DSF, 21 March 1942; William Marshall Bullitt to William Wallace Chapin, 21 March 1942, DSF MSS, Container 41.

10. DSF to William Marshall Bullitt, 2 March 1942, DSF MSS, Container 41; DSF to F. P. Gaines, 31 January 1942, DSF MSS, Container 42.

11. F. W. Boatwright to DSF, 12 June 1925, DSF MSS, Container 5. DSF to Jay Nash, 2 March 1951, DSF MSS Container 107.

12. DSF to R. S. Barbour, 4 May 1936, DSF MSS, Container 21.

13. DSF to F. W. Boatwright, 2 November 1943, DSF MSS, Container 47.

14. DSF, "A Confession of Redoubled Faith," n/d, c. 1944, DSF MSS, Container 53.

15. DSF to R. S. Barbour, 4 May 1936, DSF MSS, Container 21.

16. DSF to F. W. Boatwright, 2 November 1943; DSF, "Confession of Redoubled Faith."

17. Ruben E. Alley, *History of the University of Richmond, 1830-1971* (Charlotte: University Press of Virginia, 1977), 206-7, 222.

18. Ibid., 207.

19. F. W. Boatwright to DSF, 18 April 1935, DSF MSS, Container 21.

20. DSF to F. W. Boatwright, 19 April 1935, DSF MSS, Container 21.

21. DSF to F. W. Boatwright, 22 January 1935, DSF MSS, Container 21.

22. Ibid.

23. DSF to Inez G. Freeman, 19 July 1933, MTM MSS. Freeman reported about the "stupid party" the next day. "The ladies who were young were not fair," he wrote, "and those who were fair were not young." DSF to Inez G. Freeman, 20 July 1933, MTM MSS.

24. "Generalship with Examples," *Time*, 26 October 1942, 110.

25. Ashworth, "The Man and the Making of a Book," 24.

26. DSF, "For John Stewart Bryan—The Master of the Feast," 20 October 1943, MTM MSS.

27. M. T. McClenahan, "Manuscript," 86.

28. Ibid., 87.

29. Ashworth, "The Man and the Making of a Book," 24.

30. DSF to Inez G. Freeman, 13 July 1933, MTM MSS.

31. Hamilton, "Most Unforgettable," 153.

32. DSF, Diary, 14 December 1939, DSF MSS, Container 1.

33. Minutes, *News Leader* Current Events Class, 9 February 1933, DSF MSS, Container 98.

34. DSF to T. J. Moore, Jr., 5 December 1938, DSF MSS, Container 34. Freeman invited nine boys to join the club, and they each received the same letter as the one he forwarded to Moore.

35. James Douglas Freeman, Interview with author, 31 January 2001.

36. "Richmond's Community Christmas," *Richmond Times-Dispatch*, 20 December 1953, 6-A.

37. Rouse, *We Happy WASPs*, 47-48.

38. "Freeman's Markers," *Richmond Times-Dispatch*, 2 December 1998, L1, L6; J. Ambler Johnston, "Recollections of Douglas Southall Freeman," 6 October 1954, DSF MSS, Containers 123, 141. This eighteen-page manuscript by Johnston is inexplicably divided between two containers. The first seventeen pages are in Container 123, the last page, with Johnston's signature, is in Container 141.

39. J. Ambler Johnston, *Echoes of 1861-1961* (privately published, 2000), 7.

40. Ibid.

41. *Richmond Times-Dispatch*, 2 December 1998, L6.

42. Ambler Johnston wrote that seventy-five markers were constructed and that Freeman wrote the inscription for "over sixty." In fact only fifty-nine markers were placed, so it is possible—and very likely—that Freeman wrote all of the inscriptions. As Johnston recalls the involvement of other writers, however, it is impossible to state with certainty that Freeman is the author of each marker inscription. Johnston, "Recollections," DSF MSS, Container 123.

43. *Richmond Times-Dispatch*, 2 December 1998, L6.

44. DSF to Senator Rust, 2 July 1940, DSF MSS, Container 39; DSF to Mary Tyler Cheek, 2 August 1948, MTM MSS.

45. DSF, Diary, 31 December 1937, DSF MSS, Container 1.

46. DST to W. W. Addison, 6 April 1928, DSF MSS, Container 9.

47. DSF to Helen G. McCormack, 6 April 1931, DSF MSS, Container 18.

48. James J. Kilpatrick to Daniel E. Button, 29 July 1953, DSF MSS, Container 114.

49. Minutes, *News Leader* Current Events Class, 23 August 1920, DSF MSS, Container 177.

50. Ibid.; Minutes, *News Leader* Current Events Class, 30 August 1920, DSF MSS, Container 178.

51. Rouse, *We Happy WASPs*, 159.

52. Ashworth, "The Man and the Making of a Book," 2223.

53. "'Tramp Newspaperman,'" *New York Post*.

54. DSF, "Douglas Southall Freeman," *New York Herald Tribune*, 7 October 1951, 4.

55. Ashworth, "Some Questions and Answers," 2-3.

56. Ibid.

57. DSF, "Harbor," n/d, c. July 1933, DSF MSS, Container 20.

58. Inez G. Freeman, "Notes," n/d, c. June 1961, MTM MSS.

59. DSF to Inez G. Freeman, 28 July 1930, MTM MSS. "Andomanez" stands for Anne, James Douglas, Mary Tyler, and Inez.

60. M. T. McClenahan, "Manuscript," 59.

61. DSF to S. H. Sheib, various letters, DSF MSS, Container 20.

62. DSF to W. W. Sprouse, 16 September 1941, DSF MSS, Container 39.

63. DSF to Inez G. Freeman, 16 June 1930, MTM MSS.

64. DSF to Mary Tyler Freeman, 6 August 1930, MTM MSS; DSF to Adm. Edward Kalbfus, 2 June 1948, DSF MSS, Container 90.

65. DSF to Adm. Edward Kalbfus, 2 June 1948.

66. DSF, "Mr. Gillette—Recommendations," 21 September 1951, MTM MSS.

67. M. T. McClenahan, "My Father," 22.

68. DSF, "Spring," 19 April 1925, DSF MSS, Container 126.

69. DSF, "My Garden and I," n/d, MTM MSS.

70. "Recalling 'What a Wonderful Place It Was,'" *Richmond Times-Dispatch*, 15 April 1995, D-1.

71. DSF to Gertrude R. B. Richards, 18 December 1942, DSF MSS, Container 45.

72. Mary Wells Ashworth, "Memo on DSF for Dumas Malone," MTM MSS; Guy Friddell, "I've Laughed All My Life: Dr. Douglas Southall Freeman," *Alumni Bulletin of the University of Richmond*, Vol. XVII, No. 4 (July 1953); Mary Wells Ashworth to John Boulware, n/d, DSF MSS, Container 120.

73. DSF to Ralph Habas, 30 March 1945, DSF MSS, Container 62; "Virginia Editor Uses Civil War to Clarify War News from Europe," *Life*, 13 May 1940, 47.

74. Carl Sandburg to DSF, 21 September 1938, DSF MSS, Container 33.

75. Carl Sandburg, "Book Review," *New York Herald Tribune*, 18 June 1952.

76. Carl Sandburg to DSF, 29 April 1950, DSF MSS, Container 102.

77. Tape recording, DSF with Robert Frost, n/d, MTM MSS.

78. DSF to Ralph Habas, 30 March 1945.

79. DSF to Martha Ellyn Slayback, 28 February 1945, DSF MSS, Container 63.

80. Ibid; DSF to Charles H. Taylor, 12 December 1928, DSF MSS, Container 14.

81. DSF to Mary Tyler Freeman, 25 February 1934, MTM MSS.

82. DSF to Keen's Chop House, 20 January 1937, DSF MSS, Container 31.

83. DSF to Inez G. Freeman, 22 September 1915, MTM MSS; Anne Freeman, "Bedford Freemans," 5. Virginius Dabney, editor of the *Richmond Times-Dispatch*, once said Freeman chewed "candle wax" to help break the habit of tobacco chewing. John P. Ackerly, III, "Memorandum of Meeting with Virginius Dabney," 3 November 1995, copy provided to author by Mr. Ackerly.

84. "Lee's Biographer Leads Three Live," *Baltimore Sun*, 27 March 1938, 3.

85. DSF to Inez G. Freeman, 18 July 1932, MTM MSS.

86. DSF to Inez G. Freeman, 19 July 1932, MTM MSS.

87. DSF to James Douglas Freeman, 10 July 1934, MTM MSS; Habas, "Untitled Manuscript," 6.

88. DSF, Diary, 8 March 1937, DSF MSS, Container 1.

89. DSF, Diary, 9 December 1937, DSF MSS, Container 1.

90. DSF to Allen W. Freeman, 20 April 1940, DSF MSS, Container 36. Freeman said buying tobacco, lighting and smoking cigarettes, and cleaning up afterward, occupied eight and one-half hours per week. *Time*, 109.

91. James Douglas Freeman, Interview with author, 31 January 2001; Guy Friddell, "He Chronicled the Civil War," *Richmond News Leader*, 2 December 1968.

92. Ashworth, "Some Questions and Answers," 1-2.

93. Kilpatrick, "Freeman," 6.

94. DSF to J. O. Freeman, 19 August 1926, DSF MSS, Container 6; DSF to P. P. Bishop, 24 December 1942, DSF MSS, Container 41.

95. "WRNL Begins Broadcasting This Afternoon," *Richmond Times-Dispatch*, 14 November 1937.

96. Kilpatrick, "Freeman," 14.

97. Mallory Freeman, Interview with author, 5 February 2001.

98. Stuart Wheeler to author, 26 January 2001. Freeman's habit of walking to the microphone just as the announcer completed the introduction was also observed by reporters for *Time* magazine. "The Virginians," *Time*, 18 October 1948, 109.

99. Kilpatrick, "Freeman," 14; Scheer, "Plutarch on the James," 3; Rouse, *We Happy WASPs*, 146.

100. Kilpatrick, "Freeman," 14.

101. James Douglas Freeman, Interview with author, 31 January 2001.

102. Richard Harwell, "Introduction," *R. E. Lee* by Douglas Southall Freeman, an abridgement edited by Richard Harwell (New York: Charles Scribner's Sons, 1961), xiii; Emory Thomas, *Robert E. Lee: A Biography* (New York: W. W. Norton & Co., 1995), 13.

103. E. S. Whitlock to DSF, 19 June 1951, DSF MSS, Container 108.

104. Scheer, "Plutarch on the James," 3; "The Virginians," *Time*, 18 October, 1948, 109. *Time* reported that the critics "listen anyhow."

105. Rouse, *We Happy WASPs*, 17.

106. DSF to John Stewart Bryan, 29 June 1942, DSF MSS, Container 41.

107. DSF to Ralph Habas, 10 April 1945, DSF MSS, Container 62. The one recording of a "Lesson in Living" broadcast discovered by the author concerns the benefits of using good manners. DSF, "Lesson in Living," Tape recording, 5 November 1950, MTM MSS.

108. Scheer, "Plutarch on the James," 3.

109. Melcena West to DSF, 3 November 1929, DSF MSS, Container 13.

110. Mrs. J. B. Watkins to DSF, 21 October 1929, DSF MSS, Container 13.

111. Brantley Henderson to President, American Broadcasting System, 10 August 1947, DSF MSS, Container 78; Mrs. F. E. Nelson to DSF, 15 October 1929, DSF MSS, Container 13.

112. "A devoted father" to DSF, 23 October 1929, DSF MSS, Container 13; Mrs. E. Lee Sadler, Jr. to DSF, 28 August 1949, DSF MSS, Container 99.

113. C. T. Seavey to DSF, 26 November 1947, DSF MSS, Container 83.

114. DSF to Mrs. S. Lee Sadler, Jr., 31 August 1949, DSF MSS, Container 99.

115. Mrs. B. C. Patterson to DSF, 10 March 1946, DSF MSS, Container 71; Morris E. Tischler to DSF, 12 July 1948, DSF MSS, Container 93.

116. DSF to Mrs. B. C. Patterson, 13 March 1946, DSF MSS, Container 71; DSF to Morris S. Tischler, 12 July 1948, DSF MSS, Container 93.

117. Mrs. J. H. Turner to DSF, 26 August 1942, DSF MSS, Container 46.

118. DSF to Mrs. J. H. Turner, 27 August 1942, DSF MSS, Container 46.

119. DSF to W. F. Saunders, 31 July 1942, DSF MSS, Container 45; DSF to P. P. Bishop, 24 December 1942, DSF MSS, Container 41.
120. Mary Wells Ashworth to E. S. Whitlock, 10 December 1952, DSF MSS, Container 113.
121. Inez G. Freeman, "Notes," n/d, MTM MSS; Geneva B. Snelling, "Douglas Southall Freeman," October 1954, DSF MSS, Container 123.
122. Frances Valentine, Interview with author, 20 July 2001.
123. Margaret Lechner, Interview with author, 22 May 2001.
124. Carl Shires to Mary Tyler Cheek, 9 September 1985, MTM MSS.
125. In addition to magazine articles, "the schedule" made it into the comic "Strange As It Seems" by Ernest Hix. A sketched picture of Freeman appears in a 1949 panel—along with facts about the origination of the Fox Trot and a confusing sign in Lance County, Oregon—with the caption: "Douglas Southall Freeman, noted historian, maintains a set of books for an accurate record of his time!" Ernest Hix, "Strange As It Seems," n/d, but c. 1949, United Features Syndicate, Inc., DSF MSS, Container 97.
126. M. T. McClenahan, "Reflections," 35.
127. James Douglas Freeman, Interview with author, 31 January 2001.
128. Royall Turpin, Interview with author, 27 January 2001.
129. James J. Kilpatrick, Interview with author, 8 March 2001.
130. M. T. McClenahan, "Reflections," 35.
131. DSF to Inez G. Freeman, 19 June 1930, MTM MSS.
132. DSF to Inez G. Freeman, 17 August 1934, MTM MSS.
133. DSF, Diary, 15 July 1945, DSF MSS, Container 1.
134. DSF to A. L. Goldberg, 16 September 1946, DSF MSS, Container 68.
135. DSF to J. Alvin Russell, 11 October 1947, DSF MSS, Container 82.
136. DSF to Mary Tyler Freeman, 4 March 1934, MTM MSS.
137. Mary Tyler McClenahan, Interview with author, 4 June 2001.
138. DSF, "The Fine Art of Saving Time," 4.
139. DSF to Ralph Habas, 30 March 1945, DSF MSS, Container 62.
140. Habas, "Untitled Manuscript," 7.
141. DSF, "The Fine Art of Saving Time,"8.
142. DSF to Dr. Horsley, 28 November 1931, DSF MSS, Container 17.
143. DSF, "The Fine Art of Saving Time," 5.
144. Ibid., 9.
145. DSF to Clyde Gilmour, 1 November 1948, DSF MSS, Container 88.
146. DSF to Gaius W. Diggs, Richmond Rationing Board, 21 December 1943, DSF MSS, Container 48.
147. "Classified Ad," *Richmond Times-Dispatch*, 14 December 1943.
148. Friddell, "He Chronicled the Civil War"; Guy Friddell, "Dr. Freeman counted seconds, but always had time for others," *Richmond News Leader*, 13 May 1985; DSF to Gaius W. Diggs, 21 December 1943. It is unclear how long Freeman rode with Kenny. The best evidence is about two years.

149. DSF to Inez G. Freeman, n/d, MTM MSS.
150. Ibid.
151. DSF to Inez G. Freeman, 21 August 1934, MTM MSS.
152. Inez G. Freeman to DSF, 21 August 1934, MTM MSS.
153. DSF, "The Value of Time," 30 November 1924, DSF MSS, Container 126.
154. DSF to Inez G. Freeman, 7 August 1946, MTM MSS.

CHAPTER TEN

1. Maxwell E. Perkins to DSF, 28 September 1932, DSF MSS, Container 19.
2. DSF to Maxwell E. Perkins, 25 January 1934, DSF MSS, Container 25; *see* DSF to Maxwell E. Perkins, 29 September 1932, DSF MSS, Container 19.
3. DSF to Maxwell E. Perkins, 25 January 1934, DSF MSS, Container 25.
4. DSF to Mary Tyler Freeman, 1 February 1934, MTM MSS.
5. DSF to Mary Tyler Freeman, 25 February 1934, MTM MSS.
6. DSF to Allen W. Freeman, 25 October 1934, DSF MSS, Container 22.
7. DSF to Maxwell E. Perkins, 27 October 1934, DSF MSS, Container 25.
8. Ibid.
9. Maxwell E. Perkins to DSF, 2 November 1934, DSF MSS, Container 25.
10. DSF to Newton Baker, 31 December 1934, DSF MSS, Container 21.
11. DSF to Newton Baker, 5 January 1935, DSF MSS, Container 21.
12. DSF to Dumas Malone, 8 January 1935, DSF MSS, Container 24.
13. Dumas Malone, *Jefferson and His Time*, Vol. I, *Jefferson the Virginian* (New York: Little, Brown & Co., 1948), vii. Malone was so occupied with other matters at this time that he would devote no more than "six months" concentrated attention on Jefferson until 1943.
14. Dumas Malone to DSF, 9 January 1935, DSF MSS, Container 24.
15. Ibid.
16. "President Terms Jefferson 'Beacon' in War on Tyranny," *New York Times*, 18 May 1950, 1.
17. DSF to Dumas Malone, 10 January 1935, DSF MSS, Container 24; DSF to Maxwell E. Perkins, 12 January 1935, DSF MSS, Container 25. Freeman's thought process is clearly marked in the series of letters cited herein. There is one letter that is somewhat peculiar. On December 26, 1934, he wrote Wallace Meyer of Scribner's that "tomorrow I begin the research for another long biography." This letter seems to indicate that a decision had been made, but it comes in the midst of the letters regarding Washington, Wilson, and Jefferson. One can only conclude that Freeman thought he had made up his mind, and then started a reexamination process. DSF to Wallace Meyer, 26 December 1934, DSF MSS, Container 25. Dumas Malone went on to write a six-volume Pulitzer Prize-winning biography of Thomas Jefferson.
18. "Biography as a Pastime," *Saturday Review of Literature*, 11 May 1935, 546.
19. Ibid.
20. DSF to Maxwell E. Perkins, 28 March 1935, DSF MSS, Container 25.
21. DSF to Ernest Martin Hopkins, 5 September 1935, DSF MSS, Container 23.

22. DSF, "Adventures in Biography," Lecture III, "The New Horizons," 34, DSF MSS, Container 127.
23. DSF, "Adventures in Biography," Lecture I, "Discovery and Rediscovery," 34, DSF MSS, Container 127.
24. DSF to J. F. Jamison, 22 February 1935; J. F. Jamison to DSF, 26 February 1935; DSF to United States Printer, 2 August 1935, MTM MSS.
25. M. T. McClenahan, "A High Calling," 12; "My Father as a Writer," 39. In the former article, Mrs. McClenahan places Mrs. Freeman's comment after the release of *Lee's Lieutenants* in 1943, in the latter article, after the release of *R. E. Lee* in 1934. She confirms that the comment was made after *R. E. Lee* during the time of indecision over the next book. M. T. McClenahan, Interview with author, 1 May 2001. Freeman mentions that after he mailed the *Lee* manuscript to Scribner's, he was "in bewilderment for days." DSF, "An Address before the Civil War Round Tables of Richmond and Chicago, 7 May 1953," *Civil War Histories*, Vol. I (1955), 13.
26. DSF, *Lee's Lieutenants*, Vol. I, xv.
27. DSF, Diary, 18 June 1936, DSF MSS, Container 1; DSF to Maxwell E. Perkins, 15 July 1936, DSF MSS, Container 25.
28. Maxwell E. Perkins to DSF, 11 June 1936; DSF to Maxwell E. Perkins, 12 June 1936, DSF MSS, Container 25.
29. DSF, Diary, 14 June 1936, DSF MSS, Container 1.
30. DSF to Maxwell E. Perkins, 15 July 1936, DSF MSS, Container 25.
31. Ibid.
32. DSF, *Lee's Lieutenants*, Vol. I, xvii.
33. DSF to Maxwell E. Perkins, 15 July 1936, DSF MSS, Container 25. Emphasis in the original.
34. Ibid.
35. DSF to Maxwell E. Perkins, 7 February 1938; DSF to Maxwell E. Perkins, 15 July 1937, DSF MSS, Container 33. Beauregard and Johnston ultimately became subordinates when Lee assumed command of all Confederate forces in February 1865.
36. DSF to Maxwell E. Perkins, Bishop Collins Denny, and H. J. Eckenrode, n/d, but enclosed with letter to Maxwell E. Perkins, 29 October 1938, DSF MSS, Container 33. This letter/memo is titled "A Foreword to My Counselors" and was sent to the three mentioned individuals. Freeman's draft of the "Foreword" is in Container 142; there is no attachment to the letter to Perkins in Container 33, but the "Foreword" is referenced as an enclosure. The citations from this letter will refer to the "Foreword" and not the cover letter unless otherwise indicated.
37. DSF, "Confidential Foreword" DSF MSS, Container 242; DSF, *Lee's Lieutenants*, Vol. I, xviii.
38. Virginius Dabney, *Liberalism in the South* (Chapel Hill: University of North Carolina Press, 1932), 408.
39. Ibid., 409.
40. DSF to D. Tennant Bryan, 3 August 1952, DSF MSS, Container 109.

41. Ibid.
42. "Modern Newspapers Praised at Ceremony," *New York Times*, 19 January 1935, 15. Freeman made much the same point in his address to the American Medico-Psychological Association in May 1915.
43. Ibid.
44. *Time*, 1 April 1940.
45. "On the Death of Douglas Freeman," *Richmond News Leader*, 15 June 1953, 10.
46. Friddell, *Alumni Bulletin*, 3.
47. James J. Kilpatrick, *Fine Print: Reflections on the Writing Art* (Kansas City: Andrews & McMeel, 1993), 197.
48. Hamilton, "Most Unforgettable," 153.
49. DSF to John Stewart Bryan, 9 March 1934, DSF MSS, Container 21.
50. James J. Kilpatrick, "Deep Purple," *Miami Herald*, 17 January 1982.
51. Hamilton, "Most Unforgettable," 153.
52. John E. Leard, Interview with author, 19 July 2001.
53. Ibid.
54. James J. Kilpatrick, Interview with author, 8 March 2001.
55. John E. Leard, Interview with author, 19 July 2001.
56. James J. Kilpatrick, Interview with author, 8 March 2001.
57. Kilpatrick, "Freeman," 14-15.
58. Friddell, *Alumni Bulletin*, 3.
59. Kilpatrick, "Freeman," 13.
60. James J. Kilpatrick, Interview with author, 8 March 2001.
61. DSF to Dave E. Satterfield, Jr., 10 May 1932, DSF MSS, Container 20.
62. DSF to John Stewart Bryan, 25 May 1933, DSF MSS, Container 15.
63. DSF to Mrs. F. D. Williams, 10 April 1933, DSF MSS, Container 20; DSF, "John Stewart Bryan," 470-71, 479.
64. DSF to John Stewart Bryan, 2 October 1934, DSF MSS, Container 21.
65. "Latin: Biographer Talks It," *Milwaukee Journal*, 21 May 1935.
66. Rouse, *We Happy WASPs*, 57. James Douglas Freeman, Interview with author, 31 January 2001.
67. DSF to Amanda Kane, D. Tennant Bryan, and Stewart Bryan, Jr., 7 January 1947, DSF VHS.
68. DSF, "Memorandum," 4 January 1935, DSF MSS, Container 30.
69. Ibid. Bryan was serving as president of the College of William and Mary.
70. Ibid.
71. Freeman wrote another letter of resignation in January 1944 after he apparently took an editorial position contrary to Bryan's beliefs. It is not clear if this letter of January 13, 1944, was delivered. Within the week, the two men were corresponding on other topics with no hint of disagreement. Freeman made no notation of any trouble in his diary. DSF to John Stewart Bryan, 13 January 1944; 19 January 1944, DSF MSS, Container 53.
72. DSF, Diary, 20 June 1940, DSF MSS, Container 1.

73. DSF to Inez G. Freeman, 9 July 1940, MTM MSS.
74. DSF to Inez G. Freeman, 10 July 1940, MTM MSS. DSF, Diary, 10 July 1940, DSF MSS, Container 1.
75. Inez G. Freeman to DSF, 10 July 1940, MTM MSS.
76. DSF, Diary, 31 July 1940, DSF MSS, Container 1.
77. DSF to Eugene Meyer, 6 August 1940, DSF MSS, Container 38; DSF, Diary, 6 August 1940, DSF MSS, Container 1.
78. "Times-Dispatch" cards, Freeman File, Virginia Commonwealth University; Freeman File, Richmond Times-Dispatch Library.
79. "Times-Dispatch" cards, Freeman File, Virginia Commonwealth University.
80. Dunford, *Richmond Times-Dispatch*, 10-11. The case settled out of court.
81. DSF, Diary, 18 March 1940, DSF MSS, Container 1.
82. Dunford, *Richmond Times-Dispatch*, 256.
83. DSF to Allen W. Freeman, 21 June 1938, DSF MSS, Container 28; DSF, Diary, 26 May 1938; "Noted Editor Hurt in Wreck Near Here," n/d, no citation, DSF MSS, Container 218.
84. Ibid.
85. State highway patrolman W. H. Simpson said Freeman "was able to walk at the scene of the wreck." "Dr. Freeman, Daughter, Hurt," n/d, no citation, DSF MSS, Container 218.
86. DSF to Allen W. Freeman, 21 June 1938, DSF MSS, Container 28; DSF, Diary, 26 May 1938, DSF MSS, Container 1.
87. DSF, Diary, 29 May 1938, DSF MSS, Container 1.
88. DSF to Allen W. Freeman, 21 June 1938, DSF MSS, Container 28.
89. DSF to Inez G. Freeman, 6, 15 June 1938, MTM MSS; DSF to USF&G, 2 July 1938, DSF MSS, Container 28.
90. Mrs. Carter also received a lump sum in her own right from the insurance company. Freeman continued to send checks to Mrs. Carter, beyond the $3,500, until May 1949. DSF to Louise Carter, 18 May 1949, DSF MSS, Container 96.
91. DSF to Mary Tyler Freeman, 25 June 1938, MTM MSS. Dr. Ashworth refused payment for his services. "My love for you and Mrs. Freeman and Mary Tyler cannot be expressed," he wrote Freeman. "The number of coca colas I drank going down on the train and minor expenses amounted to nothing compared to the insurmountable help you have been to me many times." O. O. Ashworth to DSF, 18 August 1938, DSF MSS, Container 28.
92. DSF to Mary Tyler Freeman, 25 June 1938, DSF MSS, Container 34.
93. DSF to Inez G. Freeman, 5 August 1933, MTM MSS.
94. DSF to Inez G. Freeman, 3 September 1931, MTM MSS.
95. DSF to Inez G. Freeman, 9 August 1951, MTM MSS.
96. DSF to James Douglas Freeman, 26 November 1943, MTM MSS.
97. DSF, Diary, 18 July 1940, DSF MSS, Container 1. Emphasis in the original.
98. Inez G. Freeman to DSF, 3 August 1933, MTM MSS.

99. Inez G. Freeman to DSF, 3 July 1934, MTM MSS.

100. Inez G. Freeman to DSF, n/d, c. 1919-20, MTM MSS.

101. Ibid.

102. Mary Mason Holt, "Mrs. Douglas Southall Freeman," 3 December 1974, MTM MSS.

103. "The Virginians," *Time*, 18 October 1948, 110.

104. Ibid.

105. A. W. Vaughan to DSF, 22 November 1938, DSF MSS, Container 34.

106. A. W. Vaughan to DSF, 21 November 1939, DSF MSS, Container 34.

107. Maxwell E. Perkins to DSF, 6 February 1939, DSF MSS, Container 33.

108. DSF to Maxwell E. Perkins, 7 February 1939, DSF MSS, Container 33.

109. It is unclear because no letters are in the file detailing the offer or acceptance. Freeman writes as if he knew nothing about it; Vaughan writes as if it had been discussed from the beginning. Freeman later wrote Stephen Vincent Benet that he "found to my dismay that I was under contract to [publish] as part of the lecture arrangements." DSF to Stephen Vincent Benet, 29 November 1939, DSF MSS, Container 28.

110. DSF to Maxwell E. Perkins, 7 February 1939, DSF MSS, Container 33.

111. DSF to Maxwell E. Perkins, 14 February 1939, DSF MSS, Container 33.

112. DSF to Maxwell E. Perkins, 7 February 1939, DSF MSS, Container 33.

113. DSF, Diary, 11 March 1939, DSF MSS, Container 1. Carter Glass was the senior U. S. senator from Virginia. Freeman's introduction can be found in Rixley Smith and Norman Beasley, *Carter Glass: A Biography* (New York: Longmans, Green & Co., 1939), ix-xii.

114. DSF to Maxwell E. Perkins, 14 February 1939, DSF MSS, Container 33.

115. DSF, Diary, 1, 12, 17, 23 April 1939, DSF MSS, Container 1.

116. *Montevallo Times*, 27 April 1939, 1.

117. *Montevallo Times*, 4 May 1939, 1.

118. Ibid., 2.

119. "Appeal of South to Posterity Not Futile—Freeman," *Mobile Register*, 29 April 1939, 1.

120. DSF, *The South to Posterity: An Introduction to the Writing of Confederate History* (New York: Charles Scribner's Sons, 1939), 80-104; "War Not Romantic, Lecturer Says at Alabama College," *Mobile Register*, 29 April 1939, 1.

121. DSF, Diary, 27 April 1939, DSF MSS, Container 1.

122. DSF, Diary, 7 June 1939. *See also*, Diary, 4, 29 May; 14, 24 June, 1939, DSF MSS, Container 1.

123. DSF, Diary, 9 July 1939, DSF MSS, Container 1.

124. DSF to Maxwell E. Perkins, 19 July 1939, DSF MSS, Container 33.

125. DSF to Maxwell E. Perkins, 21 July 1939, DSF MSS, Container 33. Freeman offered the option of changing the subtitle to "An Introduction to the Writing of Confederate History" if Perkins judged "historiography" to be "too long a word." Whether Perkins did or not, the alternative subtitle was used.

126. DSF to Charles Scribner, 5 August 1939, DSF MSS, Container 33.
127. DSF, Diary, 6, 18 August 1939, DSF MSS, Container 1.
128. DSF to Maxwell E. Perkins, 18 August 1939, DSF MSS, Container 33.
129. Ibid. Emphasis added.
130. DSF, *The South to Posterity*, 43, 78.
131. Ibid., 202-3.
132. Ibid., 204. Freeman later wrote that he thought this segment was the "only thing . . . worthwhile" in the book. DSF to A. T. Grime, 16 August 1946, DSF MSS, Container 68.
133. Stephen Vincent Benet, "The Lost Cause in Literature," *Saturday Review of Literature*, 25 November 1939, 21.
134. William Shands Meacham, "The Writing of Confederate History," *New York Times Book Review*, 24 March 1940, 8.
135. Gerald W. Johnson, "The Lost Cause," *New York Herald-Tribune Books*, 3 December 1939. Mount Vernon, Monticello, and the Hermitage refer, respectively, to Washington, Jefferson, and Andrew Jackson. "Ashland" is in likelihood a reference to Patrick Henry who lived in Ashland, Virginia, but it should be noted that the home of Henry Clay in Lexington, Kentucky, is called "Ashland."
136. George C. Marshall to DSF, 4 March 1942, DSF MSS, Container 44.
137. Confederate secretary of war Judah P. Benjamin.
138. The 1862 Valley campaign of Thomas J. "Stonewall" Jackson.
139. Apparently a reference to William N. Pendleton, Chief of Artillery, Army of Northern Virginia.
140. DSF, Diary, 15 July 1937, DSF MSS, Container 1.
141. DSF, Diary, 29 February 1940, DSF MSS, Container 1.
142. DSF, Diary, 4 December 1937; 15 June 1938, DSF MSS, Container 1.
143. DSF, Diary, 30 April 1937, DSF MSS, Container 1.
144. DSF, "Foreword to My Counselors," 5.
145. Ibid.
146. Ibid., 5-6.
147. Ibid., 6-7.
148. Ibid., 8.

CHAPTER ELEVEN
1. DSF, *R. E. Lee*, Vol. I, xiv.
2. George C. Marshall to DSF, 3 May 1939, DSF MSS, Container 32.
3. George C. Marshall to DSF, 27 February 1940, DSF MSS, Container 38.
4. DSF, *R. E. Lee*, Vol. I, xiv.
5. DSF, "An Appraisal for John Stewart Bryan of the Situation, 28 September 1940," DSF MSS, Container 35.
6. DSF, Diary, 23 August 1939, DSF MSS, Container 1.
7. *Richmond News Leader*, 4 July 1934.
8. *Richmond News Leader*, 11, 13, 14, 17 April 1934.
9. *Richmond News Leader*, 19 March 1935.

10. DSF, Diary, 5 September 1939, DSF MSS, Container 1.
11. *Richmond News Leader*, 31 August 1938.
12. DSF to Nicholas Murray Butler, 16 September 1938, DSF MSS, Container 28.
13. *Richmond News Leader*, 13 September 1938.
14. *Richmond News Leader*, 28 September 1938.
15. *Richmond News Leader*, 7 March 1939.
16. Ibid.
17. *Richmond News Leader*, 14 April 1939.
18. *Richmond News Leader*, 1 August 1939.
19. *Richmond News Leader*, 18 August 1939.
20. DSF, Diary, 25 August 1939, DSF MSS, Container 1.
21. *Richmond News Leader*, 1 September 1939.
22. *Richmond News Leader*, 13 May 1940.
23. *Richmond News Leader*, 26, 28 April 1940.
24. "General Lee's Spokesman," *Time*, 1 April 1940.
25. *Richmond News Leader*, 21 March 1940.
26. *Richmond News Leader*, 15 January 1940.
27. "Virginia Editor Uses Civil War to Clarify War News from Europe," *Life*, 13 May 1940, 41.
28. *Richmond News Leader*, 10, 21 May 1940.
29. DSF, "Barbed-wire Horizons," Commencement Address, Marshall College, *Association of America's Colleges Bulletin*, Vol. XXVII, No. 3 (October 1941), 412.
30. Ibid., 414.
31. Ibid., 418.
32. *Richmond News Leader*, 24 June 1940.
33. DSF, Diary, 3 September 1940, DSF MSS, Container 1.
34. DSF, Diary, 27 September 1940, DSF MSS, Container 1.
35. DSF, "An Appraisal for John Stewart Bryan of the Situation, 28 September 1940," DSF MSS, Container 35, 1.
36. Ibid.
37. Ibid.
38. Ibid., 1-2.
39. Ibid., 2.
40. Ibid., 3.
41. Ibid., 4.
42. Ibid., 6.
43. Statement of Gov. James H. Price, "Virginia Defense Council," 31 May 1940, DSF MSS, Container 39, 3.
44. Ibid.
45. Wilmer Hall to DSF, 13 June 1940, DSF MSS, Container 39.
46. "Civil Protection Mobilization Plan," 7 November 1940, DSF MSS, Container 39.

47. DSF to Mrs. R. G. Boatwright, 2 January 1942, DSF MSS Container 41; DSF to Louis Jaffe, 15 August 1940; DSF to J. Edgar Hoover, 17 June 1941; J. Edgar Hoover to DSF, 24 June 1941, DSF MSS, Container 37; DSF to Governor James H. Price, 20 August 1940, DSF MSS, Container 39.

48. DSF to L. D. Glaser, 24 June 1941, DSF MSS, Container 37. Freeman served as chairman until January 1942.

49. DSF to George C. Marshall, 4 October 1940, DSF MSS, Container 38.

50. George C. Marshall to DSF, 10 October 1940; Ward H. Maris to DSF, 13 January 1941; DSF to Ward H. Maris, 15 January 1941; George C. Marshall to DSF, 17 January 1941; DSF to George C. Marshall, 18 January 1941, DSF MSS, Container 38.

51. DSF, Diary, 15 July 1941, DSF MSS, Container 1.

52. DSF to Maxwell E. Perkins, 10 September 1941, DSF MSS, Container 39.

53. DSF to Maxwell E. Perkins, 16 September 1941, DSF MSS, Container 39.

54. Ibid.

55. DSF to Allen W. Freeman, 20 October 1941, DSF MSS, Container 36; DSF to Joseph M. Hill, 17 November 1942; DSF to Judge Harry R. Howze, 24 November 1942, DSF MSS, Container 43.

56. DSF to Edward Weeks, 26 February 1940, DSF MSS, Container 40.

57. Ibid.; DSF to Gen. Sherman Miles, 21 May 1940, DSF MSS, Container 38.

58. DSF to Gen. Sherman Miles, 21 May 1940, DSF MSS, Container 38.

59. DSF, "Who's In Command," *The Atlantic Monthly*, June 1940, 744.

60. Ibid.

61. Ibid., 745.

62. Ibid.

63. Ibid., 749.

64. Ibid., 750.

65. Ibid., 751. Freeman later criticized Roosevelt for doing what he here said he would not do. Roosevelt wanted to be "Admiral of the Fleet" he wrote and needed "the truth" of Freeman's *Atlantic* article poured "into his vain head." DSF to Mrs. Tracy Lewis, 12 February 1942, DSF MSS, Container 43. That same week he wrote that "the greatest effort has been necessary to keep the President from acting, in effect, as Admiral of the Fleet." DSF to Mrs. R. N. Begien, 17 February 1942, DSF MSS, Container 41.

66. Ibid.

67. DSF to A. Willis Robertson, 8 July 1941, DSF MSS, Container 39.

68. DSF, Diary, 27 September 1941, DSF MSS, Container 1.

69. DSF to Allen W. Freeman, 1 October 1941, DSF MSS, Container 36.

70. DSF, Diary, 27 September 1941, DSF MSS, Container 1.

71. DSF, Diary, 7 December 1941, DSF MSS, Container 1; "A Silent Tower Stands Sentinel," *Henrico* (Virginia) *Gazette*, 26 November 1992.

72. John E. Leard, Interview with author, 19 July 2001.

73. DSF to Alexander Weddell, 13 December 1941, DSF MSS, Container 40.

74. DSF to George C. Marshall, 5 February 1942, DSF MSS, Container 44.
75. George C. Marshall to DSF, 16 February 1942, DSF MSS, Container 44.
76. DSF, Diary, 17 February 1942, DSF MSS, Container 1.
77. DSF to Frank McCarthy, 28 May 1942, DSF MSS, Container 44.
78. Frank McCarthy to DSF, 6 April 1942, DSF MSS, Container 44.
79. DSF, Diary, 4 October 1942, DSF MSS, Container 1.
80. DSF to Mary Tyler Freeman Cheek, 25 September 1942, DSF MSS, Container 42.
81. DSF to J. L. DeWitt, 20 October 1942, DSF MSS, Container 42.
82. DSF to George C. Marshall, 5 March 1942, DSF MSS, Container 44.
83. DSF to Frank McCarthy, 17 April 1942, DSF MSS, Container 44.
84. "Dr. Freeman Likens Leadership of Gen. Lee and Gen. Marshall," *Washington Evening Star*, 19 January 1943.
85. DSF to Frank McCarthy, 17 April 1942, DSF MSS, Container 44.
86. DSF to George C. Marshall, 22 April 1942, DSF MSS, Container 44.
87. Ibid.
88. DSF to Robert Patterson, 12 May 1942, DSF MSS, Container 44; DSF to George C. Marshall, 2 September 1943; DSF to George C. Marshall, 30 December 1943; George C. Marshall to DSF, 31 December 1943, DSF MSS, Container 51.
89. DSF to Robert Patterson, 16 October 1942, DSF MSS, Container 44.
90. Robert Patterson to DSF, 20 October 1942; Robert Patterson to DSF, 14 November 1942, DSF MSS, Container 44. *See* DSF to Radcliffe Heermance, 13 January 1943, DSF MSS, Container 50. "Through Judge Patterson, the Under Secretary of War, I have been at work on the President and got his promise to name a commission to study the return of soldiers to college after the war ends."
91. "Freeman on Town Meeting Broadcast," *Richmond Times-Dispatch*, 17 September 1942; DSF MSS, Container 46.
92. DSF to Howard Bobbitt, 11 April 1942, DSF MSS, Container 41.
93. DSF to John Atkins, 3 January 1942, DSF MSS, Container 41.
94. DSF, *Lee's Lieutenants*, Vol. I, xxii-xxvi.
95. Ibid., xxix-xxx.
96. DSF to George C. Marshall, 2 October 1942, DSF MSS, Container 44.
97. George C. Marshall to DSF, 6 December 1942, DSF MSS, Container 44.
98. Stephen Vincent Benet, "Generals in Action and Under the Stress of Action," *The New York Times Book Review*, 25 October 1942, 5.
99. Bernard DeVoto, "The Confederate Military System," *Saturday Review of Literature*, 24 October 1942, 123. There was at least one dissenting opinion. Orville Prescott, a columnist for the *New York Times*, judged *Lee's Lieutenants* to be "probably flawless" as a "final, authoritative, definitive work." "Nevertheless and notwithstanding," he wrote, "I hereby assert and certify that [it] is one of the most tiresome, ponderous, pedantic, dry, dusty, humorless, and generally dull books that ever lay in wait for the unwary reader." Orville Prescott, "Books of the Time," *The New York Times*, 19 October 1942, 19.

100.Thomas Robson Hay, "Review," *The Journal of Southern History*, Vol. 9 (February 1943), 122.
101. Branch Spalding, "Review," *American Historical Review*, Vol. XLVIII, No. 3 (April 1943), 592.
102. "Dr. Freeman Sees Parallel Problems of Leadership Between '61 and '42," *Richmond Times-Dispatch*, 18 October 1942, IV-8.
103. Maxwell E. Perkins to DSF, 9 October 1942, DSF MSS, Container 44.
104. DSF to Margaret Mitchell Marsh, 23 July 1943, DSF MSS, Container 51.
105. Ibid. The "little scene" referred to by Freeman is found in *Lee's Lieutenants*, Vol. II, *Cedar Mountain to Chancellorsville* (New York: Charles Scribner's Sons, 1943), 523.
106. DSF to William McCann, 21 June 1943, DSF MSS, Container 51.
107. DSF to Mrs. T. M. Campbell, 9 July 1943, DSF MSS, Container 48.
108. H. A. DeWeerd, "Review," *American Historical Review*, Vol. XLIX, No. 1 (October 1943), 122.
109. Bernard DeVoto, "Mr. Freeman's Continuing Study," *Saturday Review of Literature*, 29 May 1943, 26.
110. DSF to Runyon Cole, 25 February 1943, DSF MSS, Container 48. One critic of Freeman's earlier treatment of Longstreet was the general's widow. Helen Longstreet wrote Freeman and asked to be allowed "to answer your Chapters on General Longstreet" as an appendix in *Lee's Lieutenants*. "It would not be possible," she wrote, "for you to do justice to Longstreet's record." No reply is found among Freeman's papers. Helen Dortch Longstreet to DSF, 17 December 1940, DSF MSS, Container 38.
111. DSF to Runyon Cole, 25 February 1943, DSF MSS, Container 48. Freeman's reference to "the old man" is confusing. It could be to Longstreet, the subject of the letter, but the introduction of the Southern Historical Papers in the immediately preceding sentence leads one to believe that the "old man" was Jubal Early. The phrase "bitter partisan" also fits Early slightly better than Longstreet.
112. DSF to Runyon Cole, 20 April 1943, DSF MSS, Container 48.
113. DSF, *Lee's Lieutenants*, Vol. III, Appendix II, 760.
114. DSF to Lt. Col. Palmer Bradley, 2 March 1943, DSF MSS, Container 47.
115. DSF to Maxwell E. Perkins, 7 December 1943, DSF MSS, Container 51.
116. DSF to Miss Julie Duffy, 4 August 1943, DSF MSS, Container 48.
117. DSF, Diary, 9 January 1944, DSF MSS, Container 1.
118. DSF, Diary, 30 May 1944, DSF MSS, Container 1. Freeman dated his study to 1915 and the start of *R. E. Lee*.
119. DSF to Mary Tyler Cheek, 31 May 1944, MTM MSS.
120. DSF, *Lee's Lieutenants*, Vol. III, xxiii.
121. Ibid., xxiv.
122. Ibid., Vol. I, 71.
123. Ibid., Vol. III, xxiv.
124. Ibid., Vol. I, 350-51.
125. Ibid., Vol. III, xxiv.

126. Ibid., Vol. I, 602

127. Ibid., Vol. III, xxiv.

128. Ibid., Vol. II, 221.

129. Ibid., Vol. III, xxiv.

130. Ibid., Vol. II, 682.

131. Ibid., Vol. III, xxiv.

132. Ibid., 160.

133. Ibid., xxiv-xxv.

134. Ibid., 752.

135. R. H. Woody, "The Army of Northern Virginia," *The South Atlantic Quarterly*, Vol. 44, No. 1 (January 1945), 101.

136. DSF to George C. Marshall, 19 May 1942, DSF MSS, Container 44.

137. DSF to Newton Wanliss, 27 June 1944, DSF MSS, Container 58.

138. DSF to Allen W. Freeman, 27 June 1944, DSF MSS, Container 55.

139. DSF to Newton Wanliss, 27 June 1944, DSF MSS, Container 58.

140. Chester Nimitz to DSF, 25 February 1945, DSF MSS, Container 63.

141. DSF to Allen W. Freeman, 10 March 1944, DSF MSS, Container 55.

142. DSF to Douglas MacArthur, 28 December 1944, DSF MSS, Container 51.

143. DSF to Douglas MacArthur, 29 December 1944, DSF MSS, Container 57.

144. Douglas MacArthur to DSF, 12 January 1945, DSF MSS, Container 121. MacArthur's assertion that he was "of Virginia" was based on the fact that his mother, Mary Pinkney Hardy, was born in Norfolk, Virginia. Following her marriage to Arthur MacArthur (born in Springfield, Massachusetts, and reared in Milwaukee, Wisconsin), "Pinky" MacArthur returned home to "Riveredge," the Hardy homestead in Virginia, to give her first two children a Virginia birth. While preparing to make the trip a third time, she went into early labor, and Douglas MacArthur was born at the Old Arsenal Building in Little Rock, Arkansas. MacArthur stressed his Virginia roots throughout his life and is buried in Norfolk, Virginia.

145. *See* DSF to George C. Marshall, 19 May 1942, DSF MSS, Container 44; DSF to Douglas MacArthur, 12 October 1943, DSF MSS, Container 51; DSF to Dwight D. Eisenhower, 5 November 1943, DSF MSS, Container 49; DSF to Chester Nimitz, 11 January 1945, DSF MSS, Container 63.

146. George C. Marshall to DSF, 21 May 1942, DSF MSS, Container 98.

147. Dwight D. Eisenhower to DSF, 13 November 1943, DSF MSS, Container 49.

148. Ibid.

149. Chester Nimitz to DSF, 11 January 1945, DSF MSS, Container 63.

150. Douglas MacArthur to DSF, 12 January 1945, DSF MSS, Container 121.

151. Ibid.

152. DSF, "Untitled Draft of Introduction of MacArthur Article," enclosed with DSF to Douglas MacArthur, 14 May 1945, DSF MSS, Container 62. The article was not published.

153. Ibid.

154. DSF, "Address at the University of Richmond," 28 March 1946, DSF MSS, Container 65.
155. Ibid.
156. Ibid.
157. Ibid.
158. Ibid.
159. DSF to Whitney Darrow, 8 November 1945, DSF MSS, Container 60. Both MacArthur and Marshall would outlive Freeman.
160. DSF to Ernest King, 26 May 1948, DSF MSS, Container 90.
161. DSF to Raymond Fosdick, 9 April 1948, DSF MSS, Container 87.
162. DSF to James Douglas Freeman, 30 September 1943, MTM MSS.
163. Ibid.
164. DSF, Diary, 27 September 1943, DSF MSS, Container 1.
165. DSF to Douglas MacArthur, 12 October 1943, DSF MSS, Container 51.
166. DSF to Col. John Thompson, 13 January 1940, DSF MSS, Container 39.
167. DSF, Diary, 5 October 1949, DSF MSS, Container 2; DSF to Miss Beatrice Gosford, 11 March 1947, DSF MSS, Container 78.
168. "The Virginians," Time, 18 October 1948.
169. DSF to Raymond B. Fosdick, 10 May 1944, DSF MSS, Container 55.
170. Ibid.
171. Raymond Fosdick to DSF, 1 June 1944, DSF MSS, Container 55; DSF, Diary, 23 June 1944, DSF MSS, Container 1.
172. DSF to Mary Tyler Cheek, 31 May 1944, MTM MSS; DSF to Raymond Fosdick, 3 June 1944, DSF MSS, Container 55; DSF, Diary, 21 June 1944, DSF MSS, Container 1.
173. See DSF to Mary Tyler Cheek, 27 June 1944; DSF to Isaiah Bowman, 7 July 1944, MTM MSS; DSF to Raymond Fosdick, 30 June 1944, DSF MSS, Container 55; DSF to J. E. Pomfret, 6 July 1944, DSF MSS, Container 57.
174. DSF to Mary Tyler Cheek, 18 July 1944, MTM MSS.
175. DSF to John Stewart Bryan, 1 August 1944, DSF MSS, Container 53.
176. DSF to Inez G. Freeman, 10 August 1944, MTM MSS; DSF, Diary 14 August 1944, DSF MSS, Container 1.
177. DSF, Diary, 13 September 1944, DSF MSS, Container 1.
178. DSF to Allen W. Freeman, 18 October 1944, DSF MSS, Container 55; DSF to Frank McCarthy, 23 October 1944, DSF MSS, Container 57.
179. DSF, Diary, 16 October 1944, DSF MSS, Container 1.
180. D. Tennant Bryan to DSF, 5 December 1944, MTM MSS.
181. DSF, "John Stewart Bryan, 72, Publisher, William & Mary Chancellor, is Dead," Richmond Times-Dispatch, 17 October 1944, 1; "John Stewart Bryan," Richmond News Leader, 17 October 1944, 10.
182. Richmond News Leader, 17 October 1944. Compare these words about John Stewart Bryan to those used on the death of Robert E. Lee. "There he lies, now that they have shrouded him . . . one of the small company of great men in whom

there is no inconsistency to be explained, no enigma to be solved. What he seemed to be, he was—a wholly human gentleman, the essential elements of whose positive character were two and only two, simplicity and spirituality . . . religion blended with a code of noblesse oblige to which he had been reared . . . this assuredly was the great, transparent truth [of his life]." *R. E. Lee*, Vol. IV, 493-503.

183. DSF, Diary, 18 October 1944, DSF MSS, Container 1.
184. DSF to C. F. Board, 4 January 1945, DSF MSS, Container 59.
185. DSF, Diary, 5 November 1944, DSF MSS, Container 1.
186. DSF to C. F. Board, 8 February 1945; 26 July 1945, DSF MSS, Container 59.
187. DSF to Allen W. Freeman, 4 February 1946, DSF MSS, Container 68.
188. DSF to C. F. Board, 17 April 1946, DSF MSS, Container 65; DSF to Allen W. Freeman, 6 May 1947, DSF MSS, Container 78; DSF, Diary, 7 May 1947, DSF MSS, Container 2.
189. DSF to C. F. Board, 8 January 1948, DSF MSS, Container 85.
190. DSF, *Lee of Virginia* (New York: Charles Scribner's Sons, 1958).
191. DSF to D. Tennant Bryan, 26 May 1945, DSF MSS, Container 59; DSF, Diary, 8 April 1945; 22 June 1946, DFS MSS, Container 1.
192. DSF, Diary, 11 August 1946, DSF MSS, Container 1.
193. DSF to D. Tennant Bryan, Mrs. R. Keith Kane, and Stewart Bryan, Jr., 7 January 1947, Bryan Papers, Virginia Historical Society.
194. DSF to the Rev. William T. Winston, 10 February 1945, DSF MSS, Container 64.

CHAPTER TWELVE
1. DSF, Diary, 26 November 1944, DFS MSS, Container 1; "Dr. Douglas S. Freeman Opens a New Account," *Richmond Times-Dispatch*, 3 December 1944, D-6.
2. *Richmond Times-Dispatch*, 3 December 1944; "Native Daughter Comes Home to Fulfill Mission for Virginia," DSF MSS, Virginia Baptist Historical Society; DSF to Robert M. Lester, 15 August 1944, Carnegie Corporation Papers, Rare Books and Manuscript Library, Columbia University (hereafter referred to as "DSF COL.")
3. DSF to Carl W. Ackerman, 18 April 1941; Carl W. Ackerman to DSF, 25 April 1941, DSF MSS, Container 35.
4. *Richmond Times-Dispatch*, 3 December 1944.
5. DSF to Robert M. Lester, 10 April 1945, DSF COL.
6. DSF to Robert M. Lester, 12 January 1945, DSF COL.
7. DSF to Robert M. Lester, 10 April 1945, DSF COL.
8. DSF, *George Washington*, Vol. 1, xi.
9. DSF, *George Washington*, Vol. 1, xii; DSF to Robert M. Lester, 10 April 1945, DSF COL.
10. DSF, *George Washington*, Vol. 1, xii. The section on the Fairfax proprietary

proved so lengthy that Freeman removed it from the first chapter and inserted it as an appendix in Volume One. The history of Virginia became Chapter Four of Volume One. DSF, *George Washington*, Vol.1, 73-189, 447-512.

11. DSF to Andrew D. Christian, 4 December 1942, DSF MSS, Container 42.
12. DSF to Andrew D. Christian, 14 July 1944, DSF MSS, Container 54.
13. DSF to D. Tennant Bryan, 3 May 1949, DSF MSS, Container 95.
14. DSF to Frank McCarthy, 4 December 1943, DSF MSS, Container 51.
15. Ashworth, "The Man and the Making of a Book," 17.
16. DSF to Mrs. J. A. Dunleavey, 19 June 1944, DSF MSS, Container 54.
17. DSF to the Rev. George W. Sadler, 6 October 1944, DSF MSS, Container 58.
18. Ashworth, "The Man and the Making of a Book," 18.
19. DSF to Victor Wheeler, 10 March 1945, DSF MSS, Container 64.
20. *Richmond News Leader*, 2 May 1944.
21. Franklin D. Roosevelt to DSF, 31 May 1944, DSF MSS, Container 58. At his press conference, Roosevelt mistakenly gave credit for the idea to the *Washington Post*. Meyer advised the president of his mistake, and a subsequent Associated Press story corrected the version of the phrase's origination. Eugene Meyer to DSF, 27 May 1944; DSF to Eugene Meyer, 31 May 1944, DSF MSS, Container 57; DSF to Franklin D. Roosevelt, 1 June 1944, DSF MSS, Container 58; "Editor Gets Credit for Suggestion," *Richmond Times-Dispatch*, 1 June 1944.
22. DSF, Diary, 6 June 1944, DSF MSS, Container 1.
23. DSF to Allen W. Freeman, 24 August 1944, DSF MSS, Container 55.
24. DSF to Allen W. Freeman, 3 April 1945, DSF MSS, Container 61.
25. *Richmond News Leader*, 13 April 1945.
26. DSF to Inez G. Freeman, 11 August 1945, MTM MSS.
27. DSF to Allen W. Freeman, 13 August 1945, DSF MSS, Container 61.
28. DSF, "Radio Broadcast," 14 August 1945, Virginia Historical Society.
29. Ibid.
30. DSF, Diary, 3 September 1940, DSF MSS, Container 1.
31. DSF to Inez G. Freeman, 15 August 1945, MTM MSS.
32. DSF to Allen W. Freeman, 27 September 1945, DSF MSS, Container 61.
33. DSF to Inez G. Freeman, 29 September 1945, MTM MSS. Excerpts of letters from Freeman during this trip are found in DSF MSS, Container 61.
34. DSF to Inez G. Freeman, 30 September 1945, MTM MSS.
35. DSF to Inez G. Freeman, 1 October 1945, MTM MSS.
36. DSF, Diary, 3 October 1945, DSF MSS, Container 1.
37. DSF to Inez G. Freeman, 6 October 1945, MTM MSS.
38. Ibid.
39. DSF, Notebook, "Things noted but not reported in my letters home," DSF MSS, Container 3.
40. DSF to Inez G. Freeman, 6 October 1945, MTM MSS.

41. DSF, Diary, 6 October 1945, DSF MSS, Container 1; DSF to Inez G. Freeman, 7 October 1945, MTM MSS.

42. "Beaming Virginia Editor and Red Army Marshal Clink Glasses at Park Club in Budapest," *Richmond News Leader*, 18 October 1945.

43. DSF to Inez G. Freeman, 8 October 1945, MTM MSS.

44. DSF, Diary, 10 October 1945, DSF MSS, Container 1; DSF to Inez G. Freeman, 11, 12 October 1945, MTM MSS.

45. DSF to Inez G. Freeman, 12, 13 October 1945, MTM MSS.

46. DSF to Inez G. Freeman, 19 October 1945, MTM MSS.

47. DSF, Diary, 18, 19 October 1945, DSF MSS, Container 1.

48. DSF to Inez G. Freeman, 23 October 1945, MTM MSS.

49. A. Willis Robertson to DSF, 18 April 1951; DSF to A. Willis Robertson, 21 April 1951, DSF MSS, Container 107.

50. DSF to A. Willis Robertson, 21 April 1951, DSF MSS, Container 107.

51. DSF to Inez G. Freeman, 23 October 1945, MTM MSS.

52. DSF, Diary, 26, 27, 28, 29, 30, 30, 31 October 1945, DSF MSS, Container 1.

53. "Quick End to US Occupation Means Trouble, Says Expert," *Honolulu Advertiser*, 1 November 1945.

54. DSF, "Note," DSF MSS, Container 229.

55. DSF, Diary, 3 November 1945, DSF MSS, Container 1.

56. DSF to John J. McCloy, 30 September 1946, DSF MSS, Container 70.

57. John J. McCloy to DSF, 16 November 1945, DSF to John J. McCloy, 19 November 1945, DSF MSS, Container 62; DSF, "Statement of Douglas S. Freeman Before the House Select Committee on Post-War Military Policy," 14 June 1945, DSF MSS, Container 64; James Forrestal to DSF, 2 October 1947, DSF to James Forrestal, 6 October 1947, DSF MSS, Container 78.

58. Milton Caniff, "Steve Canyon," n/d, but circa 8 November 1955, MTM MSS.

59. DSF to Lewis F. Powell, 16 January 1953, DSF MSS, Container 118.

60. DSF to Richard S. Reynolds, 28 July 1948, DSF MSS, Container 92.

61. DSF to Dwight D. Eisenhower, 11 February 1946, DSF MSS, Container 67.

62. Dwight D. Eisenhower to F. W. Boatwright, 13 February 1946, DSF MSS, Container 65.

63. "Eisenhower and Nimitz, Honored by University of Richmond, Stress Need for Education on Path to Peace," *Richmond Times-Dispatch*, 29 March 1946, 1.

64. H. S. Cummins to DSF, 31 March 1946, DSF MSS, Container 67.

65. DSF to H. S. Cummins, 2 April 1946, DSF MSS, Container 72.

66. DSF to F. W. Boatwright, 2 April 1946, DSF MSS, Container 65.

67. DST to T. Justin Moore, 6 April 1946, DSF MSS, Container 71; DSF to Jack G. Holtzclaw, 10 April 1946, DSF MSS, Container 69.

68. F. W. Boatwright to DSF, 4 April 1946, DSF MSS, Container 72.

69. Theodore F. Adams to DSF, 4 April 1946, DSF MSS, Container 72.

70. T. Justin Moore, F. W. Boatwright, and O. D. Davis to DSF, 8 April 1946, DSF MSS, Container 72.

71. *See* James Weaver to DSF, 17 April 1946; Daniel F. White to DSF, 12 June 1946, DSF MSS, Container 74.

72. DSF to Dwight D. Eisenhower, 26 October 1946; Dwight D. Eisenhower to DSF, 28 October 1946, DSF MSS, Container 67.

73. DSF to Mary Tyler Cheek, 15 November 1946, MTM MSS.

74. DSF to Allen W. Freeman, 20 November 1946, DSF MSS, Container 60.

75. DSF, "Ike Gets Vote of Southern Historian," *Life*, 22 September 1952, 53.

76. DSF to Allen W. Freeman, 20 November 1946, DSF MSS, Container 60.

77. DSF to Dwight D. Eisenhower, 6 September 1950, DSF MSS, Container 101.

78. DSF to Allen W. Freeman, 20 November 1946, DSF MSS, Container 60.

79. Dwight D. Eisenhower to DSF, 12 September 1950, DSF MSS, Container 101.

80. DSF to Dwight D. Eisenhower, 10 July 1948, DSF MSS, Container 87.

81. DSF, Diary, 4 March 1944, DSF MSS, Container 1; DSF to Harry S. Truman, 7 March 1944, DSF MSS, Container 58; DSF to James Douglas Freeman, 15 March 1944, MTM MSS.

82. DSF to James Douglas Freeman, 20 March 1944, MTM MSS.

83. Harry S. Truman to DSF, 21 March 1944, DSF MSS, Container 58.

84. DSF to Mrs. G. F. Pittard, 17 October 1944, DSF MSS, Container 57.

85. DSF to A. D. Christian, 12 April 1944, DSF MSS, Container 54.

86. DSF to Harry S. Truman, 28 April 1944, DSF MSS, Container 58. Freeman's enthusiasm for Truman was matched by his contempt for the incumbent vice president, Henry A. Wallace, whom he judged to be a "jackass." DSF to A. D. Christian, 26 June 1944, DSF MSS, Container 54.

87. DSF to Mrs. G. F. Pittard, 17 October 1944, DSF MSS, Container 58.

88. DSF to Harry S. Truman, 2 February 1945, DSF MSS, Container 64.

89. Harry S. Truman to DSF, 5 February 1945, DSF MSS, Container 64.

90. *Richmond News Leader*, 13 April 1945.

91. DSF to A. Willis Robertson, 12 June 1943, DSF MSS, Container 51.

92. DSF to Horatio Bigelow, 3 June 1946, DSF MSS, Container 65.

93. DSF to W. B. Edwards, 12 December 1946, DSF MSS, Container 67.

94. Allen W. Freeman to DSF, 23 April 1946; DSF to Allen W. Freeman, 24 April 1946, DSF MSS, Container 68.

95. DSF to Gen. Bonner Fellers, 9 April 1946, DSF MSS, Container 67.

96. DSF to Horatio Bigelow, 3 June 1946, DSF MSS, Container 65; DSF to Walter S. Robertson, 12 July 1946, DSF MSS, Container 72.

97. DSF to Harry F. Byrd, 14 March 1947, DSF MSS, Container 76.

98. DSF to A. Willis Robertson, 14 March 1947; A. Willis Robertson to DSF, 17 March 1947, DSF MSS, Container 76; DSF to A. Willis Robertson, 23 April 1947, DSF MSS, Container 82.

99. DSF to Harry F. Byrd, 26 December 1947, DSF MSS, Container 76.

100. DSF to Allen W. Freeman, 3 July 1946, DSF MSS, Container 68.

101. DSF to Robert A. Taft, 9 January 1948, DSF MSS, Container 93.

102. DSF to Harry F. Byrd, 22 January 1948, DSF MSS, Container 85.

103. DSF to Harry F. Byrd, 31 January 1948, DSF MSS, Container 85.

104. DSF to Harry F. Byrd, 24 January 1948, DSF MSS, Container 85.

105. DSF to Allen W. Freeman, 3 July 1946, DSF MSS, Container 68.

106. "Dr. Freeman Suggested as Envoy to Britain," *Richmond Times-Dispatch*, 16 February 1947; Harry F. Byrd to DSF, 18 February 1947, DSF MSS, Container 76.

107. DSF to Allen W. Freeman, 17, 24 February 1947, DSF MSS, Container 78.

108. DSF to Harry F. Byrd, 19 February 1947, DSF MSS, Container 76.

109. Wilkinson, *Harry F. Byrd and the Changing Face of Virginia Politics*; Heinemann, *Harry Byrd of Virginia*; Robert T. Hawkes, "Harry F. Byrd: Leadership and Reform," *Governors of Virginia*, Edward Younger, ed. (Charlottesville: University Press of Virginia, 1982).

110. DSF to Harry F. Byrd, 22 October 1924, DSF MSS, Container 5. Freeman came to know Richard Byrd during his service on the State Tax Commission.

111. DSF to Harry F. Byrd, 8 November 1924, DSF MSS, Container 5.

112. *Richmond News Leader*, 5 August 1925.

113. Governors of Virginia are limited to one term.

114. *See* Harry F. Byrd to DSF, 29 June 1926; 27 December 1926, DSF MSS, Container 5.

115. *Richmond News Leader*, 15 January 1930.

116. DSF to Harry F. Byrd, 26 December 1928, DSF MSS, Container 9.

117. DSF to Harry F. Byrd, 10 July 1935, DSF MSS, Container 21.

118. Harry F. Byrd to DSF, 13 May 1938; DSF to Harry F. Byrd, 20 May 1938, DSF MSS, Container 28.

119. Alvin L. Hall, "James Hubert Price: New Dealer in the Old Dominion," in *Governors of Virginia*, 277, 282-85.

120. Harry F. Byrd to DSF, 16 March 1940, DSF MSS, Container 35.

121. DSF to Harry F. Byrd, 18 March 1940, DSF MSS, Container 35.

122. DSF to Rowland Egger, 4 February 1942, DSF MSS, Container 42.

123. DSF to Harry F. Byrd, 23 December 1943, DSF MSS, Container 47.

124. DSF to Harry F. Byrd, 16 September 1944, DSF MSS, Container 53.

125. DSF to Harry F. Byrd, 27 January 1945, DSF MSS, Container 59.

126. Harry F. Byrd to DSF, 20 March 1945, DSF MSS, Container 59.

127. N. Clarence Smith to DSF, 26 April 1945, DSF MSS, Container 63.

128. DSF to N. Clarence Smith, 27 April 1945, DSF MSS, Container 63.

129. DSF to S. L. Slover, 12 March 1948, DSF MSS, Container 93; DSF to Allen W. Freeman, 16 March 1948, DSF MSS, Container 88; "Gray Tells Rotarians, Educators Richmond Papers Unreasonable Toward Organization," 2 April 1948, unidentified paper, DSF MSS, Container 91.

130. DSF to Allen W. Freeman, 16 March 1948, DSF MSS, Container 88;

DSF to A. Robbins, 17 March 1948, DSF MSS, Container 92.

131. DSF to J. Budd Breidenstein, 17 March 1948, DSF MSS, Container 85.

132. Harry F. Byrd to E. R. Combs, 3 June 1941, quoted in Heinemann, *Harry Byrd of Virginia*, 122.

133. DSF to Colgate Darden, 23 February 1945, DSF MSS, Container 60; DSF to Colgate Darden, 22 January 1946, DSF MSS, Container 67.

134. A. Willis Robertson to DSF, 15 January; 8 June 1946; DSF to A. Willis Robertson, 27 June 1946; A. Willis Robertson to DSF, 9 July 1946, DSF MSS, Container 72; DSF to Francis P. Miller, 3 March 1948, DSF MSS, Container 91. Robertson would write that "no one in the State did more to convince the people of the State that I should serve them in that capacity." A. Willis Robertson to DSF, 11 September 1946, DSF MSS, Container 72.

135. DSF to Hunsdon Cary, 10 July 1946, DSF MSS, Container 66.

136. Harry F. Byrd to DSF, 16 July 1946, DSF MSS, Container 66.

137. DSF to Harry F. Byrd, 22 December 1948, DSF MSS, Container 85.

138. DSF to Harry F. Byrd, 27 January 1945, DSF MSS, Container 59. The combination of friendship and agreement on national policies led Freeman to volunteer, "as an anti-machine man" to introduce Byrd on a campaign broadcast. On July 14, 1952, after his retirement as editor, he went on a statewide radio hookup to say that "renewal of Harry Byrd's service to the American people is imperative" in order "to have government interfere as little as possible with the citizen's effort to make a decent living, to rear and to educate his children, and to maintain a respectable home." DSF, "Remarks," 14 July 1952, DSF MSS, Container 109.

139. DSF to Wallace Meyer, 17 November 1945, DSF MSS, Container 62.

140. DSF to Robert Lester, 11 January 1946, DSF COL.

141. DSF to H. N. Young, 13 March 1948; DSF to C. C. Wall, 10 April; 12 November 1948, MTM MSS.

142. Charles McDowell to DSF, 24 September 1948; DSF to Charles McDowell, 24 September 1948, DSF MSS, Container 90.

143. DSF to Alberto Tarchiani, 3 November 1947, MTM MSS.

144. DSF to Felix Frankfurter, 15 September 1947, DSF MSS, Container 78.

145. Felix Frankfurter to DSF, 7 October 1947, DSF MSS, Container 78.

146. DSF to Robert M. Lester, 11 April; 11 July 1946, DSF COL.

147. DSF to Robert M. Lester, 11 April 1946, DSF COL.

148. DSF to Robert M. Lester, 11 July 1946, DSF Col.

149. Ibid.

150. Ibid. *See also* DSF to Lloyd W. Smith, 18 February; 30 May; 27 June, 1946, MTM MSS.

151. DSF to Robert M. Lester, 19 October 1946, DSF COL.

152. DSF to James B. Munn, 18 January 1947, DSF MSS, Container 81.

153. DSF to James B. Munn, 13 November 1946, DSF MSS, Container 71.

154. DSF to Robert M. Lester, 19 October 1946, DSF COL.

155. DSF to Robert M. Lester, 14 January 1947, DSF COL.
156. DSF to Robert M. Lester, 11 September 1947, DSF COL.
157. DSF to Robert M. Lester, 14 January 1947, DSF COL.
158. DSF, Diary, 29 October 1947, DSF MSS, Container 2.
159. Mrs. George S. Patton, Jr., to DSF, 15 May 1947, DSF MSS, Container 82. "One of my husband's last letters to young George," Mrs. Patton wrote the next day to Freeman, "says 'Read all of Freeman—and then study him.'" Mrs. George S. Patton, Jr., to DSF, 16 May 1947, DSF MSS, Container 82.
160. DSF to Allen W. Freeman, 19 March 1943, DSF MSS, Container 49.
161. DSF to Robert T. Barton, 11 May 1943, DSF MSS, Container 47.
162. DSF to Robert Patterson, 1 April 1946, DSF MSS, Container 71.
163. Ibid.; DSF to Delos C. Emmons, 16 May 1947, DSF MSS, Container 77.
164. DSF to Delos C. Emmons, 20 May 1947, DSF MSS, Container 77.
165. DSF to Mrs. George S. Patton, Jr., 19 May 1947, DSF MSS, Container 82.
166. Ibid.
167. DSF, Introduction to George S. Patton, Jr., *War As I Knew It* (Boston: Houghton Mifflin Co., 1947), xviii-xix.
168. Mrs. George S. Patton, Jr., to DSF, 28 June; 24 October 1947, DSF MSS, Container 82. Carlo D'Este states in his definitive biography of Patton that Freeman "at Beatrice's instigation, would have become her husband's official biographer had he not died soon thereafter." While Mrs. Patton no doubt wanted Freeman to fill that role, it is nowhere indicated in any of Freeman's papers that he ever considered writing the biography of Patton. Carlo D'Este, *Patton: A Genius for War* (New York: Harper Collins, 1995), 806.
169. "The Virginians," *Time*, 18 October 1948, 108.
170. Ibid., 108-10.
171. *See* "A Great Figure Emerges," *Saturday Review of Literature*, 16 October 1948, 10; "Washington, Sans the Halo," *Richmond Times-Dispatch*, 17 October 1948, 12-D; Hugh T. Lefler, "George Washington: A Biography," *The Journal of Southern History*, Vol. XV (February 1948), 98.
172. Mary Wells Ashworth, "Note," MTM MSS.
173. DSF to Ben Ames Williams, 12 August 1944, DSF MSS, Container 58.
174. DSF to Miss Nicky Raitt, 3 March 1948, DSF MSS, Container 92. *See also* DSF to T. M. Downs, 9 January 1945, DSF MSS, Container 60, in which the same sentiment is expressed. "The War Between the States was one of the greatest crimes of modern times and it was perpetrated by politicians of extreme view, north and south."
175. DSF to Victor Windett, 28 July 1942, DSF MSS, Container 46.
176. Ibid.; *see also* DSF to Winston Folk, 27 April 1945, DSF MSS, Container 61, in which Freeman writes that to argue over the two terms is to "split hairs."
177. DSF to Philip Graydon Bower, 8 July 1952, DSF MSS, Container 109.
178. DSF to Miss Mary A. Bowles, 9 April 1946, DSF MSS, Container 65.
179. DSF to Niel J. Bulger, 21 September 1951, DSF MSS, Container 104.

180. DSF to Robert L. Cusick, 29 March 1947, DSF MSS, Container 77.

181. DSF to Judge Edgar Rich, 2 December 1926, DSF MSS, Container 8.

182. DSF to Sam A. Ashe, 14 March 1935, DSF MSS, Container 21.

183. *Richmond News Leader*, 12 February 1935.

184. DSF to Mrs. James H. Clower, 21 March 1935, DSF MSS, Container 22.

185. DSF to Sam A. Ashe, 14 March 1935, DSF MSS, Container 21.

186. DSF to Allen W. Freeman, 8 July 1947, DSF MSS, Container 78.

187. DSF to Allen W. Freeman, 4 November 1948, DSF MSS, Container 91.

188. DSF, "Notes on Freeman's George Washington, Volumes One and Two," n/d, DSF MSS, Container 157.

189. DSF, *George Washington*, Vol. 2, *Young Washington* (New York: Charles Scribner's Sons, 1948), 388.

190. Ibid., 389.

191. Allan Nevins, "Washington, Minus His Pedestal," *The New York Times Book Review*, 17 October 1948, 1.

192. Richard E. Danielson, "Young Washington: A Living Portrait," *The Atlantic Monthly*, Vol. 183, No. 1 (January 1949), 76.

193. "Washington: Early Days," *The* (London) *Spectator*, 13 May 1949, 654.

194. Hugh T. Lefler, "Review," *The Journal of Southern History*, Vol. XV (February 1949), 98.

195. Danielson, *The Atlantic Monthly*, 78.

196. *Saturday Review of Literature*, 16 October 1948, 10.

197. *The New Statesman and Nation* (London), 6 August 1949; Nevins, "Washington, Minus His Pedestal," 49.

198. Bernard Knollenberg, "Review," *William & Mary Quarterly*, Vol. VI (January 1949), 118.

199. Ibid., 114-15.

200. DSF to Allen W. Freeman, 3 August 1948, DSF MSS, Container 88.

CHAPTER THIRTEEN

1. DSF, "John Stewart Bryan," 454.

2. DSF to Mary Tyler Freeman, 3 July 1930, MTM MSS.

3. Mary Tyler Cheek to DSF, 14 March 1944, MTM MSS.

4. DSF to Mary Tyler Cheek, 29 July 1952, MTM MSS.

5. Mary Tyler Cheek to DSF, 9 July 1952; DSF to Mary Tyler Freeman, 14 November 1933, MTM MSS.

6. DSF to Mary Tyler Cheek, 6 October 1941, MTM MSS.

7. Mary Tyler Cheek to DSF, n/d, but Easter Monday, 1952, MTM MSS.

8. M. T. McClenahan, "Manuscript," 37.

9. Inez G. Freeman to DSF, 9 September 1919, DSF MSS, Container 6.

10. *See* DSF to Mary Tyler Freeman, 18 June 1927, MTM MSS.

11. DSF to Mary Tyler Freeman, 3 July 1930, MTM MSS.

12. DSF to Mary Tyler Freeman, 10 July 1930, MTM MSS.

13. Mary Tyler Freeman to DSF, 6 July 1930, MTM MSS.

14. DSF to Inez G. Freeman, 9 July 1930, MTM MSS.

15. DSF to Inez G. Freeman, 16 July 1930, MTM MSS.
16. DSF to Mary Tyler Freeman, 6 August 1930, MTM MSS.
17. DSF to Louisa Bacot, 10 November 1930, DSF MSS, Container 9.
18. DSF to Henry Winston Holt, 29 August 1932, DSF MSS, Container 17.
19. DSF to Mary Tyler Freeman, 17, 22 July 1930; 20 August 1930, MTM MSS.
20. DSF to Inez G. Freeman, 1 August 1932, MTM MSS.
21. DSF to Inez G. Freeman, 25 August 1932, MTM MSS.
22. DSF to Inez G. Freeman, 26 July 1933, MTM MSS.
23. Mary Tyler Freeman to DSF, 19 July 1933, MTM MSS.
24. Mary Tyler Freeman to DSF, 28 July 1933, MTM MSS.
25. DSF to Mary Tyler Freeman, 3 November 1933, MTM MSS. Emphasis in the original.
26. DSF to Mary Tyler Freeman, 14 November 1933, MTM MSS.
27. DSF to Mary Tyler Freeman, 13 March 1934, MTM MSS.
28. Ibid.
29. Mary Tyler Freeman to DSF, 18 March 1934, MTM MSS.
30. DSF to Mary Tyler Freeman, 20 March 1934, MTM MSS.
31. DSF to Mary Tyler Freeman, 4 July; 21 September; 4 December 1933, MTM MSS.
32. DSF to Mary Tyler Freeman, 10 April 1934, MTM MSS.
33. Mary Tyler Freeman to DSF, 17 April 1934, MTM MSS.
34. DSF to Mary Tyler Freeman, 18 April 1934, MTM MSS.
35. Ibid.
36. Ibid.
37. DSF, Diary, 24 November 1938, DSF MSS, Container 1.
38. Mary Tyler Freeman to DSF and Inez G. Freeman, 16 November 1938, MTM MSS.
39. DSF, Diary, 1 January 1939, DSF MSS, Container 1.
40. DSF, Diary, 12 January 1939, DSF MSS, Container 1.
41. DSF, Diary, 5 February 1939, DSF MSS, Container 1.
42. DSF, "Instruction for Traffic at Westborne June 3, 1939," DSF MSS, Container 30.
43. DSF to Sheriff T. Wilson Seay, 1 June 1930, DSF MSS, Container 30.
44. DSF, Diary, 3 June 1939, DSF MSS, Container 1; Mary Tyler noted the significance of her last few moments as his unwed daughter. "I shall never forget," she wrote, "our short ride to the church." Mary Tyler Cheek to DSF, 10 June 1939, MTM MSS.
45. DSF to Mary Tyler and Leslie Cheek, 11 November 1939, Inscription in Cheek copy of *The South to Posterity*, MTM MSS.
46. Mary Tyler Cheek to DSF, 20 November 1939, MTM MSS.
47. DSF to Mary Tyler Cheek, 6 October 1941, MTM MSS.
48. Mary Tyler Cheek to DSF, n/d, but c. August 1941, MTM MSS.
49. Mary Tyler Cheek to DSF, 13 July 1942, MTM MSS.

50. Mary Tyler Cheek to Inez G. Freeman, 3 May 1943, MTM MSS.

51. Mary Tyler Cheek to DSF, 13 August 1939, MTM MSS.

52. Mary Tyler Cheek to DSF, 25 August 1952, MTM MSS.

53. Ibid.

54. DSF to Mary Tyler Cheek, 29 August 1952, MTM MSS.

55. Ibid.

56. DSF to Mary Tyler Freeman, 14 November 1933, MTM MSS.

57. DSF, Diary, 8 September 1952, DFS MSS, Container 2; DSF to Thomas Freeman, 21 June 1928, DSF MSS, Container 10.

58. DSF to Inez G. Freeman, 3 March 1931; 4 August 1932, MTM MSS.

59. Mary Tyler McClenahan, Interview with author, 4 June 2001.

60. Frances Valentine, Interview with author, 20 July 2001.

61. DSF to Allen W. Freeman, 28 December 1945, DSF MSS, Container 61.

62. Anne B. Freeman to DSF, 1 March 1942, MTM MSS.

63. Anne B. Freeman to DSF, 18 November 1943, MTM MSS. Unfortunately, many of Freeman's letters to Anne have not been found, so it is not possible to recount his jokes.

64. Anne Freeman Adler to DSF, 26 June 1950, MTM MSS.

65. DSF to Inez G. Freeman, 8 July 1940, MTM MSS.

66. DSF to Anne B. Freeman, 2 February 1943, MTM MSS.

67. DSF to Anne B. Freeman, 8 February 1944, DSF MSS, Container 55.

68. Anne B. Freeman to DSF, 16 June 1945, MTM MSS.

69. Frances Valentine, Interview with author, 20 July 2001.

70. DSF to Mary Tyler Cheek, 8 January 1948, MTM MSS.

71. Freeman took much of the blame on himself for Anne's poor showing. "I fear I never shall forgive myself for not watching more closely her work at St. Catherine's," he wrote the dean of Vassar. "It appears now that she and any other girl could slide through St. Catherine's with as little work as they wished and with a little direction of effort." DSF to C. Mildred Thompson, 29 June 1943, DSF MSS, Container 52.

72. The first paper was an untitled history paper; the second was the previously cited "Genealogy" paper; and the third was an extensive paper on Virginia political history titled "Virginia Insurgency 1896-1917." There is no cover letter or reference to the third paper, but the text refers to "my father as a young editor" and acknowledges help in Poughkeepsie, the location of Vassar, and Richmond. DSF to Anne B. Freeman, 22 January; 12 February; 24 May; 5 November 1943, DSF MSS Container 49; Anne B. Freeman to DSF, 20 May 1943, MTM MSS; DSF to Anne B. Freeman, 20 March 1944, DSF MSS, Container 55; "Virginia Insurgency 1896-1917," DSF MSS, Container 150. It should be noted that Freeman would have, and probably did, assist his other children with any research or writing needs.

73. DSF to Anne B. Freeman, 13 April 1944, DSF MSS, Container 55.

74. DSF to Anne B. Freeman, 30 June 1949, DSF MSS, Container 97.

75. Anne B. Freeman to DSF, 5 July 1949, MTM MSS.

76. Anne B. Freeman to DSF, 25 August 1949, MTM MSS.

77. Anne B. Freeman to DSF, 28 September 1949, DSF MSS, Container 97.

78. DSF, Diary, 8 September 1952, DSF MSS, Container 2.

79. DSF, "John Stewart Bryan," 47.

80. James Douglas Freeman, Interview with author, 31 January 2001.

81. DSF to Inez G. Freeman, 5 July 1934, MTM MSS.

82. DSF to Inez G. Freeman, 29 October 1935, MTM MSS.

83. DSF to James Douglas Freeman, 13 July 1933, MTM MSS.

84. DSF to Herbert E. Hawkes, 25 July 1939; Herbert E. Hawkes to DSF, 30 August 1939, DSF MSS, Container 31.

85. DSF to John Bell Williams, 31 July 1939, DSF MSS, Container 34.

86. DSF to Leslie I. Laughlin, 13 February 1943, DSF MSS, Container 50.

87. DSF to James Douglas Freeman, 12 February 1943, MTM MSS.

88. DSF to James Douglas Freeman, 19 March; 5 April; 12 July; 13, 16, 17 August; 8 October 1943, MTM MSS.

89. DSF to James Douglas Freeman, 2 July 1943, MTM MSS.

90. DSF to James Douglas Freeman, 30 October 1943, MTM MSS.

91. DSF to James Douglas Freeman, 17 July 1944, MTM MSS.

92. Ibid.

93. James Douglas Freeman, Interview with author, 31 January 2001.

94. DSF to Allen W. Freeman, 6 January 1947, DSF MSS, Container 78; DSF to Julian P. Boyd, 12 February 1947; Julian P. Boyd to DSF, 11 February 1947, DSF MSS, Container 75; DSF to Mary Tyler Cheek, 6 January; 5 March 1947, MTM MSS. About this time, Freeman wrote a letter to "Sonny" Ashworth, the son of his friend and physician, O. O. Ashworth, and his research assistant, Mary Wells Ashworth, who was a student at Princeton. "Now that James Douglas is out of College," he wrote, "you embody my ambitions and establish my closest ties with Princeton. It is a delight always to know that you will do this in a manner worthy of your high intellectual inheritance and of your innate capacities." DSF to O. O. Ashworth, Jr., 25 April 1947, DSF MSS, Container 75.

95. DSF to Mary Tyler Cheek, 7 March 1947, MTM MSS.

96. DSF to James Douglas Freeman, 15 August 1949, DSF MSS, Container 97.

97. DSF to James Douglas Freeman, 21 April; 8 September 1950; 10 January 1951; DSF to Janice M. Freeman, 20 May 1950, MTM MSS; DSF to Allen W. Freeman, 20 November 1950, DSF MSS, Container 101.

98. DSF to James Douglas Freeman, 8 September 1950, DSF MSS, Container 101.

99. DSF to James Douglas Freeman, 22 May 1951, DSF MSS, Container 106.

100. James Douglas Freeman, Interview with author, 31 January 2001.

CHAPTER FOURTEEN

1. DSF, *George Washington*, Vol. 1, xxvi.

2. DSF, Diary, 2 November 1948, DSF MSS, Container 1.

3. DSF to Mary Brazziotti, 23 October 1948, DSF MSS, Container 85.

4. DSF to James E. Tuthill, 2 August 1948, DSF MSS, Container 93.

5. DSF to D. Tennant Bryan, 21 January 1949, DSF MSS, Container 95.

6. DSF to Allen W. Freeman, 16 September 1947, DSF MSS, Container 78.

7. DSF to Allen W. Freeman, 1 March 1949, DSF MSS, Container 97.

8. DSF to Raymond Fosdick, 23 March 1949, DSF MSS, Container 97.

9. Ibid.

10. DSF to Raymond Fosdick, 26 March 1949, DSF MSS, Container 97.

11. Raymond Fosdick to DSF, 30 March 1949, DSF MSS, Container 97.

12. DSF, "Notes," DSF MSS, Container 101, 1-2.

13. Ibid., 3.

14. DSF to Allen W. Freeman, 5 April 1949, DSF MSS, Container 97.

15. DSF to Allen W. Freeman, 3 May 1949, DSF MSS, Container 97.

16. DSF to D. Tennant Bryan, 3 May 1949, DSF MSS, Container 97.

17. Ibid.

18. Ibid.

19. D. Tennant Bryan to DSF, 3 May 1949, DSF MSS, Container 104.

20. DSF to Raymond Fosdick, 6 May 1949, DSF MSS, Container 97.

21. *Saturday Review of Literature*, 16 October 1948, 10.

22. DSF to Allen W. Freeman, 26 June 1949, DSF MSS, Container 97.

23. DSF to Allen W. Freeman, 24 May 1949; DSF to Louis Jaffe, 8 June 1949, DSF MSS, Container 97.

24. DSF to Allen W. Freeman, 3 May 1949; 20 June 1949, DSF MSS, Container 97.

25. DSF, Diary, 16 May 1949, DSF MSS, Container 2.

26. James J. Kilpatrick, Interview with author, 8 March 2001.

27. DSF to D. Tennant Bryan, 17 November 1948, D. Tennant Bryan Private Papers. Quoted here by courtesy of J. Stewart Bryan, III.

28. James J. Kilpatrick, Interview with author, 8 March 2001. Kilpatrick served as editor for seventeen years before joining the *Washington Star* and becoming one of the nation's preeminent columnists.

29. DSF to D. Tennant Bryan, 26 May 1949, DSF MSS, Container 95.

30. "Dr. Freeman Retires as Editor June 30 to Give Time to Historical Writing," *Richmond News Leader*, 25 June 1949, 1.

31. James J. Kilpatrick, "The 17 Happy Years of a Fire Breathing Editor," *Richmond News Leader*, 30 May 1992, 74.

32. "Dr. Freeman Plans to Quit as Editor," *New York Times*, 26 June 1949, 37; "Lee Biographer to Quit Paper to Write History," *Atlanta Journal*, 26 June 1949, 20.

33. F. W. Boatwright to DSF, 27 June 1949, DSF MSS, Container 95.

34. DSF to F. W. Boatwright, 28 June 1949, DSF MSS, Container 95.

35. *Richmond News Leader*, 30 June 1949.

36. DSF, Diary, 30 June 1949, DSF MSS, Container 2.

37. DSF, Diary, 1, 2, 3 July 1949, DSF MSS, Container 2.

38. DSF to Allen W. Freeman, 4, 6 July 1949, DSF MSS, Container 97.

39. DSF to Allen W. Freeman, 11 August 1949, DSF MSS, Container 97.

40. DSF, Diary, 8 July 1949, DSF MSS, Container 2. He used a similar line in a letter to Jack Wise. "Every day I tell myself that the next morning somebody is going to stand over me, shake me and say: 'Wake up, fool, and go downtown and write two columns of editorial and answer the telephone for all cranks, jackasses and politicians that call you up.'" DSF to John Dana Wise, 10 August 1949, DSF MSS, Container 99.

41. DSF to Raymond Fosdick, 15 October 1942, DSF MSS, Container 42.

42. DSF to John W. Cone, 28 October 1948, DSF MSS, Container 86; Dumas Malone, "Pen of DSF," xxvi.

43. Scheer, "Plutarch on the James," 4.

44. Mary Wells Ashworth, "Memo for Malone," MTM MSS.

45. Malone, "Pen of DSF," xxv.

46. DSF, "Don't Pity the Historical Writer," DSF MSS, Container 87.

47. "Douglas S. Freeman, One of Country's Leading Historians and Biographers, Lectures," *Sweet Briar* (College) *News*, Vol. XXIII, No. 6 (November 9, 1949), 1, 4.

48. Ashworth, "Memo for Malone," 1; "Directions for Note Taking for D. S. Freeman," DSF MSS, Container 15.

49. Ashworth, "Directions for Note Taking"; *George Washington* cards, DSF MSS, Container 193. The information from this particular card was used in *George Washington*, Vol. 5, 328. Freeman noted in footnote 43 that Trumbull "was a day in error on his chronology of September 12-15. *George Washington*, Vol. 5, *Victory with the Help of France* (New York: Charles Scribner's Sons, 1952), 328, n. 43.

50. Ashworth, "Memo for Malone," 2.

51. DSF, Diary 13, 14 July 1945, DSF MSS, Container 1.

52. Scheer, "Plutarch on the James," 4.

53. Ibid.

54. Ashworth, "Memo for Malone," 2.

55. DSF to Allen W. Freeman, 9 October 1950, DSF MSS, Container 101.

56. DSF, Diary, 27 July 1945; 21 September 1946, DSF MSS, Container 1.

57. DSF, Diary, 13 March 1947, DSF MSS, Container 1. What Freeman called "Chapter XVII" became Chapter Five in Volume Two.

58. DSF to Allen W. Freeman, 7 February 1950, DSF MSS, Container 101.

59. DSF to Mary Tyler Cheek, 14 August 1952, DSF MSS, Container 110.

60. Mary Wells Ashworth, "Notes," n/d, Mary Wells Ashworth papers.

61. DSF to M. A. McCall, 27 March 1937, DSF MSS, Container 32.

62. DSF to Lt. Roger Starr, 15 March 1945, DSF MSS, Container 63.

63. DSF to Mary Tyler Cheek, 30 June 1942, DSF MSS, Container 42.

64. DSF to Wallace Meyer, 23 June 1948, DSF MSS, Container 91.

65. Geneva Snelling, "Douglas S. Freeman," DSF MSS, Container 123, 8.

66. Ibid., 7.

67. Mary Wells Ashworth, "Prospectus on Volume VI, *George Washington*," 13 June 1953, MTM MSS.

68. Mary Wells Ashworth, "Sonnet," n/d, DSF MSS, Container 244.

69. DSF to Robert M. Lester, 11 August 1949, DSF COL.

70. Ibid.

71. DSF to Robert M. Lester, 12 April 1950, DSF COL.

72. DSF, *George Washington*, Vol. 3, *Planter & Patriot* (New York: Charles Scribner's Sons, 1951), xxviii. *See* DSF to Wallace Meyer, 11 February 1950, DSF MSS, Container 102.

73. DSF to Robert M. Lester, 12 April 1950, DSF COL.

74. DSF to Allen W. Freeman, 4 April 1950, DSF MSS, Container 101.

75. DSF to Allen W. Freeman, 11 April 1950, DSF MSS, Container 101.

76. DSF to Allen W. Freeman, 11 July 1950, DSF MSS, Container 101.

77. DSF to Mrs. George Guy, 27 July 1950, DSF MSS, Container 101.

78. DSF to Harry S. Truman, 11 April 1951, DSF MSS, Container 108.

79. Joseph Short to DSF, 2 July 1951, DSF MSS, Container 108.

80. DSF to Robert E. Vose, 17 November 1951, DSF MSS, Container 108.

81. DSF to Dwight D. Eisenhower, 6 September 1950, DSF MSS, Container 101.

82. Dwight D. Eisenhower to DSF, 12 September 1950, DSF MSS, Container 101.

83. DSF to Dwight D. Eisenhower, 13 September 1951, DSF MSS, Container 105.

84. DSF to Thomas McAdams, 6 June 1949; DSF to J. B. Woodward, 6 June 1949; DSF to Morris Sayre, 8 June 1949, DSF MSS, Container 99.

85. DSF to Morris Sayre, 8 June 1949, DSF MSS, Container 99.

86. DSF to Jay B. Nash, 2 March 1951, DSF MSS, Container 107.

87. Ibid.

88. DSF to Charles H. Wheeler, III, 6 June 1950; George Modlin to DSF, 10 June 1950, DSF MSS, Container 102.

89. DSF to George Modlin, 12 June 1950, DSF MSS, Container 102.

90. Freeman was still upset more than a year later about the university's athletic policy. He vowed he would "never give another dollar to the University of Richmond as long as this athletic policy continues." DSF to E. G. Swem, 10 October 1951, MTM MSS.

91. DSF, Diary, 22 October 1950, DSF MSS, Container 2.

92. DSF, "Memorandum," n/d, MTM MSS.

93. DSF, Diary, 14 September 1949, DSF MSS, Container 2; DSF to Mrs. Channing Ward, 27 June 1949, DSF MSS, Container 99.

94. DSF, Diary, 14 May 1951, DSF MSS, Container 2.

95. DSF to James Douglas Freeman, 22 June 1951, DSF MSS, Container 106.

96. DSF to James Douglas Freeman, 23, 28 June 1951; 18, 26 July 1951; DSF to Janice M. Freeman, 2, 18, 18 July 1951, DSF MSS, Containers 106, 111.

97. DSF to Allen W. Freeman, 7 August 1951; DSF to James Douglas

Freeman, 3 October 1951; DSF to Janice M. Freeman, 4 October 1951, DSF MSS, Container 106.
98. DSF to Allen W. Freeman, 9 January 1951, DSF MSS, Container 106.
99. Ibid.
100. DSF to S. L. Morgan, 19 January 1951, DSF MSS, Container 107.
101. DSF, "Memo," MTM MSS.
102. "Dr. Freeman at Midpoint in Life of Washington," *Richmond Times-Dispatch*, 21 October 1951.
103. DSF, *George Washington*, Vol. 3, ix.
104. "The Making of a Great Man: George Washington 1758-1778," *New York Herald Tribune Book Review*, 14 October 1951, 3.
105. "The General from Mount Vernon," *The New York Times Book Review*, 14 October 1951, 6.
106. "George Washington," *The Journal of Southern History*, Vol. XVIII (February-November 1952), 541.
107. "Planter, Burgess, and General," *Saturday Review of Literature*, 20 October 1951, 13.
108. "Washington as an Eighteenth Century Man," *William & Mary Quarterly*, Vol. IX, No. 2 (April 1952), 226.
109. "Washington as a Virginia Rebel and as American Commander in Chief," *William & Mary Quarterly*, Vol. IX, No. 2 (April 1952), 229.
110. DSF to Anne F. Adler, 29 November 1951, (marked "unsent"), DSF MSS, Container 104.
111. Ibid.
112. Friddell, *Alumni Bulletin*, 3.
113. DSF, "Outline: I've Laughed all my Life," n/d, DSF MSS, Container 128.
114. Ibid.; Friddell, *Alumni Bulletin*, 3.
115. Mary Wells Ashworth, "Note," n/d, MTM MSS.
116. DSF to Robert M. Lester, 31 March 1951, DSF COL.
117. DSF to Allen W. Freeman, 2 February 1951, DSF MSS, Container 106.
118. DSF to Gertrude R. B. Richards, 14 February; 21 April 1951, MTM MSS.
119. DSF to Edward Hummel, 18 September 1951, DSF MSS, Container 108.
120. DSF to Robert M. Lester, 4 January 1952, DSF COL.
121. Curtis P. Nettels, "The End was Yorktown," *The New York Times Book Review*, 19 October 1952, 6.
122. DSF to Allen W. Freeman, 21 January 1952, DSF MSS, Container 111.
123. DSF to Allen W. Freeman, 12 December 1950, DSF MSS, Container 101.
124. "Eisenhower for President Club Being Formed in Virginia," 8 January 1952, *Richmond News Leader*, 1.
125. Stephen E. Ambrose, *Eisenhower: Soldier, General of the Army, President-Elect* (New York: Simon & Schuster, 1983), 526-27.
126. DSF, "Ike Gets Vote of Southern Historian," *Life*, 22 September 1952, 53. Copyright 1952 Time Inc., reprinted by permission.

127. Ibid., 54.
128. Ibid.
129. Anne Freeman Adler to DSF, 4 October 1952, MTM MSS. Eisenhower repeated that statement in a speech in Richmond during the fall campaign.

CHAPTER FIFTEEN

1. DSF to Robert M. Lester, 15 September 1952, DSF COL; *see also* "Dr. Douglas S. Freeman's Trip to Europe," *Richmond Times-Dispatch*, 16 September 1952, 25.
2. DSF to Allen W. Freeman, 4 August 1952, DSF MSS, Container 111.
3. Inez G. Freeman, Diary, 25 September–8 October 1952, MTM MSS.
4. DSF, "Text of Cable," 3 October 1952, MTM MSS.
5. Inez G. Freeman, Diary, 5 November 1952, MTM MSS. Freeman had voted absentee at the U.S. Embassy in Rome. Inez G. Freeman, Diary, 16 October 1952, MTM MSS.
6. DSF, Diary, 5 November 1952, MTM MSS, Container 2.
7. Inez G. Freeman, Diary, 20 November 1952, MTM MSS.
8. DSF to Mary Tyler Cheek, 13 November 1952, MTM MSS.
9. DSF to Allen W. Freeman, 24 November 1952, DSF MSS, Container 111.
10. DSF to Dwight D. Eisenhower, 9 March 1953, DSF MSS, Container 116.
11. Geneva Snelling wrote that Freeman "refused a cabinet or diplomatic post in Eisenhower's government." If by the use of the word "refused," Miss Snelling means "preemptively declined," she is correct; if she means an actual refusal of an offered position, there is no evidence to support her statement.
12. The letter was also typed, but it is unclear which copy he mailed.
13. DSF to James Douglas Freeman, 26 November 1952, MTM MSS.
14. Ibid.
15. Ibid.
16. James Douglas Freeman to DSF, 31 January 1953, MTM MSS; DSF to James Douglas Freeman, 7 February 1953, DSF MSS, Container 116.
17. DSF to James Douglas Freeman, 19 April 1953, DSF MSS, Container 116.
18. Ibid. Freeman's disappointment was shared by his daughter Anne. "I want you to know," she wrote her father, "that I did not deliberately set out to break down J. D. But I feel that the time has come to take definite steps before he really gets in a jam. He must learn to pull his share of the load . . . We have all been hurt deeply by the young man's inability to copy with life—most of all he has been hurt." Anne Freeman Adler to DSF, 25 July 1952, MTM MSS.
19. DSF to Allen W. Freeman, 2 February 1953, DSF MSS, Container 116; *see also* DSF to Allen W. Freeman, 7 January 1953, DSF MSS, Container 116, in which Freeman asserted "that a good deal of his inertia was attributable to excessive sleep."
20. DSF to Leon Kelley, 22 April 1953, DSF MSS, Container 117.
21. DSF, *George Washington*, Vol. 6, 354.
22. William H. Higgins, Jr., to DSF, 15 August 1952, DSF MSS, Container 116.

23. DSF, "Memorandum," 20 April 1953, MTM MSS.

24. "I would prefer," Freeman wrote about these manuscripts, "that they be burned unread because I think they are very badly written. In any event, be sure they are not preserved. I think a man is entitled to have his amateurish work destroyed." Ibid., 9.

25. Freeman correctly spelled "irreplaceable" in the memorandum. The reader will recall it was spelled "irreplacable" on the sign. Ibid., 20.

26. Ibid., Addenda, 2. The author heartily concurs with Freeman's conclusion on this point.

27. DSF to Allen W. Freeman, 16 May 1953, DSF MSS, Container 116.

28. J. Ambler Johnston, *Echoes of 1861–1961*, 88.

29. Kilpatrick, "Freeman," 5.

30. Mary Tyler McClenahan, Interview with author, 4 June 2001.

31. DSF, "Directions for My Funeral, etc.," 10 June 1953, DSF MSS, Container 244.

32. Ibid.

33. Mary Tyler McClenahan, "My Father," 1.

34. Ibid., 3.

35. DSF, Diary, 12 June 1953, DSF MSS, Container 2.

36. DSF to Anne Freeman Adler, 12 June 1953, DSF MSS, Container 114.

37. DSF, "Manuscript of *George Washington*," DSF MSS, Container 167, 6-XVI-64.

38. Ibid.

39. Ibid. The published version of the last sentence was corrected to read "reluctantly would have admitted" instead of Freeman's word order in his final draft. DSF, *George Washington*, Vol. 6, 384.

40. The thirteen major works are *R. E. Lee*, four volumes; *Lee's Lieutenants*, three volumes; and *George Washington*, six volumes. The six other works are *A Calendar of Confederate Papers*, *Lee's Dispatches to Davis*, *The Report of the State Tax Commission*, *The South to Posterity*, "John Stewart Bryan" (unpublished), and *Lee of Virginia* (published posthumously). *The Last Parade* is not included because it was simply an editorial that was published.

41. DSF to Herbert Grier, 13 June 1953; DSF to J. N. Sydnor, 13 June 1953, DSF MSS, Container 116.

42. Inez G. Freeman, "Notes," MTM MSS.

43. Friddell, *Alumni Bulletin*. One wonders if this statement was in actuality an undramatic comment swollen by recollection into bombast. Friddell visited Westbourne the day after Freeman's death and interviewed Mrs. Freeman, who, no doubt, was the source of the quotation. While sounding a bit formal, it should be noted that it is consistent with Freeman's style of talking, both in private conversation and public pronouncements.

44. One of the strangest stories about Freeman arises at this moment. It is alleged that Freeman greeted Dr. Higgins "lying on his bed holding a lily in his hand." (Minutes, *News Leader* Current Events Class, 15 June 1953, MTM MSS, 5) and

joking about being ready to depart the world. Mrs. Freeman disputed the story. "I don't know the source of this misinformation, but [it] is untrue." (Inez G. Freeman, "Notes," 2) Mrs. Freeman's denial aside, it is unlikely that Freeman could have found a lily nearby or taken the time to pick one from his garden during these pensive moments. In all likelihood, he used the expression he often used about "having a lily in his hand," and the story was distorted from this comment.
45. Inez G. Freeman, "Notes," 2.
46. DSF to Dr. F. W. Burnham, 19 July 1948, DSF MSS, Container 85. Freeman made a similar reference in another letter. "I hope to live to finish [*Washington*]," he wrote, "but if I don't, I certainly want to pursue it hopefully to the last hour." DSF to James Munn, 18 January 1947, DSF MSS, Container 81.
47. Inez G. Freeman, "Engagement Calendar-1953," 13 June 1953, MTM MSS.
48. James Douglas Freeman, Interview with author, 31 January 2001.
49. Mary Tyler McClenahan, Interview with author, 4 June 2001.
50. M. T. McClenahan, "My Father," 3-4.
51. Dwight D. Eisenhower to Inez G. Freeman, 14 June 1953, MTM MSS.
52. Carl Sandburg to Inez G. Freeman, 14 June 1953; Frank McCarthy to Inez G. Freeman, 15 June 1953; J. M. Ellison to Inez G. Freeman, 15 June 1953; Mary and Chester Wilson to Inez G. Freeman, 15 June 1953; J. Earl Mooreland to Inez G. Freeman, 14 June 1953, DSF MSS, Container 124.
53. "On the Death of Douglas Freeman," *Richmond News Leader*, 15 June 1953, 10.
54. Ibid.

EPILOGUE
1. "Serene Star and Gracious Lady Who Projects Past into Today," *Richmond Times-Dispatch*, 15 January 1957.
2. Ibid.
3. DSF to Mary Tyler Freeman, 8 March 1934, MTM MSS.
4. James Douglas Freeman, Interview with author, 31 January 2001.
5. Ibid.

APPENDIX 1
1. *Report to the General Assembly of Virginia By the Tax Commission* (Richmond: The Richmond Press, Inc., 1911), vii-ix.

APPENDIX 2
1. "The News Leader's Twenty Fundamental Rules of News Writing," DSF MSS, Container 98.

APPENDIX 3
1. Gignilliat, "Freeman," 165; T. Harry Williams, "Freeman, Historian of the Civil War: An Appraisal," *The Journal of Southern History*, Vol. 21 (February 1955), 96.
2. William C. Davis, "Review of *Robert E. Lee: A Biography* by Emory Thomas," *History Book Club Review*, June 1995, 5. *See also* T. Harry Williams, "Freeman,

Historian," 96. Gary Gallagher writes that Freeman was "typically loath to acknowledge any failing on Lee's part." Gary W. Gallagher, "The Army of Northern Virginia in May 1864" in *Lee and His Generals in War & Memory* (Baton Rouge: LSU Press, 1998), 85.

3. Connelly, *The Marble Man*, 152.

4. Ibid., 147-48.

5. Ibid., 150-52.

6. T. Harry Williams, "Freeman, Historian," 96-97.

7. Frank Vandiver, "Douglas Southall Freeman," xiii.

8. Liddell Hart, "Lee: a Psychological Problem," 1.

9. Commager, "The Life of Lee," 595-96.

10. John L. Gignilliat, "A Historian's Dilemma: A Posthumous Footnote for Freeman's *R. E. Lee*," *The Journal of Southern History*, Vol. XLIII, No. 2 (May 1977), 217.

11. Robert E. Lee to G. W. Cullum, 31 July 1835, quoted in Gignilliat, "Dilemma," 221-22.

12. DSF, *R. E. Lee*, Vol. I, 134, n. 17.

13. Gignilliat, "Dilemma," 225.

14. Ibid., 226-30.

15. Donald Bartlett to DSF, 6 May 1937, DSF MSS, Container 28.

16. DSF to Donald Bartlett, 8 May 1937, DSF MSS, Container 28.

17. Donald Bartlett to DSF, 13 October 1937, DSF MSS, Container 28.

18. Ibid.

19. DSF to Donald Bartlett, 27 December 1937, DSF MSS, Container 28.

20. DSF to Milo Quaife, 20 February 1945, DSF MSS, Container 63.

21. T. Harry Williams, "Freeman, Historian," 98.

22. Connelly, *The Marble Man*, 148.

23. Allen Tate's statement that Freeman operated under "certain limitations of point of view" differs from the Williams/Connelly critique. Tate, a Southern agrarian, takes issue with Freeman's assertion that the war could have been avoided. Freeman could have made that statement, Tate argued, only by ignoring "the complicated social forces and backgrounds" that preceded the war. Tate, "The Definitive Lee," 171-72.

24. T. Harry Williams, "Freeman, Historian," 97.

25. William Garrett Piston, *Lee's Tarnished Lieutenant* (Athens: University of Georgia Press, 1987), 174.

26. DSF, *R. E. Lee*, Vol. II, 325; Vol. III, 85.

27. DSF, *R. E. Lee*, Vol. III, 150.

28. Ibid., 147-49.

29. DSF to Roy Shields, 4 January 1947, DSF MSS, Container 83.

30. Ibid. DSF, *Lee's Lieutenants*, Vol. III, xii, 757-60.

31. Gary W. Gallagher, "If the Enemy Is There, We Must Attack Him," *Lee and His Generals in War & Memory*, 66, n. 32.

32. DSF to Ben Ames Williams, 26 December 1942, DSF MSS, Container 46.

33. Ibid.

34. DSF, *R. E. Lee*, Vol. III, 81-82.

35. Gary W.Gallagher, "If the Enemy Is There, We Must Attack Him," *Lee and His Generals in War & Memory*, 61.

36. Jeffrey D. Wert, *General James Longstreet* (New York: Simon & Schuster, 1993), 258. Wert continues: "In history's glare, Lee had choices on this afternoon, but Douglas Freeman's description of him as a 'blinded giant' seems fair." Wert, 258-59.

37. Gary W. Gallagher, "Scapegoat in Victory," *Lee and His Generals in War & Memory*, 144.

38. DSF, *Lee's Lieutenants*, Vol. I, 166, n. 76.

39. Connelly, *The Marble Man*, 153.

40. Ibid., xiv.

41. Ibid., xiv-xv.

42. "The Virginians," *Time*, 18 October 1948, 108.

43. DSF, "An Address before the Civil War Round Tables of Richmond and Chicago, 7 May 1953," 10.

44. DSF, "Adventures in Biography," Lecture III, "The New Horizons," 27, DSF MSS, Container 127.

45. DSF, "What Would Lincoln Do?" *Saturday Review of Literature*, 12 February 1944, 4.

46. DSF, "Lee's Achievement in Spite of Tremendous Handicaps," *Current History*, Vol. XXIX (October 1928), 46-47.

Bibliography

Manuscripts

Douglas Southall Freeman Papers, Library of Congress
Douglas Southall Freeman Papers, Johns Hopkins University
Douglas Southall Freeman Papers, University of Virginia
Douglas Southall Freeman Papers, Museum of the Confederacy Library
Douglas Southall Freeman Papers, Virginia Historical Society
Inez Goddin (Mrs. Douglas Southall) Freeman Papers, Virginia Historical
    Society
Walker Burford Freeman Papers, Virginia Historical Society
Mary Tyler Freeman (Mrs. John L.) McClenahan Papers, Private Collection
Anne Ballard Freeman (Mrs. Royall) Turpin Papers, Private Collection
John Stewart Bryan Papers, Virginia Historical Society
D. Tennant Bryan Papers, *Richmond News Leader* Archives
Dr. O. O. Ashworth, Sr., Papers, Private Collection
Mary Wells (Mrs. O. O.) Ashworth Papers, Private Collection
Wymberley J. De Renne Papers, University of Georgia
S. C. Mitchell Papers, Virginia Baptist Historical Society
Jacob Hollander Papers, Johns Hopkins University
Carnegie Corporation Papers, Columbia University
Freeman File, Virginia Commonwealth University
Freeman File, *Richmond Times-Dispatch* Library
Scribner's Author File, Princeton University
Pulitzer Prize File, Columbia University

Interviews

Mary Tyler Freeman McClenahan
James J. Kilpatrick
J. Stewart Bryan III
Elizabeth Cheek

James Douglas Freeman
John E. Leard
Leslie Cheek III
Mallory Freeman

Robert Freeman
O. O. Ashworth, Jr.
Frances Valentine

John S. Ashworth, M.D.
Margaret Lechner
William H. Higgins, Jr., M.D.

Letters to Author

Daniel E. Button
Daniel J. Edelman
George H. Larson
Elwood N. Thompson
John R. Mayer
Philip Hamburger
Betty Ryan Wolfe

Damon M. Stetson
John Tebbel Clement
Hope K. McCroskey
Haynes W. Dugan
Robert Schulman
George R. Metcalf
Raymond Wilcove

Leonard R. Sussman
David Hellyer
Bernard S. Redmont
Edward M. Gottschall
David D. Newsom

Articles

Ashworth, Mary Wells. "Douglas Southall Freeman: The Man and the Making of a Book," in *Douglas Southall Freeman: Reflections by His Daughter, His Research Associate and a Historian*. Richmond: Friends of the Richmond Public Library (1986).

Ashworth, Mary Wells. "Prefatory Note" to *Patriot & President*, Vol. 6, *George Washington* by Douglas Southall Freeman. New York: Charles Scribner's Sons, 1954.

Blunt, Ruth H. "The Birthplace of Douglas Southall Freeman and Allen Weir Freeman." *Lynchburg Historical Society Magazine*, Vol. VI, No. 1 (1968).

Bragg, William Harris. "Our Joint Labor: W. J. DeRenne, Douglas Southall Freeman and *Lee's Dispatches*, 1910-1915." *The Virginia Magazine of History and Biography*, Vol. 97, No. 1 (January 1989).

Davis, William C. "Robert E. Lee," review of *Robert E. Lee: A Biography* by Emory Thomas. *History Book Club Review* (June 1995).

Friddell, Guy. "I've Laughed All My Life: Dr. Douglas Southall Freeman." *Alumni Bulletin of the University of Richmond*, Vol. XVII, No. 4 (July 1953).

Gignilliat, John L. "Douglas Southall Freeman." *Dictionary of Literary Biography*, Vol. 17, Clyde Norman Wilson, editor. Detroit: Gale Research Co., 1983.

Gignilliat, John L. "A Historian's Dilemma: A Posthumous Footnote for Freeman's *R. E. Lee*." *The Journal of Southern History*, Vol. LXIII, No. 2 (May 1977).

Hamilton, Charles Henry. "The Most Unforgettable Character I've Met." *Reader's Digest* (July 1960).

Harwell, Richard Barksdale. "Freeman and The South to Posterity" in *The South to Posterity*, 3rd ed., by Douglas Southall Freeman. Wendell, North Carolina: Broadfoots Bookmark, 1983.

Harwell, Richard Barksdale. "Introduction" to *George Washington* by Douglas Southall Freeman, an abridgment edited by Richard Barksdale Harwell. New York: Charles Scribner's Sons, 1968.

Harwell, Richard Barksdale. "Introduction" to *R. E. Lee*, by Douglas Southall Freeman, an abridgment edited by Richard Barksdale Harwell. New York: Charles Scribner's Sons, 1961.

Harrison, Joseph H., Jr. "Harry Williams, Critic of Freeman: A Demurrer." *Virginia Magazine of History and Biography*, Vol. 64 (January 1956).

Hawkes, Robert T. "Harry F. Byrd: Leadership and Reform," in *The Governors of Virginia*, Edward Younger, editor. Charlottesville: University Press of Virginia, 1982.

Herold, David E. *A Species of Literary Lion: Essays on Morison, Freeman, DeVoto & Becker and the Writing of History*. Master's Thesis, University of Minnesota, December 1973.

Johnson, David E. "Character Confirmed: The Life of Douglas Southall Freeman." *Columbiad*, Vol. I, No. 3 (Fall 1997).

Johnson, David E. "Freeman and the Making of *R. E. Lee*." *Civil War Society Magazine*, Vol. 68 (June 1998).

Kilpatrick, James J. "Douglas Southall Freeman, 1886-1953." *Southern Classics Library* (1982).

Kilpatrick, James J. "The 17 Happy Years of a Fire-Breathing Editor." *The Richmond News Leader* (May 30, 1992), Special Commemorative Magazine.

Link, Arthur S. "Woodrow Wilson: The American as Southerner." *The Journal of Southern History*, Vol. XXXVI (February 1970), 3.

Malone, Dumas. "The Pen of Douglas Southall Freeman" in *George Washington*, Vol. 6, *Patriot and President*, by Douglas Southall Freeman. New York: Charles Scribner's Sons, 1954.

McClenahan, Mary Tyler Freeman Cheek. "Douglas Freeman and General Lee." *Lee-Jackson Quarterly Review*, Vol. 13, No. 2 (Fall-Winter 1984).

McClenahan, Mary Tyler Freeman Cheek. "Douglas Southall Freeman: My Father as a Writer," *Richmond Literature and History Quarterly*, Vol. 1 (1979).

McClenahan, Mary Tyler Freeman Cheek. "Galatea in Richmond: Emma Gray Trigg." *The Richmond Quarterly*, Vol. 5, No. 1 (Summer 1982).

McClenahan, Mary Tyler Freeman Cheek. "A High Calling," in *Douglas Southall Freeman: Reflections by His Daughter, His Research Associate and a Historian*. Richmond: Friends of the Richmond Public Library (1986).

McClenahan, Mary Tyler Freeman Cheek. "Reflections." *Virginia Magazine of History and Biography*, Vol. 94, No. 1 (January 1986).

Nevins, Allan. "How a Great Historian Studied a Great American: The Freeman Letters on George Washington." *American Heritage*, Vol. 7 (February 1956).

Richardson, Vernon B. "Boatwright: Valiant for Truth." *Alumni Bulletin of the University of Richmond*, Vol. XVI, No. 2 (January 1952).
Rubin, Louis D., Jr. "Richmond as a Literary Capital." Richmond: Friends of the Richmond Public Library (1966).
Sandburg, Carl. "Douglas Southall Freeman: 1886-1953." *Proceedings of the American Academy of Arts & Letters and the National Institute of Arts & Letters, Second Session*, No. 5 (1955).
Scheer, George. "Plutarch on the James." *The Southern Packet*, Vol. V, No. 2 (February 1949).
Thomas, Emory M. "Rethinking Robert E. Lee." *Douglas Southall Freeman Historical Review*. University of Richmond (Spring 1994).
Vandiver, Frank E. "Douglas Southall Freeman." *Southern Historical Society Papers*, No. XIV, Whole No. LII (1959).
Ward, Harry M. "Douglas Southall Freeman: A Historian's Overview," in *Douglas Southall Freeman: Reflections by His Daughter, His Research Associate and a Historian*. Richmond: Friends of the Richmond Public Library (1986).
Williams, T. Harry. "Freeman, Historian of the Civil War: An Appraisal." *The Journal of Southern History*, Vol. 21 (February 1955).

Unpublished Manuscripts

Ashworth, Mary Wells. "Douglas Southall Freeman: A Biographical Sketch." Mary Tyler McClenahan Papers.
Ashworth, Mary Wells. "Douglas Southall Freeman: Biographical Material Prepared for Charles Scribner's Sons." Freeman Papers, Library of Congress.
Ashworth, Mary Wells. "Memorandum on Douglas Southall Freeman for Dumas Malone." Mary Tyler McClenahan Papers.
Dickson, Keith. "Douglas Southall Freeman and the New Deal: 1933-1935." Master's Thesis. April 29, 1982.
Dickson, Keith. "Peace or War: Douglas Southall Freeman and American Neutrality 1933-1936." Master's Thesis. December 1, 1983.
Freeman, Allen W. "My Brother Douglas." Freeman Papers, Library of Congress.
Freeman, Douglas Southall. "The Fine Art of Saving Time." Freeman Papers, Library of Congress.
Freeman, Douglas Southall. "John Stewart Bryan." Bryan Papers, Virginia Historical Society.
Freeman, Douglas Southall. "In the Blood." Mary Tyler McClenahan Papers.
Freeman, Douglas Southall. "Billy Walton: Governor." Mary Tyler McClenahan Papers.
Freeman, Inez G. (Mrs. Douglas Southall Freeman). "Douglas Southall Freeman: Brief Biographical Notes." Mary Tyler McClenahan Papers.

Freeman, Walker Burford. "Memoirs of Walker Burford Freeman 1843-1935." Privately published memoir.

Gignilliat, John L. "The Thought of Douglas Southall Freeman." A thesis submitted in partial fulfillment of the requirements of the degree of Doctor of Philosophy (History), University of Wisconsin, 1968.

Habas, Ralph A. "Untitled Manuscript." Freeman Papers, Library of Congress.

Hopkins, Garland Evans. "Freeman Forbears." Privately published, 1942.

Johnston, J. Ambler. "Recollections of D. S. Freeman." Freeman Papers, Library of Congress.

McClenahan, Mary Tyler Freeman Cheek. "Douglas Southall Freeman." Mary Tyler McClenahan Papers.

McClenahan, Mary Tyler Freeman Cheek. "Douglas Southall Freeman, My Father." Mary Tyler McClenahan Papers.

McClenahan, Mary Tyler Freeman Cheek. "A Quality of Love." Mary Tyler McClenahan Papers.

McClenahan, Mary Tyler Freeman Cheek. "Remarks." Mary Tyler McClenahan Papers.

McClenahan, Mary Tyler Freeman Cheek. "Tramp Newspaperman." Mary Tyler McClenahan Papers.

Meade, Robert D. "Remarks on the Unveiling of Freeman Marker in Lynchburg." Unpublished address. Mary Tyler McClenahan Papers.

Snelling, Geneva B. "Douglas Southall Freeman." Freeman Papers, Library of Congress.

Books

Alley, Reuben E. *Frederic W. Boatwright*. Richmond: University of Richmond, 1973.

Alley, Reuben E. *History of the University of Richmond, 1830-1971*. Charlottesville: University Press of Virginia, 1977.

Ambrose, Stephen. *Eisenhower: Soldier, General of the Army, President-Elect*. New York: Simon & Schuster, 1983.

Atkinson, Frank B. *The Dynamic Dominion*. Fairfax, Virginia: George Mason University Press, 1992.

Berg, A. Scott. *Max Perkins: Editor of Genius*. New York: E. P. Dutton, 1978.

Bragg, William Harris. *De Renne: Three Generations of a Georgia Family*. Athens: University of Georgia Press, 1999.

Christian, W. Asbury. *Richmond: Her Past & Present*. Richmond: L. H. Jenkins, 1912.

Coffman, Edward M. *The War to End All Wars*. New York: Oxford University Press, 1968.

Connelly, Thomas L. *The Marble Man: Robert E. Lee and His Image in American Society*. New York: Knopf, 1977.

Cutchins, John A. *Memories of Old Richmond (1881-1944)*. Richmond: McClure Press, 1973.

Dabney, Virginius. *Liberalism in the South*. Chapel Hill: The University of North Carolina Press, 1932.

Dabney, Virginius. *Richmond: The Story of a City*. New York: Doubleday, 1976.

Daniel, W. Harrison. *Bedford County 1840-1860*. Bedford, Virginia: The Print Shop, 1985.

Daniel, W. Harrison. *History at the University of Richmond*. Richmond: University of Richmond, 1991.

Dunford, Earle. *Richmond Times-Dispatch: The Story of a Newspaper*. Richmond: Cadmus Publishing, 1995.

Edmunds, Pocahontas Wight. *Virginians Out Front*. Richmond: Whittet & Shepperson, 1972.

Eisenstadt, A. S. *Charles McLean Andrews*. New York: Columbia University Press, 1956.

Flexner, Abraham. *Daniel Coit Gilman*. New York: Harcourt, Brace & Co., 1946.

Franklin, Fabian. *The Life of Daniel Coit Gilman*. New York: Dodd, Mead & Company, 1910.

Freeman, Frederick. *Freeman Genealogy*. Boston: Franklin Press, 1875.

French, John C. *A History of the University Founded by Johns Hopkins*. Baltimore: The Johns Hopkins Press, 1946.

Gallagher, Gary W. *Lee and His Generals in War and Memory*. Baton Rouge: LSU Press, 1998.

Gallagher, Gary W., editor. *Lee the Soldier*. Lincoln: University of Nebraska Press, 1996.

Gilbert, Martin. *The First World War*. New York: Henry Holt & Co., 1994.

Harrison, Henry S. *Queed*. New York: Grosset & Dunlap, 1911.

Hawkins, Hugh. *Pioneer: A History of the Johns Hopkins University, 1874-1889*. Ithaca, New York: Cornell University Press, 1960.

Heckscher, August. *Woodrow Wilson*. New York: Charles Scribner's Sons, 1991.

Heinemann, Ronald L. *Harry Byrd of Virginia*. Charlottesville: University Press of Virginia, 1996.

Jones, William Wheeler. *Of Two Virginia Gentlemen and Their McGuire's University School*. Richmond: The McGuire's School Alumni Association, 1972.

Johnston, J. Ambler. *Echoes of 1861-1961*. Privately published, 2000.

Kilpatrick, James J. *Fine Print: Reflections of the Writing Art*. Kansas City: Andrews & McMeel, 1993.

Mitchell, S. C. *An Aftermath of Appomattox: A Memoir*. Privately published, 1942.

Nolan, Alan. *Lee Considered: General Robert E. Lee and Civil War History*. Chapel Hill: University of North Carolina Press, 1991.

Parker, Lula Jeter. *Parker's History of Bedford County, Virginia*. Bedford: Hamilton's, 1954.

Piston, William Garrett. *Lee's Tarnished Lieutenant*. Athens: University of Georgia Press, 1987.

Rouse, Parker, Jr. *We Happy WASPs: Virginia in the Days of Jim Crow and Harry Byrd*. Richmond: Dietz Press, 1996.

Scruggs, Philip Lightfoot. *The History of Lynchburg, Virginia*. Lynchburg: J. P. Bell Company, 1971.

Smith, Stuart W. "Douglas Southall Freeman." *Douglas Southall Freeman: On Leadership*, Stuart W. Smith, editor. Shippensburg, Pa: White Mane Publishing, Co., 1993.

Terraine, John. *To Win a War: 1918, the Year of Victory*. New York: Doubleday & Co., 1981.

Thomas, Emory. *Robert E. Lee: A Biography*. New York: W. W. Norton & Co., 1995.

Trask, David F. *The AEF and Coalition War Making, 1917-1918*. Lawrence: University Press of Kansas, 1993.

Wert, Jeffrey D. *General James Longstreet*. New York: Simon & Schuster, 1993.

Wilkinson, J. Harvie, III. *Harry Byrd and the Changing Face of Virginia Politics*. Charlottesville: University Press of Virginia, 1968.

Books by Douglas Southall Freeman

A Calendar of Confederate Papers (editor). Richmond: The Confederate Museum, 1908.

Report to the General Assembly of Virginia by the Tax Commission (secretary). Richmond: The Richmond Press, Inc., 1911.

Lee's Dispatches: Unpublished Letters of General Robert E. Lee to Jefferson Davis and the War Department of the Confederate States of America, 1862-1865 (editor). New York: G. P. Putnam's Sons, 1915.

The Last Parade. Richmond: Whittet and Shepperson, 1932.

R. E. Lee, 4 vols. New York: Charles Scribner's Sons, 1934-35.

The South to Posterity: An Introduction to the Writing of Confederate History. New York: Charles Scribner's Sons, 1939.

Lee's Lieutenants: A Study in Command, Vol. I, *Manassas to Malvern Hill*. New York: Charles Scribner's Sons, 1942.

Lee's Lieutenants: A Study in Command, Vol. II, *Cedar Mountain to Chancellorsville*. New York: Charles Scribner's Sons, 1943.

Lee's Lieutenants: A Study in Command, Vol. III, *Gettysburg to Appomattox*. New York: Charles Scribner's Sons, 1944.

George Washington, Vols. I & II, *Young Washington*. New York: Charles Scribner's Sons, 1948.

George Washington, Vol. III, *Planter & Patriot*. New York: Charles Scribner's Sons, 1951.

George Washington, Vol. IV, *Leader of the Revolution*. New York: Charles Scribner's Sons, 1951.

460   – DOUGLAS SOUTHALL FREEMAN –

George Washington, Vol. V, *Victory With the Help of France*. New York: Charles Scribner's Sons, 1952.
George Washington, Vol. VI, *Patriot & President*. New York: Charles Scribner's Sons, 1954.
George Washington, Vol. VII, *First in Peace*. John Alexander Carroll & Mary Wells Ashworth, based on Freeman's research. New York: Charles Scribner's Sons, 1957.
Lee of Virginia. New York: Charles Scribner's Sons, 1958.

Articles and Reviews by Douglas Southall Freeman

"The Aristocracy of the Northern Neck." *The South in the Building of the Nation* by S. C. Mitchell. Richmond: The Southern Historical Society, 1909.
"Taxation Conditions in Virginia." *State and Local Taxation: Fifth Annual Conference*. Columbus, Ohio: National Tax Association, 1912.
"Publicity and the Public Mind." *American Journal of Insanity*, Vol. LXXII, No. 1 (July 1915).
"Virginia: A Gentle Dominion." *The Nation*, Vol. CXIX (July 16, 1924). Reprinted in *These United States: Portraits of America from the 1920s*, Daniel H. Borus (ed.) (Ithaca, New York: Cornell University Press, 1992).
"Lee & the Ladies." *Scribner's Magazine*, Vol. LXXVII, Part I, No. 4 (October 1925), Vol. LXXVIII, Part II, No. 5 (November 1925).
"The Ideal Ambassador." *The Outlook*, Vol. 149, No. 9 (June 27, 1928).
"Lee's Achievement in Spite of Tremendous Handicaps." *Current History*, Vol. XXIX (October 1928).
"The Confederate Tradition in Richmond." *Civil War History*, Vol. III (December 1957), originally published in *The Richmond Magazine* (1932).
"Robert Edward Lee." *Dictionary of American Biography*, Vol. 6. New York: Charles Scribner's Sons, 1933.
"Biography as a Pastime." *Saturday Review of Literature*, 12 (May 11, 1935).
"Ellen Glasgow: Idealist." *Saturday Review of Literature*, 12 (August 31, 1935).
"The Lengthening Shadow of Lee." *An Address Before Joint Session of the General Assembly of Virginia*. Richmond: Division of Purchasing and Printing, 1936.
"Who's in Command." *The Atlantic Monthly*, 165 (June,1940).
"Barbed Wire Horizons." *Marshall Review*, Vol. 4, No. 1 (November 1940).
"What Would Lincoln Do?" *Saturday Review of Literature*, 27 (February 12, 1944).
"Confederate Cabinet," a review of *Jefferson Davis and His Cabinet* by Rembert Patrick. *Saturday Review of Literature*, 27 (October 21, 1944).
"The Tonic of Southern Folklore." *American Scholar*, Vol. 19, No. 2 (April 1, 1950).
"Ike Gets the Vote of Southern Historian." *Life*, Vol. 33 (September 22, 1952).
"Washington's Hardest Decision." *The Atlantic Monthly* (October 1952).

Introductions and Forewords by Douglas Southall Freeman

"Introduction." *Memoirs of Service with John Yates Beall, CSN*, by W. W. Baker. Richmond: The Richmond Press, 1910.

"Introduction." *Homes and Gardens in Old Virginia*, by Susanne Williams Massie, editor. Richmond: Garrett & Massie, 1931.

"Foreword." *The Story of the Confederacy*, by Ralph S. Henry. New York: Bobbs-Merrill, 1936.

"In the Virginia Tradition." Introduction to *Carter Glass*, by Rixey Smith and Norman Beasley. New York: Longmans, Green and Co., 1939.

"Introduction." *The Vanishing Virginian*, by Rebecca Yancy Williams. New York: E. P. Dutton & Co., 1940.

"Introduction." *Peninsula Pilgrimage*, by Elizabeth Valentine Huntley. Richmond: Whittet & Shepperson, 1941.

"Introduction." *War Years with Jeb Stuart*, by W. W. Blackford. New York: Charles Scribner's Sons, 1945.

"Introduction." *War As I Knew It*, by Gen. George S. Patton, Jr. Boston: Houghton Mifflin Co., 1947.

"Introduction." *Lee's Centennial: An Address by Charles Francis Adams*. Chicago: Americana Home, 1948.

Selected Magazine and Periodical Articles

Bancroft, Frederic. "A Review of *A Calendar of Confederate Papers*." *American Historical Review*, Vol. XIV, No. 3 (April 1909), 623.

"Douglas Southall Freeman," *Wilson Bulletin for Librarians*, 9 (June 1935), 546.

"General Lee's Spokesman," *Time*, Vol. 35 (April 1, 1940), 44.

"Virginia Editor Uses Civil War to Clarify War News from Europe," *Life*, 8 (May 13, 1940), 41.

"The Compleat Confederate," *Newsweek*, 24 (October 9, 1944), 95.

"The Virginians," *Time*, 52 (October 18, 1948), 108.

"Virginian Goes," *Newsweek*, 34 (July 4, 1949), 54.

"Who's for Whom," *Time*, 60 (September 22, 1952), 26.

"Milestones," *Time*, 61 (June 22, 1953), 75.

"Died," *Newsweek*, 41 (June 22, 1953), 62.

"Obituaries," *Wilson Library Bulletin*, 28 (September 1953), 26.

Selected Reviews of *R. E. Lee*

Thompson, Charles Willis, "Robert E. Lee: A Final Portrait," *The New York Times Book Review* (October 14, 1934), 1.

"South's Flower," *Time* (October 22, 1934).

Hart, Liddell, " Lee: A Psychological Problem," *Saturday Review of Literature*, X (December 15, 1934).

Tate, Allen, "The Definitive Lee," *The New Republic* (December 19, 1934), 171.

"The American Civil War," *The* (London) *Independent* (December 22, 1934).

Milton, George Fort, "The Life of Lee," *The Nation* (December 26, 1934), 747.

Ramsdell, Charles, "Review," *The Journal of Southern History*, Vol. I, No. 1 (February 1935), 230.

Benet, Stephen Vincent, "Great General, Greater Man," *New York Herald Tribune Books* (February 10, 1935), 1.

Thompson, Charles Willis, "Dr. Freeman Completes His Monumental Life of Lee," *The New York Times Book Review* (February 10, 1935), 3.

"Last of Lee," *Time* (February 11, 1935).

Hart, Liddell, "Why Lee Lost Gettysburg," *Saturday Review of Literature*, XI (March 23, 1935).

Commager, Henry Steele, "New Books in Review: The Life of Lee," *The Yale Review*, Vol. XXIV, No. 3 (March 1935), 594.

Malone, Dumas, "R. E. Lee: A Biography," *American Historical Review*, Vol. XL, No. 3 (April 1935), 534.

Tate, Allen, "R. E. Lee Complete," *The New Republic* (April 10, 1935), 225.

Malone, Dumas, "R. E. Lee: A Biography," *American Historical Review*, Vol. XLI, No. 1 (October 1935), 164.

Selected Reviews of *South to Posterity*

Benet, Stephen Vincent, "The Lost Cause in Literature," *Saturday Review of Literature*, 21 (November 25, 1939), 6.

Johnson, Gerald W. "The Lost Cause," *New York Herald Tribune Books* (December 3, 1939).

Poole, Charles, "Books of the Times," *The New York Times Book Review* (December 29, 1939), 13.

Bailey, J. O., "Books of Southern Interest," *The Southern Literary Messenger* (January 1940), 63.

Meacham, William Shands, "The Writing of Confederate History," *The New York Times Book Review* (March 24, 1940), 9.

Selected Reviews of *Lee's Lieutenants*

Benet, Stephen Vincent, "Generals in Action and Under the Stress of Action," *The New York Times Book Review* (October 25, 1942).

"The Paladins of the Confederacy," *The Washington Post* (October 18, 1942).

Prescott, Orville, "Books of the Times," *The New York Times* (October 19, 1942), 19.

DeVoto, Bernard, "The Confederate Military System," *Saturday Review of Literature* (October 24, 1942), 15.

"Generalship with Examples," *Time* (October 26, 1942), 110.

Hay, Thomas Robson, "Review," *The Journal of Southern History*, Vol. IX (February 1943), 122.

Hay, Thomas Robson, "Review," *The Journal of Southern History*, Vol. IX (February 1943), 421.

Daniels, Josephus, "Saga of Military Chieftains," *The* (Raleigh) *Observer* (March 21, 1943).

Spalding, Branch, "Reviews of Books," *American Historical Review*, Vol. XLVII, No. 3 (April 1943), 592.

Brock, H. I., "The Leaders and the Men of the Confederate Armies," *New York Times* (April 4, 1943), 1.

DeVoto, Bernard, "Mr. Freeman's Continuing Study," *Saturday Review of Literature* (May 29, 1943), 16.

DeWeerd, H. A., "Review," *American Historical Review*, Vol. XLIX, No. 1 (October 1943), 121.

DeWeerd, H. A., "The Leaders Who Rode with Lee," *The New York Times Book Review* (October 8, 1944).

"Dr. Freeman Concludes Classic War History," *Richmond Times-Dispatch* (October 8, 1944), 6-D.

"American Heroes," *Time* (October 16, 1944), 99.

"Freeman's Last Volume on Lee's Lieutenants," *Philadelphia Record* (October 18, 1944).

Milton, George Fort, "The Top Command of General Lee," *Saturday Review of Literature*, 27 (October 21, 1944), 11.

Woody, R. H., "The Army of Northern Virginia," *The South Atlantic Quarterly*, Vol. 44, No. 1 (January 1945), 100.

Hay, Thomas Robson, "Book Reviews," *The Journal of Southern History*, Vol. XI (February 1945), 121.

Henry, Robert S., "Reviews of Books," *American Historical Review*, Vol. L, No. 3 (April 1945), 562.

Selected Reviews of *George Washington*

Butterfield, L. H., "A Great Figure Emerges," *Saturday Review of Literature*, 31 (October 16, 1948), 10.

Nevins, Allan, "Washington, Minus His Pedestal," *The New York Times Book Review* (October 17, 1948), 1.

"Washington, Sans the Halo," *Richmond Times-Dispatch* (October 17, 1948), 12-D.

Danielson, Richard E., "Young Washington: A Living Portrait," *The Atlantic Monthly*, Vol. 183, No. 1 (January 1949), 76.

Knollenberg, Bernhard, "George Washington, Volumes I & II," *William & Mary Quarterly*, Vol. VI (January 1949), 111.

Abernethy, Thomas Perkins, "George Washington, Volumes I & II," *Virginia Magazine of History & Biography*, Vol. 57, No. 1 (January 1949), 92.

Lefler, Hugh T., "George Washington, Volumes I & II," *The Journal of Southern History*, Vol. XV (February 1949), 98.

Miller, Perry, "George Washington, Volumes I & II," *New England Quarterly*, Vol. XXII (1949), 253.

"Washington Learns His Part," *The Times* (London) *Literary Supplement* (April 2, 1949).

"First and Last American Presidents," *The Listener* (April 14, 1949).

Pargellis, Stanley, "George Washington, Volumes I & II," *American Historical Review*, Vol. LIV, No. 3 (April 1949), 615.

"Washington: Early Days," *The* (London) *Spectator* (May 13, 1949), 654.

"George Washington," *The New Statesman & Nation* (August 6, 1949).

Hendrickson, Walter B. "A Review of Reviews of Douglas S. Freeman's *Young Washington.*" *The Library Quarterly*, Vol. XXI, No. 3 (July 1951).

Bridenbaugh, Carl, "The General from Mount Vernon," *The New York Times Book Review* (October 14, 1951), 6.

"The Making of a Great Man: George Washington 1758-1778," *New York Herald-Tribune* (October 14, 1951).

Butterfield, L. H., "Planter, Burgess & General," *The Saturday Review of Literature*, 34 (October 20, 1951), 13.

"Freeman's Life of Washington: The Middle Years," *The New Republic* (November 26, 1951).

Craven, Avery, "George Washington, Volume III," *The Journal of Southern History*, Vol. XVIII, No. 1 (February 1952), 541.

Meigs, Cornelia, Perry Miller, and Bernard Knollenberg, "Freeman's *Washington*: A Triple Evaluation," *William & Mary Quarterly*, Vol. IX, No. 2 (April 1952).

Nettels, Curtis P., "The End Was Yorktown," *The New York Times Book Review* (October 19, 1952), 6.

Pargellis, Stanley, "George Washington, Volume IV," *American Historical Review*, Vol. LVIII, No. 1 (October 1952), 128.

Lundin, C. Leonard, "George Washington: Vol. V," *The Journal of Southern History*, Vol. XIX (February 1953), 224.

Pargellis, Stanley, "George Washington: A Biography," *American Historical Review*, Vol. LIX, No. 2 (January 1954), 389.

Bridenbaugh, Carl, "After the Revolution," *The New York Times Book Review* (October 3, 1954), 6.

"Freeman's Washington Is Indispensable," *Richmond News Leader* (October 4, 1954).

Adair, Douglass, "On His Desk when He Died: Freeman's Sixth Volume on Washington," *New York Herald Tribune Books* (October 17, 1954), 3.

Bradley, Harold Whitman, "George Washington, Vol. VI," *The Journal of Southern History* (February 1955), 229.

Sears, Louis Martin, "George Washington, Vol. VI," *American Historical Review*, Vol. LX, No. 3 (April 1955), 615.

Bridenbaugh, Carl, "The Man Who Stood above Party," *The New York Times Book Review* (November 24, 1957), 1.

"A Notable Work Done," *Newsweek*, 50 (December 2, 1957), 101.

Selected Newspapers

Richmond News Leader
Richmond Times-Dispatch
Washington Post
New York Times
Petersburg Daily Index Appeal
Richmond Evening Journal
Danville Register
Montevallo (Alabama) *Times*
Mobile (Alabama) *Register*

Acknowledgments

As Douglas Freeman acknowledged his first-born child to be his eyes and his heart, so I must pay tribute to Mary Tyler Freeman Cheek McClenahan as the heart and soul of this book. I was an untested and unpublished author when I timidly approached her with the idea of a biography of her father. She quickly became, next to my wife, the project's most enthusiastic and faithful supporter. She allowed me to read thousands of her parents' letters—previously unseen by historians—and her own unpublished manuscript of recollections. She patiently and thoroughly answered all my questions, gently offered guidance and constructive criticism, and dependably opened all doors for me that might otherwise have remained closed. She read the text, but made no comments about my interpretation of her father and never once attempted to influence my conclusions. It is not fawning exaggeration to state that were it not for her loving and unswerving support, this book would not exist.

James Douglas Freeman spent a long afternoon with me discussing his complex relationship with his father. Painfully honest and utterly frank, he provided an insight and perspective unavailable from any other source.

Dr. William E. Cooper, President of the University of Richmond, embraced this project as a fitting tribute to one of the university's most illustrious alumnae and approved my appointment to the university's History Department in order that I might have the time and resources to complete the book. Dr. David E. Leary, Dean of the School of Arts and Sciences, monitored the progress of my work and never failed to write timely and encouraging notes during my months of writing. Dr. Hugh A. West, Chairman of the History Department, brought my work to the attention of the University of Richmond, developed the plan under which I would join the faculty, and was a steadfast ally of this project. It should be noted that no one at the University of Richmond read the manuscript or attempted to influence my conclusions. The involvement of the university in the writing of this book was purely magnanimous, and were it not for Dr. Cooper, Dean Leary, and Dr. West, this book would still be a dream.

Milburn Calhoun, bibliophile, physician, and president and publisher of Pelican Publishing Company, provided me the moment for which all aspiring

- *Acknowledgments* - 467

authors yearn when he accepted this manuscript for publication. He then proceeded to make it better. I also want to thank Nina Kooij, editor-in-chief, and Rachel Carner, promotions, for patiently guiding me through my first publishing experience. I am greatly indebted to my outstanding—and understanding—copyeditor, Jimmy Peacock, for his unerring eye and his "Freemanesque" editing style. While he and all the others mentioned herein deserve credit for any merits this biography possesses, I am solely responsible for any errors in it.

J. Stewart Bryan III, President and CEO of Media General Inc., wrote letters of introduction on my behalf that facilitated much of my research and allowed me access to the files of his late father, D. Tennant Bryan. James J. Kilpatrick, nationally syndicated columnist and former editor of the *Richmond News Leader*, granted me an afternoon rich with reflections on and recollections of Dr. Freeman.

Two distinguished members of the judiciary are among the best friends of this book. The Hon. J. Harvie Wilkinson III, Chief Judge of the United States Court of Appeals for the Fourth Circuit, historian, and author, has been a consistent source of encouragement during this process. The Hon. Donald W. Lemons, Justice of the Supreme Court of Virginia, "introduced" me to Dr. Freeman some fifteen years ago and was never too busy to discuss with me the most intricate and subtle facets of Freeman's personality.

When I began to work on this book, I was serving as Counsel to the Attorney General of Virginia, the Hon. Mark L. Earley. General Earley noticed my steady drift toward historical writing and graciously allowed me to accept the faculty position at the University of Richmond in order to complete this book.

At a critical junction in the early stages of this book, I was assisted by two eminent members of the Virginia State Bar, John P. "Jack" Ackerly III, Esquire, and Robert Seabolt, Esquire, who made my cause their own.

Materials on the life of Douglas Southall Freeman are scattered in depositories throughout the nation. I found the staffs, librarians, and archivists with whom I dealt to be uniformly courteous, informed, patient, and helpful. I particularly pay tribute to the staff in the James Madison Reading Room of the Library of Congress, Washington, D.C., and to the following dedicated professionals: John M. Coski of the Museum of the Confederacy, Richmond, Virginia; Margaret N. Burri, Curator of Manuscripts, and James Stimpert, Archivist, Johns Hopkins University; Michael Plunkett, Director, and Margaret Hrabe, Reference Coordinator, The Albert H. Small Special Collections Library, University of Virginia; Margaret M. Sherry, Reference Librarian/Archivist, Princeton University; Jean W. Ashton, Director, Rare Books and Manuscript Library, and William Stingone, Curator of Carnegie Collections, Columbia University, New York; E. Lee Shepard, Assistant Director for Manuscripts & Archives, Virginia Historical Society, Richmond; Mary Ellen Brooks, Director, Melissa Bush, Archival Assistant, and Chuck Barber, Assistant Director, Hargrett Rare Book and Manuscript Library, University of Georgia Libraries;

Kathy Albers, Librarian, *Richmond Times-Dispatch*; Frederick J. Anderson, Executive Director, and Darlene Slater, Research Assistant, The Virginia Baptist Historical Society, Richmond; and Eleanor Lerman, Director, Public Affairs & Publications, Carnegie Corporation of New York.

I was given invaluable assistance by many talented and indefatigable research associates. First among them is my chief research assistant, Elizabeth Robeson of Columbia University. Starting with an initial minor assignment, Elizabeth took on more and more responsibilities and duties until she became indispensable. She merits the highest praise in this area of work: namely, her research was flawless. In addition to Elizabeth, I received valuable assistance from Katherine Ferreira, Armstrong Atlantic State University; Valerie Frey, the Georgia Historical Society; Lawrence Charup, Johns Hopkins University; Robert N. Smith, the University of Georgia; and Jay McGaughy, Montevallo University.

Dr. John L. McClenahan cheerfully endured my many intrusions on his wife's time. He also offered the soundest piece of advice I received during this endeavor. "A good story," he counseled, "tells itself."

Members of the extended Freeman family graciously and unhesitatingly offered their time and recollections. I am especially indebted to Leslie Cheek III, Elizabeth Cheek Morgan, Mary A. Malhotra, Douglas Adler, Mallory Freeman, Robert M. Freeman, Royall Turpin, and Douglas Freeman II. O. O. Ashworth, Jr., and John S. Ashworth, M.D., provided many facts and papers about their parents, Mary Wells and Dr. O. O. Ashworth.

I learned very early during this process that friends were needed more than ever when writing a book. I came to rely on several for their advice and counsel. Debra L. Smith, Executive Assistant in the office of Attorney General, reviewed all my correspondence, read many parts of the manuscript, and generally provided sound advice throughout the process. I am also greatly indebted to Steve Haner, Richard Campbell, and Townsend Tucker who ruthlessly edited my first draft and offered comments that markedly improved it. I also want to thank Brett Leake, William H. Hurd, David Botkins, Siran Faulders, the Hon. R. Lee Ware, and Sam Craghead, for many instances of saying just the right thing at just the right moment. Finally there is a core of friends who were "present at the creation" and never failed to reiterate that I could do it: Anne and Bill Kincaid, Wanda and Glenn Murray, and Sharon and Steve Stells.

I never hesitated to ask questions of distinguished scholars, and they never failed to answer. My thanks goes to John L. Gignilliat; Gary W. Gallagher, John L. Nau III Professor of the History of the American Civil War, University of Virginia; William Bragg, Instructor of History, Georgia College & State University; Ruth R. Truss, Assistant Professor of History, Montevallo University; Alan Brinkley, Allen Nevins Professor of History, Columbia University; Blair P. Turner, Professor of History, Virginia Military Institute; Jonnet S. Abeles, Assistant Dean for Public Affairs & Alumni Relations, Columbia School of Journalism; Bud Kliment, Pulitzer Prize Office, Columbia

University; and Stuart L. Wheeler, Associate Professor of Classical Studies, University of Richmond.

I have been blessed with parents-in-law, Aloma and Roy Hindman, who understand their son-in-law's predilection to spend hours reading old books and who have generously contributed to that habit through the years. I have been continually blessed for more than forty years by parents, Georgia and Edward Johnson, who provided me—among countless other things—two invaluable gifts: a love of reading and the first college education in our family. I have not yet calculated their many sacrifices on my behalf, but I could not repay them in any event.

Amanda Johnson, eleven, and Sarah Johnson, eight, supported their father in ways they cannot yet appreciate. Andrew Johnson, three, reminded me to occasionally lift my head from behind the stacks. Although this book is dedicated to their mother, the best of my efforts are always for them.

Finally my wife Holly, the one who said in 1995, "You ought to write this down." Infinitely patient, understanding, supportive, loyal, and talented, she listened to me read every page, struggled with me over stubborn sentences, analyzed the book's structure, and constantly expressed the belief that her lawyer-husband could, in fact, write a book. I dedicate this book to her because it is the only thing of mine she does not already eternally own—chief among them my heart, my respect, my admiration, and my love.

While waiting for librarians to roll out boxes of manuscripts to me, I would write the initials "ICDAT" at the top of my notes. This acronym stood for Philippians 4:13 (NKJV): "I can do all things through Christ who strengthens me." If this book does nothing else, I hope it will stand as a testament to the truth of that scripture.

Index

writings of. *See* headings under
specific titles of works
writing style: 62, 141
youth: 35-39, 42
Freeman, Garland Hurt (grandfather),
16-19, 20
Freeman, Gustavus, 24
Freeman, Hamner Garland (brother),
31, 33
Freeman, Inez Virginia Goddin
(wife), 89, 113, 121, 123, 138,
171, 177, 197, 223, 227, 233, 343,
351, 355
background: 82
civic life: 243-44
courted by DSF: 83-84, 88-89,
91-92
married DSF: 101-2
relationship to DSF: 12, 113,
227-28, 233, 242-43
Freeman, James Douglas (son), 176,
211, 219, 223, 228, 337, 356
birth: 145
relationship with DSF: 177,
178, 319-22, 345-47
youth: 319
"Freeman Markers," 212
Freeman, Mary Tyler (daughter). *See*
McClenahan, Mary Tyler
Freeman Cheek
Freeman, Stephen, 20
Freeman, Thormuthis "The" Burford
(grandmother), 16, 20, 24
Freeman, Walker Burford (father),
39, 54, 56, 60, 67, 100, 160
birth and youth: 16-18
businesses of: 28-31, 33-35, 37,
38, 40
community activities: 29, 40
courtship and marriage: 29-31
death: 181-82
death of father: 19
education: 19, 21

and election of Lincoln: 20
fought for Confederacy: 15, 21-
22, 23-24, 25-27
illnesses of: 22, 23, 25
and Reconstruction: 28-29
religious beliefs: 42-43
and slavery: 17, 20, 43
surrendered at Appomattox: 27-
28
wounded: 24
Freeman, Walker Burford, Jr., (brother),
31, 33
Frost, Robert, 217

G

George, David Lloyd, 145, 168,
171
Gilman, Daniel Coit, 58
Glasgow, Ellen, 168, 217
Glass, Carter, 188, 189
Goddin, James Hinton, 81
Gordon, John B., 234
Grant, Ulysses S., 25, 162

H

Harding, Warren G., 153
Harriman, Averill, 285
Harrison, "Aunt Mary," 33, 37, 113,
309
Harrison, Henry Sydnor, 88, 96-97,
99, 106
Hemphill, J. Calvin, 90-91
Higgins, William H., Jr., M.D., 348,
351
Hollander, Jacob H., 68, 93
Hoover, Herbert, 172-73, 187
Hoover, J. Edgar, 259
Houston, Charles, 192, 198, 200, 201,
202
Hughes, Charles Evans, 121
Hundley, George J., 124-27